CONTENTS

EXPANDED CONTENTS LIST

LANGUAGE AND IDENTITY IN MODERN EGYPT

◆ ◆ ◆

EDINBURGH
University Press

This paperback edition 2015

Edinburgh University Press Ltd
The Tun – Holyrood Road
12 (2f) Jackson's Entry
Edinburgh EH8 8PJ
www.euppublishing.com

First published in hardback by Edinburgh University Press 2014

Typeset in 10/12.5 Trump Mediaeval by
Servis Filmsetting Ltd, Stockport, Cheshire,
and printed and bound in Great Britain by
CPI Group (UK) Ltd, Croydon CR0 4YY

A CIP record for this book is available from the British Library

ISBN 978 0 7486 8964 4 (hardback)
ISBN 978 0 7486 9994 0 (paperback)
ISBN 978 0 7486 8966 8 (epub)
ISBN 978 0 7486 8965 1 (webready PDF)

MAPS, FIGURES, AND TABLES

ABBREVIATIONS

Languages and varieties

CA	Classical Arabic
CB	Christian Baghdadi Arabic
ESA	Educated Spoken Arabic
ECA	Egyptian Colloquial Arabic
LCA	Lebanese Colloquial Arabic
MB	Muslim Baghdadi Arabic
MSA	Modern Standard Arabic
SA	Standard Arabic
SCA	Saudi Colloquial Arabic
TCA	Tunisian Colloquial Arabic

Other abbreviations and symbols

acc	accusative
adj	adjective
adv	adverb
asp	aspect
conj	conjugation
def	definite
dem	demonstrative
det	definite article
f	feminine
H	high, highly valued
Imperf	imperfect tense
indef	indefinite

ind	indicative
juss	jussive
L	low, lowly valued
loc adv	locative adverb
m	masculine
n	noun
neg	negative marker
nom	nominative
par.	particle
part.	participle
pass	Passive
perf	perfect tense
pl	plural
poss par	possessive particle
pr	pronoun
prep	preposition
pres	present tense
rel	relative pronoun
sub	subjunctive
sg	singular
v	verb
voc	vocative
1	first person
2	second person
3	third person

TRANSCRIPTION, GLOSSES, AND TRANSLITERATIONS

All *linguistic data* in this book is represented in Arabic script or in IPA characters:

أ		ʔ
ب		b
ت		t
ث		θ
ج		j
ح		ḥ
خ		x
د		d
ذ		ð
ر		r
ز		z
س		s
ش		ʃ
ص		ṣ

ض		ḍ
ط		ṭ
ظ		ẓ
ع		ʕ
غ		ġ
ف		f
ق		q
ك		k
ل		l
م		m
ن		n
ه		h
و		w
ى		y

The feminine ending is –a in pause and –at in construct forms. The adjectival ending is transcribed as –i: (masc.) and –i:ya (fem.), respectively.

The vowels in Standard Arabic are represented as a, i, u, a:, i:, and u:, whereas the short vowels e and o and their long counterparts e: and o: are used in transcribing dialects. Additional IPA symbols may be used where a detailed phonological transcription is necessary.

Since ʃ, θ, and ð are not used in library catalogs, all proper names and most titles (with the exception of song titles) are transliterated, according to the Library of Congress' Romanization system (see http://www.loc.gov/catdir/cpso/romanization/arabic.pdf), in order to facilitate the identification of authors and their works. In a few cases, a common conventional form has been retained in order to facilitate searching, as in "Wael Ghonim" for "Wāʾil Ghunaym."

This study uses a broad kind of transcription. However, it should be noted that the data used in this book is mainly spoken data. Thus, there is considerable variation within that data. For instance, the same word could be pronounced by the same speaker first with a long vowel and then with a short one in the same stretch of discourse. It is important for sociolinguists to capture the performance of speakers, rather than the idealized way in which words and phonemes are "supposed" to be pronounced. Thus, the aim of transcribing the data is not to idealize, but to render actual pronunciation.

Within the examples, when necessary, a forward slash denotes a short pause, while two slashes denote a long pause.

Songs

Authorized recordings of songs are difficult to come by. The data analyzed here has therefore been collected from YouTube and transcribed using the system outlined above. In the absence of a printed title, the transcribed title has been used throughout.

Glossing

For the benefit of students and researchers who are not necessarily specialized in Arabic or in all dialects of Arabic, some examples are glossed, except those in which the structure is not highlighted. In the glosses, whenever verb forms are fully analyzed, the gloss follows the translation for verbs in the perfect (which has a suffix conjugation in Arabic), whereas the gloss precedes the translation for the imperfect (which has a prefix conjugation), while the mood marking of the verb—if present—is glossed in its natural location at the end of the verb unit.

However, the glossing of examples is related to the context of the example and is not always detailed. If the example is intended to demonstrate how individuals switch between two varieties or languages and if this demonstration concentrates on specific morpho-syntactic variables (such as demonstratives, negation, tense, aspect, mood marking, and case marking), then the glossing is detailed. If, on the other hand, the example is used to demonstrate an argument that is more related to content, then the glossing is more basic. Thus, the glossing is not consistent, but rather changes in line with the change in the nature of the analysis of the data.

ACKNOWLEDGEMENTS

As I was writing this book, there were rapid changes in Egypt on many levels, and Egyptians were grappling with many issues that pertain to their identity. When asked about events in Egypt during the years 2010 to 2013 alone that possibly need a book dedicated to themselves, I always give the brief, safe, and easy answer: "it's complicated." When asked about identity issues nowadays, the answer is also, in most cases, complicated. For media-makers, the layers of identity are clearer and more demarcated. The media provides anchors during people's personal journeys to discover the self in relation to a community, a nation, and a place.

During my academic sail, there were many people who provided anchors. Scholars in the field that directly or indirectly provided support to me, sometimes through simple, straightforward feedback, sometimes by indirect inspiration, and at other times by being great friends and doing both of the above. Those great scholars and friends are not all mentioned in this acknowledgement, but some are.

Thank you to Jean Aitchison, who is, and will remain, a great academic and friend. Thank you to Abbas Benmamoun and the promising graduate students at the University of Illinois, who invited me to their first annual meeting of the Illinois *Symposium on Semitic Linguistics*, in which I presented parts of my book. Their feedback and questions were helpful. Another occasion in which I presented parts of my research in this book was another invite by Rizwan Ahmad for the *Linguistics in the Gulf* conference (LGC4) at the University of Qatar. Thanks to him and to my dear friend Irene Theodoropoulou, both of whose feedback were also very helpful.

Peter Garret graciously agreed to read Chapter 3 of my book. I thank him with all my heart for his feedback. Needless to say, any errors are my responsibility.

Keith Walters is a scholar on many levels and a person who taught me a lot, both directly and indirectly. Yasir Suleiman remains an inspiring scholar and his support and feedback made this book better.

Thank you to my dear linguist friends, Anna De Fina, Mushira Eid, Aleya Rouchdy, Teun van Dijk, Alexandra Jaffe, Barbara Johnstone, Kees Versteegh, and Ruth Wodak.

Thank you to the two anonymous readers of this book, whose comments and suggestions were essential.

My students, as usual, are my big encouragement, and their enthusiasm and interest always mean a lot to me.

During the process of preparing this book for publication, a number students and research assistants provided help. Thank you to Emily Vealy, who helped me in my preparation of the manuscript. Thank you to Sylvia Sierra and Michael Raisch.

Thank you to the Edinburgh University Press team for taking on this project. Nicola Ramsey is really a pleasure to work with on all levels. Thanks also to Eddie Clark, Jenny Peebles, and Rebecca Mackenzie. My copy editor, Elizabeth Welsh, was really one of the best copy editors I have ever worked with. As with all of the team at Edinburgh University Press, she was professional, without losing the human touch, warmth, and efficiency.

Thank you to my family, especially to Mark.

INTRODUCTION: LANGUAGE AND IDENTITY IN MODERN EGYPT

The aim of this work is to examine how language is used in Egyptian public discourse to illuminate the collective identity of Egyptians, and how this identity is then made manifest in language form and content. The data used to identify the collective identity of Egyptians in public discourse includes newspaper articles, caricatures, blogs, patriotic songs, films, school textbooks, television talk shows, poetry, and, finally, Egyptian novels that deal with the theme of identity.

Edwards (2009: 20) stipulates that "individual identities will be both components and reflections of particular social (or cultural) ones, and the latter will always be, to some extent at least, stereotypic in nature because of their necessary generality across the individual components." That is, the influence of public discourse in providing a coherent unified identity to all Egyptians is essential, even on the level of individual identity.

What concerns us here is the individual as a member of an imagined "coherent group." A collective identity may be stereotypic, exclusive, built on myths, detached from reality, and propagated by politicians or the media at different times. However, it is, indeed, this imagined identity that steers individuals into taking specific actions, endorsing others, and perhaps putting up with some. This in itself makes the study of the relationship between language and identity a pivotal task.

It has been established that language does not stand alone, but is related both directly and indirectly to social, political, historical, and other extra-linguistic factors (Spolsky 2004). However, extra-linguistic factors also need to be examined in relation to language. Thus, one cannot describe the social and political changes in Egypt without referring to the diglossic community and how code-choice reflects a political or social stand in most cases and is, in almost all cases, a reflection of an identity, whether a collective one or an individual one. In addition, identity, as we mentioned above, is the product of a community, not just an individual. A collective national Egyptian identity is no exception. While Edwards begins his book on language and identity by posing the question of what he has in common with himself as a little child in a picture, an even more challenging question would be: what does an Egyptian have in common with a statue of a Pharaoh, which is 3,000 years old,[1] especially given that this Pharaoh is supposedly a pagan, who speaks a different language altogether?

Writing a book about language and identity in Egypt is a challenging task, but a necessary one. Such work will further our understanding of the relationship between identity and language in general and also yield insights about the intricate ways in which media and public discourse more generally help shape and outline an identity through linguistic processes. Individuals express this identity through linguistic practices, including code-choice and code-switching.

I.1 Why Egypt?

Despite the fact that Egypt is the most populous Arabic-speaking country in the world, there are exceedingly few monographs on language in Egypt during the modern period.[2]

Egypt, like all Arab countries, is a diglossic community—that is, a community in which in addition to the different dialects, two varieties exist side by side, each with a different function. Ferguson (1959) called these varieties a "High" variety (in our case, Standard Arabic or SA) and a "Low" variety (here, Egyptian colloquial Arabic or ECA). There are differences between the varieties on the lexical, morphological, and structural levels. Observe the following example:

ECA:

illi:	*ʕamalu:h*	*iʃ-ʃaba:b*	*fi*	*tamanta:ʃar*	*yo:m*
rel	"do"-3mpl-pr3msg	det-"youth"	"in"	eighteen	day (sg)

ma-ḥaddi-ʃ	*ʕamaluh*	*fi*	*sitti:n*	*sana*
neg-"one"-neg	"do"-3msg-pr3msg	"in"	sixty	year(sg)

"What the young people achieved in eighteen days, no one had achieved in sixty years"

SA:

ma:	*faʕala-hu*	*ʃ-ʃaba:b*	*fi:*	*θama:niyata*	*ʕaʃara*
rel	"do"-3msg-pr3msg	det-"youth"	"in"	eight(f)	"ten"(m)

yawman	*lam*	*yafʕal-hu*	*aḥad*	*xila:la*	*sitti:n*	*sanah*
"day"-acc	neg	3msg-"do"-juss-pr3msg	"one"	"during"	"sixty"	"year"

Compare and contrast *ma-ḥaddi-ʃ ʕamaluh* and *lam yafʕal-hu aḥad* in the second part of the sentence. ECA and SA sometimes have distinct lexical choices: while *ʕamala* is also used in SA, it is construed in a much narrower sense as "to work," whereas in ECA it means "to do" in a general sense. It is also apparent that negation works differently in both varieties: where the negated verb is bracketed by *ma . . . ʃ* in ECA, SA has various negation schemes, including the pattern (lam + imperfect) for actions completed in the past. The system of numerals in SA is highly complex: for numbers between twelve and nineteen, when used with a masculine noun, the "ones" have a feminine marker, whereas the "tens" are masculine in form. In comparison, the numbers in ECA are greatly simplified. Phonological variations are not dominant in this example. Perhaps the most salient feature of many types of ECA is the replacement of q with ʔ.

In addition, Egypt constitutes more than one-third of the Arab world with a population exceeding 80 million. However, the relations between Egypt and other Arabic-speaking countries have never been without political rivalry and tensions. This is reflected in perceptions of identity in public discourse.

Since the beginning of the twentieth century, Egyptian intellectuals have oscillated between considering Egypt the leader of the Arab world, calling her, as Ibn Baṭṭūtah (d. 1369) did in the past, "the mother of the world,"[3] and emphasizing the distinctive nature of Egyptians as descendants of an ancient civilization, both geographically and historically different from other Arab countries. This contested identity—at times brought to the forefront by political and social problems—is fertile ground for a sociolinguistic study.

In discussion regarding political change in Egypt (and the Arab world at large), "identity" is constantly referenced as a driving force, both by commentators in Arabic-language media and in the English-language press. Hussein Agha and Robert Malley (2011) argue that it is not possible to understand the actions of people in Arab countries without understanding what their concept of identity "entails":

> One cannot fully comprehend the actions of Egyptians, Tunisians, Jordanians and others without considering this deep-seated feeling that they have not been allowed to be themselves, that they have been robbed of their identities. Taking to the streets is not a mere act of protest. It is an act of self-determination.

But identities also develop and acquire new meanings and positions or appeal to older and forgotten categories. In *The New York Times*, Shadid and Kirkpatrick (2011) attribute the wide spread of protests and revolts in the Arab world and the success of some of these revolts to the new meaning of national identity acquired by "Arabs":

> The revolutions and revolts in the Arab world, playing out over just a few months across two continents, have proved so inspirational to so many because they offer a new sense of national identity built on the idea of citizenship.

As for Egypt, it is not just Egyptian public discourse that constantly tries to demarcate the uniqueness of Egyptian identity, but non-Egyptian public discourse as well, as evidenced in the example below (Bender 2011):

> But, Egypt is different. The borders of the Egyptian nation have been roughly the same since the Nile River was first settled. Unlike Iraq, which never really connected its modern version with the Sumerians and Babylonians that ruled within its modern borders long ago, Egyptians continually connect themselves to their ancient and Medieval Era ancestors. Its deep, communally-shared history should serve as the mortar between the bricks of Egypt's diverse society, and that combination should help repel threats of a military takeover.

Bender does not just discuss Egypt's uniqueness compared to other countries, but relates this unique identity of Egyptians to the political future of Egypt. According to Bender, it is because Egypt has a long, well-established history that it will be difficult for the military to take over.

The relationship between language and identity in Egypt, especially after the January 25, 2011 Revolution, was also highlighted in non-Egyptian media, as in the example below (Bender 2011):

> Even before the European powers demarcated the boundaries of the contemporary Middle East during the mid-20th century, Egyptians were unique from the Bedouins migrating across the Sahara and Arabian deserts. They spoke a distinct Arabic dialect, no doubt born from the busy markets of Cairo and Alexandria. They relished their shared cultural identity that made them not just Arabs, but people of Africa and the Mediterranean Sea. They bore a sizable Coptic Christian community that had contributed to society since the pre-Islamic era. For periods throughout much of the past millennium, especially before the rise of the Ottoman Empire, Cairo was seen as the social and political capital of the Arabs. Any visitor to the great Pyramids of Giza, along the banks of the Nile River, knows that the Egyptians pride themselves in their longstanding accomplishments.

Bender classifies Egyptians as being, to some extent, different from Arabs and attempts to explain this difference by drawing upon independent variables, such as history, locality, geographical position, religion, and language. According to Bender, the fact that Egyptians spoke "a distinct Arabic dialect, no doubt born from the busy markets of Cairo and Alexandria" is one of the main reasons why they are different from others. The reference to the market streets of Cairo and Alexandria also implies that this dominant dialect is an urban one, as opposed to a Bedouin or rural dialect. The relationship between language and identity comes to the surface in this example—this is what this book will concentrate on. However, it is not non-Egyptian public discourse that will be discussed, although it has to be referred to, but Egyptian public discourse.

The Egyptian Revolution lasted for eighteen days, beginning on January 25, 2011 and ending with Mubarak's abdication on February 11, 2011 after thirty years of ruling Egypt. The protest movement in Egypt questioned the legitimacy of President Mubarak and his government and their claims to represent the Egyptian people. The demands of the opposition were encapsulated in the seemingly simple Standard Arabic slogan *al-ʃaʕb yuri:d isqa:ṭ al-niẓa:m* ("The [Egyptian] people want to overthrow the system"). As a result, the public discourse of the Revolution—both pro- and anti-Mubarak—revolved around several interrelated questions: who are "the Egyptian people"? Who represents them? What do they want?

Interestingly, many explicit statements about Egyptian identity during the revolution contained direct references to language. This is hardly surprising, given the central role of language in the construction of the Arab identity (for a thorough historical analysis of this phenomenon, see Suleiman 2003). What is new in the context of the Egyptian Revolution of 2011 is that language—as a marker of identity—became a pivotal element in the political contestation between "the people" and an autocratic regime.

To give but one example: before stepping down, Mubarak gave three speeches over a period of eighteen days. Unlike his previous speeches (see Bassiouney 2006), the three speeches were given in Standard Arabic, rather than Egyptian colloquial Arabic or a mixture of standard and colloquial. This marked choice to use SA rather than ECA did not go unnoticed by Egyptians. Mubarak was known to use ECA in his speeches; he was even criticized and accused by some intellectuals and opposition leaders of never having mastered SA. On the other hand, the former Tunisian president Bin Ali, ousted weeks earlier, was famous for using only SA in his speeches, never code-switching between Tunisian Colloquial Arabic and SA. Bin Ali, did, however, use only Tunisian Colloquial Arabic in his last speech to the Tunisian people before fleeing to Saudi Arabia on January 14, 2011. Bin Ali, in his last speech, said, in Tunisian Arabic, *fihimtuku* ("I understood you"). Mubarak made sure to never show weakness and never say *"fihimtuku"*—incidentally, a word that is pronounced almost identically in both Tunisian Arabic and ECA—and also never use ECA in his last three speeches. Egyptians, Tunisians, and Arabs more generally realized, despite not being linguists, the differences between the speeches of Bin-Ali and Mubarak. Egyptians then joked that as long as Mubarak used SA in his speeches—the authoritative language code—he would cling to power. Code-choice was fundamental, not just to define identity, but to foretell the next political step that was to be taken by the regime.

The content of Mubarak's three speeches was also important. The way that Mubarak positioned himself as serving Egypt, rather than Egyptians, smacked of vanity and detachment from reality, but was also a linguistically and politically calculated choice of intentionally abstracting himself from Egyptians and concentrating on a more important and sacred entity, which is "Egypt." That is to say, according to him, the implicit message is that Egyptians may not know what is good for Egypt, but he does. While he referred to serving Egypt for thirty years, the protestors demanded that he now listen to what "Egyptians" want. Identity was underscored and contested, and linguistic resources were manipulated by all those involved in the conflict.

The linguistic choices of the protestors, on the other hand, are worth a book by themselves; their slogans were in SA, ECA, English, and French, to name but a few. They started by chanting "leave" in SA. When Mubarak then broadcast his first speech and showed no sign of listening, the protestors used ECA and SA, saying *ʔirḥal yaʕni ʔimʃi yalli mabtifhamʃi* ("'leave' means 'go,' you who do not understand"). After the SA imperative "leave," they explained the simple word "leave" in ECA, accusing the president of not understanding their demands and failing to understand SA. By accusing him of not understanding SA, they also implicitly undermined his authority and legitimacy, as will be made clear in this book. SA has many indexes that are usually manipulated at times of conflict and transition. The imperative SA verb *ʔirḥal* was translated into English and French, as well as ECA. The protestors claimed to be the "real Egyptians," as did the small pro-Mubarak group (see Chapter 6 for a detailed discussion of the correlations between the political contestations of identity and the linguistic situation in Egypt).

I.2 Aims of this work

This book starts from the assumption that language is a resource, access to which is constantly negotiated. Blommaert (2007: 115) defines language as a "repertoire: a culturally sensitive ordered complex of genres, styles, registers, with lots of hybrid forms, and occurring in a wide variety of ways big and small." In public discourse, individuals choose from their "repertoire" to index social variables that index an identity. That is, through linguistic resources, individuals construct an identity.

The main aim of this book is to answer the following questions: what is the relationship between language and identity in Egypt, and how is this relationship manifested through language use and discussions about language in public discourse?

In order to answer these questions, one has to first answer a number of other questions, including the following two:

1. In a diglossic community such as Egypt, how do language ideology and language attitudes feed into the indexical associations and order of indexicality between different varieties and languages—that is, different codes—and how do social factors, history, politics, and language policies also feed into that linguistic process? That is, how are the associations of SA, ECA, and foreign languages applied to discussions of identity? In more general terms, can orders of indexicality better our understanding of diglossia as a linguistic phenomenon more generally and in Egypt in particular?
2. If language is considered to be a resource for individuals in a community, then what are the mechanisms of claiming access to codes or utilizing linguistic resources in Egyptian public discourse? And what is the relevance of the associations of linguistic codes to the process of stance-taking, in which speakers position themselves as Egyptians or non-Egyptians in public discourse and thus align or disalign with an object or person or group?

I.3 Setting the framework

In this section, the diglossic linguistic situation in Egypt will be outlined. The term "public discourse" will also be explained and the choice and nature of data will be discussed.

I.3.1 The linguistic situation in Egypt

Egypt's official name is *Jumhu:riyyat miṣr al-ʕarabiyya*, translated into English as "The Arab Republic of Egypt." In Arabic, the word "Egypt" comes first before "Arab," so that a literal translation would be: "Republic-of-Egypt, the-Arabic."

In order to provide some background on Egypt, I provide a few statistics here:[4]

Population: 83,688,164 (July 2012 estimate)
Ethnic groups: Egyptian: 99.6 per cent; other: 0.4 per cent (2006 Census)
Religion: Muslim (mostly Sunni): 90 per cent; Coptic Christian:[5] 9 per cent; other Christian: 1 per cent

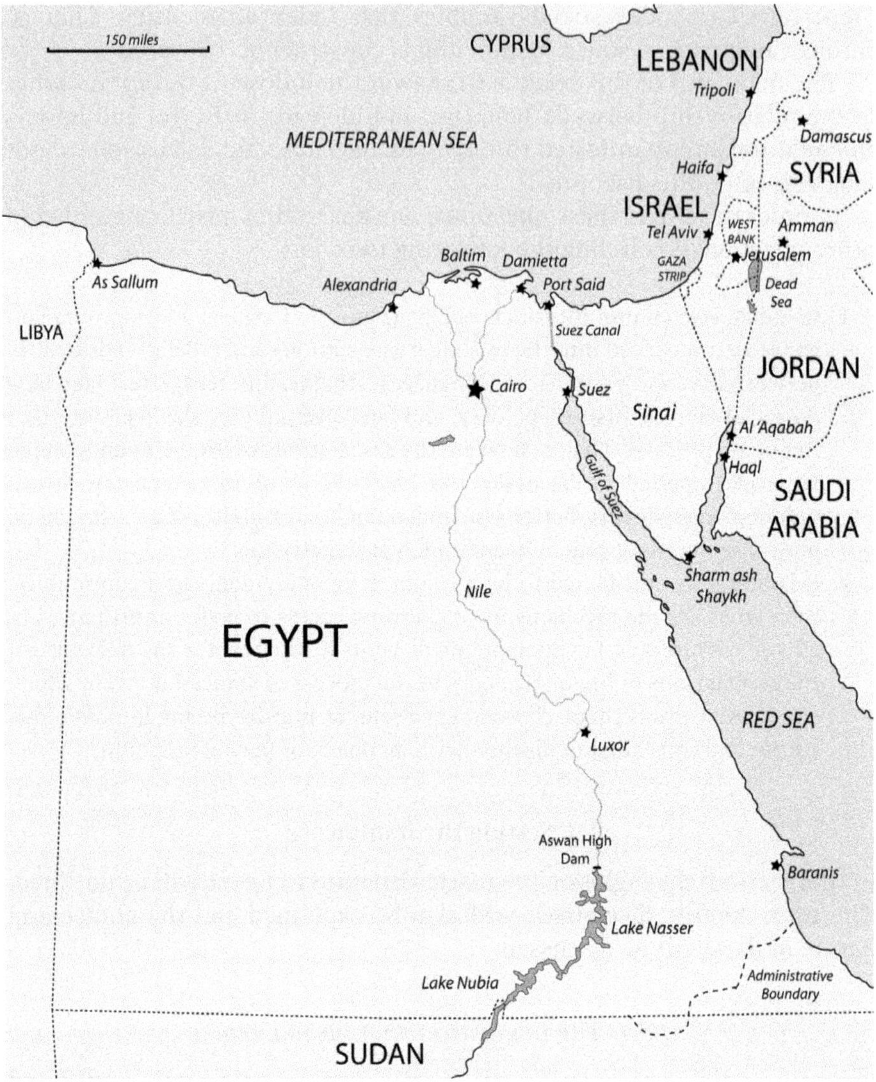
150 miles
CYPRUS
LEBANON
Tripoli
Damascus
MEDITERRANEAN SEA
Haifa
SYRIA
ISRAEL
Tel Aviv
WEST BANK
Amman
Jerusalem
GAZA STRIP
Dead Sea
Baltim
Damietta
As Sallum
Alexandria
Port Said
LIBYA
Suez Canal
JORDAN
Cairo
Suez
Sinai
Al 'Aqabah
Haql
Gulf of Suez
SAUDI ARABIA
Sharm ash Shaykh
Nile
EGYPT
RED SEA
Luxor
Aswan High Dam
Baranis
Lake Nasser
Lake Nubia
Administrative Boundary
SUDAN

Map of Egypt

Languages used in Egypt:[6]
Standard Arabic (official)
Egyptian colloquial Arabic (in most cases, this is used to refer to Cairene Arabic, but there are different varieties of colloquial in Egypt)
Nubian (ca. 50,000–170,000 speakers)
Bedja (ca. 15,000)
Siwi (ca. 6,000–22,000)
Some Armenian and Greek in Cairo and Alexandria
Colonization: 1882–1952
Official languages:
1882–1952 Arabic and English
1952– Arabic
Urban population: 43.4 per cent of total population (2010)
Rate of urbanization: 2.1 per cent annual rate of change (2010–15 estimates)

Literacy rates: (Definition: age fifteen and over can both read and write)
Total population: 71.4 per cent
Male: 83 per cent
Female: 59.4 per cent (2005 estimate)

Geography
Total area: 1,001,450 km^2
Populated area: 78,990 km2 (7.8 per cent)
Arable land: 2.92 per cent

I.3.1.1 Arabic in Egypt

The Arabs conquered Egypt around 640 CE and incorporated the country into their expanding empire. The languages used at this time in Egypt were Coptic and Greek. There is some debate about the status of Greek, but the available evidence suggests that both languages were used widely, with a preference given to Greek in contracts and official documents (Clackson 2004).

The practice of drawing up official documents in Greek survived for a limited period of time under Arab rule (and, indeed, the use of Greek letters as numerals in taxation records continued for some three centuries). However, purely Greek documents were soon supplanted by Greek–Arabic bilingual ones, which, in turn, gave way to documents written exclusively in Arabic.

In the Arab chronicles, this transition is attributed to a change in language policy during the Umayyad dynasty (661–750 CE) and to the caliph ʿAbd al-Malik ibn Marwān (685–705 CE) in particular. This caliph is often credited with implementing a consistent and effective language policy that aimed to leverage the economic and political power of the Islamic empire to change language practices and habits. Throughout history, the success of language policies is usually limited (see Spolsky 2004), but ʿAbd al-Malik is said to have initiated a policy that lead to the Arabization of not just Egypt, but the entire Near East. According to the traditional narrative, he made a drastic change in the administration of Egypt, by declaring that in order for Egyptians to keep their jobs in the administration of Egypt, they would have to learn Arabic.[7] Arabic was supposedly declared the only language allowed in what we now call government offices, and it became the language of the *dīwān*—the public register of stipends. In other words, unless Coptic speakers learned Arabic, they would be replaced in the administration by Arabs. Now the chronicles do not tell us much about the logistics of this change, and, in fact, the papyrological record suggests that the shift from Greek to Arabic was much more gradual (Hawting 2000: 63). On the other hand, the triumph of Arabic over local languages may suggest that some sort of language planning did take place, whether it was due to corpus planning or status planning.[8]

While the sources are ambiguous about the specifics of the Arabization of the administration, it is clear that ʿAbd al-Malik instituted another symbolic change that aimed to relate Arabic directly to the identity of the Islamic empire: the change in coinage. During the early Umayyad period, Muslim coinage had simply reproduced the style and iconography of Byzantine or Sassanian coinage. Under ʿAbd al-Malik, these models were abandoned in favor of a design that was purely epigraphic; henceforth, Islamic coins would not have an effigy of the ruler, but Islamic religious formulae in Arabic (Hawting 2000: 64). As Goldschmidt (2008: 5) posits, these fiscal and administrative changes would turn Coptic-speaking Christian Egyptians into Arabic-speaking Muslim Egyptians, although maintaining a Christian minority. Since then, Coptic remains a liturgical language known mainly to priests and monks, although there have always been various attempts at its revival.

By tying language to economic and political power, the Caliph succeeded in implementing its spread both faster and more effectively. There was no need to resort to extreme measures; language change was imminent, especially with a parallel change in religion. Language contact also had a pivotal role in language change in Egypt; the Arabs, when they conquered Egypt, started building inland cities, such as Fusṭāṭ, and eventually some of them settled and mingled with the Egyptians, perhaps more than Egyptian history books have previously acknowledged.

However, the question regarding why there is diglossia in the Arab world and in Egypt as an Arab country is not yet resolved. Whether Arabs all started speaking in Classical Arabic (a language similar to pre-Islamic poetry), or if Standard Arabic was ever a spoken language, and whether there was a unified "Arabic" in the Arabian Peninsula are all moot questions (see Versteegh 2001; Holes 2004). The linguistic reality is that Egypt, as with all Arab countries, is considered a diglossic community. Diglossia will be dealt with in detail in the next section. However, Egypt continuously examines the relationship between its language and identity. As noted earlier, Egypt, as part of the Arab world, is a diglossic community. In Arab countries, the official language is usually Modern Standard Arabic,[9] but there is also at least one prestigious vernacular spoken in each country.

I.3.1.2 Ferguson's definition of diglossia in the Arab world

The following is Ferguson's definition of diglossia:

> Diglossia is a relatively stable language situation in which, in addition to the primary dialects of the language (which may include a standard or regional standards), there is a very divergent, highly codified (often grammatically more complex) superposed variety, the vehicle of a large and respected body of written literature, either of an earlier period or in another speech community, which is learned largely by formal education and is used for most written and formal spoken purposes but is not used by any sector of the community for ordinary conversation. (Ferguson 1959: 336)

According to Ferguson, diglossia is a different situation from one where there are merely different dialects within a speech community. In diglossic communities, there is a highly valued H (High) variety that is learned in schools and is not used for ordinary conversations. That is to say, no one speaks the H variety natively. The L (Low) variety is the one that is used in conversation.[10] Most importantly, Ferguson claims that the crucial test for diglossia is that the language varieties in question must be functionally allocated within the community concerned (Fasold 1995: 35). Ferguson stresses that both H and L have to be in "complementary distribution functionally" (see also Boussofara-Omar 2006: 630). According to Ferguson, diglossia is a relatively stable phenomenon. Ferguson implies that if a society is changing and diglossia is beginning to fade away, this will have specific signs, such as speakers mixing between the forms of H and L, and thus an overlap between the functions of H and L occurs (Ferguson 1959: 336).[11]

Ferguson proceeds by exemplifying situations in which only H is appropriate and others in which only L is appropriate (1959: 329). According to him, the following are situations in which H is appropriate:

1. Sermon in church or mosque;
2. speech in parliament and political speech;
3. personal letters;

4. university lecture;
5. news broadcast;
6. newspaper editorial, news story, and caption on picture; and
7. poetry.

He also gives situations in which L is the "only" variety used:

1. Instructions to servants, waiters, workmen, and clerks;
2. conversation with family, friends, and colleagues;
3. radio soap opera;
4. caption on political cartoon; and
5. folk literature.

Ferguson's definition has been criticized and discussed extensively, even by Ferguson himself (see Ferguson 1996), although it is only fair to note that at that stage, Ferguson was describing a general linguistic situation; indeed, he did not set out to describe Arabic diglossia as language standardization. He was describing diglossia cross-linguistically as it relates to issues of standardization. Questions that arose from his definition of diglossia are summarized below.

How far apart or close together do the H and L need to be for a language situation to be called "diglossia"? This question was posed by Fasold (1995: 50ff.), who claimed that there are no absolute measures that can specify the distance between H and L in a diglossic community. Britto (1986: 10–12, 321) considered the same question and argued that H and L must be "optimally" distant, as in Arabic, but not "super-optimally," as with Spanish and Guaraní, or "sub-optimally," as with formal–informal styles in English.[12]

Is there only one H? Ferguson spoke only about a distinction between H and L, without distinguishing the two different kinds of H such as exist in the Arab world, where there is a distinction between Classical Arabic (CA) and Modern Standard Arabic (MSA), although one has to note that this distinction is a Western invention and does not correspond to any Arabic term. However, CA is the religious language of the Qur'ān, which is rarely used except in reciting the Qur'ān or quoting older classical texts, while MSA can be used in a public speech, for example. Ryding, in her book *A Reference Grammar of Arabic* (2005: 7), mentions that both MSA and CA are referred to as *"al-luġa al-fuṣha:"* ("the standard language"). This, in a sense, creates a shared past and present. She argues that there are few structural inconsistencies between MSA and CA. The main differences between both are stylistic and lexical, rather than grammatical. However, she posits that the journalistic style of MSA has more flexible word order, coinage of neologisms, and loan translations from

Western languages. For example, journalistic-style MSA uses the *iḍa:fa* construction (genitive "of construction") to create neologisms for compound words or complex concepts. Bateson (1967: 84) posits that there are three kinds of changes between MSA and CA. MSA is characterized by having a simpler syntactic structure and being different in lexicon, because of modern technology, and being stylistically different, due to translations from other languages and the influence of bilingualism.

There is also the question of how different is the linguistic context of countries where more than one language is in everyday use, such as in Tunisia, where some people are also fluent in French? In such countries, the term "diglossia" is too narrow for the type of situation that exists.

Ferguson considered—only to a very limited extent—the fact that there can be switching between both varieties (H and L) in the same stretch of discourse. Again, this is because he did not set out to reflect the realistic situation in Arab countries, but rather to give an idealized picture of diglossia.

Furthermore, Ferguson did not discuss the sociolinguistic significance of the competing varieties. He did not propose that social factors may have a part to play in the negotiation of choice of variety in a diglossic community in specific sets of circumstances. This may be because, as he said himself, social factors of this kind were not in fashion at the time that the paper was written. They were not considered "true science" (1996: 60). Instead, Ferguson greatly emphasized the "external situation" in determining language choice. He claimed that in certain set situations H is appropriate, while in others L is appropriate, without taking into account the possible significance of the individual in negotiating (or deliberately subverting) "socially agreed" patterns of language choice (and ultimately changing them). Having reviewed these recent reformulations and revisions to his general theory, let us now briefly review the contributions Ferguson made to the study of Arabic diglossia.

Ferguson drew the attention of linguists to the existence of two language varieties in the Arab world and the fact that people have different attitudes towards these two varieties, although the term "diglossia" had been used earlier by the French dialectologist William Marçais with specific reference to Arabic (Fasold 1995: 34).

Despite all the subsequent criticism of Ferguson's theory, his proposal that there are two poles, an H and an L, is still valid, although they both formally and functionally overlap. Indeed, Mejdell (1999: 226) posits that the H–L division still has validity. After Ferguson's article, linguists tried to refine Ferguson's concept by proposing intermediate levels, but still these intermediate levels cannot be understood unless one presupposes the existence of two "poles"—H and L. It may be that "pure H" or "pure L" does not occur very often and that there are usually elements of both varieties in any stretch of normal speech, but still one has to consider a hypothetical pure H or L, in order to presuppose that there are elements that occur from one or the other in a stretch of discourse. Ferguson himself did, in fact, recognize the existence of intermediate levels, but insisted that they cannot be described, except within the framework of H and L (1996: 59):

> I recognized the existence of intermediate forms and mentioned them briefly in the article, but I felt then and still feel that in the diglossia case the analyst finds two poles in terms of which the intermediate varieties can be described, there is no third pole.

Ferguson certainly spurred linguists to examine diglossia, but he did not provide definite answers to a great number of questions. As Walters (2003: 103) puts it:

> Our understanding of these phenomena [i.e. sociolinguistic phenomenon] would be far less nuanced than it is today had Fergie not taught us to look at Arabic as he did, looking past the norm and deviation paradigm that too often still characterizes discussions of Arabic and all diglossic languages. In so doing, he encouraged us to examine with care specific varieties and specific sets of linguistic practices as ways of better understanding the sociolinguistic processes found across speech communities that at first glance might appear quite disparate.

Note, also, that Fishman (1967), in line with Ferguson, identified specific domains to define diglossia. For example, speech events can fall under different domains, like a baseball conversation and an electrical engineering lecture. The major domains that Fishman identifies are family, friendship, religion, education, and employment (see also Myers-Scotton 2006). He also claims that these speech events are speech-community specific.[13]

I.3.1.3 The concept of prestige as different from that of standard

There has been a growing realization since the mid-1980s that variation in Arabic speech is not merely (or even mainly) a question of H interference in L. According to Ibrahim (1986: 115), "the identification of H as both the standard and the prestigious variety at one and the same time has led to problems of interpreting data and findings from Arabic sociolinguistic research." This identification is the result of applying Western research to the Arab world, without noting the different linguistic situation. In research within Western speech communities, researchers have generally been able to assume that the standardized variety of a language—the one that has undergone the conscious process of standardization—is also the variety accorded the most overt prestige.

Many studies have shown that for most speakers, there is a prestige variety of L, the identity of which depends on many geographical, political, and social factors within each country and which may, in certain circumstances, influence speech. In Egypt, for non-Cairenes, it is the prestige variety of Egyptian Cairene Arabic; for Jordanian women from Bedouin or rural backgrounds, on the other hand, it may be the urban dialects of the big cities (Abdel-Jawad 1986: 58).

In a diachronic study conducted by Palva (1982), materials from Arabic dialects spoken, recorded, and collected since 1914 in the Levant, Yemen, Egypt, and Iraq were compared. Palva examined the occurrence of phonological, morphological, and lexical items in the dialects over a period of time. He found that certain dialectal variants gradually become more dominant than the "standard" variants. For example, the glottal realization /ʔ/ of the historical /q/, which is a phonological feature of several vernaculars in the area, became widespread and dominant rather than the MSA /q/ (1982: 22–4). Holes (1983a; 1983b) discusses the influence of MSA on two Bahraini dialects from both a phonological and lexical viewpoint. Amongst other observations, he shows that the degree of influence of MSA on the speech of educated Bahrainis is dependent on the social status of the speakers. The socially prestigious Sunni speakers are not influenced much by the standard, while the speech of the low-status Shiite speakers is relatively more influenced by the standard (1983b: 448).

Abu-Haidar, in her study of the Muslim and Christian dialects of Baghdad, posits that (1991: 92):

> Apart from MSA (the H variety for all Baghdadis), CB speakers [Christian Baghdadi] use their own dialect as a L variety in informal situations at home and with in-group members, while they use MB [Muslim Baghdadi] as another H variety in more formal situations with non-Christians.

It has been realized that MSA is not the only source of linguistic prestige and that in virtually every Arab speech community that has been examined, there is a dominant L that exerts influence on the other lower-status Ls in that country or surrounding region. The reasons for its influence are various, but principle among them is factors like the socio-economic dominance of the city over the countryside (for example, Cairo) or the influence of a ruling political group (for example, the royal families of the Gulf). The dialects of these entities become a symbol of their power and exercize a potent influence over those who come into contact with them or who have to interact with speakers of these dialects.

Because this book is more concerned with attitudes, ideologies, and discourse strategies than describing the differences between Standard Arabic and Cairene Arabic as the prestigious variety, I will stick to the term Standard Arabic to include CA and MSA, since Egyptians do not make the distinction between both. I will also start with the assumption that Cairene Arabic, as spoken in some quarters of Cairo, is the prestigious variety used in Egypt. This is not to deny the real diversity of Egyptian society and linguistic practice. However, while there are diverse dialects within Egypt, as well as distinct ethnic and linguistic communities (especially outside urban areas; these include the Bedouin and Nubians), public discourse attempts to portray a unified picture of Egypt as a primarily urban civilization that emerged from the clustering of people in the cities in ancient times (this is the historical narrative that is put forward in school textbooks, among other media). It can be shown that Cairene Egyptian Arabic is the variety that is primarily used to speak about and represent "the Egyptian"; diversity is generally downplayed and undermined, while the "distinct" character of Egypt as an ancient, immutable entity—one that contains one ethnic group unified by different shared characteristics—is always in the foreground.

All this stands in contrast with linguistic realities. While one can argue that Egypt has less ethnic and linguistic diversity than some other countries in the region and that it is a centralized state built around cities rather than villages or provinces, there are still different dialects within Egypt that may carry their own covert prestige (see Trudgill (1972) for an explanation of this concept), especially in the south of Egypt. These regional dialects have deep historical roots and go back to patterns of population movement and settlement. For a more detailed map of dialects in Egypt and a historical perspective of their evolution, see Behnstedt and Woidich (1985).

I.3.1.4 Identity and code-switching in Egypt

So far, studies on diglossic switching as part of code-switching in Egypt have not directly correlated identity and code-choice using the linguistic tools adopted in this work. There are no studies that adopt the theories of stance or subject positions directly to code-switching in Egypt. There are also no studies that use orders of indexicality to explain cases of code-switching and code-choice in the Arab world. In addition, there are no studies that adopt an interdisciplinary framework such as the one adopted in this work, which regards language as a resource, access to which is unequal and negotiated. However, there are a number of studies that have indirectly alluded to the speaker's role in code-switching between SA and ECA. Some of these studies are mentioned chronologically below.

There have been a number of studies that have attempted to explain switching between ECA and SA in Egypt, whether in written or oral performance. Holes (1993) examines the relationship between language form and function in Nasser's political speeches. He attempts to explain cases in which Nasser switches between ECA and SA. Holes detects that there can be an element of conscious choice in using one code rather than another. In general, "[s]peakers are free to move up and down it [the stylistic spectrum] in accordance with what they perceive to be the moment-by-moment requirements for appropriate language use" (1993: 15). He stresses the role of the speaker by claiming that speakers always have "intentions" and "strategies," and these two factors influence their language choices at both the micro and macro levels. In a similar vein, Mazraani (1997) examines language variation in relation to three political figures in Egypt, Libya, and Iraq and how these three political leaders use language variation as a "rhetorical strategy" (1997: 25).

Mejdell (1996) examines stylistic variations in spoken Arabic with reference to recordings of the Egyptian novelist Naguib Mahfouz talking about his life, trying to explain the kinds of processes that motivate stylistic choices by matching certain discourse functions with the use of one variety rather than another. She comes to the same conclusions suggested by Holes (1993): that people often switch from SA to ECA when giving examples, explaining, rephrasing, or commenting on a previous statement in SA. She also alludes to the fact that code-choice is related to the way in which one perceives oneself, as well as to the way in which one perceives others. In a later article (Mejdell 1999), she studies the interaction between SA and ECA in the spoken performance of Egyptian academics and writers "in settings where community norms require a mode of speaking that is more formal" (1999: 228). Mejdell suggests that code-choice should be examined in relation to the speaker's change of role, vis-à-vis her or his audience (1999: 231). Mejdell concludes that she considers "the access to both varieties [SA and ECA], with the wide span of cultural and social connotations attached to them, a rich stylistic resource for speakers to use creatively" (1999: 227; see also Mejdell 2006. Note that there is no determinism here: speakers can choose how they speak, though within socially prescribed limits). Bassiouney (2006) also applied theories of code-switching including markedness theory to different forms of monologues, which include political speeches, mosque sermons, and university lectures.

In all of the studies above, identity has been referenced indirectly, but not in relation to the stance-taking process and not in direct relation to indexes. There is no study to date that does so. This book takes on this task.

I.3.2 Public discourse

This book will concentrate on data drawn from public discourse, since, as Wodak (1999: 8) contends: "Discourse constitutes social practice and is at the same time constituted by it."

Identity construction is an ongoing process; for example, in order for us to understand and analyze the way that language was employed at the time of the January 25 Revolution of 2011, we have to start as early as the beginning of the twentieth century and consider how the development of national identity and language ideology and attitudes took shape and were influenced by the relationship of Egyptians towards "the other," whether that "other" be a colonial power or a powerful neighbor-state.

Before discussing the nature of the data, I will first define public discourse.

Johnstone (2010: 36) defines discourse as follows:

> Discourse is a continual process of mutual coordination in making sense of the world; "languages" "grammars" and "identities" emerge in the course of this process, as humans' reflexivity—our ability to see what people do as an illustration of how to do it, and to arrange things in ways that encourage others to attend to these illustrations—links together sets of actions, linguistic and otherwise, into registers of conduct.

Johnstone emphasizes the fact that discourse is not just related to meaning, but to society at large, and that language is a product of the process of humans attempting to coordinate their existence in relation to actions, communities, and other individuals. Language is related directly to habits, both behavioral and linguistic.

Public discourse, on the other hand, refers to media discourse, educational discourse, political discourse, and scholarly discourse (Van Dijk 2008). Media discourse, which, in my opinion, is the main component in public discourse, refers to the organizations that produce communication devices, such as the press, cinema, broadcasting, publishing, and so on. Note that the term "media" is also used to denote the cultural and material products of these organizations and entities, such as the "forms and genres" of news and soap operas, for example, which then take the forms of newspapers, paperback books, films, tapes, discs, and so on (Lister et al. 2003: 12; Thompson 1995: 23–5).

In general terms, as Androutsopoulos (2007: 215) posits, "rather than always speaking in their 'own voice,' media performers use language to stylize an array of social identities, relying for this purpose on the cultural and sociolinguistic knowledge they assume to share with their audience" (see also Coupland 2001). According to Androutsopoulos (2007: 215), the identities constructed and assumed by media performers may be claimed by the performers themselves and also projected to their audience. It may also be "ascribed to social types in the bilingual community." That is, it may reflect a social stereotype prevalent within a particular community.

According to Lister et al. (2003), there are now new patterns of organization and production of media, such as computer-mediated communication: e-mail, chat rooms, and blogs. These new forms are commonly called "new media." The main characteristic of new media is its availability to everyone, with little or no ownership regulations or censorship. According to Eickelman and Anderson (2003: 2), new media "feeds into new senses of a public space that is discursive, performative, and participative, and not confined to formal institutions recognized by state authorities." This may explain why Lister speaks of media as "a fully social institution" (2003: 12).

In addition, a main component of public discourse is institutional discourse. Institutions are usually associated with physical buildings, such as hospitals, schools, and courts. Institutions are directly connected to powerful groups and mainly serve their interests (Agar 1985). They also produce binary roles, such as the role of the expert, who is the institutional representative and has authority, and the non-expert (client), who must accommodate and listen to institutional norms. Institutional public discourse that is relevant to this book is educational discourse, primarily textbooks, which are the main vehicle of conditioning and indoctrinating minds. Van Dijk claims that:

> like the mass media, educational discourse derives its power from its enormous scope. Unlike most other types of texts, textbooks are obligatory reading for many people, which is a second major condition of their power [. . .] The knowledge and attitudes expressed and conveyed by such learning materials, again, reflect a dominant consensus, if not the interests of the most powerful groups and institutions of societies. (Van Dijk 2008: 61–2)

However, public discourse is a process that is interactional, rather than binary. A community adds to public discourse as much as it is influenced by it. It is noteworthy, however, that as Heller (2007: 341–2) posits, at a time when we are "imagining other, more complicated and fluid ways of organizing ourselves . . . both language and identity are being commodified, often separately." This commodification of identity in public discourse is essential to this work, as well as in more general terms, since this commodification at times highlights preconceived perceptions, while at others creates them. As Coupland (2007: 118) argues, public discourse is loaded with ideological concepts, socio-cultural frames, and stereotypes. He posits that:

> the mass media certainly play an important role in reshaping the sociolinguistic environment, which is of course a matter of normalized attitudes and ideological meanings for language as well as a matter of how language forms and varieties themselves are distributed. (2007: 185)

Public discourse is an outcome of a mutual benefit relation between producers and consumers.

In this section, I have shed light on different types and genres of public discourse. It is important to know that in general public discourse, the seemingly simplistic or conversely sophisticated mirror attitudes and ideologies within a specific community, whether large or small. Audience plays a vital role in public discourse and the shared concepts and perceptions between audience and producers are essential for the success of public discourse (see also Bell 1984).

The question posed by Spitulnik (2009) is echoed throughout this work, which is basically: how can we speak of a homogenous speech community across the nation-state, where there may be millions of people who do not know each other and may not even all speak the same language? The answer lies to some extent in public discourse and, in the case of Spitulnik, specifically in mass media. When discussing the relation between speech community and mass media, Spitulnik (2009) argues the following (2009: 95):

> The repeating, recycling, and recontextualizing of media discourse is an important component in the formation of community in a kind of subterranean way, because it establishes an indirect connectivity or intertextuality across media consumers and across instances of media consumption. Returning to the earlier discussion about speech communities, then, this indicates that even for large scale societies, it is possible to speak of a density of communication and frequency of interaction in a lateral sense.

Spitulnik contends that a speech community is usually described by three features: density of communication, frequency of interaction, and shared linguistic knowledge. However, according to Spitulnik, these three features can be realized through mass media. For example, density of communication can be indirectly achieved through large-scale exposure to radio drama or soap opera. Frequency of interaction can also be indirectly achieved through the frequent and dense consumption of mass media, rather than direct face-to-face interactions. Finally, shared linguistic knowledge can be achieved by media institutions that provide "common linguistic reference points" (Spitulnik 2009: 94–5). Any speech community, whether imagined or real, requires "some experience of belonging." Linguistic practices can then create possibilities "for shared identities to be imagined" (Spitulnik 2009: 95). This connection between an imagined coherent speech community and public discourse that relates directly to identity is pertinent in this work.

I.3.3 *Choice and nature of data*

The relevance of the data analyzed was drawn from how this data is related directly to identity construction and how this identity construction is related directly to language form and content.

This book does not always provide a quantitative study, but rather focuses on producing a qualitative study of identity and language in Egyptian public discourse. As will be clear in the discussion of identity in Chapter 1, identity, as Blommaert (2005: 203–4) contends, is context dependent and involves "a semiotic process of representation," which includes symbols, narratives, textual genres, national categories, and socially constructed categories, such as age, gender, and profession. It is more appropriate for this work to include different forms and genres of public discourse that all have in common—at least, to some extent—a similar and at times stereotypical conception of an Egyptian identity.

What the data has in common is that Egyptian identity is discussed explicitly or implicitly. The analysis will concentrate on issues pertaining to the Egyptian personality, identity, and portrayals of "Egyptianness" throughout the twentieth and twenty-first centuries.

While with blogs I choose the most recent ones, with songs and novels I choose the most dominant and relevant ones from the beginning of the twentieth century through to the present. The reason for this is that blogs and novels are different forms of public discourse and so consequently have a different lasting effect on the audience. While I analyze a talk show that took place during the revolution and which aimed to cast doubt on the identity of the protestors in Tahrir Square, for example, I need to sometimes go back approximately 100 years to examine a song composed by Sayyid Darwīsh (1921), so as to show that the issues relevant to Darwīsh are still resonating in the same square where the protests took place in January 2011.

Therefore, I draw upon data from patriotic songs, novels, books, newspaper articles, films, blogs, talk shows, and poetry to show how language is used as "a set of ideologically-defined resources and practices" (Wodak 1999: 8).

While newspapers, for example, have been analyzed before as an essential form of public discourse (although not in Egypt as related to identity construction), there are fewer studies on films, blogs, novels, and patriotic songs as related to identity construction, although they are not less important.

In this book, I concentrate on specific forms of public discourse (mostly oral, for reasons mentioned below), but also written. Patriotic songs and films are the main form of oral data analyzed in detail throughout this work (Chapters 3 and 4). The main form of written data discussed in detail is novels that deal with themes of identity (Chapter 5) and also books in which language and identity are discussed together. Newspaper articles in which language and identity are discussed will also be mentioned and analyzed, especially in Chapters 2, 3, and 6. Talk shows and caricatures are discussed in Chapters 3 and 6, respectively. Poetry is discussed in Chapter 6.

Textbooks and blogs are referenced in order to give evidence at times and add new dimensions at others, but they are not analyzed systematically in this work.

It is noteworthy that the data analyzed presents mainstream public discourse to a great extent, rather than fringe or more extreme discourse, unless fringe discourse is used to contrast with mainstream discourse.

All the data in this work is selected with several factors in mind:

- Frequency: for example, how frequently the movies in question are broadcast on TV.
- Saliency: this refers to how effective or relevant this data is for Egyptians. For example, a song that is usually sung in school assemblies is salient.
- Wide scope of distribution: how available and popular the data is. A song that is available on YouTube or an article that is available and can be read by anyone for free has a wide scope of distribution.

The data covers up to the year 2013. It is essential to consider that changes to public discourse are slow, rather than sudden. This is because public discourse depends on intrinsic shared conceptions and assumptions for its appeal and maintenance over time.

In the next couple of paragraphs, I will highlight some of the reasons I decided to concentrate on these genres of public discourse.

I.3.3.1 Egyptian oral culture: films, patriotic songs, poetry

One of the main media genres analyzed in this book is the performance genre, including comedy movies, television shows, and popular music. This is because linguistically in the performance genre, speech, whether bilingual or monolingual, is subject to planning and editing (Androutsopoulos 2007: 212). In these genres, construction of identity is intentional and premeditated. Linguistic resources, including code-choice and code-switching, are built not just on linguistic realities, but on ideologies and attitudes.

Egyptian nationalism during the beginning of the twentieth century was, to a great extent, a product of oral media (see Fahmy 2011). Egyptian oral culture has always played a pivotal role in the formation of Egyptian identity in general. It is a normal part of children's learning processes in Egypt to memorize quotes from movies, slogans from patriotic songs, or excerpts of religious texts. Oral culture in the Arab world, whether in the modern or pre-Islamic world, has always been a powerful tool of communication. Poetry in the Arab world (again, whether in the standard language or the colloquial) was powerful enough that it could lead its poet to either death or perpetual fame (Holes 2011). Egypt is no exception (see Abu-Lughod 2002; Armbrust 1996). In Egypt, not just poetry, but films, songs, and other forms of oral media have always, for Egyptians, formed the crux of self-perception (Fahmy 2011). Oral media has the task of positioning the Egyptian within Egypt, on the one hand, and within the wider context of the world, on the other. As far as I know, there has not been a linguistic study on the effect of oral media on the Egyptian perception of self so far. This book attempts to fill this void.

To give but an example, Egyptian cinema started producing films with unique Egyptian traits and themes as early as 1917 (Shafik 2007). In 1939, Egyptians produced twelve films, while in 1986 Egyptians produced ninety-two films. Egyptian films have helped spread ECA throughout the Arab world as a semi-standard variety, understood by a vast number of Arabs. Film production, although a commercial endeavor, was also a powerful cultural tool that helped mold Egyptian ideologies and perceptions (see Gordon 2002; Armbrust 1996).

Patriotic songs are part of the performance genre of media (see Androutsopoulos 2007 (above)); as such, they have always formed an important role in emphasizing a strong sense of Egyptianness. There is usually a clear pattern of usage of sociolinguistic variables in patriotic songs. What is also interesting in Egyptian patriotic songs is that a great number of them are rendered in ECA. A number of recent Egyptian patriotic songs rendered in ECA are performed by non-Egyptians: *ʔumm id-dunya:* ("The mother of the world") is performed by Laṭīfah, a Tunisian female singer; *ʕaẓi:ma ya: maṣr* ("Egypt, you are great") is performed by Wadīʿ al-Ṣāfī, a Lebanese male singer; and, finally, *ana: maṣri:* ("I am Egyptian") is performed by Nānsī ʿAjram, another female Lebanese singer. What also makes patriotic songs significant for a study of language and identity is the fact that within the two main patriotic songs that place Egypt in an Arab context and in which the Arab world is called upon by singers from all over the Arab world, ECA is dominant (I refer here to *al-waṭan il-akbar* ("My greater homeland") and *il-ḥilm il-ʕarabi:* ("The Arab dream")). During the Egyptian Revolution—which was a relatively peaceful one—songs were used as a weapon to inspire individuals to revolt, but also to send a challenge to the pro-Mubarak group. The influence of songs both during and after the Revolution was mentioned on the BBC website in reference to the Palestinian singer Reem Kelani (2012). The website reads:[14]

> Palestinian singer Reem Kelani has a unique perspective on the tumultuous events in Egypt in early 2011—while in Cairo to research the music of Sayyid Darwīsh (1892–1923), she found herself watching history unfold. Caught up in the revolution, she saw Darwīsh's music taking on a new and urgent topicality, alongside the creations of contemporary songwriters [. . .] Reem recorded protestors raising their voices against Mubarak, by singing Darwīsh's songs—not only those dealing with nationalism and social justice: even love songs by Darwīsh moved protestors during the days of mass protest [. . .] The overwhelming reality was of a host of unknown and unsung singing heroes who led those around them into a musical formulation of pent-up political frustration.

From Kelani's perspective, songs have many connotations. They were reflecting the frustrations, strength, and identity more generally. As mentioned before, Egypt is not the only Arab country with a strong oral culture. Oral culture is dominant throughout the Arab world. To give an example of studies that examined code-switching in songs, Bentahila and Davies (2002) analyzed Algerian *Rai* music lyrics. They concluded that when there is switching between Arabic and French in these songs, Arabic was the matrix code. They also argued that the pattern of code-switching in these songs resembles code-mixing in an urban Algerian community. However, Bentahila and Davies did not analyze patriotic songs or *Rai* music from an identity perspective. This book takes a different approach. To my knowledge, this is the first book that studies patriotic songs and relates them directly to language and identity.

I.3.3.2 Written media: books, newspapers, novels, caricatures

This book will provide examples from newspapers, books, and also novels. While the importance of books and newspaper articles that deal with language and identity may be obvious for this work and has been analyzed before (Suleiman 2003; Bassiouney 2009), novels that deal with issues of identity have not been analyzed before from such a linguistic perspective. I will concentrate in this section on the importance of narration in identity work.

Narration can be an excellent vehicle for constructing, as well as reflecting, identity or at least a facet of it. As Georgakopoulou puts it: "narratives are seen as a privileged mode for self-construction and a unique point of entry into trans-situational features of the self and identity as those emerge in a person's ongoing life story" (Georgakopoulou

2006: 83). As a "unit of discourse" (cf. Schiffrin 1984), narratives can yield surprising insights into the way that individuals perceive themselves in relation to their community and other communities. Stories in general are a mode of defining ourselves and our attitudes and conceptions of reality (cf. Bastos and Oliveira 2006; see also De Fina and Georgakopoulou 2012). Chapter 5 tackles a number of novels that deal directly with the modern Egyptian identity within different facets of its modern history.

Books in which the main theme is Egyptian personality or identity are also relevant. Newspaper articles that relate language to identity are mentioned as well. This genre of data will highlight the salient differences between oral and written discourse in Egypt.

Caricatures and posters are a novel kind of data that are not frequently analyzed; the ones chosen for inclusion in this book, mainly mentioned within Chapter 3, are sourced from online resources. This brings us to the importance of online data.

I.3.3.3 Online media: general importance

While this book does not concentrate only on online media, it must be mentioned in this introduction that online media played a vital role in the Egyptian sense of identity during the January 25 Revolution of 2011. What differentiates online media from other forms of media is the ability to spontaneously interact and express opinions. As Greg Myers contends: "online media users produce as well as consume the content" (2010: 264).

Blogs fit this category perfectly, since, as Greg Myers argues, anyone with access to the internet can read a blog, write a blog, and post comments on a blog (see Fairclough 2000; Wright 2004). The Egyptian Revolution has been called a media revolution first and foremost; blogs, Facebook pages, and internet access were one of the main components of its success. The joke goes that when two drunkards were sitting together on the floor in Cairo, one suddenly asked the other: "What is Facebook?" The other replied: "It is something they use to get rid of presidents with."

The impact of online media is underscored in this joke and the danger that wide access to this form of communication poses on autocratic political regimes is even more apparent.[15] In fact, Mills posits that much of our understanding of "democratic processes" is dependent on the concept of "public or publics":

> Public communications are so organized that there is a chance immediately and effectively to answer back any opinion expressed in public. Opinion formed by such discussion readily finds an outlet in effective action, even against—if necessary—the prevailing system of authority. And authoritative institutions do not penetrate the public, which is more or less autonomous in its operations. (Mills 1956: 303–4)

I.4 Chapter outline

In addition to the introduction, this work has six chapters and a conclusion. Chapter 1 provides the necessary theoretical background and also sets the framework of data analysis. The term "identity," especially Egyptian identity in relation to public discourse, will be defined and explained. The chapter will then outline the adopted approach, which perceives language as both a social process and social practice (Heller 2007). This approach will then be expanded and developed to encompass theoretical methods of analyzing discourse that include positioning theory, stance, and indexicality. In order to provide a systematic mode of analysis, I will rely on what I term "linguistic resources." These resources are then divided into structural resources and discourse resources. These resources will be explained and exemplified. Code-switching and code-choice, as linguistic resources, are discussed in relation to orders of indexicality. The chapter will argue that language, for the purpose of this work, is considered both as a social variable and a resource.

Chapter 2 provides the necessary background on the formation of the modern Egyptian identity during the twentieth century. The relationship between language and identity will also be highlighted throughout. Crucial concepts that directly influence the associations of different codes will also be discussed, including nationalism, language policy, language ideology, and language attitudes. Poetry and songs will be referenced.

Chapter 3 attempts to analyze and discuss associations or indexes of codes in relation to language ideology and language attitude in Egypt, with reference to concrete examples from public discourse, including talk shows, films, newspaper articles, and books. Rather than depend on attitude surveys that are, at times, methodologically flawed and non-exhaustive, I depend on examples from public discourse, such as the attitude towards Arabic teachers in Egyptian films. These data will help explain what I refer to as "direct" and "indirect" indexes, as well as the process of indexical layering that takes place during "talk about language." Although this is not an attempt to replace attitude surveys, it is an attempt to offer a perhaps more subtle and fresh look at orders of indexicality and diglossia. This new look at language as referenced in oral and written discourse in Egypt aims to provide a more thorough understanding of language indexes in Egyptian public discourse. As with other chapters, language will be regarded as "fundamentally a social phenomenon" (Heller 2007), as part of a wider frame of historical, political, and social events, and essentially related to a process of perpetual patterning of ideologies, both linguistic and otherwise.

Chapter 4 discusses the social independent variables used in Egyptian public discourse to demarcate a cohesive and unique "Egyptian identity."

Linguistic resources outlined in Chapter 1 will be used to analyze data in this chapter, as well as in the next two chapters. Data used in this classification process includes mainly patriotic songs, but also films, textbooks, blogs, online newspaper articles, as well as print newspaper articles. In this chapter, language will also be discussed as an independent social variable—a classification category. Variables analyzed include ethnicity, historicity, locality, character traits, religion, the notion of "Arabness," and language. It will be argued in this chapter that, as a consequence of the employment of these linguistic resources in public discourse, especially patriotic songs, Egyptians are depicted as forming a large, coherent community.

Chapter 5 continues the discussion of social variables that elucidate Egyptian identity. However, this chapter will depend on a different kind of data: novels. There are four novels analyzed in detail: *Qindīl Umm Hāshim* ("The saint's lamp") (1944), *al-Ḥubb fī al-manfá* ("Love in exile") (1995), *Awrāq al-narjis* ("The leaves of Narcissus") (2001), and *Kitāb al-rin* ("The book of rinn") (2008).

The chapter will show how authors employ linguistic resources to highlight social variables attributed to Egyptian identity. These social variables include historicity, ethnicity, religion, and locality. The chapter will then focus on language as a social variable and highlight discussions of language ideologies in novels. However, the main contributions of this chapter are in showing how authors use code-choice and code-switching in dialogue within novels to both appeal to ideologies and reflect identity. The concept of orders of indexicality will be used to explain the use of code-switching in dialogue in novels.

Chapter 6 revolves around one theme: the contestation of identity before, during, and after the January 25 Revolution of 2011. As the last chapter in this book, it will act as a bridge, bringing together the layers and structures of the intricate relationship between identity and language, relating the micro and macro levels of analysis, the indexes and resources. Language as a classification category will be discussed both before and after the Revolution, and language as a resource will also be analyzed. Data in this chapter includes newspaper articles, television programs, films, and poetry. The concepts of access and resources, as well as the concept of linguistic unrest will be explained and exemplified. This acts as a concluding chapter, followed directly by the general conclusion, laying the foundation for future research and answering questions asked at the beginning of this book, as well as posing future ones.

The book will end with a general conclusion that roughly recaps all discussions and issues mentioned throughout, enunciating the contributions of this work and the framework proposed. Access to resources as a framework straddles many of the theories discussed.

I.5 Contributions of this book

This book will fill a gap in the field. To my knowledge, this is the first book that relates Egyptian identity to language. It draws upon new kinds of data and utilizes recent sociolinguistic theories to explain this data and relate it to a wider perception of a collective identity. It is also, to my knowledge, the first book that draws on such a varied range of public discourse. It deals with a crucial diglossic community that has undergone political, economic, historical, and anthropological changes during the twentieth and twenty-first centuries.

While situating identity in time and space is not a new phenomenon (cf. Herman 2010), analyzing how this is done linguistically within media, such as blogs, films, and patriotic songs, is indeed new. The book will further our understanding of the interaction between identity and language in general and will explain the enormous role played by the media in highlighting specific aspects of identity and undermining others at different times and in different circumstances. The book aims to become a model for other studies in other parts of the Arab world and the world at large. Each collective identity is unique in its own way and each nation has its way of foregrounding its uniqueness. It is almost impossible for an outsider to realize and understand this subtle yet obvious relationship between language and identity within a specific community. This book attempts to do so.

There is an urgent need for studies that relate identity to language and offer a more comprehensive and eclectic view of the relationship between language as a symbol, impregnated with ideological indexes, and the formation of a nation and or a nation-state, which feeds into identity construction. Suleiman (2011: 39) expresses this need when he posits that:

> Having read widely around the topic of the rise and progress of Arab nationalism, I was struck by how many times scholars have pointed to the importance of the Arabic language in nation building; but I was struck even more by the absence of any sustained study that explains the ways in which Arabic was used in this respect. The same is true of the role of Arabic in articulating political and social conflict in society or of the role of Arabic literature, especially poetry, in the formation of national consciousness.

Suleiman also focuses on the significance of studying the relationship between language and identity, especially in conflicts between different groups (2011: 22).

This study will attempt to do just that: to relate ideology to language and language to identity in a particular nation-state, Egypt. I propose to do this by employing sociolinguistic theories and, in the process, test these theories, modify them, and develop them. This process will involve a rigorous methodological framework that incorporates different concepts and draws upon linguistic resources in order to make the research watertight, rather than over-interpretive or subjective.

One of the main arguments of this work is that different theories of code-switching, of stance-taking as a process, or of indexicality can be understood and analyzed together within the framework of access and resources. That is, this book offers a different theoretical framework, in which theories related to identity and language can all be incorporated and articulated in a clearer fashion.

The book also offers a novel approach of studying code-switching in which codes are analyzed as resources and individuals have different levels of access to these resources. Individuals in a community may also perceive each other as sharing access to resources or not sharing access to resources. Sharing the associations of codes as resources is also essential for a community. This new perspective can explain cases of diglossic switching as part of code-switching in the data discussed in this work. The concept of orders of indexicality will be employed to provide a clearer framework of the study of diglossia in Egypt and beyond.

From a different perspective, while Arab countries are almost always lumped together, especially by outside media, into one entity called "The Arab World," this book will show that Arab countries are distinct, not just in a historical and political sense, but more importantly in the way that they perceive themselves in relation to others. As Suleiman posits, "nation-state identities have become entrenched in the Arabic speaking world" (Suleiman 2011: 51). This is true to a great extent, but also the perception of the Arab nation is called upon by public discourse at different historical stages in Egypt as part of the Arab world, as will be clear in this book.

Note that the book concentrates on Egypt, but offers examples from other parts of the world, particularly the Arab world. The aim of the work is to set the reader thinking about general issues of identity. At the culmination of this book, the reader should compare the situation in Egypt to that of his or her own country—that is, to position his or her identity in a wider context in relation to access to resources, both linguistic and otherwise.

I.6 Readers of this book

This book aims to adopt an interdisciplinary approach in analyzing the relationship between language and identity in Egypt. Although the book resorts to sociolinguistic and anthropological theories, it does so assuming no prior knowledge of the field. That is to say, the book does not assume prior knowledge of Arabic or linguistics. This will make the book accessible to a wider audience. Having said that, the book still maintains a rigorous theoretical approach to the topics discussed and data analyzed and will provide a modified framework of analysis, in which identity in public discourse is situated in a social–linguistic context. Thus, it will be of interest to sociolinguists specifically.

It should also be of interest to researchers in fields ranging from Arabic studies, linguistics, anthropology, political science, history, psychology, media, and communication.

Because of its focus on the intersection of language and identity, of private and public discourse, it will provide unique material and valuable analysis to the general public with a general interest in issues of identity, language, and culture.

I.7 Limitations of this work

Public discourse assumes that "we all agree on who we are," which is, indeed, not true. It assumes unanimity where it does not exist. However, this assumption by public discourse in Egypt is neither unexpected nor exclusive to Egypt. Fridland, when studying African-American speakers, also notices the same phenomenon, not just in public discourse, but also in research about African-Americans. She posits (2003: 6):

> The interpretation of such research, however, often assumes a unanimity among African American communities, which may obscure the fact that there are competing norms within the community which demonstrate different levels of integration and contrast within the larger community.

As Fought (2006: 148) contends, not all members of an ethnic community "behave" in the same way. Thus, it is almost impossible to expect that all members of a whole country like Egypt act in completely similar ways.

The media and public discourse more generally are supposed to provide a clear answer to a complicated question. Media has to fix an entity that is in a perpetual state of flux: identity. A collective public identity in Egypt provides a safety haven; it provides psychological stability for an ever-changing social world and an economically fluctuating state. What kept the country together for a long time may be, as Goldschmidt (2008) puts it, the loyalty to Egypt and Egyptians, rather than to a political system that was perceived by many as corrupt or archaic.

Loyalty to the "country" as such is related to how we define ourselves in relation to this entity that we call the "homeland." The definition is not always positive, but it is mostly nostalgic and refers to "the Egyptian" past and present.[16]

Notes

1. Al-Ghīṭānī in his most recent, award-winning novel *Kitāb al-rinn*—a semi-autobiography—explains how he feels detached from all his surroundings, including his immediate family. It is only with an ancient Egyptian statue that he feels any affinity. He stares at the statue, claiming that he is a close friend and relative, and relating his past to his present and future. This complete identification with a three thousand-year-old statue is of great significance.
2. Notable exceptions are the two studies by Haeri (1997; 2003); the former uses social class as a variable to analyze Egyptian society and the latter is about Egyptians' attitudes towards SA and ECA. Thus, both are markedly different in focus from the proposed study. Neither study relates language directly to identity. In addition, neither study uses the kind of data used in this book.
3. The Tunisian pop singer Laṭīfah produced a song called "The mother of the world." Of course, she sang the song in ECA. More recently, the metaphor has been challenged by Arab intellectuals. A Lebanese intellectual called Egypt "the mother of the world and the widow of cities." This postulation caused anger among Egyptian intellectuals (see ʿAbd al-Salām 2008).
4. The source for the following set of facts is the *CIA World Factbook* (unless otherwise stated), https://www.cia.gov/library/publications/the-world-factbook/geos/eg.html, accessed 14 August 2013.
5. The native monophysite Church of Egypt; see "Coptic Orthodox Church of Alexandria." In *Encyclopedia Britannica Online Academic Edition*. Online. http://www.britannica.com/EBchecked/topic/136928/Coptic-Orthodox-Church-of-Alexandria, accessed 7 June 2013.
6. See David Wilmsen and Manfred Woidich. "Egypt." In *Encyclopedia of Arabic Language and Linguistics*, ed. by Lutz Edzard and Rudolf de Jong. Brill Online 2013. http://referenceworks.brillonline.com/entries/encyclopedia-of-arabic-language-and-linguistics/egypt-COM_vol2_0001, accessed 6 May 2012.
7. The Fatimid Caliph al-Ḥākim bi-Amr Allāh is said to have threatened to cut off the tongue of Egyptian mothers who spoke to their children in Coptic. The repressive measures taken by this ruler, together with other factors, is said to have caused the quick death of Coptic. See "Coptic Language, Spoken." In *The Coptic Encyclopedia, Vol. 2*, ed. by Karen J. Torjesen and Gawdat Gabra: 604a–607a. Claremont, CA: Claremont Graduate University. Online. http://ccdl.libraries.claremont.edu/cdm/ref/collection/cce/id/520, accessed 6 June 2012. Note that that the author of this particular page writes in SA. As a linguist, one realizes that drastic measures do not have to be resorted to in order for language death to occur. Political and economic power associated with a language is sufficient to facilitate its spread, even if it means the death of other languages.

8. Language planning refers to the efforts to manage, modify, or influence the habitual practice of individuals as part of a community. There are two kinds of language planning: status planning and corpus planning. Status planning refers to the process of selecting a language or variety for use. Corpus planning is the process by which the language or variety selected is codified—that is, choices are made to standardize spelling, grammar, lexicon, and so on.
9. It is important to mention at this stage that native speakers and constitutions in Arab countries do not specify what "Arabic" refers to. However, it usually refers to Modern Standard Arabic. Native speakers also do not make a distinction between Modern Standard Arabic and Classical Arabic. For them, there is only one kind of Standard Arabic, which is called "*fuṣha:.*"
10. Note that this H and L labelling reflects, first, language attitudes among users and, second, the superposed nature of the H. Likewise, it is worth mentioning that sociolinguists may feel discomfort with these labels, since clear covert prestige attaches so strongly to the L and also since the L has sometimes been the target of attempts in Egypt and Lebanon among others to be considered the national variety. This issue of territorial nationalism as opposed to pan-Arabism will be dealt with in detail in Chapter 4.
11. Fishman (2002) defines diglossia slightly differently from Ferguson. For him, a diglossic situation is one in which roles of both varieties are kept separate; there are clear group boundaries between both languages and varieties. The access to the H variety or language is usually restricted to an outsider. He gives the example of pre-World War I European elites who spoke French or another H language or variety, while the masses spoke a different and not necessarily related language or variety. In his definition, the H variety or language is a spoken standard, while in Arabic it is not the spoken variety of any country.
12. The question of how different the two varieties should be was perhaps not the main issue for Ferguson, who was more interested in the conditions that could give rise to diglossia in the first place.
13. After Ferguson's 1959 article on diglossia, Blanc (1960), Badawī (1973), and Meiseles (1980) thought proposing intermediate levels between H and L would give a more accurate description of the situation in the Arab world. Thus, they recognized that people shift between H and L, especially when speaking, but often do not shift the whole way, resulting in levels which are neither fully H nor fully L. For a comprehensive critique of these levels, see Bassiouney (2009). Another idea that sprung from Ferguson's definition of diglossia is that of Educated Spoken Arabic, as developed by Mitchell. Mitchell claims that "vernacular Arabic (meaning dialectal/colloquial Arabic) is never plain or unmixed but constantly subject to the influences of modern times" (Mitchell 1986: 9). According to him, Educated Spoken Arabic (ESA) is not a separate variety, but is "created" and "maintained" by

the interaction between the written language and the vernacular. For a more detailed critique of this idea, see Bassiouney (2009).

14. See http://www.bbc.co.uk/programmes/b019fxjf, accessed 14 August 2013.
15. Another joke that emerged during Mubarak's trial in September 2011 is the following:
    Judge: What do you say to the witnesses' testimony?
    Mubrak: I have no comment.
    Judge: Not even a "*like*"!?
16. Independent variables, such as gender, social class, and even age will not be discussed in detail in this work, since the work aims to examine the identity of "Egyptians"—a loose and yet inclusive term. There are a number of studies that concentrate on some of these variables; Haeri's (1996) study is a case in point.

CHAPTER

1

IDENTITY AND BEYOND: SETTING THE FRAMEWORK OF ANALYSIS

Zūzū: *"What would you say to someone who does not answer a question?"*
Professor: *"If it is a question with no answer, then there is no problem if you refuse to answer it."*
Zūzū: *"Well, why didn't you answer my question?"*
Professor: *"Because it is the most difficult question in the world. 'Who are you?' Do you actually know how to answer it yourself? And by the way, why do you ask me this question Miss Zūzū?"*
Zūzū: *"Because this is the main issue here. If someone comes to speak to me, I need to know who he is first in order to know why he said what he said. Once I know who you are, I will also know what you want."*
Professor: *"I just noticed that your Arabic pronunciation is very good."*

(*Khallī bālak min Zūzū*, "Take care of Zūzū,"
Dir. Ḥasan al-Imām, released in Egypt in 1972)

Zūzū is a young Egyptian female student who comes across as intelligent, ambitious, bold, and yet tormented by her shameful family background. Her mother is an old belly-dancer who lives in a lower-class Cairene alley. While forging a different identity for herself, she is also conflicted throughout between allegiance to her old one and struggling to maintain a respectful new one. The moment she lays eyes upon the professor who will be directing a play at her university, she is swept off her feet. In a discussion session in which students write questions for the professor to answer, she writes down the apparently simple question *"man anta?"* ("Who are you?") The professor refrains from answering. She follows him to his car and engages him in the conversation quoted above.

A simple love story for some, this film was released at a critical time in Egyptian history. Behind what seems like a romantic veneer, there are pressing issues that come to the fore. Therefore, it is essential to situate this film within its socio-political context. The film was released just months before the last war between Egypt and Israel, which broke out on October 6, 1973. On June 5, 1967, the Six Day War began between Egypt, Syria, and Jordan on one side and Israel on the other. While the Israeli troops were crossing into Sinai and the West Bank, the official radio station in Cairo was claiming victory, declaring that 198 Israeli warplanes had been shot down. On June 7, Jerusalem was captured from the Jordanians by Israel, and Jordan was forced to accept a ceasefire. On June 8, Egyptian radio was declaring total victory over Israel had been achieved and that the Egyptian Army would soon be in Tel Aviv, while Israel was occupying the whole of Sinai, the East Bank, and the Suez Canal (Haag 2005). The Six Day War, as it came to be called, is considered the worst defeat ever for modern Egypt, not just because Egypt lost Sinai, but also because of the disillusionment of Egyptians towards pan-Arabism and even in general terms towards Nasser's ideals and political ideology (Sayyid-Marsot 1985). The Six Day War of 1967 is reputed to have disfigured Egyptians' perception of self for a long time, especially because years earlier Egyptians were singing their glory, both past and present. It was within the first years of Sadat's regime that the public media attempted to reconstruct an Egyptian identity and tried to overcome the shame to move forward to a brighter future.[1]

The film *Take Care of Zūzū* is an example of this process. It is certainly not surprising that the script was written by Ṣalāḥ Jāhīn (1930–86)—one of the most famous poets of Egyptian colloquial Arabic in the second half of the twentieth century. Nor is it a coincidence that the movie, released towards the end of 1972, broke a record in box office returns.

Let us return to look at the excerpt in some detail and examine the issues it addresses. The professor finds it difficult to answer Zūzū's question, "Who are you?" Is he an Egyptian, a professor, a single man from an upper-class Egyptian family or the director of the theatre play? In the movie, both Zūzū and the professor are torn between a past that they try to suppress and a present that they still do not know. It is only at the end of the film that Zūzū reconciles both parts of her identity by acknowledging her past with its shame and moves forward by forging a new, more respectful, and dignified existence. It is also at the very end of the film that the professor himself succeeds in reconciling different parts of his identity—namely, his identity as a traditional upper-class Egyptian and his rebellious identity as a young man who seeks independence and defies conventions. Although only addressed to the professor in the movie, the question "who are you?" is equally pertinent to the audience. Zūzū and the professor are no different from other Egyptians at the time: they are re-evaluating their sense of self within their country's present socio-political context.

Zūzū is supposedly a symbol of the lost generation of the 1970s—the generation of the two wars. During this time, many Egyptians grappled with pressing questions of identity. The clear message of the film is that in one's search for self, one must leave behind the past with all its accompanying shame and defeat. However, perhaps the crucial point is also not to forget the shame, much as Zūzū attempts to forget the shame of her family's background. Instead, the film urges the audience to acknowledge the past and move forward, molding a stronger, capable identity in the process.

Indeed, at the end of the film, the professor declares "we are all Zūzū." The symbol is clear and it is spelled out for the audience. What is worth noting is that Zūzū moves from being cast as an individual with a specific identity, to being cast as a generic Egyptian with a specific identity, and eventually to being cast as an archetypal Egyptian who shares aspects of her identity with all fellow Egyptians. This common connection between Zūzū as a young female student, as an Egyptian, and as a symbol of all Egyptians is significant. It suggests that the media, through the form of film, was projecting a common Egyptian identity by posing the right questions and providing the answers.

The extract above sums up beautifully a great number of issues covered in this book. Zūzū is obviously aware of the significance of the answer to her question about identity. She postulates that identity is related to the whole process of communication and interaction between individuals and groups: "Once I know who you are, I will also know what you want." In short, the content of the professor's response will facilitate her communication with him. It will also situate him within a specific social community, complete with specific perceptions and overall motives.

Zūzū positions herself as the active participant in this interaction and openly declares her intentions, addressing the professor directly with the Arabic second person pronoun *inta* ("you"), rather than the more formal *ḥaḍritak* (lit. "your presence"), which is commonly used for superiors, similar to the French *vous*. The professor resists the position he is placed in by first making an evaluative statement and then asking two more questions—the first, a challenging, rhetorical one and the second, an inquiry:

> "Because it is the most difficult question in the world, 'who are you?' Do you actually know how to answer it yourself? And, by the way, why do you ask me this question, Miss Zūzū?"

The last inquiry towards Zūzū implies that she does not have the right to ask him that question. The professor's use of "Miss" when addressing her also implies that he wants to distance himself by asserting the position of the superior, formal professor. It also juxtaposes her usage of the second person pronoun when addressing him. Essentially, he does not accept the subject position she has adopted and renegotiates their positions, placing himself as the more powerful one of the pair. By ending the conversation with an evaluative statement about her Arabic pronunciation, he implies in the process that he is more powerful and has the right to make judgments about her. He also demonstrates his control of linguistic resources, as manifested in his access and knowledge of SA proper pronunciation. By doing so, he terminates the conversation after changing his footing from the person who was asked a question to the one evaluating the speaker (see Goffman 1981; for subject positioning, see Bamberg and Andrews 2004).

It is noteworthy, however, that the professor feels trapped by Zūzū's question and her persistence. Her question intends to force him to re-examine himself. When trapped, the professor places judgment on Zūzū's Arabic pronunciation. He uses his knowledge of Arabic to place himself in a better position. His judgment is not about the content of Zūzū's words, but the way in which she pronounces them. The professor argues that since her Arabic pronunciation is so good, she will make a good actress. He manipulates language here in two different ways: his apparent knowledge of Arabic gives him leverage over her. His reference to her good pronunciation steers the discussion away from the issue of identity to the form of Arabic being used and how it is pronounced. A discussion regarding language form is more obvious and safe for him at that point.

It is clear, however, that it is language content that he cannot deal with. The professor is, like many people in the twentieth and twenty-first centuries, one who may find the issue of identity too complicated or threatening. However, public discourse continues to provide probes to help people forge an almost too clear and demarcated identity. This does not imply that public discourse imposes an identity on individuals. It simply highlights and selects, as will be clear throughout this book, specific components of identity while ignoring others, exploiting language form and content in the process by laying claim to access to linguistic resources.

While this book will attempt to give a presentation of how identity is represented through language in public discourse in Egypt, questioning one's identity, like Zūzū, and alternatively not knowing how to define oneself, like the professor, is not a new phenomenon and is not exclusive to Egypt. This in itself makes the book appealing to a wider audience.

Some fifty years prior to this movie, Egyptian author and intellectual Yaḥyá Ḥaqqī (1905 –92) made the following postulation about the intellectual pioneers of the beginning of the twentieth century (Ḥaqqī 1989: 231):

> We were worried about two issues, the issue of independence and the pressing question of who we are. I was brought up in an environment in which its priority was to search for the self. This was the main issue of this generation [meaning the beginning of the 20th century generation]; we exerted our efforts and work to understand who we are. We were aware as a generation that we have to be proud of ourselves without being arrogant but also without falling into the feeling of inferiority that was imposed on us.

The feeling of inferiority that Ḥaqqī refers to is the work of several forces at play during this period, including the power of the colonizer, Britain, and its foreign elite living in Egypt; the discrimination against Egyptians, which manifested itself in the special courts for foreigners and the segregated clubs of the British, in which Egyptians were not allowed, to name a few examples. Defining and demarcating a collective Egyptian identity was, in a way, a defense mechanism and may still be so today. Depending on historical, political, and economic factors, Egyptians, at times, distinguish themselves from France, Britain, or Israel (referring here to the 1956 war), while at other times, they demarcate their identity from that of other Arabs, who may have more economic resources and a better standard of living, but a shorter history.

Yaḥyá Ḥaqqī, whose work will be discussed in greater detail in Chapter 6, exemplifies a case of a mixed identity, which is quite typical of Egyptians, both in his time and still today. His father was Egyptian, his mother was Turkish, and yet he identified as an Egyptian only. As is clear in the quote above, his issue was not whether he himself was Egyptian, but rather what it meant to be Egyptian. In other words, he was concerned with the collective identity of Egyptians against a colonizing power and a foreign elite (that may have included his own mother), as well as the discrimination against Egyptians. The flexibility of the term "Egyptian" and what it entails are the main concerns of this book.

A much more recent example occurred about thirty years after the release of the film mentioned above. On August 1, 2010—less than half a year before the Egyptian Revolution of 2011—a young Egyptian girl, Dāliyā ʿAlī, posed a number of complicated questions on her blog. All of her questions pertained to identity and were posed in a significant language form: a mixture of SA and ECA (ʿAlī 2010):

> Who are the Egyptians? I try to understand and may God help me. It is so confusing. Is it that whoever lives in Egypt is Egyptian? Or whoever rules Egypt? Or whoever passes by? Frankly speaking I am lost. Does Egypt speak Arabic so it is an Arab country? Or a Pharaonic one? [. . .]
>
> Is language change the criterion? In such case when exactly did we become Egyptians? And why? Is it that when we were ruled by the Arabs we have

> become Egyptians and when ruled by the Romans and Byzantines we were pharaohs? And when did we change from pharaohs to Egyptians? [. . .]
>
> To be honest, it is so muddled up that I wake up at night startled. I dream that I am hanging in the air not knowing who I am so I browse the internet and books perhaps I can find an answer that will just explain to me who I am. Is this really the problem of Egypt alone? [. . .] How about Iraqis? Are they Arabs, Muslims, Romans? Or . . . or . . . it seems they have the same problem? Or even lets go a bit far, how about Americans? Is America defined as the country of the red Indians? Or a country with ethnic, religious and national diversity . . . or what? . . .[2]

In her search for answers to these pressing questions, the female author of this blog examines public discourse in the form of books and the internet, as well as anticipating receiving comments from readers. She is obviously aware of the significance of language in defining an identity and yet not sure whether it is language that distinguishes Egyptians from others. She shows some uncertainty in relating language and identity by asking whether Egypt is automatically an Arab country because Egyptians speak Arabic. She also poses the question of whether being an Arab country is an exclusive term—that is, can Egypt be Arab and Pharaonic? The concept of authenticity per se will be discussed in Chapter 3 and again in Chapter 5. Dāliyā ʿAlī even refers to issues beyond the scope of this work, such as language shift and language death.

In the extract above, ʿAlī recalls the significance of historical factors in shaping identity, but also questions the legitimacy of attributing distant historical facts to modern Egyptians. She even suggests that this may not be an issue that is peculiar to Egypt, universalizing the issues of identity and its relation to language, history, culture, and people.

To use ʿAlī's metaphor, many of us are "hanging in the air," either trying to define who we are or increase our understanding of who we are. Modern day issues of identity are pressing and immediate.

This chapter will first outline the main approach of this work and then explain the nature of identity in public discourse, with special reference to Egyptian identity. The approach of language as a social process and social practice will also be examined in relation to other concepts that provide a useful framework for analyzing identity in public discourse, including positioning theory, stance, and indexicality. The linguistic resources that I examine in order to highlight the relation between language and identity will then be outlined with examples. Code-switching and code-choice, as essential markers of identity, are both discussed within the framework of indexicality. However, main theories of code-switching, such as social arena and footing will also be briefly referenced. The work will aim to develop a conceptual framework for the study of identity in which relevant theories are modified and connected.

1.1 The main approach of this work

The question that poses itself throughout this book is: what is the essential role of language in linking the social world to identity formation?

One of the main aims of the public construction of a unified Egyptian identity is to suggest that Egyptians, with all their diversity, form a coherent community; they share the same habits, history, locality, linguistic practices, and so on.

For example, some patriotic songs in Egypt depict a mix of opposite peoples (rich and poor, educated and illiterate, urban and rural, conservative and liberal, Christians and Muslims, and so on) as if they all share the same community in an ideal world: they eat the same food, gather in the same coffee houses, celebrate the same feasts, and share the same cultural heritage, oral traditions, movies, songs, moral traits, and history (descending from the same ancestors). While unrealistic, this concept of community is promoted in most or all public discourse and is indeed what sustains a nation or nation-state.

While it is difficult to separate form and function, the intricate relationship between form and function, processes and practices will be underscored throughout this book. This work will also attempt to study identity by resorting to different socio-pragmatic theories, including mainly indexicality, stance, and positioning.

This study proceeds from the standpoint that language constitutes the weft and warp of social processes and practices and that it cannot be studied in isolation from social phenomena. Like other social variables, such as ethnicity and locality, language can be used as a resource in social interactions between individuals.

To explain further, adopting Heller's (2007) approach to language, one can argue that linguistic form is continuously linked to linguistic ideology and practice—that is, to our view of the outside world in relation to the self. In particular, code-choice can be understood as a construction of social difference (Heller 2007: 3). In the case of this work, Heller's approach is broadened not just to include cases of code-switching, but all cases in which individuals use linguistic resources in public discourse. Whenever individuals use a linguistic resource, such as pronouns or tense markers, they do so in order to take a stance, while simultaneously appealing to linguistic ideologies and practices that reflect identity.

The main argument in this work is that language in relation to identity can be systematically analyzed and explained in terms of what I call "access and resources."

The concept of access to resources—a key concept within this work—is related to the perception of language as a resource. Throughout this book and in Chapter 6 in particular, issues of linguistic resources and access to these resources will be discussed. Access to resources—linguistic ones, more specifically—are related to issues of inclusion and exclusion. These are, in turn, related to indexes of different codes and manners of positioning oneself, as well as stance-taking as a process. The main aim of constructing a distinct Egyptian identity is to decide who is included and excluded from this large community called "Egyptian." Access to codes is a determining factor. This process of inclusion and exclusion that delineates an Egyptian identity is synchronized by meta-pragmatic factors and situated within a framework. However, this process can, in fact, be creative and bold in its use of linguistic resources, even though it relies on shared perceptions, ideologies, histories, and policies of a nation-state.

In Egyptian public discourse, language is also used as a resource, in order to project a unified national identity. This happens in two different ways: language is used as a classification category; and language is used as a means for individuals to adopt different stances in public discourse, which in turn entails indexes that are associated with an identity.

The clearest evidence of the immanent role of "access to resources" as a marker of identity is in the way that Egyptian public discourse utilizes language as a classification category, as a social variable that categorizes a community, similar to ethnicity, locality, or historical context. Code-switching and code-choice are used in this case. That is, in the projection of public discourse, the code that one chooses reflects directly on how one positions her or himself in relation to others: as an insider or an outsider, as an Egyptian or as a foreigner, as an Egyptian with no affiliation to Egypt or as a loyal citizen, as a typical man in the street or as an Egyptian who does not share the same characteristics that unify Egyptians, and so on. In this scheme, for example, if one speaks Arabic, one is classified as Egyptian. However, since Egypt is a diglossic community, classification can also be dependent on which code is used and whether speakers switch between codes. Therefore, if speakers code-switch between ECA and SA or ECA and English, for example, this often carries higher orders of indexes in public discourse.

The use of language as a classification category is predicated on attitudes and ideologies more than it is on linguistic realities (this will be shown in detail in Chapters 2 and 3). This means that one cannot fully comprehend the relation between code-choice, code-switching, and identity unless one fully comprehends the order of indexicality of linguistic resources, including choice and use of different codes. In order to be able to understand the indexes of these resources, one needs to analyze the political, social, and historical contexts and processes that pertain to a specific community and how these factors helped to foster indexes.

Access to linguistic resources is negotiated at times of conflict. Let me give an example. During the Egyptian Revolution of 2011, Egyptian identity was at the center of the struggle for power as the conflict between protestors and the pro-Mubarak group escalated. The conflict was, therefore, one about public discourse and the right to represent the real "authentic Egyptian" identity.

This is exemplified in the widely publicized incident on Egyptian state television that became known as the "Tāmir from Ghamrah" episode. On February 3, 2011, a man named Tāmir appeared on a call-in program aired on the official (and hence pro-Mubarak) Egyptian state television channel, claiming that he had first-hand information to offer about the protestors in Tahrir Square. He reported that all of the people in Tahrir Square were, in fact, foreigners, who did not care about Egypt. He proceeded to explain that he, as a "real" Egyptian, had discovered this fact through observing their language use: according to Tāmir, the protestors simply did not speak any Arabic, only English.

The ways in which Tāmir positions himself and evaluates the protestors are highly significant and will be discussed in detail in Chapter 6. For the moment, it will suffice to note that Tāmir used the linguistic code adopted by protestors (or, rather, the code that he claims protestors use) as evidence that they are non-Egyptian: the protestors lack access to "Arabic." In contrast, he, on the other hand, as an authentic Egyptian, has full access to Arabic. This, then, is an example of a direct correlation between identity and code-choice.

The second point is that language as a resource in public discourse allows individuals to position themselves by manipulating linguistic resources, such as presupposition, mood and modality, use of pronouns, and so on. In public discourse, once a speaker adopts a stance using these resources, they also index social variables that, in turn, index an Egyptian identity. Through stance-taking, individuals in public discourse select, highlight, and sieve different social variables that emerge in discourse and reflect directly on the perception of Egyptians as one people. The social variables used to demarcate the Egyptian identity are both abstract and concrete. They include language, ethnicity, religion, locality (River Nile, pyramids, and so on), shared historical glory, and, finally, moral values and character traits, such as those related to generosity, courage, kindness, patience, and work ethic. The question posed is: what are the linguistic resources employed by Egyptians to index these categories and variables and to use them in times of need, such as the January 25, 2011 Revolution?

This process is illustrated by the following example, taken from a song that was produced immediately after the Egyptian Revolution of 2011, in memory of the victims of the revolution: *b-aʃabbih ʕale:-k* ("I saw you before") by Muḥammad Fu'ād (2011). In this song (the lyrics of which are in ECA), the singer positions himself as a fellow Egyptian, who shares habits, skin color (ethnicity), and communal solidarity with the victims of the revolution. This positioning takes place through the usage of different linguistic resources, which include the use of second person singular pronouns, imperatives, and references to shared experiences and familiar places.

b-aʃabbih ʕale:-k
ma:lamḥ-ak min ma:lamḥ-i:
w-lo:n-ak lo:n-u ʔamḥi:
w-ʕuyu:n-ak farḥa:ni:n

b-aʃabbih ʕale:-k
ʔul-li: w-fakkar-ni: ʔimta:
ʔana ʃuft-ak bas ʔimta:
min yo:m wala: sini:n
yimkin zama:yil madrasa ʔaw dufʕit-i: fi: l-ge:ʃ
xabaṭit kitaf-na: yo:m fi: baʕḍ w-ʔeḥna: fi: ṭa:bu:r l-ʕe:ʃ
w-la: ʔakalna: fi: yo:m sawa: ʔaklit samak fi: ʔabu: ʔi:r

I think I saw you before
Your features are just like mine
Your complexion is wheat-colored
And your eyes are full of joy
I think I saw you before
Tell me and remind me when
I saw you last, when
Was it yesterday, or years ago
Maybe we were schoolmates, or maybe from my army service
Maybe we bumped shoulders when we were in the bread line
Or maybe one day we shared a plate of fish together in Abu Qir.

In order not to fall into the trap of over-interpretation and subjectivity, the structural and discursive features will need to be analyzed in detail. In Chapter 4, I will return to this example and consider how it relates to a wider picture of Egyptian identity. That is, through language, speakers create a mental map of who is and is not Egyptian and position themselves and others on this map.

Central to my interpretation of the data is the concept of indexicality. As was mentioned earlier, linguistic resources index social variables that, in turn, indicate identity.

To sum, language has two functions in public discourse. It can be used as a classification category and as a resource in stance-taking. Language as a classification category relates directly to prevalent language attitudes and ideologies. Attitudes and ideologies, in turn, draw on the associations of different codes—that is, the indexes of different codes. Of course, the indexes themselves are ordered and do not relate only to linguistic attitudes and ideologies. They also encompass political and social features. In Egyptian public discourse, indexes mediate between linguistic forms and clear identity markers, such as ethnicity, locality, and historicity. In Chapter 2, we will therefore begin with a study of language attitudes and ideologies. In addition, the role of indexes encompasses more than just code-choice and code-switching; linguistic resources can also index positions and, thus, stances. The use of an informal pronoun can index familiarity, solidarity, and so on. To explain further, this book argues that stance-taking as a process (see Du Bois 2007; Jaffe 2009) is related directly to identity construction. In other words, speakers use language to take a stance and, by doing so, give themselves a specific identity and impose an identity on others. During the process of stance-taking, people employ linguistic resources, discourse resources, and structural resources. These linguistic resources are multi-layered and include the associations and indexes of SA, ECA, and even foreign languages. That is, this stance-taking process that reflects directly on identity construction may depend on code-switching as a mechanism that lays claim to different indexes and thus appeals to different ideologies and facets of identity.

Stance as a concept employed within this book to explain identity is studied under an umbrella of indexes. Stance is the product of linguistic resources that speakers draw upon, which are directly related to the identity that speakers endow on others or give themselves; in our case, the Egyptian identity. This book will stretch the realm of possibilities available to the sociolinguist and attempt to offer a novel way of data analysis, both in terms of the type of data analyzed and the method of analyzing it. By so doing, I attempt to add a new dimension to research on both stance and identity construction as related processes that take place at both a macro and micro level.

There are a number of methodological considerations that must be made before one begins analysis of data. In this chapter, I will set out the bases upon which this study is founded. The main approach of this work is summarized in the figure below.

In order to better clarify this concept of the process of identity formation and reflection, I will first explain specific terms and concepts that recur in this work, as well as the social approach to language adopted in this work.

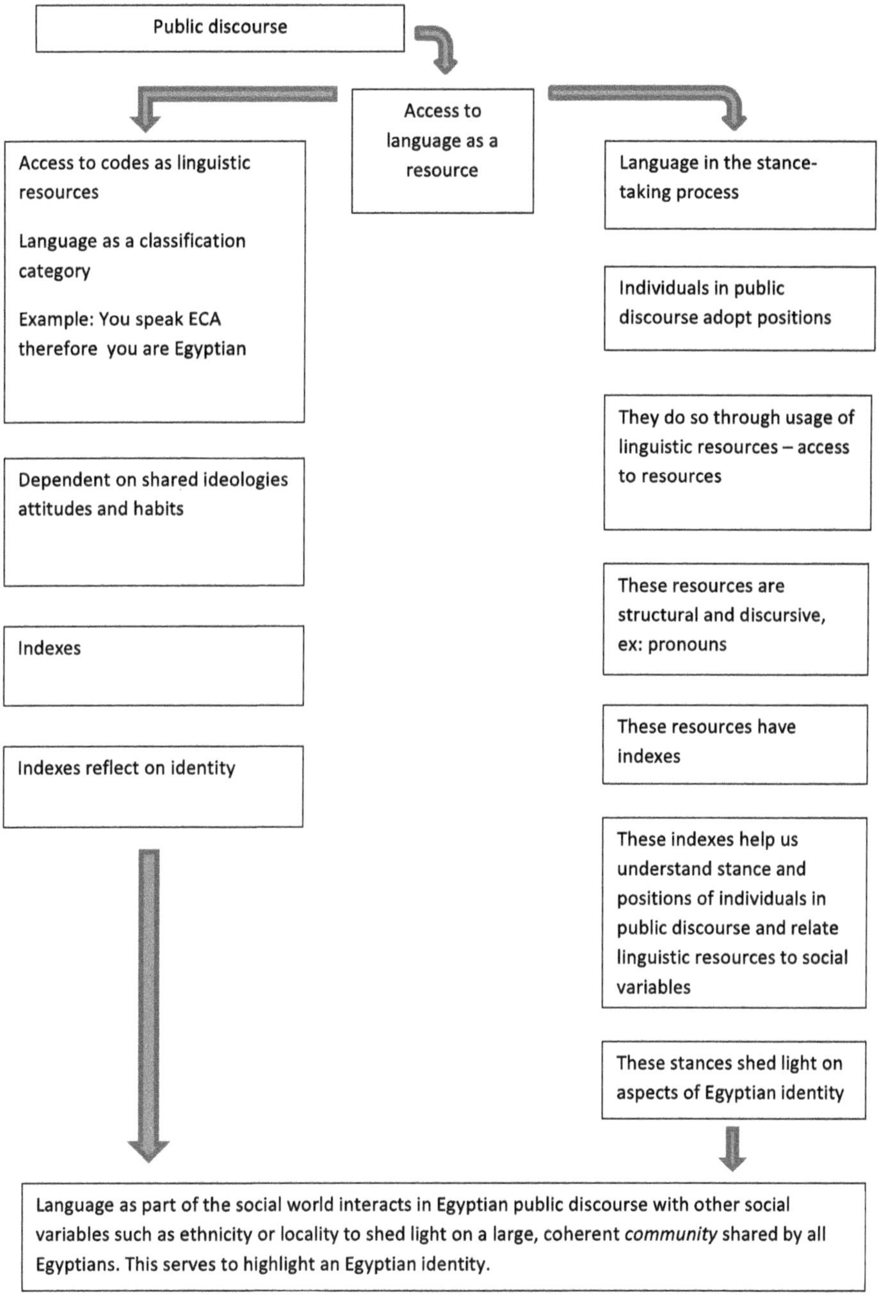

Public discourse
Access to language as a resource
Access to codes as linguistic resources
Language as a classification category
Example: You speak ECA therefore you are Egyptian
Dependent on shared ideologies attitudes and habits
Indexes
Indexes reflect on identity
Language in the stance-taking process
Individuals in public discourse adopt positions
They do so through usage of linguistic resources – access to resources
These resources are structural and discursive, ex: pronouns
These resources have indexes
These indexes help us understand stance and positions of individuals in public discourse and relate linguistic resources to social variables
These stances shed light on aspects of Egyptian identity
Language as part of the social world interacts in Egyptian public discourse with other social variables such as ethnicity or locality to shed light on a large, coherent *community* shared by all Egyptians. This serves to highlight an Egyptian identity.

Figure 1.1 Public discourse

1.2 An Egyptian identity defined

This section serves to familiarize the reader with the terms used in the literature and then provide my own definitions of terms that I will use throughout this book. The key term for this study is, of course, "identity."

Human identity is defined by Lakoff (2006: 142) as

> . . . a continual work in progress, constructed and altered by the totality of life experience. While much of the work in support of this belief concentrates on the larger aspects of identity—especially gender, ethnicity, and sexual preferences—in fact human identity involves many other categories. Identity is constructed in complex ways, more or less consciously and overtly.

Lakoff points to the variability of identity at different stages of one's life and in different contexts. In her model, one's identity is made up of more than one part. Applied to the Egyptian context, this would mean that a mother can also be a professor, a wife, an administrator, a politician, a friend, an Egyptian, a Muslim, an Arab, and so forth. As Lakoff points out, an individual is both a member of a "cohesive and coherent group," as well as an individual (2006: 142). Bastos and Oliveira (2006: 188) emphasize the fact that identity is both "fixed" and "continuous," in the sense that individuals perceive themselves differently in various situations or contexts.

Edwards (2009: 162) argues that variables, such as language group memberships, religious affiliations, and even names, are all markers of identity. A key word in Lakoff's definition is "consciously." Lakoff is aware of the intentional conscious effort to shape and maintain an identity. This effort is exerted by individuals, as well as by public discourse more generally.

Social identity has been defined as "a person's definition of self in terms of some social group membership with the associated value connotations and emotional significance" (Turner 1999: 8). The term "social identity" was coined by Turner and Brown in 1978, based on the early work of Henri Tajfel (Turner and Brown 1978; Llamas 2007). Tajfel noted how easy it was to divide people into groups on the basis of insignificant, almost arbitrary features, such as their favorite painter or even, in some cases, the toss of a coin (see Brehm et al. 1999: 146; Edwards 2009: 25). Tajfel's studies yielded surprising results about how individuals can form and maintain groups of people who did not consider themselves rivals and did not "compete for limited resources and were not acquainted with each other" (Tajfel 1978: 33–4). As Edwards contends, once metaphorical or real borders are created in a real world or in a lab, social group membership and thus social identity become indispensable (Edwards 2009: 25).

He adds that social identity rests on the idea that "we can maintain and enhance self-esteem through valued social affiliations" (Edwards 2009: 27). This identity is usually enhanced during times of danger or when threatened by outsiders. Wodak (1999: 16) adds that social identity is also assigned from the outside, by assigning individuals social features, such as age, sex, class, and so on. Usually outsiders would then form a set of expectations from these groups. Social identity is thus related to patterns of behavior or actions (Le Page et al. 1985: 181).

Collective identity, as a term, is defined in relation to social systems, groups, classes, and cultures (see Frey and Hausser 1987: 4). In other words, collective identity is dependent on how others perceive you and how you perceive yourself in relation to a social system or group. Wodak (1999: 16) finds the difference between the terms social identity and collective identity almost non-existent, since they are both dependent on perception of others and membership within a group (see also Holzinger 1993: 12).

Wodak also differentiates between personal and social identity (1999: 13). A social identity is given to an individual from outside, while the ego identity, according to Goffman (1990: 129), "is one's own subjective feeling about one's own situation and one's own continuity and uniqueness." Goffman posits that an imagined community, such as a nation, cannot have an ego identity, but can have a social one.

National identity, on the other hand, has been defined by Wodak as mainly the product of public discourse (1999: 22). She argues that:

> We assume "national identity" to imply a complex of similar conceptions and perceptual schemata, of similar emotional dispositions and attitudes, and of similar behavioral conventions, which bearers of this "national identity" share collectively and which they have internalized through socialization (education, politics, the media, sports and everyday practices. (1999: 4)

Wodak argues that national identity assumes a shared perceptual and attitudinal disposition that is the product of public discourse—that is, individuals acquire it through education, media, and everyday practices. She adds that, in this sense, a national identity is both vulnerable and impressionable.

Since this book tackles the projection of identity in public discourse, a generic, almost coherent conception of Egyptian identity is usually projected. Within the following paragraphs, I work towards the definition of identity that will be adopted throughout this book—one that is more holistic in nature and therefore encompasses our discussion of individual, social, collective, and national identity.

First, it is important to note that, for Zūzū, identity is emergent in discourse. It is reflected directly in what people say and how they position themselves. Zūzū posits: "If someone comes to speak to me, I need to know who he is first in order to know why he said what he said." Individuals produce an utterance that usually reflects a stance that reflects their identity. Identity in general and social identity in particular are viewed as the "emergent product of linguistic and other semiotic practices, a mainly cultural and social entity" (Bucholtz and Hall 2010). That is to say, identity is not a fixed entity that is reflected through language, but an entity that evolves and emerges via discourse (Bucholtz and Hall 2010: 27).

Note that while one may take issue with the distinction between collective, social, ego, and national identity, this is not the main point in question. This work will start with the assumption that when studying language and identity in public discourse, one should have a holistic approach to language that does not distinguish between social and pragmatic meaning and meaning in general (Johnstone 2010: 29). Bucholtz and Hall (2010: 25) contend that:

> Any given construction of identity may be in part deliberate and intentional, in part habitual and hence often less than fully conscious, in part an outcome of interactional negotiation and contestation, and in part an outcome of others' perceptions and representations, and in part an effect of larger ideological processes and material structures that may become relevant to interaction. It is therefore constantly shifting both as interaction unfolds and across discourse context.

Bucholtz and Hall succinctly summarize the different means of constructing an identity. An identity may be constructed consciously in public discourse and motivated by political or historical reasons, but it can also be formulated habitually and often unconsciously. Identity construction is also not only a product of individuals positioning themselves and negotiating their role in their communities, but also a product of how other communities perceive individuals from that specific community.

Identity, for the purpose of this work, has three constituents: identity is ideological, perceptual, and habitual. In this definition, ideology is considered in general, not just as language ideology. It is a shared belief system that is normalized by historical, political, and social realities and is directly and indirectly reflected in public discourse. See Wright's definition of language policy (2004: 276) for references to belief systems related to language ideology.

Ideologies may pertain to social and moral traits, as well as linguistic ones. For example, a newspaper article written by an Egyptian intellectual could claim that SA is the true language of Egyptians, ECA is just a corrupted version of Arabic that has been imposed by foreign colonizers, and that ECA has to be combatted and substituted by SA. This claim is ideological more than habitual, since different varieties of ECA are used by all Egyptians in their daily communication. Ideology is usually prescriptive rather than descriptive, especially language ideology. However, it is indeed ideology, in conjunction with perception, which helps form indexes and associations of linguistic varieties and social variables. Public discourse reflects, emphasizes, and occasionally formulates ideologies.

One has an ideology because of the way that one perceives oneself in relation to others. In other words, identity is also perceptual. The perceptual aspect of identity is related to the concept of community.

To explain this further, in Egyptian public discourse, all Egyptians tend to be perceived as forming one large community, which may then be divided into smaller segments. However, this large community encompasses all Egyptians with their religious, social, and class diversities. This is because they perceive themselves as sharing the same social variables, which include historical factors, ethnicity, locality, religious inclinations, character traits, habits, communal solidarity, cultural references, and language. While one may argue that this ideal concept of a community is far from reality, given the differences based on social class, urbanization, or even religious affiliations, it is essential to realize that the promotion of this ideal coherent community in most or all public discourse is indeed what sustains a nation or nation-state. By understanding the importance of perception, one can also understand why specific public statements could urge people to revolt or sustain a revolution (see Chapters 4 and 6 for examples).

Most individuals usually belong to a community, within which they agree on a shared "orientation towards the world" (see Eckert 2005: 16). Individuals in a community also share a tacit definition of who they are in relation to other communities of practice. A community in general can be as big as a nation-state or as small as a nuclear family. Identity—national, social, and collective—is not necessarily what one "is," but what one believes one is. It is directly related to perception of self. This perception is the product of years of conditioning by economic, socio-historical, and ethno-global contexts. This perception is also, as Wodak (1999) notes, mainly the product of public discourse. The conditioning that happens to all of us is a process that takes place as we are exposed to a number of factors, both external and specific to our own group. Insiders are usually members within the same group of individuals who share the same self-perception and differentiate themselves from others.

In the Egyptian context, Egyptians may believe that they are friendly and generous, yet we know that it is not possible that all Egyptians are friendly and generous. However, many may have this perception of themselves, because they have been taught this in school textbooks, soap operas, movies, songs, and so on. Like all of us, they have been conditioned by public discourse. One can argue that discourse in the media has a tendency to categorize and generalize (the Hispanics, the Arabs, the Muslims, the Jews, and so on), as well as to juxtapose (the West versus the East, black versus white, and so on). This raises the question of how much freedom we actually have to present ourselves and to what extent we are governed by external circumstances. Even as a scholar and researcher, one is subject to the influence of ideology as one speaks about identity. Consider, for example, the following excerpt from Goldschmidt's *A Brief History of Egypt* (2008: ix):

> Egypt is important and indeed interesting to study because of the Egyptian people. Although it is hard to generalize, most Egyptians are friendly, hospitable, patient in a crowded and hence challenging environment, and fond of cracking jokes. Devoted to their families, they believe that nothing is as important as loving one's spouse, rearing one's children wisely, caring for one's aging parents, and standing up for one's brothers, sisters, and cousins. Although Egyptians are rightly proud of their nation's history, they worry about its present and future conditions . . . The people of Egypt possess at least three identities: Egyptian, Arab, and Muslim.

While acknowledging that it is hard to generalize, Goldschmidt, in fact, describes all "Egyptians" as friendly and hospitable—both traits are individual characteristics and habits that can easily be used to identify an individual identity. Yet for Goldschmidt, the fact that these people share a nation-state called Egypt makes them prone to having these traits. Goldschmidt discusses Egyptians as people who truly share a large community. The line between national identity and an individual identity is blurred in this example. An individual who is fond of cracking jokes may be classified in Egyptian public discourse (and perhaps other public discourses) as an Egyptian. The relation between political action (or lack thereof) and individual traits such as patience are also highlighted by Goldschmidt in the following example (2008: 228): "Egyptians rebel less often than other Arabic-speaking peoples; their patience is legendary [. . .] modernization has sapped this ethos, however, and the danger of a new popular uprising is never remote." An individual characteristic such as patience is again attributed to all Egyptians. This tendency is not uncommon, although Goldschmidt's positive perception of Egyptian identity has not necessarily been the norm. In his political memoir *Modern Egypt* (1908), the former British Controller-General of Egypt, Lord Cromer, makes some generalizations about Egyptians and not all are positive. Rather than describing them as hospitable as Goldschmidt does, Cromer sees Egyptians—especially the peasants—as irresponsible when it comes to spending.

Habits are related to perception and ideology, but may also deviate from both. Identity construction is habitual, because individuals also function in the social world within a framework of tacit norms that are both linguistic and social in nature. To give a linguistic example, Egyptians may agree that a president in a formal setting will use SA. The norm for this community may be that SA is used in formal settings. Norms are also related to power and status. A president, or anyone who has power, may choose to create a different norm for him or herself, thus breaking the standard and creating a different norm that may eventually be adopted or at least expected by other members of the community. Norms, obligations, and expectations differentiate between marked and unmarked linguistic choices (see the "markedness" in Section 5 below). However, language form is not the only manifestation of the norms and obligations or shared expectations in a community. There are, of course, numerous discourse examples. Zūzū breaks the social norm by asking her professor a personal question without addressing him using the formal *ḥaḍritak* ("you"), instead writing her question addressing him with the informal second person pronoun *anta*. She therefore comes across as bolder than other Egyptian girls in the movie. The professor does not accept this violation of norms and makes this clear when he starts addressing her as *a:nisa Zūzū* ("Miss Zūzū"), thus reminding her of the social distance between them.

These three constituents of identity feed into indexes that are shared within a community. Indexes are referenced through linguistic habits and ideologies.

It is worth mentioning at this stage that in public discourse the line demarcating different facets of identities, especially individual and national, is often blurred. For example, in the introduction to this book, examples relating identity to the January 25 Revolution was discussed. In these examples, political actions are attributed to national identity. This process of attributing actions of politicians or other individuals to a citizen's national identity is not just peculiar to Egypt, but is a common practice. Consider the example of the American cruise ship that ran aground off the coast of Italy in January 2012. The Italian captain abandoned the ship before everyone was evacuated. By so doing, he broke the norm of a tacit rule of sea captains: the captain should always be the last one off the ship. However, perhaps it is less obvious that, for some people, he also cast a shadow on Italian identity. In an article in *The Guardian*, Ian Jack wrote (2012):

> The spectre now haunting Italy is that this label has stuck. "We've gone straight into the Titanic nightmare [and] Italy is once again the laughing stock of foreign newspapers," wrote a blogger, Caterina Soffici, this week. In

> Il Giornale, the columnist Cristiano Gatti wrote that the rest of the world would be delighted to rediscover "the same old rascally Italians: those unreliable cowards who turn and run in war and flee like rabbits from the ship, even if they are in command." But are either of these statements really true?

Jack continues his article with the story of Captain Smith—a British sea captain who did not abandon his ship and has the following inscription below his memorial statue in his birthplace of Lichfield: "The inscription below Smith's, says he bequeathed 'to his countrymen the memory and example of a great heart, a brave life and a heroic death,' and carries a simple instruction: 'Be British.'" Being British appears to entail acting in a specific way, having specific character traits. By this logic, the same is true for any other nationality. These examples are there to show how the individual can become synonymous with the nation in public discourse.

It is, indeed, amazing that an action of one person can influence how the identity of a country is perceived. The confusion between an individual, nation, deed, and facet of identity is not new. All this serves to illustrate that identity formation is subject to, or may be influenced by, stereotyping. In her novel *Awrāq al-narjis* ("The leaves of Narcissus") (2001), Ramaḍān writes about Kimī, a young Egyptian girl who has gone mad, because of the pressure placed on her while abroad to be all Egyptians and answer to all prejudices and perceptions of outsiders and Egyptians. Kimī says (Ramaḍān 2001: 45):

> Why do I remain something illusionary, fantastic, that is constantly under threat of being transformed into a continent in its own entirety, or an ignorant nation, or a submissive people, or even a more ancient civilization? [. . .] We Egyptians: "people in my country" who is that "we"? Precisely which "people" in that country? I am them, and I am not them, I am that "we" and I'm also "I" – just "I."

Kimī attempts to keep her individual identity different from her national one, but perceptions of outsiders makes this a futile task. In the last example in this section below, the conflict between Mubarak's regime in Egypt and the revolutionaries is reduced to a conflict about identity. This example is from the Egyptian newspaper *al-Ahrām*, published shortly after the Revolution of 2011. The example is an excerpt from an article by the poet and media specialist Fārūq Shūshah (2011):[3]

> The ex-dictator wanted Egyptians to be ashamed of their identity. But after the revolution, a new Egyptian identity was born. It is the identity of freedom, dignity, development, awakening, justice. These characteristics were all born

in Tahrir square, and in the heart of the Egyptian revolution; it is the new spirit of Egypt.

The same pattern of reducing a political conflict to a conflict of identity recurred with the ousting of President Muḥammad Mursī. Like Mubarak, this member of the Muslim Brotherhood was accused of attempting to rob Egyptians of their coherent, historical, and entrenched identity.

In an article for the newspaper *al-Yawm al-Sābiʿ*, scriptwriter Midḥat al-ʿAdl was cited saying that Egyptians would not allow the Muslim Brotherhood to "steal their identity" (see Muṣṭafá 2013). Similarly, the site *Vetogate.com* reported a statement by the manager of the Zamalek football club, who argued that the Muslim Brotherhood had already stolen Egypt's identity and that "General Sīsī realized the people's dream" (see Ḥammūdah 2013).

While this book will highlight aspects of "Egyptianness" that are related directly to national identity, it is important to keep in mind that identity, whether national, individual, or social (as was shown in the last section), overlaps. In different contexts, one appeals to different facets of identity. In the context of public discourse, identity is not just an individual identity, but a collective, national, and social one as well.

1.3 Language as a social process and practice

The social approach is developed in this work in order to examine the relationship between language and identity: language as a resource and identity as a social construct, which is ideological, perceptual, and habitual. In order to do so, one needs a theoretical framework that is both systematic and directly relevant to the social world.

The social approach adopted by Heller (2007) aims to place bilingualism within a political, ideological, and social framework. However, in my opinion, this approach can also be adopted in discussions about language in general and language variation, code-switching, and code-choice in particular. Her approach can be expanded to explain linguistic situations in bilingual, monolingual, and diglossic communities. While this book does not adopt her model completely, her model provides an alternative, more egalitarian way of viewing language in relation to nations, identities, communities, and societies.

Heller begins her approach by posing specific questions about social constructions and the individual and contends that language is one form of social practice. These questions include the following: how do we construct our world? What are the constraints we have to face? How is language essential in linking the social and moral order? Heller then posits that since language is related to nation, ethnicity, gender, class, and race, it is "fundamentally a social phenomenon" and thus our analysis of language is a form of social action. She argues that the process of social construction is long and complicated and usually within this social construction linguistic resources acquire specific values, which are connected to certain methods of interpretation: "it is always someone's notion of what counts, and someone's ability to control access both to resources and to the definition of their value, which ultimately make a difference to people's lives" (Heller 2007: 14). Public discourse, especially in the media, not only reiterates shared belief systems and ideologies, but also controls access to them.

The aim of the social process and practice approach was to move talk about code-switching, code-choice, and bilingualism in general from a micro analysis of the individual and community to a macro approach, which considers language a social practice, speakers as social actors, and boundaries as an outcome of social action. According to this approach, languages are not whole, independent systems, but are considered linguistic resources that speakers draw upon under specific conditions and circumstances. Therefore, languages have to be studied in relation to ideology, social practice, and social organization (Heller 2007: 1–2).

Accordingly, language can be defined as a set of resources that, like all resources, is distributed in unequal ways, depending on the social networks and "discursive spaces" of individuals. The meaning of these resources is related to the social organizations, historical conditions, and political situation of a community. Language is only one means of the manifestation and construction of social differences and inequality. Social conditions usually constrain and facilitate the "social reproduction of existing conventions and relations," as well as the production of new ones (Heller 2007: 15).

Heller concludes that bilingualism within a homogenized nation-state is different from real bilingualism. What actually happens with language and what we think is happening are two different things and perhaps both are closely dependent on social constructs and ideologies? A similar approach to Heller is adopted by Blommaert (2010: 180), who contends that sociolinguists need to start examining language as a resource in which "language events and experiences" preside over "language-as-form-and-meaning."

I argue that in order for us to understand the indexes of different codes, including ECA and SA, we first need to examine prevalent language ideologies and attitudes that situate different codes on a larger political and social framework. This is the subject of the next two chapters.

1.4 Theorizing identity in discourse

This section is devoted to introducing recent work on discourse theory, which addresses identity, directly or indirectly, and is pertinent to this work.

The concept of stance will be applied later to data in this book. However, the concept of stance is, to a great extent, an outcome of earlier and parallel theories that position the individual in a relation to other individuals, situations, or objects. Such concepts include that of social arena, footing, and subject positioning, all of which will be discussed below. (Note that social arena and footing has been applied to cases of code-switching and will be dealt with in Section 6, but it is important to know that it paved the way for the emergence of the concept of stance.) Second, a perhaps more general concept that is related to a macro- and micro-level of analysis of ideologies and attitudes is that of indexicality, which will also be discussed below.

1.4.1 Positioning theory

Positioning theory relies on the assumption that the process of describing one's identity is in itself a discourse phenomenon (Benwell and Stokoe 2006: 3). This is because speakers usually produce different descriptions of their identity, in which some aspects of identity are highlighted and others ignored (Bamberg and Andrews 2004; Davies and Harré 1990). This theory takes as its main task the analysis of the construction of identity between speaker and audience. Positioning refers to the method by which speakers adopt, resist, impose, and offer subject positions during an interaction (Benwell and Stokoe 2006: 43). For example, speakers can position themselves and others as victims, perpetrators, active, passive, powerful, or powerless. In the example provided at the beginning of the chapter, the professor resists and renegotiates the position given to him by Zūzū as an equal peer.

In addition, according to Cameron (2005), as people interact with one another, they adopt particular "subject positions" and also assign positions to others. Thus, when a woman talks, she assigns herself a position, such as teacher, expert, professional, and so forth. She also assigns positions to the others that she talks to; she may choose to express solidarity with them, claim distance from them, or even condescend to them. The definition of subject positions is similar to that of identity given by Bean and Johnstone (2004), who contend that identity is formed by our experiences and memories and, more importantly, by the projection of our experiences and memories on the way that we express ourselves. If having an identity requires "self expression," then individuals have to resort to all of their linguistic resources to express their identity (Bean and Johnstone 2004: 237). Bolonyai (2005: 16–17), in a study of bilingual young women, shows how young women who are bilingual intentionally and strategically use their linguistic resources to exhibit their power. They use code-choice to position themselves in a dominant position. This can be done by switching to English to show their expertise and knowledge. Switching to English is used as a control mechanism and display of power. Switching is also a means of asserting their superior identity.[4]

This theory adopts a micro and macro level of analysis in which there is a close connection between subject positions, identity, and social power relations, whether on the micro-conversational level or the macro-socio-political levels. Note that according to this theory, individuals are not passive recipients of an imposed constructed identity; rather, individuals negotiate subject positions and resist, modify, or refuse positions. The role of the individual as the main agent in the process of identity construction is still highlighted (Bamberg and Andrews 2004; Benwell and Stokoe 2006; Cook et al. 2003).

Positioning theory, as well as stance, have been criticized for presenting an abstract and, at times, exaggerated picture of the individual who may possess or lack power (see Benwell and Stokoe 2006). Related to the positioning theory is the concept of stance. In fact, stance-taking in discourse incorporates positioning as one component in the stance-taking process.

1.4.2 Stance

Stance is considered by Ochs (1992) as the mediating path between linguistic forms and social identities. To explain further, stance is a "contextualization cue" that informs interlocutors on the nature of the role that the speaker aims to project in relation to the form and content of his or her utterance—for example, choices of aspect, modals, or evidential statements can display a speaker's attitude with the claims or content of reported speech (Jaffe 2007: 56). Du Bois (2007) analyzes stance as a social action that is both a subjective and intersubjective phenomenon. According to Du Bois, stance is mainly the exposition of evaluative, affective, and epistemic orientations in discourse. As Du Bois posits: "I evaluate something and thereby position myself, and align or disalign with you" (Du Bois 2007: 163). Speakers usually position themselves and others as particular kinds of people, almost stereotypes. This positioning can then accumulate into a larger entity that we may call an identity. By studying evaluative expressions, grammar, phonology, and lexis, one can have a better understanding of the stance of a specific individual (see Bucholtz and Hall 2010: 22).

The stance triangle, as explained by Du Bois (2007: 163), is based on evaluation, positioning, and alignment. An individual evaluates an object (for example, a statement), positions a subject, usually the self, and aligns with other subjects. An individual may express doubt, cynicism, and so on, and may also show disalignment by negative yes–no interrogatives and tag questions that display doubts (Keisanen 2007: 253).

To explain further, in a single act of stance-taking, three things are achieved: evaluation, positioning, and alignment. Evaluation refers to the process in which a stance-taker "characterizes" an object of stance as having "specific quality or value" (Du Bois 2007: 143). Positioning is when the stance-taker makes her or his affective stance clear and claims certainty and knowledge. Alignment is the act of standardizing and normalizing the relation between different stances (see Du Bois 2007: 144; Damari 2010: 611).

It is noteworthy, however, that Jaffe (2009: 9) argues that personal stance is achieved through comparison and contrast with others, whether these others are persons or categories. Stance "saturates talk about others, in which speakers engage in both explicit and implicit forms of social categorization and evaluation, attribute intentionality, affect, knowledge, agency to themselves and others and lay claim to particular social and or moral identities." This will be exemplified in Chapter 6, in which ex-President Mubarak's supporters attempt to cast doubt on the identity of anti-Mubarak protestors during the 2011 Egyptian Revolution.

To explain further, stance concerns the speaker's or author's evaluation and assessment of the interlocutor's discourse object (Irvine 2009: 53). One should therefore consider language on a number of analytical scales, including linguistic features of texts, the participant role in the communicative act, and broader social categories, such as ethnicity and race (Irvine 2009: 69). Irvine also argues that an individual's choice is not always present in the stance-taking process. Irvine contends that "we say a person takes a stance, but they—and we ourselves—may also find themselves in one willy-nilly. A stance can be given or accorded" (Irvine 2009: 70).

In order to be able to interpret stance, one needs empirical evidence of conventional associations of codes and meanings gained from both ethnographic and sociolinguistic data. One also needs knowledge of a speaker's repertoire and the range of their linguistic performance. That is to say, to understand the stance being adopted in a specific moment by a speaker, interpreters need to assess the particular moment of "linguistic performance against that speaker's choices and performances in other contexts and at other moments" (Jaffe 2007: 56). I argue that understanding stance means that one should understand identity formation at multiple indexical levels. In the following paragraphs, I shed light on the concept of indexicality and how it is related to stance and identity formulation and maintenance.

1.4.3 Indexicality

Individuals use their access to linguistic resources to adopt positions that index their identity or social variables that, in turn, reflect their identity. Individuals also relate access to resources, including codes, as access to a community and an identity. Thus, the concept of indexicality is pivotal to this work.

The concept of indexicality is originally a philosophical concept that was introduced by the American philosopher Charles Sanders Pierce and later adopted into linguistics by Silverstein (2003) and Ochs (1992). It refers to ways in which an observable fact, including a linguistic one, can be considered an iconic sign if it resembles what it is taken to mean. A sign is symbolic if it is related to its meaning by convention and not resemblance. A sign is indexical if it is related to its meaning, because it mostly co-occurs with the thing that it is taken to mean. When we hear thunder, we experience lightening, rain, and a dark sky. So the sound of thunder causes us to expect a storm. Words usually acquire meaning, because they are used together with their referents. For example, a child sees his father and then hears the sentence "Daddy's here" (Johnstone 2010: 31). When a sign is taken out of context, it becomes an "arbitrary symbol" (see also Clark 1997: 590–2; Johnstone 2010). Indexical forms can imply or construct identity. The concept of indexicality involves the creation of semiotic links between linguistic forms and social meanings (Ochs 1992; Silverstein 1985). For example, an individual may imitate the dialect of an immigrant. This specific dialect, not usually used by this particular individual except in this context, is also associated with immigrants. The use of the immigrant dialect will then index a political stance for this individual (see Johnstone 2010). In another context, a speaker may communicate in a way that portrays him or her as overtly male. By doing so, this speaker is then evoking the associations attached to this particular gender, including toughness, for example, and thus acquiring a specific stance related directly to identity (see Bucholtz and Hall 2010; Johnstone 2010 for more examples). One should consider identity formation at multiple indexical levels (Ochs 1992).

In relation to linguistic structures and forms, Johnstone (2010: 21) defines an index as a linguistic form that depends on the interactional context for its meaning. Bucholtz and Hall add that "the linguistic resources that indexically produce identity at all these levels are therefore necessarily broad and flexible, including labels, implicatures, stances, styles and entire languages and varieties" (2010: 26). Indexical processes occur at all levels of linguistic structure and use (Johnstone 2010).

Indexical resources are orderly or structural in the sense that speakers can draw from a template of known, generalized associations between linguistic styles and social meanings. These are the resources that they have at their disposal to creatively re-enact or rework established indexical relationships in their speech and make sense of other people's performances. Structure and agency feed into each other in stylistic practice (Coupland 2010: 100).

Orders of indexes have been used to explain language variation and change, as well as code-switching and discourse analysis.

To avoid a circular analysis of indexicality, one has to address some crucial questions and draw borderlines between associations and meanings. The first of these questions regards how linguistic meanings attach to linguistic forms.

Collins (2011: 410) argues that indexical signs are understood in "situated encounters" in which "timing and exchange matter." According to Silverstein (2003: 193–4), in order to be able to relate the micro-social to the macro-social frames of analysis of any sociolinguistic phenomenon, one needs to understand the "integral," "ordinal degrees" of indexicality. That is, one needs to understand the concept of indexical order. Silverstein argues that any order of indexicality presupposes that there is a context with a contextual entailment that is understood relative to ideologies and schematization. That is, it is understood in accordance to an enthno-meta-pragmatic framework. Johnstone et al. (2006: 81) explain further by positing that "relationships between linguistic forms and social meaning can stabilize at various levels of abstraction or 'order of indexicality'." According to them (2006: 81), indexes can be referential—that is, the denotation of the morpheme depends on the context of the utterance. Examples of referential indexes are demonstratives and pronouns. However, non-referential indexes are usually linguistic forms that presuppose and entail social meaning. They further contend that social meaning includes *register*, which refers to situational appropriateness; *stance*, which includes certainty and authority; and *social identity*, which includes, class, ethnicity, and interactional role. First order indexes are linguistic forms that can be understood with reference to a socio-demographic identity or semantic function.

For example, we will see in Chapter 4 that in our data there is an example of a journalist who uses variables from the dialect of Alexandria as opposed to Cairo in an online article. Here are some brief examples:

Verbs	**Alexandrian**	**Cairene**
To wear	*labast*	*libist*
To drink	*ʃarabt*	*ʃiribt*
To be bored	*zahaʔt*	*zihiʔt*

According to first order indexicality, the use of this different vowel quality by the journalist presupposes that she is from Alexandria, rather than Cairo. In other words, it indexes her local identity. As Johnstone et al. (2006: 82) put it, first order indexicality is usually not noticeable, not intentional, and not performed. However, as will be clear in Chapter 4, the journalist intentionally uses these Alexandrian linguistic features. That is, in order to fully understand the significance of the journalist's usage of these variables, one needs to recognize the social meaning of being Alexandrian and also the intentionality of the journalist's usage of such linguistic forms.

Second order indexicality is usually superposed, creative, and entailing (Silverstein 2003: 220) and can be assigned an "ethnometapragmatically driven native interpretation" (Silverstein 2003: 212). Silverstein adds that the feature analyzed has usually been "enregistered." It has become correlated with a style of speech and can be used to create a context for that style. Johnstone et al. (2006: 82) add that once a linguistic form is noticeable and speakers associate it with social meaning based on shared ideologies, then it can be considered second order indexicality. Second order indexicality can help us understand the journalist's usage of Alexandrian form more comprehensibly within the particular context. The journalist wants to emphasize the shared habits of Alexandrians, as opposed to outsiders. Being Alexandrian presupposes that one is tough, helpful, and cannot be deceived easily by outsiders. However, being Alexandrian in the context of the journalist's article implies more than that. It implies a shared identity that surpasses religious differences. This, in fact, can be even better understood, once we explain higher order indexicality.

It is important to mention here that "this creative indexical effect is the motivated realization or performable execution of an already constituted framework of semiotic value" (Silverstein 2003: 194).

Third order indexicality is even more creative and performative. As Silverstein (2003: 222) contends, it creates "sites of indexical innovation that spread through analogical space." This higher indexicality exists in "a complex, interlocking set of institutionally formed macro-sociolinguistic interests" (2003: 226). In fact, the journalist's example can only be fully understood if explained within the framework of orders of indexicality. As will be clear in Chapter 4, the journalist is performing a dialect in a written text. That is, she is not only indexing that she is from Alexandria, but through indexing her origin, she also presupposes that she shares an identity with Christians and that she does not differentiate between people according to religion. It also entails that she is authentic, tough, and, first and foremost, a typical "Alexandrian." This local identity is then understood in the context of an incident that took place in 2011 in Alexandria and threatened the country with sectarian strife.

When the journalist uses the Alexandrian dialect in a written text, she is consciously imitating a "social type" (Silverstein 2003: 220). She is also depending on a shared ideological model with her audience. Johnstone et al. (2006: 84), in their work on the Pittsburghese, show how speakers draw on first, second, and third order indexicality as they decide how to talk and how to talk *about* talk.

Additionally, there is the question regarding how people agree and share an ideology. A simple answer to these two questions, according to Johnstone, is that people learn to recognize that linguistic variants have indexical meanings by being told that they do, and they continue to share ideas about indexical meaning as long as they keep telling each other about them. Ideological structures play a vital role in demarcating an identity. Usually associations between language and identity are based on cultural beliefs and values (ideologies), about the types of speakers who can and should produce particular types of utterances (Johnstone 2010: 32). Indexicality is related to habits that produce expectations linked to a context.

Talking about talk is essential in shaping second order indexicality and is the topic of Chapter 3. Since all the data in this book is performed and intentional, third order indexicality is highly significant in understanding the data more fully. In fact, in Chapter 5, a higher order of indexicality is suggested to understand the data. However, as Johnstone et al. (2006: 84) posit, "orders of indexicality are in dialectical relationships with one another." In other words, they can and do occur simultaneously in public discourse.

1.4.3.1 Indexicality, code-choice, and code-switching

Code-switching and code-choice are linguistic resources, access to which can index an identity.

Gumperz defines code-switching as "the juxtaposition within the same speech exchange of passages of speech belonging to two different grammatical systems or subsystems" (1982: 59). That is, Gumperz and later linguists working on code-switching do not restrict code-switching to switching between different languages, but include switching between different varieties and registers.

The term "code-switching" can be broad or narrow, as with all terms in sociolinguistics. What Myers-Scotton (1998) calls code-switching does not apply just to switching between different languages, but it also applies to switching between varieties of the same language. Therefore, according to her theory, diglossic switching is a kind of code-switching. She contends that

> varieties is a cover term for selections at all linguistic levels so that choices between varieties include, for example, choices of one language rather than another, one dialect over another, one style or register over another, and one form of a directive or refusal over another. (Myers-Scotton 1998: 18)

Discussions of motivations for code-switching starting from Gumperz to the present highlight identity as an essential factor in choice of code. Although not spelled out in the studies mentioned below, the means by which an individual positions him or herself in relation to an audience and a context has been referenced as a driving force in studies of code-switching. The theories that are pertinent for this work include social arena and Goffmans' concept of footing.

These theories refer indirectly to the individual's role in code-switching. The individual uses code-switching to position him or herself in a specific way—for example, as powerful, knowledgeable, and so on. This is achieved according to the norms and obligations of the community of this individual. By positioning her or himself, the individual also appeals to aspects of her or his identity.[5]

Scotton and Ury (1977) argue that there are three universal social arenas that affect discourse and code-choice: identity, power, and transaction. A speaker switches to different codes either to define the interaction taking place in terms of a certain social arena or not to define it at all. The first universal social arena is identity: a speaker switches according to the identity of the person that she or he is speaking to, as well as her or his own identity. The second social arena is power: code-switching also depends on the power dynamic of the interaction—that is, who is powerful versus who is weak, who is superior versus who is inferior. The third social arena is transaction: code-switching depends on the situation and the purpose of the speech act. A speaker may be unfamiliar with the social arena: she or he may not be sure about the status of the other person, for example. In that case, she or he uses a code that will help the speaker keep the interaction undefined. Myers-Scotton (1986: 408) gives the example of a brother and sister in western Kenya. They were conversing in the brother's shop. The sister wanted special treatment from her brother, so she used their shared mother tongue. He, on the other hand, used Swahili to show her that she was just a customer in his store. The sister chose to emphasize her identity as a "sister," rather than as just another customer in her brother's shop. She uses code-choice to do so. He, on the other hand, does not accept this identity that she assigns herself.

In this example, neither of them has power over the other, although to some extent, one can say that the sister expected to have power over the brother, because she expected to receive special treatment. The brother and sister also did not agree on the kind of transaction taking place. The brother wanted the situation to be that of a customer and shop owner, while the sister preferred a familial interaction. The brother refused to act within the social arena that the sister assigned to him and chose another one instead.

Goffman (1981) also discusses the individual as a speaker who plays different roles and uses language to mark the new role she or he plays. Each person plays different roles with different people in different situations. This is what Goffman calls "a change in footing." A change in footing is a change in the frame of an event. By "frame," he means it is a change in the way speakers perceive each other and the situation. It is noteworthy, however, that when Goffman speaks about a change in footing, he does not just refer to the bilingual, but he also refers to the monolingual, who uses different codes in different situations. For example, in diglossic communities, this can occur when there is a shift between the H code and the L code. People spontaneously manipulate their language for their own needs, changing their attitude and style frequently, and this applies to monolinguals in diglossic communities just as much as it does to bilinguals, except that in the bilingual case the change of code is more obvious.[6]

A further development in the work on code-switching is applying indexicality to cases of code-switching. Woolard (2004) explains marked choices in terms of indexes. Indexicality is again a relation of associations through which utterances are understood. For example, if a specific code or form of language presupposes a "certain social context, then use of that form may create the perception of such context where it did not exist before" (Woolard 2004: 88). If a code is associated with the authority of courtrooms and then it is used within a different context, it will denote authority. The language of the speaker would then be considered an authoritative language (Silverstein 1996: 267).

Indexicality in relation to stance has yet to be applied to diglossic switching as part of code-switching. This is what I attempt to do in this book. However, stance and indexicality have been applied to other cases of code-switching.

Jaffe (2007), in her article about code-switching between Corsican and French in bilingual classrooms in Corsica, adopts the concept of stance to examine language choice and code-switching. Jaffe argues that the teacher, whose language choice is examined in the article, projects an association between authoritative, legitimate social positions and the minority language, which in this context is Corsican (Jaffe 2007: 56).

She posits that stance is not always clear, but must be inferred from empirical studies, which provide social and historical contexts. That is, the interpretation of stance requires empirical evidence of conventional associations of codes and meanings gained from ethnographic, conversational, and sociolinguistic data. It also involves knowledge of speakers' repertoires and the range of their linguistic performance. To understand the stance being taken up in a particular moment by a specific speaker, linguists need to evaluate the "individual moment of linguistic performance" against that speaker's choices and performances in other contexts and at other moments (Jaffe 2007: 56). Thus, one has to be able to recognize the speaker's attitude, repertoire, and practices across a wide variety of domains. This is indeed true in Egypt as it is a diglossic community, which will become clear in the analysis within later chapters. Jaffe's framework of analysis depends on a study of the sociolinguistic context, which includes language shift, diglossia, language revitalization, the political and pedagogical context of bilingual education, and the teacher's explicit ideology of language choice and use. Jaffe concludes that the teacher uses the authority of her position to socialize stance and create a new set of associations between Corsican, literacy, and legitimate classroom practice. In that sense, the teacher is an active participant in imposing different associations and, eventually, even changing the conventions. The teacher is also an active participant in forming her own stance and identity. Jaffe refers to indexicality and audience design as crucial theories that help us infer the teacher's stance. This book will also explain cases of code-switching, bearing in mind orders of indexicality, stance, and access to linguistic and other resources.

1.5 Linguistic resources adopted

When discussing stance and positioning theory in Section 4, I mentioned that the main methodological problem that could be encountered when adopting positioning theory to discourse is the fact that it is too abstract and subject to personal interpretations. The same is true for stance. Irvine (2009: 54–5) posits that:

> If there is a pitfall, however, a place for "stance" to stumble, it lies in the possibility that the enthusiastic analyst may attribute too much explanatory power to individual agency in conversational interaction. So agent-centered a concept, emphasizing an individual speaker's knowledge, intentions and attitudes explicitly expressed in talk, risks producing a form of methodological individualism, such that the speaker's role in constructing social and linguistic outcomes is taken to be the only, or at least the most crucial, focus of analysis and locus of explanation [. . .] the footings, ideological positions, and social

> group memberships that inform stance are not simple or obvious assignments. They are emergent in the sense that they depend on performances and some degree of co-construction.

Stance as a process is, as Irvine argues, dependent on footings, ideological positions, and social group memberships; however, these in themselves are not necessarily clear in all situations. A study that depends on stance or positioning for analysis will have to resort to clear and concrete methods that avoid rendering a subjective or concentric analysis.

This book attempts to avoid such pitfalls by providing a more rigorous framework of explaining positions, stance, and identity. By drawing upon linguistic strategies, as well as theories of code-choice, the book attempts to provide an authentic viewpoint of the challenges faced when studying identity in general and Egyptian identity in particular, as well as the many facets of public identity present for Egyptians, which are, at times, correlated with language choice. I will depend on and expand some strategies that have been adopted from a variety of different theories, including stance, positioning, critical discourse analysis (CDA), indexicality, and markedness. I call these strategies "resources." These linguistic resources are both discourse-based and structural-based.

These resources are structured through layers of indexes that individuals acquire and use. The layers of indexes are related directly to language ideologies, as well as social, political, and demographic variables. That is, these linguistic resources are used in relation to the indexes of different codes and social variables, so that language is part of the social process that individuals engage in.

Analyzing linguistic resources is a means to an end. The end is to reach a better understanding of the agreed upon indexes that form an identity in public discourse. The linguistic resources form a micro-level of our analytical scale, which serves the macro one, that is the construction of Egyptian identity.

In addition, by adopting the social process and practice approach, the book will need to first discuss the context of linguistic resources in Egypt. This is the reason why two chapters of the book are devoted to examining the historical, ideological, and political background that creates indexes to linguistic resources. Language as a social process cannot be separated from language as a social practice and throughout the book both will occur together.

What this book will contribute is an approach that does not just concentrate on language content or language form, but relates both and shows how they can both be studied within the same framework. It is also an approach that highlights language as a social phenomenon.

This study also attempts to add a new dimension to the study of stance and thus to identity construction, in which language is an independent variable, such as religion, social class, and ethnicity, that is studied as a classification category and identity builder. Additionally, language is also the main means of taking a stance by employing linguistic resources.

It is often difficult to draw a line between structural and discourse resources, and such distinctions can at times be arbitrary. In general, the resources used to demarcate Egyptian identity in public discourse include the following:

Discursive resources

1. Mention of identification categories, such as ethnicity, locality, and shared past experiences;
2. Van Leeuwen's (1996) five categories: functionalism, classification, relational identification, physical identification, generalization;
3. nature of statements (see Gee 2010);
4. presuppositions;
5. metaphors, metonymy, and synecdoche; and
6. intertextuality and dialogicality.

Structural resources

1. Grammatical patterns—for example, nominalization, verbless sentences;
2. pronouns (see also Silverstein 1976);
3. tense and aspect;
4. demonstratives, deixis, quantification, and negation;
5. conditional sentences;
6. mood and modality; and
7. phonological, structural, lexical variation.

It is essential to mention that code-switching and code-choice as linguistic resources *straddle both* structural resources and discourse resources. This is because code-switching is obviously a social process, and, indeed, many works on code-switching reference identity construction directly as a motivation for code-choice and code-switching. One can argue that it is part-and-parcel of language as a social practice. On the other hand, code-switching is manifested in phonological, structural, or lexical variation and therefore relates to the structural resources listed above. Later, there is a section devoted to discussions of theories and methods of research on code-switching, code-choice, and diglossic switching. These resources will now be explained and exemplified.

1.5.1 Discourse resources

1.5.1.1 Identification categories

Social variables, such as ethnicity, locality, character traits, religion, and shared historical background, are essential in identity construction. We have encountered some of these before, as evidenced in the example below from the song "I saw you before":

b-aʃabbih ʕale:-k
ma:lamḥ-ak min ma:lamḥ-i:
w-lo:n-ak lo:n-u ʔamḥi:

I think I saw you before
Your features are just like mine
Your complexion is wheat-colored

In this excerpt, skin color is mentioned as an identification category that references identity. The underlying category is, of course, ethnicity.

1.5.1.2 Van Leeuwen's five categories

When expanding the function of participants, Van Leeuwen (1996) recognizes five categories of socio-semantic identification for participants:

1. *Functionalization*: this term refers to identification by virtue of what one does—for example, farmer, lecturer, and so on.
2. *Classification*: identification by virtue of what one is, including, for example, black British.
3. *Relational identification*: identification by virtue of relationships—for example, husband, brother, and so on.
4. *Physical identification*: identification by virtue of physical descriptions—for example, the red-headed woman.
5. *Genericitation*: this kind of identification makes the identity generic, rather than specific—for example, "The child develops this skill from an early age." This refers to children in general.

To give an example: al-Tūnisī, in his poem *ʔana l-maṣri:* ("I am the Egyptian") (1921), which was set to music by Sayyid Darwīsh, employs two of Van Leeuwen's five categories of socio-semantic identification—namely, functionalism and relational identification, to define himself as "*the* Egyptian." Functionalism, which refers to identification by virtue of what one does, is used by al-Tūnisī to identify "the Egyptian" as the builder of civilization and glory. This is his main function: with civilization comes fertility and science. Relational identification, on the other hand, is identification by virtue of relationships. The protagonist of the song refers to his ancestors and his relation to them, tying himself and his ancestors together (al-Tūnisī 1987: 276):

ʔana lmaṣri:/ kari:m al-ʕunṣure:n
bane:t il-magdi be:n il-ʔahrame:n
gudu:di anʃaʔu: l-ʕilm il-ʕagi:b

I am the Egyptian, of noble origin/noble stock.
I have built glory across the two pyramids.
My ancestors created great science

1.5.1.3 Nature of statements

Statements can directly reflect the identity of the speaker and audience. In a study of teenagers in a post-industrial area of Massachusetts, Paul Gee (2010: 152) uses the following categories to relate their language to their perceptions of self: *cognitive* statements, such as "I think" and "I know"; *affective* statements, such as "I like," "I want," and "I need"; *state and action* statements, which describe one's state and actions, such as "I am intelligent" and "I work hard"; *ability and constraint* statements, such as "I can get an A grade"; achievement statements, such as "I want to go to Harvard" and "I challenge myself." While the differences between achievement statements and ability and constraint statements are not always clear, this categorization, if applied even partially to public discourse in Egypt, may draw attention to tendencies in Egyptian public discourse.

I would like to add to this the category of assertive statements (see Benwell and Stokoe (2006: 179) for similar phenomena in other languages), which in Arabic can take the form of a verbless sentence in the present tense.

In the poem mentioned above by al-Tūnisī, the individual starts defining himself with a verbless sentence:

ʔana lmaṣri:/ kari:m al-ʕunṣure:n

I the-Egyptian noble the-origin
I am the Egyptian, of noble origin / noble stock.

This assertive statement is realized in the form of a verbless sentence. In this example, discourse resources interact with structural resources. As noted earlier, the differences between both are not clear cut.

1.5.1.4 Presupposition

Levinson (1983: 167) defines presuppositions as pragmatic inferences that are dependent on both context and syntactic structure. According to Benwell and Stokoe (2006: 114), presupposition "refers to the presumed knowledge a recipient needs to make full sense of a text." It usually uses cultural frames and biased assumptions that are a result of shared cultural beliefs. For example, the advertisement that says "get trouble-free holiday insurance" assumes that holiday insurance is always troubling or difficult for tourists. This presupposition cannot be understood with no familiarity of the wider context, which includes information such as: this community usually goes on holidays, they take out insurance when going on holidays, and getting insurance is typically problematic (Benwell and Stokoe 2006: 114).[7] An Egyptian may not understand this presupposition, given that he may not necessarily take out insurance when going on holiday; insurance companies in Egypt are not as prosperous or as common; and the majority of Egyptians take their holidays inside Egypt, rather than abroad. Hence, even the concept of a "holiday" is different: it may imply visiting a summer house on the beach, visiting family members in a different part of Egypt, or driving to Sinai. Note that according to Benwell and Stokoe (2006), readers may also resist a presupposition; they may misread the meaning, renegotiate it, or even reject it altogether.

Presupposition is also related to structural resources, since it can be encoded in questions such as: does your English let you down? Why are you ashamed of your English? Note that in the last example, the reader is denied the answer in the negative. The readers' "ineptitude" is built on the proposition implied in the question. To deny it is to reject the whole proposition (Benwell and Stokoe 2006: 179).

1.5.1.5 Metaphor and metonymy

Metaphor refers to the process in which one word figuratively stands for another to imply a relationship of similarities. If the same metaphor is repeated frequently, it may have a strong effect. Lakoff and Johnson (2008) argue that metaphorical representations shape our cognitive processing of events and can also serve ideological aims. Disease metaphors, for example, can be used to describe social problems or unrest (Fairclough 1989: 120).

Metonymy refers to the exchange of one word for one of its attributes—for instance, "the crown" can be used to refer to the monarch or "the university" can refer to the administrators involved in making decisions at the university.

1.5.1.6 Intertextuality and dialogicality

For the purpose of this work, intertextuality is defined as the "embedding of another's discourse" into a current one. In order for intertextuality to be effective as a linguistic resource, it must be dependent on shared knowledge of previous texts (Oropeza-Escobar 2011: 5).

For example, in a poem by the Egyptian poet Hishām al-Jukhkh, in which he addresses Egypt while adopting the stance of the protestors during the Revolution of 2011, "A bird's eye view from Tahrir Square," the poet uses intertextuality when he says "greetings from the River Nile." This phrase is, in fact, taken from a poem by Poet Laureate Aḥmad Shawqī, "Ghandī" ("Ghandi") (1931), in which Shawqī was welcoming Ghandi to Egypt as a peaceful freedom fighter, who shared with Egyptians the same aspirations and demands. Ghandi passed by Egypt on his way to India in 1931. Aḥmad Shawqī (1995 IV: 83) says:

Sala:ma n-ni:li ya: ġandi:
Wa ha:ða z-zahru min ʕindi:

Greetings from the river Nile to you Ghandi
And these flowers are from me to you.

When al-Jukhkh embeds this very same clause in his poem, he does so for a discourse function that is related directly to his stance. Intertextuality can also be used in constructing local identities and family ties (Damari 2010: 612; see also Hamilton 1996; Tannen 2007).

According to Du Bois, dialogicality

> makes its presence felt to the extent that a stance-taker's words derive from and further engage with the words of those who have spoken before—whether immediately within the current exchange of stance utterances, or more remotely along the horizons of language and prior text as projected by the community of discourse. (2007: 140)

Oropeza-Escobar (2011: 23) argues that "utterances are dialogical in that they are both responsive to the prior context and acts as context for the following contribution."

For example, in the same poem by al-Jukhkh, the poet, when addressing Egypt, clearly refers to the discourse of pro-government attackers who accused the people of Tahrir of being agents of foreign countries.

la: tatruki:him yuxbiru:ki bi-ʔannani:/ ʔaṣbaḥtu ʃayʔan ta:fihan wa muwajjaha:

Do not let them tell you that I have / become something trivial and controlled by foreigners.

There are other examples of dialogicality throughout this work, simply because identity construction is related to the perception of both insiders and outsiders, which is reflected in discourse and counter-discourse. That is, when outsiders or insiders make a claim about Egyptian identity, public discourse engages in a dialogical conversation with this insider or outsider to resist or emphasize the aspect of identity that is discussed.

1.5.2 Structural resources

1.5.2.1 Grammatical patterns: nominalization, verbless sentences

Verbless sentences in which the verb "to be" is implicit have been touched upon earlier and are a popular resource in public discourse for the factual indexes they carry in Arabic.

Nominalization is an important discourse process that frequently occurs in Egyptian public discourse, and, as Holes (2004: 320) contends, nominalization gives an objective flavor to statements. Fakhri (2012) also argues that nominalization in Arabic written discourse is used to express generic factual statements.

Related to nominalization is the transitivity framework. According to Van Leeuwen (1996), there is a relationship between transitivity and social actors, which, according to him, go beyond grammatical categories. He first posits that there are a number of socio-semantic categories relevant for the study of discourse, such as activation or passivation, which can be realized by the traditional active or passive voice, but can also be realized by possessive pronouns. For example, "my teacher" passivates me, while "our intake" activates us. For the purpose of this work, the transitivity framework will not be adopted. Grammatical structures, including nominalization, are essential in Arabic and will be referred to when relevant.

1.5.2.2 Pronouns

Pronouns are employed to create and sustain different stances and positions. They are one of the most essential markers of identity negotiation and construction.

The way that people employ pronouns, especially in addressing recipients, has implications for their interpersonal relationships and the way that the receivers are positioned (Benwell and Stokoe 2006: 115). Pronouns also decide the level of relational development (Benwell and Stokoe 2006: 119). Fairclough (1989) also argues that the way in which newspaper editorials frequently use "we" presupposes agreement with the reader and authority to speak on his or her behalf. The informal "you" can also be used as a "simulated personal address" (Benwell and Stokoe 2006: 115). Fairclough and Wodak (1997) analyze the use of pronouns by the former British Prime Minister Margaret Thatcher. For example, they argue that she used "we" ambiguously as both an inclusive and exclusive "we" that refers to the British people or political institution, respectively.

Vuković (2012) also examines how pronouns are used in parliamentary discourse in Montenegro to position politicians in relation to their audience. Another way that pronouns can be used is to create what Fairclough (1989: 205) calls "synthetic personification," which is a strategy usually adopted in advertisements to create a direct and informal relationship between the audience and the speaker by referring to the audience in the second person singular "you."

1.5.2.3 Tense and aspect

Aspect is a semantic category of a verb that describes the internal components of a verbal event. It describes an action or event as either complete, whole or incomplete, or as an ongoing process (Eisele 2006). Tense describes the time of an event as past, present, or future. It is noteworthy that tense and aspect in Arabic, especially SA, are at times difficult to distinguish. Holes (2004), for example, argues that SA is more an aspectual language than a tense one, with tense being the product of a context, rather than a verb form. Holes, however, acknowledges that SA and dialects are moving towards a tense system, rather than an aspectual one. Holes calls verbs that denote the present tense "p-stem verbs," since they are conjugated by a prefix, and he calls verbs that denote the past tense "s-stem verbs," since they are conjugated by a prefix. Aspectual markers in ECA include the b-prefix attached to p-stem verbs to indicate a continuing process. In the song and poem "Egypt speaks about itself" (1921) (analyzed in detail in Chapter 4), tense is manipulated to juxtapose the Egyptian's achievements and past to that of different invaders and colonizers.

1.5.2.4 Demonstratives, deixis, quantification, and negation

In the song "I saw you before" (2011), the singer says:

> *w-la: lamaḥtak yo:m hina tuṣrux tiʔu:l taġyi:r*
>
> Or have I seen you one day "here" screaming for change.

The singer uses the deictic marker *hina* ("here"; "in close proximity") to refer to Tahrir Square. With no knowledge of the political event of the year, his deictic marker is meaningless. With background knowledge, this deictic marker implies more than Tahrir Square. The fact that the singer uses *hina* not only implies the close proximity of Tahrir both physically and emotionally, but it also may literally imply that he is singing his song from Tahrir Square itself. The communal solidarity created throughout the song may also be the result of the physical proximity between him and the martyrs of Tahrir Square.

Negation is also used in presupposition in the song "Egypt, my love" (1967), as will be made clear in Chapter 4. Quantification in Arabic is generally expressed through quantifier nouns that precede another noun in the genitive case. Unlike in English, quantification therefore entails the creation of a category, to which the quantified noun is assigned. Among the quantifiers, *kull* stands out in that its meaning differs depending on status of the following noun; whereas with a definite noun, it conveys the sense of a full set of subparts of a single individual (*kulli l-maṣriyyi:n*), with an indefinite noun, it conveys the sense of a loose set of individual entities (*kulli maṣri*) ("each and every single Egyptian") (Hallman 2009).

1.5.2.5 *Conditional sentences*

Conditional sentences are made up of two structurally independent clauses that contain propositions such that the validity of one is dependent on the validity of another (Holes 2004: 266). For this reason, conditional sentences are used to assert positive descriptions of Egyptians, as will be clear in Chapter 4.

1.5.2.6 *Mode and modality*

Modality refers to a micro-analysis of the clause structure that concerns itself with the functional categories of statements: whether the utterance is declarative (a proposition), interrogative (a question), or imperative (a command). Modality also refers to "expressions of commitment to the truth or obligation of a proposition" (Benwell and Stokoe 2006: 112). Modal items have different grammatical forms that include adverbs, such as the English adverbs, "possibly," "certainly," "perhaps," and so on; modal verbs, such as the English "must" and "could"; participial adjectives, such as "it is required"; verbs of cognition, such as "I feel" and "I believe"; and copular verbs, such as "it seems," "it appears," "it is," and so on.

Modality, on the other hand, may express certainty and strong obligation—this is called "high modality," as in the case of "must," "should," "definitely," and "always"—or uncertainty and weak obligation, which is termed "low modality," such as "could," "possibly," "perhaps," and "kind of." Mode and modality are essential in helping us understand discourse roles—for example, our knowledge of who asks the questions. The question "who issues commands?" may be an index of "social proximity," familiarity, and involvement. It may also reflect attitude and ideology (Benwell and Stokoe 2006: 112).

1.5.2.7 Phonological, structural, and lexical variations
In order for us to better understand the role of phonological, structural, and lexical variations, they will be discussed in relation to code-switching and identity construction.

1.6 Conclusion

It has been established in this chapter that Egyptian identity as referenced in public discourse cannot be fully differentiated or separated out into individual, social, and national components. This is because of the very nature of public discourse and its tendency to generalize and homogenize, even while acknowledging differences. That is, Egyptians are perceived as forming a large coherent community, which share the same attributes, including language, ethnicity, locality, habits, and so on. Egyptian identity as such is ideological, perceptual, and habitual. That is the reason why a thorough and systematic study of identity has to depend on linguistic concepts, such as indexicality. It also has to approach language as a dynamo within an extensive cycle of political and social dynamic framework.

Language is utilized in the Egyptian context in two different yet related ways. Language can be viewed as a social variable that serves as a classification category: in this case, language is similar to other social variables, which are referenced in public discourse to negotiate an identity (ethnicity, locality, and historicity). At the same time, language can be used as a resource to provide a stance that positions individuals as either belonging or not belonging to a group.

In order to avoid falling into the trap of over-interpretation, I propose to perform a rigorous analysis of the discourse and structural resources, using examples taken from public discourse. Orders of indexes mediate between linguistic resources and social markers of identity. As Blommaert (2007: 115) contends, indexicality relates language to cultural patterns.

Indexicality can also explain cases of code-switching and code-choices between different codes. In Egyptian public discourse, language ideology, ethno-linguistic and social variables, audience, and context all coordinate together to create scopes of linguistic choices, the indexes of which are creative, performative, and unbounded.

Although Egyptians are exposed to the same ideologies, and Egyptian public discourse demonstrates how these shared perceptions are pertinent in identity construction, access to linguistic resources is not always stable or expected, but is challenged and negotiated in Egyptian public discourse, especially at times of political turmoil. Le Page et al. (1985) highlight the fact that language is a marker and maker of identity. It reveals our personal background and aspirations and "it thus metaphorically marks where we come from and where we hope to be going" (1985: 337). This is precisely what this book attempts to show. Language is a resource, the access to which is negotiated and, at times, challenged. Blommaert (2010: 38) argues that "'order of indexicality' is a sensitizing concept that should index ('point a finger to') important aspects of power and inequality in the field of semiosis." This is because forms of semiosis related to power and authority in different communities are "socially and culturally valued."

In the following two chapters, I will attempt to sketch the ideological and perceptual references of language use in Egypt, in order to understand the higher indexes of different forms. This will provide the basis for a better understanding of the use of linguistic resources in Egyptian public discourse.

Notes

1. Nasser offered his resignation on June 9, 1967, but after "spontaneous mass demonstrations implored him to remain in office" decided to stay (Haag 2005: 335). He died of a heart attack on September 28, 1970, and Sadat came to power. On October 6, 1973, Sadat launched a sudden attack on Israel. The crossing of the Suez Canal, as well as the relatively heavy losses on the Israeli side "breaks the myth of Israeli military invincibility and erases the humiliation of 1967" (Haag 2005: 347).
2. The original Arabic text of the blog follows below:
من هم المصريين . . . أحاول أن افهم وليساعدني الله في هذا فهي لخبطة ما بعدها لخبطة هل من يسكن مصر هو المصري أم من يحكم مصر أم اي حد عدي عليها بصراحة تهت هل مصر تتكلم العربية لذلك هي عربية ولا فرعونية أن كان المعيار تسمية الشعب باسم الملك. . . ولم نطب المؤرخين والكتاب من الفراعنة للعرب هل تغير اللغة هو المعيار. . . ولم ومتي أصبحنا مصريين . . . هل عندما حكمنا العرب فقط وقبلها مع حكم الرومان والبيزنطيين كنا فراعنة . . . متي تحولنا من فراعنة لمصريين بصراحة لخبطة تجعلني أقوم مفزوعة من النوم فانا احلم إني معلقة في الهواء لا اعلم من أكون فأهيم علي وجهي في النت والكتب لعلي أجد إجابة تعرفني بس أنا مين يا تري المشكلة ديه مشكلة مصر أو مشكلة تلك البقعة ما هو أنا مش عارفة اسمها إيه وها تصل لأيه يا تري العراق والعراقيين عرب أم مسلمين أم روم أم وأم ما هو ما طالنا طالهم . . . قلت ابعد شوية يا تري أمريكا تعتبر هنود أم بعدد اكبر تعددا ديني أم جنس وعرق وبلد ..
3. The article will be discussed in detail in Chapter 6.
4. Code-switching and the concept of subject positioning will both be dcalt with in more detail in the next sections.
5. Additionally, Gumperz (1982: 95) discussed for the first time the "we" and "they" dichotomy. There are two different codes used by speakers generally: the "we" code and the "they" code. The socially inclusive "we" code is associated with home and family bonds, while the socially distanced "they" code is associated with public interactions.
6. A different approach to code-switching than the one used in this book is the Myers-Scotton approach, which is briefly summarized here. Myers-Scotton

(1993) tries to explain code-switching as a universal, rule-governed phenomenon. She contends that the fact that people switch from one code to another or from one language to another does not necessarily mean that this switching has a social motivation. Code-switching in itself does not have to denote any effect, nor does it necessarily have any discourse function. Code-switching can be used as the unmarked variety of certain communities (as the normal linguistic behavior). It can be used with no particular social motivation behind it; although for an outsider to this community it does carry a social message, whereas for an insider it is the norm.

Myers-Scotton also argues that whether code-switching has a discourse function or social motivation depends on both the speaker and audience. Both are aware of what is conventionally expected from them in a community. This idea of mutual agreement concerning the expectations of audience and speaker is what differentiates marked from unmarked choices. Myers-Scotton explains what she means by markedness by proposing that "what community norms would predict is unmarked, what is not predicted is marked" (1998: 5). In other words, switching is governed by tacit social conventions.

Myers-Scotton goes further, by proposing that an ability to switch is implied in the communicative competence that all individuals possess (1998: 6). She compares this communicative competence to the grammatical competence of a language. In her theory, switching is not just a performance process, but a rule-governed competence that native speakers learn. In other words, all developmentally normal humans have the ability to learn how the community or communities that they are part of evaluate switches, whether style shifts, dialect switches, diglossic switches, or bilingual code-switching, and, likewise, they possess the ability to learn to perform, practice, and use such switches for a range of interactional purposes.

First, Myers-Scotton differentiates between using code-switching with no motivation in mind as the unmarked choice, while using it with a specific motivation in mind is the marked choice. Where the phenomenon of switching is unmarked, actual switches are more frequent and the phenomenon more predictable (one can predict that it will happen, but not how many times or where—that is, it is predictably unpredictable).

All people, according to Myers-Scotton, are equipped with the competence to assess linguistic choices. All people have a "predisposition" (1998: 6) to see linguistic choices as marked or unmarked. There is perhaps an extra message in a linguistic choice that is socio-psychological in nature. All speakers have a markedness evaluator with which to measure the markedness of an utterance, and, crucially, they learn their local community's ways of assessing markedness. They have the ability to understand that marked choices will be received differently from unmarked choices. For speakers to have this competence, they have to be exposed to the use of unmarked and marked choices. Just as exposure to grammatical structures makes people competent in a language, so exposure to marked and unmarked choices makes them competent in making and understanding linguistic choices. There is always a link between the use of a linguistic code and its effect in a certain situation; this is part of learning a language.

Within this framework, speakers as individuals make choices from within their linguistic repertoire, in order to achieve certain goals that are of significance to them. They act rationally, because they have a set of choices, and they presumably make the best choice. By "the best choice," I mean the choice that will benefit the speaker most, given the audience and the circumstances surrounding the speech event, and that involves the least effort on the speaker's part. That is to say, a speaker must calculate the costs and rewards of one choice over another (Myers-Scotton 1993: 110). "Costs" refers to the quantity of words she or he uses and the stylistic devices, and "rewards" refers to the intentional, as well as the referential, meaning that she or he conveys to the listener (see also Grice's 1975 maxims and the relevance theory of Sperber and Wilson (1986)). The speaker makes a choice that minimizes costs and maximizes rewards. Thus, speakers choose one code over another, because of the rewards that they expect from that choice, relative to its costs. So the role of the speaker is emphasized. But note also that the choice made by the speaker is connected to the audience's expectations. The speaker wants to have an effect on the audience and thus maximize her or his own rewards: the audience has certain expectations from the speaker; whether these expectations are met or not determines whether the choice the speaker has made is marked or not. That is to say, if the code used is expected by the audience, then the speaker is using an unmarked choice and does not necessarily want to have a particular effect on that audience. If, on the other hand, the speaker uses a code that is not expected by the audience, then she or he is making a marked choice for the purpose of having an impact on the audience.

Another point that I want to mention about Myers-Scotton's theory is that she recalls the fact that speakers negotiate different identities all the time. She claims that this is a major factor in code-switching: "A major motivation for variety in linguistic choices in a given community is the possibility of social identity negotiations" (1993: 111). Speakers negotiate mainly in order to reach an agreement about the mode of the interaction. They make choices either to emphasize their position or convey their own views.

7. See also Haddington (2007: 297) for an elaborate discussion of the relation between stance and presupposition.

CHAPTER

2

A HISTORICAL OVERVIEW OF THE DEVELOPMENT OF NATIONAL IDENTITY IN MODERN EGYPT WITH REFERENCE TO LANGUAGE: THE FORMATIVE PERIOD

There lie those nine or ten million native Egyptians at the bottom of the social ladder, a poor, ignorant, credulous, but withal not unkindly race, being such as sixty centuries of misgovernment and oppression by various rules, from pharaohs to pashas, have made them. It is for the civilised Englishman to extend to them the hand of fellowship and encouragement, and to raise them, morally and materially, from the abject state in which he finds them [. . .]

(Evelyn Baring, Earl of Cromer 1908: 130)

In fact, the Englishman will soon find that the Egyptian, whom he wishes to mold into something really useful with the view of his becoming eventually autonomous, is merely the rawest of raw material [. . .]

(Evelyn Baring, Earl of Cromer 1908: 131)

I am the Egyptian, of noble stock.
I have built glory across the two pyramids.
My grandparents created great science
My generous Nile is alive in the fertile valley
My ancestors have survived for thousands of years.
The universe could perish and they still remain
Shall I tell you about a lover that forced me to emigrate and leave my family and friends?
I have given my life as a gift to that lover. I cannot love another

(from the song *ʔana l-maṣri:* ("I am the Egyptian")
by Sayyid Darwīsh (1921))

The relationship between the first two quotes and the third, despite both originating from very different sources (one from a history book, the other from a play (*Shahrazād* 1921)), cannot be ignored. The first quote was produced in English, the second in mostly ECA with SA lexical items. Although never before analyzed together, it is obvious that one is a reaction to the other. The first extract (above) is from Cromer's famous work *Modern Egypt*. In his biography of Cromer, Roger Owens argues that during Cromer's time as High Commissioner, he undermined the concept of a coherent Egyptian identity. Others found that Cromer regarded Egyptians as "incapable of self-government owing to the mental deficiencies characteristic of the Oriental, a socially retrograde Islam, or both" (Lockman 2006: 217). Indeed, it would seem that, politically, it was more convenient for Cromer to provide the European outsider with a picture of Egypt as

> a mongrel nation full of peasants and sheikhs so stuck in their traditional ways that only a European outsider could bring them the law, order, water, and regular taxation they needed to make best use of their simple assets [. . .] Like the British in India, he was caught, in David Washbrook's trenchant phrase, "between inventing an Oriental society and abolishing it." (Owen 2004: 395)

Egyptian nationalists at the time were aware of Cromer's discourse and his emphasis on the concept of a disintegrated Egyptian identity. To give but one example, Aḥmad Luṭfī al-Sayyid wrote in *al-Jaridah* (1899, cited in Jibrīl 2009: 565), the leading nationalist paper of the time to which many of the country's leading figures contributed, that there was no "Egyptianness in the state school system and no study of the real political world." Nationalists responded in many ways, through political articles, protests, and books, but most importantly through a counter-discourse found within the Egyptian media: literature, theater, songs, and later films. Egyptian nationalists primarily used this counter-discourse as a defense mechanism against the real and perceived attacks of the imperialistic movement of the time, as is, indeed, apparent in their patriotic songs.

Both directly and indirectly, the British occupation of Egypt helped shape the modern manifestation of Egyptian identity. The British occupation led Egyptian nationalists and intellectuals to start questioning and renegotiating their place and role in the political and social world.

For example, the characteristics mentioned by Cromer, which in his opinion hinder Egyptians from becoming elevated to the status of the civilized Englishman, are also the same characteristics that Egyptians employ to define themselves, including traits such as generosity, spirituality, and kindness. It is important to realize that Egyptian intellectuals at the time had mixed feelings towards the British occupation and Cromer, and furthermore, there were negotiations, interactions, and communication between Egyptians and the British on different levels.

Even Ḥāfiẓ Ibrāhīm himself wrote about Cromer in both a negative as well as a positive light.[1]

As Fahmy (2011: xii) argues, during the beginning of the twentieth century, the fragmented, old, and local structures of Egyptian identity began to change into a more coherent concept of a unified community. Fahmy (2011: 19) contends that this more solid identity was made possible because of widespread ECA audiovisual material that reached a larger portion of Egyptians and helped develop a sense of camaraderie. While performances and broadcasts through audiovisual media were mainly in ECA, the role of SA as a resource that was available to some Egyptians cannot be ignored, as will be clear in the following chapters.

Although this chapter will concentrate on the formation of public identity in Egypt in the twentieth century, this is not to claim that Egyptians did not have a sense of a national identity before that or that this identity was not related to language use.

Suleiman (2008: 30) argues that language was used as a means of "textual resistance" in Egypt as far back as the French campaign (1798–1801), if not before. Mitchell (1991, cited in Suleiman 2008) discusses the response of the famous chronicler al-Jabartī (1753/4–1825) to Napoleon's communication with the Egyptians during his invasion (Mitchell 1991: 133):

> Landing at Alexandria and advancing upon Cairo Napoleon's first act had been to use a printed proclamation to the Egyptian people, prepared in Arabic by French Orientalists. Jabarti's response to this strange innovation, in a chronicle written in the midst of the crisis, was an interesting one. He began his account by copying the text of the proclamation, and followed it for several pages with a detailed list of its grammatical errors. Phrase by phrase he pointed out the colloquialisms, misspellings, ellipses, inconsistencies, morphological inaccuracies and errors of syntax of the French Orientalists, drawing from these incorrect usages a picture of the corruptions, deceptions, misunderstandings and ignorances of the French authorities.

This example is significant, since language is used to authenticate an identity. In this case, the use of SA is a symbol of sincerity and truth, while the use of bad SA is a symbol of insincerity, lack of knowledge, and deception. SA is used as an independent variable—a classification category. Access to SA indicates a sincere Egyptian identity. Access to bad SA or lack of access to SA indicates deception and a lack of knowledge of the true Egyptian character.

However, there were some historical, ideological, and political changes in Egypt during the beginning of the twentieth century that led to an increased awareness of a distinct identity. The struggle to maintain this identity was also related to a struggle to maintain SA at times and ECA at others. From a socio-political perspective, these changes are of the utmost importance. They would eventually lead to the January 25, 2011 Revolution.

Edwards (2009: 16) posits that times of transition "whether welcomed or imposed are also times of renewed self-examination." The beginning of the twentieth century in Egypt was a time of transition: transitions were at times imposed by outsiders, at others triggered by insiders.

Within a span of fifty years (from the end of the nineteenth century and into the twentieth), there were several major historical events that impacted on Egypt in ways that are still felt in the present day. These events included: the British occupation (1882–1952); the 1919 Revolution; the end of the Caliphate period and the separation between Egypt and Turkey (1923); the creation of parliamentary democracy (1922–3); the discovery of the tomb of Tutankhamen in 1922 (Suleiman 2003: 175–6); and last but most essential, the creation of Egyptian nationality on November 5, 1914. On a different level, the rise of Egypt as a cultural center and the establishment of the Egyptian press as the central press for all Arab countries greatly impacted on the language in Egypt.

This chapter will trace the historical development of identity and its relation to language up until the end of the twentieth century. In so doing, it will also shed light on essential concepts that directly impact on the indexes of different codes in Egypt, including concepts such as nationalism, language policy, language ideology, and language attitudes.

2.1 Egypt as a nation and a nation-state

Guibernau (2007: 60) defines a nation as "a human group conscious of forming a community, sharing a common culture, attached to a clearly demarcated territory, having a common past and a common project for the future, and claiming the right to rule itself." Guibernau's definition is perhaps difficult to apply to any country, since a perception of what constitutes a common culture, a common collective perspective of the future, and a common feeling of autonomy is subjective. While nationalism has been blamed as a method for fostering intolerance and exclusivity, it has also been a major factor in sustaining states and providing discontented groups with the solid ground needed to voice their claims. Edwards (2009: 201) argues that

> nationalism has proved a powerful force in the world, one that has endured well beyond the lifespan that many would have predicted. It has had important cultural manifestations. It has been a positive force, particularly in the lives of those who have felt threatened by larger or more influential neighbors.

One of the major factors in defining a nation seems to be the psychological dimension of belonging to a community. At the same time, a "nation" is often associated with a specific territory or religion. A nation may also have its way of perceiving itself in relation to history, which may or may not be an accurate perception, for a nation will have its own myths (Grosby 2005). Note also that a national identity may remain buried for years and can be resurrected at times of crises or major historical turning points (Guibernau 2007).

A nation, as opposed to a state, does not necessarily have clear borders or the legitimacy that a state may have. In other words, "[t]he state may be loosely defined as a structure that, through institutions, exercises sovereignty over a territory using laws that relate the individuals within that territory to one another as members of the state" (Grosby 2005: 22). A state may also have citizens from different nations. For example, Britain is a state with different "nations," such as the Welsh and Scottish nations (Guibernau 2007).

Egypt is considered a nation-state. A nation-state has clear borders and its members still feel that they are connected by common territory, language, and other factors. As Goldschmidt (2008: 222) phrases it, present-day Egypt "is now both a nation (an object of loyalty) and a state (a political and legal system)."[2] At the same time, it is also often construed as part of a larger "Arab nation."

During the beginning of the twentieth century, Egypt's ambivalence towards the Arab nation signals the disagreement between Egypt and its Arab neighbours in their attitude towards the ailing Ottoman Empire. Eastern Arabs in what we now call Syria, Iraq, Hijaz in Saudi Arabia, Jordan, and Palestine still believed in the Ottoman Empire, while Egyptian leaders were preoccupied with the issue of independence. The depth of the divide may be gleaned from the remarks of the Syrian Arab nationalist Sāṭiʿ al-Ḥuṣrī after he visited Egypt in 1931. To his disappointment, he had found that Egyptians did not share his Arab nationalist sentiments, nor did they consider Egypt to be part of the Arab world. Indeed, they would not even acknowledge the fact that Egypt had been part of an Arab nation in the past (Suleiman 2003: 139–40). However, al-Ḥuṣrī's reflections do not give the full picture, nor do they thoroughly account for Egyptians' attitude at the time.

On the other hand, it was, in fact, Egypt that initiated the Arab League in 1943, just twelve years after al-Ḥuṣrī's visit. The Arab League was proposed by the Egyptian Prime Minister Naḥḥās as a reaction to the Union of the Fertile Crescent States (Iraq, Transjordan, Syria, Lebanon, and Palestine), which had been proposed by Nūrī al-Saʿīd, the Iraqi Prime Minister. Naḥḥās feared that such a union would diminish Egypt's influence in the Arab world, and therefore he proposed the Arab League, which would be a league of independent Arab states. This "looser association" was organized at a conference in Alexandria in 1944. Its official existence began in March 1945 and was initially directed by the Egyptian Secretary-General, ʿAdb al-Raḥmān ʿAzzām (1893–1976). The League included Saudi Arabia, Yemen, Egypt, Transjordan, Iraq, Syria, and Lebanon, although several other countries joined later.

The "Arab nation" is still represented by the Arab League and remains headed by an Egyptian, Nabīl al-ʿArabī (from 2011 to the present). When compared to the European Union (EU), the Arab League is first and foremost an ideological construct and therefore different in many respects from the European model. Both Guibernau (2007) and Ricento (2006: 55) note that the EU is comprised of countries with different perceptions of history, different languages, and a different way of looking at the universe. Consider, for example, the differences between Greece and Sweden, such as differences in location, language, and culture. However, the EU functions relatively efficiently as a political and economic organism. The Arab League, on the other hand, is different, since it comprises "the Arab Nation." Indeed, the Arab League defines itself on its website as "an association of countries whose peoples are Arabic-speaking." Its stated objectives are to strengthen relations among the member states, coordinate their policies, and promote their interests. Guibernau (2007: 115) calls the EU a non-emotional identity. By contrast, I would call the Arab League "an ideological–emotional entity." While it is constituted primarily of Arabic-speaking countries or countries in which Arabic is the main or only official language, it also comprises countries where Arabic is not the only language used, such as Djibouti (where French is also an official language and arguably more dominant), Somalia (where Somali is both the official and most commonly used language), not to mention Berber languages in Morocco and the Maghreb in general.

2.2 The formation of modern Egyptian identity

The beginning of the twentieth century witnessed the rise of Egyptian nationalism and the appearance of prominent political figures, such as Aḥmad ʿUrabī, Muṣṭafā Kāmil, and Saʿd Zaghlūl, and intellectual figures, such as Ṭāhā Ḥusayn, Yaḥyā Ḥaqqī, and Tawfīq al-Ḥakīm. These political and intellectual figures were part of an intellectual milieu that was different from that of their parents (see Starkey 1998: 401–3). Even so, they were concerned with formulating a way of maintaining an Egyptian dignity. This dignity is only attainable if Egyptians have a distinct and special identity that places them on par with the British, on the one hand, and outsiders, more generally. These Egyptian nationalists perceived Egypt as a nation-state that deserved the pride, love, and, most importantly, loyalty of its citizens. Note that the intellectual and political elite were mostly bilingual and educated abroad, primarily in France and England (Starkey 1998: 402).

In 1901, the Jewish–Egyptian dramatist Yaʿqūb Ṣannūʿ (1839–1911) established a short-lived satirical newspaper with nationalist inclinations (Haag 2005), *Abū Naḍḍārah*, and also claimed to have coined the slogan *"maṣr lil-maṣriyyi:n"* ("Egypt for Egyptians") (Reid 1998: 223). The slogan gained increased popularity, especially after the discovery of Tutankhamen's tomb. The slogan was a simple, flexible statement that could be written in a neutral form of Arabic, realized in either SA or ECA, depending on the realization of the vowels (SA: *"miṣr lil-miṣriyyi:n"*; ECA: *"maṣr lil-maṣriyyi:n"*). Slogans of this same format are, of course, found in other countries, too, and have become rallying cries for xenophobic or fascist movements. In Egypt, however, it was a means of maintaining an identity, perceived as inferior by others, and also attacked through political and social oppression. In this context, it is interesting to consider the following statement by Ahdaf Soueif in her memoir of the Egyptian Revolution (Soueif 2012: 164):

> Omar says isn't "a girl draped in the flag of Egypt . . . etc." a typical fascist image? I say surely it's fascist only if you're powerful? We'd just got rid of the king in '52, the British in '54 – and then been attacked by Britain, France and Israel in '56. Can't we be allowed a girl in a flag?

In other words, expressions of nationalist sentiment are construed to be directed primarily against the foreign occupation, not foreigners per se. However, these distinctions need not detain us here. What is more interesting for the purpose of this chapter is the question: who are "Egyptians?" This question began to dawn on public figures in Egypt just as this slogan gained currency, appearing in public discourse more frequently than before.

To elaborate, the slogan, which smacks of nationalism, was perhaps a reaction to the status of Egyptians at the time. Egyptians were regarded as third-class citizens—the "subject race." The British and foreign elites at the time, although comparatively small in number,[3] had more political and social power than Egyptians and enjoyed special privileges. To give but some examples, there were special courts for foreigners to resolve disputes between them and Egyptians and there were exclusive social clubs for the British, in which Egyptians were not allowed to enter. Egyptians started to express a clear awareness of a different ethnic identity and different narration of history and its relation to their present.

Another element that feeds into Yaʿqūb Ṣannūʿ's slogan is the famous statement of the Egyptian statesman Muṣṭafā Kāmil (1874–1908) *"law lam akun miṣri:yan la-wadadtu an akuna miṣri:yan"* ("If I were not an Egyptian, I would have liked to be one"). The pride that Kāmil derives from, and attributes to, his being Egyptian was certainly neither shared by the British occupiers, nor the foreign elite who had more power and political, economic, and juristic rights at the time.[4]

Kāmil, like other nationalists, had to show what was so special about being an Egyptian and what being an Egyptian *meant* in the first place. When Muṣṭafā Kāmil founded the National Party in 1907, he and his cofounders were forced to define who could become a member in the new party.[5] The definition they arrived at is highly relevant for the present study: Kāmil and his colleagues declared that the National Party (al-Ḥizb al-Waṭanī) could include any person who *"man yazraʕu ʔarḍa miṣr/ wa-yatakallamu bi-luġati-ha:"* ("Whoever cultivates the land of Egypt and speaks its language"). It is supposedly an SA declaration, but can, of course, be pronounced with ECA vocalization. The significance of the definition above lies in its inclusiveness and apparent simplicity.

It is important to note that in Kāmil's days, the "land of Egypt" was not cultivated only by Egyptians. In fact, large tracts of Egypt's agricultural land were owned by Turkish landowners, even though the peasants who worked the land were mostly Egyptians. And yet, many members who joined the National Party were of Turkish origin (according to al-Ḥakīm, cited in Jibrīl 2009). This serves to show that the word "origin" itself is a more flexible term than public discourse will acknowledge. In any case, the reference to "the land of Egypt" is essential, since locality plays a pivotal role in defining identity. It is not surprising, then, that "the land" features repeatedly and prominently in Egyptian public discourse, including in the 1954 novel *al-Arḍ* ("The land") by ʿAbd al-Raḥmān al-Sharqāwī (1920–87), which depicts the attachment of Egyptian peasants to their land and their readiness to die holding on to its soil, rather than live without it. In addition, references to the "land of Egypt" occur in almost all patriotic songs, and the relationship between the River Nile, the land, and the people of Egypt is repeatedly taught to students in government schools in a variety of subjects.

This focus on "the land" is not surprising: the relation between identity and locality has been examined before in sociolinguistics, especially in approaches such as the social network approach to variation research (Milroy 1987). Land is concrete and easy to define and demarcate. It is easy to suggest that people who share a land interact frequently and share values and resources.

The second part of the definition ("and who speaks her language") is even simpler, yet it remains ambiguous. To begin with, the Arabic language is not mentioned by name. However, it is implied that Egypt's main language is Arabic, and Egyptians' language is therefore also Arabic.

However, the definition does not specify which variety of Arabic is meant, SA or ECA. One could deduce that ECA is meant, since it is the *spoken* language of Egypt, and the definition refers to speaking explicitly. However, this is not necessarily the case, given the formal nature of the declaration. It may be that both SA and ECA would be included. What is of interest in this definition is that it relates language to locality, politics, and, more importantly, Egyptian identity. It would seem that in Kāmil's mind, a person who did not speak Arabic but who cultivated the land was not eligible to be a member of the National Party. This would then exclude landowners of Turkish origin who did not master SA or ECA. Unfortunately, there are no statistics to reveal how many non-Egyptians did or did not master Arabic. Instead, one has to rely on anecdotal evidence in memoirs and history books, which largely suggest that the foreign elites in Egypt saw no need to learn or speak Arabic, because of the prevalence of European languages in use. Indeed, Kāmil himself was educated in both Egypt and France and must have been completely bilingual, since he had a French patron and wrote articles for French newspapers in France. It is also well-known that the Egyptian King Fu'ād (r. 1917–36), who ruled Egypt after the formation of Kāmil's party, was not fluent in Arabic. Technically, this would have rendered him ineligible to be a member in the National Party. In short, Arabic was not the prestigious language of the educated or the wealthy—whether Egyptians or foreigners: access to land and language together formed the real Egyptian.

It is important to note that the definition of who could join the party did not refer to religion, ethnicity, class, gender, education, age, or any other independent variable. Language and locality were the first two factors referenced as defining Egyptian identity. Of course, the word "Egyptian" was not used by Kāmil himself. Up until this point in history, Egyptians were rarely referred to collectively as "Egyptians," but were often called "*fallāḥūn*" ("peasants") instead. Even during the British occupation, the term "*fallāḥ*" ("peasant") would occur frequently in reference to Egyptians (for example, in Cromer's *Modern Egypt*). Kāmil and his colleagues employed the stereotype already in existence—namely, that Egyptians were really all peasants—to their own benefit. As peasants, they cultivated the land and spoke the language of the land; thus, they owned the land. While the emphasis on speaking the language of Egypt rendered the party an "Egyptian" one, the inclusiveness in the construct "its language" will remain for a long time. Holes (2004) contends that the diglossic situation in Egypt produced "sociolinguistic tension." Kāmil was certainly unaware of the struggle that was to take place between intellectuals in Egypt over the nature of the "true language" of Egypt, whether it is ECA, SA, or both.

In this context, it is important to note that it was only after the formation of the National Party that the Egyptian nationality was created and recognized in international law: the Egyptian nationality was created on November 5, 1914, when Britain and France declared war on Turkey, therewith bringing about the formal separation between Egypt and Turkey. Up until the beginning of World War I, Egypt had formally been part of the Ottoman Empire. In fact, the Ottoman nationality law issued in 1869 referred to Egyptians as "Ottoman subjects" (Jibrīl 2009: 565).[6] Of course, Egypt had no say in the formation of the law. Thus, until 1914, there was technically nothing called an "Egyptian nationality," nor was there any formal public recognition of Egyptians as a people.

The 1919 Revolution started shortly after the formal separation between Egypt and Turkey. It was partly triggered by the arrest of the Egyptian leader Saʿd Zaghlūl (1860–1927) and his associates by British mandate powers on March 8, 1919. Zaghlūl was exiled to Malta after he demanded full independence for Egypt from the British. Before his exile, Zaghlūl and his party circulated petitions around Egypt that Egyptians delegate him, Saʿd Zaghlūl, to represent them, in order to refute arguments by the British that he did not represent the people. Thousands of Egyptians signed the petition and, by doing so, authorized the Wafd party to speak on their behalf. This public mandate in itself made Egyptians feel more involved in the struggle for independence (Sayyid-Marsot 1977: 49).

When Zaghlūl was exiled, women took off their veils and demonstrated alongside men, including both Muslims and Copts. The revolt ended tragically, with the death of 1,000 Egyptians and thirty-six British and Indian soldiers. A month later, in April of 1919, on the recommendation of the new High Commissioner, Lord Allenby, Saʿd Zaghlūl, and his colleagues were released from detention and returned to Egypt. To Egyptians, this was one of the first times that the British had complied with their demands. This enhanced their feelings of patriotism and confidence. Saʿd Zaghlūl himself described the revolution (cited in Haag 2005: 281): "The present movement in Egypt is not a religious movement, for Muslims and Copts demonstrate together, and neither is it a xenophobic movement or a movement calling for Arab unity." Zaghlūl's statement set the stage for the public projection of an Egyptian identity, in which religion was important, but both Christians and Muslims were of equal importance, and in which "Egypt comes first." The fact that Zaghlūl clearly denied that the revolution was tied to hatred of foreigners or to a call for Arab unity emphasizes the Egyptianness of the aims of the revolution and the rise of a distinct Egyptian identity.[7]

The Revolution of 1919 was, of course, triggered by more than just patriotic feelings. It was triggered, among other things, by verbal expressions of Egyptian patriotism. One example is the 1919 song *ʔu:m ya:*

maṣri: ("Rise up, Egyptian") composed by Sayyid Darwīsh (1892–1923) with lyrics by Badīʿ Khayrī. The text of the poem is in colloquial Arabic and was published some years earlier without causing a stir. However, when set to music, it started to gain great popularity and was seen as a threat to the British and the monarchy. As a result, Darwīsh was threatened by the British with imprisonment and exile.

A bitter and yet hopeful song, it urges Egyptians to wake up and take control of their country. Although written and composed before the discovery of the tomb of King Tutankhamen, the song does refer to the glorious past and monuments of Egypt. Below is a selection of relevant parts. Note the references to religion and locality:

> Rise up Egyptian, Egypt is always calling you.
> Take my hand to victory, my victory is your duty.
> Cherish my glory, the glory that you lost with your own hands
> Every bone of your ancestors is ashamed of how fossilized you have become.
> Where are your monuments, you who polluted monuments?
> Love your house/place before you love the universe
> What is the difference between Christians, Muslims, and Jews?
> Power is in unity, in being one person and yet an army.
> Why Egyptian all your conditions are strange?
> You complain about your poverty while you tread on gold.

While aware of their glorious past, Egyptian intellectuals at the time also acknowledged Egypt's abject state and urged Egyptians to overcome their shortcomings. This bitingly critical and bitter mode is perhaps what necessitated a change, whether on the political or intellectual level.[8]

Unlike Kāmil, whose concept of nationalism referenced Islam and the Khalifate, Zhaglūl and his followers emphasized that nationalism was territorial, rather than religious. In their mind, nationalism meant "Egypt first and foremost," without regard for its neighbors or a specific religious community. As Goldschmidt (2008: 95) contends, the nationalists of the 1919 Revolution "viewed Egypt as a nation, the world's oldest, waking up after centuries of sleep [. . .] These nationalists refuted all foreign charges of xenophobia or religious fanaticism. Their first and main demand was for British troops to leave Egypt."

This concept of nationalism was to be further emphasized by later Egyptian political regimes.[9] Likewise, patriotic songs played a dominant role throughout the twentieth century; however, it is no coincidence that this particular song is in ECA. It is, after all, about Egypt and what unites Egyptians and *only* Egyptians.

Perhaps a more important manifestation of the song is the demonstration of the pride that Egyptians felt about their past and Pharaonic history as a result of the discovery of the tomb of Tutankhamen in 1922. In the Valley of the Kings at Luxor, British Egyptologist Howard Carter discovered the tomb of Tutankhamen with all treasures and the mummy untouched. The event became a sensation worldwide, and the impact on Egyptians was profound. Egyptians felt a direct psychological and racial link between modern-day Egyptians and their Pharaonic ancestors (Suleiman 2003: 176).

It is, in fact, common for nations to search the past for roots of identity. As Wodak (1999: 1) argues, "the attempts by both Austria and Italy to adorn their respective 'national pasts' with a historically highly significant archaeological find reveal a typical strategy, metaphorically described by Rudolph Burger (1996: 40) as the 'nationalist dilation of time'." Wodak adds that in British discourse, the nation is expanded mythically into a "transhistorical, and thus eternal, entity" (1999: 1). What is noteworthy, however, is that the archaeological find of Tutankhamen's tomb not only spurred on feelings of pride, but also prompted Egyptians to self-reflect and compare their glorious past to their not so glorious present. The renowned satirical colloquial poet of the time, Bayram al-Tūnisī (1893–1961), recited a poem after the discovery, which sums up the challenges, fears, and bitterness that many Egyptians felt at the time. The poem's title is *Tūt Ankh Amūn* "Letter to Tutankhamen" (referring to the discovery of Tutankhamen's tomb). It says, addressing King Tut (al-Tūnisī 1987: 25):

> In Egypt you had an army and a court.
> No country except yours can produce a mummy.
> No nation except yours can cultivate okra.
> When they entered your tomb they found you,
> Sleeping with open eyes, but in a blind country.

The irony lies in the juxtaposition of past and present: the same country that produced this magnificent mummy has nothing to be proud of, except its cultivation of a common vegetable: okra. While in the past, the king had guards and armies and slept with open eyes, in al-Tūnisī's day, the country was blind to its current situation and dependent on colonizing powers. The poem tacitly urges Egyptians to open their eyes, question themselves, search for their identity, and find their strength as a collective national group. The message that al-Tūnisī conveys is that the past may have been glorious, but the present and future seem gloomy, because Egyptians do not take action. The poem shows that while Egyptians may have been proud of the discovery of Tutankhamen's tomb, they were still aware of the challenges of their time.

Suleiman (2003) argues that as a result of this discovery, Egyptians felt they were different from other Arabs with whom they shared a language, SA. They also felt different from their co-religionists, mainly Muslims. They believed that "Egypt's great powers of assimilation . . . enabled it to absorb waves of immigrants and to stamp their mental make-up with the indelible imprint of its character" (2003: 176). However, the affinity between Egyptians and their Pharaonic past may go back even further than Carter's discovery. In 1881, villagers near Luxor discovered a large number of royal mummies of kings, such as Tuthmosis III of the eighteenth dynasty and Seti I and Ramses II of the nineteenth dynasty. As the boats carrying the mummies left the villages, local women ran along the riverbank throwing dust on their heads and screaming as a sign of mourning for their departed kings (Haag 2005: 261). The discovery of the tomb of King Tut was special, however, because it came at a time when the rise of national feelings combined with a search for a distinct identity. It was not just a matter of villagers mourning their ancestors, but of Egyptians formally identifying with their kings, their past, and what they may have in common with their ancient civilization.

It is hardly surprising, then, to find that European works on the history of ancient Egypt began to be translated into Arabic in the early 1920s. Aḥmad Effendi Ḥassan, the editor of the journal *al-Ādāb*, wrote in the introduction to his translation of a French work of Egyptology that his aim in translating had been "*muba:hatan wa-mufa:xaratan bi-miṣr, wa-ilza:man lil-ʔumam bil-ʔiʕtira:f bi-faḍl al-miṣriyyi:n salafan wa-xalafan*" ("to show pride in Egypt and oblige all other nations to acknowledge the excellence of Egyptians in the past and forever more") (Jibrīl 2009: 565).

Following the discovery of the tomb of King Tut, some intellectuals began to argue that Egyptian Arabic was the true language of Egyptians. Nīqūlā Yūsuf raised the issue in 1929: he posited that Egypt had its own environment, which was very different from the Bedouin environment in which Arabic is spoken. The "Arabic" language, meaning SA, was for him a desert language not suitable for the modern needs of Egypt (Suleiman 2003: 178). Similarly, Salāmah Mūsá (1887–1958) "declared that SA is a dead language which cannot compete with the colloquial as the true mother tongue of Egyptians" (Suleiman 2003: 182). Suleiman notes that Mūsá declared this statement not in ECA, but in SA. Suleiman further contends that Mūsá was similar to those who advocate the use of SA as a spoken language, but who never use it themselves. Mūsá was convinced that Arabs were less advanced than Egyptians, so there was no use in retaining their language. SA, according to Mūsá, was a poor language, which was artificial, difficult, and backward. He went so far as to propose the use of the Roman alphabet to write the colloquial language. Ostensibly, this would have enabled Egyptians to borrow words from

European languages and keep up with modern technology, particularly in the natural sciences (see Suleiman 2003).

However, at the same time, there were intellectuals who were quite aware of the possible dangers associated with abandoning SA altogether. Some proposed modernizing SA to make it more receptive to lexical borrowing from the colloquial and other languages. One of these intellectuals was Luṭfī al-Sayyid (1872–1963), who suggested creating a middle language between standard and colloquial. Others, like the journalist ʿAbd Allāh al-Nadīm (1844–96), warned Egyptians against abandoning the standard language. In his article "Language loss in surrendering the self," he called upon Egyptians to hold on to Arabic—meaning SA—instead of surrendering themselves to foreign languages. It is important to remember that this was all at a time when the British were emphasizing the importance of colloquial and foreign languages in schools (cf. Suleiman 2003: 174).

It is undeniable that political and cultural development had a direct impact on identity construction in Egypt. One pivotal event was the abolishment of the Khalifate in 1923 by the regime of Turkish leader Mustafa Kemal Atatürk. This brought an end to thirteen centuries in which Muslim lands had—at least nominally—been one entity. Although King Fu'ād of Egypt made a discreet attempt at becoming the leading Muslim figure and the Caliph, he abandoned the idea when he received no encouragement (cf. Haag 2005: 280–3). As a result, the issue of independence imposed itself urgently. As Yaḥyá Ḥaqqī notes: "The people [of Egypt] had to discover themselves, to establish their unity, to reach the farthest roots of their existence" (Jibrīl 2009: 563).

Far more important in terms of its linguistic impact on Egypt and the Arab world at large was the rise of Egypt as the cultural hub of the Arab world. In 1919, the first recording studio opened in Cairo; during the 1920s, several film companies began producing silent films in Egypt; and within a relatively short period of time, Egypt became the leader of Arab popular culture.

It was during this period that the Egyptian capitalist Ṭalʿat Ḥarb set up the studio complex in Cairo that was to make Egypt the Hollywood of the Arab world. Egyptian radio started broadcasting in 1932. Later renamed Radio Cairo, it eventually reached the whole of the Arab world. The cultural hegemony of Egypt led to almost all Arabs being exposed to various types of ECA. Eventually, this meant that ECA (and in particular the urban Cairene variety) became almost a semi-standard language in Arab countries and came to be understood by most Arabs who watched Egyptian films and soap operas, listened to Egyptian music, or even read Egyptian colloquial poetry (Holes 2004). Consequently, ECA gained a special status. To the present day, it remains the dialect that boosts the careers of actors or singers from Syria, Lebanon, or the Gulf throughout the Arab world.

A related phenomenon that left a lasting linguistic effect was the rise to stardom of the Egyptian singer Umm Kulthūm (1904–75), who remained an icon of Arabic culture and music for over half a century. It is difficult to overstate the importance of Umm Kulthūm. Virginia Danielson wrote about her in *Harvard Magazine*, saying: "imagine a singer with the virtuosity of Joan Sutherland or Ella Fitzgerald, the public persona of Eleanor Roosevelt and the audience of Elvis and you have Umm Kulthūm."[10]

In 1932, Kulthūm was famous enough throughout Egypt and the Middle East to start a tour through the Arab world that included Damascus, Baghdad, Beirut, and Tripoli. By 1934, Umm Kulthūm was without doubt the most famous and prestigious singer in Egypt; as a result, she was chosen to inaugurate Radio Cairo with her voice on May 31, 1934. In my opinion, Umm Kulthūm changed attitudes towards both SA and ECA and promoted knowledge of both varieties in Egypt and the Arab world at large. By singing songs in ECA that were heard from the Gulf to the Atlantic Ocean, she raised the prestige of ECA to a language of culture accessible to all Arabs. By singing both medieval and modern poetry in SA, she made SA another accessible and common code for Egyptians and all Arabs. Some of her most famous songs are medieval poems set to music, as well as poems by leading poets of the day, such as the Poet Laureates Aḥmad Shawqī and Ḥāfiz Ibrāhīm and the romantic poet Ibrāhīm Nājī. Her linguistic repertoire helped cement SA as a living language more than all of the academies combined. Egyptians, both illiterates and literates, were (and still are) repeating her songs, even if they missed some of the meanings of the SA words. In a community where oral culture plays a major role, her part in forming language attitudes and ideology cannot be ignored.

However, Egypt's cultural awakening was not only restricted to cinema and music. The beginning of the twentieth century also witnessed a flourishing of the publishing industry in Egypt. More books were published in Egypt than in all of the Arab capitals combined, and hundreds of new periodicals appeared between 1900 and 1930 (Fahmy 2011: 29–31). Not only was there an increase in the production of newspapers and magazines, but there was also an overall "expansion of the country's intellectual horizons" (Berque 1972: 356).

2.3 Language in education during the British occupation

The British—unlike the French—did not aim to assimilate their holdings in the Arab world, nor did they consider their Arab colonies part of Britain (cf. Bassiouney 2009). Consider the following quote by Lord Palmerston (d. 1865), British Prime Minister from 1855–8 and 1859–65, which summarizes the attitude of at least a part of the British establishment before the colonization of Egypt (cited in Ashley 1879, II: 337–8):

> We do not want Egypt or wish it for ourselves, any more than any rational man with an estate in the north of England and a residence in the south would have wished to possess the inns on the North road. All he could want would have been that the inns should be well-kept, always accessible, and furnishing him, when he came, with mutton-chops and post-horses.

Britain regarded Egypt as the "inns" on the road, rather than as a province or a territory overseas, and although English was declared an official language along with Arabic in Egypt, Sudan, and Palestine, Britain lacked the zeal to impose its language by force and had no investment in the linguistic situation.

That said, Egypt was occupied by Britain for seventy years, from 1882 to 1952. During this period, the British administration implemented measures to weaken the position of Arabic (Shraybom-Shivtiel 1999). First, they introduced English and French as required languages in the education system. It seems that for the British, being civilized did not entail learning English specifically, but learning and speaking a European language. According to this methodology, only a European language could be used and recognized as the language of education (Spolsky 2004). Second, they elevated the status of ECA (rather than SA) by emphasizing the distinctiveness of the Egyptian identity, as opposed to the Arab identity.

For the British, the diglossic situation was inhibiting and difficult to understand. Thus, Britain tried to raise the status of the colloquial varieties at the expense of SA. They believed that children should be educated in the language that they speak, which in Egypt would be the colloquial or vernacular. In fact, this was also Britain's policy in India, where they used the vernacular of each area for elementary education and English for secondary education (Spolsky 2004). However, Britain's encouragement of the colloquial dialects had a political dimension, too, and was linked to colonial policies.

To achieve the first goal of establishing foreign languages as the medium of education, the British administration announced in 1888 that the language of instruction in all schools was to be either French or English. Their explanation for this was that Egypt was moving towards a European style of development, and that this development was technological and scientific in nature. However, SA was seen as a language not fit for scientific writing (Jibrīl 2009). It is not surprising that during this period, Egypt's elite began to send their children to schools in Egypt, where the language of instruction was English, French, or German, (significantly, this is a practice that continues to the present day). The demands for the revival of SA were met with harsh criticism from the British and even some Egyptian elites, claiming its weakness as a living language. Its grammar and vocabulary were thought to be fossilized, while the methods of teaching SA were criticized for being tedious and difficult. Traditionally, SA was a language taught by repetition and memorization and was not considered fit for the contemporary needs of Egyptian society (Shraybom-Shivtiel 1999).

At that time of the occupation, key figures in the British administration were calling for the use of ECA as both a written language and as the official language to be used in civil affairs. Lord Dufferin, special envoy of Her Majesty's Government in Egypt and British Ambassador to the Ottoman Empire, when ordered to provide a plan for Egypt's reorganization in 1882, devoted part of his report to the problems with SA and the benefits of expanding the colloquial. At that time, foreign orientalists in the Arab world showed a strong interest in the colloquial. The Swedish orientalist Carlo Landberg wrote about the Syrian dialect, the French Louis Jacques Bresnier was interested in the Algerian vernacular, while John Selden Willmore published his classic *The Spoken Arabic of Egypt* in 1901. Orientalists started opening schools to teach the colloquial (Shraybom-Shivtiel 1999: 134) and some Egyptians seemed to be cooperating with, and encouraging, British policies. During the initial period of British rule in Egypt, the Egyptian upper classes "meekly and willingly accepted British guidance and supervision" (1999: 134).

While the British sought to weaken the usage of SA, the idea of an Egyptian national identity was being revived and shaped by other factors. This identity was not, however, always associated with SA, although for some it was and still is.

2.4 Intellectuals, politicians, and the struggle for SA

As noted above, there were repeated calls for the revival of SA. By the beginning of the twentieth century, when the process of liberation from foreign rule began and nationalist aspirations rose, Egyptian intellectuals felt a need to deal with the "issue" of SA (Shraybom-Shivtiel 1999). The first person to implement a change in language education policy was Saʿd Zaghlūl, during his tenure as Minister of Education between 1906 and 1910. He aimed at replacing English with SA as the language of instruction in schools—a crucial first step that came amidst nationalist calls for the revival of SA. The beginning of the century also witnessed the establishment of Fu'ād I University in 1908 (later to become Cairo University).

The founding committee decided unanimously that the official language of instruction would be Arabic, specifically SA.

Gradually, attitudes towards Arabic and Arabness changed (see Suleiman 2003). In the 1930s, Egyptian journalist Muḥammad ʿAllūbah declared that Egypt was an Arab country, because of the Arabic language, meaning SA. This change was reflected in the layout of his newspaper, *al-Siyāsah al-Usbūʿīyyah* ("Weekly politics"). Prior to 1930, the cover page was decorated with Pharaonic motifs, and the Islamic dates for each issue were only shown on the inside pages. Beginning in 1930, the Pharaonic decorations were replaced by caricatures, and the Islamic dates appeared on the front page (Suleiman 2003: 180).

Calls to give SA a greater role in public life went hand-in-hand with calls to reform SA itself. These included proposals to modify its grammar, script, and spelling. Some radical ideas were also proposed, such as eliminating grammatical rules entirely, dispensing with the dual, and abolishing the pronouns and suffixes of the feminine plural. Some of the suggested reforms came from the highest institution in the country: King Fu'ād himself. Though not too well-versed in Arabic, King Fu'ād was aware of its importance. He established the Academy of the Arabic Language in 1932 and intervened personally in the reform of the language. Among other things, he issued a public call for proposals for a design of capital letters in Arabic script (Shraybom-Shivtiel 1999: 136). The suggestion was met with skepticism on the part of Egyptian intellectuals and proved a failed experiment.

Despite all calls for change and reform, the linguistic situation in education did not change. As late as the 1940s, foreign languages were still the primary means of instruction, except in religious schools, which were under the direct supervision of al-Azhar University. Private schools excluded Arabic, while public schools, which were limited in number, used it in a restricted manner (Shraybom-Shivtiel 1999).

Substantial changes in education came about at the hands of two prominent intellectuals and politicians: Muḥammad Ḥusayn Haykal (1888–1956) and Ṭāhā Ḥusayn (1889–1973). The work of Azhar-educated writer Ṭāhā Ḥusayn had a profound influence on the revival of Arabic. In his book *Mustaqbal al-thaqāfah fī Miṣr* ("The future of culture in Egypt") (1938), he called for the establishment of SA in foreign schools—those schools that were run by non-Egyptians and not under government supervision (Shraybom-Shivtiel 1999). According to Suleiman (2003), Ṭāhā Ḥusayn believed that Egypt's national identity was not built on religion, but on political factors, the geographical environment, and history. On one occasion, he even exhorted the Coptic Church to ensure that it used good Arabic (meaning SA), since Arabic was part of Egypt's national identity, but was not limited to Egyptian national identity (Suleiman 2003: 194).

Ḥusayn, like Salāmah Mūsá, looked to Europe as a model and believed in the significance of the modernization of language. Yet Ḥusayn and Mūsá had different attitudes towards SA. Ḥusayn thought that "Muslims (more accurately, Muslim rulers and elites) [. . .] understood that 'religion is one thing and politics is another, and that the first basis for establishing political unity is common interests'" (quoted in Suleiman 2003: 191). He stressed the importance of language as the medium for thought and modernization. According to Ḥusayn, Egypt, with its tendency towards moderation, was to aim for integration with the West, not assimilation. In his view, therefore, one of the policies of the state should be to ensure that SA was taught in all private foreign schools in Egypt. He called for the elimination of the teaching of foreign languages at the primary level in state schools. He was well aware that SA was considered a dreaded subject, and he thought that this was so because of the focus on grammar as a teaching method (Suleiman 2003: 193). Ḥusayn also realized that there is a difference between teaching *about* language and the teaching *of* a language. Thus, the parrot-like learning style used to study grammar and rhetoric was not valid. According to him, since language should have a creative role, SA had to be simplified, without being compromised.

Ḥusayn remained an ardent supporter of SA throughout his life. He argued that if Egyptians ignored SA, they would cut themselves off from their past and their Arab literary heritage. Ḥusayn's ideas were not left unchallenged, as he encountered problems at al-Azhar where he had studied, because it claimed a monopoly on grammar teaching and teacher training.

Muḥammad Ḥusayn Haykal began his career as a lawyer and journalist. After gaining a degree in law from the Sorbonne (1912), he worked as lawyer, and then as editor for *al-Siyāsah al-Usbūʿīyah* newspaper, before finally entering public service. In 1938, he was appointed Minister of Education in the government of Muḥammad Maḥmūd. Although the government was dissolved shortly thereafter, he regained his position in 1940 and held it intermittently until 1945. Under his direction, private foreign schools were instructed to speak SA when teaching the disciplines of Arabic, Egyptian history, and geography. Still, the primary language of instruction in these schools remained a European language. However, Shraybom-Shivtiel points out that "the introduction of Arabic as a required language constituted a turning point in Egypt's national education system" (1999: 137).

When Nasser came to power after the 1952 Revolution, he began to pursue the idea of making education accessible to everyone by offering free education to the entire population and making primary education compulsory. Shraybom-Shivtiel argues that

Egypt, in its efforts to achieve national unity during the 1950s and 1960s, positioned literary Arabic (SA) at the core of its educational system and utilized it as the cornerstone in the development of the image of the young generation in the Arab World. (1999: 131)

It is certainly clear that Nasser pursued a policy of pan-Arabism and actively supported the goal of helping other Arab countries achieve independence, all the while emphasizing similarities rather than differences among Arab countries. It is only natural that SA was to play a major role as a unifying force and as a factor that defined the Arab world at that time.[11] A result of the 1952 Revolution was a change in both the attitude and approach towards Arabic. To enhance the pan-Arab movement and build a nationalist feeling among the new generation of Egyptians, schools began teaching Islamic resources, as well as Classical Arabic literature and poetry. A new image of Egypt was being formed: that of Egypt as part of the Arab nation (Faksh 1980).

Nasser himself, when addressing the United Nations on September 28, 1960, said: "We announce that we believe in a single Arab nation. The Arab nation was always united linguistically. And linguistic unity is unity of thought" (Dajānī 1973: 119–37). During this period, the calls for the simplification of SA grammar and spelling, which had been so widespread in the earlier part of the twentieth century, disappeared almost entirely. The colloquial language lost its status once more and became merely the language of daily life. In fact, SA was encouraged as the language of academics, intellectuals, and educated people. The Arabic Language Academy worked diligently to create scientific terms in SA. Universities began teaching SA, even in the scientific disciplines. In 1960, the Egyptian Minister of Education, Kamāl al-Dīn Ḥusayn, called on the Arabic Language Academy in Cairo to recommend that only SA be spoken at universities (Shraybom-Shivtiel 1999).[12]

Some have argued that during the Nasser years, SA became the spoken language of the elite in some contexts (such as lectures or formal gatherings) (Shraybom-Shivtiel 1999: 138). It is difficult to provide evidence for such a claim, but one cannot deny that SA gained a higher status particularly among the secular-minded intellectuals, eventually replacing foreign languages. If it had been an aim of the revolution to promote SA, then it was largely achieved, since SA was not just the official language of Egypt, but it also gained the status of a prestigious language, carrying political significance.[13] This, of course, is in marked contrast to the role that SA played during the period of foreign rule, which ended nominally in 1922, with four stipulations, and completely in 1952 (Sayyid-Marsot 1985).

However, the fortunes of SA remained tied to the political situation within Egypt and the Middle East at large. During the reign of Nasser, the nationalist discourse that construed Egypt's identity as distinct from that of the Arab world and emphasized the role of colloquial dialects may have been ignored or marginalized, but it was never forgotten. After Nasser's death in 1970 and particularly after the peace treaty with Israel in 1979 when Egypt was ostracized by the rest of the Arab world, the idea of a distinct Egyptian identity re-emerged forcefully. Among others, the writer Luwīs ʿAwaḍ (1915–90) called for a distinct identity for Egyptians, which should be reflected in their language (Suleiman 2003). He expressed these views in his *Muqaddimah fī fiqh al-lughah al-ʿArabīyah* ("Introduction to understanding the Arabic language"), published during the presidency of Anwar Sadat (1970–81), when Egypt "veered towards an 'Egypt first' policy in response to the Arab boycott following its peace treaty with Israel in March 1979" (2003: 198). Even in the 1940s, ʿAwaḍ had tried to separate the language factor from national identity and the political sphere. In his view, Egypt had been colonized by foreign powers for about 4,000 years, including Greeks, Romans, Arabs, Turks, and the British. He proposed that by returning to its Pharaonic past, Egypt could regain its sense of creativity. ʿAwad was quite categorical in his denial of any link between Arabic and Egyptian national identity. He even went so far as to suggest that the use of the glottal stop in Egyptian Arabic was caused by the racially bound physical constitution of the Egyptian vocal tract—a claim that is patently false (Suleiman 2003).

Although these views seem extravagant, they are clearly related to the "Egypt first" policy of the Sadat era. One also has to bear in mind that the idea of Egyptian distinctiveness and special status and even superiority that merits dignity and pride came to be the intellectual basis for education in Egypt. Starting from 1980 to the present day, Egyptian children have been taught that their affiliation is first and foremost to their country, Egypt, *then* to the nation (the Arab world), and finally to their religion (see ʿAbd al-Kāfī 1991; Khiḍr 2006). As will be shown in the later chapters of this book, the idea of an innate Egyptian genius is used time and again to reinforce the distinction between Egyptians and non-Egyptians in school textbooks.

2.5 Language ideologies, attitudes, and policies

In the previous sections, we examined statements about language by individual scholars, politicians, and intellectuals. We will now consider "official" statements of language policy, ideology, and attitude.

The current Egyptian Constitution (2012) posits in its second article that Arabic is the official language of Egypt and that Islam is the country's religion. Political indexes of SA are only understood when put into a political and historical context, with reference to previous language policies.

Language policy usually refers to "a set of planned interventions supported and enforced by law and implemented by a government agency" (Spolsky 2004: 5). The key factor in language policy is the power and legitimacy to enforce a policy. Power in this case refers to both political and economic power. Language policies always try to push an official language. For example, as was mentioned earlier, in 1888, the British language policy in Egypt undermined SA by declaring that language instruction in all schools should be a foreign language, such as English, French, or another foreign language. In doing so, they gave official status to languages that were not native and not spoken by the majority of the population. This situation was not particular to Egypt: in Algeria, the French administration went so far as to declare the native Arabic a "foreign language" (see Bassiouney 2009).

It is necessary at this point to define some terms. An "official" language is usually the language used in government offices, official contexts, and documents; furthermore, the constitution typically defines the official language. As Wright (2004: 243) puts it, it is a language with "muscles"; it is supported by the institution and by a legal written document; it is something *de jure*. A "national" language, on the other hand, is the language of cultural and social unity. It can be used as a symbol to unite and identify a nation or a group of people (Holmes 1992: 52). It does not necessarily require an official status.

Throughout this chapter, we have shown how language was referred to by Egyptians and the foreign elite. We also examined how language served to define identity and shield Arabic from outsiders. Most discussions of the importance of SA in defining an Egyptian identity were, in fact, ideological in nature. The term "language ideologies" refer to the beliefs about language and language use that prevail within a specific community and that influence language practices. Ideologies are crucial for the implementation of a language policy, since they usually form the basis for the language planning processes or for modifying language policies (Spolsky 2004: 14). Although several ideologies may exist side by side within the same country, one ideology is usually dominant.

Spolsky posits that: "language ideology is language policy with the manager left out, what people think should be done. Language practices on the other hand, are what people actually do" (2004: 15). *Where* people use a language is important in the maintenance of the language. Thus, there are domains for language use, such as home, workplace, places of religious worship, government offices, schools, and so on (Spolsky 2004: 43). Language practices are sustained in these domains.

It was shown above that SA, ECA, and foreign languages carried varying ideological associations in Egypt. These associations were not necessarily fixed, but were—and remain—politically sensitive. However, one thing remains clear: the association between SA and truth and sincerity of discourse and the association of SA and legitimate demands. This specific association emerged clearly in al-Jabartī's rejection of the French campaign at the beginning of the nineteenth century. For al-Jabartī, mastering SA was associated with legitimacy—in particular, the legitimacy of the ruler. This may seem ironic, considering that in al-Jabartī's time, a part of Egypt's ruling class would have been speakers of languages other than Arabic. This clearly illustrates the difference between practice and ideology, which can be observed throughout the Arab world and within Egypt in particular.

Related to language ideologies is the symbolic function of language, as opposed to the instrumental function of language. Suleiman (2003: 174) discusses the power of the symbol and attributes SA's long-lasting endurance to its symbolic power. As a modern example, consider Algeria, which tried to impose SA as a symbol of its identity after gaining its independence. France dominated Algeria from 1830 onwards, and Algeria was considered part of France. French had been imposed as the language of both the government and education and was therefore directly associated with the colonial power. On the other hand, French was an instrumental language in Algeria for almost a century and came into general use. The proper role of "Arabic" had been among the issues involved in the struggle for independence long before the war began. After a long and bloody struggle, Algeria gained its independence and imposed SA, in order to assert its distinctive identity. However, some have argued that the declaration of Arabic as an official language was almost purely symbolic, since there were no textbooks for teaching it, nor any instructors qualified to teach the language (see Bassiouney 2009 for more references on Algeria).

Language policies have to take into consideration both functions of language—the symbolic and instrumental—otherwise the policy will be lacking. This is not an easy task, however, especially with the instrumental function that English has worldwide, including in Egypt. Note that according to Wright (2004), a language policy will not work if it clashes with feelings of identity and ties within the community.

Walters (2006b: 651) posits that "language attitudes are psychological states related in complex ways to larger abstract language ideologies." Because of this, it is difficult to elicit the real attitude of speakers towards their language in a straightforward questionnaire. There are a number of methodological problems related to attitude. One of these problems is the representativeness of the data collected. For example, language attitude surveys in the Arab world are mostly carried out on university students or high school students; clearly, neither group represents the majority of the population in Arab countries, nor do their attitudes necessarily reflect the attitude of the masses of the population (see Bassiouney 2009). Another methodological problem is that respondents to questionnaires often answer from a *prescriptive* perspective (that is, what they think they *should* do, as opposed to what they actually do) (cf. Walters 2006b for a full discussion of methodological problems). As Walters puts it, for a methodology to be effective, the researcher has to be trained in psychology. However, such surveys are still useful as guidelines of a prevalent ideology or signs of group discontent with a specific policy.

That said, I believe that one can gain a glimpse of language attitudes by other means and less studied data (Chapter 3). Throughout this chapter, I have tried to sketch the rough outlines of the changing and often conflicting language attitudes in Egypt by adducing a variety of different data. As we have seen, the difference between language ideology and language attitude is not always clear cut: both are psychological; both are related to a belief system that may or may not coincide with linguistic reality. It has also become clear that it is essential to differentiate between language ideologies and attitudes, on the one hand, and language practices, on the other. Practices refer to the habitual selection that individuals make within their linguistic repertoire (Spolsky 2004: 9).

2.6 Conclusion

To conclude this chapter, I would like to review, once more, the ideologies related to language and identity that have emerged from the above discussion:

- Arabic and locality were used as classification categories to demarcate Egyptians and non-Egyptians (Muṣṭafā Kāmil).
- Religion remains a more multi-layered social variable than locality or ethnicity. This was clear at the beginning of the twentieth century with Zaghlūl's postulations about the 1919 Revolution and his inclusiveness of both Christians and Muslims. It will be shown in Chapter 4 that this attitude continues to prevail today.
- The role of history—particularly the history of ancient Egypt—in defining identity is evidenced clearly in Egyptian public discourse both before and after the discovery of the tomb of King Tutankhamen.
- Language was used as a resource and referenced consistently by composers, poets, and singers in their efforts to challenge, question, and reshape Egyptian identity. The beginning of the twentieth century witnessed the rise of the idea of Egyptian cultural hegemony over the Arab world. This development coincided with Egyptian political aspirations to lead the Arab world.
- Language is a defining element in discussions of "Arabness." Despite its

aspiration to lead the "Arab nation" and its pioneering role in founding The Arab League, Egypt's identity as an "Arab" nation was, and is still, contested.

These ideas will be discussed in more detail in later chapters. This chapter showed briefly how "Arabic" in its entirety has been tied to political, social, and cultural events. The different political and social movements that emerged at the beginning of the twentieth century included movements that emphasized Islam as the first and foremost marker of identity, while others emphasized Arabness as a cultural and identity category, while still others highlighted the glories of ancient Egypt as their point of reference or concentrated on the Coptic history of Egypt.

My aim in this chapter was to outline the main components that influenced the molding of modern Egyptian identity in public discourse. By doing so, I hope to provide a prelude to a discussion and examination of language indexes. This history is an essential background to a number of recurring themes in this book, such as employing language as a classification category; associating ECA and English with foreign forces; defining identity in terms of social variables that include language, ethnicity, historicity, locality, and characteristics and so on; using the process of stance-taking to highlight an Egyptian identity; and using different codes in the process.

While touching on all these topics in more general terms, this chapter also poses a number of questions, such as: what role does the concept of the "Arab Nation" play in Egyptians' perceptions of their identity? Is SA always associated with a unified Arab nation? How much do political and social factors intervene in language ideology and attitudes and, eventually, language policies? These questions are addressed throughout this book; although it is difficult to provide clear answers, these issues will be examined rigorously and with many examples.

Chapters 2 and 6 can be read together, because both chapters deal with turning points in the construction of Egyptian identity—namely, the Revolutions of 1919 and 2011, respectively. In both chapters, discussions of language and identity are so interwoven that separating them becomes an almost impossible task. It will be shown that language as a resource was manipulated at the beginning of the twentieth century, just as it was at the beginning of the twenty-first century.

In Chapter 6, we come full circle. Linguistic indexes and social variables correlate and collide, and identity is dependent on language in more than one way. However, this chapter provides the infrastructure for our discussions.

What this chapter has not tackled is how language indices are formed and maintained and how direct and indirect indexes can provide a more nuanced discussion of diglossia in Egypt and linguistic practices more generally. While it was posited that attitudes are more abstract than ideologies and, in most cases, more difficult to illicit directly, the next chapter will provide the necessary trajectory for the study of Arabic indexes.

In terms of access to resources, it was shown in this chapter that access to SA indexes sincerity of the message conveyed. However, access to Arabic in its entirety can and does index authenticity in some cases. Indexes are, of course, context dependent and ideologically charged, as will be clear in the next chapter.

Notes

1. *Wada:ʕan Kru:mir* ("Farewell, Cromer") (1907); see Ibrāhīm (1980).
2. It is also important to note that the concept of the Arab nation was, to a great extent, a reaction to foreign oppression that took place at the beginning of the twentieth century. Therefore, the nation, as such, was regarded more as a shield to protect identity, rather than as an imperialistic ideology. Rather than fall into regarding themselves as inferior, the appeal to a common language and culture was a means of cementing their existence, though largely an abstract appeal.
3. Foreign nationals in Egypt numbered between some 15,000 in the 1850s and around 200,000 just after World War I. These figures also include individuals of non-European origin, who had obtained French, British, or Italian nationality (see Krämer 1989: 8–9).
4. According to Goldschmidt (2008: 85), at the beginning of the twentieth century, European residents in Egypt were exempt from local laws and taxes at a time when taxes were being raised for Egyptians and services were being cut.
5. The party was not founded spontaneously, nor was it free from government influence. In fact, it began as a secret society headed by the Khedive ʿAbbās and brought together a group of men with a shared dislike of Lord Cromer. The founder of the movement, Kāmil, was initially a spokesman of ʿAbbās. Among its associate organizations, it had a boys' school and a newspaper (al-Liwāʾ).
6. Egyptians were referred to as "raʕiyya ʕuθma:niyya" ("Ottoman subjects") in the Ottoman Nationality Law of 1869, as ratified by the Majlis al-Nuwwāb al-Miṣrī, Lajnat al-Shuʾūn al-Khārijīyah (see Jibrīl 2009: 565).
7. Note that there was not always public consensus regarding Egypt and Egyptian identity, as Haag posits: "Political confusion between pan-Islamic and Pan-Arab affinities on the one hand and national interest on the other persists up to the present day" (2005: 253).
8. This mode is similar to the prevalent one before the January 25 Revolution of 2011.

9. However, the first two lines of the poem will be manipulated differently in modern Egypt. The official student Muslim Brotherhood blog in 2010 used the first two lines as their slogan to urge Egyptians to wake up, not in order to capture only Egyptian glory, but to capture the glory of the whole Arab and Muslim world. Another blog manipulates the text of the poem to refer bitterly to the state of corruption in Egypt directly before the January 25 Revolution of 2011.
10. See http://harvardmagazine.com/1997/07/umm-kulthum-ibrahim, accessed 4 September 2013.
11. Nasser is described by Mansfield (2003: 278) as "[a]n Egyptian who developed a genuine belief in the movement to unite the Arabs, of which he saw Egypt as the natural leader."
12. Not surprisingly, this was not heeded by students.
13. This status that SA obtained at the time may explain why Ferguson, in his analysis of diglossia (1959), mentioned that SA is the language used in mosque sermons, university lectures, and political speeches. This is not the case today, but since his article was first published in 1959, it may reflect the sentiment of that time. In addition, Badawi's levels may also reflect the *attitude* of Egyptians at the time of publication.

CHAPTER

3

"ARABIC" INDEXES AMIDST A NATION AND A NATION-STATE: IDEOLOGIES, ATTITUDES, AND LINGUISTIC REALITIES

"Do you know how to call out in Arabic,
In the name of God and my country,
– Then surely you are the Egyptian!"

(from the song *yibʔa ʔinta ʔaki:d il-masri:* ("Surely you are the Egyptian") by Laṭīfah (2001))

The Tunisian pop singer Laṭīfah has a famous song in ECA in which she defines "the Egyptian." Her main definition of an Egyptian is one who speaks Arabic. Arabic as a classification category has been discussed in the last chapter and will recur throughout the book, especially in Chapter 6, in which I discuss how the media, during the 2011 Revolution, claimed that speaking Arabic was the primary criterion for defining "the real Egyptian." However, the reference to Arabic in this song is both ambiguous and general. The sentence *b-ism illa:h wa b-ism bila:di:* ("In the name of God and my country"), when said in Arabic, is largely neutral; it is chosen intelligently to be realized almost identically in spoken SA and ECA. For an Egyptian, it does not evoke the associations of ECA, nor of SA. Tactfully, the producers of the song avoid tackling the issue of Standard Arabic versus colloquial. However, they still provide another proposition about language and identity and the close relationship between "Arabic" and the Egyptian identity, yet provide no answers about which "Arabic" is associated with identity and thus avoid the tension that occasionally exists between advocates of standard and colloquial forms of Arabic. While the book concentrates on how language is used to forge an identity, it would be a serious oversight to ignore the conflict regarding which form of Arabic is associated with Egyptian identity and whether Arabic is associated with Egyptian identity in the first place. It is usually intellectuals and not linguists who control the public discourse about language in Egypt. For this reason, linguistic habits and ideologies do not always coincide. This chapter will provide a different perspective that examines novel data in relation to language ideology and attitude.

Data used in this chapter is varied and, to a great extent, unconventional. It comes from both oral and written venues. It includes newspapers, written in English and Arabic in Egypt; two books: a political one and the other on social–psychology; films: recent and older ones; recent television interviews; caricatures and posters circulated both on Facebook and various web pages; and also a personal account from Suleiman in his book *Arabic, Self and Identity* (2011).

As was mentioned in Chapter 1, individuals use codes in two different ways. Linguistic codes become classification categories that, in this case, classify individuals as Egyptians or non-Egyptians. These categories are dependent on language indexes. During the stance-taking process, individuals use linguistic resources that include code-switching and code-choice, as well as other structural and discourse resources. These resources derive their meaning from indexes. Language ideology and attitude are essential in understanding indexes.

As will be discussed throughout this book, public discourse may use independent social variables to project an identity onto individuals, such as ethnicity, religion, locality, historical setting, cultural background, moral traits, and so on. Public discourse usually uses language form to present this identity. Going back to the interaction between the professor and Zūzū in Chapter 1, the professor, when cornered by Zūzū and pressed to give an answer to her question about his identity, resorts to language form as a safe haven that may save him from embarrassing himself by defining who he is. He comments on her beautiful Arabic pronunciation. Language form, or rather attitudes about language form, will remain the clearest of symbols that signal an identity.

This chapter will shed light on the associations of SA, ECA, and foreign languages, especially English, in Egypt. In so doing, the chapter will also discuss language as an independent variable, classification category, and marker of identity. The concept of authenticity that recurs throughout this book will also be touched upon.

This chapter will offer novel and detailed trajectories of understanding diglossia and the relation between codes and identities. The chapter will also elaborate on the concept of orders of indexes and provide the necessary background for the coming chapters.

The associations of ECA and SA are sensitive to context, whether this context is social, political, cultural, or even demographic and geographical. However, the associations of ECA and SA are also a matter of inclusion and exclusion, as well as a matter of the distribution of resources. This will be clear below. While it may be assumed that SA is a powerful resource that is not mastered by, or available to, everyone in Egypt, it will be clear from the discussion below that ECA is also a powerful resource in its own way that is not necessarily available to non-Egyptians. By analyzing less predictable data and showing how they reflect language attitudes, I aim to offer a more nuanced explanation of the associations of different codes.

To reiterate, according to Johnstone (2010: 31), indexical forms can imply and construct identity. The concept of indexicality refers to the creation of semiotic links between linguistic forms and social meanings (Ochs 1992; Silverstein 1996; 2003). By understanding the associations of ECA and SA, we can reach a better understanding of the mechanism of the stance-taking process of individuals that reflects their identity.

To repeat the example given in Chapter 1 provided by Johnstone (2010), an individual may imitate the dialect of an immigrant. This specific dialect, not usually used by this particular individual except in this context, may then index a political stance for this individual (see Johnstone 2010).

Indexes in this chapter will be regarded as not only associations that are the product of habits, but also associations that are the product of ideologies and perceptions. The traditional and untraditional forms of data analyzed in this chapter will provide evidence for this.

3.1 Diglossia and first order indexes: habits and practices

When Ferguson provided us with his definition of diglossia, he also gave examples of a number of situations in which SA is used and other situations in which the colloquial is used (1959). As we noted in Chapter 1, Ferguson was criticized for not accounting for the overlap in function between codes. I argue that Ferguson's classification can be better understood in terms of indexicality, especially first order indexes. At the time of Ferguson's article until now, indexicality has not yet been used in defining or understanding diglossia, although a closer look at orders of indexicality can help us in thoroughly analyzing data in diglossic communities. First order indexes are the product of habits, as was established in Chapter 1. Collins (2011: 409) argues that first order indexes "presuppose" fixed, contextually dependent signs. Ferguson gives situations in which SA is appropriate, such as sermons, lectures, political speeches, news broadcasts, and newspaper editorials. He also gives situations in which the colloquial is appropriate, such as conversation with family and friends, folk literature, and soap operas. There is, in fact, a semiotic link between specific situations and a specific code. This semiotic link is also the product of habits. However, this function orientation relation between code and context is not enough in understanding diglossia, although it provides a means of partially explaining code-switching. At a first order of indexes, SA is associated with formality, abstract, and distant contexts, as well as written rather than spoken contexts. ECA is associated with informality, concrete, and intimate contexts and tends to occur more in spoken than written contexts. For example, when ECA is then used in a context linked with SA, this may be to evoke the indexes of formality, distance, and so on.

However, there are other orders of indexicality that are more creative and performative. For example, "Talk about talk" and meta-pragmatic discourse are both essential in linking language use to a form of social action (Collins 2011: 409). By understanding language ideologies and attitudes, linguists studying diglossia can have a glimpse of how indexes are ordered and classified in a diglossic community.

3.2 Second order indexes: ideologies and attitudes

What I define as second order indexes are indexes that are the product of ideologies and attitudes, rather than habits. That is, these indexes do not necessarily refer to actual practices of individuals; rather, they refer both directly and indirectly to the manner in which individuals display or do not display access to codes as resources that are ideologically loaded. As Bucholtz (2009: 158) posits: "ideologies about language circulate through both explicit metapragmatic commentary and implicit metapragmatic representation."

In my definition, I would also like to distinguish between two types of processes by which second order indexes are typified—an indirect process and a direct process. As Bucholtz (2009: 158) contends, the process of typification "occurs not only in everyday interaction but also within wider-reaching cultural vehicles such as the media."

The direct variable that explains the process of second order indexes is language ideology, and the indirect variable that explains this process is language attitude.

In Chapter 2, language ideology was defined as a belief system that is also related to politics and nation-building. Language attitude was referred to as a more abstract and psychological variable. In this section, I will elaborate on these two concepts. Language attitudes are defined by Dragojevic et al. (2013: 20) as follows:

> Language attitudes are not only a product of present times, but also a reflection of complex histories of domination and subordination that, in some cases, can be traced back hundreds of years. As such, language attitudes represent a

> glimpse into the past as much as into the present, and in order to fully grasp the complex and intricate nature of languages' social meanings, we must first understand the histories, relationships, and ideologies of the people who speak them.

Dragojevic et al. stress the relationship between attitude and the social world and attitude and social variables, including historical and political variables. Attitudes are linked to ideologies on many levels. According to Garret (2010: 20), an attitude is "an evaluative orientation to a social object of some sort." This social object can be language, government policy, and so on. Attitude is a disposition that is "stable enough to be identified." Garret (2010: 228) adds that language attitude is usually influenced by dominant ideologies. He posits that there are two approaches to attitude studies—a direct approach and an indirect approach. The direct approach depends on human informants, who are aware of what is being investigated. In the indirect approach, the human informants are not aware of what is being investigated. I argue that since attitude is more abstract than ideology, an indirect approach is more effective in eliciting realistic dispositions. The public discourse data in this chapter that attempts to reveal attitudes towards different codes is intentionally chosen, because it is indirect.

Ideologies, on the other hand, provide "the organizational schema through which linguistic diversity is viewed, interpreted, and evaluated" (Dragojevic et al. 2013: 11). Language ideologies in the Arab world are direct stances about language that are usually further removed from linguistic habits than attitude and are related to self-image as much as to politics and history. This will be clear in the examples analyzed in this chapter.

In sum, the process of layering second order indexes involves direct and indirect variables. The direct variables involve language ideologies and the indirect variables involve language attitudes. The direct variables are explicit and are elicited from examples of talk about language in different forms of written and oral mediums. The indirect variables are implicit and elicited from manifestations and representations of users of different codes.

I will start with an analysis of language ideologies in which there is a direct explicit layering of second order indexes.

3.3 Direct layering of SA second order indexes

3.3.1 *Associations of SA*

3.3.1.1 SA and Islam: the legitimate and divine indexes

Religion plays a broad role in the survival of SA. But there is also the romantic belief among speakers of Arabic, as well as Muslims more generally, in the appeal and superiority of their language. Schiffman (1998: 69) points to the perceived "sacredness of Arabic." Indeed, the entry for "Koran" in *The Concise Encyclopedia of Islam* summarizes the traditional Muslim position neatly (Glassé 1989: 46):

> Muslims consider the Koran to be holy scripture only in the original Arabic of its revelation. The Koran, while it may be translated, is only ritually valid in Arabic. This is connected with the notion of Arabic as a "sacred Arabic." Language itself is sacred, because of its miraculous power to communicate and to externalize thought.

For Muslims, words are so powerful, they are divine. Indeed, to fight a curse, one has to use words—that is, Arabic words, mainly from the Qur'ān. *The Concise Encyclopedia of Islam* (1989: 46) adds that Arabic, though "originally a desert nomadic dialect, has maintained a fresh directness that makes it a more suitable vehicle than many others." He attributes this freshness to the relationship between words and their roots, to simple statements, which are the rule in the Qur'ān (cf. Wright 2004: 69). *The Concise Encyclopedia of Islam* further notes that:

> Simple statements, which are the rule in the Koran, open, under the right conditions of receptivity, into astonishing and vast horizons; the world is reduced to ripples in consciousness. These and other qualities make Arabic an incomparable medium for dialogue between man and God in prayer. (1989: 47)

Wright argues that these attitudes towards Arabic (SA) affect language policy-making in both the Arab world and the Islamic world in general (2004: 70). She contends that all language policies are culturally specific. To a great extent, this is true, although again, it is difficult to define the term "culture." Culture, in this sense, is the shared historical and geographical background of a group of people who also have the same set of values and beliefs. These beliefs may or may not be religious ones.

To give an example (albeit an older one): at the beginning of the twentieth century, as a reaction to the undermining of SA by the British in Egypt and the accusation by the British that SA was a dead language that is unfit for science, the Egyptian poet Ḥāfiẓ Ibrāhīm (1871–1932), in his poem *al-Lughah al-ʿArabīyah* ("Standard Arabic speaking") (1921), personified SA and made it defend itself. Ibrāhīm positioned SA in the role of a woman—a mother who is accused of sterility, yet who is so fertile and productive that she can encompass God's words (in Ibrāhīm 1980):

> They have accused me of barrenness in the prime of my youth.
> I would that I were barren, so that I should not suffer the words of my enemies.
>
> I have encompassed the book of God in word and meaning. And have not fallen short in any of its verses and exaltations.
>
> I am the sea; in its depths pearls are hidden.
> Have they asked the diver for my shells?
>
> I see the people of the west full of power and might.
> And many a people have risen to power through the power of their language.

In his poem about Arabic, by which he meant SA, Ibrāhīm sums up the feelings of the majority of Arab intellectuals about SA. Arab governments, in their struggle for freedom from colonizing powers, often appealed to language as a shield for their identity.[1] It is, indeed, true that the power of language reflects the power of its people. Still, the struggle is not always fair, nor is it always fruitful. However, what Ibrāhīm appeals to in order to defend Arabic is the Qur'ān—the sacred book of Muslims.

While the Qurʾān is in SA, the Coptic Bible is also in SA. Although Copts use Coptic for liturgical contexts, their religious books and the Bible are translated into SA. The late Pope Shinūdah did not just master SA, but recited poetry in it as well. However, this does not imply that SA has the same divine indexes that it has for Muslims. It may, however, have the same authoritative and legitimate indexes as the code used in the guiding books of both Muslims and Christians in Egypt.

3.3.1.2 SA as the weapon against disintegration and corruption: the pure, authoritative, unifying indexes

For Arab nationalists, the Arab world is a single entity unified by one language, one geographical territory, one culture, and similar political struggles. This holistic view of the nation does not have room for diversity, linguistic or otherwise. There is pressure to conform to this ideology, especially for intellectuals. This ideology places SA as the unifying factor and any other variety as a threat to the unity of the Arab world.

Before these propositions are discussed in detail, one needs to explain the terminology of nationhood in the Arab world: the Arabic word *ʔumma* is equivalent to "nation." The word *waṭan*, on the other hand, refers to a "country" as opposed to a nation. A common usage of *ʔumma* is to refer to *al-ʔumma al-ʕarabiyya* and *al-ʔumma al-ʔisla:miyya* ("The Islamic nation"), the latter being a universal one, rather than particular to a specific community with a shared culture and history.

In the Arab world, as is the case in the West, a nation can also be defined in terms of different factors, including but not limited to language, religion, geographical environment, historical background, colonial history, values, and so on. Linguists and intellectuals disagree as to which of these factors is the most essential. In fact, each factor is often manipulated politically at different stages throughout history. For example, the Syrian nationalist Anṭūn Saʿādah (d. 1949) held the view that the environment plays the most essential role in shaping the national character (cf. Suleiman 2003: 219).

The Arabs' perception of the Arab nation is very complicated and possibly needs a book in itself (cf. Suleiman 2003). Some Arabs perceive themselves as belonging to a single Arab nation, because they have common colonial history, they occupy a specific geographical space, they share nostalgia for a glorious past, and they speak "Arabic." The Arab nation is not a political entity, but an ideological one, the same way that the idea of "one nation, one language" is also, at times, only ideological.

However, in the twentieth century, the relationship between the Arab nation and SA has been at the forefront of government constitutions, in language academies, among Arab intellectuals, and in the media more broadly. National unity was assumed to be achieved through linguistic unity and thus multilingualism was perceived as a threat to national unity (Miller 2003: 150–1).

Note that in ancient times, the only true "Arab" was the Bedouin Arab, and kinship and lineage, as much as language, were important means of identification (Miller 2003). Miller also contends that in premodern states, there was no correlation between language and nation; the elite of a country could speak a different language from the commoners. In the Ottoman period, for example, it was religious affiliation rather than language that defined the nation. However, it is worth mentioning that the relationship between nation and language must have started earlier than the modern period in the Arab world. The fact that the elite spoke a different language is not a criterion for judgment, since the elite in some Arab countries these days frequently still speak a language other than Arabic, even if they know Arabic, as is the case in some Gulf countries, Egypt,[2] Morocco, and Algeria. Despite this, the belief in the slogan "One nation, one language" is held by many. People are not always aware of their linguistic habits. In some cases, ideologies prevail over habits (cf. the example provided by Ferguson, as discussed in Bassiouney 2009: 13).

The concept of the Arab nation as such has been accused by some intellectuals, politicians, and thinkers of promoting linguistic intolerance in the Arab world (cf. Miller 2003). Nationalism, throughout the world, has a bad reputation and has been accused, sometimes rightly, of a number of atrocities and intolerances throughout history. The murder of innocent civilians in the Balkans, Kashmir, and Kurdistan are all examples of governments or peoples who were not ready to compromise their concept of a nation (Grosby 2005: 116). Note that although Arabic is associated with Islam, the Islamic nation is a universal one where kinship, language, and territory are surpassed (Grosby 2005). The Arab nation as an ideology is built on a number of factors and prominent among them is language. Religion is not a main component in the ideology of the Arab nation, since not all Arabs are Muslims and even the Muslim Arabs are not all Sunnis. Diversity, whether economic, cultural, or historical, is still prevalent in the Arab world, and language seems like the safest haven for nationalists (see Bassiouney 2009). Note that the harshest linguistic policies towards minorities often come from secular states; Turkey is a case in point (Miller 2003: 151).

As was mentioned in Chapter 2, nationalism in the Egyptian context was an ideology related to the "protection of an Egyptian identity" that was often deemed unworthy and subordinate to a colonial one by outsiders.

For Arabs, the creation of an Arab nation was a defense mechanism against colonization and globalization. As Edwards (2009: 201) argues,

> nationalism has proved a powerful force in the world, one that has endured well beyond the lifespan that many would have predicted. It has had important cultural manifestations. It has been a positive force, particularly in the lives of those who have felt threatened by larger or more influential neighbors.

The concept of language as a unifying factor has also been promoted by Egyptian nationalists. The discussions of Egypt's identity and language are still ongoing.

Myths about what constitutes a nation are not necessarily realistic. A nation can be built on language ideologies rather than language practices, as long as the ideology is a vessel for forming a sense of belonging between members of a specific community. As was mentioned earlier, there is a psychological component to a national identity. However, I do agree with Miller that an Arab is now defined differently than during the early Islamic period. Many intellectuals in Egypt still regard Egypt as an Arab state first and foremost, regarding SA as the unifying factor. The Arabic Language Academy in Cairo remains active and the call to maintain an Arab identity against an imperialist hegemonic Western world still prevails in Egypt, as well as in other parts of the Arab world.

To give more recent examples, al-Anṣārī and al-Anṣārī in their book *al-'Urūbah fī muqābil al-'awlamah* ("Arabness in the face of globalization") (2002: 37) emphasize the relationship between the Arabic language and the Arab nation. They posit that:

> What differentiates the Arab world or the Arab nation from all other nations and states in the world is language. Statistics show that Arabic is the third biggest language, not in terms of its speakers, but in terms of the countries that adopt it as its official language. Arabic comes after English and French. However, countries that use French or English as their official language are scattered all over the world, while countries that adopt Arabic as their official language comprise one geographical entity that stretches from the ocean to the Gulf.

Al-Anṣārī, late Director of the National Archives in Egypt, took on the task of defining the Arab nation by setting its geographical and linguistic borders, later revealing his attitude towards colloquial forms of Arabic. Al-Anṣārī downplays differences between dialects in the Arab world. He mentions that it is the orientalists who pay attention to details such as the minute difference in greeting terms between *marhaba* ("Welcome!" in Gulf Arabic) and *ke:fak* ("How are you?" in Levantine Arabic), for example, which are easily understood by all Arabs. He claims that it is Western orientalists who exaggerate the differences between dialects. However, he still posits that SA is the unifying code in the Arab world.

An incident relevant to this discussion, although not concerning Egypt directly, involves the same key Egyptian intellectual during 2000 in France. The French Ministry of Education decided to offer Arabic as an optional language in some secondary schools, due to the great number of North African immigrants in France (estimated at five million). It was decided to use the main colloquial dialect of Morocco for that purpose. Nāṣir al-Anṣārī, then Egyptian Director of the Institut du Monde Arabe, sent a letter to the Minister of Education, Jack Lang (Minister of Education from 2000–2), in which he argued that teaching Moroccan colloquial Arabic instead of SA was not the best option for students. His letter argued that teaching Moroccan colloquial Arabic would not be fair to the other North Africans who did not hail from Morocco, such as Algerians and Tunisians, who have a different dialect and comprise a large portion of the North African minority. He also mentioned that since there are different dialects within Morocco, it would be problematic to choose one of them, even if it is the prestigious one, because for some speakers it may not carry the same prestige. On the other hand, teaching SA would be of more benefit to the students on many levels. First, the curriculum of Arab countries for primary education is usually similar in content. This would connect the minority group to their Arab roots and ensure that the students would have the same ability to understand news bulletins in SA, read literature in SA, and write in SA. He asked the French Minister to reconsider his decision in the light of these arguments (al-Anṣārī and al-Anṣārī 2002: 40). While al-Anṣārī was mild in his reaction, other Egyptian intellectuals were not. Egyptian scholar Yūsuf 'Izz al-Dīn (2006) accused France of religious intolerance and posited that France's policy with regard to teaching colloquial Arabic had a political dimension. Once more, he emphasized that SA gathers Arabs together, while colloquials divide them.

To give another example of the unifying associations of SA, in February 2007, the Arab League held a conference to discuss the future of SA, with an emphasis on teaching it to children. The conference was the collaborative work of many parties: the Arab Council of Childhood and Development, the Arab League (AL), the Arab Gulf Program for United Nations Development Organization, UNESCO, the Kuwaiti Fund for Arab Economic Development, and the Islamic Organization for Education, Science, and Culture (ISESCO). Under the heading "Pickled tongue," the reporter of the event for *al-Ahrām Weekly* wrote (Abdel Moneim 2007): "'The Arab Child's Language in the Age of Globalisation,' a three-day conference held at the Arab League last week, focused on the role of language in shaping identity and how to promote its unity among future generations." The Egyptian reporter of the conference wrote the following for the Egyptian newspaper *al-Ahrām Weekly* in English (Abdel Moneim 2007):

> ISESCO Secretary-General Abdel Aziz Al-Twigrii spoke of "language pollution," the condition whereby the influence of foreign languages—those of economically predominant countries—corrupts Arabic, especially among children. One study released at the conference found that the language of advertising and the commercial world has a corrupting effect—with the use of colloquial and foreign words written in Arabic script. Another, carried out on Libyan children, found that dialect and foreign expressions were far preferable among them than SA. This can undermine the language in use for 15 centuries and leave Arabs exposed to "cultural invasion"; it is a mistake to let dialect prevail at the expense of the Arabic tongue.

The last postulation in the quote—"it is a mistake to let dialect prevail at the expense of the Arabic tongue"—is indeed significant. The Egyptian reporter Abdel Moneim considers dialect, meaning the colloquial Arabic of Arab countries, to be a corrupted version of SA. SA is the "Arabic tongue," the real language; thus, dialects are not "Arabic." This postulation, coming from an Egyptian in English, ignores the fact that dialects are, in fact, the spoken languages in all Arab countries, while SA is not the spoken dialect of any of the Arab countries mentioned. Ideology, though tied closely to politics, does not always reflect reality. However, an ideology is significant, even if it is a "romantic notion" like the one mentioned here—namely, that SA can prevail and be the daily language used by all Arabs. This is because, in this case, the indexes of SA are directly influenced by ideologies as much or even more than habits. As Hill and Mannheim (1992: 382) argue, language ideology may remind us that cultural concepts analyzed by linguists are usually subjective and contentious. Language ideologies are especially used as political, religious, or social weapons in conflicts, as will become clear later in the book (cf. Schieffelin et al. 1998). In this specific article, the status of ECA is undermined.

For intellectuals and the media, SA is associated with the Arab nation, and if SA changes or loses its status, then it threatens the Arab nation, as well as the core identity of Arabs. These indexes of SA, although not reflecting language practices, as will be clear in the next chapter, are still dominant.

In sum, SA, as the language of Islam and the language of the Bible in Egypt, carries legitimacy and sacredness. It also carries power as the unifying factor in a nation that is ethnically and religiously diverse: the Arab nation.

SA remains the symbol of a larger entity—the Arab nation—and a clear means of fixing the present and the future, which seems to be changing so fast and overwhelming Egyptians and Arabs at large. By "preserving and making SA immune to change," intellectuals hope to define and demarcate their identity, so that it does not remain elusive or surrender itself to a stronger global community. It is not uncommon to try to do this, except that for Egyptians and perhaps all Arabs, identity has become more than just a common language. SA may reflect part of their identity, but not the whole.

Questions such as "where does Egypt belong?," "what is the true identity of Egyptians?," "how is this identity reflected in code-choice?," and "is it reflected in code indexes and linguistic habits?" are difficult to answer. However, the question of whether Egyptians are "Arabs" because they speak Arabic is almost impossible to answer.

There are some tendencies to perceive Egyptians as both Arabs and Egyptians, as Egyptians first and then Arabs, as Egyptians only, as Arabs mainly, as Muslims first and foremost, as Egyptians then Muslims then Arabs, and so on and so forth. When asked why they may think of themselves as Arabs, some Egyptians may refer first and foremost to the common language and then territory, history, heritage, and other independent factors. However, currently, the word "Arab" is used by Egyptians inside Egypt to refer to the Bedouin tribes that stretch across the desert areas of Egypt (Sayyid-Marsot 1985). Egyptians refer to themselves as "Egyptians." Yet again, what is additionally of interest is that it is also Egypt that promoted Arab unity and created the Arab League.

This ideology of "one language, one nation" implies that too much linguistic diversity is negative. According to the media and some intellectuals in the Arab world and Egypt, one's aim to find peace with one's self and one's nation or state can only be achieved through unity of language. In fact, the Egyptian psychologist Aḥmad 'Ukāshah published the second edition of his classic work *Thuqūb fī al-ḍamīr: Naẓrah 'ala aḥwālinā* ("Holes in our conscience: a look at our condition") (2008) only a few years before the 2011 Revolution. The book was a bestseller. Within it, the professor and psychologist analyzes the Egyptian personality and pins down negative traits of this personality, suggesting ways of changing them.

The author outlines problems that hinder the Egyptian personality from reaching political maturity. He also explains why Egyptians do not revolt and why they may be losing their identity. He highlights the dire state of Egyptian society during the 1990s and 2000s. For example, he writes about the Egyptian woman and how she needs to change certain characteristics, like greed, a lack of independence, and so on. He also writes about language, and his arguments are significant for understanding SA indexes. His section on language is called "Linguistic chaos." He argues that "language is a fundamental means of shaping national identity. The linguistic chaos that we encounter in Egypt has a clear negative effect in Egyptians' ability to express themselves, and to excel intellectually and scientifically" (2008: 48). He argues that Egyptians are not "careful" in their usage of language. In his opinion, to be able to create and appreciate culture, one primarily needs language unification. He contends that a "consistent and authentic language" is the main component for scientific development and strength of culture. It is not possible to have one language that you use at home, one for the street, one you use in songs, a fourth one for newspapers, and then one for the Qur'ān. This "chaotic" use of language and lack of uniformity leads to disintegration in thinking, a shallow culture, and the debasement of public taste. He adds that, for example, when rich Egyptians send their children to English and French schools, they are incapable of producing or being innovative in any language; he calls this *tashattut fikri:* ("disintegration of thoughts"). Even in Egyptian schools, the teaching of Arabic is in a bad state. A school graduate cannot produce proper Arabic. He adds that even decision-makers, politicians, and media-makers cannot speak a unified language. They produce a language that is neither SA nor ECA, but a mixture of both. He concludes that Egyptian intellectual maturity will not be realized, except with language unification (2008: 51). For Aḥmad

ʿUkāshah, there is only one way of speaking for everyone, and linguistic diversity of any kind leads to confusion and backwardness. A unified form of language carries psychological, moral, and political associations. This ideological stance does not, of course, reflect linguistic reality. In fact, the psychologist himself in more than one television program code-switches between SA, ECA, and English. It is ironical that as a psychologist he does not acknowledge the richness of diversity, especially linguistic diversity. However, this idea that unity of language is the only way to progress is still prevalent.

3.3.1.3 Search for linguistic stability: the preservation technique

In 2006, Yūsuf ʿIzz al-Dīn, a renowned professor and scholar, declared in the Egyptian literary magazine *Akhbār al-Adab* (ʿIzz al-Dīn 2006) that "it is our duty as Arabs and patriots to confront the conspiracy against us to weaken SA."

The call to save and preserve a language is not exclusive to Arabic. In fact, feeling threatened by language change seems to be a human trait. Aitchison (2001), in her book *Language Change: Progress or Decay?*, provides similar examples of articles written to bemoan the changing state of English. She contends that "large numbers of intelligent people condemn and resent language change, regarding alterations as due to unnecessary sloppiness, laziness or ignorance" (Aitchison 2001: 4). Aitchison adds:

> in 1986, a letter written to an evening paper complained about "the abuse of our beautiful language" by native born English speakers . . . We go out of our way to promulgate incessantly . . . the very ugliest sounds and worst possible grammar. (Aitchison 2001: 5)

See also Milroy and Milroy (1999), Maegaard et al. (2009), and Kristiansen and Coupland (2011) for similar calls to preserve languages.

While change in ECA may be resented, any change to SA is attacked viciously and considered a conspiracy against Arabic. The former Head of the Arabic Language Academy in Cairo, Fārūq Shūshah, has a program on the radio named "Our beautiful language" to introduce Arabic to its speakers and "preserve it" and save it from change. The program is in what he perceives as "pure" SA.

To reiterate, related to the indexes of power, legitimacy, and unity are the indexes of stability. There is a tendency for Arab intellectuals to regard SA as an entity that needs to be appreciated and preserved. Language change should occur at a minimum when necessary to cope with the changes of technology and science. For this specific purpose, the language academy was created.

SA and the Arabic Language Academy in Cairo, established in 1932: the preservation technique continued

The idea of creating an Arabic Language Academy sprung up first in Syria and then in Egypt at the beginning of the twentieth century and was inspired by the French Academy, which was founded in 1635. The French Academy's goals were to prescribe rules for the French language, in order to purify it and make it capable of dealing with the arts and sciences. Currently, the aim of the French Academy remains to guard the French language by producing standardized grammars and dictionaries (Spolsky 2004: 64).

There are at least five language academies in the Arab world: the Arab Academy of Damascus, established in 1919; the Arabic Language Academy in Cairo, established in 1932; the Iraqi Academy, established in 1947; the Arabic Language Academy of Jordan, established in 1976; and the Arabic Language Academy in Libya and Algeria, which has not operated.

The main purpose of all the Arabic academies is the preservation of the Arabic language and the development of Arabic to meet the needs of modern society in all domains of human knowledge (Sawaie 2006; 1986). The academies are also responsible for the creation and standardization of scientific terms (cf. Khalīfah 1977) and the Arabization of terms from other languages. An example of this from the Arabic Language Academy in Cairo is the word for "telephone," which is either *ha:tif* or *tilifo:n*, and the word for "bank," which is either *bank* or *maṣraf* (Sawaie 1986). The Cairo Academy has the following goals (Sawaie 2006: 635):

1. The maintenance of Arabic (SA) by ensuring it has new terminology for science and technology.
2. The editing of classical texts and manuscripts.
3. The compilation of dictionaries and the publishing of a journal.

Note that, currently, membership in the Cairo Academy is not restricted to Egyptians or even Arabs, but is open to all scholars who excel in maintaining SA (Sawaie 2006).

The academies base their words on *qiyās* ("analogical derivation"), which is the formation of words according to existing word patterns. This enables the academies to produce new terminology and new words from existing roots. For example, one of the forms approved by the Cairo Academy in the 1930s is the form *fiʕa:la*, which denotes professions like *ṭiba:ʕa* ("printing"), *jira:ḥa* ("surgery"), and so on. Dictionaries are then produced with the new forms.

One problem with all Arab academies, including the Egyptian one, is that since the academies lack any authority, there is no guarantee that writers in particular and society in general will follow their recommendations. In March 2007, the chair of the Cairo Academy, Fārūq Shūshah, stated in *Akhbār al-Adab*, a leading literary magazine of Egypt, that the role of the academy was diminishing, because of its lack of authority. He proposed that the recommendations of the academy should be imposed on all mass media in Egypt. Whether this is possible or not is another question (see Nūr 2007).

3.3.1.4 The authoritative indexes of SA exemplified

In this section, I provide yet again another example, this time how usage of SA carries power and how SA can be used as a resource to claim and reclaim power. Yet even so, it cannot be used in isolation, and as a variable it is related to other social variables.

In his book *Arabic, Self and Identity* (2011), Suleiman focuses on himself as both a researcher and an Arab and makes the "self" the object of inquiry. Suleiman is able to make some pertinent direct observations (mostly drawn from his experiences as a teacher trainer in Qatar), while discussing and illustrating language variation and the associations of Standard Arabic at the same time. In the narrative of his experiences as a trainer for teachers of Arabic in Qatar, Suleiman relates his interactions with a group of teachers that he nicknames "the awkward squad." His characterization of the group mixes descriptive elements with a personal evaluation of their motivations (Suleiman 2011: 49):

> [They] often end up criticizing each other the harshest, driven in this regard by their having an axe to grind or by the desire to author acts of one-upmanship for social and professional display, or for public ratification of their expertise and group affirmation of their self-worth.

Suleiman then proceeds to a linguistic analysis of his own interactions with this group. He notes, for instance, that the group was unwilling to criticize Suleiman when he intentionally abandoned case and mood marking when speaking in SA. He attributes their tolerance of an otherwise sanctioned language form to his own position of authority over them, as the professional trainer that will write a report on their performance. At the same time, Suleiman's own motivations are laid open: by choosing to speak SA rather than his own Palestinian dialect, Suleiman tries to project a particular attitude toward a shared cultural and linguistic heritage, as well as professional status (2011: 50). It is clear that his language choice is related to self-perception. He posits (2011: 56):

> I strongly feel that the state of being Palestinian is one of being an underdog in the Middle East [. . .] Speaking *fuṣḥa* [(=SA)] on my part was, therefore, a way of

> standing up for a number of underdogs in the political and cultural life of the Arabic speaking world. It was also a way of dealing with my personal marginality [. . .] It was a mode of cultural and psychological resistance against marginality in my personal life and hegemony in the public sphere.

This example as a personal study in perceptions provides a brilliantly clear illustration of how language as a resource can be used as an empowerment mechanism. While SA carries authoritative indexes that are used by Suleiman, the fact that the "awkward squad's" mastery of SA was not enough to yield them more authority means that Suleiman's status as a professor and teacher trainer is a stronger variant than his mastery of SA.

The "awkward squad," as Suleiman calls them (2011: 49), are not just common within Egypt, but in other parts of the Arab world. They use their knowledge and expertise of SA to increase their power and authority, as well as to develop their social and moral status, while undermining the status of others in the process. Claiming that someone's Arabic grammar is bad implies that the person in question has lost touch with his native language and may have a conflicted identity and is thus not fit to be in an important position. In Jordan, it is said that King Abdullah, who tends to deliver all his speeches in SA, had to receive full training in SA pronunciation before his long-awaited first speech, in which he impressed everyone with his flawless SA. The king's legitimacy and identity as a Bedouin Arab was highlighted against his identity as half-British on his mother's side. SA does have its own sacredness, but Arabic teachers do not share the honor.

3.4 Indirect layering of SA second order indexes

Negative indexes of SA are usually layered in an indirect manner and are in spoken rather than written media.

3.4.1 Negative indexes of SA

As was argued by Walters (2006b), it is difficult to elicit language attitudes by direct means. In the remainder of this chapter, I will use different forms of data, including films, books, blogs, and television interviews, to give a realistic picture of the complexity of the linguistic attitudes in Egypt. Films, in particular, are used here for the first time to shed light on Egyptians' attitude towards SA.

3.4.1.1 Complex language attitudes: the depiction of Arabic teachers in Egyptian films

Films, as a form of public discourse, frequently touch upon attitudes towards SA and on teaching and learning Arabic from a variety of perspectives. An analysis of these films will yield important insights into Egyptians' shared attitudes, beliefs, and stereotypes about (standard) Arabic and its associated indexes. The analysis will focus on the archetype of the teacher of Arabic.

As will be shown below, the figure of the Arabic teacher is a recurrent theme in Egyptian film, where he (with few exceptions, the character is male) is generally depicted as belonging to a lower class, as well as being inflexible and unyielding. This negative portrayal may reflect the aspirations of Egyptian students: nowadays, while students rush to learn English, French, and German, few aspire to become teachers of Arabic.

In Egyptian cinema, there are two important films that have an Arabic teacher in the role of a protagonist. Both films stand out with their caricature-like manner, as they portray the teachers as pedantic, inflexible "nerds" from economically modest backgrounds. Whether the films reflect reality or not is not the point. Rather, the films undoubtedly reflect a stereotype and therefore shed light on the social associations of SA. In 1949, the classic Egyptian film *Ghazal al-banāt* ("The flirtation of girls") was released in Egypt, with comedian Najīb al-Riḥānī (1890–1949) in the lead role as Ustādh Ḥamām ("Mr. Dove"), a primary school Arabic teacher. The protagonist is a poor loner, frustrated by his work in the school; his students constantly mispronounce SA words, rendering them in ECA, with different meanings altogether. For example, he asks his students to read from a children's book in which a lion is threatening a fox. A student reads the following phrase in SA:

[Lion to the fox, SA]
Ya: ablah, waylaka waylaka waylak!

"You fool, woe, woe, woe upon you!"

By changing the stress, vowelling as well as gemination, the phrase is transformed into ECA with a different meaning:

[Lion to the fox, ECA]
Ya: abla, wa-yalukk/ wa-yalukk/ wa-yalukk . . .

"Oh Miss, and he chatters, and chatters, and chatters . . ."

These mistakes do not go unnoticed by the school principal, who has been watching the class in secret. The principal expresses his disappointment with both the teacher and the students' knowledge of SA. Ustādh Ḥamām replies that the students were completely illiterate at the beginning of the year, but his protests are in vain.

His reference to the illiteracy of the students may, in fact, be a reference to the language policy of the time and the futile attempts to teach SA. Recall that during his tenure as Minister of Education (1938–45), Muḥammad Ḥusayn Haykal instructed private schools in Egypt to use SA when teaching the disciplines of Arabic, Egyptian history, and geography, while the primary language of instruction in these schools remained a European language.

In this 1949 film, Ustādh Ḥamām loses his job, but soon finds work as a private SA tutor to the spoiled daughter (played by Laylá Murād) of an Egyptian aristocrat, who has failed her Arabic secondary school exam. It turns out that his new student's knowledge of SA is pathetic, inferior even to that of his primary school students. The remainder of the film is devoted to the story of the teacher's unrequited love for his student, who is blissfully ignorant of (and cruelly insensitive to) the teacher's feelings.

For the purposes of this chapter, it is important to note two elements that are emphasized throughout the film: on the one hand, there is the poor Arabic of the aristocratic student, who does not feel the need to master SA at all. In fact, the student mockingly brushes SA aside as irrelevant in the well-known song *Abgad hawaz* "ABDCDEFG" (that is, the Arabic alphabet):

ʔin ga:ʔa Zaydun aw ḥaḍara ʿAmrun
Wa-ʔiḥna malna ʔin ʃa-lla ma ḥaḍaru:

"If Zayd comes or Amr is present,
What do we care? I hope they won't come at all!"

Ga:ʔa Zaydun and *ḥaḍara ʿAmrun* are sample sentences that have been used for centuries to illustrate grammatical concepts. By ridiculing these sample sentences, the character of Laylá rejects SA, as well as the centuries-old tradition of teaching Arabic grammar.

The second element is the awkwardness and social ineptitude of the SA teacher. The Arabic teacher lacks social standing to the extent that the father of his aristocratic student orders him to eat his lunches with the servants in the kitchen.

Years after its release, the Arabic Teachers Syndicate objected to the film on account of the lack of status and respect that is shown for the teacher, who is treated like a servant in the house of the aristocrat. What is, of course, of interest is that the teacher in the film does not object to this demeaning treatment. While the film can be analyzed from a sociological viewpoint, the linguistic component cannot be ignored.

Almost fifty years later, both themes (the irrelevancy of Arabic and the lower-class origins of its teachers) recur in another tragi-comedy by the Egyptian actor Muḥammad Hunaydī—like Rīḥānī, a famous comic actor whose fame resonates throughout the Arab world.

In *Ramadān Mabrūk Abū al-'Alamayn Hammūdah* (2008), the protagonist of the same name is depicted as a despotic Arabic teacher in a countryside secondary school, who inflicts corporal punishment on his students for committing trivial errors. As a result, his students seem to acquire a phobia of both their teacher and SA.

The visual imagery is very telling: when he starts his first class by reciting a poem by the Abbasid poet al-Mutanabbī, his class is spellbound, and one pupil is shown fainting onto his desk. When the teacher asks his class whether they understood the lines, they respond with blank stares. Like the opening scene in *Ghazal al-banāt*, this scene portrays both the ignorance of the students and the ineffectiveness of Arabic teachers.

The plot then moves on to focus on the Minister of Education, who decides to punish his son for misconduct by sending him to the provincial school, in which Ramaḍān is a teacher. The minister's son is portrayed as completely illiterate in SA. In addition, he speaks only broken ECA and constantly code-switches between ECA and English. Indeed, the young man cuts off the headmaster of his new school by replying in English to his exuberant flattery: "I don't understand you, you don't understand me. There is no point." Ramaḍan tries to discipline his new student with two tools: a leather whip and Arabic grammar. He suspends the student by his feet and forces him to analyze the grammatical structure and mood marking of Classical Arabic poetry. In naming the parts of speech, the student uses the English word "verb" instead of the Arabic *fi'l* ("verb") and is consequently whipped for the mistake. When it becomes clear that Ramaḍān has transgressed against a member of the highest social class, he expects to be severely punished himself. Instead, the Minister of Education appoints him to a post at a private school, in order to impose discipline on the ill-bred offspring of the upper class. Armed with Arabic grammar, Ramaḍān succeeds in imposing some degree of order and eventually becomes a mentor to a group of teenagers. The film eventually loses itself in a trivial side-plot of Ramaḍān's marriage to a Lebanese singer and dancer, but it remains important for its depiction of the archetypal Arabic teacher.

The film is, of course, full of hyperbole, but it can be taken as a depiction of the fear that SA inspires in students, of the total irrelevance of SA teaching, and of ineffective teaching methods. It is highly significant that throughout the film, the students are not shown to substantially improve in their knowledge of SA. They do, however, display a changed attitude toward the teacher of Arabic—one that is marked by fear of the draconian punishments that he might inflict. At the same time, the social inequality between the teacher and his upper-class students is highlighted. Despite his iron grip on the students in the classroom, the teacher remains powerless against them and their parents.

It seems that 50 years after the film *Ghazal al-banāt*, Egyptians have come full circle: despite the reforms of the 1950s and 1960s and an ideology that promoted SA at the time, learning SA still does not carry much prestige for the majority of Egyptians. Both films portray the same problems. SA in both films is regarded as difficult and not necessarily useful. It is also associated with the pre-modern lifestyle, the countryside, the lower classes, and rigid teachers.

The more recent film sends a foreboding message by showing the language practices of rich Egyptian youths. When the son of the Minister of Education uses code-switching, he positions himself as a symbol of a new generation of rich Egyptian youth who may one day lead their country and whose identity is completely separate from SA and its associations. It is no coincidence that the student in the film is the son of the Minister of Education, yet he is not even educated in Egyptian public schools (which the minister oversees). Education in foreign language schools has indeed become the norm for children of the upper classes, who consequently feel as familiar with English as they do with Arabic. In this respect, the film is a realistic portrayal of the education system in Egypt in all its complexity and the issues relating to identity that arise within this system.

When the Arabic teacher and the student fail to communicate or find a common ground, the student addresses his teachers not in ECA, but in fluent American English. In fact, throughout the film, the character of the student is contrasted with that of the teacher: both are Egyptians and yet both represent a different facet of Egyptian collective identity; one is traditional, conservative, and well-meaning, yet rigid, whereas the other is Westernized, untraditional, careless, and, at times, aimless. The characters and their identities are not portrayed positively, and both characters are symbolically juxtaposed through their use of language and lack of communication.

Similar themes recur in other films. For example, the fixation with grammatical rules was depicted in a film that was released during Nasser's presidency in 1963, when the official ideology of the state focused on the idea of the Arab nation and the promotion of SA. The film *al-Aydī al-nāʿimah* ("The soft hands") is a didactic one that extols the virtue of working with one's hands. It tells the story of a destitute Egyptian aristocrat after the 1952 Revolution, who is forced to accept a professor of Arabic grammar as a lodger in his palace when he can no longer afford to pay his servants.

Among other things, the film depicts the prevailing attitude towards Arabic in general and its indexes. The unemployed professor of Arabic grammar has lost his perspective: he is so immersed in contemplating a linguistic example (whether the noun following the particle *ḥattá* should be in the accusative or genitive) that he loses sight of the essential question of how to earn a living. Arabic for him is reduced to one ambiguous sentence that takes over his life. However, this is shown to be a sterile, useless pastime: the people around him do not share his passion for Arabic grammar and view him as eccentric.

The destitute former prince has lost all his money to the nationalization movement and retains only his palace. What he and the Arabic professor share is that both are unemployed. The prince befriends the professor, whom he respects for having a PhD, although the prince himself is ironically illiterate in SA. Although the prince speaks ECA, he frequently code-switches between SA and French.

The prince begins to search for a job, but fails because he does not know how to read and write in Arabic. He then falls in love with the daughter of an Egyptian worker, who volunteers to teach him Arabic. Because of his love for her, he also learns more about Egypt and his language. The fact that her father is a member of the working class is, of course, significant.

At the end of the film, both the prince and the professor discover the virtue of honest work. The Arabic professor ends up working as an actor and gives up his search for a clear grammatical rule: his pronunciation may be good, but he selects a practical use for it. The prince becomes a tour guide, because of his proficiency in English and French.

The representation of Arabic grammar is not positive in this film. On the other hand, Arabic is shown in a positive light for practical reasons. In other words, it is not the abstract grammatical rules or the obsession with grammar that count in mastering SA. The fixation of Arabic specialists on minute details of the language is criticized and ridiculed in public discourse.

It is quite clear that SA may carry its own power as the authoritative and legitimate code, but in the context of Egyptian society, mastering SA does not necessarily come first among social variables. One's social status is the product of so much more than mastering SA; if SA and other social variables are compared, SA is bound to lose in the face of more powerful variables, such as class and professional status.

I will demonstrate this by giving two more examples from the films analyzed above. In the film *Ramadān Mabrūk Abū al-ʿAlamayn Hammūdah*, the Arabic teacher is outraged when another of his students, the son of the Minister of the Interior, uses the nominative case when the genitive is required. He sets out on his bicycle for the house of the minister, in order to complain, but is arrested by a squadron of bodyguards and badly beaten. Upon being released from hospital, he declares that if the Minister of the Interior wishes to decree that the nominative should be the only case used in Arabic, he just has to say so.

In the older film, Hamām attempts to teach the spoiled daughter of the Pasha about the verb *ka:na* and its "sisters" (that is, verbs that behave like *ka:na* ("to be" in the perfect tense)). The Pasha decides to add another word to the "sisters of *ka:na*," thereby changing a grammatical tradition of more than a thousand years. The teacher yields by saying: "If you as Pasha say so, then it must be true."

These two examples illustrate that although SA carries authoritative indexes, this authority is easily overridden by other social variables—in particular, social status. The following figure shows the manner in which the indexes of SA were deduced. SA associations were based on ideologies, perceptions, and linguistic habits. The data used in this chapter to shed light on linguistic ideologies include: poetry; books: political books about the Arab nation and psychology texts; and newspapers: both English and Arabic. The data used to indicate the perceptions of Egyptians include films depicting Arabic teachers and also an example from Suleiman's book (2011) regarding his experience as a teacher trainer in Qatar. Linguistic habits referred to in this section include the Qur'ān; the Bible; religious textbooks; literature: classic, modern, and other SA domains.

To recap, first order indexes are the product of linguistic habits. The SA domain includes religious texts, such as the Qur'ān and the Bible, as well as religious textbooks or devotional works; literature: classical, modern prose, and poetry. SA second order indexes are the product of ideologies and attitudes.

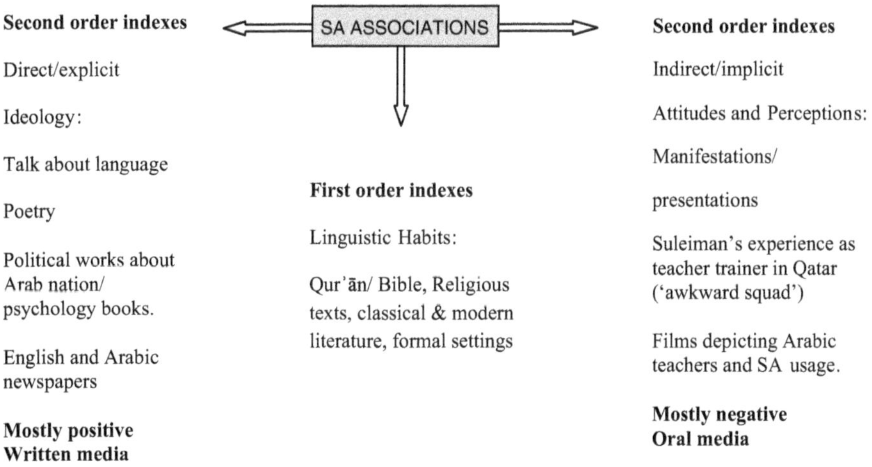

Figure 3.1 SA indexes

3.5 ECA indexes: first order and second order

ECA domains include informal settings, films, conversations with families and friends, and so on. These associations form first order indexes of ECA—linguistic habits. However, ECA, like SA, has second order indexes that, in our case, are more positive ones and are related mostly to indirect language attitudes, rather than explicit references to language ideologies.

3.5.1 Direct and indirect layering of ECA second order indexes

In this section, I will turn to the associations of ECA. As was alluded to in the previous chapters, ECA sometimes carries negative indexes; some Egyptian intellectuals have considered ECA a corrupt version of SA and a potential disintegrating factor for the Arab nation. However, Egyptians' attitude towards their dialect is not necessarily reflected in the attitude of the intellectuals, nor is it dependent on it. In previous studies, such as that conducted by Blanc (1960), in which he examines inter-dialectal communication, he concludes that Egyptians, when interacting with other Arabs, are the least accommodating when leveling their colloquial towards SA or any other colloquial. Whether this is true or not is a moot point and needs more study. Some of the earlier studies are now dated, and what was true at that time may not be true today. However, the conclusions of Blanc give us cause to pause. As was shown in the last section, SA does not just possess positive associations; in particular, by studying unconventional data such as films, it is clear that the associations of SA are not only multi-layered, but also more complex than they would seem at first sight. The almost smug attitude of Egyptians towards their dialect is related to two essential factors that are a prerequisite for us to understand the associations of ECA—namely, the market force factor and aspirations of cultural hegemony. Both factors are, of course, related. By "market force," I refer to the fact that Egyptians comprise about one-third of the inhabitants of the Arab world. Therefore, they form the prime audience and market for the media. Egyptians have also immigrated to other Arab countries by the millions over the past few decades.

The Egyptian economy might have seemed to be faltering during the thirty years of Mubarak's presidency. But directly before the revolution, it was considered the third largest economy in the Arab world after Saudi Arabia and the Emirates. This is, of course, not reflected in the income of the vast majority of the eighty-five to 100 million Egyptians, of which some 20 per cent live below the poverty line. Within the pan-Arab market, Egypt has been supplying labor to rich Gulf countries, in addition to Libya, Algeria, Jordan, and Yemen, for decades, including both unskilled workers and highly trained professionals, such as professors, teachers, doctors, and engineers. Up until now, Alexandria University has maintained a satellite campus in Beirut and Cairo University has had a campus in Khartoum. This dispersal of Egyptian professionals and workers occasioned the spread of the Egyptian dialect or dialects. Because their teachers at school, their doctors, and their bankers are Egyptians, other Arabs are exposed to Egyptian dialect(s). The question of how much Egyptians accommodate their dialect and appearance to members of their host countries is not our concern here and may be related directly to power relations. That is, a worker is more likely to accommodate their dialect and appearance than a professor and so on and so forth. What concerns us here is that the sheer number of Egyptian immigrants caused the exposure and familiarity of different Arabs with ECA. This familiarity may explain why Egyptians do not feel the urge to accommodate their colloquial. It may also partly explain why ECA is considered a semi-standard in the Arab world (cf. Holes 2004).

However, the main factor in the spread of ECA and the pride and confidence that Egyptians have towards their dialect is Egypt's cultural hegemony within Arabic media for almost a century. That said, it is essential to also realize that exposure to Levantine Arabic has increased dramatically among Egyptians recently, due to popular soap operas that are available via satellite television. The same is true of exposure to Gulf dialects. This, however, has not changed the attitude of Egyptians towards their dialect: Egyptians still strive to achieve cultural hegemony, and Egyptian films are still hitting box offices throughout the Arab world. In order for us to understand the powerful associations of ECA, I will resort to unconventional data of a kind that has not been analyzed before. I will provide examples of the "Egyptianization" process that non-Egyptian actors, singers, and artists go through in order to appease an Egyptian audience. I will also show what the challenges are for those who refuse to go through this process.

3.5.1.1 ECA and cultural hegemony: the Egyptianization process of non-Egyptian actors and singers

Najwá Karam is a well-known Christian Lebanese singer and one of the few singers who openly declared that she would never sing in any dialect except her own (that is, Lebanese), including Egyptian and Gulf dialects. No Gulf country took this as an offence, but Egyptian producers and media-makers were livid. Karam was attacked by Egyptian newspapers, magazines, radio, and television. On more than one occasion, she was asked to explain her declaration and provide justifications. In response to attacks by the Egyptian media, Karam convened a news conference to explain her position[3] and made a number of significant public statements about Egyptian singers. She first explained that she did not master

ECA, and while other Lebanese singers may be proficient in ECA, she simply could not sing in a dialect that she had not mastered. When asked whether she might lose all of her Egyptian audience as a consequence, she replied: "There are also those who like the Lebanese dialect in Egypt. I appreciate the singer who values his own dialect and his own country." With her statement, Karam rendered the issue a patriotic one. According to this perspective, there are those who sing only in their dialect and therefore appreciate who they are and what their country is, and there are those who do not. Karam then accused Egyptian *jiha:t* ("bodies") (possibly the Ministry of Culture) of prohibiting Egyptian singers from singing in any other dialect except Egyptian.[4] She also issued a direct challenge by stating that she would sing in Egyptian Arabic only if ʿAmr Diyāb (a famous Egyptian pop singer) sang in Lebanese.[5] On another occasion, she again emphasized the fact that, for her, singing in Lebanese was a reflection of her love for her country.

Karam was also apologetic at times when attacked by Egyptian media. She said on one occasion that she did not mean to offend Egyptians, but only meant to be generous by asking them to sing in her dialect: "It is like asking someone to come to visit you," she declared.

Karam was accused by the Egyptian media of being a mediocre singer, who would never become famous, because of her refusal to sing in other dialects. She was also accused of being a fanatic, who does not appreciate diversity and the global nature of art. The reaction in the Egyptian media clearly showed that Egyptians somehow associate musical fame with singing in Egyptian Arabic. Egyptian Arabic, for them, is the gateway to fame and fortune. Interestingly, the same idea was confirmed by Karam herself, who accused fellow Lebanese singers of using ECA in order to become famous (see the article cited above in elbadil.com). The attack provoked counter-attacks in the Lebanese media, as is clear in the following extract from an article posted in 2011 on the website *Anazahrah.com*:[6]

لكنّ "أم الدنيا" التي ترفض الانفتاح على اللهجة اللبنانية، تعتبر أنّ رفض نجوى الغناء باللهجة المصرية إهانة كبرى لمصر. إذ أنّ بعضهم يعتبرون أنّ مصر ما زالت بوابة العبور إلى النجومية كما كانت منذ خمسين سنة. في وقت انقلبت فيه الموازيين وأصبحت بيروت والخليج بوابتي العبور إلى جمهور متعدد الثقافات والجنسيات، بقيت مصر منغلقة على ذاتها، ترفض الانفتاح على الآخرين أو القبول بإزاحتها من الصدارة في صنع النجوم غير المصريين. علماً أنّه في عصر البث الفضائي، يمكن لأي مغنية درجة عاشرة إصدار أغنية وتصويرها فيديو كليب لتصبح بين ليلة وضحاها أشهر من نار على علم.

But the "mother of the world" that refuses to open up to Lebanese Arabic considers Karam's refusal to sing in Egyptian an offense to Egypt.

Some [journalists] still think of Egypt as the gateway to fame like it was 50 years ago. This is not true anymore; Lebanon and Gulf countries are the gateway to an audience that is diverse in both nationality and culture. Egypt has remained closed upon itself, refusing to open up to what others are doing, and refusing to abandon its place in making non-Egyptian stars. While now, with satellite channels, any singer can make it in a day by having his video clip broadcast all over the place.

While we will not analyze this article in detail, the writer assumes that Egyptians wrongly consider themselves the center of the world. Note that the phrase "mother of the world," a common appellation for Egypt, is placed within quotation marks, presumably in order to cast doubt on Egypt's role as such. The Lebanese journalist assumes that Egyptians' fixation on their dialect (ECA) and attempts to pressure non-Egyptians to use it stem from Egyptians' perception of themselves as the cultural center of the Arab world. ECA reflects past and present aspirations of cultural hegemony. This cultural hegemony is not just dependent on the numerous films, songs, and soap operas produced in Egypt, but is also dependent on the historical and political past of Egypt.

By refusing to sing in ECA, Karam spurred an argument in both the Egyptian and Lebanese media about power, control, identity, and, of course, language. Karam had to justify and explain her stance, but this event made her famous in the process.

As I have pointed out, Karam explicitly acknowledged the role of ECA in the "making" of stars. In a way, ECA is more than the prestigious code in Egypt, since Arab singers, actors, and even writers who want to carve out a niche for themselves in the Egyptian market often feel that they have to learn ECA. Nānsī ʿAjram, another Lebanese singer, not only sang in ECA, but performed Egyptian patriotic songs in ECA. When asked by Lebanese media why she did so, ʿAjram referred back to the Egyptian singer and composer Sayyid Darwīsh, who influenced the whole Arab world, and then she posited that art transcends borders. An artist has to be ready to sing in all dialects.

The question remains: why do Egyptians and the Egyptian audience specifically find it so fascinating if non-Egyptians play the part of Egyptians and speak ECA fluently? There appears to be a huge market for non-Egyptian actors in Egypt. It somehow appeals to the Egyptian ego when a Syrian pretends to be Egyptian or, even better, when he pretends to be an Egyptian from the south, speaking in a *ṣaʿīdī* dialect of Upper Egypt. It is no coincidence that the Syrian actor Jamāl Sulaymān played the role of a *ṣaʿīdī* more than three times in four years in Egyptian soap operas, not only mastering ECA, but also mastering the southern dialect of Egypt. He then played the role of a man from Port Said and spoke the dialect of that town. The Egyptian audience seems to enjoy this and thus have created a demand for non-Egyptian actors to play roles in which they must use atypical Egyptian dialects. The Tunisian actress Hind Ṣabrī also played a character from Upper Egypt, as well as many varied roles, including that of a lower class Cairene, again with a distinct dialect. The actor who played the role of Egyptian King Farouk in the famous eponymous soap opera was a Syrian, Tayyim Ḥasan. The same actor also starred in the soap opera *ʿĀbid Kirmān* (2011), in which he played the role of a Palestinian double agent, who speaks in ECA and pretends to be Israeli. When asked in the soap opera how he came to speak ECA so well by the Egyptian Army officer, he answers (as is expected, since the script is written by an Egyptian) that as a child he was so fond of Egyptian films, songs, and soap operas that he picked up the dialect from watching and listening to them.

All this leads to discussion of an example of the Egyptianization process undertaken by non-Egyptian actors. I will explore this by providing examples from two interviews (one in 2008; the other in 2010) by the same actor, the Jordanian ʿIyād Naṣṣār.

ʿIyād Naṣṣār became known in Egypt after his lead role in the Syrian SA production *Abnāʾ al-Rashīd* ("Sons of al-Rashid") (2006)—a serialized costume drama that chronicles the life of Hārūn al-Rashīd and his two sons. He was then asked to play various small roles in Egyptian films and soap operas until 2008, when he landed his first main role in an Egyptian soap opera. By this time, he had mastered ECA, in order to play the role. But not only did he have to master ECA to play a main role in an Egyptian soap opera, he also had to master ECA in order to conduct interviews on Egyptian talk shows. In the 2008 interview, he was pressured by the announcer to speak in ECA and was only allowed to switch to Jordanian Arabic for novelty's sake. Note the following example, all of which is in ECA, unless marked in bold. This interview took place on the well-known Egyptian television program *al-Sahrah taḥlá* "A pleasant evening" on the main Egyptian satellite channel.[7] The program is broadcast live and accepts calls from viewers. The interviewer was a young female announcer. During the program, the Jordanian actor was also accompanied by his Egyptian scriptwriter. The following interaction took place in ECA.

Egyptian female interviewer: "How did you learn to speak Egyptian Arabic so well?"

Script author: "In fact, when ʿIyād arrived in Egypt his accent [in ECA] was not like that at all. But he said to me that in a month he would be very fluent."

Interviewer: "So what did you do in that month?"

Jordanian actor: "You know in the Levant, because of Egyptian TV series we really understand Egyptian Arabic, but understanding vocabulary is one thing and being able to pronounce words correctly is another. I mean, the spirit of talking. So I started listening carefully to people speaking in Egyptian, I started training myself by recording myself and listening to it later and correcting my mistakes. There was vowelling on the script, but sometimes I had to write the pronunciation of a word above it in red in English letters to make sure I get it right. When I was working on the series I refused to take any calls from Jordan or use any other dialect in order not to confuse myself."

Interviewer: "So please answer the next question in Jordanian Arabic . . ."

Naṣṣār complied with her request. The way that the interviewer frames her first question implies that to be able to master ECA in such a short time is a big achievement for him. This achievement is clearly the result of hard work and resolution. The presupposition is that Naṣṣār has mastered ECA. The scriptwriter emphasizes the fact that it was not easy for the actor, since he did not know how to pronounce ECA properly before coming to Egypt. Mastering ECA is construed as a prize to be won by hard work, and Naṣṣār willingly accepts this idea. Before Naṣṣār explains how he managed to gain fluency in ECA, he explains the difference between a passive knowledge of a dialect and usage of this dialect. He mentions that he could always understand ECA, like "all other Arabs in the Levant," but he could not produce it himself. He also diplomatically acknowledges the dominance of Egyptian television series and thus the Egyptian media in the Levant, and by doing so he ensures his popularity with the Egyptian audience. The actor proceeds to explain the tools that he used to learn ECA. Though not a linguist, he basically used a rough phonetic transcription to help him pronounce the vowels correctly, using what he calls "English" letters (that is, Latin script). To check his pronunciation, he practiced with a recorder. The methods he used are, in fact, not very different from methods used by French students of Spanish, for example, who learn by imitation, trial and error, and practice.

The fact that the interviewer then asks him to speak in Jordanian Arabic is interesting. It could imply that Egyptians are not as familiar with Levantine Arabic as Jordanians are with Egyptian Arabic. We might call this an instance of uneven bilingualism (see Bassiouney 2009). Hence, she wants to present him speaking in Jordanian Arabic as an exciting feature. It could also be to highlight his linguistic achievement in being able to differentiate and master two Arabic colloquials so well.

The attitude of the Egyptian interviewer towards ECA and the pressure on the actor to conform to ECA norms is apparent in the next example from the same interview. A transcription is used, since there is code-switching, and the non-Egyptian Arabic is marked in bold. The context is as follows: a female Syrian fan calls in and asks to speak to

"Mr. 'Iyād" in Levantine Arabic. The Syrian fan then asks him about his films and soap operas in Syria. The Jordanian actor attempts to reply in Levantine dialect:

Jordanian actor: *Aflaːm/ ma fi fi mintiʔat iʃ-ʃaːm...*

"Films, in the Levant there are no ..."

Announcer interrupts: *ʔiḥki bil-maṣri:*

"Speak in Egyptian Arabic!"

Jordanian actor smiles and continues: *Musalsalaːt ʕamalt aktar/ wi inti ʕarfi inni nawʕiyyat il iʕlaːm fi ʃ-ʃaːm bi-tkuːn tarixiyya/ wi nni ayyi fannaːn ḥatta law bi-ykaːbir beːnuh wi beːn nafsu ʕaːrif inni dixuːl maṣr ha-yiʔaddim luh kitiːr/ wi da bil-nisba li ayyi fannaːn ḥaʔʔi maʃruːʕ wa fin-nihaːya da fi maṣla-hit il-ḥaːla l-diraːmiyya l-ʕarabiyya.*

"I have done more soap operas than films in Syria. You know in Syria the kind of soap opera you do are usually historical. Also any actor even if he denies it to himself knows what it means to him to enter Egypt. This to any Arab actor is a legitimate right and at the end this is for the benefit of drama in the Arab world."

Interviewer: *tiftikir eːh illi yixalli l-fannaːn yikaːbir innu yiʔuːl inni maṣr miḥaṭṭa muhimma bil-nisbaː luh.*

"Why do you think an actor would refuse to acknowledge that being in Egypt is an essential part of his career?"

Jordanian actor: *Mumkin li-ʔannu lam tutiḥ luh il-furṣa innu yaʔti li-maṣr [...]*

"Perhaps because this actor never had a chance to come to Egypt in the first place [...]"

Fan: *inta gazzaːb awi bil-lahga l-masriyya*

"You are really attractive when you speak Egyptian Arabic."

The status of ECA as the language of Egyptians who aspire for cultural hegemony is apparent in this example. The actor receives a phone call from a Syrian and reverts back to his Levantine dialect to answer her, probably unconsciously so as to accommodate her and because it is his mother tongue. He starts with a marked negative marker in Levantine Arabic *ma fi* ("there is no"), as opposed to the ECA *ma-fiː ...ʃ*. Before he has a chance to finish his sentence, the interviewer interrupts him, ordering him to speak in Egyptian Arabic. Strangely, she uses the impera- tive Levantine form *ʔiḥki* ("speak"), rather than the Egyptian equivalent *itkallim*; it is not entirely clear why she does so. Ironically, it could be that she, too, unconsciously accommodates to the discourse of the Syrian fan. It could also be a conscious message that his speaking ECA is a choice, even if he masters another dialect. In other words, she may be signalling that she chooses ECA, although she could speak to him in Levantine.

The actor is swift in his reaction. Not only does he switch back to ECA, but he also feels the need to flatter his Egyptian audience. He does so by confirming the Egyptian belief that Egypt is, in fact, the center of Arab culture, if not also the "mother of the world." The interviewer picks up this thread and shows an interest in his propositions about Egypt. She asks him why anyone would doubt the importance of the Egyptian market. His reply aligns him completely to Egypt and Egyptians as he posits that the scorn of those sorts of people is usually due to sour grapes: they, meaning other actors or singers (which statement would, of course, include Najwá Karam), do so because they never had a chance to visit Egypt. Note that in his last sentence about actors not having a chance to visit Egypt, he uses the SA negative construction *lam tutiḥ luh il-furṣa*. This switch may be to emphasize the importance of the last proposition.

His attempts to please his Egyptian audience by speaking positively about Egypt—and, more importantly, doing so in ECA—pay off when the Egyptian female fan flirtatiously comments that he is "very attractive" when he speaks ECA. An Egyptian actor may not be as attractive, but a Jordanian flattering Egyptians' ego is, of course, much more interesting and fascinating. When the fan makes the proposition that ʿIyād Naṣṣār is attractive (the same word is used to denote "sexy") when he speaks in ECA, she acknowledges his efforts and achievements and also rewards him for mastering her dialect. Needless to say, the same sentence would not have been used to compliment an Egyptian using ECA. It is the fact that the actor is Jordanian that renders him "sexy" when he speaks in ECA.

The interview above was conducted in 2008. Since then, ʿIyād Naṣṣār's popularity as an actor has steadily risen in Egypt, and he even was cast in the role of Ḥassan al-Bannāʾ—the controversial Egyptian founder of the Muslim Brotherhood—in the television series *al-Jamāʿah* ("The brotherhood") (2010). The fact that Egyptian producers chose a Jordanian actor to play such an important Egyptian figure is telling.

In 2010, Naṣṣār was invited to another interview on the well-known talk show *al-ʿĀshirah masāʾan* ("Ten o'clock") with Muná al-Shādhilī—a show somewhat comparable to Oprah Winfrey's.[8]

Muná starts her interview with Naṣṣār by congratulating him for undertaking the task of playing such a controversial role as that of al-Bannāʾ. In his introduction, she uses a mixture of SA and ECA, while

Naṣṣār sticks to ECA throughout the interview. When he pauses and stumbles after some minutes, his host interrupts to inform him that he is allowed to speak in Jordanian Arabic, SA, or ECA—whatever code that he feels more comfortable with. Naṣṣār, however, has learned his lesson well: he replies quickly in ECA that he feels more comfortable in ECA, since he has been in Egypt for a while and now even thinks in ECA.

The dominance of ECA is not new, but has been a continuous theme in the Egyptian media for several decades. Even at the zenith of Arab nationalism in Egypt when SA was promoted under Nasser, ECA did not lose its status. In fact, there is more than one sign that there were even stronger attempts at establishing Egypt's cultural hegemony across the Arab world. Nasser himself, when addressing Egyptians and the Arab nation, used both ECA and SA, possibly a first in Egyptian political history. It may not have been his intention to elevate the status of ECA, but rather to produce the utmost effect possible on his audience. However, the very fact that he did not feel bound to use SA is sufficient to reflect the familiarity and ease with which Egyptians use ECA. Another sign of the pervasive influence of ECA is found in the language of films of this era, particularly those films that had nationalist undertones, such as *Wā Islāmāh* ("Woe to Islam") (1961) and *Nāṣir Ṣalāḥ al-Dīn* ("Saladin") (1963). The title of the latter was, of course, intended to allude to Nasser himself, thereby establishing a comparison between Saladin and Nasser. In the movie, Saladin uses a mixture of ECA and SA, while all other characters, including the Crusaders, do not use SA. An even more interesting and intriguing example of ECA dominance is in the film *Jamīlah Būḥrayd* ("Djamila Bouhired") (1959). The film dramatizes the life of Algerian nationalist and revolutionary Jamīlah Būḥrayd, who was imprisoned and tortured by the French during the Algerian War. Her story became a symbol of Algerian resistance and the struggle for independence, in which Egypt gave political support to Algerians against the French.

This film was directed by the famous director Yūsuf Shāhīn, while the screenplay was written by Naguib Mahfouz. It is absolutely fascinating to see that in the film, all Arab Algerians and French are depicted as speaking ECA. Even by Egyptian standards, it was awkward to depict Arab Algerians as speaking ECA, but to let the French characters in the film also speak ECA is even stranger. One would have expected that the French would speak in SA, in order to render the linguistic divide between the French and Arabic more obvious. In fact, this is a common device that has frequently been used in Egyptian cinema: the audience will assume that the French has been "translated" into SA. This language choice cannot be left unnoticed. The fact that the producers did not feel the urge to depict any linguistic diversity is highly significant and illustrates the dominant role that ECA has played in the media.

It is clear from the examples above that the associations of ECA and SA cannot be presented in terms of a simple dichotomy, where ECA is only associated with being Egyptian and SA is only associated with being Arab. Egyptians' attitude towards ECA is much more complex and is related to Egyptians' perception of themselves as much as their perception towards the Arab world in general. Perceptions of the role that Egypt plays in the Arab world are, of course, influenced and shaped by the media.

In Egypt, perhaps more than in any other Arab country, the tension between SA and ECA has been highlighted by a number of intellectuals, some of whom express a preference for the symbolic significance that the colloquial carries. In August 2006, Christian Egyptian billionaire Najīb Sawīris launched a new private satellite channel called O-TV. At the outset, an editorial decision was made that the channel's distinctive feature was to be its use of ECA for all domains, including news broadcasts. This domain, in particular, had been associated exclusively with SA.

O-TV represents a businessman's ambitious plan to provide an audience with an "authentic" rendering of facts. ECA is employed to reflect political opposition, honesty, freshness, and innovation. Note that in the period prior to the fall of Mubarak, ECA was increasingly employed in opposition newspapers as a symbolic resistance mechanism. The underlying logic is that if SA represents the official language of the government, then to resist the government, people use ECA; if SA is the language of government officials who are older and perceived as more corrupt and inflexible, ECA is the language of the youth (O-TV) and portrays a new, different Egypt. Language and politics are thus closely intertwined.

However, the example of O-TV also shows that perceptions and realities are very different categories. As with all linguistic issues that deal directly with people and societies, things are sometimes fuzzy—for example, writers who think they are using ECA may, in fact, be using SA. Even though O-TV claims that they are using ECA, they are also using SA (Doss 2010). Auer (2005) poses the crucial question: where does one draw a line between one language and another when they are both being used together? In Egypt, this line or border is often blurred incidentally, because of the similarities between both varieties, or deliberately, as in the lines from the song at the beginning of this chapter.

3.5.1.2 ECA as an "authentic" code: implicit language attitudes

Whereas SA seems to be associated with legitimacy and authority—for the reasons discussed above—there is evidence to suggest that ECA is associated with authenticity. However, the concept of authenticity as such is at times difficult to associate consistently with one code. In the last section, I showed how O-TV presented itself as an "authentic Egyptian channel" and therefore chose ECA as its code, even for domains that were previously associated with SA. In its publicity, O-TV refers to itself as a "100 per cent Egyptian" channel.

There are other examples in which the media implies that ECA is the authentic code. For example, consider some recent films, which focus on individual identities. Perhaps not surprisingly, a number of such films were released shortly before the 2011 Revolution. These films include *Ḥasan wa-Murquṣ* (2008), *Tīr inta* (2009), *'Asal aswad* (2010), *Thalāthah yashtaghalūna-hā* (2010), *Lā tarāju' wa-lā istislām* (2010), and others. The dominant theme in all these films is the search for an identity on the individual level.

In their quest for an identity, the protagonists of these films manipulate their linguistic resources. From a linguistic viewpoint, these films provide insights to the associations of different codes.

I will focus on one film specifically, *Thalāthah yashtaghalūna-hā* ("The three manipulate her") (2010). This film chronicles one year in the life of Nagībah, a young Egyptian girl who is manipulated by different political groups. Nagībah is a hard-working lower middle-class Egyptian girl who scores 101 over 100 in her secondary school exam. The film focuses on her journey to find an identity as she enrolls in university. Nagībah—meaning "intelligent" in Arabic—is accustomed to memorizing books from cover to cover, including their page count and the type of paper, yet she has never learned to think for herself or make her own choices. She memorizes all of her school books (which are in SA) and recites them on more than one occasion without understanding them, sometimes even in inappropriate linguistic situations.

For example, when she achieves the highest score in the whole country on her A level exam, she is invited by the Egyptian television to speak about her experience; she then starts reciting the general advice given to students on the back cover of school books (which is also in SA): one should wash one's hands carefully, smoking is bad for your health, and so on.

When Nagībah is confronted with university life, she is at a loss, because she is not used to dealing with real life situations. She is then manipulated by three men in turn, each with different political affiliations and aims. The first man she is attracted to is a liberal upper-class student who makes a habit of failing his exams; the second is a communist; and the third is a religious fundamentalist. One by one, Nagībah adopts three different identities, each with its own linguistic choices. There are, of course, clear political overtones to the film, but these are beyond the scope of this book. Nagībah's linguistic choices in her search for an identity are of importance here.

When Nagībah adopts the identity of a liberal upper-class girl, her language changes to constant code-switching between English and ECA, enriched with slang expressions. Her style of dress also changes, and she starts wearing fashionable but revealing Western clothes. As a communist political activist, she quotes books in SA and switches between SA and ECA. Her dress code is jeans and a t-shirt. Finally, when Nagībah adopts the identity of a religious fanatic, she employs mostly SA and covers herself in a black *abāyah*.

Ultimately, the protagonist realizes that these borrowed identities are not "her" and decides to choose for herself what she really is. When she declares that she has finally found herself, her linguistic choice is pure ECA.

The film clearly establishes a link between ECA and authenticity, for while Nagībah pretends to be something she is not, she uses more SA and English.

In the film *Tīr inta* ("You fly") (2009), the same theme is adopted. This time, the protagonist is a shy veterinarian who uses magic to adopt different identities, in order to please the girl he loves. As in the previous film, his language changes from one code to another as his character changes, from code-switching between ECA, a leveled version of Gulf Arabic and English, to the dialect of Upper Egypt, and so on. It is only when he "finds" himself—and speaks in ECA, Cairene—that his love is requited. This idea that in order to be oneself, one must speak Cairene, ECA, recurs in all recent films about identity. I believe that this is a reflection of a prevalent attitude in Egypt towards ECA.

Another kind of data that is not analyzed in detail in this book, but that is essential in any analysis of language is cartoons, caricatures, and posters. There were many of these before, during, and after the revolution. I will concentrate on three specific ones here.

These examples are important in more than one way. The main methodological problem with work on code-switching is that it can be over-interpretive and subjective, as well as the fact that the argument can become circular. That is, unless one establishes associations of different codes first, interpreting the reasons for code-switching and code-choice could become arbitrary.

Caricatures are unique, as they provide clear associations. In the first caricature, Egypt is shown as a woman dressed in the Egyptian flag. The caricature refers to an incident in 2012, in which a female activist was dragged through the street by Egyptian soldiers during a demonstration and stripped and beaten in the process. The incident caused uproar in Egypt, while the attitude of the Muslim Brotherhood and the Salafist groups was harshly criticized, since they did not condemn the incident strongly enough.

Figure 3.2 *al-Fatāh al-mastūrah bint Miṣr*
("The well-protected girl, daughter of Egypt")

Figure 3.3 *Ibʿadū ʿannī* ("Go away!")

Figure 3.4 *Yallā nikammil*
("Let's go forward together")

In the drawing, the Muslim Brotherhood and Salafist representatives are shown speaking in SA, declaring that the victim did not belong to their respective groups. The personified Egypt replies to both by taking the woman in her arms and declaring in ECA: "This is my daughter." In other words, the caricature provides an example of inclusion and exclusion. Egypt speaks in ECA, while both groups that are built on exclusion are represented as speaking in SA. The message is clear: Egypt speaks ECA, while those who use SA position themselves as distinct from "her."

In the second caricature, Egypt again speaks in ECA. She is dressed in the Egyptian flag as usual and walks in despair, while the different political factions in Egypt run after her. She declares in ECA: "You are not my children, I do not know you."

The campaign poster of the Freedom and Justice Party—the political arm of the Muslim Brotherhood—shows a "typical," good-looking Egyptian girl who wears a headscarf. The text says in ECA: "Let's change (Egypt) together." Note that although the caricature discussed above showed the Muslim Brotherhood speaking in SA, their party chooses ECA for its own political advertisements. What we have in all three examples is a conflict about language as a resource—in this case, ECA. The underlying implication in each instance is that whoever "owns" ECA is the "real Egyptian."

On a broader scale, ECA is associated not only with authenticity, but also with other social resources: it is manipulated in political conflicts to cast doubt on the affiliations of specific political groups and as an inclusion and exclusion device. While the examples chosen for this section are all recent, the association between ECA and authenticity is not just the product of the recent revolution, but dates back much earlier than 2011.

In her book *Ibn al-balad*, Sawsan Messiri (1978: 1) explains what this anthropological concept means, historically, from the beginning of the twentieth century, if not before. She argues:

> In some contexts, "Ibn al-Balad" is employed by Egyptians to refer to themselves as Egyptians. In this use the word seems to be synonymous with the term miṣrī (Egyptian).

She goes even further by claiming that not all Egyptians are *ibn balad* "sons of the country" and that the Egyptian nationality, although a necessary prerequisite, is not sufficient to make someone *ibn balad*. In her view, there is a tacit understanding that a true *ibn balad* has no foreign ancestors up to three generations in the past (ethnicity) and speaks Egyptian Arabic (not foreign languages, broken Arabic, or SA). She also refers to the expression *kallimni: bil-baladi:* ("speak to me *baladi*")—that is, speak to me in a clear language that is not ambiguous or convoluted, not philosophical and not in SA, a language understood by everyone (1978: 2).

In his book about national identity in Egypt during the beginning of the twentieth century, Fahmy (2011: 170) also elaborates on the concept of "*ibn al-balad*" by arguing that:

> Only an authentic *ibn* or *bint al-balad* (son or daughter of the country) would use Egyptian Arabic and grasp its multiple meanings and nuances and hence participate in this new-produced colloquial culture.

Note the use of the term "authentic" by Fahmy. Both Messiri and Fahmy—although not linguists—associate ECA with authenticity and with being a "real, local Egyptian," as opposed to being a foreigner or a fake. In other words, associations of ECA with authenticity appear not only in popular culture, but have been argued from both an anthropological and historical viewpoint, not only a linguistic one.

From a linguistic viewpoint, authenticity is, however, a complex concept (Coupland 2007) and will be revisited in Chapters 5 and 6 with more examples.

Before I conclude this section, I would like to mention a unique and highly relevant example in which Arabic—ECA specifically—indexes an authentic Egyptian identity, despite political tensions. In January 2013, the Muslim Brotherhood spokesperson and prominent political figure ʿIṣām al-ʿAryān issued a controversial and interesting invitation to the Egyptian Jews in Israel to come back to their country, Egypt, and live there as Egyptians. His ultimate goal was, of course, to show how tolerant and inclusive the post-revolution Egypt is. The Egyptian media responded to his invitation with surprise and caution, but his invitation also brought the attention of media producers to Egyptian Jews who are still in Egypt. There are currently less than 100 Jews in Egypt. However, the handful of Jews who do still live in Egypt were, for the first time in decades, talked about and interviewed on television. On the program *Bi-tawqīt al-Qāhirah* ("Cairo time") broadcast on the Drīm channel on January 3, 2013, the announcer spoke, and invited Egyptian Jews to speak, about their "Egyptian identity." In fluent ECA, the Jews that were interviewed spoke about their quintessential Egyptian identity and referred to language as a resource that they share with all Egyptians, in addition to other resources. Albīr Aryīh, a senior member of the dwindling Jewish community in Egypt, declared in Egyptian Arabic: "Some Jews were Egyptians before 1948; they speak Egyptian and eat Egyptian." Albīr's reference to linguistic habits and food is highly relevant. His reference to ECA as the exclusive Egyptian code is also essential. Mājdah Hārūn was also interviewed in the same program. Hārūn, who is now sixty-three years old, is one of the few Jews left in Egypt. Her father was a well-known Egyptian nationalist and author of a book on the Jews of Egypt. She declared in ECA that: "My grandfather did not even speak any language except Arabic." Her grandfather's lack of access to any other code is a clear marker of his authentic Egyptian identity. Religion as a complex variable will be discussed in the next chapter. However, these explicit mentions of Arabic as a classification category are further proof of its associations with an Egyptian identity.

In this section, the associations of ECA have been discussed with examples from films, interviews, caricatures, posters, and newspapers. The perceptions of Egyptians towards ECA have been revealed, and the positive second order indexes of ECA as rendering Egyptianness have also been discussed. Perceptions and attitudes are essential for understanding indexes in most cases, and the linguistic habits of Egyptians as media-makers and producers have also been highlighted. Ideologies that associate ECA with fame and a lack of knowledge of ECA with narrow-mindedness mainly target non-Egyptians and are another means of exclusion and inclusion (see Chapter 6 and the Conclusion).

3.6 English indexes: linguistic habits and prestige

In the preceding sections, I have repeatedly alluded to foreign languages and their associations in public discourse, which are not necessarily positive. However, while in some ideologies foreign languages may be considered a divisive, colonizing force, the power and allure of foreign languages and their relation to social prestige in Egypt cannot be ignored. I will refer briefly to the linguistic reality of Egypt in this section.

It is well-known that Egypt is a country that is dependent to a great extent on tourism for its economic growth. It has been reported that the largest group of foreign tourists are, in fact, from the UK. According to the American University in Cairo Career Advising and Placement Services (CAPS) office, the number one criterion for finding a decent job is being able to demonstrate proficiency in English (cf. Russell 1994: 147). In addition, since Sadat adopted the open-door economic policy, Egyptians have been very keen on learning English.

While there are clear economic advantages to learning foreign languages, there are vast differences among the population in the acquisition of these languages, due to the nature of the education system. There is a clear gap between the elite and the majority of the population, because the elite can afford to send their children to private schools, in which they learn English, French, or German, whereas the masses can only afford to send their children to state schools, in which Arabic is the main language of instruction. With Egypt in the 2000s moving towards a capitalist system and privatizing most of the companies owned by the government, knowledge of SA is downplayed and knowledge of English specifically is becoming a necessity. Since the government during the 2000s failed to provide jobs to young Egyptians, the private sector started to set the rules. Due to privatization, a whole generation of employees that once worked for the government has been forced into early retirement, with the result being that a new generation is poised to take over. For this generation, SA does not play a major role.

A new phenomenon in Egypt is the great number of private universities that are opening up beside the American University in Cairo (AUC) and the steady increase in private schools that are not supervised by the Egyptian Ministry of Education, in which SA is not taught at all. Thus, there is a new generation of Egyptians who are highly educated and who speak ECA, but who are illiterate in SA, because their private schools do not teach SA. This seems the most pressing problem in Egyptian education today. Walters (2006b: 660) discusses the influences of a globalized economy—which is based on Anglo-American capitalism that seems less focused on culture or politics and more focused on economic and market factors—on the linguistic situation in Arab countries.

When it comes to scholarship and technology, computer manuals, for example, are written in English, and scholars who want to be recognized internationally have to publish in English. It appears that even France, with its systematic language policy, cannot stand in the face of the spread of English within French society (Spolsky 2004). More than twenty years ago, Crystal (1987: 358) contended that "over two-thirds of the world's scientists write in English, three quarters of the world's email is written in English, of all the information in the world's electronic retrieval systems 80% is stored in English" (see also Luke et al. 2007). Arab societies are following what Fishman calls their "common sense needs and desires" and these needs are not necessarily related to their colonial past (1996: 639). There are changes affecting the world at large, whether social, political, or economic, and they are related directly to globalization. Language is just another domain in which these changes are reflected (cf. Bourdieu 2001).

As for education in Egypt, the discrepancy between the majority of the population and the elites, private and public schools, and universities will remain a problem. English, French, and (to a lesser extent) German will remain the languages of the elite and the educated in Egypt.

That is not to say that English is viewed favorably by everyone. During a parliamentary session in March 2012, a *salafī* MP declared that English was there to colonize Egypt. He suggested that English be banned from schools, so that Egyptians could go back to their true identity. As was to be expected, the declaration was criticized and ridiculed by other Egyptians. The following joke circulated in its aftermath:

A woman speaking to her female friend:
Woman (in ECA): "They found two persons in a dark alley in Cairo . . ."
Female friend: "What were they doing?"
Woman: "I can't even say, I am so ashamed! They were speaking English!"

The declaration of the MP and the subsequent joke both show how language is used as an exclusion/inclusion device and as a resource that is both manipulated and disputed in public discourse.

While linguistic habits and linguistic realities associate English with positive indexes, linguistic ideologies do not do so. That is, second order indexes of English are negative.

3.7 Discussion

In this chapter, I have attempted to lay the foundation for a systematic analysis of data that will take up the next three chapters. Chapter 2 touched upon concepts such as language policy, language ideologies, and language attitudes, as well as linguistic realities. Through an analysis of some unconventional and new examples, Chapter 3 tries to find the connection between language form and its associations. Contexts that mention language explicitly reflect language ideologies; contexts that refer to manifestations of language reflect language attitudes.

Linguistic associations play a double role: when language is used as a classification category, then the associations of linguistic codes have to be previously shared and classified in a specific community. When language is used as a resource to adopt a stance and code-switching is one of the strategies used by individuals during this stance-taking process, then again the associations of codes are of pivotal importance.

In this chapter, the associations of both SA and ECA as well as the significance of English have been discussed.

Indexes of SA and ECA are ordered and in different contexts can be positive or negative. For a thorough understanding of indexes, one does not just resort to linguistic habits, but to ideologies and perceptions, even when ideologies do not adhere to habits. In fact, there are examples in Chapter 6 in which the second order indexes of ideologies prevail over those of linguistic habits. Similar to identity, indexicality as a concept is ideological, habitual, and perceptual.

We noted that SA has associations with the realm of the divine, authority, and legitimacy, which are the result of the fact that SA is the language of the Qur'ān, as well as Islamic texts more generally.

The Arabs' attitude towards SA has always related unity of language to unity of a nation. This may explain the different attempts to stabilize and preserve SA. If SA were to be varied or if there was language variation more generally (that is, the use of dialects), then this may be perceived as a sign of disintegration on a political, social, as well as a moral level. The language academies' role is therefore to preserve "Arabic." Intellectuals have been calling for a "pure," rather than a "corrupt" language. The search for a pure, unified, coherent form of SA is still ongoing. However, the indexes of SA as the ideal form are also prevalent. However, we have seen that SA also carries negative indexes. The depiction of Arabic teachers in Egyptian films is never completely positive and their fixation with grammatical errors and the pure form of Arabic has been mocked and criticized in Egyptian comedies. Teachers of Arabic are depicted as belonging to lower social classes and as inflexible and narrow-minded. Becoming an Arabic teacher in Egypt is not a prestigious choice, and mastering SA does not guarantee employment (Haeri 1996). On the contrary, it is English that carries social prestige and the prospect of good employment, although it may not carry positive indexes in relation to Egyptian identity. It is clear that SA may have authoritative indexes, but other social variables may be more influential in some contexts.

ECA, on the other hand, is associated with the cultural hegemony that Egyptians have (or believe they have) over the Arab world. ECA has positive indexes for many Egyptians, and mastering ECA may be the gateway to fame and fortune for any non-Egyptian actor or singer. And yet, the clear admiration that Egyptians have towards their dialect and the perception of some intellectuals that ECA is a corrupted version of SA are paradoxical and clear proof of the discrepancy between ideologies and attitudes, on the one hand, and ideology and habits, on the other. Egyptian intellectuals oscillate between being ardent defenders of SA as the only language of Arabs and highlighting ECA as the distinct language of Egyptians that differentiates them from all other Arabs. Nevertheless, ECA carries both prestige and authenticity. Being a "real" Egyptian also means speaking in ECA.

Though authenticity is a complex notion, as Coupland predicts (2007), the fact that when Egypt or "real" Egyptians are depicted in caricatures ECA is used is significant evidence that "authenticity" is located in the use of ECA.

To sum up, both SA and ECA carry negative as well as positive indexes. Both are part-and-parcel of Egyptian identity. In this sense, Egyptians are once more left "hanging in the air," as the blogger in Chapter 1 phrases it. Their public collective identity may or may not be easy to identify, but their attitude towards language—as with most people in a diglossic or bilingual community—is paradoxical.

The nature of the discourse also yields different associations of both codes. Venues in which SA is heavily used—such as newspapers, books, and language academies—show a positive attitude towards SA and a negative one towards ECA. Commercial, oral discourse, such as films, songs, and television interviews, have a different, more nuanced, and less positive attitude towards SA. In fact, in these venues, ECA usually fares better.

The following points aptly summarize the discussions in this chapter. First order indexes are related to linguistic habits. Second order indexes are related to ideologies and attitudes. In written data, talk about SA refers to language ideology and is mostly (in our data) positive, direct second order indexes. ECA is represented in a negative light, ideology, and direct second order indexes. However, in oral data, manifestations of SA can be negative, language attitudes, indirect second order indexes. When it comes to ECA, oral data also talks about ECA in a positive light, language ideology, and direct second order indexes. Manifestations of ECA are also positive, language attitudes, indirect second order indexes. Foreign languages, especially English, can be perceived negatively or positively, depending on the context. In direct ideological contexts, they are usually associated with colonial powers (direct second order indexes). However, linguistic habits show the opposite. English is a prestigious code to learn, although not in relation to Egyptian identity.

Wright (2004: 225) posits that "[l]anguage is a robust marker of group membership and one that is not easily changed." Egyptians are still struggling with how to define themselves, both as a group and individually, and how to belong to a group while still projecting a different identity. Language is at the heart of this struggle. The instinct to belong is what nations are usually built on (Grosby 2005). Egyptians, perhaps like everyone else, are also struggling with the ideology of what they are "supposed to be" and what they "really are." It is not easy to separate both and perhaps one should not attempt to, since both forge an identity.

Notes

1. Wright (2004: 224) discusses how communities who are suffering, or who have suffered, from colonization consider language an "identity marker."
2. In the documentary film *Four Women of Egypt* (1997), a female Egyptian professor, who was then about fifty years old, claimed that she only spoke French to her family and Arabic to the servants and that when she read the Qur'ān for the first time it was in French, not Arabic. It is common for rich families in Egypt to address their children in English and employ nannies who only speak English at home.
3. "Najwā Karam takshif asrār ʿadam ghināʾihā bi-al-lahjah al-Miṣrīyah." See http://www.anazahra.com/celebrity/news/article-8934, accessed 4 September 2013.
4. "Najwā Karam: Ghināʾ al-fannānīn al-Lubnāniyīn bi-al-lahjah al-Miṣrīyah

lil-shuhrah wa jihāt bi-Misr tamnaʿ al-Miṣriyīn bi-al-ghināʾ bi-al-lahjah al-Lubnānīyah." See http://elbadil.com/%D9%86%D8%AC%D9%88%D9%89-%D9%83%D8%B1%D9%85-%D8%BA%D9%86%D8%A7%D8%A1-%D8%A7%D9%84%D9v%81%D9%86%D8%A7%D9%86%D9%8A%D9%86-%D8%A7%D9%84%D9%84%D8%A8%D9%86%D8%A7%D9%86%D9%8A%D9%86-%D8%A8%D8%A7%D9%84%D9%84/, accessed 4 September 2013.

5. "Najwā Karam: sa-ughannī bi-al-lahjah al-Miṣrīyah idhā ghannā ʿAmr Diyāb aw Anghām bi-al-Lubnānīyah." See http://www.elcinema.com/news/nw678915001/, accessed 4 September 2013.
6. Rihāb Dāher writing for *Anazahrah.com* from Beirut in an article dated January 22, 2011. "Najwā Karam bi-lā tārīkh min dūn al-lahjah al-Miṣrīyah." See http://www.anazahra.com/celebrity/features/article-9401, accessed 4 September 2013.
7. A transcript of the interview is available at: http://www.facebook.com/note.php?note_id=22504433455, accessed 4 September 2013.
8. Recordings of the interview abound on YouTube; for example: http://www.youtube.com/watch?v=nR9miLBuj8k, accessed 4 September 2013; a transcript is available at: http://www.facebook.com/note.php?note_id=22504433455, accessed 4 September 2013.

CHAPTER

4

SOCIAL ATTRIBUTES OF EGYPTIAN IDENTITY

"My wife is American. I can apply for US citizenship but I didn't, not even the lottery. Many people want to leave, though. We have to restore dignity to all Egyptians. We have to end corruption. No more theft. Egyptians are good people. We are a beautiful people. Please, everyone, this is not a time to settle scores, this is a time to build our country."

(Wael Ghonim in an interview on O-TV, February 7, 2011)[1]

This quote is from Wael Ghonim, the Egyptian Google executive and blogger, whose page "Kullunā Khālid Saʿīd" ("We are all Khalid Said") helped trigger the protests that led to the toppling of President Mubarak. It is taken from a television interview broadcast on the eve of his release from prison, where he had been held on accusations of fomenting revolt. The statements by Ghonim undoubtedly struck a chord with the masses of protesters in Egypt and gave renewed momentum to the protest movement; this is evidenced by the wide publicity given to his appearance on the Egyptian channel Drīm.[2] In this chapter, I will clarify why Ghonim's statements appealed to Egyptians. In particular, I will focus on the messages of authenticity, perseverance, and patriotism that Ghonim was able to convey and examine the indexes and stances used in Egyptian public discourse.

From a sociolinguistics perspective, Ghonim appealed to a sense of community that encompassed all Egyptians and was based partly on perception, partly on habits. While Mubarak appealed to *Egypt* as an abstract entity in SA, Ghonim appealed to *Egyptians* in ECA. He referred to them as "a good people," a people who should be proud of their identity, and a people who should work to restore dignity. This appeal came at a critical moment during the eighteen days of the revolution, when some were ready to let Mubarak finish his term and depart after six months. It was rewarded with another, larger million-person march, which eventually led to the toppling of Mubarak and his regime. In the quote above, Ghonim—unlike Mubarak—adopted the stance of the "fellow Egyptian" whose conceptions of Egyptianness were shared by others. He portrayed himself as a fellow Egyptian who suffered from oppression and kept his head high in spite of it. More importantly, he showed communal solidarity by breaking into tears once he heard of the death of his fellow Egyptians during the uprising.

In his television interview, Ghonim appealed to his Egyptian compatriots by sharing myths and perceptions of what it entails to be an Egyptian. These perceptions will be examined in detail in this chapter. I will show that one of the main assumptions of Egyptian public discourse is that Egyptians, despite their diversity in education, wealth, religion, and so on, comprise a large, inclusive community. This community is also built on ideologies of Egyptianness; these perceptions include specific social variables, such as historicity, ethnicity, locality, character traits, religion, and language. As Coupland (2010: 101) argues, conceptions of a community in general are usually defined in "subjective terms" associated with social and moral values, such as trust, solidarity, and mutuality, as well as with pragmatic considerations of people occupying a specific space and taking part in "conjoined activity." Similarly, Cohen (1985) contends that people construct community symbolically, making it a resource and repository of meaning, as well as a "referent of their identity" (Cohen 1985: 118).

I argue that Egyptian public discourse renders this conception of a cohesive community of Egyptians by making use of stances. For these stances to be successful, the members resort to linguistic resources. This process of stance-taking will be discussed and illustrated throughout this chapter. The last section ("Discussions") will outline particular features of public discourse, especially patriotic songs. For example, the tendency to adopt both epistemic and affective stances by singers is common in Egyptian public discourse. The tendency to also use what Fairclough (1989: 205) calls "synthetic personification" is similarly common. These and other tendencies are discussed and explained in detail in the last section of this chapter.

Orders of indexicality and access to resources are essential in understanding Egyptian identity, as will be clear in this chapter.

This chapter begins with a detailed description of the social variables that public discourse builds upon to mark Egyptians as one community, thereby creating a sense of an Egyptian identity experienced by the majority of Egyptians. These social variables are different in nature and are hierarchical. They include variables that one might call the backbone of Egyptian identity: historicity, locality, and ethnicity. Religion as a social variable is a complex one, as will be clear in the discussion in this chapter, and is treated differently in public discourse than the backbone variables. Language, too, can be regarded as a social variable and will be examined as such.

The result of Egyptians believing that they share a common history, environment, and ethnicity is the Egyptian character. Egyptians, as a community, are portrayed in patriotic songs as sharing character traits, habits, and a strong sense of communal solidarity. Some of these habits and characteristics are variable and flexible, unlike the backbone variables.

Last but not least, "Arabness" will be considered as a variable that is significant in any discussion of Egyptian identity and character. I will address this in the last section.

4.1 Nature of the data

Before I proceed to the analysis, let me begin by explaining the nature of the data analyzed in this chapter. The chapter will concentrate on patriotic songs,[3] in which the relevant independent social variables (mentioned above) are referenced. This chapter will also refer to other forms of public discourse, including newspaper articles, blogs, online articles, and films. The songs are selected according to the following criteria:

1. They deal directly with one or more aspect of Egyptian identity.
2. They are not songs that are tied to a specific occasion or person. That is, the songs selected do not include songs that praise Nasser as a leader or praise the achievements of Mubarak, and so on. There are a number of songs here that relate to political events, but they also deal directly with identity.
3. The songs selected are popular in the sense of being "well-known." If old, the songs must have survived until the present and continue to be recognized and enjoyed today. This is difficult to measure, and I rely on my first-hand knowledge of Egypt to some extent. However, I also interpret the presence of a song on YouTube as evidence of its current popularity, and I measure popularity by the number of times that these songs have been viewed online. In addition, I am guided by the number of times that these songs are broadcast, both on state and private satellite channels.

During the Egyptian Revolution of 2011, there were different movements that employed singing as a peaceful and motivating "weapon." Songs that were popular during this period in time are analyzed and highlighted, since it is in times of political turmoil that identity comes to the fore. In addition to patriotic songs, this chapter includes a section devoted to analysis of significant online articles, films, textbooks, and newspaper articles.

4.2 The backbone: historicity, ethnicity, and locality

Built on my examination of data, I argue that historicity, locality, and ethnicity form the backbone of discussions of Egyptian identity in public discourse. These variables have been referenced in almost all discussions of identity in public discourse from the beginning of the twentieth century up until now. In fact, some intellectuals argue that it is, for example, because of Egypt's location and historical background that Egyptians possess specific traits, such as patience and perseverance. These backbone variables occurred very early on during the formation period, as referred to in Chapter 2. They have also reoccurred since then, not just in songs, but also in textbooks, novels, and films.

4.2.1 Historicity

Public discourse manipulates linguistic resources in Egypt to argue that historical achievements as manifested in local monuments, including Pharaonic ones, Coptic ones, and Islamic ones, have helped delineate Egyptian identity. The monuments "prove" Egyptians' ability to overcome hurdles and survive intact: Egyptians are ethnically linked to their ancestors; they are dark and of noble origin. This increases their capabilities, rather than hinders their progress. Egyptians share a local area called Egypt, which has pyramids and the Nile and has not changed for thousands of years. This large local area shelters a people who share a large community. These public ideologies are indexed and called upon when needed.

For the purpose of this work, historicity is defined as the reliance on past historical achievements to provide legitimacy, authority, authenticity, and credibility to a contemporary community. In fact, this strategy of relating past and present to a national identity, according to Wodak, is common practice. Wodak (1999: 1) posits that "the attempts by both Austria and Italy to adorn their respective 'national pasts' with a historically highly significant archaeological find reveal a typical strategy, metaphorically described by Rudolph Burger (1996: 40) as the 'nationalist dilation of time'." This dilation of time in an Egyptian context refers to the complete identification between Egyptians, both past and present, in public discourse. Wodak adds that the British also do this by "mythically" stretching the nation into a transhistorical entity that is also an eternal one. Again, this is true in Egyptian public discourse and is especially highlighted during the formation of the modern Egyptian identity referred to in Chapter 2.

The following is a recent example—namely, a 2012 edition of a seventh grade history textbook that deals with ancient Egypt and contains a section on Pharaoh Ahmose I (ca. 1550–25 BCE). This Pharaoh is credited with driving out the Hyksos invaders from Egypt, and, indeed, the textbook discusses the Hyksos in two separate tables. The first section of the table shows how the Hyksos *harmed* Egyptians, while the other section discusses how the Hyksos were influenced by the Egyptian civilization, as in the following example (Yūsuf and Wahbah 2012a: 158): "With time the Hyksos were influenced by the Egyptian civilization. They started adopting Egyptian names, wearing Egyptian clothes and speaking the ancient Egyptian language." It is interesting to note that the textbook refers to names, clothes, and language as markers of identity and also as evidence of the dominance of Egyptians, even as they were under occupation. The following note is highlighted in blue within the book (Yūsuf and Wahbah 2012a: 158): "Note, my son: Egyptians are people who preserve their identity and culture; That is why Egyptians influenced invaders but were not influenced by them." This last statement is addressed to the student, referred to here as "my son." The note is for the Egyptian student to relate to both Egypt's past and present. The verb form of "*yuḥa:fiẓ*" ("preserves") denotes a continuous state, rather than a past action, which would be expressed by the perfect form "*ḥa:faẓa*" ('preserved").

The authors of this textbook take it for granted that "the Egyptian" has not changed much since the Pharaonic era several thousand years ago. The textbook presents the core identity of the Egyptian people as unchanging throughout history and highlights Egyptians' ability to overcome challenges in order to survive. This is an isolated example, but references to history or "lessons from the past" recur throughout the curriculum. It is, therefore, no surprise that public discourse continues to reiterate this argument, too. In my opinion, history is the first component of Egyptian identity construction in public discourse, and it is the most important one, simply because of the common recurrence of references to historical achievements. Note that these historical references allude not only to the Pharaonic past, but also include the historic contributions of Egypt to Islamic scholarship, as manifested through the great university and mosque of al-Azhar.

In the eighth grade textbook (Yūsuf and Wahbah 2012b: 133), Lesson 4 has the following title: "The greatness of our Islamic civilization in establishing a political and social system." Islamic civilization is attributed to Egypt as much as to other Arab countries. The pronoun "our" renders Egyptians the owners of this civilization, as much as they are the owners of the ancient and Coptic ones.

To give another example, the recent song *Alla:h Alla:h* ("God, God")

(2010) by Kuwaiti singer Rāshid Masharī al-ʿAffāsī deals with Egyptians' contributions to Islam. There are other examples of Egypt's contributions to Christianity highlighted in public discourse in different contexts, such as the historical event of Christ and Mary seeking refuge in Egypt.

In the following section, I analyze two songs in detail, both of which were written by famous poets and both of which came out in the year 1921, two years after the 1919 Revolution. The first song is in ECA and its lyrics were written by the well-known colloquial poet Bayram al-Tūnisī (1893–1961). The text of the second song was written in SA by the celebrated poet Ḥafiẓ Ibrāhīm (1872–1932). I have selected these songs for good reasons. Both songs relate Egypt's past to its present, both form a counter-discourse to the discourse of the British occupation, and both mirror the nationalist sentiment current at the time. In my opinion, these songs lay the foundation for all discourse on Egyptian identity.[4] However, in each text, the stance of the poet is different: just as the poets position themselves differently, they differ the linguistic code that indexes these different stances.

In Chapter 2, I discussed how the formation of modern Egyptian identity was, to some extent, a reaction to the British occupiers' stance towards Egyptians as the "subject race." One could argue that the discourse on Egyptian identity was formed by a reaction against the British representative, Lord Cromer, in particular. Cromer blamed the lack of innovation and stagnation of Egyptians on their previous despotic rulers, from Pharaohs to Pashas. According to him, Egyptians never had a chance to grow up. This idea was reiterated in other discourses during his time and was met with an Egyptian counter-discourse. A late example of that counter-discourse would be Yaḥyā Ḥaqqī's novel *Qindīl Umm Hāshim* ("The saint's lamp") (1944).

The reason why these two songs in particular were once again popular during the Egyptian Revolution of 2011 is the fact that Cromer's discourse was to a great extent echoed in the speeches of Hosni Mubarak and his deputy, Omar Suleiman. In more than one statement, they accused Egyptians of not being ready for democracy, which of course implies that they are immature. While Cromer blamed history for the political state of Egypt, Egyptians relied on history to prove their achievements and maturity. Their argument was that since "we" built the pyramids and managed to have a long-lasting impact on humanity and world history, we can govern ourselves. Then, as now, no distinction was made between the Pharaohs and the mass of the people. In Egyptian Arabic, the term *fara:ʕinah* ("Pharaohs") is used to denote ancient Egyptian society as a whole. Rather than proving the abject state of Egyptians, history was used as proof of the stamina, greatness, and unperishable nature of Egyptians—and, therefore, Egypt. If Egypt survived so many invasions, it can weather this crisis and all future ones. The two poems or songs merit detailed analysis, since they form the frame for so many patriotic songs to come.

(1) ***ʔana l-maṣri:*** **("I am the Egyptian") by Sayyid Darwīsh (1921)**
ʔana l-maṣri:/ kari:m al-ʕunṣure:n
Bane:t il-magdi be:n il-ʔahrame:n
godu:di anʃaʔu: l-ʕilm il-ʕagi:b
wi magra: n-ni:l fil wa:di il-xaṣi:b
lahum fi l-dunya: ʔala:f is-sini:n
wi yifna: l-ko:n wi humma mawgu:di:n
wa ʔaʔu:lik ʕala lli xalla:ni/ ʔafu:t ʔahli wi ʔawṭa:ni
ḥabi:b ʔawhabti-lu ru:ḥi/ li-ġe:ru la ʔami:l

I am the Egyptian, of noble stock.
I have built glory across the two pyramids.
My grandparents created great science
My generous Nile is alive in the fertile valley
My ancestors have survived for thousands of years.
The universe could perish and they still remain
Shall I tell you about a lover that forced me to emigrate and leave my family and friends?
I have given my life as a gift to that lover. I cannot love another

Bayram al-Tūnisī is well-known as a colloquial poet whose poems were sung by a number of famous singers during his lifetime. As I have tried to show above, this specific song is pivotal in many ways. Originally, it formed part of the play *Shahrazād*, which premiered in 1934 (al-Tūnisī 1987: 286). In the play, the Egyptian character introduces himself to a woman who is an outsider with little knowledge of Egypt or Egyptians. She is depicted as curious and, to some degree, filled with admiration of this Egyptian man. The Egyptian defines himself in general terms and does not mention his name. As an Egyptian, he comes across as a knowledgeable, confident achiever. This confidence and knowledge are depicted through linguistic resources. As an outsider, she gives him the chance to elaborate on what it means to be Egyptian. The message is that Egyptians all share the same timeless characteristics.

Two lexical references that are essential in situating the Egyptian in a specific time and place are the River Nile and the pyramids. By referring to both, the poet demarcates a territory for the Egyptian—a territory as old as the pyramids and the Nile. Drawing on Van Leeuwen's (1996) five categories of socio-semantic identification, one finds that al-Tūnisī uses both functionalism and relational identification to define himself. Functionalism, which refers to identification by virtue of what one does, is used by al-Tūnisī to identify the Egyptian as the builder of civilization and glory. This is the Egyptian's primary function, for with civilization comes fertility and science. Relational identification, which is identification by virtue of relationships, is also used in this song, for al-Tūnisī refers to ancestors and the character's relation to them. He and his ancestors are tied together. The first two factual statements come in the form of two verbless sentences:

ʔana lmaṣri:/ kari:m al-ʕunṣure:n

I the Egyptian, noble stock

This device is common in songs and will appear in several other examples below. The lack of verbs renders the two propositions as assertions of common knowledge. This is followed by a cluster of factual statements about Egypt's achievements. The first verb used in the song is in the perfect tense:

Bane:t *il-magdi be:n il-ʔahrame:n*

I built glory across the two pyramids

This perfect tense renders the definiteness of the action. It is, without doubt, the Egyptian who has built glory. Although the verb is in the perfect tense and refers to the building of civilization, it is used in reference to the modern Egyptian. The Egyptian, by using a verb in the perfect tense to describe a complete action simultaneously positions himself beyond time. Tense and aspect are extremely relevant in this song. Throughout the song, there is no distinction between modern and ancient. This is rendered through the use of aspect. The verbs used in the first part of the song are verbs of action used in the perfect tense ("built," "established," and so on). The Egyptian is the doer, the agent. The statements are statements of achievement. These two perfect verbs are then contrasted with the participle that denotes continuity:

wi yifna: l-ko:n wi humma ***mawgo:di:n***

The universe could perish and they still remain

Metonymy is also employed. The universe could perish and "they still remain," referring to their ancestors, but meaning their monuments. In other words, the universe will eventually perish, but Egyptians will live on in their monuments, alluding again to the ancient Egyptian civilization as opposed to the civilization of the colonizer. The text implies that the "civilized" colonizer may perish, while the Egyptian civilization will remain. This complete identification between the past and present Egyptian and ancient Egyptian monuments has become a recurrent theme in public discourse.

However, the pronoun "they" is ambiguous, as it may refer to the ancestors, but could also refer to Egyptians more generally. The Egyptian then becomes transhistorical—a survivor in spite of everything.

The position of the Egyptian changes to a more intimate one when he addresses the woman using the second person feminine pronoun. He does not define himself anymore, but tries to tell the woman that admires him what brought him there and forced him to leave Egypt.

wa ʔaʔu:lik ʕala lli xalla:ni/ ʔafu:t ʔahli wi ʔawṭa:ni
ḥabi:b ʔawhabti-lu ru:ḥi/ li-ġe:ru la ʔami:l

Shall I tell you about a lover that forced me to emigrate and leave my family and friends?
I have given my life as a gift to that lover. I cannot love another . . .

It may be significant that the speaker of this text is addressing a woman throughout—significantly, a woman who is an outsider. The fact that the speaker is Egyptian provides the opportunity to define what being Egyptian means, particularly vis-à-vis a non-Egyptian. The linguistic form is also meaningful: as an Egyptian, the character of the play speaks in ECA, although the woman whom he addresses is certainly not Egyptian. However, the use of ECA adds authenticity and intimacy to his message. Dialogicality is also employed by al-Tūnisī in this song, but this feature will be discussed in detail with reference to the next song.

miṣr tataḥaddaθ ʕan nafsi-ha: ("Egypt speaks about itself") by Umm Kulthūm (1921)

Ḥāfiẓ Ibrāhīm's classic poem *miṣr tataḥaddaθ ʕan nafsi-ha:* ("Egypt speaks about itself") still resonates in Egypt in the present day. Set to music, it was sung by the greatest Egyptian singer of all time, Umm Kulthūm (1898–1975). Grave but majestic, the song was called upon at every important turn in Egyptian history, such as the 1952 Revolution, the 1967 defeat, 1973 victory, and, most recently, the 2011 Revolution. The original text of the poem is much longer than that of the song and was first recited as part of a celebration at the Intercontinental Hotel in Cairo to mark the boycott of negotiations with the British by Adlī Yakin Pasha, who had also simultaneously resigned from the government.[5]

Although the song is exclusively in SA, it is memorized by a great number of Egyptians. While the message of this song is similar to the one by al-Tūnisī, the stance and code-choice are different. Both songs argue that Egyptian history stands witness to the Egyptian's character, ethnicity, and, more generally, identity. However, while in the first song the poet addresses a woman who is an outsider and tells her about Egypt in ECA, in this song the poetic voice personifies Egypt and makes her speak for "herself" about her achievements; importantly, she does so in SA. The stance of Egypt is different from that of "the Egyptian." While the Egyptian needs to index his or her authenticity in ECA, Egypt does not need to do so. The very fact that Egypt speaks renders her authentic. What Egypt needs to show through her stance is her power, authority, and legitimacy.

The poet uses metonymy to let Egypt speak from a position of power, but it is the Egyptian people that are implied as having built glory and survived. The use of personification emphasizes this fact. The poem argues that because of the long history of Egypt and sheer fact that it has survived, one has enough reason to believe that her children, the Egyptians, are mature and strong enough to rule themselves.

Egypt is portrayed as positioning herself as a confident, proud, sophisticated, and mature entity. Pronouns are used to index this position. Egypt refers to herself, as well as to the colonizer. However, the non-Egyptians are referenced in a non-specific manner, both in passing and in general terms. All of these features undermine this "other." Egypt is referenced in the first person feminine singular and the "other" is referenced in the third person plural "they." This renders the other insignificant and not special in any way compared to the uniqueness of Egypt and, thus, Egyptians.

(2) *miṣr tataḥaddaθ ʕan nafsi-ha:* ("Egypt speaks about itself") (1921)
waqafa l-xalqu yanẓuru:na gami:ʕan kayfa ʔabni: qawa:ʕida l-magdi waḥd-i:
wa buna:tu l-ʔahra:m fi: sa:lif id-dahri: kafawu:ni: l-kala:m ʕinda t-taḥaddi:
ʔana ta:gu l-ʕala:ʔi fi: mafraq iʃ-ʃarqi wa dura:tu-hu faraʔidu ʕiqd-i:
ʔin magd-i: fi lʔu:laya:-ti: ʕari:qin man la-hu miθl ʕu:liya:-ti: wa magd-i:
ʔana ʔin qaddara l-ʔila:hu mama:t-i: la: tara: aʃ-ʃarqa yarfaʕu r-raʔsa baʕd-i:
ma: rama:ni: ra:mi wa ra:ḥa sali:man min qadi:min ʕina:yatu l-la:hi gund-i:
kam baġat dawlatun ʔalayya: wa ġa:rat θumma za:lat wa tilka ʔuqba t-taʕʕdi:
ʔinna-ni: ḥurratan kasartu quyu:d-i: raġma rukb al-ʕida: wa qaṭaʕtu ***ʔid-i:***
ʔa:tura:-ni: wa qad ṭawaytu ḥaya:t-i: fi: ***mi:ra:sin*** *lam ʔabluġ al-yawm rushd-i:*
ʔa-min al-ʕadli ʔanna-hum yaridu:n al-ma:ʔa ṣafwan wa ʔan yukaddar wardi:
*ʔa-min al-ḥaqqi ʔanna-hum yuṭliqu:n al-***ʔuðdi** *min-hum wa ʔan tuqayyida* ***ʔuðd-i:***
naẓar al-la:hu l-i: fa-ʔarʃad abna:ʔ-i: fa-ʃaddu: ʔila: l-aʕala: ʔayya ʃadd-i:
ʔinnama: l-ḥaqqu quwwatun min quwa: ad-diya:n ʔamḍa: min kulli ʔabyaḍin hindi:

> All of creation stood watching, how I build the foundations for glory by myself.
> The builders of the pyramids eons ago saved me from having to speak when challenged.
> On my head I wear the crown of the whole east, and its pearls hang around my neck
> My glory is ancient and rooted in the very beginnings. Who has glory and beginnings like mine?
> For if God decrees my death, you won't see the East raise its head after I've gone
> No invader ever left my land intact for the care of God is my warriors.
> Many a country transgressed against me, and attacked me, but then ceased to exist—and this is its punishment for transgression.
> For I am free and I've broken my bonds, in spite of being ridden by the enemy—I've cut my reigns
> Do you believe that I, who have spent my life in a continuous struggle, have not come of age yet?
> Is it fair that they want to have their water pure, while they muddy my spring?
> Is it right that they let their reins run free, while they keep my wrists in chains?
> God looked to me while I am guiding my sons, and they pulled upwards with all of their might
> But righteousness is a power belonging to God, mightier than the sword.

Some of the discourse and structural resources used in this song include: dialogicality, pronouns, aspect, tense, achievement and assertive factual statements, and mention of specific categories that are essential in identity construction in Egyptian public discourse. These categories include local sites, such as the pyramids. The pyramids are not just important as a local site, but as a surviving witness to glory. There is also mention of religion in a generic manner.

In the first factual statement, aspect and tense are crucial:

> *waqafa l-xalqu yanẓuru:na gami:ʕan kayfa abni: qawa:ʕida l-magdi waḥd-i:*
>
> All of creation stood watching, how I build the foundations for glory by myself.

The first verb, *waqafa* ("stood"), is in the perfect tense. It refers not only to mankind, but to all of creation, which stood in amazement while Egypt built her civilization. What is significant here is the verb of action, *abni:* ("I build"), which is used in the imperfect. It would have been theoretically possible to say *banaytu* ("I built"), but the emphasis here is that Egypt is still building its glory, that it is an ongoing process. The contrast between the stative verb *waqafa* ("they stood") and the verb of action ("I build") is also important.

Another contrast is between speaking and not speaking. Egypt posits that she does not have to speak when challenged, since her actions—as manifested in monuments, such as the pyramids—are witnesses to her power.

> *wa buna:tu l-ʔahra:m fi: sa:lif id-dahri: kafawu:ni: l-kala:m ʕinda t-taḥaddi:*
>
> The builders of the pyramids eons ago saved me from having to speak when challenged.

The first rhetorical question repeats again as a direct reply to the claim of the British that Egypt was not capable of ruling itself and was in need of the help and protection of Britain. Dialogicality is therefore a crucial feature in this song. Ibrāhīm was acutely aware of the British discourse of his time; in fact, he refers to it in more than one of his poems. In his farewell poem to Cromer (*Wada:ʕan Kru:mir*) ("Farewell, Cromer") (1907)), he accused Cromer of calling Egyptians intolerant and portraying Middle Eastern peoples as naïve, crude, and incapable of invention or creation (Ibrāhīm 1980: 26–7). The present poem contains a similar reply to colonial discourse:

> *ʔa:tura:-ni: wa qad ṭawaytu ḥaya:t-i: fi: mi:ra:sin lam ʔabluġ al-yawm rushd-i:*
>
> Do you believe that I, who have spent my life in continuous struggle, have not come of age yet?

The construction of this rhetorical question is again dependent on the contrast of aspect and tense: *qad ṭawaytu* ("I have spent") with the perfective particle *qad* implies definiteness, completion, and conjures up an existence that reaches deep into the past. The definiteness of experience renders the accusation of immaturity absurd.

The negated verb *lam ʔabluġ* ("reached") is in the perfect. Note, however, that it is only the negative marker *lam* that carries the perfective meaning, while the verb form itself is identical to the imperfect. These factors combine to form a contrast with *al-yawm* ("today"), which refers to the present and reinforces the (false) claim that Egypt had not reached maturity *yet*. The English translation cannot capture the contrast in tense between the past and present that occurs in Arabic.

The identity of the accusers who make this claim of immaturity is not revealed, although the covert reference to the discourse of British and that of Cromer in particular would not have been lost on the audience. Indeed, it would seem that the poet chooses to dismiss colonizing powers summarily, as a way of belittling their importance:

kam baġat dawlatun ʔalayya: wa ġa:rat θumma za:lat wa tilka ʔuqba t-taʕʕdi:

Many a country transgressed against me, and attacked me, but then ceased to exist—and this is its punishment for transgression.[6]

The challenging tone is sustained throughout the poem, as in this set of rhetorical questions:

ʔa-min al-ʕadli ʔanna-hum yaridu:n al-ma:ʔa ṣafwan wa ʔan yukaddar wardi:
*ʔa-min al-ḥaqqi ʔanna-hum yuṭliqu:n al-**ʔuðdi** min-hum wa ʔan tuqayyida **ʔuðd-i:***

Is it fair that they want to have their water pure, while they muddy my spring?
Is it right that they let their *reins* run free, while they keep my wrists in chains?

These questions enhance the conversational style of the song, which aims at convincing the audience (which is mostly Egyptian) of the glory and power of Egypt and, thus, Egyptians and also stands in contrast to the first factual statements. Again, the colonizers are referred to by the pronoun *hum* and are not specified. This ties in well to the main argument of the poem—namely, that Egypt had many colonizers who never influenced her and failed to destroy her identity. This recalls the same argument in the history textbook discussed earlier.

Not only is Egypt ancient and strong because of its achievements, but she also has God on her side. There is no reference here to a specific religion, whether Islam or Christianity, but rather the reference is made to God in general. As we will see later in the chapter, this technique is repeated in many songs.

naẓar al-la:hu l-i: fa-ʔarʃad abna:ʔ-i: fa-ʃaddu: ʔila: l-aʕala: ʔayya ʃadd-i:
ʔinnama: l-ḥaqqu quwwatun min quwa: ad-diya:n ʔamḍa: min kulli ʔabyaḍin hindi:

God looked to me while I am guiding my sons, and they pulled upwards with all of their might
But righteousness is a power belonging to God, mightier than the sword.

It seems clear that the whole poem or song is a counter-argument to a prevailing sense of superiority in the discourse of foreigners and the British occupiers. Echoes of such a counter-discourse can still be heard today. One noteworthy example was Mubarak's interview with ABC's Christiane Amanpour on February 3, 2011 (at the height of the 2011 Revolution), in which he argued that Obama did not understand Egyptian culture, and Egyptians were not ready for democracy. Mubarak advanced these arguments as the reason why he could not give up his post, postulating that if he left, Egypt would fall into chaos. The newly appointed Vice-President Omar Suleiman reiterated this very same discourse on February 6, 2011. The reply of the Egyptian masses came in the form of more protests (and more singing) in Tahrir Square. The songs analyzed in this chapter were songs that accused both Mubarak and Suleiman of not understanding Egyptians; a recurrent idea running through these songs was that because of their long history, Egyptians were mature enough to take control of their future. Again, identity was called upon to wage a war. We will be looking in detail at the dynamics of the conflict in Chapter 6 below.

4.2.1.1 Recurrent themes in nationalist songs

While stance and language choice are different in the two songs analyzed above, both songs highlight three essential props of Egyptian identity: history, locality, and ethnicity. History is manifest in reference to the pyramids in both songs, and locality is manifest in reference to the Nile and the pyramids. Ethnicity is referenced in both songs: in the first song, the Egyptian comes from a noble origin (that is, ethnicity is related to common descent); the same is true for the second song.

The main argument of Egyptian public discourse—as manifested in both songs—is that Egyptians have the pyramids and the Nile, both of which have stood witness to Egypt's great civilization. It is the modern Egyptians' ancestors who built the pyramids and benefitted from the Nile. The modern Egyptian is their grandchild, therefore she or he is as "noble" as they are. She or he is also different from the "white man," perhaps even superior to him.[7] With regards to locality, the argument goes that Egyptians still share the Nile and the pyramids; they see them every day and therefore they are part of who they are: they form and influence their habits and characteristics. History, ethnicity, and locality thus form the Egyptian identity and shape its characteristic traits. For example, the common belief that Egyptians possess a lot of stamina is a product of their long history. They are depicted as invincible and strong; as patient, but never defeated.

The following examples from more recent songs that are as popular as the two analyzed above will serve to prove these assertions and enhance the points discussed above. In the following example, I argue that history, locality, and Egyptian character traits are closely tied.

(3) *maṣr hiyya ʔumm-i:* ("Egypt is my mother") by ʿAfāf Rāḍī (1976)

fa:t-ak nuṣṣu ʕumr-ak ya: illi: ma:-ʃufti maṣr
da t-ta:ri:x fi: maṣr w-il-haram fi: maṣr w-il-karam fi: maṣr

Half of your life **was wasted**, if you haven't seen Egypt.
All of history is in Egypt, and the pyramids are in Egypt, and generosity is in Egypt.

The female singer positions herself as the Egyptian expert on Egyptian identity. She addresses the outsider who has never seen Egypt, expressing her pity at his or her great loss. In so doing, she also evaluates Egypt and Egyptians. The outsider misses the rich history of Egypt, the pyramids (locality and history), and the generosity of Egyptians (in other words, "typical" character traits are presented as a consequence to location and shared history). The outsider is referenced to as "you, who has not seen Egypt." Negation is used to address this outsider, to emphasize her or his loss:

ya: illi: ma:-ʃufti maṣr

[lit.] you, who not seen Egypt.

Then the next assertive statement is verbless:

da t-ta:ri:x fi: maṣr w-il-haram fi: maṣr w-il-karam fi: maṣr

all of history [is] in Egypt and Pyramids [are] in Egypt and generosity [is] in Egypt

This lack of verbs, also found in the song *ʔana: l-maṣri:*, is a common resource used to denote and emphasize the sincerity or commonsensical nature of the statement. References to history, ethnicity, and character traits also occur as linked in the following example:

(4) *il-maṣriyyi:n ʔahumma* ("Here are the Egyptians") by Yasmīn al-Khayyām (1980)
il-maṣri fi ʔayyi tari:x mila:di: aw higri:
wi fi ayyi zama:n wi maka:n huwwa huwwa l-maṣri: (2)
l-asmar abu ḍiḥka truddi l ro:ḥ
taʕrafu: min be:n milyo:n insa:n

The Egyptian of any era—be it the Christian or the Muslim one—
of any time, or place, he is the very same Egyptian.
The dark-skinned one, with a hearty laugh:
You can recognize him among a million people.

The idea of "the" Egyptian defeating time or existing beyond time is even more apparent in this example. The singer again takes the stance of the knowledgeable Egyptian who evaluates other Egyptians and refers to "the" Egyptian in the third person masculine singular. This entire strophe does not include any verbs. It posits as a given that the Egyptian at any age and time is the same. The pronoun *huwwa* is repeated twice for emphasis and to highlight the uniqueness of the Egyptian. The text states explicity that throughout the ages, the typical Egyptian is dark-skinned and endowed with a humorous nature. He is so unique that you would recognize him even before a million others.

The use of ECA possessive form *l-asmar abu ḍiḥka truddi l ro:ḥ* ("the dark-skinned one with a hearty laugh") attributes the hearty laugh to the dark-skinned Egyptian. It is easy to see that the entire strophe consists of a cluster of definite, emphatic factual statements.

Before I turn to discussion of ethnicity in more detail, I would like to mention an article written in SA in *al-Shurūq* newspaper on December 23, 2011 entitled *Aḥfād aḥfād Khūfū* ("The great-grandchildren of Khūfū [Cheops]").[8] The author of the article, Jalāl Amīn (b. 1935), a famous Egyptian author and thinker, refers to a short story by Aḥmad Bahjat entitled "The grandchildren of Khūfū." The short story laments the abject state of Egyptians in the 1960s[9] and how the grandchildren of such a great king have been reduced to a state of stagnation and resignation. Jalāl Amīn then addresses Aḥmad Bahjat in a dialogical way and posits that, now, the great-grandchildren of Khūfū, the young revolutionaries of the 2011 Revolution, and their continuing struggle and fighting during December 2011 have proven that they are worthy of their great-grandfather and deserve to be his grandchildren: they are resourceful and strong and possess the stamina needed to change Egypt for the better.

I mention this article to show how historicity carries the same indexes in the Egypt of 2011 that it carried in the Egypt of 1901. Authenticating identity through history is an ongoing process in Egypt. Whether this will change in the coming years is not yet clear, but so far it continues to be utilized.

4.2.2 Ethnicity

Ethnicity has been referred to in the examples in the last section. As with most variables, it does not occur alone, but is accompanied by other variables, such as historicity, locality, or character traits. Ethnicity, although different from race as will become clear below, is a flexible concept. I will first start by defining ethnicity and then discussing it in relation to Egypt.

Ethnicity is a crucial variable in a great number of places within the world at large and in parts of the Arab world in particular. In some cases, the definition of ethnicity is too flexible, as it can include differences built on nationality or religious affiliation; in other cases, it can be built on skin color. For example, Al-Wer's work on variation in the speech of Jordanians and Palestinians in Jordan used the term ethnicity to refer to the historical and national differences between both groups (Al-Wer 2002: 66). In a number of cases in the Arab world in particular, the lines between nationality and ethnicity are blurred, especially in public discourse. Egypt is a case in point. Davies and Bentahila (2006: 59) also argue that both ethnicity and nationalism can be considered "as points on a continuum." Degrees of self-awareness, organization, mobilization, or ideologization can all be factors that distinguish nationalism and ethnicity (cf. Connor 1978; Edwards 1985; Fasold 1995; Paulston 1994).

According to Davies and Bentahila (2006: 58), ethnicity is "an analytical concept used to describe the bonds which lead certain people to identify themselves as a group." This bond could be an ancestral lineage. Fishman (1977: 17) describes this bond as a paternity bond. Fishman posits that "ethnicity is, in part, but at its core, experienced as an inherited constellation acquired from one's parents as they acquired it from theirs, and so on back further and further, ad infinitum." In Egyptian public discourse, ethnicity is related to an ancestral bond, usually a paternal one that is substantiated by skin color. However, the images that usually accompany patriotic songs show different Egyptians, with different skin colors, mostly with black to brownish hair, but always from different parts of Egypt, including the urban, rural, rich, poor, educated, and illiterate. This inclusive attitude may seem to contradict the perception of Egyptians as all dark-skinned and descending from "the Pharaohs." Such problems in grasping ethnicity are not peculiar to Egypt (see Fought 2006 for other examples). As with most social variables, perceptions of ethnicity are to a great extent subjective.

The definition of ethnicity by Fishman (1977: 17; see also Edwards 2009: 162) relies on patrimony and ancestral lineage. He also posits that

> ethnic identity is allegiance to a group—large or small, socially dominant or subordinate—with which one has ancestral links . . . this can be sustained by shared objective characteristics (language, religion, etc.), or by more subjective contributions to a sense of groupness, or by some combination of both. Symbolic or subjective attachments must relate, at however distant a remove, to an observably real past.

Perhaps this explains why ethnicity as a variable does not occur by itself, but usually in addition to another variable, as in the examples mentioned above. In Egyptian public discourse, ethnicity is combined primarily with the variables of language, history, and locality, since in Egypt there is more than one religion.

There are a number of moot issues related to ethnicity, including the issue of whether one can acquire or lose an ethnicity. Note that according to Fishman, this bond can be lost; in other words, it is not inherent, thus one can acquire or lose an ethnicity. This may not be necessarily true in the Arab world (see Bassiouney 2009) or in Egypt. Another issue is the arbitrary nature of public discourse in dealing with issues of ethnicity. While being inclusive is a positive attitude, it can also be a negative one. For example, in Egypt, Nubians or Bedouins may want to be perceived as ethnically different, but are usually lumped together in the same ethnic group with urban and rural Egyptians, as they are characterized by their "dark skin." These issues need further study and data in order to analyze them in the future.

It is noteworthy, however, as mentioned earlier, that the concept of ethnicity is associated with skin color in Egypt. To a great extent, this is related to the attitude towards different colonizing powers, including the Mamluks (depicted with lighter skin); the Ottomans (depicted with lighter skin); and finally the British (who considered Egyptians to be of a different race at the time). Rather than denying their differences, Egyptians in public discourse emphasize them and use them as an empowering tool. Their dark skin marks them as Egyptians, from a different and nobler ethnic origin. Again, this issue needs to be dealt with in more detail, but it is not the topic of this book. Rather, the aim of this section is to show how Egyptians in public discourse used the linguistic resources available to them to demarcate this ethnicity and create a general community in the process. There are a number of resources used in the following examples, including direct reference to color during the stance-taking process of singers in patriotic songs and, more importantly, choosing non-Egyptian singers to sing to Egyptians, which allows the singer to adopt the stance of the outsider and emphasize traits of Egyptians, including skin color. This last technique—a common one—is significant.

I will discuss the examples in this section chronologically, beginning with one of the most popular Egyptian patriotic songs, which was sung by Shādiyah during the 1960s and on through to the 1980s, when Shādiyah finally retired. The song is so popular that it was sung regularly by protestors in Tahrir Square during the 2011 Egyptian Revolution.

(5) *ḥabibt-i: ya: maṣr* ("Egypt, my love") by Shādiyah (1967)

ya: ḥabibt-i: ya: maṣr ya: maṣr
ma: ʃa:f-ʃ ir-riga:l is-sumr iʃ-ʃuda:d
fo:ʔ kulli l-meḥan
w-la: ʃa:f il-ʕina:d fi: ʕuyu:ni l-wila:d
w-tiḥaddi: iz-zaman
w-la: ʃa:f ʔiṣra:r fi: ʕuyu:n al-baʃar

bi-yiʔu:l ʔaḥra:r w-la:zim nintiṣir
ʔaṣl-u ma-ʕadda:-ʃ ʕala: maṣr

He who hasn't seen those dark-skinned men
Who rise above any tribulation;
And he who hasn't seen stubbornness in the eyes of children,
Nor the challenge of time,
And he who hasn't seen a resoluteness in the eyes of men,
That says: "We're free and we must be victorious!";
Such a one has never been to Egypt.[10]

The singer, Shādiyah, positions herself as the knowledgeable lover of Egypt. The song starts with the singer describing how beautiful and lovely Egypt is (this is the chorus). Then the singer starts with negation to denote both definiteness to her message and factuality. She addresses an outsider who does not know Egypt or Egyptians. Since this someone never came to Egypt, she or he never witnesses dark strong men or the stamina of the Egyptians. This technique of conjuring up an ignorant outsider is common. According to Shādiyah, Egyptians are so unique that character traits such as stamina will not be found, except among Egyptians themselves. This evaluation of Egyptians is done through the usage of a number of linguistic resources. Presupposition as a discourse resource is salient in this song, since the singer, as the all-knowing Egyptian, presupposes that Egyptians are dark-skinned and resilient. Not only does she presuppose this, but she also presupposes that it is only Egyptians who possess these traits. The structure of the song is as unique as Egyptians. The song is formed of a cluster of negative statements, followed by an explanation of the reason why these statements are negated.

ma: ʃa:f-ʃ ir-riga:l is-sumr iʃ-ʃuda:d
fo:ʔ kulli l-meḥan
[. . .]
ʔaṣl-u ma-ʕadda:-ʃ ʕala: maṣr

He who hasn't seen those dark-skinned men
Who rise above any tribulation
[. . .]
Such a one has never been to Egypt

The verb is in the third person and is negated by the ECA markers *ma- ʃ*. The verb is then repeated twice and negated before we know the reason why this third person masculine singular did not witness or see these things; it is because he has never been to Egypt.

This kind of factuality, hyperbolic statements, and confident stance are frequent in patriotic songs. Ethnicity is mentioned in relation to skin color. Character traits, such as toughness and stamina, are also mentioned. Location is mentioned as part-and-parcel of the character traits and ethnicity of Egyptians. The outsider did not see the dark-skinned men, nor did he see the Nile and the trees. An Egyptian community of practice is depicted with a special ethnicity, locality, and character traits.

(6) *maṣr hiyya ʔumm-i:* ("Egypt is my mother") by ʿAfāf Rāḍī (1976)
maṣri hiyya ʔumm-i: nil-ha: huwwa damm-i:
ʃamsa-ha: fi sama:r-i: ʃakla-ha: f mala:mḥ-i:
wi-ḥatta lo:n-i: ʔamḥi: lo:n xe:rik ya maṣr

Egypt is my mother: Her Nile is my blood;
Her sun gives me my tan, and you can see her in my features.
Even my wheat color is the color of your goodness, Egypt[11]

This song, which is mentioned in the section about historicity, also references skin color as a marker of identity. The relation between Egypt and the Egyptian is apparent in this song. There is interaction between locality and ethnicity and, later in the song, between history and characteristics (see Example 6 above).

The use of a verbless cluster of sentences adds to the factuality and definiteness of the propositions: "Egypt is my mother, in my features." Egyptian features are mentioned three times. The Egyptian is "tanned" and dark, and it is implied that it is a blessing to be dark. Fought (2006: 6) argues that phenotype or the grouping of physical features relevant in the "ascription of race" is pivotal in some communities' categorization. Race can also be defined as different types of human bodies with cultural and social significance (Fought 2006: 224).

Again, the singer ʿAfāf Rāḍī positions herself as a true Egyptian, who addresses Egypt occasionally, as in "*wi-ḥatta lo:n-i: ʔamḥi: lo:n xe:rik ya maṣr*," where the second person suffix *ik* ("your") is used to emphasize that goodness and blessings are attributes of Egypt.

For the sake of clarity, I will repeat another example that was analyzed in the first section.

(7) *il-maṣriyyi:n ʔahumma* ("Here are the Egyptians") by Yasmīn al-Khayyām (1980)
il-maṣri fi ʔayyi tari:x mila:di: aw higri:
wi fi ayyi zama:n wi maka:n huwwa huwwa l-maṣri: (2)
l-asmar abu ḍiḥka truddi l ru:ḥ
taʕrafu: min be:n milyo:n insa:n

The Egyptian of any era—be it the Christian or the Muslim one—
of any time, or place, he is the very same Egyptian.

The dark-skinned one, with a hearty laugh:
You can recognize him among a million people.

Again, in this example, ethnicity is tied to history and character traits.

Note that songs sung by non-Egyptians about Egyptians comprise more than one-third of patriotic songs. In the following example, the popular Lebanese singer Nānsī ʿAjram adopts the stance of the admirer of Egyptians. This is a frequent stance that aims to convince the audience of the truth regarding claims about Egyptians. The assumption here is that if the claims are made by knowledgeable non-Egyptians, they are supposedly more objective.

(8) *ana: maṣri:* ("I am Egyptian") by Nānsī ʿAjram (2006)
ana masri:
law saʔalt-ak ʔinta maṣri: tiʔul-li: ʔe:h
tuʔul-li: maṣri: ibni maṣri: w-ibn maṣr Alla:h ʕale:h
ʔul-ha: bi-ʔaʕla: so:ṭ wi-rfaʕ ra:s-ak li-fo:ʔ
ʔana maṣri: w-ʔabu-ya: maṣri:
bi-sama:r-i w-lo:n-i: maṣri:
w-bi-xiffit damm-i: maṣri:
w-kulli maṣri: Alla:h ʕale:h

If I asked you if you're Egyptian, what would you say?
You'd tell me: "I'm Egyptian, born of an Egyptian, and how wonderful is an Egyptian!"
Say it as loud as you can, and raise your head up high
I'm Egyptian, and my father is Egyptian,
In the tan of my skin I'm Egyptian
And in my humor/light-heartedness I'm Egyptian
And how wonderful is every Egyptian.

While Egyptian singers can sing in ECA or SA, non-Egyptian singers have more choices. They can also sing in their different colloquials. Code-choice is significant in both the song above and other songs. Nānsī ʿAjram chooses to sing in ECA, while other non-Egyptians, in particular Dīnā Ḥāyik (in *maṣr ʔumm al-dunya:*, "Egypt, mother of the world") (2010), sing about Egypt in Lebanese Egyptian Arabic. Mājdah al-Rūmī sang the poem of the Lebanese poet Jurj Qardāḥī, "The dark-skinned" (implying Egyptian) woman in SA (*samra:ʔ*) (1996). For the most part, the songs about Egyptians by non-Egyptians are in ECA.

Nānsī ʿAjram opens her song with a question to an Egyptian and recalls the song by al-Tūnisī and Darwīsh, "I am the Egyptian, of noble origin." Remember that "I am the Egyptian" was supposedly a situation where an Egyptian man addresses a non-Egyptian woman. The echo of this song may be lost to some, but the main props of Egyptian identity discussed in the previous section are called upon. Nānsī ʿAjram then uses the imperative to ask the Egyptian to define himself as an Egyptian of an Egyptian lineage (ethnicity) and encourages him to be proud of it. She, in fact, *orders* him to be proud of his Egyptian heritage. Not only does the singer position herself as confident and all-knowing, but by using the imperative she also emphasizes the position that should be adopted by the Egyptian: that of being proud. Her evaluative statement at the end of this part is also generic: "w-kulli maṣri: Alla:h ʕale:h." The use of the quantifier *kull* ("all") followed by an indefinite singular noun refers to each and every Egyptian and, again, adds definiteness to the uniqueness of Egyptians.

Mājdah al-Rūmī, the famous Lebanese singer, sings her song *samra:?*, originally a poem, in SA. In fact, she positions herself as the poet—a Lebanese man infatuated by a dark Egyptian woman. Again, there is a direct reference to color in the song.

(9) From *samra:?* ("Dark-skinned woman") by Mājdah al-Rūmī (1996)
samra:? ka-layl is-sahra:ni
wa-ka-ṭallati bint is-sulṭa:ni

Dark-skinned like the wake of night,
like the gaze of the Sultan's daughter.

Fought (2006: 6) argues that "most works on race and ethnicity acknowledge the important roles of both self-identification and perceptions and attitudes of others in the construction of ethnic identity." This is true in the Egyptian case as well. Not only do we have Egyptian singers who sing about Egyptian identity, but we also have non-Egyptians who do so, including singers from Algeria, Tunisia, Saudi Arabia, Syria, and Lebanon. It is interesting that ethnicity and especially color are mentioned positively, mostly by Lebanese singers, as well as Algerian ones; it is possible that peoples from both countries are perceived by Egyptians as having a lighter skin color.

4.2.3 Locality

In the last two sections, locality has been referred to as one of the main components of this broad community called "the Egyptians," who mainly share a demarcated space (Egypt). The importance of locality in relation to both identity and language has been highlighted in Milroy's work on Belfast (1987) and in other sociolinguistic studies, including

Eckert (2005). As Casey posits: "places not only are, they happen" (1996: 27). As is clear in Example 7, a place "happens" because it influences our perception of who we are, what history we share, and which linguistic choices we take. Basso (1996: 57) contends that "places and their meaning are continuously woven into the fabric of social life."

The Nile and the pyramids are two demarcating sites in the construction of Egyptian identity that do not just exist, but have meaning and indexes. Other local historical places, such as al-Azhar Mosque (in the discussion of the history textbook), are also mentioned. This is indeed apparent in patriotic songs. As with ethnicity and historical references, locality is tied to other independent variables and may also contribute to the perception of the large community sharing specific characteristics. Place names are also necessary for conjuring ideologies, habits, and perceptions.

As Basso (1996: 76) argues,

> because of their inseparable connection to specific localities, place names may be used to summon forth an enormous range of mental and emotional associations – associations of time and space, of history and events, of persons and social activities, of oneself and stages in one's life.

To put it differently, places and their names carry indexes.

It is only to be expected, therefore, that there are frequent references to the Nile and the pyramids as well as other places in patriotic songs, as the following chart illustrates.

The River Nile is referenced in the following examples from songs mentioned above.

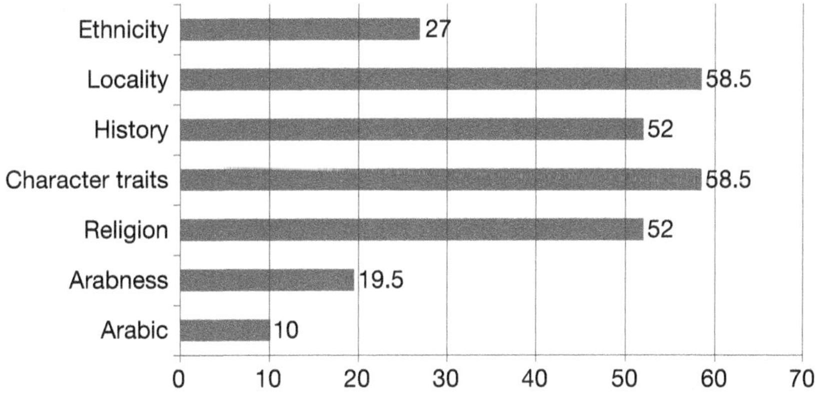

Figure 4.1 Attributes of identity (per cent)

(10) From *ḥabibt-i: ya: maṣr* ("Egypt, my love") by Shādiyah (1967)
wa-la: ʃa:f in-ni:l f-ʔaḥḍa:n iʃ-ʃagar
wa-la: simaʕ mawa:wi:l fi: laya:li: l-ʔamar [. . .]
ʔaṣl-u ma-ʕadda:-ʃ ʕala: maṣr.

And who hasn't seen the Nile enveloped by trees
And hasn't heard ballads in moonlit nights . . .
Such a one has never been to Egypt.

This song was analyzed in the sections about historicity and ethnicity, in which presupposition is used to emphasize the distinctive nature of Egyptians. The addressee, who has never been to Egypt, has not seen the Nile enveloped by the trees. As was mentioned earlier, locality in this song as manifested in the River Nile is related to ethnicity and character traits, such *as stamina* (see the analysis above).

(11) From *maṣr hiyya ʔumm-i:* ("Egypt is my mother") by ʿAfāf Rāḍī (1976)
maṣri hiyya ʔom-i: nil-ha: howwa damm-i:

Egypt is my mother. Her Nile is my blood.

Again, in this song, which was analyzed before, the singer defines Egypt in two verbless statements, positing Egypt as the mother and the River Nile as the blood that runs through all Egyptians. In the next lines, ethnicity is also conjured.

The 1983 song "What does 'homeland' mean?" provides a more sophisticated picture of the intricate relation between identity, locality, habits, and religion. The song ends a film that tells the story of a group of Egyptians who decide to immigrate to the USA. The Egyptians, after a tough experience in Romania on their way to the USA, decide to seek the help of the Egyptian embassy and return home. Egypt is never portrayed in a purely positive light and the characters all supposedly seek a better future in the land of dreams (USA). The singer, who portrays the main character, is a poor, semi-educated, mundane Muslim Egyptian worker with some positive traits (honor and chivalry) and some negative ones (that is, he searches for women to satisfy him and shows a great amount of jealousy towards the educated doctor in his group). The moment that they reach Egypt, the worker sings the song that is of interest to us. The song reveals his search for identity after his ordeal, and although his future in Egypt is still uncertain and perhaps even worse than when he left, his gradual discovery of his identity is made clear in the structure of the song, which starts with a question and ends with the thrice-repeated proposition: "This is what a homeland is."

The main character, who is clearly from a working-class background with little education (if any), appeals to specific events and places that are not just specific to Egyptians, but also to lower-class Cairenes. The song reads as follows:

(12) *yaʕni: ʔe:h kilmit 'waṭan'* ("What does 'homeland' mean?") by Muḥammad Fu'ād (1983)

yaʕni: ʔe:h kilmit waṭan?
ʃa:y bi-l-ḥali:b ʕala: ʔahwa fi: ḍ-ḍa:hir hina:k.
nismit ʕaṣa:ri: is-sayyida w-de:r il-mala:k
yaʕni: ʔe:h kilmit waṭan?
naʃʕit roṭu:ba fi: l-gida:r
walla: ʃamsi mġarraʔa bard in-niha:r
walla: ʔummak walla: ʔuxtak walla: ʕasa:kir dufʕitak
wa-r-ramla na:r . . .

What does "homeland" mean?
It is tea with milk in a café in al-Ḍāhir district.
It is an evening breeze in [the neighbourhood of] Sayyidah [Zaynab mosque] or of the Monastery of the Angel.
What does "homeland" mean?
It is humidity condensing on the wall, or drenching sun lighting up the cold of day;
Or your mother, or your sister, or the soldiers of your draft year for army service,
Or the scorching sand . . .

The song starts with the singer contemplating the question of what a homeland means, and, again, there are no verbs in the first few lines of the song. His answer is depicted as a truism, clear to any other Egyptian. A homeland, to the singer, is the habit of "drinking tea with milk in a coffee house" in the al-Ḍāhir area—an over-populated, poverty-stricken area in Cairo. Drinking tea is a process specific to him, but it is also common amongst all Egyptians, as is sitting in coffee houses. The singer depends on the idea that even if people do not do these activities, they are at least familiar with them. The singer targets an audience who needs to know, but who is also familiar enough to be able to appreciate the importance for such a ritual. The word *ḥali:b* (rather than *laban* ("milk")) is associated with local Cairene lower-class dialects; by using this colloquial term, the singer shows that language and locality are intertwined.

Here it is not just the Nile or the pyramids that demarcate locality, but the breath of air in the afternoon in a specific quarter of Cairo. By moving from the particular details to more general ones he ensures that the audience will identify with him. Through his song, he creates visual images of the places and hopes that perhaps the audience came from there or passed by these areas on their way to work or for a night out with friends or even in their travels through Cairo. The highly specific concrete locales add authenticity to the context. As Pagliai (2003: 50) argues, references to places by name implicate recognition and shared memories.

The singer positions himself in a similar fashion to Ghonim in the first quote in this chapter; he is a fellow Egyptian who experiences Egypt or Cairo par excellence, with its local cafes, mosques, and churches. The pronouns used indicate this stance that is adopted by the singer. There is also reference to "your mother, your sister." "You," as a fellow Egyptian, may share his contemplations and questions about his identity. Locality is depicted in relation to community habits and relations between members.

The use of structural resources such as deixis is also significant: *hina:k* ("there") depicts Daher as a near place. The proximity of the place will also reflect the proximity of the identity. Complete identification will occur between the Egyptian and the singer as an Egyptian, for they are literally close. As will be discussed in more detail in the section on religion, the chosen place names refer to places of worship for both Christians and Muslims. Both areas (*is-sayyida* and *de:r il-mala:k*) are over-populated lower-class areas in Cairo, concrete areas; the first is associated with Islam, because it refers to the presence of a mosque, while the second is associated with Christianity, because it refers to a monastery. However, in both, Christians and Muslims live side by side. Even if the listener is from a higher class, the identification is still there. They both may suffer in this shared community, but overall the community is coherent and strong.

In the last song analyzed in this section, the singer is the young female Egyptian Shīrīn. The singer positions herself as the knowledgeable Egyptian, and in an informal conversational style, she addresses a singular generic male who may be Egyptian, but who does not appreciate Egypt or Egyptian identity. The audience, addressed again with singular second person pronouns, has the potential to be an insider, but at this moment remains an outsider. The singer evaluates Egypt for this Egyptian outsider.

(13) *ma-ʃribt-iʃ min ni:l-ha:* ("Didn't you drink from her Nile?") by Shīrīn (2008)

ma-ʃribt-iʃ min nil-ha: ṭabb garrabti tiġanni-l-ha:
garrabti fi: ʕizzi ma tiḥzan timʃi: fi: ʃawariʔ-ha: w-tiʃkil-ha:
ma-mʃit-ʃi fi-ḍawa:ḥi:-ha: ṭayyib ma-kbirti-ʃ fi:-ha:
wa-la: lak ṣu:ra ʕa-r-ramla ka:nit ʕa-ʃ-ʃaṭṭi bi-mawa:ni:-ha:
dawwar guwwa:k tilʔa-ha: hiyya iṣ-ṣuḥba wi-hiyya l-ʔahl

ʕiʃrit balad-i: bi-tibʔa: nisyan-ha: ʕal-ba:l muʃ sahl
yimkin na:si: li-ʕinn-ak fi:-ha:
muʃ waḥṣa:-k wa-la ġibti ʕali:-ha:
bas illi mgarrab w-fariʔ-ha: ʔa:l fi d-dunya: ma fi:ʃ baʕdi:-ha:

Haven't you drunk from her Nile? Well, have you tried singing to her?
Have you tried, in your deepest sadness, to walk in her streets, singing and complaining to her?[12]
Haven't you walked through her neighborhoods? Okay haven't you grown up in her?
And don't you have a picture of yourself on the beach in one of her ports?
Search within yourself: she is your friend, and she is your family.
The family bonds in my country are not easy to forget.
Perhaps you forgot because you are living in her:
You haven't missed her and you haven't left her.
But those who have tried to leave her say that there's nothing else like her in the world.

Negation is used here to ask questions that presuppose specific facts about Egyptians and Egypt. If you drink from the Nile, you must appreciate Egypt. If you walk around its streets and go to its beaches, then you must appreciate Egypt. This song in its depiction of place is more generic than in "What does 'homeland' mean," with the reference to the Nile, but then also to general ports, which could be Port Said, Alexandria, Suez, and so on. There is also reference to Egypt's suburbs, which could be rich or poor areas. This general reference aims to appeal to a wider audience. Local identification such as the Nile, streets, and ports conjures up different images for different Egyptians.

It is noteworthy that Egyptian textbooks, especially history and Arabic books, emphasize the importance of space as a defining factor in Egyptian identity. In an Arabic lesson for first and ninth graders, it is emphasized that Egyptians built their civilization by rallying around the River Nile. The lessons also posit that Egyptian characteristics such as generosity, religiousity without intolerance, and humor mixed with melancholy are all products of Egyptians occupying places around the River Nile and interacting together in a dense context (al-Muʿallim textbook for Arabic (2012), both for the first and ninth grade). As Secor argues in his study of Turkish textbooks, schools can be viewed "as prime sites of identity formation and boundary creation, become implicated in the everyday construction of citizenship" (Secor 2004: 360).

Locality in general is essential in the formation of identity and is usually connected to other variables, such as habits, history, and ethnicity. Local places index history, as in the case of the Nile, the pyramids, the al-Azhar Mosque, a monastery, or a church. They are also associated with family and friends, with religion, and even with the weather. The singers position themselves as knowledgeable individuals who speak to outsiders, yet they really target an insider who shares the same associations, presuppositions, and indexes.

ECA is primarily used in the songs discussed above. Resources used include presupposition, verbless sentences, pronouns, mention of place names, questions, negation, quantification, and deixis. Some of these resources are used to render an informal conversational style to the songs and make the arguments more convincing. Some resources, such as presupposition, are used to emphasize the truthfulness of propositions and arguments. Other resources, such as place names, are there to demarcate identity, as well as to physically demarcate where this identity is located. Blommaert (2005: 221) highlights "the importance of space and spatial references as organizing motifs in narratives, emphasizing how space provides a framework in which meaningful social relationships and events can be anchored and against which a sense of identity can be developed." Locality is a major point of reference that triggers a community. In fact, Johnstone (2004: 69) argues that "[r]egions have come to be seen as meaningful places, which individuals construct, as well as select, as reference points. Identification with a region is identification with one kind of 'imagined community'." Since spaces are meaningful to individuals and serve as points of reference, living in a specific place and sharing the same historical background and perceptions of ethnicity also leads to communal solidarity. This solidarity is built on the assumption that people who share a space, history, and ethnicity also share habits, character traits, and language. That is the reason why character traits, habits, and communal solidarity are referred to as the outcome of sharing a location, history, and ethnicity. Because all of these social variables are related, it is necessary to organize them in a hierarchical fashion, in order to understand how they are employed in public discourse. Members and non-members of this space are then identified and granted various kinds of attributive qualities—for example, character, style, preferences for food, and even specific modes of behaviour.

This is why in our discussion historicity, ethnicity, and locality are discussed as the origins and backbone of Egyptian identity. Throughout this discussion, character traits such as generosity have also been referred to. These traits will be discussed below.

4.3 The outcome: habits and characteristics

Egyptians are portrayed in patriotic songs as kind, humorous, chivalrous, generous, resilient, and hardworking. As members of one community, they also eat the same food and share the same customs. As was shown when discussing ethnicity, locality, and historicity, the character traits of Egyptians are in most cases yoked to one or more of the backbone variables. As with all variables, habits and characteristics are connected to prevalent discourses. When Cromer gave his stance on Egyptian characteristics, the Egyptians' reply came in the form of poems and songs. When Egypt was defeated by Israel in 1967, Egyptians again demonstrated their resilience through the song "Egypt, my love" (analyzed above). When the former President Mubarak declared in an interview with the American news channel ABC (February 3, 2011)[13] that President Obama does not understand the nature of Egyptians and that if he, Mubarak, were to leave there would be chaos, Egyptians' dug out their resources and their response came in the form of a song by Shādiyah, "Egypt, my love." Additionally, Egyptians developed slogans, such as "if you have a Ph.D in stubborness, we have a Ph.D in patience." To a great extent, discussions of characteristics and habits are entrapped by a counter-discourse defense mechanism. However, ideologies shared by Egyptians are also a product of years of education, patriotic songs, and reiterated perceptions from both insiders and outsiders.

I will refer here to two songs mentioned before, "Egypt, my love" and "What does 'homeland' mean?" In "Egypt, my love," the stamina of Egyptians is mentioned. This is the very same song sung by protestors in Tahrir Square throughout the eighteen days of the 2011 Revolution. The hypothetical audience that does not know Egyptians was implied as Mubarak, since he, according to the protestors, did not realize how much resilience and resoluteness Egyptians have. The outsider was, in fact, another Egyptian who failed to understand his fellow Egyptians. This is, indeed, important, since the outsider does not necessarily have to be a foreigner or a foreign power. An Egyptian identity can be contested, and an Egyptian who does not show that she or he shares the same ideologies, perceptions, and habits could be considered an outsider.[14]

In "What does 'homeland' mean?" relational categories, such as one's relation to one's family, are also mentioned within the definition of what a homeland is. In fact, relational categories that index communal solidarity often occur in patriotic songs, in which Egyptians are portrayed as warm and family-loving individuals that form an organic community.

The song also references habits that Egyptians share and relationships with fellow Egyptians who form a community. Pronouns are used to refer to "you," "your" mother, "your" sister, and "your" army fellows,[15] in order to indicate a practice that they share. Even references to the hot weather of Egypt recall their communal Egyptian heritage and perceptions about Egypt's weather. It is indeed interesting that the singer mentions the mother first and then the sister. In more than one part of the Arab world, the female relatives carry the traditions and culture.

They are also the preservers of unity and solidarity, and in some cases they also preserve the language, as in the case of Morocco, where Berber is preserved by older, mostly illiterate females (see Bassiouney 2009). The singer positions himself as the fellow Egyptian who shares specific memories of places, people, weather, and patterns of behavior with all Egyptians. Even the melancholic mood of Egyptians is mentioned as a memory that one carries with him or herself. In other words, the singer is addressing one male Egyptian who symbolizes all Egyptians.

In the following song, communal solidarity is again called upon. Like before, the singers (four in this case: two men and two women) address one male Egyptian who epitomizes all Egyptians. The four singers are the all-knowing Egyptians, who adopt a positive stance towards Egypt and Egyptians and explain to an outsider what it means to be in Egypt.

(14) *yibʔa ʔinta ʔaki:d fi: maṣr* ("Surely, you are in Egypt") by Various Artists (2001)

Lamma tila:ʔi: fi: garḥ-ak ʔalf ʕe:n bakiya ʔale:-k
w-tila:ʔi: farḥ-ak zaġari:d w-zi:na ḥawa:li:k (2)
w-be:t-ak il-basi:ṭ yitḥawwil ʔaṣr, wi-lxe:r guwwa:-h ma:-lu:-ʃ ḥaṣr
yibʔa: ʔinta ʔaki:d ʔaki:d fi: maṣr

If in your misery you find that a thousand eyes are crying for you,
and in your joy you find that happiness and decorations are all around you;
if your simple house transforms into a palace, and the goodness inside of it has no limits,
Then surely, surely you are in Egypt.

The structure of this song is significant. It is entirely in the form of conditional sentences. For example:

lamma tila:ʔi: fi: garḥ-ak ʔalf ʕe:n bakiya ʔale:-k
[. . .]
yibʔa: ʔinta ʔaki:d ʔaki:d fi: maṣr

When you find in your misery a thousand eyes crying for you
[. . .]
Then surely you are in Egypt.

The conditional sentences are made up of two structurally independent clauses that contain propositions, and the validity of one depends on the validity of the other (Holes 2004). This structure is adopted throughout the song, in which more than one proposition is, in fact, dependent on "you" being in Egypt. This proposition asserts the uniqueness of Egyptians and their character traits. The use and repetition of modality to express certainty in *ʔaki:d ʔaki:d* ("for sure") adds emphasis to the proposition. The usage of conditional sentences and modality in this song as structural resources asserts the proposition that communal solidarity is the natural behavior of Egyptians.

The next example is worth noting, since Egypt is again defined in a number of verbless sentences. This time, this is done not just for a few sentences, but for almost the entire song. Verbs are a subordinate part of the clause, but the main clause has an implicit verb "to be." The female singer positions herself as the all-knowing Egyptian who offers the proposition that there is something beautiful about Egypt. Her positive stance towards Egypt and Egyptians is apparent in her evaluation of what these beautiful things are. Note that the first quote of this chapter by Ghonim reiterates the same meaning. It is worth mentioning that when violence erupted after 2011, the proposition of Egyptians being warm and good has been occasionally challenged by Egyptians themselves, both in public discourse, as well as privately. This is a popular song that is at times challenged by Egyptians and at other times adopted and believed.

(15) *fi:-ha: ḥa:ga ḥilwa* ("There's something beautiful about her") by Rihām ʿAbd al-Ḥakīm (2010)

Maṣr hiyya ṣ-ṣubḥi badri: maṣri ṣo:t il-fagri yiddan
sobiya fu:l ṭaʕmiya koʃari do:m baṭa:ṭa suxna giddan
maṣri ʔawwil yo:m il-ʕi:d ʕiddiyya bomb w-libs gidi:d
fanni si:ma: w-ġuna w-tiya:tru:
ḥaflit tala:ta f-sinima: metro:
mawa:ʔid ar-raḥma:n wi-fawani:s ramaḍa:n
muslim fi: be:t misi:ḥi fiṭru:
tarni:ma la:yiʔa ʕala: daffi ġana:
fi:-ha: niyya ṣafiya fi:-ha: ḥa:ga dafiya

Egypt is the early morning. Egypt is the sound of the call to dawn prayer.
It is sobia, beans, falafel, koshari, doum, and a really hot sweet potato.
Egypt is the first day of the holiday, your holiday gift, candies and new clothes.
It is the fine arts of cinema, singing and the theater,
a three o'clock show in the Metro Cinema.
It is the food prepared for the poor and the lanterns in Ramadan,
A Muslim breaking his fast in a Christian home,
and a Christian hymn ready to be sung and played.
There is something pure, something warm about her.

In this example, which does not contain any verbs, Egypt is defined in terms of food, habits, festivals and holidays, and also religious tolerance. The communal solidarity is emphasized in the relationship between the Christians and Muslims who share each others' festivals. The list of food items includes falafels, beans, sobia, doum, and sweet potatoes, all of which are quintessentially Egyptian specialities.

The existential adverb that has been used, *fi*, is again a typical ECA construction that is repeated to indicate that Egypt and Egyptians possess warmth and good intentions.

It is noteworthy, however, that when praise for Egyptians comes from outsiders who are also insiders (that is, who have the knowledge and expertise of insiders, such as singers from other Arab countries, especially if this praise comes in ECA), then it, indeed, has more appeal and credibility. Code-choice is also relevant here: when a singer from another Arab country sings in ECA, she or he is accommodating Egyptians (for a discussion of accommodation theory, see Beebe and Giles (1984) and subsequent work by Giles), in order to express admiration and solidarity. However, when Nānsī ʿAjram, the famous young Lebanese singer, sang the song *ana: maṣri:* ("I am Egyptian") (2008) for Egypt in ECA, she was criticized in Lebanon by some of the Lebanese media for not singing in her own dialect, as well as for not singing to Lebanon first before Egypt. This linguistic tension crops up from time to time. In "I am Egyptian," Agram expresses her positive stance towards Egyptians. She admits that since she drank from the Nile, she decided to sing to Egypt, appealing to the Egyptian belief that if you drink from the Nile, you surely come back to Egypt. She is an outsider who chooses to become an insider, because of her admiration for Egyptians. She demonstrates her insider's knowledge of Egyptians by mentioning categories such as dark skin, humor, drinking from the Nile, and so on.

The following song by the famous Emirati singer Ḥusayn al-Jāsimī has a similar message.

(16) *ʔagdaʕ na:s* ("The best people") by Ḥusayn al-Jāsimī (2010)
ʔisʔalu kull in-na:s mi:n humma ʔadgaʕ na:s
humma l-maṣriyyi:n
ya ʔarḍ aṭyab na:s
kullik dafa wi ʔiḥsa:s
ḥafaẓik rabb il-ʕa:lami:n

Ask everyone, who are the most chivalrous people
They are the Egyptians
You, the land of the kindest people
You are full of warmth and feelings.
May God protect you!

The quantifier *kull* and superlative construction *aṭyab na:s* in these lines again emphasizes the idea that Egyptians are the most chivalrous and kind people. Note the mention of the concept *gadaʕ* mentioned in Chapter 3 to describe Egyptians, which refers to chivalry, courage, and so on. Once more, the song is made up of a cluster of verbless sentences. Adjectives are lumped together to refer to Egypt and Egyptians.

It is noteworthy, however, that Egyptian character traits were not always presented by Egyptians themselves in a positive light. As was the case at the start of the twentieth century, Egyptians at the beginning of the twenty-first century have also been questioning and challenging their identity and sometimes admitting faults and paradoxes. This echo of the age of the formation of modern Egyptian identity detailed in Chapter 2 has yet to be studied in detail, even after a number of years. In a number of songs, Egyptians often find fault or issue with their fellow Egyptians, but nevertheless they are forced to accept them. Sometimes Egyptians' bad habits are also mentioned in public discourse, and the current condition of Egyptians is juxtaposed to that of their ancestors. In fact, referring to bad habits as well as good ones may add more vividness and authenticity to the depiction of Egyptians. As Pagliai (2003: 64) posits: "Then, would the absence of that sting make us happier, or just more bored and dull people." What is interesting, however, is that throughout the twentieth century and up until today, the backbone variables are never challenged by Egyptians. There is, for example, no claim that Egyptians are not descendants of their ancient ancestors, nor is there a claim in patriotic songs that Egyptians do not share one ethnicity. The relation to ancestors is complex. As authors and poets at the beginning of the twentieth century argued, modern Egyptians should be ashamed of themselves, because they cannot attain the same glory of their ancestors; however, this argument is based on the presupposition that the ancient Egyptians are their ancestors. What could be questioned and criticized are the habits and characteristics of the modern Egyptian, but not her or his past ethnic origin or local area.

Here follows a song that was popular before the 2011 Revolution in Egypt. This song was edited on YouTube with accompanying images and videos to show the abuse by police officers during protests prior to 2011. The song plays in the film *'Asal aswad* ("Black honey") (2010), which tells the story of an Egyptian–American who returns to Egypt in search of an identity, but instead faces cruelty, corruption, and the stagnation of the Egyptian people. In this song, the position of the singer is not a positive one. He refers to Egypt's state as bittersweet or "black honey/molasses." While Egyptians may still be warm, they can also be cruel. While they may be generous, they can also steal your money in more than one way, whether by asking for bribes, tricking you into paying more, or physically stealing it. Egyptians may be helpful, but they can also be unfair. Unlike the other songs discussed previously, there are no verbless sentences, no definiteness or assertions. The song ends with a question by the singer, which demonstrates the confused stance. Again, a conversational style is adopted, as the singer addresses a fellow Egyptian who may have the same frustrations.

(17) *ʕasal ʔiswid* ("Black honey") by Rihām ʿAbd al-Ḥakīm (2010)
bi-tisraʔ-ak wi-tsallif-ak
ẓalm-a:k wi-barḍu bi-tinṣif-ak
ʔizza:y fi: ḥudn-ik malmumi:n wi-ʔinti: ʕala: ḥa:l-ik kida

She robs you blind, but lends you what you need.
She oppresses you, but defends you, too
How can we all be gathered in your embrace when you carry on this way?

The difference between the stance of this singer and the others discussed previously are clear. Unlike the other singers, there is no definiteness or clear answers. The singer uses the ECA aspectual marker *bi* to express continuity in the following verbs:

bi-tisraʔ (she steals from you)
bi-tinṣif (she defends you)

This ongoing paradoxical process adds doubt and confusion to the stance of the singer, but as other singers have, she addresses a single male who represents all Egyptians. She then addresses Egypt as a female who embraces them, yet continues to be unfair. The final rhetorical question emphasizes the doubt expressed by the singer.

A similar, earlier song released in 1987, *nifsi:* ("I wish"), is sung by the male singer Īmān al-Baḥr Darwīsh, who also refers to Egypt as a mother holding a child. However, the child constantly fears and mistrusts this mother, rather than loves and trusts her.

The following chart shows the most dominant character traits that reoccur in patriotic songs.

In the previous sections, historicity, locality, ethnicity, Egyptian habits, characteristics, and communal solidarity have all been discussed. In the next section, religion is discussed in detail. The complex nature of religion as a social variable and marker of identity and the linguistic resources manipulated by public discourse in discussions of religion merit a thorough discussion.

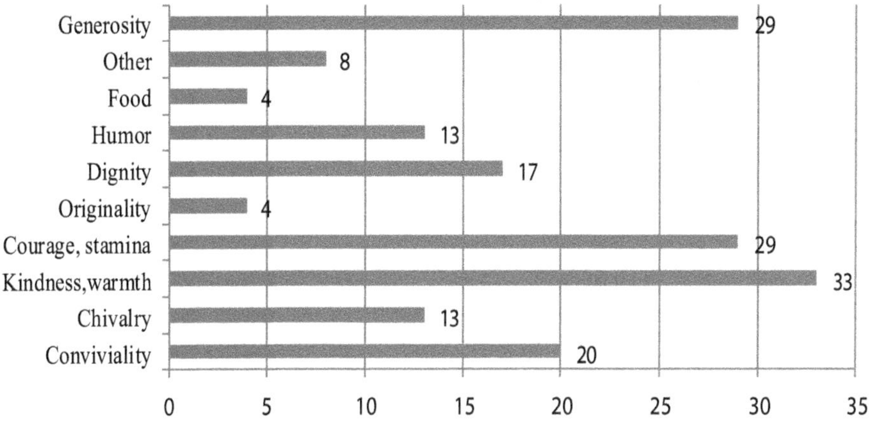

Figure 4.2 Subcategories: character traits

4.4 Religion: dilemmas of foregrounding and backgrounding in public discourse

Religion plays a vital role in defining an identity in the Arab world in general and in Egypt in particular. Two of Egypt's Arab neighbors—Lebanon and Iraq—have suffered from violent religious struggles. These religious struggles are not even necessarily the product of two religions existing side by side, but involve two sects of the same religion (Sunnis, Shiites, and so on). Egypt has, for some time, been on the alert out of fear of a similar destiny—strife based on religious distinctions between Muslims and Christians. Language, as part of the social processes and practices, has played an essential role in portraying a unified Egyptian identity.

In Egypt, public discourse tackles the thorny issue of religious differences by using two strategies: foregrounding and backgrounding. That is, in public discourse, religious differences are undermined and religion as a general belief system is highlighted. Religion is foregrounded as an essential inclusive and holistic concept that brings all Egyptians together. Examples of this are found in patriotic songs, as will be discussed below. However, religious differences between Christians and Muslims in Egypt are backgrounded as trivial and not determinant in identity formation. This will be clear in the analysis of online articles and films, as well as patriotic songs. To promote these two concepts, public discourse employs linguistic resources and orders of indexicality. To elaborate, public discourse attempts to give the following messages to Egyptians:

1. Both groups, Muslims and Christians, share the same linguistic practices; they have equal access to linguistic resources. These practices are the

product of location, class, education, and other social variables that do not include religion. The image conveyed is: we speak the same language or code, therefore we belong to the same community, therefore we are the same people, regardless of our religious affiliations. By so doing, this discourse also undermines religious differences. The argument is that language variation, apart from religious context-dependent lexical morphemes, is not dependent on religion as an independent variable, since all Egyptians share the same community.[16]

2. Religion is important, since most Egyptians take religion seriously and are regular attendants at mosques and churches. However, the strife between both religious groups is non-existent, since they are of the same ethnic group, share the same history, and live in the same location. They worship the same God. Egypt is mentioned in both the Bible and the Qur'ān (historicity). The image conveyed is that both Christians and Muslims form one large holistic community, which is comprised of many small communities and, therefore, one Egyptian identity. Egyptians' religion is a main part of their identity, but is subordinate and dependent on the main three social backbone variables of historicity, ethnicity, and locality.

In order to discuss this in detail, reference to social networks, community of practice theory, and variationist approaches to language will be discussed. Stance-taking processes and linguistic resources manipulated in public discourse will also be discussed. In order to convey these two points, public discourse utilizes different structural and discursive linguistic resources, as will be clear below.

4.4.1 A different approach to data

The question of the ideological connotations of linguistic variation in the Arab world is long overdue. As Suleiman (2011) argues, while correlating linguistic variables with sociolinguistic ones, such as gender, class, and ethnicity, linguists analyzing the Arab world neglect issues related to the symbolic function of Arabic and the relation between Arabic, self, and the formation of identity in the socio-political world. These issues, according to Suleiman, are essential for a thorough understanding of language change and variation in the Arab world. Cameron (1997: 59–60) criticizes variationist research for a different reason; he argues that variationist research usually falls into the trap of "correlational fallacy," by which one independent variable is tied sometimes arbitrarily to a linguistic one in a causal link. As Benwell and Stokoe (2006: 27) explain, one can never be sure of the "implicit assumptions" of such variables: "A person may speak with a pronounced Scottish accent, but we cannot be confident that this is an expression of 'Scottish identity'."

In public discourse, the ideological component is prevalent. Occasionally, we have a case of someone admitting to speaking an Alexandrian dialect, in order to emphasize an Alexandrian identity that is also an Egyptian one, as in the example analyzed in detail below. What distinguishes public discourse data from variationist research data are the ideological and indexical elements. The causal link between language and identity is, in fact, underpinned sometimes; at times, linguists yoke linguistic variation with social variables with no consideration given to indexes.

The kind of data analyzed in this section is significant in a number of ways: media reflects to a great extent the way that we want to be perceived by others and how we perceive ourselves. This kind of data is, of course, not spontaneous; it is revised and edited. It reflects directly on ideologies and indexes shared by producers and audiences. Identity is directly influenced by these indexes, as was discussed in Chapter 1.

Public discourse and the media in general, especially Egyptian films, play on stereotypes. Linguistic variation, due to class and location, are common in the Egyptian media. There are soap operas that deal exclusively with southern districts in Egypt and use the dialects from these regions. In fact, a number of recent films juxtapose the way Egyptians and other Arabs speak, sometimes poking fun and exaggerating the speech of Gulf Arabs, as in the film *Sāḥib ṣaḥbuh* ("A friend's friend") (2002). Muḥammad Hunaydī's film *ʿAndalīb al-Duqqī* ("Nightingale from Duqqī") (2007) goes as far as imitating pidgin Arabic in Dubai as spoken by an Indian (who is, in fact, an Emirati actor). That is, linguistic variation is part-and-parcel of humor, characterization, and plot more generally. Having mentioned this, the fact that the Egyptian media emphasizes that religion is not a variable that influences linguistic variation is significant. It reflects language attitude and ideology, and it also suggests that both Christians and Muslims belong to the same group. Although this may be a reflection of reality to a great extent (as will be clear below), public discourse deliberately uses lack of variation to negate any differences between Christians and Muslims that are due to religion. It is important to emphasize again that there is no study to date that correlates linguistic variation in modern Egypt with religion.

In the next section, I will offer a fine-grained analysis of a written article posted online in the newspaper *Youm7* ("Seventh day") on January 4, 2011, directly after the bombing of the church in Alexandria on New Year's Eve 2011 and less than a month before the January 25 Revolution. The article is written by Ghādah ʿAbbūd (ʿAbbūd 2011), who writes from Alexandria and sheds light on the relationship between religion, language, and identity in Egypt on various levels. This article indexes language as directly related to identity and group membership.

I will then refer to another online article that also indexes language as related directly to identity. Following this, I will refer to the depiction of language variation (or rather the lack of linguistic variation) between Muslims and Christians in Egyptian films and how this directly reflects on language attitudes and ideologies in Egypt. It also, more importantly, reflects directly on the lack of associations between linguistic variation and religious differences.

4.4.2 First claim in public discourse: linguistic variation is not dependent on religion

Work on language variation in the Arab world usually correlates an independent variable, such as religion, social class, or ethnicity, to a sociolinguistic variable. A sociolinguistic variable, according to Milroy (1987: 10), is "a linguistic element (phonological usually, in practice) which co-varies not only with other linguistic elements, but also with a number of extra-linguistic independent variables such as social class, age, sex, ethnic group, or contextual style." This concept was, in fact, developed by Labov. Walters adds that "empirical studies of sociolinguistic variation in the Arab world have, like quantitative studies in the west, generally been studies of phonological variation" (1996: 184). The reason why their interest is mainly related to phonological variables is that phonological variables occur frequently. They are also less salient than lexical or morpho-syntactic variables in many ways and thus are less subject to consistent conscious manipulation. Sound change was the major concern of historical linguistics traditionally (cf. Walters 1988).

Religion as an independent variable does not seem to influence linguistic variation in Egypt, at least on a phonological level. Apart from religious lexical references and names, both Muslims and Christians share social networks and linguistic varieties. Of course, not all Egyptians speak the same variety, but independent variables, such as social class, locality, and even gender, are more salient and consistently influential than religion. In my opinion, this is because religious groups do not necessarily form communities of practice in Egypt.

This is primarily due to limitations of space–population density in Egypt, as Cairo, per square mile, is one of the highest in the world. The population density is 31,727 inhabitants per square kilometre for the city of Cairo. Egyptians, because of demographic and geographic settings, live in dense and multiplex networks. Networks can be described in relation to density and multiplexity. A dense network is one in which a large number of people are linked to each other through ties of kinship, occupation, specific voluntary group membership, and so on. For example, in certain areas, there are youth gangs that spend a lot of time together and belong to the same club and neighborhood (Milroy and Gordon 2003: 118–23). A network can also be multiplex, in that the same person, for example, is connected to another as a co-worker, neighbor, kin, and so on—that is, in several ways. Both density and multiplexity are efficient indicators of the pressure to adopt the norm of a community. They act as "norm enforcement mechanisms" (Milroy 1987: 50).[17] This is also evident in Egypt,[18] although the mechanism is also manipulated by public discourse, in order to downgrade religious differences as a driving force that shapes the public identity of Egyptians.

Bayat (2010: 199) argues that in Egyptian society, people of different faiths intermingle all the time. Bayat posits, regarding the lower-class area of Shubrá in Cairo:

> Followers of both faiths invariably stressed deep interfaith friendships, in particular among youths of the same sex. Beyond the schools where peer groups are formed, neighborhoods and apartment buildings are places where youngesters establish deep affinity. Male youngsters spend a great deal of time on the street corners, strolling, chatting, seeing movies, sitting in coffee shops, or playing soccer, sometimes very late at night. But young females, both Muslims and Christians, are likely to join together in the privacy of homes to build close associations.

Before I delve into the first point, I would like to shed light on studies of religion as an independent variable in the Arab world. This knowledge will better our understanding of the relationship between these categories in Egypt and will also explain why public discourse highlights linguistic norms that are common among Christians and Muslims.

It is common knowledge that Islam, Christianity, and, to a lesser extent, Judaism are the primary religions among the populations of the Arab world. At the same time, these religions are divided into different sects.

Like other social variables, religion does not stand in isolation, but is connected to other categories. In the Arab world specifically, religion is closely connected to the political system of each country. Religion is important in terms of language variation and change, only in the sense that it can create a close-knit community whose members feel, for one reason or another, that they are united by it.[19] Political factors are highly important in many communities in the Arab world and may be intertwined with religion in many cases.

Studies that have concentrated on religion in the Arab world as an independent variable that has direct linguistic implications include Holes' studies of Bahrain (1983a; 1983b; 1984; 1986), in which he highlights significant factors in language change and variation in this country.

These factors are related to the phonological variations between the Shiite Baharnas and the Sunni Arabs. Holes (1984) predicts a change in progress towards the Sunni dialect. In another study that concentrates on religion, Abu-Haidar (1991) examines the differences between what she calls "Muslim Arabic of Baghdad (MB)" and "Christian Arabic of Baghdad (CB)." Her study is different from a great number of studies on language variation, since it explores not only phonological variables, but also syntactic and semantic ones. Khan (1997) studies the Arabic dialect of the Karaite Jews in the Iraqi town of Ḥīt on the Euphrates, 150 km west of Baghdad. Khan, like Holes and Abu-Haidar, provides the historical background of the community that he studies, as well as its current status. But unlike Abu-Haider and Holes, Khan does not try to examine language change in progress, but rather to describe the dialect and record it. Abu Haidar is perhaps the only one who mentions linguistic differences within the Christian community of Bagdad, although she does not concentrate on the diglossic situation.

Other studies that concentrate on religion include studies on Bethlehem in Palestine by Spolsky et al. (2000), in which they indicate that Christian speakers, both women and men, tend to use more urban features, like the glottal stop, than do Muslim speakers, who tend to use SA /q/. Blanc's 1953 study of the Northern Palestinian Arabic dialect used by Druze remains a classic, unique study, mainly because there are very few if any studies that concentrate on linguistic variation in the speech of Druze (cf. Walters 2006a for other references).[20]

Miller (2004) explains religion as a variable by positing that in most Arab cities religious minorities used to live in certain areas and thus developed different linguistic models, as in Baghdad and Fes. Different religious communities kept their unique vernaculars for centuries and did not acquire the dialect of the Muslim community. This was due to a degree of segregation, but also to the fact that the Muslim urban Arabic dialects were not associated with power, because political power was in the hands of foreign rulers up until the beginning of the twentieth century. Only recently has there been any political change. An additional cause is the demographic changes that have taken place in different parts of the Arab world.

Egypt has the largest Christian minority in the Arab world (mainly Copts, but some Anglicans and Catholics, Russian and Greek Orthodox), estimated between six to ten million, which is equal or more than the population of countries such as Jordan, Israel, or Tunisia. While Egypt is a highly centralized, over-populated country, this also means that, in most cases, Christians and Muslims live in the same buildings and have contact with each other in dense and multiplex ways, perhaps more than in other Arab countries that have different religious sects.

However, this does not mean that religious tension does not erupt from time to time, due to different factors.[21] What is, indeed, important is that this dense and multiplex social network has led language variation in Egypt, especially phonological and syntactic variation, to be based on locality, class, gender, and factors other than religion. That is to say, in the southern part of Egypt, both Christians and Muslims will speak the same distinct southern dialect; in Cairo, both groups will speak Cairene; and in other parts of Cairo, both groups of different social classes will again share the same linguistic features. In Alexandria, both Copts and Muslims use different vowel qualities from their Cairene co-religionists. Religion is not as essential a variable in influencing language variation or change as it is in Bahrain, Iraq, or Lebanon. While there are no studies that back this claim, the mere lack of studies that concentrate on religion as an independent variable in Egypt—a variable that affects language change and variation—provides the necessary backing, since there may be nothing salient to study. In addition, Haeri's (1996) classic work on gender and social class in Cairo does not refer to religion as an essential variable in linguistic variation.[22] However, this chapter does not attempt to answer the question of whether or not there is linguistic variation based on religion in Egypt, but rather the question of how does public discourse tackle language and religion as markers of identity in Egypt.

I argue that public discourse deliberately uses the lack of linguistic variation based on religion in Egypt to index the shared identity of all Egyptians. It is no coincidence that language is referenced in films and articles when discussing religion in Egypt.

4.4.2.1 Article analysis

The article analyzed below is highly significant. While it may perhaps be possible to perform dialects and talk about them, in Arabic and in the Arab world it is difficult and uncommon to write in a local dialect. This is because of the absence of standard orthography and the defective writing system of Arabic. In this article, the journalist not only shows morphological, syntactic, and lexical variation, but also phonological variation by using Arabic vowel marks.

I argue that when the journalist uses the Alexandrian dialect in a written text, she is consciously imitating a "social type" (Silverstein 2003: 220). She also references a shared ideological model with her audience. I also argue that the journalist does not just index that she is from Alexandria, but also indexes that the fact that she is from Alexandria presupposes that she shares an identity with Christians and that locality as manifested in linguistic performance is more salient as a social variable than religion. The importance of this article lies in the way that it opens new trajectories for research on the use of local dialects in written media.

(18) *Anā iskandirānīyah ḍidd al-irhāb* ("I am Alexandrian and against Terrorism") by Ghādah ʿAbbūd (2011)[23]
آه أنا إسكندرانية، ركبت الترام من بكلة لمحطة الرمل وأتمشى هناك للصبح، أنا اللى لما ينزل فيلم جديد بقطع تذكرة فى سينما مترو، أنا اللى بوقف على القمة عشان أوقف تاكس وقبل ماركب أقوله "الابراهيمية ياسطة؟ بس أكتر من 5 جينى ما تلاقيش، "أنا اللى كل ما أقابل واحدة جميلة وسابغة شعرها كله أشقر أسألها، "هو انتى من بحري؟" ترد عليا "عرفتى منين؟" أجاوبها، "من لون شعرك!" أنا اللى فى الصيف بتمشى فى المعمورة وأتصور جنب الجسر فى المنتزة، أنا اللى بقول لَبست، شَربت، زَهقت، وبنطق "كوسة"، "كووسة،" ولما القاهراوية يستغربوا كلامى، أقول بفخر "أصل أنا ملاكى اسكندرية".
أنا اللى باكل الفول من "محمد أحمد"، وأنا اللى بزاحم الناس عشان أشترى "جيلاتى عزة"

ʔa:h ʔana ʔiskandaraniyya/ rakabt al-tra:m min bukla li-maḥaṭṭit al-raml wa atmaʃʃa: hina:k l-al-ṣubḥ/ ʔana illi: lamma yinzil film gidi:d baʔṭaʕ tazkara fi sinima metru, ʔana illi baʔuf ʕala l-ʔimma ʕaʃa:n ʔawʔaf ta:ks/ wa ʔabla ma-arkab ʔaʔu:l-u l-ibrahimiyya ya sṭa/ bas ʔaktar min xamsa gini: ma talaʔi:-ʃ/ ʔana illi: kul ma ʔaʔa:bil waḥda gami:la wa sa:bġa ʃaʕr-ha kull-u ʔaʃʔar ʔasʔal-ha/ huwa ʔinti min baḥri:/ tiruddi ʕalay-ya:/ ʕarafti: mine:n/ ʕaga:wib-ha:/min lo:n ʃaʕrik/ ʔana illi fi l-ṣe:f bitimʃi fi l-maʕmu:ra wi ʔatṣṣawwar ganb il-gisr fil montaza/ ʔana illi: baʔu:l labast/ ʃarabt/ zahaʔt/ wi b-nṭaʔ ko:sa/ ku:sa/ wi lamma l-qahrawiyya yistaġrabu kla:mi:/ ʔaʔu:l bi-faxr/ ʔaṣil ʔana mla:ki: ʔiskindiriyya/
ʔana illi: ba:kul l-fu:l min maḥammad aḥmad/ wi ʔana illi: biza:ḥim al-na:s ʕaʃa:n ʔaʃtiri: jila:ti ʕazza/

Yes. I'm Alexandrian—I ride the tram from Bolkly to Raml Station and I stroll around there in the morning. I'm the one who, when a new movie comes out, I get a ticket for Metro Cinema. I'm the one who stands in the intersection to flag down a taxi and before I get in I say to the driver, *Ibrahimia, driver. . . but you won't get more than five pounds!* I'm the one who, every time I see a pretty girl with her hair dyed all blond, I ask her, *so you're from Bahari?* She responds to me, *How did you know?* I answer her, *From the color of your hair!* I'm the one who walks around in Mamoura in the summer taking pictures of the side of the bridge in Montazah. I'm the one who uses my Alexandrian accent to say *I wore, I drank, I got exhausted*, and *zucchini*, rather than the Cairene way of saying it. When the Cairenes think how I talk is weird, I say proudly, *Here I am, made in Alexandria.*
I'm the one who eats beans from Muhammad Ahmad, and I'm the one who fights my way through the crowd to buy ice cream at Azza's.

This is an article about language, first and foremost. There are a number of studies that show how speech about, and performance of, local dialects is usually associated with a local and authentic identity. Such work includes the studies conducted by Johnstone and Baumgardt (2004) on Pittsburgh, Pennsylvania, where talk about identity is often related to talk about local dialects. While it may be perhaps possible to perform dialects and talk about them, in Arabic and in the Arab world it is difficult and uncommon to write in a local dialect, showing phonological variations and not just syntactic or morphological ones. While writing colloquial Arabic in Egypt has become more common, writing in a newspaper in and about a local dialect of colloquial Arabic is almost unheard of. This is what makes this article unique and relevant to this study. It will not only provide a novel analysis of the relationship between identity, language, and religion, it will also provide an example of ways in which writers can reflect local dialects in Arabic in public written discourse.

The article starts with the word "yes" to conjure up an imagined argument between her, the writer, and the terrorist who bombed the church in Alexandria on New Year's Eve. This imagined argument provides the chance she needs to position herself as an Alexandrian. Throughout the article, the author positions herself as the "authentic" Alexandrian and the terrorist as an outsider who neither understands the Alexandrians, nor is successful in driving a wedge between the Muslims and Christians of Alexandria in particular. ʿAbbūd's stance is clear throughout the article by the use of the pronouns "I" and "we." Furthermore, by referring to the terrorist as the outsider, she aligns herself completely with Alexandrians, who may have different names, which may also entail different religions, but who speak in the same way and thus belong to the same community of practice. A community of practice as defined by Eckert (2005: 16) is

> [a]n aggregate of people who come together on a regular basis to engage in some enterprise. A family, a linguistics class, a garage, band, roommates, a sports team, even a small village. In the course of their engagement, the community of practice develops ways of doing things—practices. And these practices involve the construction of a shared orientation to the world around them—a tacit definition of themselves in relation to each other, and in relation to other communities of practice.

Most individuals usually belong to a community of practice, in which they agree on a shared "orientation towards the world" (see Eckert 2005: 16). Individuals in a community of practice also share a tacit definition of who they are in relation to other communities of practice. This is directly related to their perception of self.

ʿAbbūd also argues that "we" live in a dense and multiplex community—that is, literally dense, due to lack of space, and dense in the sense that we share activities and local habits. Throughout, the terrorist is a foreigner, an outsider who is challenged by the author.

> ما محمد وما يكل إخواتي، وخديجة ومارى كمان إخواتي، أخدنا اسكندرية من الأنفوشى للعصافرة، بنزعل
> مع بعض لما مصر تخسر ماتش، ونهيّص الدنيا مع بعض لمّا الأهلى يكسب، دول اللى كانوا جنبى وحواليّا،

همّا الإرهابيّين الكفرة دول فاكرين يوقعوا بينى وبين ليندا؟ طبعاً لأ، ليندا ومارى وجون عارفيني، بنقسّم اللقمة سوا، وحافظين نفس الإفيهات من المسرحيات والأفلام بنضحك عليها سوا،
لا أنا ولا فيرجنين يتضحك علينا، وازاى يكون، واحنا الاسكندرانية نفهمها وهيا طايرة، إحنا كلنا عارفين إن اللى هدد أمننا، وسوّلت له نفسه إنه ممكن يخوّفنا، واحد مش مننا، لا عمره سمعنا بنتكلم.

ma maḥammad wi maykil ʔixwa:ti:/ wi xadi:ga wi ma:ri kama:n ʔixwa:t-i:/ ʔaxadna: ʔiskindiriyya min al-anfu:ʃi: lil-ʕaṣṣafara/ (. . .) linda wi me:ri: wi jon ʕarfini:/ biniʕssim il-luʔma sawa:/wi ḥa:fizi:n nafs il-ʔifi:ha:t min l-masraḥi:ya:t w al-ʔafla:m/ biniḍḥak ʕale:ha sowa:/
la ʔana wala virji:n yiddaḥak ale:na/ wi ʔiza:y yiku:n wi ʔiḥna il-iskandara:niyya/ nifhamha wi hiyya ṭayyra/ ʔiḥna kullina ʕarfi:n inni lli haddid ʔamnina/ wi sawwalat lahu nafsu innu mumkin yixawifna/ wa:hid miʃ minina. Wala ʕumru samaʕna binitkallim/

My siblings are both Muhamad and Michael, and Khadiga and Mary are my siblings, too. We walked around Alexandria from Anfushi to Asafara (. . .) Linda and Mary and John know me. We break bread together, and we memorize the same quotes from plays and films that we laugh at together. Neither I nor Virginia can be deceived. Whoever threatened our safety and thought he will frighten us is an outsider. Someone who never heard us speak.

There is direct reference to language and the Alexandrian variety specifically as an index of identity and also as a natural outcome of sharing one's community of practice. The Alexandrians share the same community of practice, because they go to the same places, such as Mamura; they take the same tram to stations; they also share the same cultural inferences, such as, for example, if a woman dyes her hair blonde, she must be from Bahari. We are informed that they also share the same jokes, food, and cultural heritage, which includes films and plays.

Throughout the article, Christians are never referred to as "Christians"; instead, names are used as metonyms to refer to Christians. This technique is used to undermine the differences between both religious groups, who may have different names, but who "speak" the same language variety. In fact, we can only infer that the speaker is a Muslim when she says: "Neither I nor Virginia can be deceived. Whoever threatened our safety and thought he will frighten us is an outsider. Someone who never heard us speak." The fact that the speaker mentions herself and Virginia (a Christian name) as the group that could not be deceived by the outsider implies that she is a Muslim. The outsider cannot separate her, as a Muslim, from her sister community member Virginia, who is a Christian, since they speak the same language.

In this article, there is clear reference to language as an independent social variable throughout: the author manipulates the resources available to her to position herself as an Alexandrian that is against terrorism and whose community has members of two religions. It is noteworthy, however, that the fact that Ghada positions herself in such a way with direct reference to linguistic variables peculiar to the Alexandrian dialect does not mean that she herself uses these variables. As Johnstone (2007: 66) contends: "claiming to be a speaker of the local dialect is not the same as being one in the sense that linguists usually have in mind; it does not require anything more than knowing a few local-sounding words." Whether Ghādah actually uses Alexandrian dialect is a moot point. Her perceptions and ideologies are what are essential in this analysis.

4.4.2.2 Structural resources

Note that writing an article in ECA that also refers to a different variety used specifically by Alexandrians is not an easy task.

The author uses two strategies: first, she uses the Arabic writing system when possible to denote linguistic variation between Alexandrians and Cairenes, as when she writes:

> أنا اللى بوقف على **القمة** عشان أوقف **تاكس** وقبل ماركب أقوله "الابراهيمية ياسطة؟ بس أكتر من 5 **جينى** ما تلاقيش،
>
> *ʔana illi baʔuf ʕala l-ʔimma ʕaʃa:n ʔawʔaf ta:ks/ wa ʔabla ma-arkab ʔaʔu:l-u l-ibrahimiyya ya sṭa/ bas ʔaktar min xamsa gini: ma talaʔi:-ʃ/*
>
> I'm the one who stands in the intersection to flag down a taxi and before I get in I say to the driver, *Ibrahimia, driver . . . but you won't get more than five pounds!*

The words featured in bold type are typical Alexandrian forms. While القمة is written with a q, it should be pronounced with a glottal stop. The word itself, which means "intersection," is not used by Cairenes. Here the author has to rely on the shared assumptions of her readers in rendering the right pronunciation of the word *l-ʔimma*, which is written as *l-qimma*. The Alexandrian pronunciation of the word ta:ks (taxi), as opposed to the Cairene taksi:, is easy to render in written form, since the writer had only to eliminate the last vowel. So instead of writing the Cairene تاكسي, she writes it without the final long vowel i:, as تاكس. Also the word for pound is written in Cairene as جينيه, *gini:h* with a final e:h sound, which is again easy to render in Alexandrian by eliminating the final h. So in the article, it is written as جينى, *gini:*.

The author uses Arabic vocalization to ensure that the reader realizes the different phonological differences between Cairene Arabic and Alexandrian Arabic, such as:

> لَبست، شَربت، زَهقت، وبنطق "كوسة"، "كووسة،

The *fatha* as used in these words marks them as Alexandrian, rather than Cairene.

Cairene would use a long close mid back vowel */o:/* in pronouncing *ko:sa* ("zucchini"), rather than the long closed back vowel *u:* used by Alexandrians, as in *ku:sa.* In the following first person singular s-stem (perfect) verbs, Alexandrians use an open front vowel */a/*, rather than the Cairene closed front vowel *i.*

Verbs	**Alexandrian**	**Cairene**
To wear	*labast*	*libist*
To drink	*ʃarabt*	*ʃiribt*
To be bored	*zahaʔt*	*zihiʔt*

According to first order indexicality, the use of this different vowel quality by the journalist presupposes that she is from Alexandria, rather than Cairo. That is, it indexes her local identity. As Johnstone et al. (2006: 82) puts it, first order indexicality is usually not noticeable, not intentional, and not performed. However, the journalist intentionally uses these Alexandrian linguistic features. That is, in order to fully understand the significance of the journalist's usage of these variables, one needs to recognize the social meaning behind being Alexandrian and the intentionality of the journalist's usage of such linguistic forms.

Second order indexicality is usually superposed, creative, and entailing (Silverstein 2003: 220) and can be assigned an "ethnometapragmatically driven native interpretation" (Silverstein 2003: 212). Silverstein adds that the feature analyzed has usually been "enregistered." It has become correlated with a style of speech and can be used to create a context for that style. Johnstone (2007: 82) adds that once a linguistic form is noticeable and speakers associate it with social meaning based on shared ideologies, then it can be considered second order indexicality. Second order indexicality can help us understand the journalist's usage of Alexandrian form more comprehensibly within the context. The journalist wants to emphasize the shared habits of Alexandrians, as opposed to outsiders. Being Alexandrian presupposes that one is tough, helpful, and cannot be deceived easily by outsiders. However, being Alexandrian in the context of the journalist's article implies more than that. It implies a shared identity that surpasses religious differences. This, in fact, can be even better understood once we explain higher order indexicality. It is important to mention here that "this creative indexical effect is the motivated realization or performable execution of an already constituted framework of semiotic value" (Silverstein 2003: 194).

Third order indexicality is even more creative and performative. As Silverstein (2003: 222) contends, it creates "sites of indexical innovation that spread through analogical space." This higher indexicality exists in "a complex, interlocking set of institutionally formed macro-sociolinguistic interests" (2003: 226). In fact, the journalist's example can only be fully understood if explained within the framework of third order indexes. The journalist is performing a dialect in a written text. This is innovative as well as unique within the context of the written medium. That is, not just to index that she is from Alexandria, but to index that the fact that she is from Alexandria presupposes that she shares an identity with Christians and that she does not differentiate between people according to religion. It also entails that she is authentic, tough, and, first and foremost, a typical "Alexandrian." This local identity is then understood in the context of an incident that took place in 2011 in Alexandria and threatened the country with sectarian strife.

When the journalist uses the Alexandrian dialect in a written text, she is consciously imitating a "social type" (Silverstein 2003: 220). She is also depending on a shared ideological model with her audience. The forms that the journalist uses are also salient and immanent (cf. Johnstone et al. 2006). In their work on "Pittsburghese," Johnstone et al. (2006: 84) show how they draw on first, second, and third order indexicality as they decide how to talk and how to "talk about talk."

4.4.2.3 Discourse resources

One can apply Van Leeuwen (1996) identification categories directly to this article:

1. Functionalization: this term refers to identification by virtue of what one does; ʿAbbūd says that she is an Alexandrian who takes the tram from a specific location to another. She also goes to Cinema Metro. She takes a taxi and only pays five pounds.
2. Classification: this term refers to identification by virtue of what one is, including, for example, that ʿAbbūd is implied to be a Muslim, although she never mentions it. She does, however, include names that recall both Muslims and Christians and men and women, such as Muhammad and Michael, Khadiga and Mary.
3. Relational identification: this term refers to identification by virtue of relationships. She refers to both Mohammed and Michael as her brothers.
4. Physical identification: this term refers to identification by virtue of physical descriptions. She infers, due to her Alexandrian cultural knowledge, that the woman who dyes her hair blonde is from the Baḥarī quarter. This is essential, since it is easier for her to infer the place where the woman comes from, rather than the woman's religion from her appearance.
5. Genericization: this kind of identification makes the identity generic, rather

than specific. ʿAbbūd generally references Alexandrians in general throughout the article and does not refer to Christianity or Islam.

She concludes her article as follows:

(19) *da ʔeḥna w il-mursi: ʔabu l-ʕabba:s niġsilu:ku/ wi ninaʃʃaru:ku:/ maʃʃu: min ʕandina/*

(I swear by Mursī Abū al-ʿAbbās that we will wash you and leave you to hang out to dry (i.e. "we will beat the hell out of you"), get out of our country.)

The article ends with her oath to the Sheikh Mursī Abū al-ʿAbbās, an Alexandrian Sheikh whose mosque and shrine are located in the Baḥarī district at the heart of old Alexandria. This sheikh is commonly used in oaths and can be considered the "patron saint" of the city. The intention is to teach the terrorists a lesson, and once again the author uses salient phonological Alexandrian features, such as:

niġsilu:ku/ wi ninaʃʃaru:ku:

(we wash you and hang you out to dry)

These features are utilized, as opposed to Cairene features:

niġsilku:/ wi ninaʃʃarku:

in which the vowel *u:* is totally omitted.

This usage of salient Alexandrian phonological features that, in fact, are associated with local lower-class Alexandrians (a variety of fishermen in films) carries covert prestige (Trudgill 1972), conveys authenticity, and suggests a close network. It is easy to maintain one's vernacular in close-knit communities in spite of cultural pressure. However, when networks are weakened, then language change is often triggered (Milroy 1987). ʿAbbūd's argument, indexed in her language choice, is: "because we have such a close-knit network it is impossible for the outsider who lacks competency and knowledge to drive a wedge between us." She plays on the concept of social networks to the utmost. The article is written to a Christian and Muslim audience, but mainly targets the Christians who were intimidated by the bombing. The comments from readers posted on the website come mainly from Christians who appreciate her stance. Her message, if we examine the comments posted, succeeds in appealing to the large community of practice through language indexes. The phonological variables that she emphasizes have clear meanings to Egyptians, especially to Alexandrians.

In this analysis, I attempted to show how variables "mean"—that is, how they index—ideologies, attitudes, and identity on different levels. I will now refer to a different kind of data; data from variationist research that is not ideological in nature, but dependent on empirical quantitative data analysis.

For the sake of comparison, I would first like to show some of the phonological differences between the Baharna Shiite dialect and the Arab Sunni dialect. I will also include the realization of the phonological variable in SA. The variables studied are *j* and *q*.

Table 4.1 Realization of SA variables /j/ and /q/ by Sunnis and Shiites in Bahrain (after Holes 1986: 34)

SA	Shiites	Sunnis
j	*j*	*y*
q	*q*	*g*

A salient variable such as the SA *q* realized differently because of religious differences is not found in Egypt. If we take the same variable, then it is realized, roughly speaking, by all urban centers in Egypt as *g* and in rural areas as /j/ (see Woidich and Behnstedt 1985).

The importance of the article analyzed above lies in the meanings it attributes to linguistic homogeneity between religious groups. Religion plays a significant role in the construction of identity, but religious differences are not a defining element in the way people speak in Egypt. Religion may be a salient marker of identity, but religious differences as manifested linguistically are not as salient as class differences and local differences and so on.

Another online article worth mentioning is a blog posting that appeared after the Salafis' tensions with Copts.[24] The blog was written by a Muslim to poke fun at fanatic Muslims and also to minimize the exaggerated putative differences between Christians and Muslims in Egypt. The blog begins by addressing the fanatic, saying "my brother and sister the fanatic." Then the blogger starts ridiculing the differences between Christians and Muslims and the attitudes of fanatics. While we will not go into this article in detail, the first question asked of the fanatic is worth mentioning here for its satire and apparent alignment, but in reality disalignment, with the fanatics.

(20)
ʔaxi: al mutaʕaṣṣib ʔuxti al-mutaʕaṣṣiba
hal ga:rak yaqu:l ṣaddaqni: badalan min an yuqsim bi-Lla:h

hal yaqu:l wa ʕalaykum al-sala:m wa la: yazi:d ʕalay-ha wa raḥmat Alla:h wa-baraka:tuh

My brother the fanatic, my sister the fanatic:
Does your neighbor say "Believe me" instead of swearing by God's name?
Does your neighbor reply to your greeting with "And peace be upon you," without adding ". . . and God's mercy and God's blessing"?

The Muslim blogger pokes fun at the few lexical differences between Christians and Muslims that may be exaggerated by fanatics. He satirically asks the fanatic a rhetorical question about whether his neighbor does not swear but instead says "believe me," due to the fact that some religious Christians refrain from using the name of God in vain. Note the reference to "your neighbor" to again put emphasis on the close physical proximity of both religious groups. The Christian may also avoid saying one or two words associated with Muslim greetings. These little lexical differences are supposedly deemed by the fanatic to show identity differences. The blogger aims to ridicule the exaggerated and unfounded projections of differences between Christians and Muslims by resorting to linguistic lexical differences that he deems unimportant. The blogger frames his blog in the form of an advertisement and after asking the questions says: "if you answer yes, then you need our program of how to get rid of your Christian neighbor!" Throughout, the blogger addresses the fanatic in the male second person singular, synthetic personification. In this case, synthetic personification is used to imitate the style of advertisements more generally.

In the next paragraphs, I will show how Egyptian films manipulate the lack of linguistic variation between both religious groups to intentionally highlight shared practices, rather than differences. Three films are mentioned: *Amrīkā shīkā bīkā* (1983), *Hammām fī Amstirdām* (1999), and *Ḥasan wa-Murquṣ* (2008).

Amrīkā shīkā bīkā ("America: a fake dream") (1983)

In the film *America: A Fake Dream*, a group of desperate Egyptians decide to immigrate illegally to the USA. They end up in Romania with no money and no future. The group is comprised of a variety of Egyptians from different walks of life: an educated lower-middle class girl who is searching for a better future, an aged teacher, a medical doctor, laborers, and an old prostitute who wants to find a cure for her daughter's kidney disease. The two main characters, Aḥmad (clearly a Muslim name) and Fu'ād, are different. Aḥmad is a lower-class laborer, while Fu'ād is a medical doctor. Tension increases between them, especially when they compete for the attention of the girl in their group. However, they eventually realize how similar they are: both of them are poor, desperate, and humiliated. Eventually, they reconcile. Throughout the film, there is no mention of the religion of any of the group members. The aged teacher dies in Romania and they all discuss how to bury him. They decide to bury him in an arbitrary spot and start praying for him. When Fu'ād starts his prayer, the audience realizes for the first time that he is Christian. There was nothing in Fu'ād's appreance, language, or even neutral name to indicate this. Only during the burial scene, which occurs towards the end of the film, does the group in the film, as well as the audience, realize this. Aḥmad then asks, surprisingly in ECA, the redundant question: "You are Christian, Fu'ād?" The surprise of Aḥmad is a reflection of the lack of indication of any differences. Aḥmad then hugs Fu'ād in a didactic scene meant to undermine any differences. The surprise is intentional, and the fact that we and the main character in the film are left in the dark as to the religion of Fu'ād is a manipulation of the common variable shared by all Egyptians, including linguistic habits.

Hammām fī Amstirdām ("Hammām in Amsterdam") (1999)

Code-choice and identity are also conspicuous in the blockbuster film *Hammām fī Amstirdām* ("Hammām in Amsterdam"). This film strikes a chord with Egyptians, because it deals with issues that affect a great number of Egyptians: poverty, immigration, and the issue of identity more generally. The protagonist, Hammām, played by the comedic actor Muḥammed Hinaydī, is the Egyptian par excellence: he is poor, yet generous, humorous, resourceful, and persistent. When he is dumped by his fiancée and faces frustration at home, he decides to immigrate to the Netherlands to visit an uncle whom he has never seen. Once there, he faces discrimination and arrest as he undergoes a number of adventures. In the meantime, he is struck by the loose network that his uncle has with his Dutch family, wife, and children compared to the close relations that Hammām has with his own friends and family in Egypt.

Throughout the film, Hammām is on the brink of failing, but never does. In fact, at the end, he becomes rich and marries a Moroccan–Dutch girl—a rags to riches story. He starts by sharing a house with other poor Arabs and an Egyptian from the south of Egypt (a "*saʿīdī*"), and he has a good relationship with them all. However, there is only one character in particular who is always there for him—a man who protects him, helps him, and finally becomes his partner in his restaurant. This man, Adrian, is another Egyptian from Cairo, but unlike Hammām, he is a Christian. Hammām and Adrian (played by Aḥmad al-Saqqā) form the most constructive and close relationship throughout the film. While Hammām is by nature sympathetic to all those around him and while there are moments when he calls on the Arabs who share the house with him to forget their differences and start anew,[25] it is only Adrian with whom he trusts and confides. Even the southern Egyptian Muslim does not share this affinity and solidarity with Hammām. It is only the Cairene Adrian who stays with Hammām until the end.

The way that the audience is introduced to Adrian is significant on more than one level. When Hammām arrives in the Netherlands, his passport is stolen. He ends up in the police station, struggling to speak English to the police officer, becoming frightened and confused. He starts muttering to himself in Egyptian Arabic when a Moroccan illegal immigrant hears him and says in Moroccan Arabic:

ma-tqul-ʃi innak maṣri:

"Do not tell them that you are Egyptian"

Hammām replies bitterly in Egyptian Arabic:

ʔaʔuluhum e:h/ hulandi:

"What shall I say then? That I am Dutch?"

Realizing that it is impossible for him to change his identity, given that he does not speak the language nor does he look Dutch, Hammām insists that he is Egyptian and eventually regains his passport. That night, he becomes curious about a nightclub that he has seen. He enters the nightclub and the waitress starts putting things on his table while he is mesmerized by the show of acrobats. She then asks for money in English. He replies (the English words are in bold type):

***bill** e:h ana maṭalabtiʃ ḥa:ga inti lli kullu ʃwayya tiḥuṭṭi:li/ **no moni:**/ ana maṭalabtiʃ ḥa:ga*

"What **bill**? I did not order anything. You kept putting things in my table. **No money.** I did not order anything."

The waitress then signals for two bouncers to beat him up. Note that the two words that he utters in English are "bill" and "money." He shouts for help in Arabic, saying:

ya gidʕa:n maḥaddiʃ ʕarabi: hina/ soʕu:di: kowe:ti: ʕira:ʔi: suda:ni: ayyi li:bi: iwʕa: yala ana maṣri: ya gidʕa:n/ iwʕa: yala ana maṣri: ya gidʕa:n/

"Lads, are there no Arabs here? A Saudi, a Kuwaiti, a Sudanese, any Libyans? Get away from me, kid! I am Egyptian, lads! (he shouts:) Get away from me, kid! I am Egyptian . . . lads!"

He appeals to *gidʕa:n* (chivalrous Egyptians) in ECA, while shouting out that he is Egyptian.

When Adrian first notices Hammām, Adrian's Dutch girlfriend turns his face away from the scene and asks him to finish his drink. But once Hammām again appeals to *gidʕa:n* and says that he is an Egyptian, Adrian cannot refrain from interfering. So far Adrian has not spoken, so Hammām and the audience do not know that he is Egyptian. Adrian puts himself at risk by hitting the bodyguards, in order to help "the Egyptian." Hammām says:

ʔiddi:lu/ ayywa

"Yes, give it to him!"

Hammām does not have the physique or strength of Adrian, so he remains in the background while the fighting goes on, commenting in both Arabic and English. His evaluation of Adrian comes in English when he says: "Good man." When the fighting intensifies and there are too many men against Adrian, Adrian takes out a knife. The men all step back, and Adrian leaves with Hammām and his girlfriend. Hammām latches on to Adrian and follows after him, saying in English (the English words are in bold type):

"Mr. thank you very much. Thank you very very much.
I am Hammām. Whats your name? Where you go?"

Adrian then speaks his first words in the film and they are in ECA:

ʔirkab wi miʃ ʕa:yiz dawʃa

"Just get on the motorcycle and shut up."

Hammām is taken by surprise by the Egyptian Arabic and shouts in joy:

taḥya gumhu:riyat maṣr al-ʕarabiyya
Hamma:m miga:hid ʃaʕba:n

"Long live the Arab republic of Egypt
I am Hammām Mujāhid Shaʿbān'."

Adrian only utters few words: his name (which of course identifies him as a Christian to an Egyptian audience) and an order to Hammām:

Adriya:n
irkab baʔa.

"Adrian.
Now sit [on the motorcycle]."

Adrian has been part of a gang and involved in shady business, but his relation to the somehow naïve and well-meaning Hammām develops into a close friendship. It is Hammām who eventually pulls him up at the end and asks him to be his partner.

Throughout the film, Adrian wears a cross. Once or twice, Hammām is behind him and Adrian thinks that he is one of the gang sneaking up behind him, so he takes out his knife, but Hammām shouts in Arabic: "Long live the Arab Republic of Egypt!" By so doing, he appeals to the national identity that they both share and the language they both understand.

In other words, Arabic and Egypt are what the men both share. More specifically, they share an Egyptian identity that is highlighted in the Netherlands. Locality on a more specific level is also essential, which is similar to ʿAbbūd's article analyzed above. Both Adrian and Hammām are from Cairo and they share more than one social variable, a common code being one of them. In fact, despite their religious differences, they both have more in common as Cairenes than Hammām does with an Egyptian Muslim from Upper Egypt with whom he shares a house. On more than one occasion, the Egyptian from Upper Egypt acts in ways that lead Hammām to laughter and surprise. Once more, the local, specific identity is highlighted.

In the above example, Hammām uses English when he speaks about money, as well as when he evaluates Adrian. When he appeals to the chivalry of a good man, Arabic (ECA, in particular) is used. ECA indexes an Egyptian identity not built on religion, but rather on chivalry and solidarity—two traits that are absent in the foreigners throughout the film. It is, of course, intentional that Adrian is Christian and that Hammām feels both safe and exhilarated the moment he hears Egyptian Arabic. Once more, public discourse deliberately pinpoints the importance of sharing linguistic practices.

Ḥasan wa-Murquṣ ("Hasan and Murqus") (2008)

The last film we analyze here is *Ḥasan wa-Murquṣ*.[26] The "Ḥasan" of the title is, in reality, the Coptic priest Būluṣ, who runs into a conflict with

Christian fundamentalist groups. When he and his son narrowly escape an assassination attempt, the security agency provides him and his family with false identities as Muslims and relocates them to al-Minyā—a well-known hotbed of Islamic extremism and sectarian strife.

Murquṣ, on the other hand, is a pious Muslim, whose brother was involved with a terrorist group. After his brother's death, Murquṣ is harassed by the organization, and the state security agency arranges to disguise him and his family as Coptic Christians recently returned from America.

In al-Minyā, Būluṣ and his family find it easy to pass as Muslims; Būluṣ renames himself Ḥasan, while Būluṣ' wife takes off her cross and dons a long headscarf. Indeed, it is not long before Ḥasan/Būluṣ acquires a reputation as a learned Muslim sheikh, and the people in the village credit him with the extraordinary ability to perform miracles.

When the simple-minded villagers ask him to give the sermon at their mosque for the Friday prayer, "Ḥasan" is at a loss. When the villagers begin to ask his opinion about Islamic law, he always resorts to two questions: "What does the Prophet say?" and "What does religion say?" The audience interprets these as rhetorical questions designed to test their knowledge, thus, with very little effort on his part, he manages to impress them as a learned Muslim sheikh.

Eventually, Hassan becomes so successful in his impersonation of a popular Muslim leader that he becomes a focal point for rebellion against the government and is arrested as a terrorist suspect.

In the meantime, Murquṣ, the Muslim, has managed to pass himself off as a Christian. A pious Muslim at heart, he does not attend church. This raises concerns among his Christian neighbors that Murquṣ may not be a devout Christian. However, his basic religious affiliation is never called into question and, more importantly, his language never arouses suspicion or betrays him. Indeed, both Hassan and Murquṣ speak Cairene Arabic. Apart from a few lexical expressions that the would-be Christian Murquṣ does not know (*karbaniyūt* "Christian engagement") and Murquṣ's inadvertent quoting of the Qur'ān, there is nothing that reveals their true religious identities.

On more than one occasion in the film, the differences between both are blurred. At least twice they exclaim that their destiny is the same, especially when both are harrassed by the police and arrested without a valid reason. In the film, both the preachers in the mosques and the churches code-switch between ECA and SA (see Bassiouney 2006 for studies on code-switching in mosque sermons).

To recap, public discourse in Egypt foregrounds linguistic homogeneity as an indexical resource for Egyptians and negates the relationship between linguistic diversity and religious diversity. The established indexical relationship in Egyptian public discourse between language and religion is next to nothing. Stylistic practices of both parties are dependent more on their small or big community of practice, rather than on their religious affiliation. Language is used in public discourse as a marker of a unified, large community of practice that embraces both Christians and Muslims. Differences between both religious groups are limited to religious vocabulary and liturgical language, confined to the context of the church or mosque.

Language can also be a salient feature that can be brought to the forefront, especially in times of conflict, to indicate that sectarian tensions are unfounded and that Christians and Muslims are of one communal group. Sharing the same language also indicates sharing the same food, habits, morals, historical background, ethnicity, and location; it indicates living in a close-knit community. Language is impregnated with indexes.

In Egyptian films, personal names are used as metonyms to indicate religious affiliations and undermine religious differences. Metonymy refers to the exchange of one word by one of its attributes—that is, "the crown" can be used to refer to the monarch and "the university" can refer to the individuals involved in making decisions at the university (Benwell and Stokoe 2006). Metonymy is used in films, online articles, and (as we will see in the next section) patriotic songs to downplay religious differences. The message of public discourse is that we, Egyptians, are all Copts, but some of us are born Christians. This is an arbitrary fact, not a conscious choice, and therefore should not be foregrounded. The reference to this difference will be through personal names. In *Ḥasan wa-Murquṣ*, when the Christian Būluṣ feels threatened by the police officer, he says: "I will not change my name." This means that he will not change his religion. By mentioning names rather than religion, the differences are undermined. The paradox of names is that the choice of names by Muslims and Christians in Egypt in fact highlights religious identity and is not meant to undermine it. Parents attempt to impose a religious identity on children by choosing traditional religious names for them. This ensures that the child will always belong to a specific religious group. There are, of course, families that choose neutral names. Public discourse tends to regard names as less significant in identity construction, thus ignoring how important they are for identity in general. In public discourse, the indexes of names come as subordinate to those of language form and code-choice.

In general, indexes of language form as evidence of an Egyptian identity come before those of religion as an independent variable in the hierarchical ladder.

It is worth mentioning, however, that the question of whether Christians and Muslims vary in their usage of SA and ECA has not been examined in detail yet. The fact that Lūwis ʿAwaḍ, who called for the use of ECA in writing in Egypt, is Christian may be a mere accident or a reflection of an ideology. Salāmah Mūsá, a Muslim, also made a similar call (see Chapter 3). Since SA is not spoken except in specific contexts, it is not mentioned when discussing linguistic variation. SA is the language of the Qur'ān, but it is also the language of the classical heritage of Egyptians. The Bible is translated and read in SA in Christian churches. A church sermon is officially in SA (except the Coptic part) and so is a mosque sermon; both Christian religious scholars and Muslim religious scholars use code-switching between SA and ECA in a similar fashion. Although this topic has not been examined in detail, it is worth mentioning here for the sake of thoroughness.

In August 2006, a Coptic Christian multimillionaire launched a new private satellite Egyptian channel called O-TV. The channel's distinctive feature is its use of ECA for all domains, even in news broadcasts—a domain associated exclusively with SA. As expected, there were Egyptians who were in favor of the idea of using ECA in the news and claimed that this was the only channel that highlighted Egypt's distinct identity. However, the fact that the channel is owned by a Coptic Christian who uses ECA was not considered without scepticism from others. For the first time, blogs started discussing the pros and cons of using ECA in Egyptian news broadcasts. The Muslim Brotherhood website accused the channel of targeting an audience of rich Egyptian youth and encouraging the breakdown of language in Egypt. Using ECA in the news was regarded as a conspiracy—an unpractical one, for that matter, since it is difficult to read the news in colloquial, and it almost requires more effort to read the news in colloquial than in SA (Kamāl 2008). The tentative association of Copts with ECA (as the "true" Egyptians) and Muslims with SA (as the Arabs who immigrated to Egypt after the Arab conquest in the seventh century) is ignored in Egyptian public discourse, but reappears from time to time, both inside and outside Egypt. However, the fact that the late Pope Shinūdah would write his weekly article in *al-Ahrām* newspaper in SA at a time when Muslim and Christian journalists switch between both is significant.

Yet the fact that both religious groups live in close proximity and share many political, social, and economic challenges is an important and highlighted aspect of identity. Whether the conjuring up of a lack of linguistic variation between different religious groups in Egypt is enough to defuse the spectre of sectarian strife is, of course, a moot point. But once again language is used as the linchpin for an identity that is supposed to be a coherent and holistic one.

To recap, public disourse deliberately manipulates shared resources between Christians and Muslims to show that they belong to the same community. These resources are both linguistic and meta-linguistic ones. In the three films mentioned, the intrinsic identity of the main characters is that of being "Egyptian." Apart from wearing a symbol of their religion or mentioning a name that categorizes them as belonging to a specific religion, there is nothing in their appearance or language that indicates their religion. Wearing a cross or specifically Muslim attire is something that can change and can be confusing, as in the case of the film *Ḥasan wa-Murquṣ*. However, linguistic resoruces are more engrained, so are backbone variables: ethnicity, historicity, and locality. In the film *Hammām fī Amstirdām*, variables are reduced to linguistic ones in the first scene between Hammām and Adrian. Adrian's attire does not single him out as an Egyptian and his Dutch girlfriend confuses the audience and Hammām even more. It is only when he utters his first words in ECA that the audience (and Hammām) begin to realize how similar both protagonists are.

In ʿAbbūd's article, social variables are referenced as well, but linguistic ones are treated as core identity markers and are emphasized throughout. In her article, orders of indexicality are implicit. In the films, code-switching is occasionally used and linguistic habits are always referenced.

In the following section, the second point is discussed in relation to patriotic songs specifically.

4.4.3 Second claim of public discourse: Egyptians are religious, but religious differences between Christians and Muslims are not salient

This section describes how religion features in patriotic songs.

Religion as a social, independent variable is essential in defining Egyptian identity. However, religious differences are undermined in public discourse. This is done using a number of strategies.

Religion is indicated in different ways in 52 per cent of the songs analyzed. The strategies employed to refer to it render it in a more neutral, holistic, and inclusive manner. In 52.5 per cent of cases, religion is alluded to in a neutral manner with no reference to a specific religion. Examples of this are propositions that imply that God is with Egypt, God protects Egypt, we pray to God, and so on. When songs refer to specific religions, they usually refer to both Christianity and Islam and they do so indirectly by using place names or proper names. When both religions are mentioned in a song, there is mention of how Egypt is special for both religions, even referencing the religious scripture. There are examples in which the name of a famous monastery and famous mosque are mentioned. There are also references to how Egypt is mentioned in both the Bible and the Qur'ān and is, thus, a special and holy place.

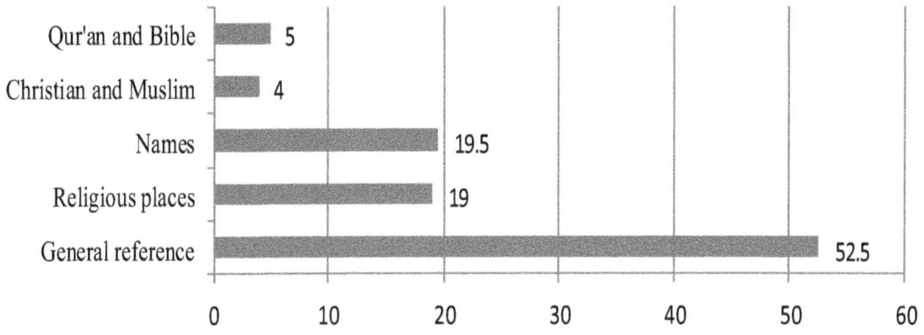

Figure 4.3 Subcategories: religion

Mention of local areas in reference to religion occurs 19 per cent of the time, while mention of proper names in reference to religion occurs 19.5 per cent. The mention of the Qur'ān and the Bible is 5 per cent. Direct reference to Christians and Muslims occurs only twice in the forty-eight songs analyzed and almost a century unfolds between the songs.

Reference to religion occurs in the song mentioned above in Chapter 2, "Rise up, Egyptian," in which the singer says: "What is the difference between Christians, Muslims and Jews? They all come from the same ancestors." This indicates that ethnicity comes before religion. The other mention is in a more recent song, *fi:ha: ḥa:ga ḥilwa* ("There's something beautiful about her") (2010), analyzed below, which declares emphatically that what characterizes Egypt is a Muslim breaking his Ramadan fast in a Christian house—an example of love and tolerance between different religious groups. Other than these examples, the words "Christian" and "Muslim" are not mentioned. This is done intentionally to downplay differences.

Religion, as with other variables, does not occur exclusively as a marker of identity, but in relation to other variables, especially the backbone variables, such as locality, ethnicity, historicity and so on. This technique is again to downplay differences and highlight other shared variables that establish Egyptians as members of a large community of practice.

The following examples demonstrate how religion is referenced in patriotic songs. In the song analyzed in Section 1 (above), *miṣr tataḥaddaθ ʕan nafsi-ha:* ("Egypt speaks about itself"), religion is referenced through Egypt's perspective, and God's support to Egypt and its children the Egyptian is described. God is on Egypt's side, and Islam and Christianity are not mentioned as distinctly different religions. This technique is echoed again in the 2010 song *balad-i:* ("My country") by Muḥammad Fu'ād, when he says: "We believe in the one God, and we are all one." This inclusiveness, as was stated earlier, marks more than half of the references to religion in this type of public discourse.

4.4.3.1 Neutral mention of God

Note, again, the following example from the SA song *miṣr tataḥaddaθ ʕan nafsi-ha:* ("Egypt speaks about itself"):

> *naẓar alla:hu l-i: fa-ʔarʃad abna:ʔ-i: fa-ʃaddu: ʔila: l-ʕala: ʔayya ʃadd-i: ʔinnama: l-ḥaqqu quwwatun min quwa: ad-diya:n ʔamḍa: min kull ʔabyaḍ wa hindi:*
>
> God looked to me while I am guiding my sons, and they pulled upwards with all of their might
> But righteousness is a power belonging to God, mightier than the sword.

Egypt's stance is a powerful, confident one and so is the Egyptian's stance, because of factors such as historicity discussed above and also because of God's support. When righteousness is mentioned, it is used in a superlative construction that places it above the weapons of the invaders. Quantification is also used in *kull ʔabyaḍ wa hindi:* to add definiteness to the power of fairness and righteousness, which surpasses the power of weapons. This reference to God also targets an Egyptian audience that is to a great extent religious, regardless of whether they are Christians or Muslims. Egypt positions herself in direct relation to God by ascribing the trait of righteousness to herself, which is one of the traits of God. This allows Egypt and Egyptians to gain credibility and strength.

4.4.3.2 Mention of local areas that reference religion

In the song "What does 'homeland' mean?," location, habits, and religion are connected to reflect an Egyptian identity.

> **(21) From *yaʕni: ʔe:h kilmit 'waṭan'* ("What does 'homeland' mean?") (1983)**
> *yaʕni: ʔe:h kilmit waṭan⸮ʃa:y bi-l-ḥali:b ʕala: ʔahwa fi: ḍ-ḍa:hir hina:k.*
> *nismit ʕaṣa:ri: is-sayyida w-de:r il-mala:k*
>
> What does "homeland" mean?
> It is tea with milk in a café in al-Daher district.
> It is an evening breeze in [the neighbourhood of] Sayyidah [Zaynab mosque] or of the Monastery of the Angel.

To reiterate, the place names chosen refer to places of worship for both Christians and Muslims. Both areas are distinct, over-populated, lower-class areas in Cairo. The implication is that in both areas, Muslims and Christians suffer from hot weather, poverty, and oppression, and that is why they are driven to immigrate to the USA. In the film that plays the song, "America, a fake dream," as discussed above, a Muslim and a

Christian are both driven to emigrate. They share a community of practice in which they suffer, but which is coherent and strong overall.

4.4.3.3 Relating religion to other social variables
In the following example, history, religion, locality, and character traits are mentioned together to refer to Egyptians.

(22) *yibʔa ʔinta ʔaki:d fi maṣr* ("Surely you are in Egypt") (2001)
lamma tila:ʔi: il-kini:sa gawwa-ha: da:fi w-ʔaṣi:l w-kulli rukni fi:-ha ʃa:hid ʕa-t-tari:x
hina: l-miṣi:ḥ wi-l-ʔaðra ʕa:ʃu bi-s-sini:n fi-wusṭ na:s-ha: w-ʔahli-ha: iṭ-ṭayyibi:n
da kala:m girgis w-ʕamm naṣr
w-yibʔa: ʔinta: ʔaki:d ʔaki:d fi: maṣr

When you find the church, and inside its air is warm and pure, and its every nook and cranny is a witness to history;
—here is where the messiah and the virgin lived for years among these kind people;
Those are the words of Girgis and Uncle Naṣr—
Then surely, surely you are in Egypt.

The stance of the singers in this song is discussed in detail in Section 2. The church here is not just a Christian institution; it is also a witness to history and to the characteristics of Egyptians, such as warmth and kindness. The reference to Christ and Mary's trip to Egypt appears often in patriotic songs as a proof of the kindness and special status of Egyptians. The fact that both Christians and Muslims agree on the same version of the story is also manipulated to emphasize that they are, after all, one people. They share the same history of religion, which renders Egypt a special place. Using names to reference religion (metonymy) is also a common technique.

4.4.3.4 Clear mention of religious categories
As was discussed earlier, obvious mention of religions occurs only twice in about 100 years: once in the song mentioned both above and in Chapter 2, *ʔu:m ya: maṣri:* ("Rise up, Egyptian") by Sayyid Darwīsh (1919), and once in a song from 2010, *fi:-ha: ḥa:ga ḥilwa* ("There's something beautiful about her") by Rihām ʿAbd al-Ḥakīm. This song has been analyzed already in this chapter. In this song, which is comprised mainly of a cluster of verbless clauses, the "beautiful things" in Egypt are summarized, including the tolerance and love between Christians and Muslims who share food in the same house.

4.4.3.5 A typical example to recap discussion

Before concluding this section, I would like to provide an analysis of one recent and essential example that summarizes all the points discussed so far—an example related directly to the January 25 Revolution. Interaction between religion, ethnicity, and a community of practice are apparent in this example. This song was released as a dedication for the martyrs of the Egyptian Revolution in February 2011.

(23) *b-aʃabbih ʕale:-k* ("I saw you before") by Muḥammad Fu'ād (2011)

b-aʃabbih ʕale:-k
ma:lamḥ-ak min ma:lamḥ-i:
w-lo:n-ak lo:n-u ʔamḥi:
w-ʕuyu:n-ak farḥa:ni:n

b-aʃabbih ʕale:-k
ʔul-li: w-fakkar-ni: ʔimta:
ʔana ʃuft-ak bas ʔimta:
min yo:m wala: sini:n

yimkin zama:yil madrasa ʔaw dufʕit-i: fi: l-ge:ʃ
xabaṭit kitaf-na: yo:m fi: baʕḍ w-ʔeḥna: fi: ṭa:bu:r l-ʕe:ʃ
wa-lla ʔakalna: fi: yo:m sawa: ʔaklit samak fi: ʔabu: ʔi:r
wa-lla lamaḥtak yo:m hina tuṣrux tiʔu:l taġyi:r
[. . .]
yimkin fi: le:la wiʔift-li: w-ʔana ʕaṭla:n ʕa-ṭ-ṭari:ʔ
saʔalti ʕan-ni: fi yo:m w-ʔana maxnu:ʔ ḥa:sis biḍ-ḍi:ʔ
sa:yibni: le:-h miḥta:r kida ma:-taʔu:l-li: tiṭlaʕ mi:n

huwwa ʔinta ʔaḥmad w-la: girgis w-la: ṣo:t malayi:n
wa-lla ʔinta wa:ḥid ṣidur-u ḍa:ʔ min iẓ-ẓulmi w-iẓ-ẓalmi:n
wa-lla ʔinta ba:ʕt-ak rabbi-na: ta:xud bi-ʔi:d malayi:n

b-aʃabbih ʕale:-k
ya: lli: ḍaḥi:t bi-ru:ḥ-ak ya: wa:ḥid minni-na:
w-sa:yib ʔahl-ak w-na:s-ak ʕalaʃana kulli-na:
ya: ʃahi:d ʔinta maka:n-ak fi-l-ganna muʃhina:

ka:n nifs-i bas ʔaʔu:l-lak ʔinta ma-ruḥti-ʃ hadar
dilwaʔti: sot-na: ʕa:li: w-xala:ṣ xof-na ʔinkasar
baʔa fi:-h fi: ʔulub-na: raḥma w-lelna: fi:h ʔamar

b-aʃabbih ʕali:-k

I think I saw you before
Your features are just like mine
Your complexion is wheat-colored
And your eyes are full of joy

I think I saw you before
Tell me and remind me when
I saw you last, when
Was it yesterday, or years ago

Maybe we were schoolmates, or maybe from my army service
Maybe we bumped shoulders when we were in the bread line
Or maybe one day we shared a plate of fish together in Abu Qir'
Or have I seen you here one day, screaming for change

(. . .)

Maybe one night you stopped to help me when my car broke down on the highway.
You asked about me one day when I was sad, stifled and anxious.
Why do you leave me confounded?—Do tell me: Who are you?

Are you Ahmad or Girgis or the voice of millions?
Or one who is sick and tired of oppression and the oppressors?
Or where you sent to us by God, taking the millions by the hand?

I think I saw you before:
You, who sacrificed your life, oh one of us,
And you left behind your family and your people for the sake of all of us.
Oh, you martyr, your place is in heaven, not here!

I only wanted to tell you that you did not go in vain.
Now our voice is raised, and our fear is finally broken.
Mercy has stayed in our hearts, and a moon remains in our nights.

I think I saw you before.

This song is unique in more than one way. In terms of stance, this is one of the few songs in this study in which the singer addresses an audience who is not an outsider or an ignorant and unappreciative insider. In fact, the singer appeals to the communal solidarity that he has with the "martyr" as a fellow Egyptian. The martyr is quintessentially Egyptian—he shares the color, features, and also the habits of Egyptians, including such characteristics as joy and humor (his eyes are happy), as well as kindness and generosity in helping others. He is an Egyptian because of his color and ethnicity, his habits (like eating fish in Abu Qīr), his locality (he goes to areas such as Abu Qīr, al-Azhar), and finally his character traits: helpful, warm, and kind.

The martyr is a symbol: he is the Egyptian everyman. The fact that this martyr has to leave his family behind—a difficult decision for an Egyptian, whose community is an essential part of his or her identity—is referred to specifically as a big sacrifice. The singer's evaluation of the martyr and the situation is also essential. He posits that the martyr did not die in vain, but has changed something in all Egyptians.

The singer starts with a direct statement addressed to the martyr (we do not yet know that he is a martyr). The pronouns used—*inta* ("you"), not *haḍritak* (lit. "your presence," formal you)—emphasize the informality of the relationship between the singer and the martyr, whose name he does not know. The men do, however, share so many Egyptian characteristics that it is easy for the singer to identify with the martyr completely. The use of the ECA aspectual prefix in *b-aʃabbih ʕali:-k* renders this process of trying to identify with the martyr an ongoing process. The martyr is never identified, because he is all Egyptians in a way. The use of modality, as in *ga:yiz* ("perhaps"), *yimkin* ("perhaps"), highlights the nonspecificity of this Egyptian man (the martyr) and raises him up to become the symbol of Egyptian identity. The singer also implies that the martyr died in Tahrir Square where the singer was singing.

wa-lla lamaḥtak yo:m hina tuṣrux tiʔu:l taġyi:r

Or have I seen you here one day, screaming for change

The singer uses the deictic marker *hina* ("here" for close proximity) to refer to Tahrir Square. With no knowledge of the political events of the year, his deictic marker is meaningless. With background knowledge, this deictic marker implies more than Tahrir Square. The fact that the singer uses *hina* not only implies the close proximity of Tahrir to him both physically and emotionally, but it also may literally imply that he is singing his song from Tahrir Square. This communal solidarity created throughout the song may also be the result of the physical proximity between him and the martyr.

The question addressed directly to the martyr and followed by the imperative "tell me who you are" again emphasizes both the nonspecificty of this individual and yet the familiarity between the martyr and the singer.

sa:yibni: le:-h miḥta:r kida ma:-taʔu:l-li: tiṭlaʕ mi:n

Why do you leave me confounded?—Do tell me: Who are you?

Names are mentioned to refer to religion in the question:

huwwa ʔinta ʔaḥmad w-la: girgis w-la: ṣo:t malayi:n

Are you Ahmed or Girgis or the voice of millions?

We, in fact, are left in the dark as to whether this martyr is Christian or Muslim. The religious differences are reduced to differences in proper names, yet the habits, characteristics, features, and skin color are all the same. The question adds nonspecifity to this martyr and undermines any potential religious differences. The song moves from the individual man with dark skin who appears to be a typical Egyptian to a martyr—a general term to refer to all who died to symbolize the demands of all Egyptians. The singer moves from the specific to the general, from doubt to certainty.

b-aʃabbih ʕale:-k
ya: lli: ḍaḥi:t bi-ru:ḥ-ak ya: wa:ḥid minni-na:
w-sa:yib ʔahl-ak w-na:s-ak ʕalaʃana kulli-na:
ya: ʃahi:d ʔinta maka:n-ak fi-l-ganna muʃ hina:

I think I saw you before:
You, who sacrificed your life, oh one of us,
And you left behind your family and your people for the sake of all of us.
Oh, you martyr, your place is in heaven, not here!

The vocative *ya:* is used to define the martyr. He is "one of us" who sacrificed himself and left his family and community behind for "our sake." The song then moves from direct questions to the martyr to assertive statements about "'him." He is one of us. His sacrifice is not in vain.

The song ends with the proposition that the proper place for this martyr is heaven, not earth. The proposition comes in the form of a verbless sentence and negation is used to add definiteness to the place of the martyr.

ya: ʃahi:d ʔinta maka:n-ak fi-l-ganna muʃ hina:

Oh, you martyr, your place is in heaven, not here!

Dialogicality is indeed employed here. During the 2011 Revolution, the pro-Mubarak group accused the protestors of treason and of working for foreign agencies. The assertion of the proper place of the martyr is a direct reply to the accusations against the protestors.

In this song, the stance of the singer is that of the fellow Egyptian. The singer moves from doubt to certainty regarding precisely which Egyptian is this martyr. Knowing his name may enable the singer to demonstrate the Egyptian characteristics that he shares with this unidentified Egyptian. The singer then realizes the futility of his attempts to uncover the identity of this Egyptian and realizes that the Egyptian is a symbol of every Egyptian. While the song starts with the stance of the singer as familiar with the martyr as a specific individual, the song ends with the martyr as a symbol of all Egyptian martyrs, including both Christians and Muslims. However, the fact that this martyr is God-sent to Egyptians implies that God is on their side. The singer appeals to Egyptians' religiosity without distinguishing between Christians and Muslims: both are martyrs, both love their country, and both will go to heaven. He uses two common techniques: Christian, Muslim, personal names, as well as generic mention of God to include both religions and undermine differences between them.

There is complete identification with the martyr throughout, as is apparent in the use of deixis, modals, aspectual markers, negation, pronouns, propositions, assertive statements, and mention of identity categories, such as color, names, habits, and character traits. The stance of the singer is positive towards the martyr throughout.

In patriotic songs, linguistic resources are used to reflect Egyptian identity in different ways, but also to emphasize the inclusiveness of this identity of both Christianity and Islam. Through adopting different stances, singers have shown how important religion is by stating that God is on their side, without highlighting differences between the Christian or Muslim God or other key distinctions. While tensions do rise every now and then, public discourse does not undermine one religion or the other, but in fact highlights religion generally as an essential part of the identity of Egyptians. Public discourse undermines differences between Muslims and Christians inside Egypt, almost emphasizing the distinctive cohesive relationship between the Christians and Muslims of Egypt as different from other parts of the Arab world and the world at large.

The identity of Egyptians as Arabs and the direct role that language choice plays in identity construction in patriotic songs will be discussed in detail in the next sections.

4.5 Arabic language as an independent social variable

Arabic as an independent variable and marker of identity is mentioned only four times in patriotic songs and, as with other variables, is not mentioned in isolation, but in conjunction with other variables, such as ethnicity, history, and locality. However, during times of upheaval and political tension, language is called upon usually as one of the main markers of identity in the Arab world and in Egypt specifically. Chapter 6 tackles this issue in more detail and discusses how language is manipulated as a resource and an independent variable. Although Arabic as an independent variable is mentioned only a few times, the context in which it occurs renders it essential. Consider the four examples below.

(24) *al-waṭan il-akbar* ("My greater homeland") by ʿAbd al-Ḥalīm Ḥāfiẓ, Shādiyah, Sabāḥ, Wardah, Fāyizah Kāmil, and Najāt al-Ṣaghīrah (1960)
il-ṣo:t ṣo:tak ḥurri w-ʕarabi:
miʃ ṣada: ʃarʔi: wala ṣada: ġarbi:

Your voice is free and Arab
It does not have echoes of the western or Eastern bloc.

In this song, a number of singers from different parts of the Arab world sing to and about the Arab nation, *al-waṭan il-akbar* ("the greater homeland"). It is highly significant that all participants in the song sing in ECA. The Egyptian female singer Shādiyah refers to the voice of this Arab homeland. This reference is not just to Arabic as a language, but to Arabic as rendering a unique political identity different from the Eastern and Western Bloc of the time. Nasser was a propagator of the non-alignment policy and encouraged the Arab world to join the Non-Alignment Movement.

Shādiyah addresses the greater homeland—the Arab nation—in the singular masculine second person; this (synthetic) personification emphasizes the intimacy between Shādiyah, an Egyptian, and her fellow Arabs. Shādiyah refers to "Arabic," an inclusive term that refers to both dialects SA and ECA. This may index her authenticity and spontaneity in evaluating the nature of the Arab nation, which is a unique nature, because of language and political non-alignment. The use of ECA, as was implied before, may be a natural outcome of the Egyptian production of the song or an implication of the political domination that Nasser aspired to.

(25) From *yibʔa ʔinta ʔaki:d il-maṣri:* ("Surely you are the Egyptian") by Laṭīfah (2001)
tiʕraf bil ʕarabi tina:di:
b-ismi Lla:h wi b-ismi bila:di:
nu:r lil-ʕa:lam yisri:
yibʕa ʔinta aki:d il-maṣri:

Do you know how to call out in Arabic,
In the name of God and my country,
"Let light shine forth to the world!"
—Then surely you are the Egyptian!

In this song, female Tunisian pop singer Laṭifah sings in ECA, with lyrics that define "the" Egyptian. She starts her song with questions addressed to Egyptians, the answers to which determine their identity. The questions presuppose that Egyptians speak Arabic, worship and believe in God (note the generic and neutral mention of God), and love their country. She positions herself as the knowledgeable outsider who also masters the code, ECA, as a sign of her knowledge and identification with Egyptians. Modality is also used in this song to highlight the uniqueness of Egyptians. The assertive statement above is again in the form of a verbless sentence (*ʔinta aki:d il-maṣri:* ("Surely you are the Egyptian")), while the question–answer structure of the song renders the whole postulation factual and directly related. The singer addresses the Egyptian in the second person singular masculine: *tiʕraf/ ʔinta* ("you (2 m. sg.) know"/"you"). Mention of Arabic is again inclusive, although the song—just like the previous one—is in ECA. What is, indeed, worth mentioning is the leveling that takes place in the statement:

b-ismi Lla:h wi b-ismi bila:di:

In the name of God and my country

This statement is rendered almost in the same way in ECA and SA, given that most spoken SA does not include case and mood marking.

(26) *il-ḥilm il-ʕarabi:* ("The Arab dream") by Various Artists (1998)
Min ʔayyi maka:n fil ʔarḍ
Na:ṭig bi-lisa:n iḍ-ḍa:ḍ
Wi b-ʔaʕla iṣ-ṣu:t wi-nabḍ
bi-nʔu:l il-wiḥda mila:d

From any place on earth
that speaks the language of the *da:d* [i.e. Arabic],
with a loud voice, and the beat of our heart
we say that unity is birth.

In "The Arab dream" (analyzed again in the next section), singers from different parts of the Arab world take a positive stance towards the Arab nation, but their statements are mostly general and do not pertain to a specific place or people. Although they speak about the Arab dream, the only reference to a unifying factor in the song is the reference to language and the Palestinian struggle. This is unlike the song "My greater homeland," in which there were references to each Arab country by name and the struggle of each country towards the colonizing powers.

The singer who refers to Arabic as a unifying factor is a Saudi male singer, which is clear by the phonological salient realization of SA *q* as *g*—a Bedouin feature, rather than an urban glottal stop. In this song, language is the defining factor. It is related to the confidence and strength of the voice that calls for unity. Unity is defined in a verbless assertive statement:

bi-nʔu:l il-wiḥda mila:d

We say that unity is birth

The Egyptian aspectual marker *bi-* is used by the Saudi singer to denote the continuity of the state of unity and to emphasize the fact that "we" all still believe in this unity. The fact that the Saudi singer uses an ECA aspectual marker is significant and may just refer to the production of the song, which is dominated by Egyptians, or to a cultural hegemony that Egypt aspires to. Using the salient Bedouin feature, *g*, and the Egyptian aspectual marker may indicate the intentional mixing of codes to blur differences between Arabs. It is also interesting that it occurs when language is called upon as a social variable. It may imply that even with dialectical differences, Arabs still speak Arabic and are therefore "one."

I will conclude this section with the following song, which combines almost all variables discussed in the chapter. The poem or song is in SA, sung by the famous Lebanese singer Mājdah al-Rūmī.[27] For a change, the song refers to a female Egyptian, rather than the typical male that is generally used. The poet, a Lebanese man, is fascinated and mesmerized by the Egyptian woman. He starts describing the Egyptian woman and then narrates an echoing conversation between them, in which the Egyptian woman asks him whether he will forget her. She then starts defining herself in a manner that echoes that of al-Tūnisī in 1921, "I am the Egyptian"—the song that was analyzed at the beginning of this chapter.

The poet, an outsider, has a positive stance towards the Egyptian woman and starts with a number of assertive statements, again constructed in the form of verbless clauses.

(26) *samra:ʔ* ("Dark-skinned woman") by Mājdah al-Rūmī (1996)
samra:ʔ ka-layl is-sahra:ni wa-ka-ṭallati bint is-sulṭa:ni (2)
samra:ʔ
min farḥati ʔarḍin ʔazaliyya
min rannati ʕu:din ʃarqiyya
laftatu-ha: l-xiffa
xuṭwatu-ha: ir-raqṣa
lahjatu-ha: l-miṣriyya
(. . .)
wa-tusa:ʔilu-ni: hal tansa:-ni:
hal taðkuru dawman ʕunwa:n-i:
(. . .)
ʔana bintu n-ni:l wa-zahu: ij-ji:li bi-kul jami:lin talqa:-ni:
fi: qamar il-layli wa-mawj il-baḥari wa-ʃams iṣ-ṣaḥra: tara:-ni:
fi: wajhi d-dunya: katabu:-ni: li-luġa:t id-dunya: naqalu:-ni:

wa-ʔiʃta:qu: li: wa-ʔaḥabbu:-ni:
ʔana lastu ʔimraʔatan ʕa:di:ya
ʔana miṣriyya

She is dark like the sleepless night; like the visage of the Sultan's daughter;
Dark,
From the joy of the land of eternity,
From the tune of an oriental lute,
Her gestures are light and joyful,
Her steps are a dance,
Her accent is Egyptian.
She asks me, "have you forgotten me?"
"Will you always remember my name?"
I'm the child of the Nile and the pride of my generation; you'll find me in all beauty
In the moon of the night and the waves of the sea and the sun of the desert, you'll see me.
They wrote about me in the face of earth and translated me to all languages
I am not an ordinary woman, I am Egyptian.

The first variable that describes the Egyptian girl is her dark, tan skin color, which marks her ethnicity. In his description and evaluation of her, he mentions her origin: the Egyptian girl springs from a land that is eternal—a reference to historicity. She is also the product of the music of the East. There is reference to her as joyful, which perhaps also means humorous. The variable that distinguishes her specifically as Egyptian is her Egyptian dialect, as opposed to other dialects in the Arab world, including that of the poet and the singer. This is the first and the only time that Egyptian Arabic, rather than the more inclusive term "Arabic," is mentioned in patriotic songs. The fact that the poem is in SA makes the contrast clear. In this case, ECA is a social variable that distinguishes Egyptians from other Arabs.

When the Egyptian woman speaks, she does so in SA, asking whether the poet will forget her. This is a clear example of how perception plays a pivotal role in identity construction. In this case, the poet was perhaps unwilling to switch to ECA to prove that this is the language she speaks. So the words of the Egyptian woman are in SA, but she is still perceived as speaking in ECA. She then starts defining herself and mentions the River Nile (locality), just as al-Tūnisī did in his classic "I am the Egyptian." However, when the Egyptian woman defines herself, she also refers to language, and she does not refer to Arabic only, but to all world languages. She prides herself in being important to the extent that she has been written about in all languages. In a way, she, as al-

Tūnisī did, positions herself as a transhistorical being, who is essential for humanity or for the history of all humanity. She implies that she was written about because of her ancestors' historical achievements. The negation at the end asserts her uniqueness. Again, it comes in the form of a verbless sentence. Note that the poet claims the Egyptian woman speaks in ECA, although his claim is in SA. She claims that she has been transformed and transmitted into all world languages and her claim is also in SA. This renders her beyond time. SA indexes this generality and inclusiveness.

This example also shows how public discourse reiterates the same concepts of Egyptians' identification with their past achievements or what Wodak (1999) calls dilation of time. When defining herself to a sympathetic outsider, as al-Tūnisī did years ago, the Egyptian woman refers to historicity, locality, and her uniqueness as an Egyptian. She refers to what we called the "backbone." The outsider poet refers to ethnicity and habits.

Although mentioned rarely in patriotoic songs, language remains an essential factor in identity construction, as will be clear in the next two chapters. Language comes to the forefront at times of conflict. Usage of ECA in general may reflect attempts at cultural hegemony and the mention of the distinctive dialect of Egyptians is a reflection of uniqueness.

4.6 The "Arab" component in the "Egyptian" identity

Questions such as "are Egyptians Arabs" crop up from time to time, and they are often strongly tied to political events. To give an example, while in 2010 Egyptians and Algerians both accused each other of not being "Arab enough" because of a football match between them, this was forgotten in 2011 after the Jasmine Revolution in Tunisia. In this instance, Egyptians emphasized their solidarity with fellow Tunisians and aimed to follow suit and revolt. During upheavals, Egyptians in public discourse promote themselves as either the core of Arabness (as was the case in the 1950s, 1960s, and, to a great extent, in 2011) or not Arab at all (as at the end of the 1970s, 1980s, and the beginning of the 1990s when Egypt was ostracized by the Arab world, because of their peace with Israel). For a full discussion of this fluctuating attitude, see Suleiman (2004; 2011). In this section, songs that deal directly with the Arab aspect of Egyptian identity or that consider Egypt as part of a bigger Arab entity will be discussed. What is interesting about these songs are the concrete facts mentioned to render Egypt Arab and the choice of code between ECA, SA, or both. Before starting this discussion, I would like to appeal to a quote repeated in a work by Jamāl Ḥamdān (Ḥamdān 1981: 507–8):

> Without linguistic unity, a people does not really have any unity at all.
> [. . .]
> Ethnicity is simply another attribute, a third dimension that supports national unity.
> [. . .]
> Arabness is a cultural concept, not an ethnic concept. If we want to measure the degree of Arabness of Egyptians then we cannot measure it according to ethnicity. Arabness is not about how much Arab blood Egyptians have, but how much Arabic is used in Egypt. The measurement of Arabness is not ethnicity, but language. If Arabs succeeded in Arabizing Egypt culturally, Egypt had succeeded in egyptianizing the Arabs that settled in it.

The role of language in this quote is highly emphasized, but there is no claim that Egyptians share the same ethnic identity as other Arabs (which is why ethnicity is one of the backbone variables). In fact, this claim is never made in any song analyzed in this study, even those songs that identify completely with other Arabs. Language is always at the forefront of such discussions, as is a shared history of manipulation by outsiders, usually a colonizing power or the Palestinian–Israeli conflict.

Note that in this quote, Egypt's cultural hegemony is mentioned and will be reflected in the choice of code in the songs analyzed.

It is noteworthy that on its official webpage, the Arab League defines itself as comprised of countries in which Arabic is the official language. This includes countries that perhaps at first sight do not seem Arab, such as Djibouti and the Comoros Islands. Arabic, rather than religion or ethnicity, is the main unifying factor for all Arabs. It is implied that SA is what is meant by "Arabic." This also explains why proposals to make a colloquial dialect an official language of a country are met with fear and shock by Arab intellectuals. However, the role of SA, as opposed to the colloquial dialects, is more complex than it seems at first.[28]

Code-choice plays a pivotal role in this section. The first two songs referred to are the two most prominent ones regarding Arab unity. One was produced in 1960, the other in 1998. To date, there have been some attempts to produce more songs about Arab unity, especially after the Arab Spring, but none have been as popular as the two mentioned above.[29] What both songs have in common is that they have Egyptian writers, producers, and composers, but they have singers from all parts of the Arab world.

In the 1960 song "My greater homeland," the Arab world is referred to as *al-waṭan il-akbar* ("the greater homeland"). The singers take turns and each address the great homeland as one entity in the masculine singular second person. There is familiarity and direct conversation between the singers and the great homeland.

This song includes singers from Syria, Lebanon, Algeria, and Egypt and is one of the few songs about Arab unity that also has Arab singers from different countries. They all sing in Egyptian Arabic, rather than their own dialects or, as may be expected, SA, which is the neutral inclusive dialect. Whether this language choice is also a reflection of Egypt's aspirations of political hegemony at the time or is just an outcome of the production conditions is difficult to know. However, it is clear that ECA was considered a semi-standard at the time, and it was not considered by the producers as a hindrance to the success of the song in the Arab world at large.

This song is about the Arab world; the unity among different Arabs who share a common history of manipulation by colonizers; and Arabs who aspire to reach better future—these features are significant in more than one way.

First, most Arab countries are mentioned, including Gulf and North African countries, in addition to Syria, Iraq, and Lebanon. Names of Arab countries act as a unification mechanism. Furthermore, the use of only one dialect, ECA, is important and perhaps expected, since at the time Egypt considered itself as the leader in Arab unity. The Arab world is not referred to in this song as a nation, but as a great country or homeland, something even closer than a nation. ECA acts as the intimate familiar code for this close and informal relationship among Arabs in the Arab world. These indexes of ECA were not uncommon at the time and often went hand-in-hand with the indexes of SA as the unifying language of all Arabs, as well as the language of Arab intellectuals.

To reflect on language attitude at the time, I will mention two films that deal with the theme of Arab unity, both of which were produced in Egypt. Two films that echo political unification under Nasser are *Wā Islāmāh* ("Woe to Islam") (1961) and *Nāṣir Salāḥ al-Dīn* ("Saladin") (1963). The former is about the Mongol invasion of the Arab world and Egypt's role in confronting the Mongols and eventually defeating them, while the latter deals with Saladin and his role in unifying Arabs to confront the Crusaders. The parallelism between Saladin and Nasser is clear to an Arab audience, even from the title of the films. *Wā Islāmāh* is mainly in ECA, whereas *Nāṣir Salāḥ al-Dīn* is also predominantly in ECA, but contains insertions from SA. On more than one occasion, Saladin himself speaks in a leveled form of ECA, as do his soldiers and the English, French, and other foreign kings in the film. The dominance of ECA is not a coincidence in both films, as the indexes of ECA are called upon as the authentic intimate code. Additionally, Egyptian politicians at the time considered Egypt the heart and natural leader of the Arab world—the use of ECA reflects this underlying stance. Political hegemony is reflected in the hegemony of ECA, rather than the neutral SA.

Because all Arabs and, significantly, the foreigners in the films and song speak primarily in ECA, the public discourse of the time highlighted the Egyptians' sincere role as the defenders of the Arab cause. This complete identification of all Arabs with ECA, as reflected in the public discourse of the time, was to an extent lost after Nasser's death.

In the first song about Arab unity, "My greater homeland" (1960), all of the singers use ECA. In the song "The Arab dream," on the other hand, there are some features from other colloquial dialects, even though the structure of the lyrics, as well as the chorus, is in ECA. However, code-switching to different dialects, especially on the phonological level, does occur. In both songs, the dominance of ECA may also imply an aspiration of cultural hegemony. By speaking about Arabs and portraying all Arabs as not only understanding ECA but also speaking it, the producers index ECA as a semi-formal code at the same level or slightly subordinate to SA. Note the difference between the 1960 song in ECA only and the 1998 song where phonological features from other colloquial dialects are used. In both songs, language is not just used to index attitudes and ideologies, but is used as a social variable, part-and-parcel of the social world.

A more recent song takes a more subtle, different stance, although Egypt's attempts at linguistic hegemony are still clear. The song "The Arab dream," which was discussed above, does not mention location as a unifying factor as "My greater homeland" did, nor does it mention the historical struggles against colonizing powers as a unifying factor, but mentions language and the Palestinian struggle as the unifying factors. The code used in this song is more innovative. There are, again, singers from different parts of the Arab world, including singers from the Gulf, unlike in "My greater homeland" where the Gulf was mentioned by non-Gulf singers. The song's refrain, sung by a chorus, is in ECA. There are salient ECA phonological features, such as the use of *g* instead of *j* in *ga:yiz*, which only Egyptians use. The chorus addresses "us," Arabs, everywhere. Location is undermined and language is highlighted. The song thus appeals to Arabs who immigrated to non-Arabic speaking countries, such as in the film *Hammām in Amsterdam*. However, it is not SA that is the unifying language, but all colloquial dialects of Arabs, although these dialects are leveled for the purpose of this song (on leveling, see Bassiouney 2007). While there are singers from most parts of the Arab world, they attempt to use a leveled code, in which clear phonological features of their variety is used, although the whole structure of their lines is modified to be understood by Arabs not familiar with their variety. The song is thus leveled towards ECA structure. Each singer uses his or her own phonological repertoire to give the whole song a more authentic flavor. Note the use of /g/ to realize the SA /q/, rather than the ECA glottal stop.

Singers, one by one, evaluate the Arab dream and position themselves as experts in the Arab world. They also address a male second person singular, who symbolizes all Arabs.

(27) From *il-ḥilm il-ʕarabi:* ("The Arab dream") (1998)
ʔagya:l wara: ʔagya:l ha-taʕi:ʃ ʕala: ḥilmi-na:
w-illi: niʔu:l-u l-yo:m maḥsu:b ʕala: ʕumri-na:
ga:yiz ẓala:m il-le:l yibʕid-na: yo:m ʔinnama:
yiʔdar ʃuʕa:ʕ in-nu:r yu:ṣal li-ʔabaʕd sama:
da ḥilmi-na: ṭu:l ʕumri-na:
ḥuḍni yaḍumi-na: kuli-na: kuli-na:

*el-ḥilm ma:-hu: mustaḥi:l ma: da:m taḥ***gi:g***-u muba:ḥ*
w-il-le:l law ṣa:r ṭuwi:l ʔaki:d min baʕd-u ṣaba:ḥ
ku:n ʔinta b-kulli ma: fi:-k ʔin ka:n li:-k w-la: ʕale:-k
ḥa:wil jarrab w-bi-tu:ṣal ʃaraf it-tajruba yikfi:-k

Generation after generation, we will live according to our dream.
What we say today is recorded throughout our lives.
The night's shadow may separate us, but:
The ray of light can reach the farthest sky.
That's our dream, all our life long:
An embrace that takes us in, all of us.

A dream does not remain impossible, as long as realizing it is within our grasp.
For even if the night is long, it is always followed by morning.
Be yourself, with everything that you are,
With your mistakes and your achievements.
Try, experience, and you'll arrive:
The honor of the experience is enough for you.

Note the following factual statement, in which phonological and syntactic features of Gulf Arabic are used:

el-ḥilm ***ma:****-hu: mustaḥi:l* ***ma: da:m*** *taḥ***gi:g***-u muba:ḥ*

A dream does not remain impossible, as long as realizing it is within our grasp.

The negation is used to assert the fact that a dream is still possible, and the statement comes in the form of a verbless sentence in Gulf Arabic.

What the two songs discuss is the Arab nation, yet they address this issue differently. The first song mentions the struggle against the colonizers as the unifying factor and then provides place names as concrete evidence of the unifying struggle. The singers address the great homeland and its "people" more generally.

In "The Arab dream," the singers take a similar positive stance and position themselves as the experts and use synthetic personification. However, they all urge the Arabs to rise up and capture the dream. However, the dream is never concrete, and the whole song can be about any place and any country, not necessarily the Arab world specifically. If not for mention of language and the Palestinian struggle, there would be nothing specific about this song that refers to Arabs. The Palestinian struggle is referenced by the mention of children who carry stones and nothing else. The singers expect an Arab audience to understand associations of this image. When broadcast, the song was played over images of Palestinian children and the Palestinian strife, but did not include images of other Arab countries.

After the Arab Spring, there would seem to be more concrete material for songs about Arab unification. However, this new solidarity between Arabs so far is not built on the common SA, nor is it built on struggles against colonizers, but rather it is built on struggles against copycat dictatorial regimes and the perception of the "Arab" as yearning for freedom and justice. One attempt has already been made in a song combining Tunisians and Egyptians singing together, *niḥlim* ("We dream") (March 2011a). The Tunisians sing in their colloquial with no leveling and the Egyptians do the same. The song is not popular, as of this moment of writing.

Another Egyptian song, *aḥla: ʃaba:b* ("The best youth") (2011b), refers to the struggles against dictatorship in Tunisia, Syria, Yemen, Libya, Bahrain, and Egypt. Again, these are all songs that are not yet popular throughout the Arab world. What they have in common is that they are not in SA. "The best youth" is in ECA, while "We dream" code-switches between ECA and TCA (Tunisian Colloquial Arabic). What is, indeed, interesting in "We dream" is that, unlike "The Arab dream," the chorus in this song sings in TCA, not ECA. The word *niḥlim* ("to dream") is pronounced in TCA, rather than in the ECA pronunciation, which involves a different vowel quality, *niḥlam*. As expected, the song is a Tunisian–Egyptian co-production. This lack of leveling may be because Tunisians initiated the Arab Spring and thus it may add more authenticity to the song. That is, since it refers to the young people in both countries, it is supposed to realistically present the language of these young people.

The two songs examined above are about Arabs, whereas the following song deals with Egyptian identity and Arabness as *part* of this identity. The example mentioned here comes from an Egyptian classic, *ṣo:t bila:di* ("The voice of my country") (1980).

(28) From *ṣo:t bila:d-i:* ("The voice of my country") by Various Artists (1980)
ṣo:t ʃaʕbi maṣri: wi ʔaʕẓam ma fi:h
ʔayyi axxi ʕarabi yiʕu:zu yilaʔi:h

It is the voice of the Egyptian people,
and the best thing about them is
that if any Arab brother needs them [i.e. the Egyptians]
he'll find them.

Egyptians are first referred to as "the Egyptian people," but the pronouns for "them" (that is, the Egyptians) and his "brother" (the Arab) are both in the singular to emphasize the intimacy between both: they have a one-to-one relationship of brotherhood. Egyptians are positioned as the helpers or givers. The lines above presuppose that Arabs are brothers, but that "we" are Egyptian and that it is the Arab who will need the Egyptian. The verbless clause emphasizes that the Egyptian will always be there for his Arab brother.

This is another song that addresses Arab unity, but that also depicts the competition between different Arab identities and nationalities. Code-choice plays an essential role in this song. This is a song in which an Egyptian woman, Amīnah, and a Lebanese man, Hishām, brag about their identity as manifest in their history and in the achievements of artists, singers, and other prominent figures of their countries. Thus, historicity forms the backbone of their argument. In the video clip that accompanies the song, the Egyptian singer appears in Pharoanic clothes, while the Lebanese singer is dressed in Phoenician attire. Amīnah refers to the River Nile as her father (locality) and the pyramids as her mother (historicity); Hishām refers to Baalbek (locality and historicity) as his mother and Jabal Ṣini:n (Mount Sannine) as his father (locality, historicity). Their ethnic identity is therefore explicitly related to their ancestors and their land. They both reference the cultural legacy of their respective countries through the mention of singers, such as Umm Kulthūm for Egypt and Fairuz for Lebanon. Tension rises over the course of the song, and it seems that a physical conflict will break out between them: the video clip depicts an Egyptian Army (dressed in the Egyptian *galabiyya* typical of the countryside) and the Lebanese Army (in Lebanese Bedouin attire). However, the conflict dissolves in a second when Amīnah mentions that she has always loved Beirut, whereupon Hishām also confesses that he always loved Egypt or Cairo. The affinity between a Lebanese and an Egyptian springs from their emotional attachment to each others' locations.

What is, indeed, interesting in this song are the codes that are employed. As far as I know, this is the only song in which code-switching and language choice is used directly to symbolize both identity and conflict.

To begin with, Hishām sings in Lebanese colloquial Arabic and Amīnah sings in ECA up until the end of the song, at which point

Amīnah accommodates her code phonologically to Lebanese colloquial Arabic and Hishām accommodates to ECA. Both then acknowledge their love and admiration of each other's country. Divergence and convergence as two processes related to code-switching are manipulated: when they compete with each other, each singer uses their own dialect, but when they reach out for each other, they also converge towards each other's dialects.[30] Note the following example:

(29) *balad-na: (maṣri:ya w-ṭabaʕ-i: ʔa:si:)* ("Our country [I'm Egyptian and I'm harsh]") by Hishām al-Ḥājj and Amīnah (2010)
(singers: A = Amīnah, H = Hishām)

A: *maṣriyya w-ṭabʕ-i: ʔa:si: w-fi: l-ʃaʔa:wa: ma:-li:-ʃ*
ya: ḥaggi law kunti na:si: zayyi maṣr la: ma:-fi:-ʃ

H: *jba:l w-ḥala: w-msku: tura:b w-dahab rana:n*
ya:ba: siti di:-ni: w-ma: fi: mitil lbina:n

A: *a:h ya: wadd ya: gami:l ma:-bala:ʃ kutr ik-kala:m*
da ʔabu:-ya nahr in-ni:l w-ʔumm-i: hiyya l-ʔahra:m

H: *ba-ʕalb-ak hiyyih ʔimm-i: w-bayyi jabal ṣini:n*
faxar id-di:n ʕamm-i: jidu:d-i: l-fini:ʔiyyi:n

A: "I am an Egyptian, not to be toyed with and do not accept nonsense.
In case you forget, old man, there is no place like Egypt!"

H: "Mountains, sand and Gold, my dear the mistress of the world is Beirut and there is no place like Lebanon"

A: "Hey, handsome, stop bragging!
My father is the Nile and my mother the Pyramids."

H: "My mother is Baalbek, and my father is Mount Sannine.
Fakhr al-Dīn is my uncle, and my ancestors are the Phoenicians."

Note Amīnah's frequent use of the salient realization of *ji:m* as /g/ in Egypt. This does not happen in any other country. She addresses Hishām with his last name and pronounces it in a quintessentially Egyptian way: *hagg* rather than *ha:jj*. When she refers to him again as *gami:l* ("handsome"), she again realizes it with the salient ECA /g/. Later in the song when they reconcile, she refers to him by his first name and starts using LCA phonological features. Note this example:

A: ʕa:rif ana minisni:n baʕsaʔ hawa: bayru:t
H: ya ḥilwit il-ḥilwi:n ana bi-maṣr bamu:t
A: ya: hiʃa:m ʔana b-aʕʃaʔ bayru:t
H: w-il-la:hi ya: ʔami:na ʔana ʔilli: bi:-ki: b-amu:t

A: "You know, for years I have loved Beirut."
H: "You, the most beautiful of them all, I adore Egypt."
A: "Hishām, I do love Beirut."
H: "By God, Amīnah, I die for you."

Note that Amīnah uses *minisni:n* ("for years"), rather than the Egyptian form *min sini:n*. This accommodation on her part to the phonological repertoire of LCA is countered with Hishām's use of the ECA lexical expression *ya ḥilwit il-ḥilwi:n* ("you, the most beautiful of them all"). This mutual display of solidarity is also apparent in the change of terms of address. Their stance has also changed: whereas in the first part, both took a stance as confident, knowledgeable, and competitive Arabs, the pair now position themselves as Arabs who are still confident in their historicity, ethnicity, and oral legacy, but who also show solidarity in their admiration of each other. This stance is apparent in the indexes of their code-choice and terms of address.

It is interesting that SA is not used as the neutral code. Instead, accommodation to the code of the other is employed. It would seem that leveling and accommodation are important in emphasizing an "Arab" identity, and that in the context of these songs, it is the colloquial dialects that unite Arabs, rather than the neutral SA.

An example that is worth mentioning to conclude this section is a recent parody of the song *al-waṭan il-akbar* ("My greater homeland"), which was broadcast on CBC—an Egyptian private channel—on the Egyptian version of the Jon Stewart show, al-Barnāmig ("The programme"), featuring Bāsim Yūsuf. The parody used the same music and costumes as the original, with Bāsim Yūsuf in the role of the conductor (the role played by the composer Muḥammad ʿAbd al-Wahhab in the 1960 original). The parody was broadcast on the April 5, 2013. Within a month, it had more than six million views on YouTube alone. This song is not about the Arab world, but about the unequal relationship between Egypt and Qatar. There were claims at the time within Egyptian media that Qatar had lent Egypt three billion dollars, and rumors ran wild that Qatar was to buy the Suez Canal or even rent the pyramids. Instead of listing Arab countries that were influenced by the Egyptian Revolution as the 1960 song does, the parody lists Cairo streets and laments the abject state of Egypt, who has to beg money from Qatar. Here are some of the lines from the parody:

(30) *qaṭar-i: ḥabi:b-i:* ("My beloved Qatar") by Bāsim Yūsuf (2013)
qatari: ḥabi:bi il-axi al-azġar
yo:m wara yo:m amwa:luh b-tiktarr
inta kibi:r wa kbrar kiti:r min il xali:g kulluh
min il-tari:x kulluh ya qatari:

My dear the Qatari, my younger brother
Day after day his money increases
You are so big, bigger than all the Gulf
Bigger than all history.

The original of this part (from *al-waṭan il-akbar* ("My greater homeland")) is the following:

Waṭani ḥabi:bi al-waṭan il-akbar
Yo:m wara yo:m amga:du b-tikbar
(. . .)
Inta kibi:r wa akbar kiti:r min il-wugu:d kulluh
Min il-khulu:d kullu

My dear homeland, the greater homeland
Day after day your glory increases
(. . .)
You are big, bigger than all the universe
and bigger than eternity.

Note that Qatar is referenced as the "younger brother"—the reference is, of course, an allusion to the size of Qatar. The song also mentions history and the pyramids. Again, historicity, the physical size of Egypt, and its current abject state are all essential facts in understanding the parody. There is no contestation that Egypt owns "history" and may now sell such a precious part of its identity to Qatar, because of its current economic crisis. See the example below:

bi:ʕ lil-qatari: wi xudd min xe:ru
bi:ʕ lu-alharam wi bni: itne:n ġe:ru

Sell to the Qatari and take from his money
Sell him the Pyramids and build two more.

In this song, Egyptians are lamenting their abject state and also the fact that they do not have political hegemony anymore in the Arab world; they do not serve as an inspiration to other countries, as they did at the time of the original song. The parody is a reaction to the political status quo. In my opinion, the parody only serves to show that the social attributes discussed are immanent, visible in the mind of Egyptians as attributes that were real aand concrete. They may, of course, disagree as to which part of their history is more valuable, but they take for granted their historical backing.

4.7 Discussion and conclusions

4.7.1 "The paradox of the knowledgeable Egyptian": discursive and structural resources

It is obvious that this chapter is largely descriptive in nature. On the one hand, it aims to show how Egyptians define themselves in public discourse. Patriotic songs have been used as an example of public discourse, because of their importance and popularity in highlighting and reasserting certain core conceptions. What I hope to have quite clearly shown is that historicity, ethnicity, and locality form the backbone of discourse on Egyptian identity and that there is a remarkable continuity and consistency in the use of these themes since the beginning of the twentieth century, when they were first used as markers of identity. In the study, these themes regularly co-occur with references to Egyptian character traits, habits, and communal solidarity.

During the stance-taking process of singers, discursive and structural resources are used. However, more importantly, a recurring strategy used in patriotic songs will be discussed below in relation to Bell's audience design framework. Bell (1984: 197) argues that linguistic variation is the outcome of individuals responding to an audience. That is, speakers "design their style to their audience. An audience includes addressee, third persons' auditors and overhearers" (1984: 145). In Bell's discussion on the language of mass communication, he refers to two essential concepts: initiative style and referee design. Initiative style creates the relationship between "communicator and audience." That is, instead of responding to a matter of fact relation between communicator and audience, initiative style creates and establishes this relation. On the radio, for example, communicators may use style as an "expressive instrument" to signify a shared identity between communicator and audience or in some cases to mark a different identity, an ingroup, or an out group identity (1984: 192). Referee design is defined by Bell as divergence from the addressee towards an absent referee group (145). This design is common in media in which the third persons, overhearers, and auditors are ideal, absent, and untangible in most cases, and there is usually no direct feedback from them. In these cases, speakers manifest their ingroup solidarity to this ideal absent group through language.

The paradox of media language according to Bell is that while communicators take the initiative in most cases, they are still completely dependent on the audience for their livelihood and survival. Bell (1984: 193) states that this paradox can be resolved

> when we see that communicators persuade by using language as an expression of shared identity with the audience (. . .) ideally, the audience will regard a

mass medium as its voice. The best communicators (and leaders) thus make the people's voice their own, and their voice the people's.

In the songs analyzed in this book, there is a general tendency for singers to position themselves as knowledgeable arbiters on Egypt and Egyptians and to provide a positive evaluation of what it means to be Egyptian. Interestingly, the lyrics often target an addressee that either does not know or may not be fully convinced of Egyptian positive identity markers. To reference this positive stance, the singer uses various linguistic resources and also repeats lexical identification categories that already carry indexes for her or his audience. Positioning the addressee as either an outsider or a reluctant insider is essential to be able to argue the positive aspects of Egypt.

This positioning happens through the use of different resources that include mainly what Fairclough (1989: 205) calls "synthetic personification," which is a strategy usually adopted in advertisements to create a direct and informal relationship between the audience and the speaker in the advertisement (see Nordquist 2010). This technique highlights the conversational style of the songs, as well as the informality and sincerity of the singer and his or her evaluated object—that is, Egyptian identity. When a colonizer or an aggressive outsider is referenced in a song, third person is often used instead of second person, as in the case of "Egypt speaks about itself." In this example, Egypt refers to colonizers in the third person plural. In the case of the song *ḥabibt-i: ya: maṣr* ("Egypt, my love"), the person who does not understand Egyptians is referred to in the third person singular. In my view, this manipulation of pronouns is intentional and attempts to undermine the aggressive, unfriendly, unsympathetic outsider, while appealing to the insider or a sympathetic outsider. One might argue that outsiders are divided into two categories: those with knowledge and those without; those who are important (referred to with a second person pronoun) and those who lack power and influence (referred to in the third person). This style of positioning is artificial, of course, since the singer appeals to ideologies already shared by his audience. These ideologies and perceptions are difficult to understand or appreciate for non-Egyptians, especially the hyperbole of the glory of Egypt, both past and present.

One other striking technique that is frequently used is verbless clauses to render propositions about Egypt and Egyptians. In fact, there is one song that has only one verb (*fi:-ha: ḥa:ga ḥilwa*) and compensates by repeating the existential adverb *fi:ha* throughout. The fact that Arabic has an implicit construction for the verb "to be" is manipulated to the utmost. Assertive statements and statements of achievement are also prevalent in the data analyzed. This suggests that throughout the songs, what Du Bois (2007: 171) calls epistemic stances and evaluative stances are more common than affective ones. Indeed, the singers' highlighted position as knowledgeable arbiters was demonstrated above. There are a number of examples that include elements of affective stance (as in, "Beautiful, my country," "Egypt, my love"), but in my view, the epistemic stance prevails, while other forms of stance appear as a consequence. This is significant, because it suggests that in the process of defining identity, epistemic stances are perceived of as more convincing.

Dialogicality is essential on different levels. I began with the assertion that identity formation is the outcome of a perpetual dialogical process in which discourses interact and collide. Public discourse is, therewith, also dependent on dialogical processes. As Du Bois (2007: 171) argues, stance "comes into existence in its natural environment of dialogic interaction." That is, a community's shared norms, expectations, ideologies, and, therefore, indexes are an essential component of this stance-taking process. This is also the reason why this kind of data would not be appreciated by someone who is not familiar with the indexes and previous dialogues. This is what I call the "the paradox of the knowledgeable Egyptian" who may use epistemic stances frequently to a supposedly ignorant outsider, but who, in fact, can only address an insider who shares the dialogical context. I have tried to demonstrate that most, if not all, patriotic songs reference a dialogue on national identity that has been part of Egyptians' communicative knowledge and perceptions.

4.7.2 Code-choice and orders of indexicality

Throughout this chapter, there were examples of code-switching in which first, second, and third order indexes were used. The example of the online article by ʿAbbūd is a case in point. By consciously using the Alexandrian dialect in a written medium, ʿAbbūd is appealing to a local identity that transcends religious differences. When Hammām in the film *Hammām in Amsterdam* switches between Arabic and English, he is not just trying to communicate. He is appealing to the second level indexes of ECA, authenticity, communal solidarity, and the "chivalrous nature" of Egyptians. Again, the common linguistic resources shared between Christians and Muslims are intentionally highlighted.

By sharing access to the same linguistic resources, Egyptians from different religious groups are portrayed in public discourse as sharing a unified identity—an Egyptian one. In fact, even a lack of access to resources can render one more authentic. In the article by ʿAbbūd, the fact that she does not use Cairene Arabic, but attempts to stick to Alexandrian Arabic even in a written text places emphasis on her authentic local dialect as more essential than religious differences.

Although code-switching does not occur often in patriotic songs, it did occur in the set of data only in inter-dialectal communication with Arabs from different parts of the Arab world. In these cases, ECA indexed an authentic, unique Egyptian identity; in other cases, such as in "The Arab dream," it indexed cultural dominance. Both ECA and Lebanese Arabic were employed by Amīnah and Hishām to index the uniqueness of their respective national cultures, while accommodation was used to show solidarity by both.

SA was used in the song "Egypt speaks about itself" to index Egypt's powerful, legitimate stance, while ECA was used to index authenticity in the song "I am the Egyptian." However, when the Lebanese poet Jurj Qardāḥī describes an Egyptian girl and even conjures up a conversation with her, he does so in SA. The reason may be that the Lebanese poet does not need to prove his Egyptian authenticity, nor is he obliged to accommodate to ECA. Indeed, it would seem that the poet used SA as a technique to contrast "her" quintessential Egyptian Arabic and the neutral SA used to describe her. These are all examples in which first and second order indexes are employed.

An important finding in this chapter is the fact that a significant portion—that is, 30 per cent—of the songs that reference Egyptian identity are sung by non-Egyptians. I believe that this is related to the perception of the outsider: when Egyptian identity is described by a knowledgeable outsider, it carries more credibility and adds the element of objectivity. These outsiders do not write their own lyrics, of course, and as a consequence completely accommodate Egyptian Arabic to index their admiration, solidarity, and respect for the cultural hegemony of Egypt.

On the other hand, there are also a couple of songs in other dialects (Saudi and Lebanese, respectively) that praise Egyptians. This code-choice has its advantages. While not necessarily expressing and approving the cultural hegemony of Egypt, the singers provide a yet more objective depiction of Egyptians, because they are outsiders who clearly do not assimilate totally with Egyptians (as is, perhaps, expected), but who still display admiration and respect. Indexes are again hierarchical, complex, and multi-layered. Throughout this chapter, code-choice and code-switching have straddled both functions of language—language as a classification category and language as a means to indicate a stance—and thus provide a perspective of Egyptian identity.

This brings us back to our initial proposition: language directly and indirectly indexes an identity that is built on shared ideologies, perceptions, and habits. Public discourse processes and reprocesses ideologies shared by Egyptians through a stance-taking process. If these ideologies, such as those of ethnicity and historicity, are not shared by the audience, the songs are devoid of meaning.

4.7.3 Social variables attributed to Egyptian identity

As shown in the examples above, public discourse enhances the perception of Egyptians as forming a large community that encompasses many small ones. This large community shares habits, assumptions about others, as well as character traits (such as humor, generosity, kindness, and communal solidarity). By and large, Egyptian public discourse provides a coherent and emphatic portrayal of shared identity, but one also encounters examples in which this identity is challenged. There are examples in which Egypt's current or past actions are questioned and in which Egyptian identity does not necessarily incorporate only positive traits. Such challenges seem to occur at times of political awakening in particular. At the beginning of the twentieth century, Bayram al-Tūnisī provided numerous examples in his work. At the beginning of the twenty-first century, Egyptians were again harshly criticized in public discourse, as we have seen in the examples in this chapter and will see again in the following one. However, even if positive traits of Egyptian identity are called into question, the backbone variables of historicity, ethnicity, and locality are not challenged. On more than one occasion, the backbone variables are used as part of the argument to criticize the abject state of Egyptians, as in al-Tūnisī's poem "Letter to Tutankhamen" (al-Tūnisī 1987: 276).That is, there are more nuanced aspects of public discourse than first meets the eye.

The social variables attributed to Egyptian identity in public discourse are summarized in these points:

- Historical achievements of Egyptians throughout history render the modern Egyptian strong, resilient, patient, and kind. This historical authenticity and superiority of "the Egyptian" is attributed to his ancient Egyptian, Islamic, and Coptic history—a history in which the Egyptian past and present are discussed as one.
- Because the Egyptian is a direct descendant of her or his ancient Egyptian ancestors, Egyptians all share one ethnicity. This ethnicity may be manifested in skin color and ancestral lineage.
- Egyptians all share one local area called Egypt, marked by the River Nile, the pyramids, and other religious and historical monuments.
- What Egyptians share are perceptions of their historical achievements, their one ethnic origin, and the local area they share in public discourse. Because of these three variables, they are also considered one large community. This community then shares specific habits—linguistic and social—and also character and moral traits. These habits include sharing food, socialising, and being generous and kind to fellow Egyptians. Communal solidarity is highlighted in public discourse.

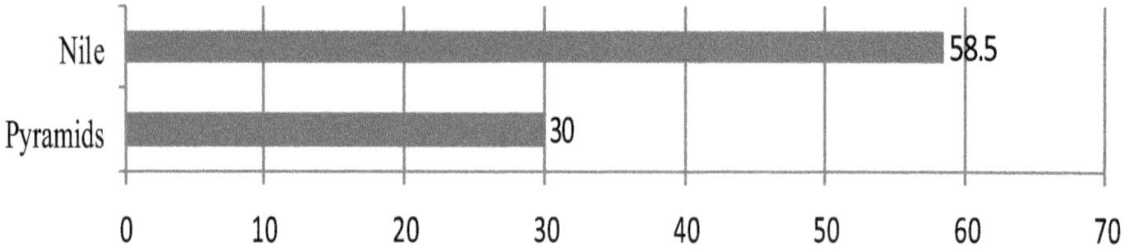

Figure 4.4 Subcategories: locality

- This communal solidarity—an outcome of sharing one's community—is more salient than religious differences. Public discourse tackles religion in a complex and twofold way. While highlighting the fact that Egyptians are by nature religious, public discourse also undermines the differences between Christians and Muslims as two distinct religious groups. The fact that there is no significant linguistic variation built on religion as an independent social variable is highlighted continuously in public discourse. Linguistic resources, together with backbone and outcome variables, make up the Egyptian. Religion is an outcome variable, but linguistic resources are then treated as backbone variables, as an essential fixed part of Egyptian identity.

Language as a social variable and marker of identity has also been discussed and illustrated with examples. As a related issue, the complex "Arab" component of Egyptian identity was also examined. This chapter argues that in patriotic songs, newspaper articles, and films, linguistic resources are employed to index attitudes and ideologies through a stance-taking process. Language as a classification category and a resource can and does become treated as a backbone variable.

However, while public discourse is at pains to depict a coherent and holistic community of Egyptians, it cannot prevent the outbursts of questions and challenges to this holistic approach. Egyptian identity can be contested, too. Indeed, the Revolution of 2011 witnessed the fiercest challenge to the coherence of "Egyptians." While the state media branded the protestors in Tahrir Square "non-Egyptians" both metaphorically and literally (as will be discussed in detail in Chapter 6), the pro-democracy protestors branded the pro-Mubarak group as traitors, lacking in Egyptianness. However, before I discuss the events of 2011, I will first show examples of the relationship between identity and language in Egyptian novels. Genre of discourse is highly significant in our analysis, and while patriotic songs tend to give a positive stance of Egyptian identity, novels do not give such a clear-cut stance, instead providing a definitely less positive one.

There are questions that this chapter poses and that are not fully answered. The questions that were alluded to in the Introduction are posed again in this chapter, which are: how seriously do Egyptians take these claims about their identity? How much do they believe them? Who propagates Egyptian public discourse? Will public discourse change with the political situation in Egypt? As was mentioned in Chapter 1, public discourse is an outcome of a mutual benefit relation between producers and consumers. Producers depend on consumers for their living. Producers are affected by school textbooks, dialogicality and intertextuality, political affiliations, and the very nature of the country and its make-up. For example, with a large Christian minority, it would seem unlikely and unpractical for mainstream public discourse to favor one religious group over another or to highlight religious differences. Mainstream public discourse is produced by diverse individuals with different agendas, but these individuals are already the product of discourse. They have been conditioned by their schooling, by watching television, by reading history books, and by repeating and rehashing existing discourses. Or, to put it bluntly, in public discourse, audience and producer usually simmer in the same sauce.

However, the fact that concepts and ideologies are shared between producers and consumers does not mean that they are not occasionally questioned, challenged, and even ridiculed. We have had examples in which Egyptians challenged the homogenous and perfect picture of the Egyptian community; in Section 5, there is the parody of the perfect homogeneous Arab nation.

The concept of access to resources was also referenced in this chapter. When ʿAbbūd in her article sticks to Alexandrian only and refuses to show any knowledge of Cairene Arabic, she is also proving that a lack of access to linguistic resources can be a sign of authenticity. In the poem and song *samra:ʔ*, the Egyptian girl is described as speaking in Egyptian Arabic and nothing else. This concept will be developed more in Chapter 6.

The idea that I wish to retain from this chapter is that identity is constructed through the accumulation of linguistic and non-linguistic associations. Analyzing linguistic resources in this chapter—and indeed in this book as a whole—is a means to an end. The end is to reach a better understanding of the commonly agreed indexes that shape identity in public discourse. I would like to conclude this section with the following quote by Collins (2011: 404):

> Categories of gender or generation, of class or religion, are not deterministically operating at all times in uniform ways. Instead, they are evoked and brought into interaction; sometimes they are enforced, sometimes resisted, but always as part of a process.

That is, public discourse, during the continual process of identity construction, highlights, sieves, and selects categories—highlighting some, ignoring others, and sometimes conjuring up some that never existed before.

Notes

1. In an interview on O-TV. A partial transcript was posted online at: http://techcrunch.com/2011/02/07/wael-ghonims-first-interview-after-jail-release-video/, accessed 21 August 2013.
2. The recording of this interview was posted all over the internet and viewed hundreds of thousands of times. Excerpts from the recording were translated and widely commented upon in the worldwide press. See, for example, the commentary in *The New Yorker* of February 8, 2011. Available at: http://www.newyorker.com/online/blogs/closeread/2011/02/wael-ghonim.html, accessed 21 August 2013.
3. See also the Introduction for an explanation of the choice of data. The songs referenced or analyzed in this chapter are listed in the Appendix.
4. It is noteworthy and indicative of their importance that these two songs in particular were sung repeatedly during the 2011 Revolution and shared widely online.
5. See the introduction to the poem in Hafiẓ Ibrāhīm, *Dīwān Ḥāfiẓ Ibrāhīm* (Cairo: al-Hay'ah al-Miṣrīyah al-ʿĀmmah lil-Kitāb, 1980), Vol. II, p. 89.
6. With this summary statement, the poet effectively equates the British with the Hyskos, who were discussed above in the context of school textbooks. Given that almost all traces of the civilization of the Hyskos have vanished throughout the centuries, while Egypt's civilization has endured, this statement includes an overt taunt to the British that their empire, too, would vanish, as a punishment for transgressions against Egypt.
7. The word "white" is used in the poem to refer to a sword, but the connotations of the word go beyond that use.
8. See http://www.shorouknews.com/columns/view.aspx?cdate= 23122011&id=732c8921-12ac-4c29-90ef-84b23c860159, accessed 21 August 2013.
9. Compare to the poem by al-Tūnisī in Chapter 2.
10. A joke was made about this song in 2013, because of the political and economic turmoil in Egypt. The joke uses the picture of the singer and quotes the lines: "Such a one has never been to Egypt." It follows this with a face of a laughing man and the comment: "Such a lucky man! He saved himself."
11. "Wheat colored" refers to the dark skin color of Egyptians and is mentioned frequently in patriotic songs.
12. This song has been used in Egyptian jokes in 2013. Because of the lack of security, Egyptians ridiculed the claims of the singer. One joke quotes the lines: "Have you tried, in your deep sadness, to walk in her streets, singing and complaining to her?" The lines are then following by a picture of a laughing man who says: "I tried and was mugged!"

13. See http://www.youtube.com/watch?v=NtpamD9Jx3g, accessed 21 August 2013.
14. See Chapter 6 for examples.
15. Military service is mandatory for all Egyptian men.
16. During the Coptic Christmas of 2012 and amid tensions between Salafist groups and Copts, Egyptian Muslims chose their wording carefully when congratulating Copts on their religious feast. Public discourse used terms such as "To the Egyptian Christians of Egypt, to our brothers the Christians of Egypt and from an Egyptian Muslim Copt to an Egyptian Christian Copt." All statements were there to highlight similarities and minimize differences.
17. Milroy and Gordon highlighted the concept of social networks. Their definition of networks is as follows: "An individual's social network is the aggregate of relationships contracted with others, a boundless web of ties which reaches out through social and geographical space linking many individuals, sometimes remotely" (2003: 118).
18. In Damascus, unlike Cairo, there are specific quarters that have been historically linked to Christians. In Iraq, there are quarters or cities that are predominantly inhabited by Shiitis and others by Sunnis. In Beirut, the city is divided into an east Christian part and a western Muslim one. Although in Cairo there are areas in which a large number of Christians reside, such as Shubrā, the Muslim population is also dense in these areas (see http://weekly.ahram.org.eg/2005/741/eg11.htm for a brief history of the area).
19. Religion may be regarded in the Arab world as an essential part of one's identity, perhaps more so than in the West. However, as a factor that influences language variation and change, it may be equal in importance to other factors, like ethnicity. This varies from one community to another.
20. Tomiche (1968: 1178–80) tried to distinguish the Jewish dialect spoken by the Jewish community of Alexandria and Cairo until the 1960s from other dialects. He states that the Jewish dialect was characterized by the absence of emphatics and the use of *n-* and *n-u* for first person singular and plural imperfect. According to Miller (2004), this claim was refuted by Blanc (1974), who prefers to call this dialect a non-standard Cairene Arabic, which is shared by other groups. For example, the *n* is one of the North African features, as well as a feature of other areas of Egypt—namely, the western delta and the western oases (see Behnstedt and Woidich 1985). In fact, coming from Alexandria myself, I know that the use of *n-* and *n-* . . . *-u* for first person singular is a characteristic of Alexandrian Arabic and not just limited to a specific religion.
21. These factors are not the subject of this book.
22. Some of the work that examines class as a variable includes Haeri's study of the phonological change of urban middle-class women in Cairo who had a stable urban vernacular (1996). One of the phonological variables she concentrates on is palatalization. She found that variables associated with upper

middle-class women tend to become prestigious norms associated with refinement (see Chapter 4, Section 4.7.2).

23. January 4, 2011. See http://www.youm7.com/News.asp?NewsID=330103, accessed 6 June 2013.
24. See http://www.werakak.com/archives/8686, accessed 21 August 2013.
25. It is, indeed, interesting that Hammām uses the song "The Arab dream" analyzed in this chapter to call for Arab unity.
26. The film contains a reference to the famous play *Ḥasan wa-Murqus wa-Kūhīn* ("Hassan, Mark and Cohen"), which was first performed by Najīb al-Rīḥānī in 1941 and made into a screenplay in 1954. The protagonists, Hassan, Mark, and Cohen, are all Egyptians with different religious backgrounds: as their names reveal, the first is a Muslim, the second is a Christian, and the third is a Jew. They jointly own a pharmacy and together humiliate and abuse the poor Egyptian worker in this pharmacy. This continues until the worker inherits a large sum of money. The three then start manipulating him and try to persuade him to marry one of their daughters.
27. Mājdah al-Rūmī, a female, takes the stance of a male poet who is infatuated by the Egyptian girl. This is not uncommon. ʿAbd al-Wahhāb, the classic Egyptian composer and singer, also took the stance of a woman in the SA song *ʔa-yaẓunnu* ("Does he think"). This can happen in SA, but not in ECA.
28. See Chapter 3 for a discussion of this role.
29. This is based on YouTube listeners and the frequency of broadcasting them on different satellite channels.
30. See Beebe and Giles (1984) on accommodation theory.

CHAPTER

5

IDENTITY AND NARRATION IN EGYPT

My passport is Egyptian. I defend it. What is it that I am trying to defend? Whatever loyalties I have are judged suspicious in advance. What am I defending? My passport? My language? My faith? This is a religion, I say, that took from and build upon your religion. That's all there is to the matter.

From *Awrāq al-narjis* ("The leaves of Narcissus")
by Sumayyah Ramaḍān (2001: 76)

In Ramaḍān's novel *Awrāq al-narjis* ("The leaves of Narcissus"), Kīmī, an Egyptian upper-class girl, travels to Ireland to study for a doctorate in English literature. Kīmī's sense of identity is to a great extent influenced by her experience; when abroad, Kīmī is forced to explain who she is in relation to Egypt. Those around her stereotype her as an Egyptian, an Arab, and a Muslim. Whether she likes it or not, Kīmī is also forced to defend the identity of Egyptians more generally. As was mentioned in Chapter 1, identity is subjective, as well as ideological and habitual. In fact, although she is not overly religious, in the extract above she explains how her religion, Islam, is related to Christianity. In her painful search for one coherent identity for all Egyptians, she loses her mind and ends up in an asylum. In despair, she claims that it is impossible to summarize the "people of Egypt" in a few words or even within the space of a book. However, Kīmī's only hope of recovery towards the end of the novel comes when she returns "home." It is only when Kīmī defines her home and, thus, her identity in relation to Egypt that she is at last able to recover.

To return to the extract above, Kīmī is not sure what she tries to defend when foreigners attack her for being an Egyptian Muslim. However, she does not have any doubts that she has to defend her passport, which for her represents her Egyptian identity. Her confusion begins when she questions which aspect of this identity is dominant. She then contemplates language and religion as two markers of her Egyptian identity.

Language as a social variable has been discussed in previous chapters and will, again, be referenced frequently throughout this chapter. In fact, Ramaḍān is not the only author whose protagonist directly relates language to identity. In the following sections, I will shed light on other authors whose novels connect language to identity and in the process make postulations about diglossia and linguistic diversity more generally.[1]

Some eight novels are mentioned in this chapter, of which four are analyzed in detail. The four novels analyzed have the following factors in common: the protagonists embark on a journey—whether real or imagined—and are then forced to tackle issues of identity imposed upon them; they are forced to explain their own identity in relation to others. As Blommaert (2005: 203) contends, "when abroad, we discover ourselves talking a lot about that country, living up to its stereotypes, defending its values and virtues, and in return receiving flak because of the mistakes it made or makes." As was discussed in Chapter 1, being an uprooted Egyptian in a foreign land also means that the Egyptian identity, with all accompanying stereotypes and ideologies, is highlighted and brought to the forefront.

In all four novels, social variables that demarcate Egyptian identity are present, while code-switching is employed as a linguistic resource that reflects a stance related to identity. In sum, they are novels that deal with themes related to Egyptian identity in the twentieth and twenty-first centuries.

The novels analyzed in detail are:[2]

Qindīl Umm Hāshim ("The saint's lamp") by Yaḥyá Ḥaqqī (1944)
al-Ḥubb fī Al-manfā ("Love in exile") by Bahā' Ṭāhir (1995)
Awrāq al-narjis ("The leaves of Narcissus") by Sumayyah Ramaḍān (2001)
Kitāb al-rinn ("The book of rinn") by Jamāl al-Ghīṭānī (2008)

Other novels referred to in passing are:

al-Ayyām ("The days") by Ṭāhā Ḥusayn (1929)
'Uṣfūr min al-sharq ("A bird from the East") by Tawfīq al-Ḥakīm (1938)
al-Bāb al-maftūh ("The open door") by Laṭīfah al-Zayyāt (1960)
al-Watad ("The tent peg") by Khayrī Shalabī (1986)
Qismat al-ghuramā' ("The debtor's share") by Yūsuf al-Qa'īd (2004)

This chapter starts by explaining the importance of narration in discourse about identity. Section 2 will concentrate on language as a social variable that demarcates identity. Other social variables are also mentioned briefly. The study will show how authors also employ linguistic resources to highlight these variables.

However, the main contribution of this chapter will be to show how authors use code-choice and code-switching in dialogues. This chapter poses the question of why writers in Egypt use SA in dialogues or why they alternate their usage of SA and ECA. If literature, as Eid (2002b) posits, is supposed to reflect the reality outside of the stories, then one would expect most, if not all, dialogues to be in colloquial. I will argue that writers use code-choice and code-switching between SA and ECA in dialogues as a device that does not *reflect* real patterns of language use, but rather *redefines* and *reconstructs* different stances for the protagonists with different people in their lives. This reconstructed stance can be understood by reference to the indexes of SA and ECA and therefore adheres to the public perception of "an Egyptian." Since I deal with authors that employ code-switching between ECA and SA in dialogues to reflect different stances, I exclude authors like Mahfouz (who refused to use ECA in dialogues as a matter of principle, considering literature a vehicle only for SA), as well as authors like ʿAbd al-Quddūs (who mostly employed ECA in dialogues).

Note that studies that concentrate specifically on dialogues from a linguistic perspective are rare. Arab writers deal with the diglossic situation differently and reflect in their language use both their political and social stances, as well as the identity of their protagonists. Therefore, before I start my analysis, I will outline how different Egyptian novelists deal with linguistic diversity and specifically how they deal with the diglossic situation by providing different stances adopted by Egyptian authors towards language. That is, I will show the ideological framework of some Egyptian authors and discuss how talk about language reflects second order indexes of different codes.

5.1 Importance of narration in identity work

Narration is a significant part of public discourse. Through narration, authors reproduce public discourse and at times challenge or try to change it. In most cases, authors themselves are the product of this discourse, and they may present different facets of it through both their characters and plot.

Narration can be an excellent vehicle for constructing, as well as reflecting, identity or at least a facet of it. As Georgakopoulou puts it: "narrative is seen as a privileged mode for self-construction and a unique point of entry into trans-situational features of the self and identity as those emerge in a person's ongoing life story" (2006: 83). This is because

> if selves and identities are constituted in discourse, they are necessarily constructed in stories. Through storytelling, narrators can produce "edited" descriptions and evaluations of themselves and others, making identity aspects more salient at certain points in the story than others. (Benwell and Stokoe 2006: 137)

To elaborate on this further, Garner (2007: 44) discusses features that are essential in any narrative. Garner states that narratives usually involve a recounting of personal experience, whether it is of the narrator or protagonist. Narratives also contain temporality, which is a set of distinct events that occur in chronological order towards a culminating point. Narratives have a plot, a frame of events. Narratives also have three communication aims: entertainment, instruction, and the construction of personal identity (2007: 46). The last aim is what concerns this chapter.

Narratives form an important aspect of how the self is constructed and negotiated. The audience of a narrative, who are usually community members, will then examine the nature of the social and physical contexts of the narrative—in other words, which events are selected? What do these events contribute to the perception of the self of the narrator and protagonists and his or her audience? What does it say about narrators and protagonists' beliefs and attitudes (see Garner 2007).

As a "unit of discourse" (cf. Schiffrin 1984), narratives can yield surprising insights into the ways that individuals perceive themselves in relation to their own community and other communities. Stories in general are a mode of defining ourselves, our attitudes, and our conception of reality (cf. Bastos and Oliveira 2006). The notion of the true self lurks behind discourse.

Although novels are a written form of narratives, they still shed light on cultures and societies in relation to the self. As Garner (2007: 46) posits, narratives are "a rich though still underexplored field for sociolinguistics." This chapter will show how authors employ language to discuss identity. As Harrison (1998: 248) explains, "identity is generated through culture, especially language."

5.2 Social variables that mark the Egyptian identity

In this section, language as a social variable is discussed. However, it is also essential to mention other intertwined variables, such as ethnicity, historicity, religion, and locality. This will be done briefly in Section 2.2.

5.2.1 Language as a social variable

In this section, protagonists' stance towards language and identity in Egyptian novels is discussed. Through their protagonists, authors attempt to depict a picture of society, as well as a picture of language attitudes and ideologies. If these attitudes and ideologies are not those of the authors, then they are those of the characters who represent facets of Egyptian identity and are portrayed by the authors. These stances on language will at times echo second order indexes discussed in Chapter 3. It is noteworthy also that these stances reflect direct, rather than indirect, indexes about codes. Dialogues, on the other hand, will show how indexes are manifested indirectly, rather than directly. The search for self is a recurring theme in Egyptian novels of the twentieth and twenty-first centuries and is related directly to language as a marker of identity (Jibrīl 2009).

In the following chronological examples, protagonists in novels make clear references to language and relate it to identity. In some cases, language as a social variable is yoked together with religion, history, and locality.

In Ṭāhā Ḥusayn's autobiographical novel *al-Ayyām* ("The days") (1943), the student of the Dār al-ʿUlūm (the secular academy) says to the member of al-Azhar (the religious university) (Jibrīl 2009: 566),

> "Who are you to know about science? You are just an ignorant who knows nothing except grammar and jurisprudence . . . you have never heard a lesson about the history of the pharaohs. Have you ever heard the names of Ramses or Ekhnaton?"

In this example, knowledge of history as an identity marker is placed before knowledge of Arabic grammar. It is more prestigious to study history. Recall the portrayal of Arabic teachers and the attitudes towards them discussed in Chapter 3. Tawfik Al-Ḥakīm also confesses that in his search for identity he had to go back to "our old alley [. . .] and traditional blue galabiyya" directly after the 1919 Revolution (Jibrīl 2009: 566).

As was mentioned at the beginning of this chapter, in Ramaḍān's novel *The Leaves of Narcissus* (2001), Kīmī's sense of identity at the beginning of the novel, when she is in Ireland working on her doctorate, is extremely conflicted. The conflict within Kīmī is caused partly by her identification with more than one language, English and Arabic, especially but not only ECA. Kīmī declares that all languages are her languages and that is why she has no language; likewise, all countries are her countries, which is also why she has no home. Kīmī does not regard linguistic diversity in a positive light. In fact, it is this diversity that confuses her. In this case, Kīmī is similar to the psychologist in Chapter 3, who blames Egyptians' lack of creation and stagnation on, what he terms, linguistic chaos. At one point in the story, she even claims to be illiterate in all languages. This shows how access to more than one code can, in fact, imply a disintegrated identity, given the ideological weight given to linguistic unity in identity construction. In that case, having the luck to have more available resources than others in the community is also taken against the speaker. It implies that the speaker is different and does not share equal resources with the community. That is, access to more resources is not always looked upon ideologically in a positive light.

Both Kīmī and the psychologist believe in the concept that one identity equals one language. In the case of Kīmī, she does not have a choice. Even if she masters English, she is still regarded as an "Egyptian" by non-Egyptians. That is, as a social variable, language comes next after ethnicity, locality, and historicity in her case. Ironically, Kīmī is not just regarded as an Egyptian, but her putative identity straddles all Muslim countries, including Iran. While she does not share a language (Kīmī speaks Arabic, while Iranians primarily speak Persian or Turkish dialects) or location with Iran, she is perceived as sharing a religion with Iranians and therefore as belonging to their "community." It would seem that for the "outsiders" in Ireland, religion is the salient social variable that marks identity. For Egyptians, in public discourse, the issue of religion is a complex one.[3]

Her attitude towards other Arabs, Africans, and the Irish is also complicated. When her Irish friends make fun of Libya and its political system, she feels the urge to say that Egypt is not Libya, that it is very different. Nevertheless, she also feels offended by their remarks and, to a great extent, she feels an affinity with the Libyans, given that they share a language. While she may consider herself only Egyptian, others in Ireland do not distinguish Egyptians from Libyans, nor from Iranians.

The protagonist claims in despair that it is impossible to summarize "people of Egypt" in a few words, sentences, or even books. Note again the following example—entirely in SA—in which her Irish colleagues attack her (2002: 76):

> "This passport that you folks carry—Why it's soaked in blood!"
> So I (Kīmī) defend it. "My passport is Arab, not Iranian."
> "All of you over there hate Jews. Racists!"
> My passport is Egyptian. I defend it. What is it that I am trying to defend? Whatever loyalties I have are judged suspicious in advance. What am I defending? My passport? My language? My faith? This is a religion, I say, that took from and build upon your religion. That's all there is to the matter.

Kīmī is not sure what she tries to defend—that is, which aspect of her identity is being attacked and which aspect is perceived in a negative way. She then lists different aspects of the identity that she tries to defend. This list includes: a passport (a national identity), a language (a marker of this identity), and a faith (another marker of this identity).

Once in the asylum, Kīmī declares in SA that she has been reduced to a "thing" with no characteristics (2002: 62):

> A thing, nothing more. Without voice, without story, indeed without language. A body that hears and sees only [. . .] how do you resist your fate through writing if writing is your fate? I clutch my pen. Before me, the white page takes on the blurred outlines of a phantom. I see small black letters in a highly ornate font: hospital for Mental and Nervous Disorders. Even if I knew how to write, my language would be unreadable: all languages are foreign and the tongue of my people is suitable only for telling stories.

Kīmī tries to write her own story, but is unable to. She says simply that the tongue of her people—meaning ECA—is only fit for *telling* stories, not for writing them. Her language, ECA, is not to be read by anyone. In her state of mind, it is difficult for her to write in any other language except her mother tongue, what she refers to as "the tongue of my people." The possessive pronoun "my" makes her the owner of the people and also of the tongue. However, she is the owner of a deficient language in which she cannot express herself, a language that, to a great extent, she looks down upon. Her conflict with herself is amplified by the diglossic situation in Egypt. Her split identity may even be the result of this diglossic situation.

While Kīmī may feel this way, it is not clear whether the author shared these views. Ramaḍān managed to keep her narration in SA and switch between ECA and SA in her dialogues. Whether this was done with significant or insubstantial effort is difficult to determine. However, what is clear is that language in the case of Kīmī is related directly to her state of mind. Her inability to write her story in her mother tongue and declare what "all Egyptians are" is significant on many levels. Kīmī's ideology is shared by many. The author, unlike Kīmī, challenges these ideologies and uses indexes of SA and ECA creatively in her work.

The schizophrenia that she suffers from is also reflected in the split of language that is difficult for her to overcome, a spoken language that is not taken seriously, and a formal language that she cannot master or utilize while in her state of psychosis.

An even more recent example, in which the diglossic situation in Egypt is again related to identity, is in al-Qaʿīd's novel, *The Debtor's Share* (2004). Al-Qaʿīd's novel boldly tackles the hidden religious prejudices between Muslims and Christians inside Egypt. Muhrah, a Muslim second-rate actress, divorces her Muslim ex-general husband and initiates an affair with a poor, young Christian man who is half her age. When describing and criticizing her ex-husband Mustafa, who remains a distant friend of hers until the end, she says in SA (2004: 140):

> Mustafa is still Mustafa. He did not change. He still has two tongues in his mouth, two hearts in his chest. A tongue that speaks for him and a tongue that speaks against him. A heart that speaks for him and a heart that speaks against him. When he speaks sincerely his words are in colloquial. A colloquial that was the only variety he knew and used in narration before. But once he starts speaking what they dictate to him, then he speaks in the language of books, and his words become comic!

This extract reflects Muhrah's tension and ambivalent feelings towards both SA and ECA. Muhrah, like Kīmī, does not perceive diglossia in a positive manner. Diglossia for her is a reflection of a split personality, although Muhrah and Kīmī's attitudes towards ECA are different. While Kīmī is ashamed of her deficit code that is not fit to write with, Muhrah considers ECA the authentic code. Both indexes of ECA were discussed in Chapter 3, as well as the belief that correlates unity of language to coherence of identity.

Muhrah considers Mustafa's switching between SA and ECA in different contexts and with different people as a sign of his falseness and perhaps inauthenticity. For Muhrah, the language that speaks from the heart is ECA.

The concept of authenticity and how ECA indexes it is worth a section on its own. However, there is no doubt that even if some consider ECA deficient, shameful, or unable to be used as the sole vehicle of novels, it does however carry all the indexes of authenticity. This will be apparent in the case studies analyzed in this chapter. Al-Qaʿīd himself wrote one novel exclusively in ECA (for example, *Laban al-ʿuṣfūr* ("Bird's milk") (1994)). However, the fact that the novel was not widely read in Egypt or elsewhere made him return to using SA in narration and ECA in some, but not all, dialogues. For al-Qaʿīd, his audience—primarily Arabs not specifically from Egypt—needed SA in order to fully understand and appreciate his work. The market forces reigned in his particular case.

I would now like to recall the example of Dāliyā ʿAlī in Chapter 1, who raises a number of questions about the relation between language and identity, especially in relation to historical events and perceptions. Ghīṭānī, in his novel *Kitāb al-rinn* ("The book of rinn") (2008), faces the same issues. The author tries to relate the identity of his protagonist to that of his ancient Egyptian ancestors. This is difficult for him, given that the ancestors did not speak the same language. He then resorts to names—a linguistic feature—in order to do so.

In this work, language as a social variable is discussed from a different perspective, as it is discussed in relation to names. Upon reaching the age of sixty, the protagonist embarks on a physical and mental journey in a final search for his true identity. Realizing that his previous searches were futile, he delves deeper into himself, as well as into the external world, for a meaning to his existence. For him, language is both a means to try to understand his present social context, as well as his past one, and it is an achievement, because in language lies the relation between past and present, history and context; in language lies the nature of the self. The relation between him and his ancestors is manifest in the importance of names for both. For him, it is only names that remain from history, like the name of the town Akhmim (which referred to the ancient Egyptian god Min, a reference that is now lost).

According to him, the reason why names in themselves are enough is that it is almost impossible to reveal the whole truth about things. While we may know the name of a town, we know nothing about what took place in the town throughout history. Memories and people accumulate for thousands of years, to the extent that understanding them all becomes a futile task.

Al-Ghīṭānī is not sure which code is associated with his identity. Is it the ancient Egyptian language that he does not understand, or the Standard Arabic that he uses for narration, or is it Egyptian colloquial, which is barely mentioned at all? The main problem for al-Ghīṭānī is that while his affiliation is to his Pharaonic ancestors, he fails to understand their language; in fact, he even fails to remember the names of places that once belonged to his ancestors. In his failure to understand or remember, he loses his identity. Once he remembers the ancient Egyptian names, his identity is complete. It is by writing down the ancient Egyptian names in Arabic letters and memorizing them that he reaches his completeness. His inability to understand the ancient Egyptian language and his affiliation to his ancestors is paradoxical and he realizes this. Al-Ghīṭānī's stance reminds us of that of Dāliyā ʿAlī in Chapter 1, who poses the questions regarding what it means to be Egyptian and which language is associated with being Egyptian. He asks: how can you feel affiliated to people that you do not share a language with? How can you identify with ancestors, when you cannot even decipher their names? These are questions that echo throughout Egypt, both in the past and still today.

Al-Ghīṭānī's solution is ingenious. One needs to memorize the names. Names are what are left. One needs to write them down, spell them out in whatever language one uses, even in Standard Arabic, but most importantly one needs to keep remembering them, in order to reach ones true identity. Al-Ghīṭānī uses SA not because it is related to his Pharaonic identity, but because it is the best vehicle for communication.

For the protagonist, loss of identity is directly related to loss of language. If a language does not make sense, is not understood, or is not coherent, then our existence and identity are lost.

Language, in this case, is reduced to the knowledge of names. When names are coherent entities, they are also related to other social variables, such as historicity, and as such can help in identity recognition. In his search for identity, the protagonist also realizes the importance of names[4]—unlike Shakespeare in *Romeo and Juliet*, in which Juliet declares (II, ii, 1–2):

> "What's in a name? That which we call a rose
> By any other name would smell as sweet."

In other words, al-Ghīṭānī does not believe that it is the smell of the rose that distinguishes it and gives it its character, but rather that it is, in fact, its name. For him, names are what will remain in the collective memory of individuals, as well as from history. Even names that cannot be traced back to their roots anymore are still important in defining identity.

It is also names that connect him as an Egyptian to his ancestors—the ancient Egyptians—and even though he cannot understand their language, he can still spell their names. Because it is difficult for him to gather all of names in his memory, he cannot feel whole yet (al-Ghīṭānī 2008: 20):

> Perhaps I realized then that only my name will remain of my existence. Only names will remain from all creatures. Only names will remain from all roads, from what is born and what will blossom, from what will end and what will bid us farewell, from what is near and what is far. The power of names determines the truth. The power of names proposes the solution and makes everything possible.

For the protagonist, names are powerful on their own, even if devoid of literal meaning. He then spells out the name of Akhmīm, one of the largest towns situated on the east side of the Nile in Upper Egypt, in SA. The name is derived from the ancient Egyptian name *xnt.j-Mnw* ("Khenti-min"). In Modern Standard Arabic, "Akhmīm" is a five-letter word. Spelling out each letter draws our attention to the importance attached to names throughout the book. Once he hears the name of the town, he feels that something has been engraved inside his soul, even before visiting the town. This example summarizes the power that names have in abstraction (2008: 5):

> Akhmim: A, K, H, M, I, M
> Something sank in once I heard the name, even before I visited the town regularly, even before I settled temporarily there during my departure, just before I headed towards the eastern bank. There is significance in the utterance, in writing the name.

The title of the novel is, in fact, incomprehensible to an Egyptian. While the Arabic word *kitāb* is readily understood as "book," the meaning of *rinn* or *rann* cannot be immediately recognized. It is only on the seventh page of the novel that the reader encounters an explanation of the word *rinn or rann*, which signified "name" in ancient Egyptian. By keeping the reader in the dark about the title of the novel, the author emphasizes the point that meanings are not essential in identity construction.

Consider the following example (2008: 7):

> The Egyptian Sīdī Dhū al-Nūn was knowledgeable; he could decipher hieroglyphics, or as the Arabs used to call it "The birds pen." I pronounce the utterance sometimes in its old version, "rinn." "Rinn" means "name," and name means "rinn." There is something attached to it, to the town [Akhmim]. What is left hidden is more than what is obvious.

It is mainly ancient Egyptian names that move him, as well as ancient Egyptian statues and ruins. In the following example, the author emphasizes once more that the meaning may change, but the name becomes the only significant symbol of identity (2008: 48): "If this bank that I am crossing was not called the 'West Mountain,' it would be different." In the following example, the author again highlights the importance of names in shaping his identity as a descendent of the ancient Egyptians (2008: 71):

> A name adds features to its holder, whether this holder is a human, an animal, a bird a plant or an inanimate matter. No one can imagine the universe without names or colors. In fact, we cannot distinguish colors without using names. If the East had a different name, it would have different features. The same is true for night and day.
>
> Names appear first, before creatures. A name will remain when things perish, only if we memorize it. Were names created before things then?

His main problem, and the main reason behind why he is embarking on his journey, is because he has started forgetting names (2008: 61):

> The universe is only a memory and memory is only names. Thus, forgetting names may signal senility. When I was young I used to go to a weekly meeting organized by a prominent scholar. I was lucky enough to meet him and hear his views and arguments. Although we were different in age and experience, he was welcoming to anyone who seeks knowledge. He came nearer to me while I was in the meeting, as if he noticed something about me. He was the knowledgeable scholar Amīn al-Khūlī, may he rest in peace.
>
> I can see him now from the void that surrounds me. He approaches me and

> then passes by. I see him at the heart of the Sunday meeting. He did not leave behind a lot of books, but a lot of disciples. Although I only met him during the Sunday meetings, I consider myself one of his disciples. I can see him with my mind's eye trying to remember the name of someone. He used to touch his forehead and say, "it seems I am beginning to forget. The first thing that drops of our memory is names."
>
> During the last years, before all the reasons for my departure were revealed to me, I started forgetting a lot of names. I even sometimes see the meaning, the features, the voice, but not the name. I try in vain to remember it. Some people realize this when they meet me and ask, "Do you know who I am? It seems you do not remember me."
>
> At first I used to be ashamed of myself and would not admit my forgetfulness, but after the re-occurrence of the incident repeatedly, I started to take the initiative in asking, "remind me who you are. It is possible to forget."
>
> More than once, I uttered the sentence that I heard half a century ago.

At the end of the novel, the protagonist or writer realizes that unless he gathers in his mind all names, his entity is not whole (2008: 125):

> I do not know what happened to names [. . .] Names are drifting in no particular direction. If we recall them, the universe is complete. If they are absent, the universe vanishes [. . .] That night, I came running in spite of the time difference, my hands on my chest as if in surrender. During that night, letters, colors and creatures were scattered. They were all scattered and we do not know in which language, in which dialect, in which look or signal and in which string that had been struck. In the scattering of letters lies my annihilation and in the coherence of letters lies my completion and the end of my strife. (2008: 125)

The revelation comes to him when he realizes, first, that he is part of a bigger historical entity, which is the entity of ancient Egyptians, and also when he realizes that unless he discovers all of the names, he cannot attain inner peace. Note that al-Ghīṭānī's description and definition of names strikes a chord in all Egyptians. He manages to capture an essentially Egyptian concept, which regards names as magical and sacred. To clarify this point, I would like to refer to a scholarly work that concentrates on names as the vehicle of examination. Eid (2002a), in a study that compares and contrasts obituaries in Egypt, Iran, and the USA over the span of fifty years, mentions the fact that women's names are lost when they die in Egypt; they are always referred to as the wife of, daughter of, sister of, mother of, and so on. Eid, an Egyptian scholar, emphasizes that in obituaries, women's names are frequently not mentioned at all. In a way, she also emphasizes the importance of names in her study. However, her study brings us to a crucial point that has to be mentioned regarding how Egyptians perceive names (cf. Bassiouney 2009). Egyptians in general are superstitious and believe that one can inflict pain on someone by invoking his mother's name. Specifically, a mother's name is used in the practice of magic in Egypt, as well as when casting a curse on someone. Because of this, names, especially women's names, are still hidden and sacred. For al-Ghīṭānī, names connect us to our ancestors and identify us as Egyptians. For him, names are sacred, devoid of literal meaning.

As McConnell-Ginet (2003: 69) posits, how we label ourselves and others is significant, because it can "offer a window on the construction of gendered identities and social relations in social practice," adding that referring to others is not just a basis for conveying information, but also for maintaining the social structure of a community (2003: 72).

Note that the use of names have been referred to before in this book, particular as regards undermining the differences between Muslims and Christians within patriotic songs. In these cases, names were perceived as not carrying any significant connotations of identity. For al-Ghīṭānī, the opposite is true. However, the protagonist in al-Ghīṭānī's novel does not refer to names that distinguish Muslims from Christians, but to names that place the Egyptian in a direct ethnic and historical relation to her or his ancestors.[5]

5.2.1.1 Discussion

The examples in this section relate back to our discussions of code indexes and order of indexicality. Similar to the psychologist in *Thuqūb fī al-ḍamīr: Naẓrah ʿalá aḥwālina* ("Holes in our conscience: a look at our condition") (ʿUkāshah 2008, see Chapter 3), Kīmī's disturbed psychological state is related to her knowledge of more than one code. She suffers from schizophrenia, which is directly related to this "linguistic chaos," as the psychologist in Chapter 3 calls it. Also, Muhrah, in *The Debtor's Share*, makes her own stance clear when describing Mustafa. She also does not believe that speaking two codes and switching between codes is a positive, enriching linguistic habit. In the examples cited above, the language ideology of some intellectuals that relates one identity to one code was prevalent. But again, ideology in this case does not conform to habits. In fact, all evaluations of the linguistic situation in the above examples were in SA. While this is the ideology of protagonists and perhaps some authors, authors use the diglossic situation to their utmost advantage. They use code-switching and code-choice between ECA, SA, and even foreign languages as a linguistic resource, as will be clear in Section 3.

Language as a variable was discussed in relation to other variables and in Kīmī's case because of outsiders' perceptions that religion and ethnicity were more dominant than language in identity classification.

Al-Ghīṭānī, in his novel the *The Book of Rinn*, addresses the issue that is raised periodically in Egypt of how people can identify with their ancestors when they do not share a language. Al-Ghīṭānī uses the power that names possess in Egyptian history as a sacred entity for some to relate language to identity. However, this holistic identity is not only a Muslim one, but mainly an ancient Egyptian one.

Language in the Arab world more generally is loaded with symbols and ideologies that do not conform to realities in most cases. In a different vein, Suleiman (2011) discusses that through their narratives, we can speculate on the attitudes of authors of Arab origin who write in English. The authors in question are Edward Said, Leila Ahmed, Moustapha Safouan, and Amin Maalouf. Suleiman discusses those sections of the texts in which Arabic is indexed directly to the self and pays particular attention to the associations of standard and colloquial Arabic. He argues (2011: 141):

> The data in this chapter shows the complexity of the language-self link in the Arabic-speaking world. They also show the Arab "obsession" with language as a cultural product and as a symbol of belonging and alienation, of closed and open meanings, of despotism and freedom and of dictatorship and democracy [. . .] It is like a barometer: It registers the state of the nation and those who belong to it, whether at home, in exile or in the diaspora.

This is, indeed, true in novels written in Arabic as well.

The establishment of second order indexes discussed in Chapter 3 is echoed in Kīmī's stance towards language. However, there is more to the use of code-switching than the establishment of second order indexes. In this genre of public discourse, some authors go beyond the use of first and second order indexes to creatively establish a higher third order index that, at times, challenges expectations. This third level index conveys the main ideas of the novel more effectively and less traditionally.

In the next section, I will briefly show how other variables discussed in this book are tackled in novels.

5.2.2 Other social variables: historicity, ethnicity, religion, and locality

Other social variables discussed earlier in this book also occur in the novels analyzed in Section 3. The first novel that is analyzed deals directly with issues of identity in Egypt during the first half of the twentieth century, *Qindīl Umm Hāshim* ("The saint's lamp") by Yaḥyá Ḥaqqī (1944). The story is about Ismāʿīl, who originally comes from Sayyidah Zaynab, a historical and overpopulated lower-class area of Cairo. The area was named after the mosque, which has the tomb of Zaynab, the

Prophet's granddaughter. Ismāʿīl grows up in this area and then is sent by his parents to study medicine in the UK. His parents spend every penny they have on his education, but when he returns to Egypt, Ismāʿīl is a changed man. He is acutely aware of the abject state of both medicine and society in Egypt and is sharply critical of everything around him. As an eye doctor, he is shocked to discover that his cousin Fāṭimah uses oil to treat her eye disease in the belief that the oil coming from the lamp of the mosque of Zaynab will cure her. Ismāʿīl is appalled and tries to cure her with modern medicine, but Fāṭimah, to his surprise, becomes blind. At this point, Ismāʿīl evaluates his life and chooses to embrace his Egyptian identity with all its pitfalls. He only manages to cure Fāṭimah when he also understands and appreciates her beliefs. He fails when trying to change the Egyptian identity. Instead, he is forced to change himself. He realizes that in embracing an identity, one should not compare between states, cultures, East, or West. An identity is not a rational calculation, but an emotional state of belonging.

Ḥaqqī, the author himself, posits that he was the product of the first generation of the twentieth century—the generation that was searching for a distinctive identity different from that of the colonizing powers (see Chapter 1). Ismāʿīl, at the end of the novel, realizes the strength, stamina, and special characteristics of Egyptians. His perception of the Egyptian collective identity changes to become more like that of intellectuals at the time. This perception portrays Egyptians as people who throughout history managed to overcome hurdles and despite their deficiencies and disadvantages have remained resilient. His usage of historical references as support for his perception of Egyptians is again not different from songs analyzed in previous chapters. Ḥaqqī does not render a romantic identity of Egyptians, nor an idealized one. Ismāʿīl himself has his faults, not only is he arrogant and self-righteous, but he is a womanizer as well.

Ethnicity and historicity are intertwined in Ḥaqqī's novel, as well as others. However, Ḥaqqī, as in patriotic songs, does mention the skin color of Egyptians specifically. Throughout the novel, the dark skin of Egyptians is emphasized in contrast to the whiteness of Ismāʿīl's girlfriend and colleagues in the UK. In fact, an essential character in the novel is never mentioned by name, but is described by her physical identification as a dark-skinned girl. This girl is a prostitute who seeks the help of Umm Hāshim, and she is also the first love of Ismāʿīl, the woman whom he fantasized about as a teenager and longed for constantly. Ismāʿīl feels a mixture of sympathy, lust, awe, and respect for this prostitute. She is also the catalyst who brings about his moment of enlightenment. She succeeds where he fails, as will be clear below. She appears in the novel twice, and in both instances she is only identified by her skin color. Ismāʿīl himself is also referred to by Ḥaqqī as dark-skinned. Mary,

Ismāʿīl's British girlfriend, also refers to him by his physical appearance as "the dark-skinned man from the East."

In *The Saint's Lamp*, historicity and the Egyptian "belief system" are discussed together as two essential social variables that reflect identity. The Pharaonic past is referred to throughout the novel, but it is also made clear that Egypt's long history—whether Islamic or Pharaonic—bestows upon the Egyptians certain qualities, such as strength and resilience. Once more, "the Egyptian" is depicted as transcending time. Once more, there is complete identification between Egyptian past and present, both themes that we have already encountered in songs such as "Egypt speaks about itself" and "I am the Egyptian."

As was established in Chapter 1, identity is ideological, perceptual, and habitual. The way in which Egyptians are perceived by both insiders and outsiders is essential in identity construction. That is also why novels in which the protagonist undertakes a journey outside of Egypt are thought-provoking.

Ismāʿīl's British supervisor says to him (Ḥaqqī 1944: 62):

أراهن أن روح طبيب كاهن من الفراعنة قد تقمصت فيك يا مستر إسماعيل. إن بلادك في حاجة إليك، فهي بلد العميان.

"I bet the spirit of some pharaonic doctor priest has materialised in you, Mr. Ismael. Your country is in need of you, for it is the land of the blind."

The metaphor of blindness has been dealt with earlier. However, the fact that the professor regards Ismāʿīl as a descendant of the ancient Egyptians is, indeed, relevant. The declarative, assertive statement is emphasized even more by the use of the perfect tense preceded by the untranslatable particle *qad* in *qad taqammaṣat* ("has materialized"). The professor is certain that Ismāʿīl is affiliated to his ancestors. Note also that Ismāʿīl's professor addresses him, unlike all his relatives in the old quarter of Cairo who seem to have an informal relationship with Ismāʿīl, with the formal term of address "mister."

The professor's stance towards Egypt is clear in this evaluative statement. He considers Egypt an ancient country, the country of the Pharaohs. He also considers Egypt in need of Egyptians educated abroad who can cure "her" of her blindness. "It is the country of the blind," the professor declares. His declaration is perhaps not that different from the declaration of intellectuals, who at the time were trying to carve out a niche for Egypt globally.

In the next three examples, Ismāʿīl's perception of Egyptians is through their history. The first two examples show his negative stance towards Egyptians, while in the last example, he experiences his moment of enlightenment and thus his stance is more positive as a result (1944: 112):

هذا شعب شاخ فأرتد الى طفولته. لو وجد من يقوده لقفز الى الرجولة من جديد في خطوة واحدة فالطريق عنده معهود و المجد قديم، و الذكريات باقية

His was a people who had grown old and reverted to childhood. Were they to find someone to lead them, they would spring back to a state of vigour once again at a single bound, for the road was familiar, and their ancient glories and old memories were intact. (= 1973: 82)

Ismāʿīl's evaluation of Egyptians starts with the SA demonstrative *ha:ða:* to refer to all Egyptians. The use of this demonstrative places him outside this group, as the external evaluator of the state of Egyptians. However, the statement "[t]his was a people who had grown old and reverted to childhood" also presupposes that Egyptians have a long history and that their present is the product of this long history. Their relationship to time is measured by this history. Indeed, the assumption that Egyptians are ignorant, naïve, and simple when compared to their European counterparts was prevalent at the time.

The last three declarative statements in this part are in the form of three verbless sentences. The use of verbless sentences in which the verb "to be" is implicit emphasizes the factual nature of the statements:

فالطريق عنده معهود
for the road was familiar
و المجد قديم،
and their ancient glories
و الذكريات باقية
and old memories were intact

While accusing Egyptians of being naïve and simple, Ismāʿīl also gives them credit for their long, impressive history and states emphatically that this long history gives them enough strength to be able to reach maturity again in a single leap. There is no doubt in Ismāʿīl's mind that the modern Egyptian is a descendant of the Pharaohs and of the different civilizations that she or he made, whether Islamic, Coptic, or ancient. Throughout the novel, the people of Egypt are referred to in the third person singular.

The same theme of relating past and present is reiterated in the next two examples (1944: 113):

و لكن لالا..لو اسلم نفسه لهذا المنطق لأنكر عقله و علمه. من يستطيع أن ينكر حضارة أوربا و تقدمها، و ذل الشرق و جهله و مرضه؟ لقد حكم التاريخ و لا مرد لحكمه، و لا سبيل الى ان ننكر أننا شجرة أينعت و أثمرت زمنا ثم ذوت.

But no, he told himself, were he to surrender himself to such a way of thinking he would be refuting his mind and his knowledge. Who can deny Europe's civilization and progress, and the ignorance, disease, and poverty of the east? History had passed its verdict and there was no going back on that verdict, no way of denying that we are a tree that flourished and bore fruit for a time and then withered. It is quite unthinkable that life might invade it anew. (= 1973: 82)

Ismāʿīl's conflicted stance towards Egyptians is clear in this part. He starts with repeating "no" twice. Then he asks another rhetorical question. However, what is, indeed, significant in his evaluation of Egyptians in this part is the change in the usage of pronouns—for example, "we." While in the last example, the people of Egypt were referred to with the third person singular pronoun, in this part they are referred to using the first person plural pronoun. Ismāʿīl is not an external evaluator of Egyptians anymore; he is an Egyptian himself. The argument that Ismāʿīl cannot resolve is not whether Egyptians are descendants of the ancient Egyptians, but rather whether the Egyptians' civilization is over. The presupposition throughout is that there is an ethnic and historical relationship between Egyptians and their ancestors. That is, ethnicity and historicity, two backbone variables, are not disputed.

In this last example, Ismāʿīl once more relates Egyptians to their history. However, in this part, his stance is not negative, but is, in fact, positive. He once more, as in the first example, relates to Egyptians as an outsider and objective evaluator, but this time he expresses his admiration of Egyptians' resilience and strength (1944: 116):

ما يظن ان هناك شعبا كالمصريين حافظ على طباعه و ميزته رغم تقلب الحوادث و تغير الحاكمين. (ابن البلد) يمر أمامه كأنه خارج من صفحات الجبرتي. أطمأنت نفس اسماعيل و هو يشعر ان تحت اقدامه ارضا صلبة. ليس امامه جموع من اشخاص فرادى، بل شعب بربطة رباط واحد: هو نوع من الايمان، ثمرة مصاحبة الزمان و النضج الطويل على ناره. و عندئذ بدأت تنطق له الوجوه من جديد بمعان لم يكن يراها من قبل. هنا وصول فيه طمأنينة و سكينة و السلاح مغمد. و هناك نشاط في قلق و حيرة، و جلاد لا يزال على اشده و السلاح مسنون. و لم المقارنة؟ ان المحب لا يقيس و لا يقارن و اذا دخلت المقارنة من الباب، و لى الحب من النافذة.

He did not think there was a people like the Egyptians, with their ability to retain their distinctive character and temperament despite vicissitudes of the times and the changes of rulers. It all passed in front of the average Cairene like something out of the pages of al-Gabarti's chronicles. Ismāʿīl began to be at peace with himself and to feel that there was solid ground under his feet. There were no longer hordes of individuals in front of him but a whole people united together by a common bond, a sort of faith, the fruit of a close association with time and a long process of maturity. At this, the faces began to speak to him anew with meanings he had previously not noticed. Here was an arrival of tranquility and peace, and the sword was sheathed. In Europe, activity was undertaken in a state of anxiety and agitation, with the sword ever drawn. But why should one compare? The lover does not measure or compare: if comparison enters by the door, love takes flight out of the window. (= 1973: 84)

In this part, there is reference to *ibn al-balad*, which is translated here as "the average Cairene," whereas the literal translation would be "the son of the country." For an Egyptian, the term has significant connotations, as was discussed in Chapter 3, one of which is authenticity.

The use of deictic in this passage is noteworthy:

هنا وصول فيه طمأنينة و سكينة و السلاح مغمد.

Here was an arrival of tranquility and peace, and the sword was sheathed.

This first word, "here," may refer to both physical and mental proximity: "here," as in Egypt, the Sayyida Zaynab quarter, and "here," as in his state of mind, he managed to find peace from within. The factual statement is again verbless. Ismāʿīl himself does not have a conflicted stance towards Egyptians and Egypt anymore, but has reached peace. He now embraces his Egyptian identity, both physically and mentally: physically, by staying in the quarter and establishing himself there; and mentally, by making peace with Egypt.

It is noteworthy, however, that authors of the same period had a similar stance towards history as an identity marker.

While acknowledging the importance of religion in Egyptian life, Egyptian public discourse also tends to undermine differences between Muslims and Christians. This novel is a case in point. In fact, while Ismāʿīl is a Muslim, the belief system described by him to refer to his family and community is culturally entrenched and may not necessarily reflect the lives of Muslims, as opposed to Christians. At least, there is no indication of this in the novel. In fact, this belief system is so entrenched in the identity of the Egyptian, trying to destroy it may result in the destruction of all Egyptians. Ismāʿīl claims that his people believe in idols and worship them. Superstition, which is prevalent in this novel, does not reflect religion as such, but rather a belief system shared by all Egyptians. Note the following example (1944: 102):

استيقظ. استيقظ من سباتك و أفق، و افتح عينيك. ما هذا الجدل في غير طائل؟ و الشقشقة و المهاترة في سفاسف؟
تعيشون في الخرافات، و تؤمنون بالاوثان، و تحجون للقبور و تلوذون بأموات!

"Wake up!" he would have said. "Wake up from your slumber, come to, and open your eyes. What is this useless dispute? This prattling and altercation about trifling matters? You live in a world of fables and you believe in idols, you make pilgrimages to graves and you seek refuge with the dead." (= 1973: 77)

The stance of Ismāʿīl in this example is that of the knowledgeable, enlightened outsider, who evaluates the community in front of him. He disaligns himself completely from his community and their beliefs. He, in fact, employs linguistic resources, which includes the use of the imperative, repetition, pronouns, and rhetorical questions.

He addresses "the Egyptian" with the singular second person masculine pronoun in the imperative verb *ʔistayqiẓ* "wake up!," which is repeated twice. This synthetic personification is a common technique in patriotic songs as well. In fact, like the stance of the singer in patriotic songs, Ismāʿīl's stance is that of the all-knowing. However, unlike the singers in patriotic songs, his stance is not positive towards Egyptians. Ismāʿīl is also not addressing an outsider to tell him or her about the Egyptian. He is addressing Egyptians directly. The order for Egyptians to wake up was, as we have seen, a recurrent theme at the time and occurred in patriotic songs. The metaphor of blindness was also common at the time, as is clear in the poem of Bayram al-Tūnisī (in "Letter to Tutankhamen"). The twice-repeated imperative denotes the powerful position that Ismāʿīl adopts. His rhetorical questions show his indignation. The content of this example also reveals the stance of Ismāʿīl towards Egyptians in his area. In his last proposition, he addresses Egyptians in the second person plural, rather than singular. It is a general declarative statement about their abject state, but the use of the plural here, rather than the singular, may also denote his contempt. They are not special, but they form an anonymous group of people who worship idols (1944: 117):

هو تعالى فسقط!
أين انت أيها النور الذي غبت عني دهرا؟ مرحبا بك! لقد زالت الغشاوة التي كانت ترين على قلبي و عيني. فهمت الآن ما كان خافيا علي. لا علم بلا ايمان. انما لم تكن تؤمن بي، انما ايمانها ببركتك أنت و كرمك و منك. ببركتك أنت يا أم هاشم.

"Oh light, where have you been all this time? Welcome back! The veil that descended over my heart and eyes has been raised. Now I understand what had been hidden from me. There is no knowledge without faith. She didn't believe in me; her whole faith was directed to your blessing, your loftiness, and your gracious favor, O Umm Hāshim." (= 1973: 84)

After Ismāʿīl's moment of enlightenment, he provides a declarative statement in the form of a verbless sentence: "there is no knowledge without faith." He then addresses Umm Hāshim for the first time with second person pronouns. His relationship to Umm Hāshim is now different. It is more informal and intimate. The second person pronouns demonstrate this. It is noticeable that Ismāʿīl does not refer to Islam specifically in this example. The superstition and customs of people in this area are associated more with an entrenched belief system than with a specific religion. In fact, he accuses them of being pagans. The word faith is both inclusive and neutral. Although the setting and context in this novel are more Islamic, the idea of the novel is to emphasize the belief system as such, rather than the beliefs of Muslims or Christians.

It is also difficult to separate locality from ethnicity and historicity. In the novel, Ismāʿīl, after his shift, is ready to accept all the negative characteristics of his community members, because he belongs to the same quarter as them. Note the following example (1944: 118):

تعالوا جميعا الى! فيكم من آذاني، و من كذب علي، و من غشني، و لكني رغم هذا لا يزال في قلبي مكان لقذارتكم و جهلكم و انحطاطكم، فأنتم مني و أنا منكم، و أنا ابن هذا الحي و أنا ابن هذا الميدان. لقد جار عليكم الزمان، و كلما جار و استبد، كان إعزازي لكم أقوى و اشد

> "Come to me, all of you. Some of you have done me harm, and some of you have lied to me and cheated me, yet even so there is still a place in my heart for your filth, your ignorance, and your backwardness, for you are of me and I am of you. I am the son of this quarter, the son of this square. Time has been cruel to you, and the more cruel it is the stronger my affection is for you." (= 1973: 85)

The imperative here is used to show his familiarity with members of this quarter. When Ismāʿīl destroys the lamp of Umm Hāshim, members of the community attack him and try to kill him. Sheikh Dardīrī then asks them to stop. He appeals to two things that may save Ismāʿīl: the fact that he belongs to the same quarter and the fact that he is the son of Shaykh Rajab (1944: 105).

اتركوه! انني اعرفه. هذا سي اسماعيل ابن الشيخ رجب من حتتنا. اتركوه. ألا ترون انه مريوح

> "Leave him!" He said. "I know the man—it's Ismāʿīl, the son of Sheikh Ragab. He's one of us. Let him be. Don't you see he's possessed?" (= 1973: 78)

This appeal to relational identification (Van Leeuwen 1996) is essential, as is the appeal to the local area that they all share. Both variables make Ismāʿīl a member of this community, and both save his life. Using the term of address "Sheikh" to refer to the father of Ismāʿīl renders him a respected man in the community.

In *The Leaves of Narcissus*, Kīmī, the female protagonist, is not confident about her identity. She expresses a conflicted stance throughout most of the novel. As a female Egyptian student abroad, she is confronted with prejudices, stereotypes, and negative perceptions.

Ramaḍān, like Ḥaqqī, contrasts Kīmī's skin color to that of people in Ireland, the country in which she studies. Egyptians' dark color is emphasized as being different from white Europeans. In other words, ethnicity as manifest through skin color is prevalent in this novel. Kīmī has an affair with an Irish man in the novel, and the day after they make love Kīmī comments on his skin color (2001: 39):

> In her room, on the small bed, she studied the long pale languid body. She had never liked white flesh: it had always seemed to hint of flabbiness. Before this. And it had never happened that she'd known a man untouched by the purifying blade of circumcision. Yet, he left her synonymous with gentle radiance and rich fulfillment.

It is clear from this extract that Kīmī bases some of her prejudices on the different skin color of whites. She then confronts these prejudices as she studies the physical differences of her lover.

Historical backing is also prevalent in this novel. Kīmī identifies with the history of Egypt, Pharaonic, Islamic, and modern. In fact, when Kīmī attends a lecture about modern Egyptian history, she feels uncomfortable. She first feels that her history has been stolen from her, as it is analyzed by outsiders. Because her history has been stolen, the outsider has intruded on her identity, and she is not sure whether she has also become an outsider herself. However, her perception that Egypt is the cradle of civilization remains constant throughout the novel. Her belief in the relationship between history and identity is apparent throughout. Note this example (2001: 36–7):

> "اين من كل هذا مصر؟ و عدت اراجع عنوان المحاضرة: كان كما قرأته من قبل، كان عن تاريخ مصر الحديث! اه يا كيمي، قصة لم تجمع و لم تسرد و لم تغن الا مشرذمة. استلبوك فصاروا منك، هل صرت انت منهم؟ [. . .] فاذا سئلت قالت: مصر مهد الحضارات، فاذا هزأ احدهم كما هزأ نيكولوس بعد زيارة ليبيا، اضافت،
> -هكذا قال برستيد.
>
> And where among all this is Egypt? I reread the title of the lecture. Yes, I had read it correctly the first time: the subject was the history of Egypt! Ah, Kīmī, black soil, mother of nations, a story gleaned and narrated and sung only in echoes. They plundered you and became part of you. Have you now become part of them? [. . .] and if the questions come, she answers "Egypt is the cradle of civilization," and if any one jokes, as Nick did after his visit to Libya, she then adds, "that's according to Breasted." (= 2002: 34)

Kīmī refers to herself by using her proper name. Her name, in fact, is an ancient Egyptian word for "black land," which signifies Egypt. As Mehrez explains,

> Finally, it is important to note that the diminutive name of the protagonist Kīmī is very close to the word Kīmīt that denotes Egypt (the black earth) in

> ancient Egyptian. It may therefore be said that Kīmī's search for meaning on a personal level, through writing, is also a search for a collective one, "perhaps." (Mehrez 2001)

Again, both ethnicity and history are prevalent. Kīmī identifies with her Pharaonic and Arab traditions. The conditional sentence in this part shows her stance, as she aligns herself with Egypt's history, but she is also unsure as to how she can prove the validity of her claim. She then resorts to her professor's words about Egypt. Having been attacked before as an "Arab" affiliated in one way or another to Libya, she is careful and ashamed. Note the conditional conjunction in the passage quoted above:

فاذا هزأ احدهم كما هزأ نيكولوس بعد زيارة ليبيا، اضافت،
-هكذا قال برستيد

> If anyone jokes, as Nick did after his visit to Libya, she then adds, "that's according to Breasted!" [her professor]

The conditional particle *iða* in SA denotes confirmation. Someone is bound to make fun of her, like Nick did. When this happens, she will resort to the outsiders' perception of Egypt to make a more valid argument.

What is, indeed, interesting about this specific novel is the way in which social variables are multi-layered and hierarchical. Kīmī, who does not come across as a particularly observant Muslim, is stereotyped throughout in the role of the traditional Muslim woman. That is, for the outsider, her gender and religion are much more salient as identity markers than her linguistic skills and education. Kīmī masters English, but this does not make her Irish or English, Catholic or Protestant—without these attributes, the outsiders consider her to be the stereotype of the uneducated, submissive Muslim woman. Note the following example, in which her Irish colleagues attack her (2001: 76):

> "What a life you Muslim women have! What a religion! Fascists. Nazi. You remind us of how some people once behaved here—but we've rid ourselves of all that! Look at yourselves. You remind us of our own past."
> "This passport that you folks carry—Why it's soaked in blood!"
> So I (Kīmī) defend it. "My passport is Arab, not Iranian."
> "All of you over there hate Jews. Racists!"
> My passport is Egyptian. I defend it. What is it that I am trying to defend? Whatever loyalties I have are judged suspicious in advance. What am I defending? My passport? My language? My faith? This is a religion, I say, that took from and build upon your religion. That's all there is to the matter.

Identity is reduced, for Kīmī, to that of a Muslim woman. However, Kīmī, in fact, refers to her traditions during the eastern Easter, which are the same traditions of Copts in Egypt. While Kīmī tries to prove that her religion is not different from theirs, she is also forced to define herself in relation to their accusations. The interaction between Kīmī and her Irish friends has a pattern. They are on the attack, she is on the defense. They use adjectives to describe all Muslims, such as old-fashioned (the implication likely being a criticism of the position of women in the Islamic community), violent, racist, and backward. She attempts to explain similarities between Islam and Christianity. She attempts to be inclusive, while they are more exclusive. Kīmī is then forced to also define a distinct Egyptian identity.

For Ismāʿīl, religion is a belief system, while for Kīmī it is outsiders who impose on her a distinct view of religion, rather than her holistic inclusive view of religion. Locality also interacts with perceptions of identity. Kīmī posits (2001: 45):

> I am African, too. Why do I remain something illusionary, fantastic, that is constantly under threat of being transformed into a continent in its own entirety, or an ignorant nation, or a submissive people, or even a more ancient civlization? [. . .] "We Egyptians," "people in my country" [. . .] who is that "we"? Precisely which "people" in that country? I am them, and I am not them, I am that "we" and I'm also "I"—just "I."

Kīmī's juxtaposition of herself in relation to "we," Egyptians, is important in her search for a collective identity. Kīmī is forced to identify with all Egyptians by outsiders. Whether she likes it or not, she represents her country and all of its peoples once she goes abroad.

When asked to define her homeland, Kīmī is unsure about how to do so. She finds it difficult to summarize a homeland in a few words. She is then forced to be one individual representing an entire homeland. Kīmī then refers to places and language as two markers of this homeland.

In al-Ghīṭānī's *The Book of Rinn*, the protagonist's journey is inside Egypt, and his main affiliation is to the ancient Egyptian ancestors. The protagonist's solitary confinement is a choice on his part, as a means to reach a better understanding of himself and his environment (2008: 20):

> فى مستهل ليلتى الأولى، أطل فضولى العتيق: كيف سأعتاد ظلام الجبل، كيف أتقى وحوشه وهوامه؟، غير أننى تدثرت بنفسى، انطويت على حالى، فلم يمسسنى خوف، ولم تسر عندى رجفة، أمرى مع العتمة قديم، العلامة الكبرى عندما أمضيت ليلة كاملة داخل الهرم الأكبر.
>
> At the beginning of my first night I was wondering how I will put up with the darkness of the mountain, how I can protect myself from the illusions and

> monsters of the darkness. I covered myself with myself. I shrank into myself. I was immune to fear and I did not tremble. I am used to darkness, since the night that I have spent inside the pyramids.

Al-Ghīṭānī refers to a night he spent inside a pyramid, in order to again reach a better understanding of himself. His journey takes place on a mountain (this has religious, biblical connotations). He also undertakes a similar journey, in which he searches for himself inside a pyramid, an ancient Egyptian location that he perceives as his completely. He also compares the darkness in the mountains to the darkness inside the pyramid, where he once spent a whole night. Darkness is associated with graves, which in this context makes sense, since the pyramid was used as a grave. Thus, his journey relates to the hereafter. His journey also relates to the journey of ancient Egyptians up the Nile to Thebes after death. While the protagonist does not establish any meaningful relationships with anyone around him, including his wife and children, he does establish an affinity with an ancient Egyptian statue (2008: 94):

أما سى نجم رع فصحبة وعشرة وملاطفة.
يغلب على مرقده اللون الأصفر الصريح الواضح، كل ألوان المرقد خصبة، طازجة كأنها بُسطت بالأمس،

> Senedjemibra is a companion, a good old friend and we share mutual affection. His tomb is mainly bright yellow. All the colors of the tomb are fresh and fertile as if painted yesterday.

The author, when he refers to the ancient Egyptian statue, uses a verbless factual statement. The fact that the colors of the statue are fresh also implies that the relationship is ongoing between the protagonist and his ancestors.

5.2.2.1 Discussion

When discussing social variables that mark identity in novels, linguistic resources were employed. These resources include, first and foremost, the use of pronouns, as well as the use of presupposition, identification categories, assertive statements, rhetorical questions, terms of address, adjectives, deixis, negation, and demonstratives. Language as a social variable interacts with other variables, including locality, ethnicity, religion, and historical backing.

Note also, that for outsiders, variables are organized in a different fashion than for insiders. While in Egyptian public discourse "religion" as an identity marker is either neutralized or rendered inclusive, in the case of *The Leaves of Narcissus* the outsider's perception of Egyptian identity is based mainly on religion; in fact, on one particular religion, Islam.

In the discussion of language as a social variable, it was clear that the protagonists tended to share second order indexes discussed in Chapter 3. There was also the emphasis on the unity of language as a reflection of a sound and coherent identity. Access and lack of access to language as a social resource was also highlighted.

In terms of access and resources, identity construction is a continuous struggle; a struggle of both inclusiveness and exclusiveness. Pronouns, such as we, them, and I, are salient in this struggle. Social variables are an essential part of this struggle. This struggle is twofold. First, there is the perception of outsiders; of "us" and "them," which are mutually exclusive—for example, "their" religion, "our" religion, "their" language, "our" language, "their" history, "our" history, "their" ethnicity, "our" ethnicity, and so on. Second, there is the struggle between insiders regarding which part of history, religion, and ethnicity should be included. For example, which historical era is quintessentially Egyptian: the ancient Egyptian era or the Islamic one? Which segment of religion defines Egyptian identity: Islam only or also Christianity? Or is it the inclusive aspects of both, as is clear in patriotic songs? Novels do not provide definite answers, but force the readers to think and in the process emphasize the ideological and perceptual aspects of identity.

5.3 Code-choice and code-switching as a linguistic resource: evidence from dialogues in Egyptian novels

In this section, I will focus on the ways that novelists employ code-choice and code-switching in dialogues to highlight the identities of their different protagonists. This study is the first of its kind to approach code-switching in dialogues as a linguistic resource that directly reflects identity construction. This relationship between code-choice and identity is articulated through stances adopted by protagonists and indexes of different codes. Concepts such as language ideologies, attitudes, and linguistic habits are indirectly referred to and evoked.

Before I elaborate on this point, I will provide a general background, which is necessary in order to appreciate the role of code-switching as a linguistic resource. I will first shed light on the attitude of Egyptian authors towards using SA and ECA in literature more generally. I will then outline studies of literature that take language as their focal point. Then I will provide my data analysis.

5.3.1 Diglossia and literature: authors' stance

Authors have their linguistic stances. Some prefer to use only SA in their novels, whether in dialogues, narration, or internal monologues. Others prefer to code-switch between SA and ECA, and yet others prefer to write exclusively in ECA, although those authors are few and far between. As well as using code-choice to position themselves and their protagonists and to reflect their attitudes not just towards language, but in most cases towards their own self and others, authors also use code-choice to position their protagonists in different contexts.

In this section, I would like to elaborate on and give an overview of the way that authors position themselves and their characters and also the way that authors reflect their own ideologies and attitudes towards language and identity continuously in their work.

Ḥaqqī, like most writers, had to make a linguistic choice of either writing in SA only, mixing SA and ECA, or writing in ECA. Ḥaqqī (1944) mentions that he considered writing in colloquial, but found SA more eloquent as the code that unites Arabs and as the line that binds past and present. However, Ḥaqqī, as with a number of authors, does mix SA and ECA, especially in dialogues.

One form of language often associated with the Egyptian playwright Tawfīq al-Ḥakīm's plays was widely referred to as "third language" (Somekh 1981: 74). This language was supposed to conform to the syntactic rules of SA and avoid lexical and morphological choices that are either saliently vernacular or saliently SA (Cachia 1992: 414). This third language would then enable the play to be performed in more than one Arab country without any modification. Ḥakīm discovered early on that use of dialect may hinder his plays from being performed in other Arab countries (Somekh 1998; Holes 2004; for a general discussion of diglossia in literature, see Cachia 1967).

As far as novels and short stories are concerned, the writer Yūsuf Idrīs claimed that he was mainly interested in depicting a realistic and concrete picture of Egyptian society in both plot and language, so he used both ECA and SA in his dialogues. His use of SA in dialogues was usually to juxtapose specific characters with others (Holes 2004: 305). For example, he used SA to satirize authority figures, as he did in *Jumhūrīyat Faraḥāt* ("Farahat's republic") (1956), in which a policeman in a poor quarter of Cairo takes a statement from an illiterate young woman and asks his questions in SA. The woman does not understand what he says. In *al-Laḥẓah al-ḥarijah* ("The critical moment") (1958), Idrīs makes his Egyptian characters speak in ECA and his British characters, who are supposed to speak in English, speak SA.[6]

Using vernacular in literature is more than just the construction of an identity of a protagonist; it also reflects the attitude, political affiliations, and ideologies of an author. This is the case for Yūsuf Idrīs, whose use of the colloquial is to express his sympathy for the socialist system advocated by Nasser (cf. Holes 2004).

An author who refused to use the colloquial in his dialogues and even in his narration is the Egyptian Nobel Prize winner Najīb Maḥfūẓ. In a letter to Luwīs ʿAwaḍ dated 1988, Maḥfūẓ discusses the diglossic situation in Egypt (Maḥfūẓ 2006: 21): "Language duality is not a problem but an innate ability. It is an accurate reflection of a duality that exists in all of us, a duality between our mundane daily life and our spiritual one." It appears that for Maḥfūẓ, literature is confined to the domain of spirituality and that SA is therefore its appropriate vehicle. However, Maḥfūẓ's later style shows "underlying dialectal structure and rhythm" (Holes 2004: 309). Somekh (1998: 191) calls his style in dialogues "colloqualized fuṣḥā," which is described as sentences that appear as SA, but with interwoven features of dialects. Such features may be lexical in nature, as when an ECA proverb is translated into SA. This "colloqualized fuṣḥā" is characteristic of the work of both Najīb Maḥfūẓ and ʿAbd al-Raḥman Munīf.

However, when illiterate characters in Maḥfūẓ's novels speak in SA, this, according to Holes (2004: 309), "requires a suspension of disbelief." Thus, Maḥfūẓ does not try to depict reality in his dialogues or at least linguistic reality. This is the case with most writers, as we have seen. And yet, the choice of code clearly serves a purpose, as this study will show. Unlike Maḥfūẓ, authors such as Tawfīq al-Ḥakīm, Yūsuf Idrīs, Iḥsān ʿAbd al-Quddūs, and Ḥaqqī—to name but a few—choose to use both ECA and SA in their novels, mainly in dialogues. The first author who took the initiative in 1960 of writing a novel in which the dialogue, including the internal monologue, was only in ECA is a woman. Laṭīfah al-Zayyāt (b. 1923), though not the first woman in Egypt to write novels, has been considered one of the first major feminist writers of the century in the Arab world at large. Her novel *al-Bāb al-maftūh* ("The open door") appeared in 1960, breaking both old and new rules in writing. *The Open Door* chronicles the political and sexual coming-to-awareness of a middle-class girl in the Egyptian provinces. Al-Zayyāt has called it "an attempt to capture her own vision of the world as she was growing into adulthood" (al-Zayyāt 2000: xxiii). A novel mainly about identity, history, politics, gender, and class, *The Open Door* was applauded as a genuine work that reflects social reality; however, it was also looked upon with skepticism, if not disdain, by the defenders of SA or, as Suleiman (2011) calls them in a different context, "the awkward squad," who considered it the work of a "woman" writer who may never have mastered SA. It was, indeed, the work of a woman writer, but a politically active one with a Leftist inclination. Al-Zayyāt had the courage and vision to explore and experiment with language further than anyone before her. While al-Sharqāwī—a socialist like al-Zayyāt—experimented with pure colloquial in his dialogues in his acclaimed novel *al-Arḍ* ("The land") (1953), al-Zayyāt took the use of colloquial a step further. For al-Sharqāwī, colloquial was the best option for an authentic portrayal of peasants and their lives. For al-Zayyāt, on the other hand, colloquial was the best option for an authentic portrayal of a middle-class family and, in particular, of Laylá, the daughter of the family, who struggles to find her own identity and adopt a different ideology from that of her community (see the remarks by Booth in al-Zayyāt 2000).

Unlike al-Sharqāwī and others before him, al-Zayyāt used ECA in both internal monologues and external dialogues, although not in narration. In the preface to her translation, Booth argues (al-Zayyāt 2000: xxvi–ii):

> This dominance of the colloquial enhances al-Zayyāt's portrayal of the mundane, of the everyday as a political arena, more specifically of the interrelationships between the gendering of expectations and behavior on the one hand, and the politics of national liberation on the other. It seems to me that this deployment of language can be seen as a feminist act, as basic to al-Zayyāt's production of what is unquestionably a feminist text in its assumptions, its authorial stance, as well as in its subject matter. In its very structure and language, the novel questions the culture's consignment to the margins of, first, female experience and articulation; second, the mundane as literary subject; and third, the language that is the medium of everyday experience. And her colloquial is lively, precise, female: characters emerge in their choice of expression.

Booth also explains how difficult it is for translators to render diglossia in English.

One could argue that the use of ECA by al-Zayyāt is similar to the use of ECA in opposition newspapers in Egypt (see Ibrahim 2010). However, both are different forms of media, and both need to be studied thoroughly first.

However, it is wrong to assume that ECA is associated with women writers and SA with men. In fact, some authors—although not necessarily women authors—have taken the form of the novel even further by producing ECA novels, mainly during the Sadat and Mubarak eras, rather than the era of pan-Arabism under Nasser. *Laban al-ʿuṣfūr* ("Bird's milk") (1994) by Yūsuf al-Qaʿīd is a case in point. The novel is critical of society and attempts to provide a realistic picture of the dire political and social situation in Egypt.

5.3.2 Studies of diglossia in literature

Diglossia in literature has been examined by a small number of linguists. For example, Abdel-Malek conducted a study on the influence of diglossia in the novels of Yūsuf al-Sibāʿī. According to him (1972: 141), the development of the "novel" genre in Arabic literature in the early twentieth century resulted in considerable tension between H (SA) and L (ECA). In response to that tension, he claims that a new linguistic style appeared in Arabic prose literature (developed by Yūsuf al-Sibāʿī and others). Abdel-Malek's idea of a mixed written style is similar to the idea of "Educated Spoken Arabic" (ESA) (cf. El-Hassan 1978), although he specifies no clear rules to define this style. Rosenbaum (2000) studies the occurrence of a mixed style SA and ECA in texts written by Egyptians—a phenomenon that seems to be gaining in popularity. He states that a mixed written style, involving clear shifts between H (SA) and L (ECA), breaks the "rules, old and new, of writing in Arabic, but does not encounter any serious opposition in Egyptian culture, probably because Egyptian readers have been accustomed to seeing ECA forms in print already for decades" (2000: 82).

Eid (2002b) analyzes the narration and dialogues of eight short stories by Egyptian female writers. Eid contends that the dialogue, which is expected to reflect the reality outside of the stories, is not necessarily in ECA. However, she also refers to the phenomenon of "colloquialized *fuṣḥā*," without using the term. She notices that in writing in general, there is no marking of short vowels, which means that in most cases there are no phonological differences between SA and ECA varieties. She concludes that in both narration and dialogue, the line between SA and ECA is blurred, due to the ambiguity of both clear syntactic markers and vowels. Eid also acknowledges cases of switching between ECA and SA in dialogues. Eid argues that writers use both SA and ECA in their dialogues, sometimes with a discourse function, as when Laṭīfah al-Zayyāt used SA for internal monologues and ECA for external dialogues, thus highlighting that there are two separate worlds, an internal one and an external one.

It is noteworthy, however, that most of the studies done on the language of dialogues have their own limitations, at least to some extent. First, the phenomenon of third language and "colloquialized *fuṣḥā*" have not been studied systematically in a manner that would allow rules and patterns to be deduced, whether structural rules, morphological rules, or lexical ones. There is a need for a study that attempts to highlight common recurrent patterns of using SA or ECA in dialogues, whether in relation to one author or different ones. In addition, few studies have tried to relate the identity of the protagonists to their code-choice. It is necessary to have more studies that apply linguistic theories to literature and examine how these could help broaden our understanding of language use in literature. This study tries to do so, although on a small scale.

5.3.3 Code-choice and code-switching as a linguistic resource: applications

This study will concentrate on the code used by the authors in dialogues. Although narrations may or may not be completely written in SA, dialogues are essential to study for a number of reasons. While it is expected, although not always preserved, that narration should be in SA, conversations that reflect real life should be in ECA. Conversations in Egypt between family, friends, colleagues, and even between an employee and his or her employer are typically in ECA. Additionally, conversations in different contexts that include the home, such as visiting friends or sexual intimacy, are in ECA. There are instances when an employee has to use SA as part of her or his work—for example, the employee is a lawyer and the context is a courtroom. Although there are no explicit surveys that show exactly the percentage of SA and ECA usage, one can depend on a different kind of medium of comparison, soap operas. Conversations in soap operas in Egypt are in ECA. Again, except in limited contexts, conversations tend to be in ECA and sometimes in ECA with insertions from SA. Soap operas are supposed to reflect reality, and the script is written to be performed orally and broadcast. Literature, especially the novel, is in most cases also a reflection of reality and a mirror of social, political, and personal problems. However, they are not written to be performed orally.

In the novels discussed in this section, the codes ECA and SA are used by authors in dialogue as a linguistic resource that reflects identity. That is, in dialogues or conversations, one would expect speakers to speak mainly in ECA, especially in dialogues between family and friends. If novels are supposed to reflect linguistic habits, then dialogues should be in ECA. However, as was clear in the last section, the use of language in novels is not necessarily tied to habits, but rather to ideologies, perceptions, and attitudes. That is, it is tied to higher levels of direct and indirect indexes. What is, indeed, essential is the manner in which authors use indexes of different codes to establish the stance of their protagonist and by so doing reflect the identity of this protagonist through her or his stance towards people and objects. That is, novels as a kind of public discourse are different in nature from patriotic songs or films. In novels, authors do not have to adhere to linguistic reality and they tend to use the diglossic situation to their advantage as a resource to convey their message and establish the identity of their protagonists. While linguistic diversity may be viewed as a negative aspect of Egyptian culture, it is, in fact, a complexity that is manipulated by authors. This diversity can be understood best if analyzed in relation to code indexes and stance-taking as a process. The next couple of examples will clarify this proposition.

To reiterate, in order to leave an impact on their audience, authors have to appeal to the tacit norms framework referred to in Chapter 1. It was argued in Chapter 1 that identity is habitual, because individuals function in the social world within a framework of tacit norms that are both linguistic and social in nature. This framework helps codes acquire their indexes. Authors work within this framework not to reflect linguistic reality in their dialogues, but to reflect stances and identities.

However, authors paradoxically still adhere to concepts such as linguistic unity and regard language diversity as chaos. That is, their ideologies and practices collide. However, this collision is perhaps expected, given the public discourse that they have been exposed to. One could also interpret their use of switching as an innovative process, in which they are establishing different tendencies or challenging old ones.

To recall, Collins (2011: 410) contends that indexical signs are interpreted in situated encounters, in which timing and exchange matter. That is, the context and genre are essential for us to grasp the full meaning of indexes. When authors switch in a dialogue between SA and ECA in a context that, realistically speaking, would be in one code, they are, in fact, using third level indexes to perform and create stances, a general impression of characters, and, ultimately, identity. This will be clear in the analysis below.

5.3.3.1 Analysis

In Ḥaqqī's novel *Qindīl Umm Hāshim*, Ismāʿīl, the main protagonist, has a number of conversations with his family and neighbors. He also overhears a number of monologues and dialogues. These conversations are not all in the same code.

It is essential to mention here that in the film adaptation of *Qindīl Umm Hāshim*, all of the dialogues are in ECA. That is, the linguistic diversity of the novel is lost.

In the novel, when Ismāʿīl speaks to his foreign girlfriend, their conversations are in SA. Note the following example, in which Mary, his British girlfriend, provides an evaluative statement about life (1944: 87):

يا عزيزي إسماعيل. الحياة ليست برنامجا ثابتا، بل مجادلة متجددة.

"My dear Ismail, life is not a fixed program, but an ever-renewing debate."

Of course, one would expect Mary to have addressed Ismāʿīl in English, but the author "translates" the statement into SA. Unlike Mary, Fāṭimah, his Egyptian cousin, speaks only in ECA and never takes a stance or even gives her opinion about any issue.

Fāṭimah is, as we see from the beginning of the novel, turning blind. Her eyes worsen throughout and while she seems to be resilient and patient, she is also simple-minded and naïve. An orphaned cousin, Fāṭimah lives with Ismāʿīl and his parents. She is expected to marry Ismāʿīl; indeed, as a teenage girl, she spent hours staring at him, while he studied. Ismāʿīl does not have any respect or admiration for her. Just like his inability to understand the Egypt that he comes back to, similarly, he cannot understand Fāṭimah. He returns to Egypt as a duty towards his parents, who have spent a fortune to educate him in the UK, but he also has to marry Fāṭimah as a duty to his parents.

Indeed, it is no coincidence that his professor calls Ismāʿīl's country the country of the blind. Before he leaves Egypt, Ismāʿīl is unaware that Fātimah has sick eyes and comes back to find her almost blind. Fāṭimah clearly represents "Egypt" throughout the novel. When she resorts to the old tradition of using oil from the lamp of the Prophet's granddaughter to cure her blindness, she almost turns blind, but when she submits to Ismāʿīl's modern medical attempts to cure her, she does become blind. Fāṭimah is only cured when Ismāʿīl's stance towards his country changes. While still aware of his fellow Egyptians' deficiencies, he starts to identify with them, as well as with the old quarter where he lives. He then decides to use both the lamp and the medicine. Thus, by showing respect towards her beliefs and the beliefs of his family and friends, he also manages to leave an impact on them and cure them.

Fāṭimah speaks less than most characters in the book. Fāṭimah is mostly addressed by Ismāʿīl in ECA, and we encounter her reply only once in the book. Again, it comes only in ECA (1944: 62):

قومي نامي يا فاطمة
لسة بدري ما جاليش نوم

> "Get up and go to sleep, Fāṭimah."
> "It's still early—I'm not sleepy yet." (= 1973: 48)

Fāṭimah is never an active participant. Things happen to her, others make decisions for her, but she patiently and stoically accepts everything. Her relationship with Ismāʿīl is not a partnership, but rather, as Ḥaqqī puts it, the relationship between a master and his slave. However, it is Fāṭimah's blindness that makes Ismāʿīl realize his ignorance and weakness. Although she never takes a stance, by turning blind, she makes him realize his limitations. Her ability to see at the end of the novel also makes him realize the importance of believing and respecting his culture. Ismāʿīl struggles with his Egyptian identity throughout and by submitting to the world that Fāṭimah represents and marrying her at the end, he is also succumbing to Egypt. On more than one occasion, Fātimah represents Egypt, which is highlighted by her speaking only in ECA. Although she speaks very little, she shows power and resilience. Fāṭimah is also illiterate and naïve, which represents the deficiencies of both Egyptians and the associations of ECA, which are not necessarily all positive. Like "Egypt," she may be authentic, but she is far from ideal.

When Ismāʿīl, towards the end of the novel, realizes the importance of the Egyptians' belief system, he also addresses Fāṭimah for the first and last time in SA (1944: 118–19):

تعالي يا فاطمة! لا تيأسي من الشفاء. لقد جئتك ببركة أم هاشم! ستجلي عنك الداء، و تزيح الأذى، و ترد إليك بصرك فإذا هو حديد. . .

و فوق ذلك، سأعلمك كيف تأكلين و تشربين، و كيف تجلسين و تلبسين، سأجعلك من بني آدم.

> "Come here, Fāṭimah. Do not despair of being cured. I have brought you the blessings of Umm Hāshim. She will drive away your illness and restore your sight as good as new."
>
> He pulled at her plait of hair as he continued to speak. "And on top of that, I will teach you how to eat and drink, how you should sit, and how you should dress—I'll make a lady of you." (= 1973: 86)

Ismāʿīl's patronizing tone with Fāṭimah is clear in the content of his discourse, as well as in the form. He takes the stance of the authoritative doer; this stance is reflected in his code-choice of SA with its authoritative indexes, as well as in the linguistic resources he uses. Ismāʿīl starts with the imperative: "Come here, and do not despair." Both imperative verbs ("come" and "do") reflect his authority over her. He then uses the future marker *sa-* to list what will happen to Fāṭimah once she uses the oil of Umm Hāshim, as well as what *he* will do to her once she regains her sight. He positions himself as the powerful and knowledgeable superior with the code-choice of SA. His patronizing tone is clear in his last statement. Here is its literal translation: "I will make you human." Yet Fāṭimah is a thermometer of both his success and failure. When she turns blind, he fails; when she is cured, he succeeds. It is noteworthy, however, that he also refers to the religious divine indexes of SA when he claims:

و ترد إليك بصرك فإذا هو حديد. . .

> "restore your sight as good as new."

This is, in fact, a direct reference to the Qurʾān in verse 22 of Surah Qāf. Intertextuality is employed here as a discursive resource to add power and authority to his statement.

Ismāʿīl is not the only character who uses SA in the novel. Interestingly, the dark-skinned prostitute whom Ismāʿīl fantasizes about as a teenager and who visits the shrine of Umm Hāshim to ask for her blessing is only depicted as speaking in SA (1944: 50):

> يا أم هاشم : يا ستارة على الولايا، لا تغضي عينيك و لا تشيحي بوجهك. تمد إليك يد مسترحمة فخذيها. إن الله طهرك و صانك و أنزلك الروضة. و إن قلبك لرؤوف. إذا لم يقصدك المرضى و المهزومون و المحطمون، فمن غيرك يقصدون؟ إذا نسينا فاذكري أنت! متى يمحي المقدر على؟ أيرضيك أن جسدي ليس مني، فما أشعر بالألم و هو ينهشه نهشا. ها هي روحي على عتباتك تتلوى و تتمرغ مصروعة. تريد أن تفيق. منذ غادرني رضا الله و أنا كالنائم يركبه الكابوس، يقبض في يد واحدة على الموت و الحياة! رضيت لحكمه و أسلمت نفسي، و لن أضيع و انت هنا معنا. أفيطول الأمد، أم رحمة الله قريب؟ نذرت لك يوم يتوب المولى على أن أزين مقامك الطاهر بالشموع.خمسين شمعة، يا أم هاشم يا أخت الحسين!
>
> "O Umm Hāshim, O you who shields women, deflect not your gaze, turn not your face away. The hand of one who seeks mercy is stretched toward you, so take hold of it. God has purified you, has sustained you, so take hold of it. God has purified you, has sustained you and has put you down in His garden, and your heart is compassionate. If the sick, the defeated, and the broken have not sought you, then who else should they seek? If we have forgotten, let you at least remember! When will that which has been destined for me be wiped out? Here is my soul at your threshold, felled to the ground, twisting, and writhing and wanting to recover. Since God's grace has left me, I have been like someone asleep and pursued by nightmares, clutching at life and death with a single hand! I consented to His judgment and handed myself over, and I shall not be lost so long as you are here with us. Will it be long, or is God's mercy close at hand? I have made a solemn vow to you that the day when the lord shall make me turn from sin I shall decorate your holy shrine with candles, with fifty candles, O Umm Hāshim, O sister of al-Husayn." (= 1973: 60)

This is an example of the use of third order indexes, as defined in Chapters 1 and 3. Within the contextual framework of this novel, this use of SA is both creative and challenging, but also simultaneously reflects second order indexes. The prostitute implores Umm Hāshim to help her find the right path. She refers to Umm Hāshim with her relational identification, the sister of Ḥusayn, the Prophet's grandson. Although SA (as is clear from the content of the message, as well as from the indexes discussed in Chapter 2) indexes the prostitute's seriousness and reverence for Umm Hāshim, it does not contradict the intimate, emotional relationship that the prostitute has with Umm Hāshim. The prostitute refers to Umm Hāshim as the one who shields women. Her stance towards Umm Hāshim is that of the powerless supplicant towards the powerful yet merciful woman. Umm Hāshim is also an active doer: she shields women. She therefore has power. The prostitute feels comfortable enough with Umm Hāshim to command her to look at her and not ignore her. She even argues with her using a rhetorical question: "If the sick, the defeated, and the broken have not sought you, then who else should they seek?"

After this supplication, the dark-skinned girl then kisses the fence of the shrine, a sincere kiss from her heart. The narrator, Ismāʿīl's nephew, says: "Who knows that Umm Hāshim did not kiss her back from behind the fence?" (1973: 80) Again, realistically speaking, the prostitute, who is illiterate, would not have spoken to Umm Hāshim in SA. However, the author uses the indexes of SA to reflect the stance of the prostitute towards Umm Hāshim and her power. The reader is struck with the choice of code of the prostitute, as opposed to that of Fāṭimah, for example. The perceptive reader is then left to contemplate the choice and its relevance.

A dialogue that employs code-switching between ECA and SA to the utmost to reflect the conflicted relationship between Ismāʿīl and his mother is the one below. When Ismāʿīl sees his mother putting oil in the eyes of Fāṭimah, he is outraged (1944: 99–100) (SA is set in bold):

ما هذا يا مي؟

هذا زيت قنديل أم هاشم. تعودت أن اقطر لها منه كل مساء

لقد جاءنا به صديقك الشيخ درديري. انه يذكرك و يتشوق اليك. هل تذكره؟ أم تراك نسيته؟

حرام عليك الأذية. حرام عليك. **انت مؤمنة تصلين فكيف تقبلين أمثال هذه الخرافات و الأوهام؟**

صمتت امه...

اسم الله عليك يا اسماعيل يا بني. ربنا يكملك بعقلك **هذا غير** الدوا و الأجزا. **هذا ليس إلا من بركة أم هاشم.**

أهي دي أم هاشم بتاعتكم هي اللي ح تجيب للبنت العمى **سترون كيف أداويها فتنال على يدي أنا الشفاء الذي لم تجده عند الست أم هاشم.**

يا أبني ده ناس كثير بيتباركوا بزيت قنديل أم العواجز جربوه و ربنا شفاهم عليه. إحنا طول عمرنا جاعلين تكالنا على الله و على أم هاشم.ده سرها باتع

انا لا اعرف أم هاشم و لا أم عفريت.

والده: **ماذا تقول؟ هل هذا كل ما تعلمته في** بلاد برة؟ **كل ما كسبناه منك أن تعود إلينا كافرا؟**

"What's that, mother?"

"It's oil from the lamp of Umm Håshim. Every evening I pour some of it into her eyes. Your friend Sheikh Dardiri brought it to us. He remembers you and longs to see you again. Do you remember him, or have you forgotten him?"

"You should be ashamed of yourself at the harm you're doing." He shouted at his mother at the top of his voice "Shame on you! **And you a believer who says her prayers, how can you accept such superstitions and humbug?"**

"I take my refuge in God." and then said to him, "God protect you, my son Ismael. May the lord keep you in your right mind. **This is nothing to do** with medicine, though. **This is just the blessing of Umm Håshim."**

"So this is Umm Hāshim, the one that will make the girl blind! You'll see how I'll treat her and how I'll cure her when Umm Hāshim failed."

"My son, many people seek blessings through the oil of Umm Hāshim, the mother of the destitute. They tried it, and the lord cured them through it. All our life, it is God and Umm Hāshim that we put our trust in. her secret powers are invincible."

> **"I know neither Umm Håshim** nor Umm of the fairies!"
> Father: **"What are you saying? Is this what you learned** abroad? **Is all we have gained to have you return to us an infidel?"** (= 1973: 74)

In this example, three orders of indexicality are used simultaneously. The question asked by Ismāʿīl is in SA. The fact that Ismāʿīl asks a question in SA positions him in the authoritative role (second order index). The mother's answer also comes in SA. She attempts to accommodate to him in more than one way. First, she uses the same code as his question. Second, she uses relational identification (Van Leeuwen 1996) when she reminds him of his friend Sheikh Dardīrī. She, unlike him, is at pains to find a common ground and uses all of her linguistic resources to do so. By reminding him of his friend, she is also reminding him of his identity as a native in this place with friends and family, a dense and multiplex network. Ismāʿīl does not accept the identity that his mother tries to impose on him. His stance is different from hers in relation to the place and people around them. This stance is reflected in his code-choice and the indexes of this choice. After his mother's reply in SA, Ismāʿīl's reply comes unexpectedly in ECA. He refuses to accommodate to her and wants to highlight their differences, rather than similarities. His first exclamation is in ECA: "You should be ashamed." Then he proceeds in SA with its authoritative indexes to reprimand his mother for using the oil. SA places him in the more powerful position. The rhetorical question at the end of his statement shows the degree of his indignation at the use of the oil to treat Fāṭimah's eyes.

The mother is taken by surprise and is silent for a while, then starts to flatter him and explain why she uses the oil in Fāṭimah's eyes. She starts in ECA, this time to evoke its intimate associations, but then code-switches to SA. The demonstratives used by the mother are in SA for emphasis and to evoke the seriousness and sacredness of her beliefs. She wants him to understand what Umm Hāshim means to them. He fails to identify with her beliefs and conceptions. His reply comes first in ECA, which demonstrates that his stance towards Umm Hāshim is different from his mother's, as is clear through his use of pronouns. He says: أهي دي أم هاشم بتاعتكم ("This is that Umm Hāshim of yours"). This use of the clitic pronoun كم -kum as a structural resource in addition to code-choice as another linguistic resource highlights his stance towards both Umm Hāshim and his local community. The use of ECA in this context is to undermine the importance of Umm Hāshim as a sacred figure. He evokes the negative ECA indexes, as opposed to the positive ones. This is clear in the content of his discourse and is reinforced by his use of the pronoun "your." He disaligns himself totally from his mother's (and the community's) beliefs and, therefore, from their identity as Egyptians more generally. When he then proceeds to mention what he is capable of doing to Fāṭimah, he does so in SA with all its powerful indexes. The mother tries to again explain what Umm Hāshim means to them, doing so using ECA.

The mother starts with the vocative "my son" to remind him of the relationship that they share—that of son and mother. It is only expected that she would then use the less formal, more intimate ECA code.

Her use of linguistic resources here includes the use of quantification in "many people" to show that this belief in the power of Umm Hāshim is not just her belief. Also, the use of the ECA aspectual marker *b-* in بيتباركوا ("they seek her blessing") denotes the commonality of Umm Hāshim's blessing. His reply comes in SA and starts with the pronoun, followed by the SA negative marker *la:* in "I do not know." Ismāʿīl refuses to acknowledge the power of Umm Hāshim. The second part of his proposition is in ECA and may seem to them almost blasphemous. His lack of respect towards Umm Hāshim is not just reflected in his use of words to refer to her, but also in his use of ECA.

The father overhears this blasphemy and interferes. The father's indignation and shock are reflected in his code-choice, as well as his rhetorical question:

> His Father: "**What are you saying? Is this what you learned** abroad? **Is all we have gained to have you return to us an infidel?**"

The father replies in SA to reflect the seriousness of Ismāʿīl's mistake in cursing Umm Hāshim. He only switches to ECA when he refers to "abroad." This switching may also reflect his lack of respect for what Ismāʿīl has learned while abroad. The last question presupposes that his parents expected him to learn something from studying abroad, to gain something. The fear is that this did not happen.

Again, it is clear that the switching between both codes reflects the mounting tension between son and mother, Ismāʿīl and his community, and Ismāʿīl and his country. This mounting tension is understood more thoroughly by understanding the higher third level index that is employed. This dialogue, unrealistic as it is, is innovative and it is part of the creative process of the author.

I would like to explain this example using a different model and referring to a similar example that occurred in the data of Myers-Scotton (1986). The model I want to refer to is the social arena examined by Scotton and Ury (1977). According to Scotton and Ury, there are three universal social arenas that affect code-choice: identity, power, and transaction. A speaker switches to different codes, in order to define the interaction taking place in terms of a social arena or to keep it undefined. The first universal social arena is identity: a speaker switches according to the identity of the person that she or he is speaking to and his or her own identity as well. The second social arena is power: code-switching also depends on the power that one has over others or the power that others have over one another. The third social arena is transaction: code-switching depends on the situation and the purpose of the speech act. A speaker may not be sure about the social arena: for example, she or he may not be sure about the status of the other person. In that case, she or he uses a code that will help keep the interaction undefined. Myers-Scotton (1986: 408) gives the example of a brother and sister in western Kenya, who were conversing in the brother's shop. The sister wanted to receive special treatment from her brother, so she used their shared mother tongue. He, on the other hand, replied in Swahili to show her that he was treating her as a customer in his store. This shows that speakers may use code-choice in order to emphasize aspects of their identity. Whereas the female speaker in the example chose to emphasize her identity as a "sister" (rather than that of a customer in her brother's shop), the male speaker does not accept the identity that she assigns herself. It is obvious that the brother and sister do not agree on the kind of transaction taking place. The brother refuses to act within the social arena that the sister assigns to him and chooses another one instead. This interaction suggests that the sister expected to have power over her brother and, therefore, to receive special treatment—a better price, a better cut of meat—but in the end, his power as shop keeper prevails over her power as his sister.

The dialogue in Ḥaqqī's novel can be analyzed in similar terms. In the example of the interaction between Ismāʿīl and his parents, there is also no agreement over power, transaction, and identity. This is reflected in both the content of the dialogue, as well as the code used.

However, the difference between Myers-Scotton's example from Kenya and the extract from this novel is that the former is real, while the latter is fictional. There can be no doubt that if the imagined dialogue had occurred in real life it would have been in ECA throughout. In fact, in the film based on the novel, it is in ECA. In other words, the fictional dialogue does not reflect language use in a real-life situation, but it does reflect realistic social interactions and power struggles by drawing on the underlying indexes of different codes. I contend that authors use their knowledge of ECA and SA indexes as a stylistic device to highlight identity. Without knowledge of the indexes of both codes, authors would fail to have the right effect on their readers. In this hypothetical context, both readers and authors have an established first and second order of indexes in place, and the reader is challenged by the use of the higher index to perform stance and reflect identity.

A relatively more recent novel is *al-Ḥubb fī Al-manfā* ("Love in exile") (1995) by Bahāʾ Ṭāhir. The novel examines the life of a journalist, who works as a correspondent for an Egyptian newspaper in a European country. Throughout the novel, the protagonist evaluates his life and achievements and suffers from frustration caused by his exile and a sense of uselessness. The reader soon comes to realize that the journalist has been sent to Europe to be removed from the media in Egypt. A middle-aged divorcee, the journalist is a symbol of a generation that has been oppressed and marginalized, both in Egypt and abroad.

Unlike Ismāʿīl in Ḥaqqī's novel, the unnamed protagonist's search for identity is not successful. While Ismāʿīl ends up embracing his Egyptian collective identity with all its problems, the search for identity in Ṭāhir's work ends in utter failure. The protagonist or narrator defines himself in relation to the historical events of the Nasser era and Nasser's ideology. He believes that Egypt is part of the Arab world and that the Arab world (or *umma*, "Nation") is worth fighting for. With Nasser's defeat in 1967 and subsequent death in 1970, the narrator's dreams are shattered. His relational identification to Nasser remains, but it is never effective. Subsequently, the narrator fails to establish any other fruitful relational identification, except with his two children. Eventually, he only identifies with his daughter, not even with his son.

Ṭāhir's novel sheds light on a phase in the construction of Egyptian collective identity during which Egyptians supposedly considered Egypt as, first and foremost, an Arab country, during which they were fully engaged in promoting independence movements in other Arab countries, as well as Palestinian liberation efforts. As the examples below show, the author employs code-switching to reflect the failure to belong and the loss of Arab identity, due to the policies of Sadat and Mubarak. The conflicted, detached identity of this particular Egyptian character, as a symbol of a whole generation of Egyptians, is reflected in the dialogues that he conducts with individuals around him and the code he uses to address these individuals.

Although the journalist dies at the end of the novel, his death comes as a release from all the defeats and disturbances that he endured. In the end, he says (Ṭāhir 1995: 254):[7]

لم أكن متعبا. كنت أنزلق في بحر هاديء..تحملني على ظهري موجة ناعمة و صوت ناي عذب.
و قلت لنفسي: أهذه هي النهاية؟ ما أجملها! و كان الصوت يأتي من بعيد. و كان الصوت يكرر يا سيد..يا سيد!..و لكنه راح يخفت و راح صوت الناي يعلو.
و كانت الموجة تحملني يعيدا.
تترجرج في بطء و تهدهدني..الناي يصحبني بنغمته الشجية الطويلة الى السلام و الى السكينة.

I wasn't tired. I was sliding into a calm sea, carried on my back by a soft wave and the sweet melody of a flute.
I said to myself, "Is this the end? How beautiful!"

The voice was coming from far away, saying, "Sir, sir!" but it kept getting lower as the sound of the flute kept rising.
The wave was carrying me away.
It was undulating slowly and rocking me. The flute was accompanying me, with its long, plaintive melody, to peace and tranquillity.
(= Ṭāhir 2001: 277)

The protagonist has numerous conversations with his young European girlfriend, who, he claims, repeats Arabic words like a parrot. She does not speak any Arabic, but instead speaks possibly German or French. His communication with her is written in the novel in SA. This is not, in fact, surprising. The girl interacts with him in a foreign language, and he, the author, "translates" this interaction into SA. Since translation is usually made into the standard language and not the colloquial one, it comes as no surprise that he uses SA. As mentioned above, this is a standard device used to represent foreign-language speech in Arabic films.

However, when the narrator interacts with his only male Egyptian friend, who is the same age as him and suffers very similar problems, the dialogue is also set in SA. Note the following example (1995: 104–5):

قلت: اذن على اي شيء تلومها؟
أخذ يحك جبينه بيده ثم قال: هل قلت أنا اني ألومها؟ كل ما قلته اني أحبها.
و سكت مرة أخرى قبل أن يقول:أنا عائد الآن من عندها . . . من البدء . . . لم أكن استطيع ان اقاوم . . . كرت سنوات عمري كله و تلخصت الحياه كلها في شيء واحد. اني اريد هذه الجميلة لي. أريدها هنا و أريدها الآن . . .
-ثم ماذا ماذا حدث؟ . . .
-لم يحدث شيئ.
-كيف؟
-قلت لك لم يحدث شيء! لا تسألني كيف كانت تمسك بيدي و نحن في التاكسي. تقبض عليها و تنشج . . . و كانت هي تلهث مغمضة العينين و تحاول التخلص من ثيابها و هي بين ذراعي و تقول بهمس متوتر: نعم، نعم، قبلني هكذا، هكذا هيا.

"So what are you blaming her for?" I said. He began to rub his forehead with his hand and said, "Did I say that I blame her? All I said is that I love her."
He fell silent again before saying, "I've just come back from her house . . . from the beginning . . . I couldn't help it. The years of my entire life surged and all life was epitomized in one thing: I want this beautiful woman for myself. I want her here and I want her now . . ."
—"Then what? What happened?"
—"Nothing happened."
—"How?"
—"I told you nothing happened. Don't ask me how. She was holding my hand in the cab, gripping it convulsively. I kissed her face and every inch of her and

> she was panting, her eyes closed, trying to get out of her clothes while in my arms, whispering tensely, 'Yes, kiss me like that, like that, come on.'"
> (= 2001: 112–13)

In the above example, his friend explains his inability to perform sexually with a girl. The subject is very intimate and one would certainly not expect this interaction to take place in SA in real life. However, the author chooses not to use any ECA at all. He is, in fact, laying claim to three orders of indexicality; first and second order indexes of ECA include intimacy and informality and since both are absent, ECA is not used. Third order indexes are used, because within the contextual framework of this interaction and the topic of discussion, ECA would have been used, but it is not utilized by the author. That is, the author takes indexes a step further to construct an overall picture of the identity of the protagonist.

Meanwhile, in another interaction between the protagonist and a young Egyptian waiter who eventually turns to fanaticism, the author also uses SA for the interaction. Note the following example (1995: 224):

سألت يوسف: و لكن ما علاقة الامير بذلك؟
الأمير افهمني اشياء كثيرة يا استاذ، اشياء كانت غائبة عني . . .

> —"What does the prince have to do with it?" I asked Yusuf.
> —"Prince Hamid explained many things, *ustaz*, things that were not clear to me."
> (= 2001: 248)

When interacting with foreigners, SA is always used. This extends to other Arabs, who speak different dialects. In fact, when interacting with a corrupt Arab prince, the whole interaction is in SA (1995: 160):

ضغط على يدي و هو يقول: حمدا لله على السلامة. كنت مشغولاً عليك . . .

> The prince repeated as he looked at me, "Thank God you are well. I was actually worried about you . . ."
> (= 2001: 170)

One might think that the whole novel is, in fact, in SA, and that is the reason why conversations are also in SA. Given that there are a number of famous authors who choose to use SA only as a political statement, one would, indeed, expect this from Bahā' Ṭāhir. However, what is really of interest is that this is not, in fact, true.

It appears that SA is used as a detachment device to reflect the feelings of exile and nostalgia that dominate the novel. The protagonist, in fact, fails to establish any sound and happy relationship with any of the characters, except for his children. There is not one single instance in the novel when the protagonist seems to belong anywhere. He neither belongs to the European country in which he resides, nor to Egypt. His relationship with the young European woman is doomed to fail, while his male friend ultimately disappears, the young Egyptian waiter turns into a fanatic, and the prince from the Gulf stands for everything he hates and fights against.

One can contrast the protagonist's failed interactions with strangers with his more personal conversations with his children (1995: 88):

- ألو يا بابا؟
- أيوه يا حبيبتي . . . ازيك يا هنادي؟
- هلكانة من المذاكرة، و الدنيا حرّ جدا
- معلهش شدي حيلك يا هنادي هانت . . . الإمتحان الاسبوع الجاي، مش كدة؟
- أيوة. إدعي لي يا بابا . . . .

جائني صوت خالد عميقا ووقورا و هو يقول بالفصحى:

- السلام عليكم
- و عليكم السلام يا خالد . . . إزيك يا ابني؟
- الحمد لله يا بابا . . . و انت ازاي صحتك؟ كويس ان شاء الله؟

—"Hello Dad?"
—"Yes, love. How are you, Hanādī?"
—"Studying is killing me. It's very hot here."
—"It's okay. Hang in there, Hanādī. The exams are next week, right?"
—"Yes. Pray for me, Dad."
Khalid's voice was deep and dignified as he said in formal Arabic,
—"Peace be upon you."
—". . . and you too, Khalid. How are you, son?"
—"I am fine, thank God. And you, how's your health? I hope it's fine, God willing."
(= 2001: 96)

Only the narrator's children can touch his heart. Moved by hope and agony, the protagonist asks his daughter—in ECA—never to change, to always remain as innocent and in love with life (1995: 188):

- خلاص يا هنادي. انا فهمت خالد انك تخرجي و تروحي النادي وقت ما انت عايزة. لكن طبعا لازم تاخدي اذن ماما . . .
- بس كدة . . . انت تأمر . . . باي باي . . .
- استني دقيقة يا هنادي
- ايوه يا بابا
- باقول ايه يا هنادي «سكت لحظة ثم قلت» ارجوك يا هنادي..خليك زي ما انت و اوعي تتغيري.

—"Okay Hanādī, I told Khalid that you can go out and can go to the club whenever you want, but of course you have to get your mom's permission . . ."
—"Is that all? That's so easy, bye bye . . ."
—"Wait a minute, Hanādī."
—"Yes, Daddy?"
—"Tell you what, Hanādī." I paused for a moment then added: "Please, Hanādī, stay as you are. Don't change." (= 2001: 206–7)

Note the following explanation that comes from his son, concerning banning his sister from going to the club (1995: 187):

- يا بابا اصل النادي فيه مساخر و فيه شباب فاسدين و انا . . .
- اي حتة في الدنيا فيها ناس فاسدين و فيها ناس كويسين. سيبها تتعلم بنفسها و تحمي روحها . . .
- اذا كنت انا الراجل بطلت اروح النادي. هي تروح؟ حضرتك حتدلعها زي ماما و تسمع كلامها اول ما تنزل لها دمعتين؟

—"Well, father, immoral things take place at the club and there are bad young men and . . ."
—"There are bad people and good people every place on earth. Let her learn on her own and protect herself . . ."
—"If I, a man, have stopped going to the club, how can you expect me to let her go? Are you going to spoil her just as mom does and every time she sheds two tears?" (= 2001: 206)

The dialogue here is in ECA, like in the previous example. The tone in the latter is very intimate, whereas in this last example the protagonist perceives that his son is also drifting away from him. He lays claim to the indexes of ECA, including feelings of intimacy and harmony that are not frequently present in the novel. It is precisely because of his unhappiness and agony that he dies happily at the end.

The concept of indexicality can once again help clarify the use of code-switching and code-choice in this novel. As was shown above, the protagonist does not speak in just one code throughout the novel. This implies that the use of the other code (ECA) is to juxtapose his stances to different people around him. That is, code-choice positions him in relation to others and aligns or disaligns him with objects and individuals. When the protagonist uses SA in dialogues that—realistically speaking—should be in ECA, he calls upon third order indexes of both ECA and SA in different contexts. In this novel, mostly SA negative connotations are called upon, for SA is associated with formality and even detachment (first and second order indexes). SA is also used to "translate" foreign languages. When SA is then used to depict the conversation between the protagonist and his close Egyptian friend, it still denotes foreignness on the part of the protagonist: he is a stranger to himself, as well as to his closest friends. The same code is used for two different contexts, but with the same indexes. On the other hand, the use of ECA is associated with informality and intimacy, and both of these indexes are called upon when the protagonist converses with his children. The estrangement that prevails throughout the text is absent from these short dialogues; these conversations are only phone calls and are never face-to-face meetings. Thus, although his children are far away in terms of physical distance, they are emotionally close to him. He is also detached from his inner self and can only reach it by bridging the distance, as he does in the case of phoning his children.

As was mentioned above, indexicality is related to stance-taking, while stance-taking is related directly to identity construction on the part of the protagonist. Going back to the concept of subject positions as developed by McConnell-Ginet (2004), one could say that the protagonist adopts a particular subject position with all people around him, except his own children. This subject position is that of a formal distant acquaintance and is expressed through the indexes of SA. Throughout most of the novel, the protagonist has a problem achieving reconciliation with his inner self. His last plea to his daughter comes in ECA, as he entreats her never to change.

The third novel analyzed in this section is *Awrāq al-narjis* ("The leaves of Narcissus") by Sumayyah Ramaḍān (2001), which follows the story of Kīmī, as discussed above. Its female protagonist, Kīmī, who suffers from a psychological illness, embarks on a forced search of identity in Ireland, where she studies for a PhD. Most of Kīmī's conversations are either in SA or a mixture of ECA and SA. There is only one character in the novel that addresses, and is addressed by, Kīmī in ECA—namely, Āminah. Āminah is a servant from the countryside who accompanies Kīmī throughout her life, even in the asylum, and is portrayed as Kīmī's alter-ego.

Kīmī has a conflicted relationship with everyone around her, but is able to confide in Āminah, who provides her with a "home": Āminah smells like Kīmī's mother, tells Kīmī stories, believes in Kīmī, and also shares Kīmī's secrets and frustrations.

Below is an example of Āminah interacting with Kīmī (Ramaḍān 2001: 23):

لكنها تنتفض فجأة
"و النبي انت فاضية و مقعداني جنبك أحكيلك، أوعي كدة يا شيخة، و انت تعطلي المراكب السايرة، أنا ورايا شغل".
و لا تتركني مع اني رأيت الباب يغلق وراءها. و تظل تحكي، أكاد أراها رأي العين، حتى الآن و أسمعها تحكي. حكاية الملك الاطلسي. و لما تنتهي تقول: "بس و عليه، كنت هناك و جيت، حتى العشا ما تعشيت"
لا اذكر أني رأيتها تأكل إلا في مناسبات ضئيلة جداً. كانت تأكل و كأنها لا تأكل. تعيش وسطنا و لا اعلم متى

تدخل الحمام، متى تبدل ملابسها. اصحو فتكون في كامل هيئتها و أنام و هي في كامل هيئتها. و تشع منها دائما رائحة الصابون و كولونيا 555. أذكرها الآن و كأنها ماتتز
أخاف ان اكون قتلتها؟ لو كتبنا الناس يموتون؟

Abruptly she gives her body a shake. "Look here, now! You've got nothing to do, you get me sitting here next to you telling you stories, and the next thing you know—you'd keep sailing ships from leaving harbor, you would. I've got work to do."
But she doesn't leave me, even though I saw the door close behind her. She goes on talking. I can all but see her, almost as if she were before my eyes, even now; I can hear her narrative and the story. The tale of al-malik al-atlasi, king of the Atlas Mountains.
When she comes to an end, she chants, "That's all, that's it. I was there and came here on my own feet, not even dinner did I stop to eat."
I don't remember seeing her eat, ever, except on very rare occasions. She ate as if she wasn't eating. She lived in our midst and I never knew when she used the bathroom or when she changed her clothes. By the time I woke up in the mornings she was already dressed for the day, and when I went to sleep at night she was still fully dressed. She always gave off the smell of soap and cologne no. 555. When I recall her now, it's as if she is dead. I'm afraid. I am afraid I killed her. If we write people, do they die?
(= Ramaḍān 2002: 18)

Āminah is almost not human, but rather acts as a symbol of a home that Kīmī never reaches. It is possible that Āminah is also, like Fāṭimah in *Qindīl Umm Hāshim*, the "authentic Egypt." The fact that Āminah consistently uses ECA in her interactions with Kīmī calls upon the informal, intimate, and authentic indexes of ECA (first and second order indexes).

By the way of contrast, Kīmī addresses her mother in SA, and her mother replies likewise in SA (2001: 89):

بجانب السرير جلست امي، و عندما فتحت عيني كانت تبتسم مشجعة:
-سوف أجيء لك بشيء تأكلينه يجب ان تأكلي الآن و تستريحي.
-قتلته، أرئيت؟ قتلته. لو كنت رأيت عينيه و انا امزق كارت الفيزا، لم ادفع القربان، انا القربان، عندما لا ادفعني يموت احدهم دائما.
صوتها عاقل، واضح و بسيط في تعامله مع الكلام:
- لم تقتلي احدا. لم يحدث شيء. انت متعبة قليلا، هذا هو كل ما في الامر.

Next to the bed sat my mother. When I opened my eyes she smiled encouragingly.
"I'll bring you something to eat. You must eat now, and rest."
"I killed him, did you see? I killed him. If you had seen his eyes as I was ripping up the credit card, you would have known that I did not pay enough. I am offering. When I don't pay with myself, someone dies. Every time."

Her voice is wise and even. Clear and simple in its use of words.
"You did not kill anyone. Nothing happened. You're a bit tired, that's all there is to it."
(= 2002: 85)

In the next example, Āminah, unlike Kīmī's mother, addresses Kīmī in ECA, and Kīmī declares in ECA that she wants to go home. Āminah replies that Kīmī is already home and she embraces her. The example implies that Āminah is home or, in other words, that Āminah is Egypt (2001: 100):

مالك يا حبيبتي؟ كنت بتضحكي من دقيقة بس
-عايزة اروح يا آمنة، زهقت.
[. . .]
- انت في بيتك يا كيمي، هنا بيتك و انت دلوقت وسط اهلك و ناسك.
- انت ليه رحتك برتقال؟
- كنت بعصر برتقال.
[. . .]
كيف استحوذت آمنة على رائحة امي؟

"What's wrong, love? Just a minute ago you were laughing."
"I want to go home, Amna. I'm tired of this."
[. . .]
"You are at home, Kīmī, this is your home, honey, and you're in your own family, your own folk, dear."
"Why do you smell like oranges?"
"I was squeezing oranges?"
[. . .]
My mother—she is the smell of oranges. How did Amna take over that smell?
(= 2002: 94–5)

The three women addressed in ECA in the last three novels are depicted as "authentic" Egyptians: Fātimah is naïve and illiterate, but is also the one who passively measures the success or failure of Ismāʿīl; Hanādī, the daughter of the protagonist in *Love in Exile*, represents everything that is beautiful in Egypt and has the most meaningful relationship with him; Āminah is the "home" that can and does save Kīmī in *The Leaves of Narcissus*. What these female characters have in common is that they are depicted as speaking in ECA. What is more, their ECA is juxtaposed with the SA of other characters, such as Ismāʿīl's parents, the narrator's friends, and Kīmī's mother. I believe that the female characters' use of ECA is highlighted deliberately by the authors, in order to invoke the "authentic" indexes of ECA, which were discussed in Chapter 3.

The theme of estrangement recurs in al-Ghīṭānī's novel *Kitāb al-rinn* ("The book of rinn") (2008), the last novel analyzed in this section. Here, too, the protagonist fails to establish a close relationship with people around him, including his wife and children. Again, the language form reflects this alienation, as everyone is addressed by the protagonist in SA, except one "person"; in fact, this dead person is now an ancient Egyptian statue.

It is worth noting that the conversations are intentionally short to convey the protagonist's feelings of detachment that he suffers from the beginning to the end of the novel. For example, the protagonist has a short conversation with an acquaintance whose name he has forgotten. The conversation is represented in SA. As was noted earlier, this does not reflect reality, but rather a fictional, imagined universe, since in reality Egyptians would not speak to their acquaintances in SA. In another example, the protagonist is addressed by a young man in a museum (2008: 66):

أفاجأ به يميل نحوى، يقول بتأنٍ:
«إذا كنت جئت تسأل عن العلمٍ، فلا علم هنا،
وإذا كنت تبحث عن مقصد سعيك فأنت تاركه هناك،
وراءك..»

> He bends towards me suddenly and says slowly, "If you come seeking knowledge, there is no knowledge here. If you are searching for your aim, know that you left it there, behind you."

It is noteworthy, however, that code-switching occurs only once in the entire novel, and only once does the narrator use ECA, rather than SA. This happens when he is faced with an ancient Egyptian statue of Pharaoh Senedjemibra in the museum. The protagonist comments that this statue, to him, represents a long-lasting friendship, familiarity, and mutual affection. In fact, this is the only instance in the novel in which the protagonist expresses these feelings towards anyone, whether dead or alive (2008: 94):

أما سى نجم رع فصحبة وعشرة وملاطفة.
يغلب على مرقده اللون الأصفر الصريح الواضح، كل ألوان المرقد خصبة، طازجة كأنها بُسطت بالأمس،

> Senedjemibra is a companion, a good friend and we share mutual affection. His tomb is mainly bright yellow. All the colors of the tomb are fresh and fertile as if painted yesterday.

The narrator then addresses the ancient statue in ECA and seems to believe that he listens to him attentively (2008: 94):

عندما بدأت الفهم، ابتسمت، كنت أقف بمفردى متطلّعا إليه، خاطبته وكلى ثقة أنه يصغى..
«طبعاً يا عم، شغل المعلم لنفسه..»
أتوقف أمام الجانب الشرقى، أسعى معه أثناء حصاده القمح فى حقول يارو، الجنة الأبدية، [. . .] زوجته بردائها الأبيض خلفه، حقول يارو تتخللها قنوات المياه، تحيط بها كالإطار، هذا طبيعى، لابد من أنهار فى الجنة

> When I started to understand, I smiled. I was standing alone watching him. I addressed him with all confidence that he hears me, "Yes of course mate, you are the masterpiece of the craftsman himself aren't you?"
> I stand on the eastern side. I go with him to reap wheat in Yārū's fields, the eternal paradise [. . .] I can see his wife with her white garment behind him. There are water canals that go through Yārū's fields. The canals surround it as a frame. This is natural. There must be rivers in paradise.

The feeling of solidarity between the protagonist and the statue is reflected in the narrator's code-choice, as he positions himself as the friend of Senedjemibra. It would seem that the protagonist reaches an understanding of his identity once he identifies with the ancient statue, which is made to represent more than just an ancestor; he is both a friend and family member. For once, the protagonist does not feel detached from his surroundings, but in fact seems part-and-parcel of them and a continuation of the existence of the statue. The fact that this process of identification is expressed in ECA clearly demonstrates that intimacy and solidarity are primary indexes of ECA.

5.3.4 Discussion

This chapter examines a different kind of public discourse—namely, written discourse. Unlike patriotic songs, this material is perhaps less accessible to everyone. However, it is also a kind of public discourse that is essential in its own right. First, it reinforces the associations and linguistic indexes discussed in the earlier chapters. It can be shown that Egyptian authors share the ideologies and attitudes of most Egyptians and operate within the same tacit framework of norms. What sets novels apart is that their authors can manipulate linguistic indexes and appeal to them to construct the identity of their protagonists.

The second point that makes this kind of public discourse relevant is that authors in their dialogues do not reflect realistic linguistic habits. They construct a different linguistic context, in which ideologies, attitudes, and perceptions are more prominent. Language is abstracted from its function for communication to a social variable.

Authors who adhere to one code in dialogues are not the main concern of this chapter. It is, in fact, authors who creatively switch between different codes employing orders of indexicality in the process that concern us here. The audience or reader in this case is challenged and motivated to follow the lead of the author in deciphering indexes at different levels and reflecting on identity more generally. By using three orders of indexicality simultaneously, authors show how unique the genre of the novel is in Egypt and the Arab world more generally.[8]

Third, unlike in patriotic songs and Egyptian films, dialogues in novels seem to contain more instances of code-switching and code-mixing. This is not to deny that there is code-switching between SA and ECA in films and songs, but the degree and frequency is less. As we have seen, the use of ECA and SA is related to indexes of authenticity, familiarity, and solidarity. In other instances, code-switching reflects a struggle for authority and power.

For example, in the classic Egyptian novel *al-Watad* ("The tent peg") (1986) by Khayrī Shalabī, a powerful, rural, illiterate mother holds her family together. Although her husband is alive, he is never in the foreground, as decisions are made mainly by the mother. The mother's power is reflected through her code-choice: in the last chapter of the novel, the uneducated peasant mother, Fāṭimah, is represented speaking in SA, while her children reply to her in ECA, although we know that this could not have happened in reality. It would be almost impossible for an uneducated, peasant woman on her deathbed to start speaking pure SA. Similarly, her son's replies are always in ECA, since he does not have any power over his mother. Note the following example, in which the eldest son tries to placate his mother by telling her not to take what his young brother said seriously:

-صلي على النبي يا حاجة بقى [[. . . سيبك منه هو يعني الكلام عليه جمرك؟

"Invoke God's blessing on the Prophet, *ḥajja*, please do not think of what he said. He is just saying nonsense. His words do not count."

The statement is in ECA. By asking her to invoke blessings on the Prophet, he takes initiative in the reconciliation process, which the mother seems to refuse by replying in SA. The mother then starts telling her children her life story and achievements; all of this is done in SA:

-لقد دخلت هذه الدار وهي مجرد جدران..كانوا لا يوافقون على زواج أبيكم مني..و كنت وحيدة أبوى . . . و
لم أكن فلاحة . . . فزرعتهما أشجاراً و خضروات..و قال جدكم لأبيكم كيف تتزوج بنت أرملة لا عائلة لها؟

"I had come to your grandfather's house when it was just walls. They did not approve my marriage to your father. I was an only child and I was no peasant then. Since then, I have planted trees and vegetables. Your grandfather then asked your father how he can marry a mere widow with no family."

The mother calls upon the authoritative indexes of SA. Her language choice reflects her identity, which is that of a dominant authoritative figure. When the novel was made into an Egyptian television series, the mother was depicted—realistically—as speaking in a rural dialect of ECA, not in SA. As was mentioned before, the same is true for the film based on *Qindīl Umm Hāshim*, in which most characters are shown as speaking in ECA. In fact, the scene that depicts the conflict between Ismāʿīl and his mother is taken directly from the novel and the dialogues are converted to ECA. It is important to note that in the screenplay, SA was *not* used to reflect the tension mounting between Ismāʿīl and his mother. Instead, other paralinguistic devices were used, such as facial expressions. Such devices are, of course, impossible to employ in a novel. All of this serves to prove that novels are significant for the way in which they use different orders of indexicality.

In more than one example above, ECA was associated with a woman who represents Egypt. This is perhaps predictable, given the discussion of ECA associations above. While ECA also has some negative associations (ignorance, naivety, and illiteracy), it is also—and perhaps primarily—associated with intimacy and authenticity. Conversely, SA is associated with authority, sacredness, seriousness, and power, but it is also associated with detachment and conflict (see Chapter 3 for more details).

5.3.4.1 Authenticity, second discussion

Authenticity has already been touched upon above. I have tried to show that although it is a complex concept, it is a fundamental component of ECA indexes. Note that Coupland (2007) discusses the concept of authenticity more generally and contends that vernacular authenticity is based on beliefs about ontology, "how language really is" (2007: 181). He then questions the assumption that standards are "inauthentic." According to him, "standard" languages are described by variationists (such as Labov) as "imposed," as a "deviation from real natural," and as "orderly vernaculars." However, Coupland then suggests that the same argument could be used by users of standard, who "constructed 'standard' varieties to be more ontologically real, historic, coherent, consensual and valuable—in short, as more authentic" (2007: 182). In other words, each side may feel that they have "authenticity" on their side. Yet we can accept neither as truly authentic.

However, in the introduction to this book, the difference between a standard and prestige as pertaining to the Arab world has been discussed. This difference does not correlate to the standard in other languages. The linguistic situation in Egypt as part of the Arab world is also complex. Depending on the individual stance and context, both SA and ECA may be considered authentic. However, ECA in the Egyptian context tends to be related more to being a "typical *ibn balad* ('son of the country') Egyptian." SA may also be related to how sincere one's message is. Linguistic ideologies are an essential part of determining the associations of different codes. Context and audience or reader, as the case may be, is also essential.

Because of its religious associations discussed in Chapter 3, SA is depicted as "sincere." "Sincere," here, is in the sense of truthfulness in some contexts and faithfulness in others. For example, if a president or king fails to speak in SA on formal occasions, this may imply that he is not a real, faithful Arab. Recall the example of al-Jabartī above, in which he uses the French scholar's lack of proficiency in SA to mark his insincerity. His grammatical mistakes in SA are taken to imply a deceptive attitude towards Egyptians. In the next chapter, SA will be employed by the poet al-Jukhkh to express his devotion to Egypt. This demonstrates how SA is associated with sincerity and faithfulness in relation to a cause or country in specific contexts. ECA is authentic, because it is associated with quintessential Egyptian variables. To elaborate, the indexes of SA and ECA need to be examined in relation to two different dimensions. That is, the questions asked should be: how does code-choice reflect on the person's identity and how does code-choice reflect on the person's discourse? When a speaker uses ECA, Egyptians may judge him or her as a typical Egyptian, with Egyptian character traits. In other words, the person's identity is judged. When a speaker uses SA to make a statement, one should evaluate the statement as truthful or faithful relevant to the speaker's affiliations. That is, the audience judges the speaker's sincerity in relation to what he proposes or states. This does not always work, of course. In the spring of 2011, when Mubarak chose to address Egyptians in SA in his last three speeches, he was appealing to the indexes of SA or attempting to convey sincerity and truthfulness in his stance. However, in that particular case, the political circumstances were more powerful than linguistic codes; that is, deeds were more important than words. In the following chapter, I will turn to a detailed analysis of language use during the Revolution of 2011 and show how all sides—both pro-Mubrak and pro-democracy groups—manipulated the indexes of SA and ECA during a time of conflict. In order to understand the indexes of SA and ECA more thoroughly, one has to regard both as resources that speakers may or may not have access to. The concepts of access and resources are discussed more thoroughly in the next chapter and again in the Conclusion.

5.4 Conclusion

This chapter provided examples from literature—a different kind of public discourse—to show how identity is constructed and emphasized.

What the chapter also provides is a snapshot of how, during the twentieth and twenty-first centuries, the discourse about Egyptian identity has continued to be dependent on the same variables, although at times with a different focus. What this kind of data has in common with patriotic songs, for example, is the use of the same social variables to construct identity. These variables include ethnicity, historicity, locality, religion, and character traits.

Language as a social variable is a salient marker of identity in all of the novels discussed. In fact, ideologies about the unity of language and unity of identity were discussed again in this chapter. However, literature deals with social variables differently.

Unlike in patriotic songs, protagonists are less sure and less positive. Questions pertaining to one's individual identity—as opposed to a collective Egyptian one—come to the fore in literary texts. Protagonists in novels are not always all knowledgeable, nor do they address a less knowledgeable audience. All in all, the stances given to literary characters are dynamic, rather than static. In the examples above, the protagonists all evolved into "Egyptians" over the course of the narratives, but did so only after a long struggle with the self. However, the "end product," the Egyptian, is similar in ideologies and attitudes to the end product in textbooks and patriotic songs.

As was shown in some of the earlier chapters, religion as a defining element of identity is highly complex. However, religion is a salient identity marker in Ramaḍān's novel. Gender, a variable that was not discussed in public discourse about identity, emerged as a prominent element in novels. In Ramaḍān's novel, the perceptions of outsiders placed the Egyptian identity in relation to religion, first and foremost, rather than language. The continuous struggle for a coherent identity also involves a struggle of inclusiveness and exclusiveness on different levels.

Another difference between patriotic songs and novels is the manipulation of code-switching as a linguistic resource. The relationships between the protagonists and individuals in their lives are commonly qualified by the use of code-switching. Of course, this is an unrealistic depiction that places literature in a special category of discourse: a form of discourse in which the diglossic situation is constantly being manipulated in relation to orders of indexicality.

For protagonists, identity is the product of self-perception. It is also the product of communal solidarity or a lack of it. The relation between protagonists and other individuals in their lives determines their identity to a great extent. That is, the ways in which these relationships are constructed and deconstructed reflect directly on their identity, both as Egyptians and individuals.

Notes

1. It is important to note that the questions raised in this chapter are different from those asked in literary theory. There is no reference here to the artistic or literary merit of the novels. My analysis focuses on descriptions of linguistic structures. As a sociolinguist, I pose questions such as: "What are the mechanisms through which language interacts with society and culture and our inner mental and emotional life?" (McConnell-Ginet 2011: 80)
2. If the novel has been translated and published in English, the translation will be used in the examples.
3. Perhaps the fact that Kīmī studies in Ireland specifically is also significant. It could be that in Ireland, where religious tensions between Catholics and Protestants persist, perceptions of the self are directly related to religion. This proposition is not mentioned directly in the novel, but may be worth investigating in future studies, especially because outsider's beliefs can influence insider's perceptions of identity markers.
4. Jamāl al-Ghīṭānī (b. 1945) is one of the most prominent contemporary Egyptian writers. This novel is an autobiographical account of a semi-imaginary journey to search for truth and reality, which is paralleled by the ancient Egyptian idea of the journey to the hereafter. At the end of his journey, the protagonist realizes that it is only by gathering together all names can he feel whole again and reach peace from within. Since this aim is not yet attainable, his search, striving, and journey will have to continue. While he attempts the process of gathering names, he also recognizes his affiliation to his ancestors, the ancient Egyptians. This is not the first autobiographical work by al-Ghīṭānī, as his "classic" works (*Tajallīyāt* ("Revelations") (1990), as well as his series *Dafātir al-tadwīn* ("Record-books") (1996–2010)), were also autobiographical. The most salient autobiographical feature in this novel and the others is his use of real names when referring to friends and relatives, as well as his use of real incidents from his own life and actual historical facts (cf. Fadl 2008). By explaining the importance of names in his life and in the lives of all Egyptians, al-Ghīṭānī helps us understand how Egyptians perceive themselves in relation to their history, surroundings, and aspirations.
5. The final chapter (Chapter 5 "Names, self, identity, and conflict") applies the findings of the preceding chapters to an analysis of personal names, trade names, and toponyms. The data includes name lists, web-based materials, self-reported data, and literary compositions. Suleiman discusses the symbolic associations of names with reference not just to the Arab world, but also to other Middle Eastern countries, including Israel, Turkey, and Iran. One of the points discussed is the fact that Christians in Jordan tend to choose Arabic names for their children, while in Egypt this is not the case. In Suleiman's analysis, this is due to the way in which Christians choose to conceptualize themselves in either place.

6. Using the vernacular in dialogues is not only restricted to Egypt, but is a phenomenon in the whole Arab world. The Iraqi writer ʿAbd al-Malik Nūrī is a case in point (see Somekh 1998).
7. See the study by Bassiouney (2006), which examines monologues, as opposed to dialogues. In monologues, the speaker has more freedom to use ECA, SA, or both together.
8. It would be essential to study authors' styles in different novels and examine the pattern of code-switching by different authors. However, authors will continue to surprise readers.

CHAPTER

6

THE POLITICS OF IDENTITY AND LINGUISTIC UNREST: THE CASE OF THE EGYPTIAN REVOLUTION

(Scene: Cairo, Egypt, 1259 CE)
Mongol messenger: *"Where is the woman who rules Egypt?"*
Prince Qutuz: *"Do you mean to say you are not up to date with the news? You missed one of your spy's messages? The great queen is dead."*
MM: *"And where is prince Aybak?"*
PQ: *"He is also dead."*
[silence]
MM: *"Where is prince Aqtāy?"*
PQ: *"Is that why you are here? Because all of these people are dead?"*
MM: *"You mean to say they have all been murdered."*
PQ: *"The information you received about Egypt's late rulers is correct."*
MM: *"So who should I speak to if I want to address the Egyptian people?"*
[long silence]
PQ: *"You can speak to me."*
MM: *"But who are you?"*
PQ: *"I am a citizen of Egypt. Talk."*
MM [starts reading]: *"From the master of armies and the destroyer of nations, the victorious chief commander Hulagu. We know how weak your country is . . ."*

(From the film *Wā Islāmāh* ("Woe to Islam") (1961), which deals with Egypt's fight against the Mongol invasion in 1259 CE)

The quote above is one of the most famous quotes in Egyptian cinema. The MM implies to Qutuz, the Mamluk leader, that Egypt has lost all its leaders and is in a very weak position. He challenges him with the famous sentence: "So who should I speak to if I want to address the Egyptian people?"

The Mamluk prince, Qutuz, then declares himself the new Egyptian leader. When asked about his identity ("who are you?"), he humbly replies, "I am a citizen of Egypt," and then uses the imperative form "talk" to show the Mongol messenger that Qutuz, as a citizen of Egypt, is now occupying a powerful position and can command him. This quote is worth considering for a number of reasons: it was referred to throughout the 2011 Revolution and up until the present day. It was used in cartoons and jokes to satirize political figures both during and after the revolution. The quote, although supposedly spoken in the thirteenth century, is in ECA. All of the speakers featured within this quote communicate in ECA, including the Mongol messenger. Qutuz, who claims to represent Egyptians as a citizen from Egypt, is ironically not ethnically Egyptian in the actual historical scenario or in the film. Qutuz is reputed to be from a dynasty of Turkic Mamluks. He, however, is a Muslim who speaks ECA in the film. The fact that he lived in Egypt for a long time, became sympathetic to its plight, and mastered ECA renders him Egyptian. His linguistic code and religion seem sufficient reasons for the purpose of the film to portray him as Egyptian. Perhaps this may also suggest that at times of political turmoil the role of language in defining an identity is inflated.

A very similar situation occurred in Egypt at the time of the January 25, 2011 Revolution—a revolution that supposedly derived its momentum and strength from being a leaderless revolution. Because it was a leaderless revolution, it was also a revolution in which identity issues were in the forefront, prompting questions such as "who should I speak to when I want to address the Egyptian people?" Being Egyptian was also called into question: who was the "real" citizen of Egypt, as opposed to the one who pretended to be? Who really cared about Egypt? The words "authentic," "real," and "legitimate" became keywords. The core identity of Egyptians and their authenticity was at stake and the media was ready to provide many propositions. Language was used as an identification variable to differentiate between Egyptians and non-Egyptians and as a stylistic device through which to discuss identity, verify it, and cast doubt upon it. It was a question of citizenship and rights, as well as a question of laying claim to linguistic resources and varieties. Language was also used to justify a lack of democracy at times and the legitimacy of protestors at others. Issues of linguistic resources and access to them were disputed. Issues of inclusion and exclusion were also prevalent.

Throughout this book, it has been clear that language feeds into politics through identity construction. This chapter provides examples to round out the discussion so far regarding the relationship between language, identity, and politics. The politicizing of identity and language that took place in Egypt both before and after the January 25 Revolution provides a rich environment for linguistic analysis on many levels.

As Gee (2010: 7) contends, language is, in essence, political:

> Politics is not just about contending political parties. At a much deeper level it is about how to distribute social goods in a society: who gets what in terms of money, status, power, and acceptance on a variety of different terms, all social goods. Since, when we use language, social goods and their distribution are always at stake, language is always "political" in a deep sense.

Note also that talk about language is part of the weft and warp of social upheavals and political change. At times of political upheaval, language is always employed to produce the greatest possible impact on the masses. But codes are also pitted against each other, both carrying their own indexes, and at a time of conflict over political hegemony, there is also a linguistic power struggle over who has access to the powerful code—who controls the political arena by mastering and producing SA, for example. Taking control of one's political fate is closely related to controlling one or two linguistic varieties or codes. By favoring one code over the other—in some cases, SA—one also excludes one group of Egyptians and favors another and finds justification for political elitism. Our concern is not just with how language is employed by different institutions or rebels, revolutionaries, and opposition leaders, but how language is related directly to political conflicts.

The diglossic situation in Egypt has been manipulated politically on more than one level, as will be clear below, while also simultaneously providing linguistic richness, as was shown in the preceding chapters. The linguistic situation in Egypt has been illuminated by non-linguists, who sense the significance of language in forging an identity or denying one. Politics and language have never been more intertwined than at the time of the Egyptian January 25 Revolution.

If we agree with Heller's (2007) postulation that language is a social process and a social practice, then the process of relating political conflicts and language to identity and the practice of linguistic choices are to be discussed together as one and the same system.

Access to these linguistic codes and resources is highlighted throughout this chapter. In the process of identity construction, an exclusion–inclusion pattern of display takes place. Language as a social phenomenon is a resource that is partially projected as distributed unequally, as is the case with most social resources. But more importantly, language as a social phenomenon is dependent on ideological factors, which may or may not adhere to linguistic reality. The assumption is that Egyptians share the same indexes of codes. Therefore, when a group or individual claims to have access to a specific code—for example, SA—this group or individual also attempts to position themselves as more powerful or in a better position than others who may have limited or no access to it. In most instances of political conflict, linguistic ideologies supersede linguistic reality and ordered indexes of different codes are then of pivotal importance. This will be clear throughout this chapter.

This chapter is organized chronologically. It aims at highlighting discussions of language as a social variable in Egypt directly before, during, and after the January 25, 2011 Revolution. Stance-taking processes that speakers engage in so as to adopt an identity are also discussed and are directly related to the indexes of different codes. The first section in this chapter will outline, first, how linguists in the Arab world at large and Egypt in particular have referred to language to explain and justify negative social and political phenomena. The section will then concentrate on an article about Arabic by the former Speaker of Parliament, Fatḥī Surūr, which was published ten months before the 2011 Revolution. I show how diglossia has been used to justify and, at times, explain the lack of democracy in Egypt prior to the revolution. I also show how laying claim to all the indexes of SA is a means of acquiring both political legitimacy and national credibility.

Unlike Section 1, Section 2 shows examples of linguistic manipulation that took place *during* the revolution, rather than after or before. It was during the revolution that the state media attempted to cast doubt on the identity and motivations of the protestors in Tahrir Square. The conflict was not one-sided, and the protestors in Tahrir Square counter-attacked the state media through poetry and other means. In this section, it becomes clear how language is referred to and manipulated so as to position individuals as "real or not real Egyptians." Examples used in this section include media talk shows and poetry. In this section, Egyptian identity is contested; language as a social variable and code-choice as a stylistic device and resource that sheds light on stance and, thus, identity is at the core of this conflict.

Section 3 will show how SA indexes are used to lay claim to political legitimacy and the credibility of the revolutionaries, rather than the pro-Mubarak group. In this section, I will analyze an article by Fārūq Shūshah that was published directly after the revolution's successful ousting of Mubarak. The article stands in sharp contrast to the one by Surūr: while the author of this article adopts a positive stance towards SA, much like Surūr, it relates SA to the identity of Egyptians, although in a very different way. In the analysis, I will also refer to the code used by the Supreme Council of the Armed Forces (SCAF) to address Egyptians on Facebook and the controversy surrounding the Egyptian Constitution of 2012.

6.1 Language as a scapegoat: unequal access to resources

I will begin with linguistic explanations for the lack of democracy in Egypt before the revolution, as well as for other socio-political problems, with particular reference to the work of Haeri (2003). For the sake of thoroughness, I will refer to other parts of the Arab world, in which linguists also relate political and social problems to the diglossic situation. I will then provide a concrete example of a former Egyptian politician's stance towards SA and his underlying assumptions about Egypt's political status quo at the time.

6.1.1 Linguistic explanations for the lack of democracy prior to the revolution

Linguistic resources, as Heller (2007) posits, are social entities that are distributed unequally in one or more communities. Applying this to Egypt and the Arab world more generally, one could conclude that SA is an exclusive code mastered only by a few intellectuals and not the mass population of the Arab world, simply because it is not a spoken language and is in more than one way different from the colloquials of Arab countries. This unequal distribution of language resources in Egypt and the Arab world more generally has led linguists to relate language directly to the political status quo in the Arab world, including Egypt. Without exaggeration, the diglossic situation became basically a scapegoat for almost all political and social problems in the Arab world, starting with illiteracy and the unequal distribution of wealth and going as far as the lack of democracy.

For example, McFerren (1984: 5) identified diglossia as the cause of the failure of Arabization in North Africa: "Diglossia remains the single greatest impediment to Arabization in the Maghreb." Benrabah (2007a: 226) claims that the enforcement of SA as the only official language in Algeria is the main cause of the rise of fanaticism, civil war, unemployment, and the failure of the education system. He adds that the regime in Algeria is "an authoritarian regime allergic to pluralism whether cultural, political or linguistic" (Benrabah 2007a: 248), because the regime seems to prefer one subgroup over all others. Benrabah's claims make his political stance clear and do not just reflect a linguistic stance. It is, indeed, difficult to remain neutral when discussing language as a social variable. It would be simplistic to think that multilingualism would solve all problems in Algeria, including unemployment, poverty, fanaticism, and political frustration (see Bassiouney 2009). In the case of Algeria, the linguistic situation reflects the political tension, rather than creates it. It is easier for intellectuals to be outspoken about linguistic diversity—a safe topic compared to other political ones. That is, in these cases, language is used as the scapegoat. The conflict regarding distribution of resources in these cases is reduced to a conflict about access and the distribution of different linguistic codes.

Before discussing SA as a social variable, I would like to explain more about the political situation in Egypt prior to the revolution. Before the January 25 Revolution in Egypt, there was virtually no participation of Egyptians in the political sphere. There was one dominant ruling party, the National Party, which controlled the country and which was headed by the president. The Speaker of Parliament, Fatḥī Surūr, was also the legislator for this party. One of the main reasons for the revolution was the forging of the 2010 elections, in which the National Party won with an overall majority as expected.

To some extent, this political situation was clear to sociolinguists studying Egypt prior to the revolution. Haeri is a case in point. Haeri, in her study *Sacred Language, Ordinary People* (2003), has attempted to shed light on language attitudes in modern Egypt. Her argument was that the main problem in Egypt is that Egyptians are custodians of SA, rather than owners of it. SA is the language of religion, the holy book of Muslims, but it is not necessarily mastered by the majority of Egyptians. When discussing diglossia in Egypt, Haeri reached the following conclusions (2003: 151):

> Beyond its use for religious purposes, most Egyptians find speaking and writing in classical Arabic difficult, especially given the dire state of pre-college education. The official language thus acts as an obstacle to their participation in the political realm. There is of course no suggestion here that this is the only reason for absence of democracy in Egypt. But the language situation makes a strong comment on the nature of politics in that country. There seem to be deeply entrenched political interests in having classical Arabic to be the sole official language.

While acknowledging the relationship between religion and SA, Haeri partly explains the lack of democracy in Egypt at that time by resorting to the diglossic situation. The main argument of her work is that it is owners of language who can feel at ease with it and eventually master it. Egyptians may not master SA, nor have an easy relation to SA and, eventually, to part of their identity. Haeri calls this a "highly uneasy relation to the self" (2003: 152) that develops in Egyptian children, because they grow up to hear that the language that they speak is "bad" and has no grammar. In a parallel fashion, Egyptians do not own their country or the decision-making mechanisms within it, since they are regarded as "ignorant, or perhaps unfit to choose and decide." They are "ignorant," according to the illiteracy rate, but more importantly because of their uneasiness towards SA—the official language of the government. This work provides a useful attempt at explaining the political situation from a linguistic viewpoint. However, at times, it seems to unintentionally emphasize ideological points promoted by the National Party about access to SA and participation in the political arena, as will be clear below.

It is noteworthy however, that Buṭrus Ghālī, former Secretary-General of the United Nations, almost came to the same conclusion just days before Mubarak was ousted. In the television program *al-ʿĀshirah masāʾan* ("10 o'clock") on the Drīm channel (February 8, 2011),[1] Ghālī claimed that in a country in which the illiteracy level is so high, democracy does not work. He added that one needs first to prepare Egyptians for democracy—that is, educate them. While not touching upon diglossia, he indirectly blamed a lack of knowledge of SA for the lack of democracy and also used education as a criterion for classifying communities as fit or unfit for democracy. In more general terms, he implied that Mubarak was right when he claimed that Egyptian culture was not ready for democracy. However, Ghālī tried to put it in more objective terms, using education as a variable. SA is the language of education and literacy, and as long as it is not mastered by all Egyptians, they may not have access to the mechanisms "necessary" to be democratic. The solution may not necessarily be to raise levels of literacy in SA, but according to some it may be to abandon SA altogether and start teaching ECA.

As expected, Haeri's work has been criticized mainly by Arab intellectuals for a number of reasons, all of which are ideological. Although she was at least right in claiming that there is no democracy in Egypt, her linguistic explanation for the lack of democracy and her tacit conclusion that SA as a sacred language rather than an ordinary usable one may be the reason for the lack of democracy and various other problems was what made her book provocative for Arab intellectuals (see Walters 2006b). Blaming SA and promoting ECA is always like stirring up a hornet's nest. Note again that the call to use colloquial instead of SA in education has been promoted by colonizing powers, especially the British, in Egypt. This call is associated in the minds of native speakers in general and intellectuals in particular with colonization and orientalist thinking. When the call for using the colloquial instead of SA in writing and school subjects comes from non-Arabs, the skepticism is even greater (cf. Walters 2006b). For Arabs, such calls are considered a conspiracy to divide the Arab nation. It is SA that, as Walters (2006b: 656) puts it, "is the glue holding the Arab culture and the Arab world together." Hypothetically, if each Arab country started using their own colloquial in domains in which SA were used, then in fifty years, all Arab countries would be detached from SA and the common SA literature that is read by all Arabs would be incomprehensible for a young generation trained only in colloquial. Whether Arabs would still understand each other is difficult to predict. Possibly some of them would still be able to communicate, since Arabic satellite channels are now broadcast worldwide with all dialects of the Arab world. Taking the side of ECA is, in fact, for Arab intellectuals, like trying to fix the identity of Egyptians as a non-Arab identity. It is considered a threating proposition to Egyptians' sense of belonging to a wider entity of "the Arab nation."

However, it is also important to note the fact that ECA is being employed politically to reflect opposition (see Ibrahim 2010), honesty, freshness, and, in a sense, innovation. Still, journalists who may use ECA to write articles against the government may also be the same journalists who may be wary of a non-Arab imposing a linguistic ideology in which ECA is prevalent.

Haeri was right in relating diglossia to democracy and stale political systems. However, unlike Haeri, I argue that this relationship is not necessarily because of linguistic habits, but rather because of linguistic ideologies and perceptions. Some politicians can and do use a patronizing tone when speaking to the masses, because they believe that the masses have a limited knowledge of SA. They use their expertise in SA to legitimize their political system, almost in the same way that priests in ancient Egypt monopolized certain aspects of knowledge to empower themselves. This does not imply that politicians actually master SA, nor study it, nor even really truly believe in its superiority. It only means that politicians manipulate the sacred status of SA for their own ends. It is important to realize that for Haeri as a linguist, SA does not necessarily carry only positive indexes, whereas those politicians who discuss SA draw on positive indexes only.

In this section, it was shown how linguists may blame diglossia for social and political problems in the Arab world at large and Egypt in particular. It is essential to realize that linguists studying the Arab world are not without their own ideologies. As with any social phenomenon, the study of language in society is impregnated with social and political associations.

In the next section, I will show in more detail the stance of Egyptian politicians towards SA, with examples from other forms of public discourse, including newspapers and films.

6.1.2 Linguistic justifications for the lack of democracy in Egypt

Former Egyptian politician and Speaker of Parliament Fatḥī Surūr was perhaps the most influential legal expert and legislator during the latter part of the Mubarak era. After the Revolution of 2011, he was imprisoned on charges of corruption. On March 10, 2010—some ten months before the revolution—he wrote a series of articles for *al-Ahrām* newspaper on the topic of the "Arabic language," one of which, analyzed here, is entitled *al-Lughah al-ʿarabīyah fī al-dustūr* ("The Arabic language in the constitution"); *al-Ahrām* is a state-owned newspaper that was consistently pro-Mubarak and functioned as a propaganda organ for the ruling National Democratic Party. The article therefore provides an example of what might be called "institutional discourse." After the revolution, *al-Ahrām* changed its political alignment, as will be clear in the example provided in the last section of this chapter.

In Surūr's article, his stance towards SA and the constitution is that of an expert. Surūr positions himself as powerful because of his knowledge of SA and goes so far as to assign himself the role of the guardian of SA and the Egyptian Constitution, since they, according to Surūr, go hand-in-hand. He even discusses the differences between SA for specific purposes (the language of law) and SA for public consumption (the language of the constitution). By lamenting the dire state of SA, he takes the stance of the legislator, politician, Arabist, and protector of Egypt's identity as a Muslim Arab country.

In his article, Surūr reiterated some of the most common concepts in the institutional public discourse about language, such as the idea that Egypt is an Arab country and that its official language and the language of the constitution is SA; since the second amendment of the constitution also proclaims Islam as the main religion, it is natural that the language of the Qur'ān should be the language of the constitution.

Surūr argues in detail that language should not be above the people and that simple, straightforward SA was therefore the language of the constitution. While acknowledging that there is a difference between the language of the constitution and the language of law, he insists that the constitution is written in a language accessible to everyone. In his view, this SA is different from the language of law codes, which is more specialized and perhaps uses more jargon, which may be obscure to the masses. He adds that the constitution should use the language that is functional within the community, rather than proclaim its principles with a language that is not used. Surūr's argument is that since the constitution is written by the people, then the people with their language come first. The constitution should also be common knowledge to everyone who can read Arabic. Surūr adds that if there is a problem for SA at the moment, then it should be dealt with before it affects legislative law (legal texts). Surūr also argues that the spirit of law is language and that if language—as the medium of laws—is subject to change and decay, then so is the law.

Because of his official function, Surūr was seen as the mouthpiece of the government. The opinion expressed in this article is therefore more than simply a private statement. Since it was published in a state newspaper, it comes across as an official opinion, which reflects the government's stance towards SA. He demonstrates the direct relationship between language, identity, and politics, assuming that a constitution defines a nation-state. Note that this article is one of a series of articles by Surūr, in which he discussed the problems facing SA and the importance of learning and teaching SA.

وتدفعنا أهمية اللغة العربية في التعبير عن ذاتيتنا الثقافية, مقترنة بالأزمة التي يمر بها التعامل مع هذه اللغة إلي معرفة حكم الدستور حول هذه اللغة.
الدستور هو الذي يحكم مسيرة حياتنا العامة ويحدد المقومات الأساسية لمجتمعنا.. والنظرة إلي اللغة العربية في الدستور نظرة تنقب عن الشرعية الدستورية التي تحكم استخدام لغتنا.. تلك الشرعية التي أقام أركانها الشعب المصري حين وضع دستوره لكي يحدد مسار حياته ويضع دعائمها [. . .]
كما أوضح الدستور دعائم مكانة اللغة العربية داخل الدولة حين نص في مادته الثانية علي أن الإسلام دين الدولة, وهو ما يبرز العلاقة بين لغة الدولة وعقيدتها الدينية الرسمية بوصف أن اللغة العربية هي لغة القرآن الكريم [. . .]
وجاء كل ذلك متفقا مع مبدأ اعتنقه الدستور وهو الانتماء القومي للشعب المصري حيث نصت الفقرة الثانية من المادة الأولي من الدستور علي أن الشعب المصري جزء من الأمة العربية. فهذا النص يحمل في طياته تأكيدا علي أن اللغة العربية هي لغة الشعب المصري. ولما كان وجود الشعب يسبق وجود الدولة, فكان منطقيا أن يتحدد مركز اللغة العربية في الدستور مع تحديد الانتماء العربي للشعب المصري في مادته الأولى [. . .]
وإذا كان الخطر الذي يواجه اللغة العربية الآن يهب من التآكل العام للغة الفصحي وغياب الإلمام بها وبمفرداتها وترادفاتها وتراكيبها ومعانيها ونحوها وصرفها, إلا أن هذا التآكل العام لا تحتمله المواد القانونية والقضائية. فالفصحي هي قوام الأحكام وأساس صياغة الفكر القانوني عامة.

The importance of Arabic language in expressing our cultural identity, and the current crisis in dealing with this language force us to consider what the constitution has to say about this language.

The constitution is what determines the course of our lives in public, and what sets down the basic rules of our society. If we examine the use of Arabic in the constitution we realize the constitutional legitimacy that governs the use of our language. The legitimacy of the constitution and of Arabic springs from the Egyptian people who have set down this constitution to govern the course of their lives and to lend it support [. . .]

The constitution also identifies the factors supporting the position of the Arabic language within the state, since it states, in its second article, that Islam is the religion of the state, thereby highlighting the relation between the language of the state, and its official religious creed, in describing the Arabic language as the language of the Holy Qurʾān [. . .]

All this is in keeping with the principle embraced by the constitution, regarding the national identity (lit. *intima:ʔ qawmi:* "national belonging") of the Egyptian people, since section two of article one states that the Egyptian

> people are part of the Arab nation. This text carries within it an affirmation that the Arabic language is the language of the Egyptian people. Given that the Egyptian people preceded the state in its existence, it is logical that the position of the Arabic language in the constitution is incorporated in the definition of the Arab identity of the Egyptian people in its first paragraph.
>
> The danger to the Arabic language now stems from a general erosion of the standard language (*al-lughạ al-fuṣḥa:* "the eloquent language") and a lack of control on its vocabulary, its synonyms, its structures, its meanings, its grammar and its morphology. Legal and judicial texts cannot support such a general erosion of language. The standard language is the foundation of legal rulings, and the basis for legal thought in general.

This article, apparently about the importance of SA, is loaded with political connotations. In this first example, Surūr presupposes the following: first, there is a crisis for SA, but the constitution is legitimate and is a reference point that can help us solve this crisis for SA. His postulation is that the constitution is legitimate, because it is the voice of the people; it is written by the people for the people. This assertive statement may appear to emphasize the legitimacy of SA, while it, in fact, also asserts the legitimacy of the constitution. This legitimacy is, indeed, emphasized, since the constitution had been modified several times before to allow Mubarak to run for president multiple times. In other words, what seems like an innocent article about language is, in fact, about political justifications and ideologies.

Surūr then relates language directly to identity, both a religious identity and a national identity. By so doing, he positions himself as the protector of this identity, who fears its loss with the crisis facing SA. If there is no crisis, then he will lose his role. If there is no crisis that involves people's lack of ability to understand and read, then this may also imply that people were directly involved in putting together their constitution and reading it, which, as was said earlier, is a blatant lie in this case. That is, if SA is alive and thriving, then there is no justification for the alienation between the Egyptian people and their constitution. Needless to say, his article is all in SA. The claim that Egyptians do not have access to SA is a pretext for their lack of political participation in this case. By claiming that he cherishes the language of the Qur'ān and the Arab nation, he positions himself as both the owner and guardian of this powerful language. Other Egyptians may be custodians, rather than owners. That is one reason why he (and not "them") is in power. By relating SA to knowledge of Islam, he implicitly endows himself with more authority.

He then adds that the main problem currently facing SA is the deterioration of its vocabulary, syntactic constructions, grammar, and lexical connotations. He claims that legislators cannot afford to lose their SA, if their job is to enact meaningful laws. This erosion poses a serious challenge, because the legitimacy of the government derives from it. That is to say, Surūr explicitly acknowledges that authority, sovereignty, and legitimacy are all indexes of SA. The article ends with the following assertive statement:

فالفصحي هي قوام الأحكام وأساس صياغة الفكر القانوني عامة.

> The standard language is the foundation of legal rulings, and the basis for legal thought in general.

This statement comes in the form of a verbless sentence, which shows his epistemic stance. As a law expert, he underlines the importance of SA. By showing his awareness of the importance of SA, he legitimizes both himself and his position.

Throughout his article, Surūr adopts an epistemic and evaluative stance, whereas there are no expressions of affective stances. This stance and the indexes of his alignments feed into his identity as an Egyptian who is more knowledgeable about SA and constitutional law than other Egyptians. With this knowledge and access comes his natural position of power. SA legitimizes his Egyptian identity and feeds into his political one.

However, the question remains: what was the linguistic reality in Egypt before the revolution? Does his article actually reflect the linguistic or political reality? As regards the latter question, the answer is no.

While Surūr is right in claiming that almost no Egyptians ever bothered to read or be concerned with the constitution before the revolution, the reasons for this are not due to their linguistic abilities, but to their belief that the constitution does not represent them. It is more common for educated Egyptians to read the Qur'ān, newspapers, magazines, and, more recently, bestseller novels than to read the constitution. Literate Egyptians' knowledge of SA is definitely superior to their knowledge of the constitution. Thus, it is not because people's skill in SA is disintegrating that they did not read the constitution.

In the political satire farcical film *ʿĀyiz ḥaqqī* ("I want my rights") (2003), the economically struggling protagonist, who wants to buy a flat in order to marry his girlfriend, stumbles across the constitution and reads a section which says that everything inside Egypt "belongs to the people of Egypt." Not knowing exactly what the postulation means and feeling that it may change his life for the better, he goes to his lawyer friend and asks him about what the postulation means. The lawyer explains to the protagonist that the clause in the constitution refers to the rights of all Egyptians to own everything in the land of Egypt: all buildings, monuments, government-owned hotels, institutions, and even the pyramids. The protagonist then gleefully claims that he did not realize how rich he was until that day. He then starts a popular movement among his fellow citizens—who do not understand the meaning of the constitution's language until it is explained to them—to sell their stake in national property.

It is highly ironic that Surūr should emphasize how accessible the constitution ought to be to the people because it is written in simple and clear SA, while in reality the constitution was simply irrelevant to the concerns of the people, and the public was not interested in reading it. The fact that the protagonist in the film "I want my rights" seeks the help of his lawyer friend to decipher the meaning of the clause (which is in SA) implies that SA is associated more with the government than with the people. However, the attitude towards SA is more complicated than that, as was shown before and will be discussed in this chapter.

Readers' comments on the article were all positive, which is not surprising, given that *al-Ahrām* is a state-owned newspaper and consequently strictly pro-government. What is of interest here is that all readers commended Surūr for relating SA to the essence and identity of Egyptians, and two out of the six comments mentioned Canada and the UK as two countries that have taken measures to improve their national standards in literacy in English. One commenter mentioned the fact that Canada asked non-native students of English to reach a competent level of English before resuming their study of engineering, while the other commenter presented the example of Winston Churchill as a politician whose English was eloquent and expressive and suggested that Egyptian politicians should learn from this example and should likewise be fluent in SA.

Yet another (perhaps expected) comment was provided by one person who lamented the degraded state of SA used in the Egyptian Parliament and the "bad grammar" used by many of its members. Surūr's article managed to placate some of the "Arabic militants"—what Suleiman (2012) calls "the awkward squad," who derive their social power from their knowledge of SA—but obviously not the majority of Egyptians.

While indirectly blaming the linguistic situation for the fact that very few Egyptians read the constitution, he also clearly undermines ECA and forcefully encourages the people of Egypt to master SA, in order to understand their rights and obligations by reading their constitution. Note that the whole article concentrates on the famous second article of the constitution, which states that Egypt is a Muslim country, it is part of the Arab nation, and Arabic is the official language.

After the January 25 Revolution, there was a referendum in which Egyptians voted on the changes made to the Egyptian Constitution (March 2011)—the first democratic process that Egyptians have taken part in for sixty years. This is another reason why Surūr's article is essential. The second article of the constitution in particular was debated at length by the majority of Egyptians. There was no disagreement about Arabic being the official language of Egypt (at least, not at this point), but there was disagreement about Islam being the official religion of the state. Intellectuals called for a secular state, although the majority voted for keeping the second article intact, but agreed on the modifications on the constitution that limit the term of the president and allow for a freer and more flexible way of voting.

What is of importance is the fact that the modified texts of the constitution were available and discussed in coffee houses, universities, social gatherings, over the internet, on billboards, banners, and on Facebook pages. There was no mention, whether in newspapers or any other forms of public discourse, of any linguistic difficulty experienced by anyone—whether literate or illiterate—in understanding the meaning of the constitutional language. Note the following quote from the *Washington Post* (Dobson 2011) about the referendum over the constitution after the 2011 Revolution:

> Another thing has changed, too: The political life of Egypt has reawakened. Friday night I walked by outdoor cafes in downtown Cairo. The only topic of conversation was today's vote. Friends were debating this and that clause of the constitutional amendments. Family members were trying to persuade each other to either vote yes or no. Just before midnight the streets leading to Tahrir Square were filled with people holding up posters and placards doing last-minute political canvassing. In one of its sillier gestures, the Egyptian military issued an order on Wednesday forbidding media outlets from printing or discussing anything about the constitutional referendum that might sway opinion. As if Egyptians needed to rely on journalists to sway opinion? As one activist told me, "These days everyone is a constitutional expert."

Surūr's article shows how when he cast legitimacy over himself as a law legislator and constitution expert, he manipulated the linguistic situation. The reason why people do not read the constitution is not because of SA and their education or lack of it, but because it simply did not matter before: they had no political power, so reading the constitution was irrelevant. Diglossia was not their main problem: their main problem was the stale political system. Perhaps linguists and Arab intellectuals need to revise their ideas about diglossia. What Egyptians are taught to believe about their knowledge and access of SA is not true. And, arguably, what they are taught to believe about themselves—that they are not good enough to understand SA or the constitution—is also not true.

We may also be underestimating the average Egyptian's tacit knowledge of SA. As linguists, we know that there are different ways to master a language; while most Egyptians would find it difficult to speak SA without preparation, to write in SA without any grammatical mistakes, or to decipher the vocabulary of medieval poetry, the average Egyptian does not have a problem understanding modern spoken SA (as found in news broadcasts or translated television series, for example).

The point is: language is burdened with a conflict that it did not create. Religion is also usually burdened with conflicts that it did not create or maintain. But language is, indeed, manipulated even more. It is our main means of expressing ourselves and, in some cases, of casting doubt on other "selves," as the next section will show.

6.2 When identity is contested: who are the "real" Egyptians and what language do they speak?

The 2011 Egyptian Revolution was also a media war. The main question behind the media war was "who was the 'real Egyptian' and what does she or he want?" Does the "real Egyptian" want to change the regime? Or are the couple of million people in Tahrir, no more than a couple of million, who do not represent the entire Egyptian people of 85 million or more? While there were protests throughout the country, the media feud concentrated on Tahrir Square. Indeed, all over the world, news broadcasts likewise concentrated on the same square. The Egyptian state television and other pro-government satellite channels tried to ignore the whole protest movement for as long as possible. On January 25, while protests raged throughout the country, the Egyptian channel broadcast cooking programs. While Aljazeera and the BBC, for example, covered the protests in detail, the Egyptian media pretended that there were dozens of protesters in Tahrir Square, rather than millions.

When the government media finally talked about the protest movement, they tried to cast doubt on both the motivations and core identity of the protestors. Their attack on the identity of the people at Tahrir Square mainly employed language as an independent variable—as a passport photo, so to speak. Their equation was simple: whoever speaks Arabic is Egyptian and whoever does not is not Egyptian, although there are some who may, of course, attempt to pass as Egyptians by speaking Arabic.

The media war during the 2011 Egyptian Revolution needs a book by itself. However, in this section, I will discuss three clear and representative examples in detail. The three examples present three different forms of public discourse; what they all have in common is the fact that they all occurred while a political struggle was taking place. These struggles were mostly peaceful, but at times they turned bloody, as they did on February 2 and 3, 2011, two days before Mubarak abdicated. They also all directly discuss "the Egyptian identity."

The first example is from a special program from Nile TV that covered current affairs in Egypt during the protest movement. During a part of the program, the presenters accepted and discussed calls from viewers. The example analyzed is a partial transcript of a live call-in from a viewer named Tāmir on February 3, 2011, who purported to present a first-hand account of the identity and motivations of the people in Tahrir Square.

The second example is from a talk show, *al-Ḥayāh al-yawm* ("Life today"), on the al-Hayāh channel on February 5, 2011, in which the revolution was discussed by a conservative Egyptian actress (who is unusual in that she wears a headscarf—a significant sign of her conservative stance). In the example analyzed, she discusses the identity of the protestors in Tahrir Square.

The third example is different in form, since it is a poem that presents the point of view of the protesters in Tahrir Square and defends their identity and motivations. However, this poem was distributed widely during the revolution. Directly after being broadcast on Abu-Dhabi TV on February 8, 2011, the poem was uploaded on YouTube, shared through Facebook links, and eventually became a symbol of the revolutionary discourse.

While the first two examples cast doubt on the identity of the protestors in Tahrir Square by giving verdicts about their linguistic abilities, in the third example, the poet uses language to reclaim "the Egyptian identity" for himself and all those in Tahrir Square. Although poetry is a different kind of public discourse, the distribution of specific poems (and especially this one) underscores their importance in the discussion of identity.

The aim of this study is twofold: first, this study shows how speakers use public discourse in order to construe language as an independent variable similar to religion, social class, and ethnicity—a variable that is studied as a classification category or an identity builder. The examples below will show how language "is talked about," as well as how it is used to reflect identity.

Second, the study argues that stance-taking as a process is directly related to identity construction. In other words, speakers use language to take a stance and by doing so give themselves a specific identity and impose on others a different one. During the process of stance-taking, people employ linguistic resources, discourse, and structural ones. These linguistic resources include the associations and indexes of SA, ECA, and even foreign languages. That is, this stance-taking process, which directly reflects upon identity construction, depends on code-switching as a mechanism that lays claim to different indexes and thus appeals to different ideologies and, eventually, different facets of identity. Therefore, I refer again to indexicality (Woolard 2004; Johnstone 2010), which can further our understanding of code-switching as a resource that is employed in the process of stance-taking. By so doing, I attempt to add a new dimension to research on both stance and identity construction as related processes.

To reiterate, when relating the concept of stance to variationist research, Kiesling (2009: 173) argues that there is a methodological problem with coding stance. He contends that "there is a general problem in such work of coding stances" (Kiesling 2009: 173). Stance in general, not just in variationist research, is a concept that is, at times, subjective and difficult to quantify. I attempt to partially solve this problem by concentrating on specific linguistic resources, as will become clear below.

Bearing in mind that language is a social process and practice and by applying theories discussed in Chapter 1 that relate identity to stance-taking processes, I argue that speakers use linguistic resources to take a stance and by so doing reveal an identity or cast doubt on other identities. Linguistic resources also demonstrate access to codes that may index authenticity in some cases and legitimacy in others.

6.2.1 Data analysis

As was established in Chapter 1, identity—be it national, social, or collective—is not necessarily what one "is," but rather what one believes that she or he is. It is directly related to self-perception. This perception is the product of years of conditioning by economic, socio-historical, and ethno-global contexts. This perception is also mainly the product of public discourse. The conditioning that happens to all of us is a process that is unintentionally enacted by a number of outsiders and insiders. Insiders are usually members of a group of similar individuals who share the same self-perception and differentiate themselves from others by indexing their common traits. Outsiders do not share or appreciate the perceptions, ideologies, and habits of these community members.

As was discussed in Chapter 1, the media's main task is to categorize and generalize: the West versus the East, the black versus the white, the Hispanics, the Arabs, the Muslims, the Jews, and so on. This is exactly what occurs in the first two examples discussed below.

6.2.1.1 Tāmir's attack on the identity of the protestors

The first example is a famous, or rather infamous, example of a man who only gives his first name and his supposed whereabouts: "*Tāmir min ġamra*" ("Tāmir from the district of Ghamrah in Cairo") claims to have experienced first-hand encounters with people in Tahrir Square.

He phoned Nile TV to participate live in the current affairs program on February 3, 2011. Tāmir and the announcer discussed the identity of the protestors in Tahrir Square and both agreed that these protestors were not "real Egyptians" and therefore did not represent what Egyptians wanted or demanded. Note that throughout the call, Tāmir was in tears and sometimes had to stop speaking altogether, in order to control his crying.

Tāmir: *il-balad itbahdilit wi ʔiḥna s-sabab/ʔiḥna ḥanitkitib fit-tari:x in ʔiḥna s-sabab/la wallahi la//*
Announcer: *ʔismaḥ li ʔinta bi-tʔu:l fi magmuʕa:t guwwa bi-timnaʕ in-na:s mil-xuru:g. il-magmuʕa:t* ***do:l*** *sawa:ʔ kanu maṣriyyi:n ʔaw aga:nib/ tiʔdar/ timayyiz il-maṣriyyi:n* ***do:l*** *aw il-aga:nib* ***do:l*** *ginsiyya:t muʕayyana/*
Tāmir: *humma aga:nib bi-yitkallimu ingliʃ langwidje kuwayyis giddan/mafi:ʃ ḥaddi bi-yitkallim ġe:r al-ingli:ziyya guwwa/mawgudi:n maʕa:na ṭu:l il-waʔt/ bilʕaks kanu bi-yiʔu:mu yitẓahru maʕa:na/ bi-yuʕudu yiʕmilu maʕa:na il-flayerz wi kulli ḥa:ga/la:kin guwwa illi bi-yiwaggih . . . [cries] ʕalaʃa:n bukra itḥaṭṭilu slo:gan b-innu yibʔa/yo:m il-xala:ṣ//yo:m il-xala:ṣ min e:h*
Announcer: *Tayyib ʔusta:ði ʔana ʔaqaddar lak* ***da****/la:kin mumkin aṭlub minnak ṭalab/*
Tāmir: **[Cries]**
Announcer: *ʕustað ta:mir/biḥaʔʔi xo:fak ʕala* ***ha:ða*** *l-waṭan innak tilabbi:h/ inta fi ġamra dilwaʔti/*
Tāmir: *ah ya fandim/ʔana tiʕibt ʕalʃa:n akallimkum/miʃ kull in-na:s ḥatiʔdar tikallimku/*
Announcer: *ʔismaʕni bas/*
Tāmir: *ʕalʃa:n xaṭri:/ana miḥta:g it-tilifizyo:n/bi-gaddi miḥta:g il-maṣriyyi:n bi-gadd/*
Announcer: *ʃarrafna fi qana:t in-ni:l/inta ʔa:rif wi kull in-na:s ʕarfa inn* ***ha:ðihi*** *layla wa* ***ha:ðihi*** *ẓuru:f hiya ẓuru:f daqi:qa giddan/ʕayzi:n niʕraf e:h illi bi-yihṣal guwwa. Wi ʕayzi:n nismaʕ minnak min ḥadd ka:n guwwa/ḥadd ġayyu:r ʕala maṣr/ḥadd ġayyur ʕala l-balad/*
Tāmir: *ṣaʕb ʕalayya/*

T: "The country has been wrecked and we are the reason. History will record that we are the reason. No, really no."
A: "Allow me, you say the groups that are inside [Tahrir Square] stop others from getting out of the square? These groups, are they Egyptians or foreigners? Can you distinguish between them? Can you distinguish their nationalities?"
T: "They are foreigners. They speak 'English language' very well. No one speaks any other language except English there [Tahrir Square]. They are with us all the time. In fact they even protest with us. They even do with us the flyers and everything. But inside the one who controls and drives them . . . [cries] They prepared a slogan for tomorrow saying that it would be 'the day of riddance.' Riddance of what?"

A: "Okay, Sir [lit. 'my professor'], I appreciate this from you. But can I ask you for a favor?"
T: [Cries]
A: "Mr. Tāmir, I ask you by your love for this country that you answer my request. You are in Ghamra now?"
T: "Yes, sir. I had a hard time trying to call you. Not everyone will be able to call you."
A: "Please allow me . . ."
[Tāmir interrupts]
T: "Please for my sake, I need the [government] TV. I need the real Egyptians."
A: "It will be a pleasure to host you on Nile TV. You know and everyone knows that this night and these circumstances are very serious. We need to know what happens inside Tahrir Square. We need to hear from you, from someone who was inside the square, someone who cares about Egypt, someone who cares about this country."
T: "It is difficult for me to come."

If we apply Du Bois' stance triangle (2007), then we note that Tāmir disaligns himself from the people in Tahrir Square. He positions himself as the well-informed Egyptian sufferer, who posits that the people in Tahrir Square, because of their linguistic practices, are not Egyptians (an evaluative statement). Both Tāmir and the announcer have the same stance. Through discourse resources and structural resources that include presupposition, stance adverbs, adjectives, tense, pronouns, negation, deixis, rhetorical questions, and code-switching, they attempt to achieve their aim, which is mainly to influence the wider audience to adhere to their stance as the real Egyptians who love Egypt and care about its future.

Tāmir also uses both discourse and structural resources to attack the core identity of the protestors in Tahrir and position himself as the "real Egyptian," who thus represents the millions of Egyptians that did not go to Tahrir Square, but stayed at home to watch the events. What distinguishes Tāmir from these Egyptian bystanders is that he "was" in Tahrir Square and, supposedly, has first-hand knowledge of what happened there, although he was helpless to stop it.

In his first factual statement, Tāmir comes across as a caring, wise Egyptian: "the country has been wrecked and we are the reason." The tense changes in this statement from past to future: this is what took place, and what will come is even worse. History will blame us for being so passive. The pronoun *ʔiḥna* is repeated twice to juxtapose "the Egyptians" from the others, who are foreigners that pretend to be Egyptians. Tāmir employs the "we" and "they" dichotomy discussed by Gumperz (1982) throughout and uses code-switching to emphasize this dichotomy. The announcer then asks Tāmir to distinguish between the Egyptians and non-Egyptians in Tahrir Square:

> **Announcer**: *ʔismaḥ li ʔinta bi-tʔu:l fi magmuʕa:t guwwa bi-timnaʕ in-na:s mil-xuru:g. il-magmuʕa:t* ***do:l*** *sawa:ʔ kanu maṣriyyi:n ʔaw aga:nib/ tiʔdar/ timayyiz il-maṣriyyi:n* ***do:l*** *aw il-aga:nib* ***do:l*** *ginsiyya:t muʕayyana/*
>
> **A**: "Allow me, you say the groups that are inside [Tahrir Square] stop others from getting out of the square? These groups, are they Egyptians or foreigners? Can you distinguish between them? Can you distinguish their nationalities?"

In this part, the announcer uses ECA lexemes and structure. It is notable that the ECA plural demonstrative *do:l* ("those") is repeated three times. There are no SA features in this part. Tāmir starts to answer the announcer's query about whether they are foreigners or Egyptians by using the pronoun *humma* ("they"). The juxtaposition becomes clearer in this part. He starts relating language directly to identity. Language is regarded as a classification category, rather than a communicative one, as an independent variable, such as religion or ethnicity. He says: "they are foreigners, they speak English very well." The adverb is followed by an adjective, *kuwayyis giddan* ("very well"); both are used to emphasize that the protesters can by no means be Egyptians. Their mastery of English is impeccable. The fact that Tāmir code-switches to English himself, saying "English language," puts him in the position of the fair assessor of their linguistic capabilities. He has also mastered English, so he can judge whether they are foreigners or Egyptians. Code-switching is used as a structural strategy to clarify his stance and legitimize his statements. The first and second indexes of English are also clear in this example: it is simply the language of past colonizers and foreigners (second order indexes). It is also a language that is easily understood and accessible (first order indexes), therefore these foreigners are dangerous: they can appeal to masses of people, and "these foreigners" do not necessarily come from an English-speaking country. They could be (as was implied in other state-sponsored television programs) trained in English, but work in, or otherwise come from, Iran, Qatar, Israel, or even Hamas—all of which were accused by the Egyptian media at that time of stirring and backing the revolution.

Tāmir uses ECA negation after this statement. He uses the existential negative construction "no one speaks anything but" to confirm his previous statement. Rather than use English again when saying "English language," he repeats his statement in ECA and refers to English in SA, not in ECA or English. He could have said *ingli:zi*, but he says *ingli:ziyya*. He then refers to the slogan that will be used the day after: *yo:m il-xala:ṣ* ("day of riddance"). The English word "slogan" is used, rather than the

Arabic *ʃiʕa:r*. Again, this brings to mind the indexes of English. Another structural strategy that he uses is the rhetorical question: "riddance of what?" The rhetorical question implies that there is really no problem. It is the protestors who created this problem.

The announcer's affective statement *ʔana ʔaqaddar lak da* ("I appreciate this from you") clarifies his stance. He not only believes Tāmir, but appreciates his love for his country. What is really noteworthy is the marked phonological use of the SA "q," rather than the ECA glottal stop in *ʔa**q**addar* (the verb "to appreciate"). Although the whole statement is in ECA (including, again, the ECA demonstrative *da*), the use of SA /q/ clearly marks the stance of the announcer. The term of address "my professor" is endearing, but also prestigious. The announcer does not, even for a moment, doubt Tāmir or argue with him. He not only agrees with him, but bestows upon him the status of the expert who should be appreciated. This, in itself, will, after the revolution, be criticized ruthlessly by opposition media.

Tāmir then bursts into tears and cannot answer the announcer's question. So the announcer repeats his demands, this time using presupposition and code-switching:

> **Announcer**: *ʕustað ta:mir/biḥaʔʔi xo:fak ʕala* ***ha:ða*** *l-waṭan innak tilabbi:h/ inta fi ġamra dilwaʔti/*
>
> **A**: "Mr. Tāmir, I ask you by your love for this country that you answer my request. You are in Ghamrah now?"

The announcer presupposes that Tāmir loves this country. This is why he asks him through his "love for this country" to answer his request. For the first time, the announcer uses the SA demonstrative, *ha:ða* ("this"), when he refers to Egypt as "this homeland," laying claim to the authoritative indexes of SA, indicating that this homeland is not a laughing matter and is not to be tampered with. It has to be respected and protected. It is Tāmir who is the one that loves "this" country—the protestors do not care about it. They, in fact, want to harm it, since they are not even Egyptians. The announcer then attempts to verify Tāmir's whereabouts by asking "You are in Ghamrah now?" By so doing, he again adds credibility to Tāmir's statements. Tāmir exists, he is real, and he is now in Ghamrah after leaving Tahrir Square.

Tāmir replies that he is, indeed, in Ghamrah and then refers to his personal experience of his difficulty in telephoning the show. The use of the personal pronoun "I" is followed by reference to other people who may fail to call in. When the announcer tries to interrupt him, Tāmir breaks down completely and starts pleading with the television station and also with what he calls "the real Egyptians":

Tāmir: *ah ya fandim/ʔana tiʕibt ʕalʃa:n akallimkum/miʃ kull in-na:s ḥatiʔdar tikallimku/*
Announcer: *ʔismaʕni bas/*
Tāmir: *ʕalʃa:n xaṭri:/ana miḥta:g it-tilifizyo:n/bi-gaddi miḥta:g il-maṣriyyi:n bi-gadd/*

T: "Yes, sir. I had a hard time trying to call you. Not everyone will be able to call you."
A: "Please allow me . . ."
[Tāmir interrupts]
T: "Please for my sake, I need the [government] TV. I need the real Egyptians."

With these final statements, Tāmir positions himself as the one who really cares about Egypt, but is helpless to stop what is happening. For Tāmir and the announcer, the dichotomy between "us" and "them" is now complete: we are passive Egyptians; they are simply not Egyptians at all. The announcer then code-switches again to SA and uses two SA demonstratives (presented in bold):

Announcer: *ʃarrafna fi qana:t in-ni:l/inta ʔa:rif wi kull in-na:s ʕarfa inn* ***ha:ðihi*** *layla wa* ***ha:ðihi*** *ẓuru:f hiya ẓuru:f daqi:qa giddan/ʕayzi:n niʕraf e:h illi bi-yihṣal guwwa. Wi ʕayzi:n nismaʕ minnak min ḥadd ka:n guwwa/ḥadd ġayyu:r ʕala maṣr/ḥadd ġayyur ʕala l-balad/*

A: "It was a pleasure to host you on Nile TV. You know and everyone knows that this night and these circumstances are very serious. We need to know what happens inside Tahrir Square. We need to hear from you, from someone who was inside the square, someone who cares about Egypt, someone who cares about this country."

The SA demonstratives are used to index the seriousness of the situation that Egypt is in ("this night" and "these conditions"). The announcer's marked choice of pronouncing *daqi:qa* with the SA */q/*, rather than the ECA glottal stop, is also worth noting and, again, emphasizes the announcer's concern for Egypt in such difficult circumstances.

The conversation between Tāmir and the announcer concludes in a dramatic fashion when Tāmir says tearfully, "it is difficult for me," followed by the line being cut. Playing on the emotions of Egyptians was part of the media war; language and identity were the two main weapons.

6.2.1.2 Actress Shuʿayb's postulations of the "fake" identity of the protestors in Tahrir Square

An even more linguistically interesting claim was made by Egyptian actress ʿAfāf Shuʿayb on the current affairs talk show *al-Ḥayāh al-yawm*

("Life today"). The protests were discussed and the identity of the protestors was evaluated. On February 5, 2011, Shuʿayb—who is seen as a mother figure in the Egyptian media, due to her recent performance in the role of a mother—used her appearance on the talk show to cast doubt on the identity of the protestors in Tahrir Square. When asked by the announcer to say what she thinks of the people in Tahrir, Shuʿayb claimed that the people in Tahrir were not "Egyptians." However, she used a conspiracy-driven theory and a slightly more subtle argument than Tāmir. Note the example below:

> *Shuʿayb: ṭabb dilwaʔti ig-gizi:ra ṭu:l in-naha:r bi-tʔu:l/ fi wa:ḥid gabu:h ma:sik farx abyaḍ/ ʔiddulu ʔalam filumastar wi ʔalu:lu ʔiktib no muba:rak/ landan bi-tḥa:wil tidarrab wila:d ʕala il-lahga il-maṣriyya wi tgibhum kulluhum lo:n baʃritna/ miʃ illi huwwa il-lo:n il-ʔabyad bitaʕhum/ bi-tgibhum min kulli ginsiya:t/ bi-tdarrabhum ʔizza:y yirkabu dabba:ba/ wi ʔizza:y yiʃi:lu: il-ʕaskari: il-maṣri: min id-dabba:ba wi yirkabha huwwa/ ʕaʃa:n fi ḥarb qa:dima/*

> S: "Okay now Aljazeera channel claims all day that . . . they brought someone with a white sheet of paper and they gave him a crayon and asked him to write on it 'no Mubarak.' London tries to train young men in the Egyptian dialect and they choose them all with our skin color, not with that white color of theirs. They are from all nationalities. London trains them on how to drive tanks and how to take out the Egyptian soldier from the tank and drive it, because there is a war coming."

ʿAfāf Shuʿayb's proposition is that the people in Tahrir are simply not Egyptians, but people who look like Egyptians. In addition to this, the argument that they have been trained in London to master colloquial Arabic rather than SA. This not only brings to mind the colonizers' manipulation, but also the colonizers' language policies and ideologies. The British occupation of Egypt (1882–1952) encouraged and promoted colloquial Egyptian Arabic; the first Egyptian Arabic grammar was published in 1901 by Wise, a British linguist (see Bassiouney 2009). In the minds of most Egyptians and many Arabs, when foreigners encourage colloquial Arabic, it is a disintegrating device used to divide the Arab world and, more importantly, to erase the national Arab identity. It is no coincidence that these foreigners are trained in Egyptian Arabic. This implies more than simply the fact that they are foreigners: they are foreigners that are there to colonize, divide, and rule.

ʿAfāf Shuʿayb uses ethnicity as it is reflected in skin color and language as it is reflected in the colloquial language of the protestors as two independent but related factors. She differentiates between "our" color and "their" color, "our" language and "their" language. According to her, what Britain attempts to do is trick "real" Egyptians into believing that there are "other Egyptians" protesting and taking action against the government. Britain manages to trick Egyptians by ensuring that these foreigners have the same identity verification and classification variables as Egyptians: they are dark-skinned and they speak ECA.

Shuʿayb positions herself as all-knowing. She employs linguistic resources to clarify her stance, such as the ECA aspectual marker b-prefix in verbs such as *bi-tḥa:wil* ("tries to"). This indicates that this process is still occurring and that we must try to stop it. By referring to her skin color as different from the British white color, she emphasizes the fact that she is Egyptian. She then finally ends with the declarative proposition "there is a war coming," again positioning herself as the expert, "real" Egyptian. The actress switches to English only once when she says "no Mubarak." This is indeed significant, because it is the sentence that is written on the flyer by an anonymous person, who was driven to write it—in English—by "someone with bad intentions." This implies that whoever is against Mubarak works with foreign powers and may either be a non-Egyptian or a traitor. The only opposition to Mubarak is referred to in English, with all its negative second order indexes discussed above and in Tāmir's example, rather than in Arabic. She then uses the salient SA phonological feature /q/ in her last proposition *ʕaʃa:n fi ḥarb qa:dima* ("because there is a war coming"), again making SA a marked choice that indexes seriousness and knowledge. If there is a war coming, this is really serious, but she seems to be the one with all this knowledge.

What she shares with Tāmir is the use of code-switching to English, the casting of doubt on the core identity of the protestors, and, more importantly, the clear knowledge of what really takes place, as opposed to what may seem to take place.

6.2.1.3 The revolutionaries fight back: laying claims to SA authoritative indexes

During the 2011 Egyptian Revolution, the well-known Abu Dhabi television competition *Amīr al-shuʿarāʾ* ("The prince of poets")—a program that selects the best Arabic poet of the year for a prize of a million dollars—was broadcast on air. The competition was fierce, especially between Egyptian poet Hishām Jukhkh and a Yemeni poet. Jukhkh could not attend one of the episodes, due to the events in Egypt at the time. However, he appeared unexpectedly in the penultimate episode on February 8, just days before Mubarak abdicated. Before reciting his contribution to the competition, he said—in a southern Egyptian dialect of ECA—that although he only had two minutes, he would like to observe a moment of silence for the martyrs of the revolution. He then began reciting a poem in SA, which contained a clear reply to accusations and attacks on the identity of the people in Tahrir. While Jukhkh is a poet who uses both ECA and SA in his poetry, sometimes code-switching between both in the same poem, he chose to authenticate the identity of the Egyptians in Tahrir Square in SA. By using SA, he reclaimed the possession of "the real Egyptian." Through his code-choice and language content, he presented himself as the "real" Egyptian, as if to declare forcefully: "I have now spoken. My language is not English, and it is not even ECA. It is the authoritative SA, with all its powerful indexes." His emphasis was on the access that he has to SA. Again, first and second order indexes were employed.

No sooner did Jukhkh recite the poem, than it was distributed on YouTube, Facebook, Twitter, and thousands of blogs; it was viewed on YouTube more than one million times in a week. The poem started to act as a counter-attack by the pro-democracy protestors and sympathizers. One day after Mubarak's abdication, the same recording of the poem was broadcast with images from the revolution on Nile TV—ironically, the same channel that several days earlier had broadcast the famous call by Tāmir discussed above. The sudden change of attitude of the Egyptian media needs a book by itself. However, the message and language form of the poem *Mashhad ra'sī min maydān al-taḥrīr* ("A birds-eye view from Tahrir Square") (Jukhkh 2010) provides an important example of how language can be used to reclaim an identity through a stance-taking act by using structural and discourse resources, including intertextuality and dialogicality.

Xabbiʔ qaṣa:ʔidaka l-qadi:mata kullaha/ wa-ktub li-miṣra l-yawma ʃiʕran miθlaha:
La ṣamta baʕda l-yawmi yafriḍu xawfahu/ fa-ktub sala:ma ni:la miṣra wa ʔahlaha:
ʕayna:ki ʔagmalu ṭiflatayn tuqarrira:n/ bi-ʔanna ha:ða l-xawfa ma:ḍin wa- ntaha:
ka:nat tuda:ʕibuna l-ʃawa:riʕu bil-buru:dati wa-l ṣaqi:ʕi/ wa lam nufassir waqtaha:
kunna nudaffiʔ baʕḍana fi: baʕḍana/ wa nara:ki tabtasimi:n nansa: bardaha:
wa ʔiða ġaḍibna kaʃʃafat ʕan waghaha:/ wa ḥaya:ʔuna yaʔba: yudannisu waghaha:
la: tatruki:him yuxbiru:ki bi-ʔannani/ mutamarridun xa:na l-ʔama:nati ʔaw saha:
la: tatruki:him yuxbiru:ki bi-ʔannani/ ʔaṣbaḥtu ʃayʔan ta:fihan wa muwajjaha:
fa ʔana ʔibn baṭnik wa-bnu baṭniki man ʔara:da wa man ʔaqa:la wa man ʔaqarra wa man naha:

ṣamatat fulu:lu l-xa:ʔifi:na bi-jubnihim/ wa jumu:ʔu man ʕaʃaqu:ki qa:lat qawlaha:

Hide all your old poems, and write to Egypt today poetry that is good enough for her.
There is no silence after today that will impose its fear. So write greetings from the river Nile to Egypt and its people.
Your eyes are like the most beautiful girls that have now decided that this fear is a past that is now over.
Streets were flirting with us with their coldness and frost and we did not mind then.
We used to warm ourselves with each other and when we saw you smile, we forgot our coldness.
And when we did become angry, she showed her face and then our awe made us stop and not mar her face with our anger.
Do not let them tell you that I am a rebel who betrayed you or forgot you.
Do not let them tell you that I have become something trivial and controlled by foreigners.
I am the son of your womb (your son) and the son of your womb is the one who wants, who deposes, who asserts and forbids.
The crowd of the cowardly is now silent and the masses of those who love you have said their word.

The poem starts with the imperative: "hide all your old poems." The verb "hide" is in the first person singular. Verbs used throughout this poem to refer to Egyptians are verbs of action. The first two imperative verbs are "hide" and "write." Unlike Tāmir, the poet positions himself as the active, powerful Egyptian that can and will change Egypt. Negation is used in the first declarative statement of the poem:

La ṣamta baʕda l-yawmi yafriḍu xawfahu

There is no silence after today that will impose its fear

The statement presupposes that before today, Egyptians were silent and thus cowardly and passive. This is no longer the case. After this declarative statement, another imperative verb ("write") is repeated again, denoting the new state of "action" that Egyptians are in. The poet orders himself to write.

The poet resorts to intertextuality when he says "greetings from the river Nile." This phrase is, in fact, taken from a poem by Poet Laureate Aḥmad Shawqī, entitled "Ghandi" (1931), in which Shawqī welcomes Ghandi to Egypt on his way to India. In the poem, Shawqī hails Ghandi as a peaceful freedom fighter, who shares with Egyptians the same aspirations and demands. It begins:

Sala:ma n-ni:li ya ġandi:
Wa ha:ða z-zahru min ʕindi:

Greetings from the river Nile to you, Ghandi
And these flowers are from me to you.

By referring to Shawqī, one of the most powerful poets of his time, and the particular poem that deals specifically with Ghandi, Egypt, and the struggle for independence and freedom, the poet relates Egypt's present to its past. He also explains indirectly that the struggle for freedom is not a betrayal of stability, but a continuous process. By referring to Shawqī and quoting from him, he also adds legitimacy and importance to his message. It is as if he says: "my poetry before that event is not good enough. I have to write poetry that is as grand as the event but I first have to borrow from a grand poet who also witnessed a great struggle for freedom."

The poet addresses himself and then later addresses Egypt using the typical female metaphor, since Egypt is also feminine in Arabic. The shift from the poet addressing himself and later describing himself as one of the people in Tahrir and then addressing Egypt as a woman with beautiful eyes shows the intimate relationship that he has with Egypt. He is definitely not a foreigner who speaks English, nor is he a foreigner who is trained in colloquial Arabic. He is an Egyptian who addresses his beloved country in perfect SA, although in intimate and direct statements. He starts explaining what he and the people in Tahrir used to do. It was hard for him to spend freezing nights at the square, but knowing that Egypt was happy made him do it. The use of aspect in this part is important. The poet uses the auxiliary verb *kunna* followed by a verb in the imperfect to denote continuity in the past:

kunna nudaffiʔ baʕḍana fi: baʕḍana/ wa nara:ki tabtasimi:n nansa: bardaha:

We used to warm ourselves with each other and when we saw you smile, we forgot our coldness.

This verse presupposes that Egypt, as a woman, approves of his decision to protest and strike in Tahrir. When he is fed up or angry, Egypt shows its smiling, encouraging face, endorses his decision, and he is then able to endure the challenging situation.

The female metaphor is emphasized with facial details, such as smiles and eyes. Yet Egypt is also a chaste woman, who is sacred enough for the protestors to feel ashamed for displaying their anger in front of her. Although the metaphor of Egypt as a woman is an old one, employing it here to show intimacy, respect, and, more importantly, love towards Egypt is essential as a device to refute arguments that people who protest "do not love Egypt." He then entreats Egypt not to listen to the cowardly by saying:

> *la: tatruki:him yuxbiru:ki bi-ʔannani/ mutamarridun xa:na l-ʔama:nati ʔaw saha:*
> *la: tatruki:him yuxbiru:ki bi-ʔannani/ ʔaṣbaḥtu ʃayʔan ta:fihan wa muwajjaha:*
>
> Do not let them tell you that I am a rebel who betrayed you or forgot you.
> Do not let them tell you that I have become something trivial and controlled by foreigners.

This imperative statement in which the poet forbids the woman Egypt from listening to "them" reflects again his intimate, direct relationship to Egypt and also situates him and Egypt on one side and "them," who accuse him of treason, on the other. He clearly aligns himself with Egypt and its "real sons" and disaligns himself from those who accuse the people of Tahrir of treason and being without character or aim. The real Egyptians are himself and others at the square.

It is worth mentioning that Jukhkh had produced an earlier poem, *Goḥā* ("Goha") (July 30, 2010), in which he also addresses Egypt angrily and yet lovingly. The poem is not in SA, but is a mixture of SA, ECA, and his own southern colloquial dialect. In fact, his southern dialect prevails in the poem. Although both poems are similar, in the sense that both address Egypt as a woman whom they care about, his poem before the revolution was an angry, frustrated cry from an Egyptian to an Egypt that is represented as a woman who seems to be either indifferent or forced to act in a cruel manner. The poem is translated below and is in pure ECA:

أنا اللى زارعك دهب
بتاكلينى سباخ
[. . .]
بعتينى علشانهم
وعنيكى معصوبة
ياهلترى خاينة
ولا زيى مغصوبة

I have sown you with gold
but you feed me dung.
[. . .]
You have blindly
betrayed me for their sake.
I wonder whether you are treacherous
Or, like me, oppressed by them?

The fact that he chooses to address Egypt in pure SA in the poem analyzed in this section makes his choice a well thought out decision with a specific aim, which is, as was stated earlier, to lay claim to all the authoritative and credible indexes of SA.

Dialogicality is also used in this poem. According to Du Bois, dialogicality

> makes its presence felt to the extent that a stance-taker's words derive from and further engage with the words of those who have spoken before—whether immediately within the current exchange of stance utterances, or more remotely along the horizons of language and prior text as projected by the community of discourse. (2007: 139)

Lempert (2009), in a study of US presidential candidate John Kerry's stance-taking during a 2004 debate, shows how Kerry took stances and positioned himself as a person of conviction, indirectly addressing attackers who accused him of "flip-flopping." This is exactly what the poet does in this poem. It is clear that he is addressing the pro-government attackers who accused the people of Tahrir of being agents of foreign countries and of not being Egyptians in the first place. The poem is an attempt to reclaim his identity as an Egyptian after this identity was attacked and distorted by others. This act of stance-taking on the poet's part would not have been as effective if it were not expressed using SA with all its indexes. It is noteworthy, however, that this poem may have directly addressed the accusations of Tāmir and ʿAfāf Shuʿayb discussed above. The poem repeats the verb *yiwaggih* ("control" or "drive") used by Tāmir in the example above in the form of a participle *muwaggah* ("foreign-controlled"). The poet's reply is:

> *la: tatruki:him yuxbiru:ki bi-ʔannani/ ʔaṣbaḥtu ʃayʔan ta:fihan wa muwajjaha:*
>
> Do not let them tell you that I have become something trivial and controlled by foreigners.

Note again that Shuʿayb in the example above claims that the foreigners in Tahrir Square are fluent in Egyptian Arabic and have been trained in London. She clearly attempts to recall to the minds of average Egyptians the British occupation of Egypt and the linguistic struggle that took place between the British calls for the use of ECA and the Egyptian intellectuals' insistence on preserving SA as the language of the Qu'ran and Arab identity more generally. By reciting the entire poem in SA, the poet refutes Shuʿayb's argument directly and reclaims SA as the language of the revolutionaries, rather than of the cowardly. By employing intertextuality with reference to the poem by Shawqī, in which he welcomes

Ghandi and his struggle against the British, the poet again replies directly to the accusations of Shuʿayb. The struggle of Egyptians in Tahrir is, in fact, similar to their past struggle against the British. Rather than working with foreigners, these Egyptians are again struggling for freedom, much like they did at the beginning of the twentieth century and as the Indians did through Ghandi. They also recall Ghandi's struggle as a peaceful one.

There are two dominant themes in this poem: the metaphor of Egypt as a woman who is cherished and the recurrent theme of speaking versus silence.

Silence is first mentioned with a negative construction: "No silence after today." Rather than saying "I will not be silent after today," using a negative marker and a verb, the poet uses nominalization, a negative marker *la:* followed by a noun, to indicate the definiteness of this new stance of never keeping quiet after today. Silence is again mentioned in the last line of the poem, in which the now-silent cowards are juxtaposed with the lovers of Egypt who spoke up.

The verb *ṣamatat* ("to stop speaking," "keep silent") and the verb *qa:lat* ("to speak") are both in the perfect form: the action is complete and the future is decided. The stance of "them" and "us" is also clear. While the "they" keep silent, the "us" (that is, those who love their country) speak up: *Qa:lat qawlaha:* ("said their word"). Now *qawla-ha:* refers to deeds as well as words; in other words, speaking is associated with action. Note that Suleiman (2012: 205) argues that in the Arabic grammatical tradition, speaking also implies action. So, literally, by speaking up, Egyptians have already taken action. Again, the poet positions himself as the active lover who takes a stance. This stance is reflected in what he says, his language form, and also his actions. While he spent the night in the cold recalling the face of beautiful Egypt, the cowardly group ran out of words.

Rather than portray himself as innocent of the crimes that the media accuses him of, the protestor–poet uses the powerful, authoritative indexes of SA to position himself as the authentic, reliable, and brave Egyptian. SA, again, has moral values associated with it. When the protestors are denied their identity, they fight back. The poet pleads with Egypt to believe that he has lost neither his character, nor his identity. He is not, however, helpless. He has spoken up and his words, unlike in his other poems, are in SA.

6.2.1.4 Discussion

This study aims to provide a fresh look at the relationship between language and identity in a diglossic community during a politically challenging time as well as the relationship between stance-taking as a process and identity construction. Throughout this section, language was regarded as a social process, as well as a social practice. These functions of language cannot be separated (see Heller 2007).

Linguistic resources acquire indexes by being associated with specific domains. In Chapter 3, I gave a glimpse of the layering of indexes process that takes place continuously in public discourse. Indexicality is an integral part of language as a social practice and process. Furthermore, language ideology and second order indexes were called upon in the three examples discussed. In the first example, the speaker uses and refers to English to cast doubt on the identity of protestors. The speaker appeals to the indexes of English and language ideologies associated with English as the language of the British colonizers. In the second example, the Egyptian actress uses the attitude and ideology surrounding foreigners who learn colloquial Arabic and promote it, rather than Standard Arabic, to again cast doubt on the Egyptian identity of the protestors. According to her, they are foreigners who came to conquer and their language variety, ECA, is the one promoted by the British Empire in the past. Note that, according to her, they are trained by the British.

In the third example, the poet, obviously aware of the state of the media argument, chooses to position himself as the "real Egyptian" by using SA with its powerful, authoritative, and nationalistic indexes. To reiterate, with no knowledge of the linguistic resources available for Egyptians and the indexes of SA, ECA, and English, one would miss the significance of the code-choice and the direct reference to the "language" used by all three speakers.

In terms of indexicality, while ECA has been associated with intimacy, informality, and affection, the poem shows that when a poet wants to combine indexes of SA and ECA, then SA will dominate by default. When trying to express his intense love for Egypt as well as his authoritative powerful stance, the poet uses SA, rather than ECA. SA domains are, for him, more pressing and, by prioritizing his indexes, SA indexes supersede ECA indexes. The same poet, as was noted above, addressed Egypt in ECA and in an Upper Egyptian ("ṣaʿidī") dialect in several other poems prior to the 2011 Revolution. Sometimes he even addresses Egypt angrily, and when he does so, he still uses ECA, rather than SA. In addition, in the first two examples, language was construed as an independent variable—a passport photo, so to speak. Whoever speaks Arabic is Egyptian and whoever does not is not Egyptian. There are some who may, of course, attempt to pass as Egyptians by speaking colloquial Egyptian Arabic. This "linguistic verification technique" is, of course, not new. It is reported that in Poland in 1312, there was a supposed German-led revolt at Cracow against Lokietek. Although the revolt was not successful and was put down, anti-German sentiments developed. The instigators were then tried and their guilt was determined by whether or not they could correctly pronounce such Polish words as *soczewica* ("lentil"), *kolo* ("wheel"), and *mlyn* ("mill"). Those who mispronounced any of these words were judged to be either German or Czech and deemed guilty (Grosby 2005: 70). Language, in this example, is also employed as a classification and verification category to cast an identity on individuals or, conversely, to rob them of one.

In this section, I concentrated on different examples that contribute to our understanding of stance-taking linguistic processes as a means of identity construction. According to Du Bois' stance triangle, positioning oneself is an important angle in stance-taking. The study argues that code-switching can be a choice that enables people to position themselves within a wider context and community. SA, ECA, and English have different indexes and all of these indexes can and, indeed, are employed in public discourse, not only to appeal to an audience, but also to position and situate oneself in relation to one's country, political affiliations, and identity in more general terms and to align or disalign with a specific group. While language form plays a pivotal role in this section, other linguistic resources have also been employed, including structural and discourse resources, such as mood, tense and aspect, pronouns, negation, deixes, metaphor, presupposition, dialogicality, and intertextuality. The last two resources, dialogicality and intertextuality, do not just depend on previous shared assumptions and knowledge, but are also dependent on shared ideologies and attitudes that may be related directly to language, as was clear in the third example discussed.

It is worth mentioning, however, that discussion of language and manipulation of linguistic devices in these examples does not aim to reflect the way Egyptians communicate or the way Egyptians interacted in Tahrir Square, but rather the way language was employed in public media discourse. There is no implication as to whether people in Tahrir spoke SA or English or ECA.

What I have also shown in this section is the struggle that involves access to codes as resources. Tamer makes claims about the lack of access of protestors to the Egyptian code, ECA or SA. He also demonstrates his access to English, as well as ECA. The actress also demonstrates her access to English and claims that the protestors have "stolen" access to ECA, in order to trick Egyptians into believing that they are also Egyptians. In the poem, the poet does not just demonstrate his access and knowledge of SA, but uses its powerful and legitimate indexes.

So far in this chapter, it has been made clear that during times of political turmoil in Egypt, in different forms of public discourse, there was struggle over the control and access to language as a resource. In the next section, we will see another example of this struggle.

6.3 How should I address Egyptians? Reclaiming access to SA after the revolution

In the last section, I showed the conflict surrounding who is and who deserves to be a "real" Egyptian. This conflict was tied to language content and form. It was also a linguistic territorial conflict, in which SA was the point of contention: whoever owned SA, owned legitimacy and credibility. This conflict, in fact, does not really have anything to do with who masters SA. It is a conflict about SA as an independent social variable, much like ethnicity, religion, or class, and not a conflict about SA as a linguistic variable in the first instance. That is, it is not about the essence of SA as a language, but about attitudes and ideologies towards SA. First, before the revolution, the Speaker of Parliament claimed ownership of SA—the language of the constitution and law, the language that gave legitimacy to Mubarak and his party. In fact, the whole article was supposedly about the importance of SA, but the underlying aim of the article was to underscore that the constitution is written by the people and that it is therefore legitimate. SA was used as a pretext to imply and also presuppose this claim. Surūr's attitude may not necessarily reflect the practice of the political elite in Egypt. The elite in Egypt do not, in fact, need to master SA (see Haeri 2003).

I have already shown that during the 2011 Revolution, language was used as both a linguistic resource and an independent variable. It was used to verify identity and also to produce the utmost effect on the consumer—the other Egyptian, who may not have made up his mind yet regarding which camp she or he belongs. After the 2011 Revolution, pro-revolution intellectuals and, more importantly, pro-SA intellectuals such as Shūshah reclaimed SA as the language of the protestors and rebels, rather than the language of Surūr or the National Party. Shūshah, an ardent defender of SA and once the head of the Arabic Language Academy in Cairo, is a famous poet and announcer and is still a member of the aforementioned academy. His famous radio program "Our beautiful language" has been broadcast for several decades now and is a landmark of Egyptian radio. The program is conducted in SA to discuss SA lexical variables and SA grammar and rhetoric in a fashion more accessible to the general public. Shūshah's stance towards SA is well-known in Egypt and the Arab world at large. He is one of the few intellectuals who intentionally and exclusively uses SA in all public appearances.

Shūshah's article (2011) discussed below was published in *al-Ahrām* newspaper, the same newspaper in which Surūr's article was also published, two months after the 2011 Revolution (March 27, 2011). The article is, as expected from Shūshah, in SA. It is titled: "The language of the youth of the revolution." As was noted earlier, *al-Ahrām* newspaper is an example of institutional discourse. It is a pro-government newspaper that is also linguistically conservative, since ECA is not used in it as much as in opposition newspapers (see Ibrahim 2010). In this article, Shūshah contradicts Surūr. He argues that it is because of the National Party (which Surūr belonged to) that SA deteriorated. Shūshah argues that SA is, in fact, the language of the revolution. Indeed, the young people of Egypt chanted the slogan الشعب يريد اسقاط النظام ("The people demand the fall of the regime") in SA. Note that this is almost the same slogan used in Tunisia and that it was later adopted in Yemen, Libya, and Syria. In that sense, SA did, indeed, unify all Arabs in their demand for liberation from their oppressive regimes.

Shūshah contends that the language of the revolution, SA, was elevated, dignified, and sophisticated. He argues that when young Egyptians shouted "we, the people, demand the fall of the regime," all of their calls were in perfect Arabic, SA—a Standard Arabic that reflects their determination and patriotism. The National Democratic Party in Egypt was in the habit of using ECA in its slogans as a means of degrading Egyptians, dealing with them as illiterates, simple-minded, crude, and naïve. The party had very low expectations of Egyptians and they falsely portrayed Egyptians as poor and ignorant. Shūshah adds that in Egypt both literates and illiterates, cultured and uncultured, understand SA and appreciate it. This is because SA reflects their national identity and sense of belonging to Egypt. As a result of the revolution, Egyptians have regained their national language in a natural and unpretentious way. According to him, these Egyptians will also create a new linguistic environment suitable for the new Egypt.

Before giving a detailed example of Shūshah's article, it is essential to state that Surūr and Shūshah had different motives in writing about SA as related directly to the Egyptian identity. While both relate SA to Egyptian identity, Surūr uses his expertise in SA to legitimize the constitution, his party, and his political position as Speaker of Parliament. In claiming that SA was in crisis and that he was the detector of this crisis who can also explain its repercussions, he also adopted a powerful stance as the sincere, knowledgeable law-maker. Shūshah's stance is different, although his attitude towards SA is similar to Surūr's. In expressing his admiration of the young Egyptians who demanded the overthrow of the regime, through both epistemic and evaluative statements, Shūshah aligns himself with the revolution and disaligns himself totally from the National Party and Mubarak's regime. His discussion of the linguistic choices of the revolutionary young Egyptians implies his admiration for them. His stance towards SA, which is a well-known stance in Egypt and was the same stance both before and after the revolution, is highlighted again in this article. The presupposition is that SA has social and moral indexes and is an elevated and prestigious code that is understood by most Egyptians who took a political stance against Mubarak. That is, for both Surūr and Shūshah, SA has the same moral and social indexes. However, the group that has access to SA is different for both. For Surūr, SA is in crisis because people ignore it and he, as a member of the National Party, knows its importance and masters it. For Shūshah, SA fell into crisis because of the political group that chose to use a crude and vulgar code when addressing Egyptians. This crisis is now over, because Egyptians have reclaimed their usage of SA and, with it, their identity. Both had been stolen by the National Party, the party of the regime.

This is a case when there is disagreement about the distribution of resources. There is also a renegotiation of the distribution of linguistic resources. While Surūr claims that he, as a legal expert, has access to SA and that there is a crisis in the usage of SA because most Egyptians do not have access to it, Shūshah posits that Egyptians always had access to SA, but were denied this access by the National Party, who chose to address them in a vulgar ECA. That is, the National Party claimed that Egyptians did not have access to SA and therefore they did not have access to the associations of SA, including mainly political awareness. This renegotiation of resources is, indeed, significant. It can happen with other social variables, such as ethnicity, as was the case in Shuʿayb's claims about people who pretended to be Egyptian. Again, it does not reflect reality, but rather a conflict that is both political and ideological in nature.

Shūshah's stance towards SA and admiration of the revolution are the two main points highlighted in the article:

حين هتف شباب مصر في أول أيام ثورتهم بالهتاف الذي رددته الملايين من ورائهم: الشعب يريد إسقاط النظام وما يتضمنه من حرص علي لغة عربية صحيحة, ثم بعد أن تتابعت نداءاتهم وشعاراتهم علي مدي الأسابيع المتصلة, في لغة سليمة تفجر بها شعورهم الوطني الفائر وعزمهم المتقد

The young people of Egypt in the first days of the revolution chanted the people demand the overthrow of the regime. Millions echoed their call. This chant shows a care on their part to use a correct form of Arabic. Then their chants and slogans in the following weeks were all in a proper language. Their strong patriotic feelings and their burning zeal were expressed with this language.

Shūshah makes a number of evaluative statements about the youth of Egypt during the revolution and their linguistic capabilities. Their chants throughout the revolution were in an elevated form of Arabic, SA. Unlike Shuʿayb and Tāmir, who both claimed during the revolution that the people in Tahrir Square were not Egyptians, Shūshah does not just claim that they are Egyptians, but also that they can use an elevated form of SA. To recap, Tāmir claimed on Egyptian television that the protestors spoke only English, therefore they were not Egyptians. Shuʿayb, the Egyptian actress, claimed that the protestors were foreigners trained in London to master ECA. According to her, their slogans were also written in English. Shūshah claimed the opposite of both. He claimed that ECA was, in fact, used by the National Party, not the revolutionaries. In giving his opinion of their SA, he also positions himself as the SA expert. This in itself empowers him and places him in an elevated position that can then enable him to judge others.

> وجدت نفسي تسترجع الشعارات التي رفعها الحزب الوطني في مؤتمراته السنوية الأخيرة, التي ادعي فيها رجاله التعبير عن فكر جديد ورسالة جديدة إلي الشعب.
>
> I found myself remembering the slogans of the national party conferences in the last few years, in which members of the national party claimed to express new ideas and new messages to the Egyptian people.

Shūshah now compares the young Egyptians of the revolution who had a sincere message delivered in SA slogans to members of the National Party who claimed to use a novel mode of expression, but who, in fact, used a degraded form of language that reflected their lack of respect for Egyptians.

> أن الأمية الكتابية والقرائية لم تعد حاجزا يفصل بين المواطن والمعرفة, التي يستطيع الحصول عليها بالاستماع والمشاهدة, وأن الأمية الحقيقية الآن لم تعد تلك المرتبطة بالقراءة والكتابة, بل هي البعيدة عن استخدام وسائل الاتصال الحديثة والناتجة عن العزلة والانقطاع عن مؤثرات الحياة والمجتمع. لكن شعارات شباب الثورة ونداءاتهم وولافتاتهم التي جاءت في صورة لغوية صحيحة لم تجيء هكذا مصادفة, وإنما هي المعادل الموضوعي الحقيقي لما في أعماقهم من انتماء إلي الوطن ومن هوية قومية, اكتسبت لغتها القومية بصورة عفوية وغير مفتعلة. وهو ما يؤكد أن الفطرة السليمة والنزوع السليم ينتج عنهما لغة سليمة, وأن افتقاد الانتماء الوطني والحس القومي الذي انتقدناه لدي بعض قطاعات الشباب قبل ثورة الخامس والعشرين من يناير كان هو المسئول عن انحدار المستوي اللغوي الذي يتخذونه لغة خطاب وتواصل.
>
> The inability to write and read is no longer a barrier now between the citizen and knowledge, for he can gain knowledge by listening and watching. Real illiteracy is not now related to writing and reading but is the inability to use modern communication technologies as a result of being cut off from the rest of society and social life.
>
> The slogans of the youth of the revolution, their chants and signs—which were cast in a correct form of language—were not created by accident. They were the concrete result of their deeply rooted patriotism and national identity. Their language acquired a nationalist spirit spontaneously without pretense. This proves that sound intuition and natural disposition find their expression in correct language, and that a lack of National identity and patriotic spirit—which can be seen in a part of our youth before the January 25th Revolution—were the reason for the degradation in the level of the language which they adopted as language of communication.

The argument is that both literates and illiterates, cultured and uncultured, understand SA and appreciate it. SA reflects the protestors' national identity and sense of belonging to Egypt. They have regained their "national language" in an authentic and unpretentious way. They will also create a new linguistic environment suitable for the new Egypt. SA is related to the intuition of Egyptians, to the sincerity of the message, and, more importantly, to the way Egyptians identify with each other and with Egypt. If they care about Egypt and their national identity, they use SA. If they do not do so, they use ECA (or, more specifically, a degraded form of ECA).

> وكان المثير للحزن والسخرية معا, اختيار الحزب الحاكم لشعارات صاغها من صاغها من عقول الحزب المفكر في لهجة عامية سوقية, ظنا منه أن الشعار بهذه الطريقة يكون أكثر قدرة علي الذيوع والانتشار ومخاطبة الجماهير [. . .]
> إن ثورة الخامس والعشرين من يناير, جديرة بهذا الدور الوطني والقومي في مجال اللغة, جديرة باجتثاث حالة التردي والإسفاف التي سيطرت علي الوطن في عقوده الثلاثة الأخيرة, وزادها سوء الفكر المتخلف لقادة الحزب الوطني البائد الذين رأوا في ابتذال اللغة وسوقيتها سبيلا إلي استهواء الجماهير والسيطرة عليها وترويج شعاراتها. لكن الجماهير أسقطت فيما أسقطته هذا الفكر السوقي, وهذا التوجه الذي يكشف عن خواء العقل, وسيطرة الجهالة والجهلاء.

> It was both sad and ironic to see that the ruling party chose slogans—created by whatever intellectual minds the party had—which where phrased in a vulgar dialect, thinking that slogans of this type would be most likely to spread and proliferate, and affect the masses [. . .]
> The 25th of January Revolution is worthy of this national and patriotic role in the realm of language; it is worthy of eliminating the state of linguistic vulgarity, regression, and triviality that controlled our country throughout the last three decades, a state which was made even worse by the backward way of thinking of the National Party, which perceived the pollution and vulgarity of language as a way to attract the masses, to control them, and to make them adopt their slogans. However, the people have toppled, among other things that were toppled, this vulgar mode of thinking, and this ideology that reflects an intellectual vacuum, and the dominance of the ignorant and ignorance [. . .]

Shūshah assigns SA moral indexes. SA is the language of intelligence, as opposed to the language of stupidity, naivety, and crudeness—all of which are characteristics of the previous government and the National Party. SA also carries values such as liberty, political awareness, and sophistication. By addressing Egyptians in ECA, the National Party underestimated Egyptians and their capabilities. The National Party patronized Egyptians, rather than respected them. Shūshah's attitude and propositions are summarized below:

1. He presupposes that by choosing ECA, the National Party implies that Egyptians are naïve and ignorant. That is, he ignores the solidarity and intimate indexes of ECA discussed throughout this book. He may have chosen to highlight specific negative indexes of ECA, but he, more importantly, claimed that the National Party intentionally barred Egyptians from access to SA.
2. As with a number of intellectuals, he claims that the National Party intentionally corrupts language. He equates the corruption of language to the corrupt system of a country. That is, as two social variables, language and politics are equal, according to him. The linguistic and political arenas are parallel.
3. He assumes that people have removed this vulgar thinking in eighteen days. A drastic language change or code-choice has taken place in the same way that a political change has taken place.
4. The moral values of SA and ECA are clear: one is vulgar and crude, the other is clear and sophisticated.
5. The pro-Mubarak group seems to be working against SA, while the revolutionaries use SA to reclaim their identity.

Remember that SA is associated with legitimacy, as discussed in Chapter 3. Note that Mubarak's three speeches before his abdication were all in SA. That is, he did not address Egyptians in ECA with its negative and positive indexes, but demonstrated his access to the legitimate code, SA.

6.4 When linguistic ideologies prevail

Shūshah shares the same ideologies and indexes of Tāmir, Shuʿayb, Jukhkh, and Surūr. Although they may all be involved in a political conflict and although they all may disagree about Egypt's political future, they all share the same linguistic ideologies, the same tacit norms. They seem to agree that identifying with fellow Egyptians and being patriotic implies access and usage of SA, the sincere and national code. As with Shuʿayb and Tāmir, Shūshah, albeit with different aims and intentions, accuses whoever does not use SA or an elevated form of Arabic as betraying the Egyptian identity.

Again, the question posing itself throughout this chapter is: "what language did the protestors really use?" Is it English, as Tāmir claims in Section 2? Is it colloquial Egyptian Arabic, as Shuʿayb claims in the same section? Or is it SA, as Shūshah claims? In fact, the protestors used "all" languages and codes available to them. Some banners were in French, others were in English or Arabic, parallel to the Tunisian ones, all saying "leave." The protestors started by chanting in SA *ʔirḥal*, which means "leave." When Mubarak delivered his speech on January 28, 2011, in which he declared that he would remain to serve Egypt and ensure its security and safety, the protestors in Tahrir Square modified their slogan and code-switched between SA and ECA, chanting *ʔirḥal yaʕni ʔimʃi/ yalli ma-b-itifhamʃi* ("'Begone!' means 'Go!,' you who doesn't understand"). They explained their SA slogan in ECA, accusing Mubarak in the process of not mastering SA—that is, of being less patriotic and less sincere. This is the same argument that Jabartī used centuries earlier when he accused the French of being deceitful because of their lack of good SA grammar. All linguistic means possible were used to put pressure on Mubarak to leave. By demonstrating their access to different codes, the protestors also demonstrated their control of resources, both linguistic and otherwise.

What, in fact, happened throughout the political conflict and, indeed, continues to occur today is that Egyptians, who mostly share a tacit norm and a linguistic ideology, use these shared ideologies to undermine their political opponents. They disagree about politics, but the core linguistic belief system among them is similar to a great extent. One has to remember that ECA carries positive indexes as well. The linguistic indexes of both codes, as was argued in Chapter 3, are complex. In caricatures, Egypt is mainly portrayed as speaking in ECA.

The Supreme Council of the Armed Forces (SCAF) in Egypt also had to make their linguistic choices, as well as political alignments and disalignments. They declared that they were on the side of the people from the very beginning. Not used to giving statements and reluctant to do so, they realized early on that without communicating effectively with the people, it would be difficult to regain stability. They also must have realized that the official government television channels had lost their viability, both before and after the revolution. The Supreme Council of the Armed Forces (SCAF) first started broadcasting a number of statements on Egyptian television. Then, a few days after Mubarak's departure from office, they decided to mainly concentrate on Facebook, reputedly the mechanism responsible for bringing Mubarak down. Their Facebook page displayed Egypt's flag, and they started addressing Egyptians periodically after an event took place or when there was a Muslim or Christian festival. Sometimes they reassured Egyptians, sometimes they provided an agenda for the future, and sometimes they replied to rumors. The armed forces only addressed Egyptians in SA, drawing on all the legitimacy and credibility that it carries. Their first declaration began with the address: "From the armed forces of Egypt to the honest sons of Egypt and the honest young Egyptians of the revolution and the martyrs, may God rest their souls of the revolution . . ." In their Facebook declarations, they mostly begin with the address: "a declaration from the armed forces to the great people of Egypt and the great youth of the revolution." SA places them in a powerful, legitimate position. The recurrent form of addressing Egyptians as "the great people of Egypt" is meant to appeal to Egyptians' egos and also acknowledge the important task of the armed forces in protecting these great people.

The armed forces have taken over representing Egyptians directly after the revolution, in the same way that Qutuz came forward in the example at the beginning of this chapter, saying that he, as a citizen of Egypt, represented Egyptians. Qutuz made this claim in ECA, appealing to the authentic associations of ECA and capturing the identity of the *ibn al-balad*, the son of the country who always speaks in ECA (see Chapter 3). SCAF was not just one man, but more than twenty men. Their aim was to appeal to the legitimacy of their position as representing Egypt after the revolution. That is, while acknowledging that Egyptians are great, they also appealed to the legitimate indexes of SA. They wanted their Facebook statements to be associated with truth. They were in SA—and good SA, for that matter. Although placing themselves in a powerful position by assessing Egyptians as great people (an evaluative statement) and addressing the youth of the revolution also as great (another evaluative statement), they also wanted to ensure that whatever they said would be truthful and, thus, valuable. They, as the revolutionaries, the National Party, and all Egyptians, understand the ideologies and indexes of SA and ECA.

6.5 Linguistic unrest: the war over access to resources

What we have, at times of conflict, is a group of individuals who think that resources are not distributed equally. These resources include political resources, social resources, economic resources, and, at times, linguistic resources. Revolutionaries usually challenge the way that resources are distributed and demand a more fair distribution. They aim to renegotiate this distribution. While doing so, they also renegotiate access to codes as resources. This renegotiation is more symbolic in nature than a reflection of actual access to linguistic codes. The result of this negotiation is usually a challenge to identity that manifests itself through a challenge of language practices. Again, this challenge does not always reflect linguistic reality.

What is meant by linguistic unrest is the struggle that involves access to, and distribution of, linguistic resources. This struggle has been exemplified throughout this book with different forms of public discourse. At times of political turmoil, there is also an ideological conflict that manifests itself in the way that individuals classify each other and position themselves. They classify and position themselves by judging different linguistic codes and varieties. They also position themselves by using different resources, including code-switching and code-choice between different codes and different varieties.

While using linguistic resources to challenge, contest, or highlight an Egyptian identity is a linguistic reality, talking about language as a classification category is a linguistic projection of reality that is mainly ideological in nature.

Political unrest can be both associated with particular locations and also particular codes. During the Revolution of 2011, there were a frequent number of evaluative statements about who was the real Egyptian who cared about Egypt. Tahrir Square, as a local place, symbolized the political struggle against Mubarak. Other areas were also sites of pro-Mubarak demonstrations on a much smaller scale. Locations eventually carried indexes, such as the following areas of Cairo: Muṣṭafá Maḥmūd, pro-Mubarak and later pro-SCAF, ʿAbbāsiyyah. In November 2012, two more locations emerged representing two more social and political groups: Ittiḥāadiyya (where the president's palace is located) represented liberal or revolutionary protestors; and Cairo University represented the Islamists and pro-Morsi (Egypt's current president) group. Places and access to those places became symbols of affiliations and ideologies. Judgments about the language of these places were also part of this conflict. The public space "serves as a tool in the hands of different groups for the transmission of the messages as to the place of different languages in [. . .] geographical and political entities and for influencing and creating de facto language realities" (Shohamy 2006: 11). Laying claim to different locations was also part of the conflict. To give yet another example, Masbīrū ("Maspero")—the office of the official television channel—was frequently a focal point of conflict and sometimes bloody altercations, as in the case of the Copts' demonstrations in October 2011. Maspero as a place represents pro-government discourse, but was used by the Copts, who wanted (in this particular case) to revise access to resources and lay claim to an essential resource. Locations and linguistic codes were variables at a time of political unrest. People moved to demonstrate in different places, to lay claims to different codes, and, in the meantime, the unrest became both physical and linguistic.

Language as a social variable was similar to dress code, social class, and ethnicity, although different in importance and level of saliency in different domains. The people in Tahrir Square were accused of pretending to be Egyptians, because they had a dark skin color (challenge to ethnicity). They were also later accused of being riffraff, because of their dress code. They were accused of being lower class, uneducated, and so on. Social variables were an essential part of the conflict and places were also centers (focal points) for media wars. SA specifically with its ideological indexes was the main code used to legitimize different groups. Some of the accusations about people in Tahrir were as follows:

1. They do not speak Arabic. They do not have access to Egyptian codes.
2. They pretend to be like us, speaking colloquial with its negative indexes, and they pretend to have our ethnicity, because of their skin color. They stole access to one of our codes.
3. They use foreign languages, especially English—the language of past colonizers and American political hegemony. They have access to the wrong codes.

Pro-democracy groups and poets used SA as a resource to add weight and legitimacy to their demands, as in the example of the poem analyzed in this chapter.

Before the 2011 Revolution, SA was used to justify a lack of democracy. For example, Surūr claimed that SA was in crisis; therefore people were linguistically incapable of having a democracy, since they could not even read their own constitution. SA was also used to presuppose that the National Party and, with it, Mubarak's regime were legitimate and chosen by the people. The people wrote their constitution—a rather contradictory statement to that above, since if the people wrote their constitution, then they should be able to read it as well.

After the revolution, Shūshah, an ardent defender of SA, justified his positive stance towards SA by claiming that it was, in fact, the language of the revolutionaries. For both Surūr and Shūshah, the role of ECA in identity construction and political participation is ignored and indirectly undermined.

Language as part-and-parcel of political conflicts has been studied before by Suleiman, specifically in his book *A War of Words* (2004). However, it has not been studied in relation to Egypt before or during a revolution or in relation to a political turmoil in Egypt specifically. This study offers a novel way of relating language to political conflicts and identity. In the approach adopted in this work, language is simultaneously a resource and a social variable. As such, members involved in a political conflict will usually resort to language to reclaim their identity. In some cases, SA is seized as a trophy by the winners of the political conflict. Whoever has access to SA is the legitimate and true Egyptian and thus is the person who should also rule the country.

Note that in all the examples in this chapter, language was addressed as a social variable. Ideologies were at work to the utmost. When it is language that is put into question, ideologies take over. When other social variables are contested, such as religion, ethnicity, and so on, then SA is not necessarily called upon as the marker of Egyptian identity. As was shown in previous chapters, authenticity is also associated with ECA. What distinguishes the examples analyzed in this chapter is the sensitive nature of the topic of political turmoil.

Despite its negative indexes, SA remains the most obvious symbol of political legitimacy. Claiming to master SA and judging the way that others use SA positions individuals in the role of the powerful and sincere Egyptian.

I would like to recall an example mentioned in Chapter 1, in which the professor, when at a loss as to how to answer Zūzū about his identity, ignores the content of her question and concentrates on her Arabic pronunciation. Surūr, when justifying the political system at the time, also concentrates on the crisis facing SA. He explains in detail the second amendment of the constitution, which claims that SA is the official language, while ignoring the main problem, which is that the constitution has been modified many times to accommodate the previous president. Shūshah also concentrates on the language form of the revolutionaries, rather than whether their demands have been met. While his intentions are better, his focus is the same. Language was at times the scapegoat, while at other times it was a means of holding a conflict by proxy (see Suleiman 2004).

Jabartī's example, which took place centuries ago and in which "grammar"—that is, form of language—was essential in evaluating the credibility and intentions of outsiders, has been echoed recently in Mubarak's historical trial. Mubarak was sentenced to life in prison by an Egyptian judge on June 2, 2012. The first sentence of its kind to an Arab president, the judge's verdict was followed on air throughout the Arab world, if not the world at large. However, the Egyptians were disappointed with the acquittal of other dominant figures in Mubarak's system, as well as the acquittal of his two sons. Egyptians rushed to Tahrir Square to express their frustrations and doubts about the judicial system in Egypt and this judge's verdict in particular.

A prominent satirical journalist and announcer Ibrāhīm ʿĪsá expressed his doubts about the judge's independence and impartiality through resorting, once again, to language form. He did so through his program, which was broadcast on air on O-TV on June 2, 2012.[2] Note that courtrooms are the domain for SA, and judges build their evidence through laws written in SA. Therefore, their SA is supposed to be impeccable. ʿĪsá expressed his doubts by pointing out all the grammatical mistakes and SA mispronunciations made by the judge while giving his verdict. ʿĪsá then said that there had been "a linguistic crime" committed, first and foremost. Throughout his program, ʿĪsá attempted to cast doubt on the intentions of the judge, as well as his general knowledge. The judge's lack of access to perfect SA was, for ʿĪsá, an indicator of his lack of credibility as a judge and also, in the process, his lack of sincerity and professionalism. Access to SA in this case is a necessity, rather than an asset.

When a group or individual lay claims to SA, they may, in fact, be taking possession of legitimacy, political or other. They may also be excluding another group that has limited or no access to SA. SA as a resource becomes essential in the political pattern of display of exclusion and inclusion. This is true, as was shown above, before, during, and after the revolution. In fact, this process of laying claim to resources and access to them is ongoing.

Almost two years after the revolution, the controversial new Egyptian Constitution was approved by the constituent assembly on November 30, 2012. The assembly's meetings were all broadcast on air on an official Egyptian channel. The constitution was controversial, because a number of politicians, activists, and intellectuals opposed the domination of Islamists in the constituent assembly. However, the constitution was passed in a referendum held on December 15 and 22, 2012, with approximately 63.8 support. This 2012 Constitution then replaced the 1971 Constitution, as well as the 2011 amendments to it. Although the articles of the constitution were discussed and broadcast on television, some intellectuals objected to holding a referendum on the constitution in which both literates and illiterates voted. Again, the passive knowledge of SA by illiterates and the shared vocabulary and structures of ECA and SA were ignored.

On December 9, 2012, the acclaimed Egyptian author and political activist ʿAlāʾ al-Aswānī (b. 1957) made his views known.[3] According to the Masrawy News website, al-Aswānī wondered: "Would the Muslim brotherhood agree to exclude illiterates from voting in the referendum and also agree to stop buying votes with oil and sugar?" Al-Aswānī then defended his suggestion by arguing that "excluding illiterates from voting is not racism but respect for the democratic process. How can an illiterate discuss the constitution?" He continued: "the Brotherhood and Salafis use ignorance and poverty to push illiterates to vote for anything they want in the name of Islam. They also buy their votes with oil and sugar." Al-Aswānī emphasized that he respects illiterates and would like to help them by educating them, but he still posed the question of how one could vote on a constitution that one cannot read.

Al-Aswānī's position was criticized by many, including intellectuals and professors who supported the new constitution. Although his intentions may have been well-meaning, Al-Aswānī, as some other intellectuals and scholars had done before him, hit a nerve. Some understood his proposition as insinuating that all those who said yes to the constitution are ignorant in some way or another.

To recall, Surūr justified a lack of political participation in Egypt by claiming that SA is in danger because many fail to master it. Haeri, in a more scientific manner, attempted to explain a lack of democracy by suggesting that SA is a sacred language not mastered by many. Almost two years after the revolution, al-Aswānī suggested that the democratic process in Egypt is not moving in the right direction, because of the limited or complete lack of access to SA by a specific group, illiterates. In the case of al-Aswānī, democracy should privilege a group of people who have access to education and SA. That is, especially when it comes to voting on the constitution, with no access to SA, the democratic process is not complete. Al-Aswānī also echoes Ghālī's claims at the beginning of this chapter and during the 2011 Revolution. Once more, democracy, a political process, is yoked to SA, a linguistic code.

It is worth mentioning, however, that al-Aswānī shares the same ideologies and indexes of not only Surūr, but also Shūshah, Tāmir, Shuʿayb, and Jukhkh. That is, in spite of all their political conflicts, all of the Egyptians studied here seem to share the same linguistic indexes of SA, at least to some extent. Access to SA is a prerequisite to legitimacy and political weight. This in itself is essential. What they do not agree on is who has access to SA and who does not. In addition, they also do not agree on who assumes that the other lacks access to SA and who does not assume so. That is, the conflict regarding access to resources did not subside or end after the 2011 Revolution in Egypt. In fact, it is just at its onset.

However, access to ECA can also be essential for a political figure, as the satirical female poet Īmān Bakrī claims in her famous ECA poem "Qualities of the future president" (2012). The poem was recited weeks before the presidential election in Egypt in May 2012. The poet Īmān Bakrī had a different linguistic demand from the coming president. In her poem (2012), the colloquial satirical poet says:[4]

Yiku:n maṣra:wi:/ w-miʃ bara:ni manaʕrafu:ʃ
Yurṭun waya:ya tirya:ni/lawindi:/ wida:ni matifhamhu:ʃ

We want him Egyptian, not a fake outsider we do not know.
Who would then speak to us in whatever gibberish/language that my ears would not understand.

What she means is that she wants to have access to his ideas and thoughts. She wants his code to be "inclusive" for all those who master ECA, not just for those who master SA or a foreign language. She also wants him to be an "ibn balad" ("son of the country")—that is, a typical Egyptian who speaks clearly, so that "all" have access and all understand. She demands an authentic, inclusive president who does not leave behind some Egyptians simply because they do not understand or share his resources. It is not just language that she refers to. But, as usual, it is language that is mentioned—a symbol of entrenched conflicts and ideologies. Bakrī is concerned with an Egyptian issue and, as such, it is ECA that she emphasizes.

Although this book is about Egypt first and foremost, this "exclusion and inclusion pattern of display" is, of course, not peculiar to Egypt. In fact, a relevant example to our discussion is one from Morocco. The Arab world has twenty-four countries and they all, except for four African countries—Chad, Comoros, Djibouti, and Somalia—have Arabic and only Arabic as their official language (see Bassiouney (2009: 211) for a list of Arab countries and official languages). After the 2011 Revolution in Egypt, the King of Morocco took preemptive steps to show that, unlike the rulers of Tunisia, Egypt, and Libya, he was ready to compromise. He declared on June 17, 2011, that he would make some amendments to the constitution. These changes would mainly ensure that the king is also a citizen in the country and that he will yield some of his powers to the parliament and government. More importantly for this book, he was the first North African ruler to actually add another language, Tamazight, next to Arabic as an official language. The gesture was not just to show his linguistic awareness, but also to show that he was ready to be inclusive and share resources. Tamazight is not just a Berber language used by a significant proportion of Moroccans. Forty per cent of Moroccans speak a Berber language. This is also a resource that was denied and ignored for a significant period of time, access to which also symbolizes inclusion in the political arena. The King of Morocco correctly predicted the coming conflict regarding unequal access to resources, including linguistic ones, so he took the unprecedented step of introducing another official language in addition to Arabic. It is not a coincidence that this gesture was accompanied by other political concessions. As a resource, language is part of the social practices and processes of individuals, communities, and nations.

Notes

1. See http://youtu.be/Tml9rX9Uv78, accessed 30 August 2013.
2. See http://youtu.be/RGv6sII7SZQ, accessed 30 August 2013.
3. See http://www.masrawy.com/news/Egypt/Politics/2012/December/9/5455445.aspx, accessed 30 August 2013.

تساءل الأديب علاء الأسواني، هل يقبل الإخوان إذا ما وافقت القوى المدنية على تمرير الاستفتاء بشرط أن يستبعد الناخبين الأميين، وتوقيع عقوبة الحبس لمن يشترى الأصوات بالزيت والسكر.

وأوضح الأسواني أن قصر الانتخاب على من يعرف القراءة ليس عنصرية إنما هو احترام للديمقراطية متسائلاً: ''كيف يناقش الدستور أميين››.

وأكد عبر تغريده على موقع التواصل الاجتماعي ''تويتر'' أن تلك الشروط تحرم الإخوان ممن وصفهم

بجمهورهم الأساسي قائلاً: ‘‘ الإخوان والسلفيون يستغلون الجهل والفقر و يدفعون الأميين للتصويت لأى شيء باسم الإسلام ويشترون اصواتهم بالزيت والسكر››.
وتابع قائلاً: ‘‘يصاب تجار الدين بالهستيريا عندما نشترط القراءة والكتابة فيمن يصوت على الدستور و السبب انهم يستغلون جهل الناس وفقرهم ليصلوا الى الحكم››.
واختتم الأسواني تغريداته قائلا: ‘‘كيف يصوت إنسان على دستور لا يستطيع قراءة مواده››، مؤكداً أن احترامنا للأميين يكون بأن نعمل على تعليمهم وليس بان نتركهم فريسة لاستغلال لمن وصفهم بتجار الدين.
9/12/2012

4. A recording of her recitation is available in multiple versions, including: http://www.youtube.com/watch?v=YVdZ22imnYQ, accessed 30 August 2013.

CHAPTER

7

CONCLUSIONS

This book aims at providing a theoretical framework to study identity in public discourse.

- Identity is defined for the purpose of this work as a social construct that is ideological, perceptual, and habitual.
- In order for us to understand the relationship between language and identity, one must first regard language as both a social variable and a social resource available to individuals. As a social variable and resource, it is also dependent on the shared norms of the community and on the ideological, perceptual, and habitual aspects of identity as a social construct.
- Egyptians are perceived in public discourse as forming one large community. This community shares a tacit norm mechanism that enables its members to decipher indexes, both linguistic and meta-linguistic.
- Linguistic indexes occur at different orders and, depending on the context, can be challenged or modified.
- Public discourse may attempt to provide a fixed, coherent facet of Egyptian identity. However, some aspects of this identity are sensitive to socio-political changes. Social variables can be classified even further into backbone variables and outcome variables. In the right context, language is a backbone variable in Egypt, especially ECA.

7.1 The twofold function of language in identity construction

The question posed at the start of this work was: what is the essential role of language in linking the social world to identity formation?

It was first argued that Egyptian identity, when depicted in public discourse, cannot be fully differentiated or separated out into individual, social, or national components. This is due to the very nature of public discourse and its tendency to generalize and homogenize, even while acknowledging differences.

In Egyptian public discourse, language is used as a resource, in order to project a unified identity for Egyptians as a coherent community sharing similar perceptions, ideologies, and habits. This is achieved through two means: language is used as a classification category and as a means for individuals to adopt different stances in public discourse that, in turn, entails indexes that are associated with an identity.

Public discourse utilizes language as a classification category, as a social variable that categorizes a community, similar to ethnicity, locality, or historical context. Code-switching and code-choice are used in this case. That is, in the projection of public discourse, the code that one chooses directly reflects on how one positions her or himself in relation to others: as an insider or outsider, as an Egyptian or a foreigner, as an Egyptian with no loyalty to Egypt or as a loyal citizen, as a typical man in the street or as an Egyptian who does not share the same characteristics that unify Egyptians. In this scheme, for example, if a person speaks Arabic, she or he is classified as Egyptian. However, since Egypt is a diglossic community, classification can also be dependent on which code is used and whether speakers switch between codes. If speakers switch code between ECA and SA or between ECA and English, for example, this often carries specific indexes. These indexes occur at different levels and can be either direct or indirect.

The use of language as a classification category is predicated on attitudes and ideologies as much as on linguistic realities. This means that one cannot fully comprehend the relationship between code-choice, code-switching, and identity, unless one fully comprehends the indexes of different codes. In order to be able to understand the indexes of different codes, it is necessary to analyze the political, social, and historical contexts and processes that pertain to a specific speech community and study how these factors helped foster indexes.

The second point is that language as a resource in public discourse allows individuals to position themselves by manipulating linguistic resources. The linguistic resources adopted in this book include discursive resources and structural resources. Discursive resources include: mention of identification categories, such as ethnicity, locality, and shared past experiences; Van Leeuven's (1996) five categories: functionalism, classification, relational identification, physical identification, and generalization; nature of statements (Gee 2010); presuppositions; metaphors; metonymy; intertextuality; and dialogicality. Structural resources include grammatical patterns: for example, nominalization, verbless sentences; pronouns (see also Silverstein 1976); tense and aspect; demonstratives, deixis, quantification, and negation; conditional sentences; mood and modality; and phonological, structural, and lexical variation. Code-switching and code-choice are both a discursive and structural resource. I also argue that code-switching can be a resource that enables people to position themselves within a wider context and community.

7.2 Social variables and linguistic resources: how are Egyptians defined in public discourse?

7.2.1 What does being an Egyptian mean?

In public discourse, specific social variables are attributed to Egyptian identity. These include what have been called backbone variables and outcome variables. Backbone variables are not usually challenged as defining concepts; these include ethnicity, historicity, and locality. Outcome variables are usually the result of the combination of backbone variables and include character traits, moral dispositions, and communal solidarity—these outcome variables can be challenged and their truth contested at times of political and social turmoil.

To elaborate, public discourse argues that the historical achievements of Egyptians throughout history render the modern Egyptian strong, resilient, patient, and kind. This historical authenticity and superiority of "the Egyptian" is attributed to her or his ancient Egyptian, Islamic, and Coptic history—a history in which "the Egyptian," both past and present, are discussed as one and the same. The achievements of Egyptians are then taken as proof of their capacity for progress and success and as a reason for maintaining their pride and dignity. These achievements of ancestors could also be used to highlight the inefficiency of the present Egyptian and spur her or him on to take more positive action, as was the case at the beginning of the twentieth century and again at the beginning of the twenty-first century. Because the Egyptian is a direct descendant of her or his ancient Egyptian ancestors, Egyptians all share one ethnicity. This ethnicity may be manifested in skin color and ancestral lineage. Egyptians also all share one local geographic area called Egypt, which is marked by the River Nile, the pyramids, and other religious and historical monuments.

Because Egyptians share these three social variables in addition to language, they are considered to form one large community, even among different religious groups (Muslims and Christians, in particular). This community is perceived to share specific habits, as well as linguistic, social, character, and moral traits. These habits include sharing food, socializing, being generous and kind to fellow Egyptians, and being patient and resilient. Egyptians are also distinguished by their communal solidarity. This communal solidarity—an outcome of sharing one community—is more salient than religious differences. Public discourse tackles religion from a complex and multi-layered perspective. While highlighting the fact that Egyptians are, by and large, religious, public discourse also undermines the differences between Christians and Muslims as two distinct religious groups. Public discourse argues that apart from lexical variation that pertains to liturgical items, there is no significant linguistic variation built on religion as an independent social variable in Egypt. Indexes of the religious sectarian divide are undermined, while indexes of linguistic unity as a marker of communal unity are emphasized. Egyptians are depicted as sharing backbone and outcome variables, and religion is a special variable that does not fall neatly into either category. Religion is then either dealt with in a neutral or holistic way; there is either indirect mention of both religions of Christianity and Islam or no mention of a specific religion, but a neutral mention of God. Language as a social variable and a resource will be discussed in detail in Section 4.

7.2.2 How are linguistic resources used? What are the salient tendencies?

Note that there is a remarkable continuity and consistency in the use of social attributes since the beginning of the twentieth century in Egypt, when they were first used as markers of identity. In the data analyzed throughout this book, including patriotic songs, these themes regularly co-occur with references to Egyptian character traits, habits, and communal solidarity.

Language indexes an identity that is built on shared ideologies, perceptions, and habits. Public discourse processes and reprocesses ideologies shared by Egyptians through stance-taking. If these ideologies, such as those of ethnicity and historicity, are not shared by the audience, the data is void of meaning. The ideologies and perceptions are difficult to understand or appreciate for non-Egyptians, especially the hyperbolic expression of Egypt's past and sometimes present glory.

In this book, different genres of public discourse were studied. In the patriotic songs studied, public discourse enhances the perception of Egyptians as forming a large coherent community that encompasses many small ones. This large community shares habits and assumptions about insiders and outsiders, as well as character traits (such as humor, generosity, kindness, and communal solidarity). By and large, Egyptian public discourse provides a coherent and emphatic portrayal of shared identity, but there are examples in which this identity is challenged.

There are instances in which Egyptian's current or past actions are questioned and in which Egyptian identity does not necessarily incorporate only positive traits. Such challenges seem to occur at times of political awakening, in particular. At the beginning of the twentieth century, Bayram al-Tūnisī criticized Egyptians numerous times in his work. At the beginning of the twenty-first century, Egyptians were again harshly criticized in public discourse. On more than one occasion, the backbone variables were used as part of the argument to criticize the abject state of Egyptians, as in al-Tūnisī's poem "Letter to Tutankhamen."

In patriotic songs, linguistic resources are employed to index attitudes and ideologies through a stance-taking process. There is a general tendency for singers to position themselves as knowledgeable arbiters on Egypt and Egyptians and to provide a positive evaluation of what it means to be Egyptian. Interestingly, the lyrics often target an addressee who either does not know or may not be fully convinced of what it means to be an Egyptian. To reference this positive stance, the singer uses various linguistic resources and also repeats lexical identification categories that already carry indexes for her or his audience. Positioning the addressee as either an outsider or a reluctant insider is essential to argue in favor of the positive aspects of Egypt.

This positioning happens through the use of different resources that include mainly what Fairclough (1989: 205) calls "synthetic personification." This technique highlights the conversational style of the songs, as well as the informality and sincerity of the singer and his or her evaluated object—that is, Egyptian identity. When a colonizer or an aggressive outsider is referenced in a song, the third person is often used instead of the second person, as in the case of *miṣr tataḥadaθ ʕan nafsi-ha:* ("Egypt speaks about itself") by Umm Kulthūm (published as a poem in 1921) when Egypt refers to colonizers in the third person plural or in the case of the song *ḥabibt-i: ya: maṣr* ("Egypt, my love") by Shādiyah (1967), in which the person who does not understand Egyptians is referred to in the third person singular. In my view, this manipulation of pronouns is intentional and intends to undermine the aggressive, unfriendly, unsympathetic outsider, while appealing to the insider or sympathetic outsider. One might argue that outsiders are divided into categories: those with knowledge and those without; those who are important (referred to with a second person pronoun) and those who lack power and influence (referred to in the third person). This style of positioning is artificial, of course, since the singer appeals to ideologies already shared by his/her audience. These ideologies and perceptions are difficult to understand or appreciate for non-Egyptians.

One other striking technique used frequently is the use of verbless clauses to express propositions about Egypt and Egyptians. In fact, there is one song *fi:-ha: ḥa:ga ḥilwa* ("There's something beautiful about her") by Rihām ʿAbd al-Ḥakīm (2010) that includes only one verb (*b-tzi:d*, "increases"), compensating for this by repeating the existential adverb (*fi:-ha*, "there is") throughout. The fact that Arabic has an implicit construction for the verb "to be" has been manipulated to the utmost.

Assertive statements and statements of achievement are also prevalent in patriotic songs. This suggests that throughout the songs what Du Bois (2007: 171) calls epistemic stances and evaluative stances are more common than affective ones. It is true that there are a number of examples that include elements of affective stance (as in, "How lovely is Egypt," "Egypt, my love"), but in my view, the epistemic stance prevails, while other forms of stance merely appear as a consequence. This is significant, because it suggests that in the process of defining identity, epistemic stances can be more convincing.

Dialogicality is essential on different levels. I began with the assertion that identity formation is the outcome of a perpetual dialogical process, in which discourses interact and collide. Public discourse is also dependent on dialogical processes. That is also the reason why patriotic songs would not be appreciated by someone who is not familiar with the indexes and previous dialogues. This is what I call the "the paradox of the knowledgeable Egyptian" who may use epistemic stances frequently to a supposedly ignorant outsider, but who, in fact, can only address an insider who shares the dialogical context. The complexity of media language, according to Bell (1984), is that while communicators take the initiative in most cases, they are still completely dependent on the audience for their livelihood and survival. Bell contends that

> communicators persuade by using language as an expression of shared identity with the audience [. . .] Ideally, the audience will regard a mass medium as its voice. The best communicators (and leaders) thus make the people's voice their own, and their voice the people's. (1984: 193)

I have tried to demonstrate that most, if not all, patriotic songs and poems reference a dialogue on national identity that has been part of Egyptians' communicative knowledge and perceptions. In Chapter 6, for example, when the poet al-Jukhkh starts addressing Egypt in SA, it is also clear that he is involved in a dialogue with pro-government attackers who accused the people of Tahrir of being agents of foreign countries or even of not being Egyptians in the first place. In this dialogue, he asserts his identity as a very patriotic Egyptian.

In addition, while public discourse is at pains to depict a coherent and holistic community of Egyptians, it cannot prevent the outbursts of questions and challenges to this holistic perception. Egyptian identity can be contested, too. Indeed, the Revolution of 2011 witnessed the fiercest challenge to the notion of the coherence of "Egyptians." While the state media branded the protestors in Tahrir Square as "non-Egyptians," both metaphorically and literally, the pro-democracy protestors branded the pro-Mubarak group as traitors and lacking in Egyptianness.

On the other hand, Arabic as an independent variable and marker of identity is mentioned only four times in patriotic songs and, as with other variables, is not mentioned in isolation, but in conjunction with other variables, such as ethnicity, history, and locality. However, during times of upheaval and political tension, language is usually called upon as one of the main markers of identity in the Arab world, specifically in Egypt. Chapter 6 tackles this issue in more detail and discusses how language is manipulated as a resource and an independent variable. Although Arabic as an independent variable is mentioned only a few times, the context in which it occurs renders it a backbone variable.

Although rarely mentioned, language remains an essential factor in identity construction. Language comes to the forefront at times of conflict. Usage of ECA in general may reflect attempts at cultural hegemony and mention of the distinctive dialect of Egyptians is a reflection of uniqueness.

In the poem *samra:ʔ* ("Dark-skinned woman") (1996) by the Lebanese poet Jurj Qardāḥī, an Egyptian girl is referred to by her Egyptian dialect as a distinctive feature. The poem, written in SA, was later set to music and sung by the famous Lebanese singer Mājdah al-Rūmī.[1] For a change, the song refers to a female Egyptian, rather than a male, which gender is generally utilized.

In novels, we encounter a different kind of public discourse that sheds light on Egyptian identity and also more frequent use of higher levels of orders of indexicality, as will be discussed below. What this kind of data has in common with patriotic songs, for example, is the use of the same social variables to construct identity. These variables include ethnicity, historicity, locality, religion, and character traits. Language as a social variable is also a salient marker of identity in all of the novels discussed. In fact, ideologies about the unity of language and the unity of identity were tackled again in Chapter 5. However, literature deals with social variables differently. Unlike in patriotic songs, protagonists were less sure and less positive. Questions pertaining to one's individual identity, as opposed to a collective Egyptian identity, came to the forefront. Protagonists were not always knowledgeable, nor were they addressing a less knowledgeable audience. Their stances were dynamic, rather than static. They evolved into "Egyptians" towards the end of the novels, but after a long struggle with the self. However, the end product was similar in ideology and attitude to the end product depicted in textbooks and patriotic songs, as was mentioned in various chapters. Note, also, that for outsiders, variables are organized in a different fashion than for insiders.

While religion as a variable was, to a great extent, dealt with in a complex way in Chapter 4, it became more salient as an identity marker in Ramaḍān's novel *Awrāq al-narjis* ("The leaves of Narcissus") (2001). Gender, a variable that was not discussed in public discourse about identity, emerged as prominent. In Ramadan's novel, the perceptions of outsiders placed the Egyptian identity in relation to religion, first and foremost—and to one particular religion, Islam—rather than language. The continuous struggle for a coherent identity also involves a struggle of inclusiveness and exclusiveness on different levels.

To recap, when discussing social variables that mark identity in novels, linguistic resources were employed. These resources include, first and foremost, use of pronouns, as well as use of presupposition, identification categories, assertive statements, rhetorical questions, deixis, negation, and demonstratives.

7.3 Theorizing indexes and identity in the Egyptian context

This work attempts to provide an alternative framework for understanding and studying diglossia, in which the concept of orders of indexicality is eminent. However, the concept is, to some extent, modified to account for the linguistic situation in Egypt as part of the diglossic Arab world. Indexes are classified as direct or indirect and as first, second, and third order indexes.

First order indexes reflect linguistic habits that have been established over time and explain Ferguson's classification of different functions of the H and L varieties or the standard and colloquial codes. There is, in fact, a semiotic link between specific situations and a specific code. This semiotic link is also the product of habits. SA is formal; ECA is informal. SA is associated with abstract, religious, legal, public, written discourse, while ECA is associated with concrete, daily life situations and oral discourse.

To recall, Collins (2011: 409) argues that first order indexes "presuppose" fixed, contextually dependent signs. Ferguson describes situations in which only SA is appropriate, such as sermons, lectures, political speeches, news broadcasts, and newspaper editorials. He also describes situations in which the colloquial is appropriate, such as conversation with family and friends, folk literature, and soap operas. However, when a situation occurs in which the speaker is supposed to use SA, but ultimately uses ECA, this can be because the speaker wants to claim the indexes of ECA in a particular incident.

However, this is not enough to explain cases of code-switching or code-choice in public discourse, nor is it enough to explain the highly eminent ideological aspects of discussions about language in Egypt and the Arab world at large.

Second order indexes refer to "Talk about talk" and what Collins (2011: 409) refers to as meta-pragmatic discourse, which is essential in linking language use to a form of social action (2011: 409). By understanding language ideologies and attitudes, linguists studying diglossia can have a glimpse into how indexes are layered and ordered in a diglossic community.

What I define as second order indexes are indexes that are the product of ideologies and attitudes, rather than habits. That is, these indexes do not necessarily refer to actual practices of individuals, but instead they refer both directly and indirectly to the manner in which individuals give or deny access to codes as resources that are ideologically loaded. As Bucholtz (2009: 158) posits: "ideologies about language circulate through both explicit metapragmatic commentary and implicit metapragmatic representation."

In my definition, I would also like to distinguish between two types of processes by which second order indexes are typified: an indirect process and a direct process. As Bucholtz (2009: 158) contends, the process of typification "occurs not only in everyday interaction but also within wider-reaching cultural vehicles such as the media." In order for us to understand the second order indexes of different codes including ECA and SA, we first need to examine prevalent language ideologies that situate different codes in a larger political and social framework.

The direct variable that explains the process of second order indexes is language ideology, and the indirect variable that explains this process is language attitude. Direct indexes tend to be written, rather than oral. Indirect indexes are manifested in different domains and genres of public discourse, such as movies and blogs. While language ideology reflects SA in a positive light, indirect indexes show the negative indexes of SA. On the other hand, ECA is talked about directly in both a positive and negative manner. The positive manner tends to be in oral public discourse, and the negative manner tends to be in written discourse. Indirectly, ECA also carries positive and negative indexes, but positive ones prevail.

I have attempted to analyze unconventional and new examples to find the connection between language form and its associations. Contexts that mention language explicitly reflect language ideologies; these, in turn, reflect the associations of codes. Linguistic associations play a double role: when language is used as a classification category, then the associations of linguistic codes have to be previously established in a specific community. When language is used as a resource to adopt a stance and code-switching is one of the strategies used by individuals during this stance-taking process, then again the associations of codes are of pivotal importance.

In Chapter 3, the associations of both SA and ECA, as well as the significance of English, have been discussed. We noted that SA has associations with the realm of the divine and with legitimacy, which are the result of the fact that SA is the language of the Qur'ān, as well as Islamic texts more generally. These associations are the result of linguistic habits: the fact that Muslims recite the Qur'ān frequently in their prayers and that in some domains individuals have to use SA, such as in laws, the Egyptian Constitution, Islamic jurisprudence, and the Christian Bible. However, Egyptians take these associations a step further by regarding SA as a sacred language, a powerful one. Ideologies may not necessarily be reflections of habits. For example, some intellectuals still regard ECA as a corrupt version of SA, although they use it in their daily lives. Other intellectuals regard SA as an endangered language that needs to be preserved and protected against the invasions of colloquials. The Arabs' and Egyptians' attitude towards SA have always related unity of language to unity of a nation. This may explain the different attempts to fix SA and preserve it. If SA were to be varied or if there was language variation more generally, then this may be perceived as a sign of disintegration on a political, social, as well as moral level. Therefore, the language academies' role is to preserve "Arabic." Intellectuals have been calling for a "pure," rather than a "corrupt," language. The search for a pure, unified, coherent form of SA is still ongoing.

In Chapter 6, we have seen how intellectuals can have opposing political views, but agree in terms of their linguistic ideologies. The articles by Shūshah and Surūr are a case in point. They both agree on the positive indexes of SA that denote legitimacy and sincerity. However, Shūshah was pro-revolution, and Surūr was pro-Mubarak regime.

Bearing in mind the content and context of a stretch of discourse, SA seems to endow an utterance with truth value. An utterance is sincere and morally sound if delivered in SA. However, this is sensitive to the content of what is said. That is, if a speaker uses SA in the domain of intimacy with his wife, he may be regarded as insincere. But if SA is used in the context of professing affiliation to a country or an identity associated with a country, then it carries different, more positive indexes.

Indexes are more complex than they seem at first. We have seen that SA also carries negative indexes. The depiction of Arabic teachers in Egyptian films is never completely positive, and their obsession with grammatical errors and the pure form of Arabic has been mocked and criticized in Egyptian comedies. Teachers of Arabic are depicted as inflexible, narrow-minded, and belonging to lower social classes. Becoming an Arabic teacher in Egypt is not a prestigious choice, and mastering SA does not guarantee a good job (Haeri 1996). These perceptions of the social prestige attributed to SA are related not just to a linguistic environment, but also to a social one. In fact, it is English that carries social prestige and the prospect of a good job. But when habits and ideologies collide, ideologies may prevail.

English provides the perfect example. While Egyptians rush to master English and teach it to their children, when someone is depicted as speaking English, her or his Egyptian identity is contested. In Chapter 3, there was an example of a student who code-switches between English and ECA in the film *Ramaḍān Mabrūk Abū al-ʿAlamayn Ḥammūdah* (2008); similarly, in Chapter 6, we discussed how Tāmir from Ghamrah accused the protestors in Tahrir Square of speaking in English.

ECA is also associated with habits and perceptions. Because of the dominance of the Egyptian media during the twentieth century, Arabs in different countries were exposed to ECA perhaps more than any other colloquial language. Due to the linguistic habits of the media, ECA became prevalent in Arab public discourse. This led Egyptians to perceive of ECA as almost a standard code that is also a symbol of their cultural hegemony. ECA was also associated with Egyptians' perceptions of their hegemony, due to their sheer numbers and control of media for a long time.

The complexity of indexes lies in the differences between first and second order indexes—habits, on the one hand, and ideologies and attitudes, on the other. While Egyptians perceive of their dialect in a positive light, some intellectuals still think that ECA is a corrupted version of SA. Context is, again, what distinguishes between the positive and negative indexes of ECA.

ECA also carries "authenticity." Being a "real" Egyptian means speaking in ECA. Being a real Egyptian is different from being sincere and truthful. A real Egyptian possesses certain character traits and perceptions, but does not necessarily tell the truth all of the time. This was clear in examples presented in Chapter 6, in which the poet al-Jukhkh had to use SA to prove that the protestors in Tahrir Square were true to their cause and to Egypt. In other cases, Egypt is predicted as speaking in ECA. The authentic Egypt addresses her children in ECA.

In addition, the nature of the discourse also yields different associations regarding both codes. Venues in which SA is heavily used—such as newspapers, books, and language academies—show a positive attitude towards SA and a negative one towards ECA. Commercial, oral discourse, such as films, songs, and television interviews, has a different, more nuanced, and less positive attitude towards SA. In fact, in these venues, ECA usually fares better.

In the Egyptian context, one has to differentiate between authenticity and sincerity, both of which terms are extremely close in meaning. Because of its religious associations, as discussed in Chapter 3, SA is depicted as "sincere." Sincere, here, is in the sense of truthfulness in some contexts and faithfulness in others. For example, if a president or king fails to speak in SA on formal occasions, this may imply that he is not a real, faithful Arab. In the example of al-Jabartī, as discussed in Chapter 2, al-Jabartī uses the French peoples' lack of proficiency in SA as a marker of their insincerity. Their grammatical mistakes in SA are taken to imply a negative attitude towards Egyptians. That is, SA is associated with sincerity and faithfulness in relation to a cause or a country. ECA is authentic, because it is associated with quintessential Egyptian variables. To elaborate, the indexes of SA and ECA need to be examined in relation to two different dimensions. That is, the questions that are asked should be: how does code-choice reflect the person's identity? And how does code-choice reflect on the person's discourse? When a speaker uses ECA, Egyptians may judge him or her to be a typical Egyptian, with Egyptian character traits. That is, the person's identity is assumed. When a speaker uses SA to make a statement as a marked code, then one should evaluate the statement as truthful in relation to the speaker's affiliations to a homeland. That is, the audience judges the speaker's sincerity in relation to what he proposes or states. This does not always work, of course. When Mubarak chose to address Egyptians in SA in his last three speeches, he was appealing to the indexes of SA—the sincere and truthful evaluation of his stance. However, in that particular case, the political variables were more salient than the linguistic ones; deeds were more important than words.

Sticking to one code is also associated with unity and the preservation of a coherent national identity. Similar to the psychologist in Chapter 3, in the novel *Awrāq al-narjis* ("The leaves of Narcissus") (2001) by Sumayyah Ramaḍān, Kīmī's disturbed psychological state is directly related to her knowledge of more than one code. She suffers from schizophrenia, which is related to this "linguistic chaos," as the psychologist calls it. Muhrah also makes her stance clear in *Qismat al-ghuramāʾ* ("The debtor's share") by Yūsuf al-Qaʿīd (2004) when describing Mustafa. She also does not believe that speaking two codes and switching between codes is a positive, enriching linguistic habit. In the examples above, the language ideology of some intellectuals was prevalent and relating one identity to one code was also salient. But again, ideology in this case does not conform to habits. In fact, all evaluations of the linguistic situation in the above examples were in SA. While this is the ideology of protagonists and perhaps some authors, authors use the diglossic situation to their utmost advantage. They use code-switching and code-choice between ECA, SA, and even foreign languages as a linguistic resource to maintain a higher level of indexes.

The complexity of attitudes and ideologies clearly emerges from the discussions in Chapters 2 and 3: it is shown that Egyptian public discourse references highly nuanced indexical systems. These are reflected in a rich linguistic landscape that is usually condensed into clear identity markers, such as ethnicity, locality, and language.

To give an example, during the beginning of the twentieth century, "Arabic" and "locality" were used as classification categories to demarcate Egyptians from non-Egyptians—in other words, to specify who is eligible to join the National Party (see Chapter 2). Language was used as a resource and referenced consistently by composers, poets, and singers in their efforts to challenge, question, and reshape the Egyptian identity.

Second order indexes help explain cases of code-switching and code-choice, according to the nature of the data. In Chapter 4, code-switching occurred in the set of data only in inter-dialectal communication between Arabs from different parts of the Arab world. In some songs, ECA was mentioned and or used to index an authentic, unique Egyptian identity, such as *samra:ʔ* ("Dark-skinned woman") (1996); in other cases, such as in "The Arab dream," it indexed a cultural dominance. Both ECA and Lebanese Arabic were employed by Amīnah and Hishām in their efforts to index the uniqueness of their respective national cultures, while accommodation was used to show solidarity.

The role of religion and code-choice was discussed further with examples taken from the film *Hammām in Amsterdam*. I have shown that ECA with its local varieties (and not SA) are used to index an Egyptian identity that transcends religious differences. In an indexical hierarchy, language, in addition to other backbone variables, will come first, before religion.

Turning now to the indexes of SA, we have seen that SA was used in the song *miṣr tataḥadaθ ʕan nafsi-ha:* ("Egypt speaks about itself") by Umm Kulthūm (1921) to index Egypt's powerful, legitimate stance, while ECA was used to index authenticity in the song *ʔana l-maṣri:* ("I am the Egyptian") by Sayyid Darwīsh (1921). However, when the Lebanese poet Jurj Qardāḥī in the poem and song *samra:ʔ* ("Dark-skinned woman") (sung by Majidah el Roumi in 1996) describes an Egyptian girl and even conjures up a conversation with her, he does so in SA. The reason may be that the Lebanese poet does not need to prove his Egyptian authenticity, nor is he obliged to accommodate to ECA. Indeed, it would seem that the poet used SA as a technique to contrast "her" quintessential Egyptian Arabic and the neutral SA used to describe her. The fact that she is such a phenomenon that her unique Egyptian identity is transmitted to all languages and all peoples makes SA the more appropriate language of transmission and translation.

An important finding in Chapter 4 was the fact that a significant portion of the songs that reference Egyptian identity are sung by non-Egyptians. I believe that this is related to the perception of the outsider: when Egyptian identity is described by a knowledgeable outsider, it carries more credibility and adds to the perception of objectivity. These outsiders do not write their own lyrics, of course, and, as a consequence, accommodate 100 per cent to Egyptian Arabic to index their admiration, solidarity, and respect of the cultural hegemony of Egypt.

On the other hand, there are a number of songs in other dialects (Saudi and Lebanese, respectively) that also praise Egyptians. Examples of this are *maṣr ʔumm id-dunya:* ("Egypt, mother of the world") by the Lebanese female singer Dīnā Hāyik (2010) and *ʔagdaʕ na:s* ("The best people") by the Emirati male singer Ḥusayn al-Jāsimī (2010). This code-choice has its advantages. While not necessarily expressing and approving of the cultural hegemony of Egypt, the singers provide a more objective depiction of Egyptians, because they are outsiders who clearly do not totally identify with Egyptians (as is expected), but who still display admiration and respect for them.

Third order indexicality is both creative and performative. As Silverstein (2003: 222) contends, it creates "sites of indexical innovation that spread through analogical space." This higher indexicality exists in "a complex, interlocking set of institutionally formed macro-sociolinguistic interests" (2003: 226). In Chapter 4, there was an example of a journalist, ʿAbbūd, who used an Alexandrian dialect in a written text in an opinion article published in the online newspaper *Youm7* on January 4, 2011. This is innovative, as well as unique, within the context of the written medium. That is, she was able to index that she is from Alexandria, as well as indexing the fact that being from Alexandria presupposes that she shares an identity with Christians and that she does not differentiate between people according to religion. It also entails that she is authentic, tough, and, first and foremost, a typical "Alexandrian." This local identity is then understood in the context of the church bombing that took place during 2011 in Alexandria and threatened the country with sectarian strife.

When the journalist uses the Alexandrian dialect in a written text, she is consciously imitating a "social type" (Silverstein 2003: 220). She is also depending on a shared ideological model with her audience. The forms that the journalist uses are also salient.

In Egyptian novels, some authors go beyond the use of first and second order indexes to creatively establish a higher third order index that, at times, challenges expectations. This third level index conveys the main ideas of the novel more effectively and less traditionally. To recall, Collins (2010: 410) contends that indexical signs are interpreted in situated encounters in which timing and exchange matter. That is, context and genre are essential for us to grasp the full meaning of indexes. When authors switch in a dialogue between SA and ECA in a context that, realistically speaking, would be in one code, they are, in fact, using third level indexes to perform and create stances, a general impression of characters, and, ultimately, identity.

In novels, the manipulation of code-switching as a stylistic device is at its zenith. The relationship between the protagonists and different individuals in their lives was depicted through the use of code-switching—an unrealistic depiction that places literature in a special category of discourse, a discourse in which the diglossic situation is manipulated to the utmost. For protagonists, identity is the product of perception, but also relationships between themselves and others. The manner in which these relationships are constructed and deconstructed directly reflects on their identity, both as Egyptians and individuals.

This relation between code-choice and identity is articulated through stances adopted by protagonists and indexes of different codes. Concepts such as language ideologies, attitudes, and linguistic habits are indirectly referred to and evoked.

That is, while linguistic diversity may be looked upon as a negative aspect, as was clear in Chapters 3 and 5, it is, in fact, a richness that is manipulated by authors. This diversity can be understood best if analyzed in relation to orders of indexicality and stance-taking as a process.

To reiterate, in order to leave an impact on their audience, authors have to appeal to the tacit norm framework referred to in Chapter 1. It was argued in Chapter 1 that identity is habitual, because individuals function in the social world within a tacit norms framework that is both linguistic and social in nature. This tacit norms framework helps codes acquire their indexes. Authors work within this framework not to reflect linguistic reality in their dialogues, but to reflect stances and identities by manipulating this framework.

However, protagonists are depicted by authors as also, paradoxically, still adhering to concepts such as linguistic unity, and regard language diversity as chaos. That is, their ideologies and practices collide. However, this collision is perhaps expected, given the public discourse that they have also been exposed to.

Indirect indexes can also reflect an identity. One theoretical aim of this work is to stretch the concept of indexicality, so that it is not just related to indexes associated with different forms of language, but indexes associated with different linguistic resources: social indexes, political ones, socio-pragmatic ones, and meta-pragmatic ones. To elaborate, there are indexes related to forms or codes of language and indexes related to language as a structural and discursive resource. For example, linguistic resources can also index positions and, thus, stances. The use of an informal pronoun can index familiarity, solidarity, and so on. Both types of indexes feed into identity construction. In public discourse, individuals use their access to language as a resource in two different ways: individuals in public discourse adopt positions or stances. They do so through their usage and access to linguistic resources, which are structural and discursive in nature. These resources carry indexes that relate linguistic resources to social variables, which, in turn, index identity. They also use access to codes as a classification category to define who belongs and who does not belong to the community of authentic Egyptians.

Note that, as was established in Chapters 2 and 3, access to linguistic resources and codes is related to language ideologies and attitudes and, more importantly, to language as a resource, access to which is negotiated and contested.

7.4 An alternative framework: access and resources

Identity construction is a continuous struggle—a struggle of inclusiveness and exclusiveness. Pronouns such as we, them, and I are salient in this struggle. Social variables are an essential part of this contestation. This fight has different facets. First, there is the perception of outsiders, of us and them, which are mutually exclusive—for example, "their religion," "our religion," "their language," "our language," "their history," "our history," "their ethnicity," "our ethnicity," and so on. Second, there is the struggle between insiders regarding which segment of history should be included, which segment of religion, which segment of ethnicity, and so on. For example, which historical era is quintessentially Egyptian? The ancient Egyptian era only or the Islamic one? Which segment of religion defines Egyptian identity? Islam only or Christianity as well? Or is it the inclusive aspects of both, as is clear in patriotic songs? This book does not provide definite answers, but challenges the reader to consider the answers and, in the process, articulates the ideological and perceptual aspects of identity.

Identity, as well as language, is a highly social phenomenon, sensitive to socio-political struggles. Throughout this book, issues of linguistic resources and access to them were discussed. Issues of inclusion and exclusion were also dominant. The main aim of constructing a distinct Egyptian identity is to decide who is included and who is excluded from this large community called "Egyptians." In most cases, religion cannot be a criterion of inclusion and exclusion in a country with a large Christian minority, but other variables can, including language, ethnicity, locality, character traits, and moral dispositions. There were numerous examples in this book of what I term an "exclusion–inclusion pattern of display" by individuals in public discourse. This is defined as a pattern in which individuals display their stance of belonging or not belonging to a community and also display their stance towards other individuals as belonging or not belonging to a community and nation. Individuals use social variables, including language, in this pattern of display. For example, Arabs who do not master ECA will not be able to have a career in the Egyptian cinema and soap opera industry. Egyptians who do not master SA may be perceived by some politicians as unable to read the constitution and thus may not be able to practice democracy. Egyptians who use ECA when they could have used SA in the public arena may be making negative assumptions of the abilities of their fellow Egyptians to participate in a democratic process or may want to appeal to a positive aspect of ECA. At times of turmoil, there is usually a dispute about the distribution of resources and language is part of this struggle. In order for the struggle to be meaningful for the majority of Egyptians, there has to be shared language indexes. To explain further, while political and social ideologies in Egypt are varied, there has to be a tacit norm of the indexes of different codes and social variables, in order for the discussion of language to be both meaningful and effective during a political struggle. In Chapter 6, we saw how both Surūr and Shūshah, who wrote articles related to SA in the same official Egyptian newspaper, *al-Ahrām*, agree on the importance and positive indexes of SA. However, their conceptions about who has access to SA were totally different and so were their political affiliations.

While Surūr claims that he, as a legal expert, has access to SA and that there is a crisis in the usage of SA, because most Egyptians do not have access to it, Shūshah posits that Egyptians were always exposed to SA, but were denied access to it by the National Party. That is, the National Party claimed that Egyptians do not master SA and therefore they do not have access to the associations of SA, including mainly political awareness. In this case, there is disagreement about the distribution of resources, but not about linguistic ideologies. There is also an attempt by Shūshah to renegotiate the set distribution of linguistic resources.

When the identity of protestors in Tahrir Square was contested, language was the focal point of the struggle. The exclusion and inclusion pattern of display was played with full force. Whoever does not speak Arabic cannot be Egyptian, although whoever speaks ECA could be a deceitful non-Egyptian who stole access to an Egyptian code. When the poet al-Jukhkh wanted to reclaim Egyptian identity for the protestors, he used SA with its legitimate indexes. That is, he demonstrated his access to SA.

At times of conflict, there is always a group of individuals who think that resources are not distributed equally. These resources include political resources, social resources, economic resources, and, at times, linguistic resources (see the example of the King of Morocco in Chapter 6). Revolutionaries usually challenge the way that resources are being distributed and demand to renegotiate this distribution more fairly.

While doing so, they also renegotiate access to codes as resources. This renegotiation is more symbolic in nature than a reflection of actual access to linguistic codes. The result of this negotiation is usually a challenge to identity that manifests itself through a challenge of language practices. Again, this challenge does not reflect language reality. However, throughout this struggle, there may still be consensus to some extent about the indexes of codes shared by all opponents.

In Chapter 6, the concept of "linguistic unrest" was introduced. Linguistic unrest refers to the way that different codes are manipulated during times of political turmoil. On an individual or national level, it can also refer to challenges to the indexes of codes. During times of political turmoil, there is also a conflict that manifests itself in the way that individuals classify each other and position themselves. They classify and position themselves by evaluating different linguistic codes and linguistic varieties. They also position themselves by using different resources, including code-switching and code-choice, between different codes and different varieties.

Note that although using linguistic resources to challenge, contest, or highlight an Egyptian identity is a linguistic reality, talking about language as a classification category is a linguistic projection of reality that is mainly ideological in nature.

Times of conflict are highly essential in linguistic struggles. There are cases in the book in which access and resources were either explicitly or implicitly negotiated. This is what is referred to as linguistic unrest. When the Lebanese singer Najwá Karam refused to use ECA as a resource for inclusion and fame in Egypt, she was frowned upon by some Egyptians. She shunned their tacit linguistic or ideological norm by refusing access to what some Egyptians perceive as an important resource. Her perceptions are different. She considers LCA an important resource. But in Egyptian public discourse, mastering ECA for a non-Egyptian means access to fame and admiration by Egyptians. The opposite is not true for Egyptian actors or singers who sing in another dialect, although these are highly uncommon. Interestingly, when Egyptians participate in Gulf soap operas, they use their own ECA and play "an Egyptian," as in the Kuwaiti soap opera Ablah Nūra (2008), featuring the Kuwaiti actress Hayāt al-Fahd, who plays the role of a headmistress in a Kuwaiti school. Teachers in this school come from different countries in the Arab world and speak their own dialect; for example, the Egyptian teacher speaks ECA, the Syrian teacher speaks in Levantine Arabic, and so on.

The ideology discussed in Chapter 3 that correlates unity of language to a coherent identity is salient in data found in this book. In public discourse, access to too many linguistic resources may reflect a disintegrated identity. In Chapter 3, the psychologist Aḥmad ʿUkāshah in his book *Thuqūb fī al-ḍamīr: naẓrah ʿala aḥwālinā* ("Holes in our conscience: a look at our condition") (2008) lamented the linguistic diversity of Egyptians, who seem to have lost their positive traits as a result. The character of Kīmī in the novel *Awrāq al-narjis* ("The leaves of Narcissus") by Sumayya Ramaḍān (2001) is made to say that she masters *too many* languages and as a result cannot achieve a coherent identity. In the novel *Qismat al-ghuramāʾ* ("The debtor's share") by Yūsuf al-Qaʿīd (2004), the same sentiment is echoed by Muhrah about her ex-husband, who switches between SA and ECA (see Chapter 5).

In fact, when the journalist ʿAbbūd in her online article (ʿAbbūd 2011) discusses terrorism and potential sectarian strife in Alexandria, she resorts to the exclusion pattern of display to keep out all non-Alexandrians who do not share the same perceptions, habits, and linguistic resources with the authentic Alexandrian. Having access to the salient Alexandrian features only is a way to overcome terrorism and sectarian violence. That is, lack of access to resources renders an individual more authentic. Access to resources may render an individual less authentic or more powerful, depending on the context.

In that case, having access to more available resources than others in the community also places the speaker at a disadvantage in relation to his or her identity. It implies that the speaker is different and does not share equal resources with the community. That is, access to more resources is not always looked upon ideologically in a positive light. Recall the example, mentioned in Chapter 3, of Jews in Egypt who authenticate their Egyptian identity by mentioning that they simply do not have access to any other language except Arabic, ECA. They even lack knowledge of Hebrew.

This ideology of positive, limited access to resources is not peculiar to Egypt. Hoffman (2006: 146) posits that in Morocco, it is, in fact, rural Berber women who remain monolinguals, mastering Berber languages only, not Arabic, and that they therefore remain a symbol of authenticity, carrying the burden of culture and tradition.

Display of access to resources is context dependent, as well as participant dependent. It depends on the framework of a public context, as well as the manner in which speakers position themselves. Similar to showing off education, a new car, or a new house, showing off knowledge of English in a context in which speakers do not have the same access to it implies a lack of identification with the community and a less positive stance towards members of this community.

The following two questions were also addressed: what linguistic resources do Egyptians and other Arabs share? Which linguistic resources are non-Egyptian Arabs expected to access?

In patriotic songs, it was clear that when Egyptians refer to themselves as part of the Arab world, language is referenced as the main resource shared by all. While ideologies of SA as a unifying factor may still prevail, access to linguistic resources is more nuanced. On more than one occasion in patriotic songs and films about Arab countries, ECA is used to portray both Egyptians and non-Egyptians. In fact, we have a film, *Jamīlah Būrayd* ("Djamila Bouhired") (1959), that is in ECA, but that supposedly takes place in Algeria in the 1950s concerning Algeria's struggle for independence. SA is not used even to refer to foreigners in this film.

For Egyptians in public discourse, access to ECA may imply access to the Arab world. But also by imposing ECA as the code of all Arabs in some cases, Egyptian public discourse attempts to redistribute resources, so that ECA is more dominant and powerful on both a social and political scale. Refusing to acknowledge the importance of ECA as a resource may then lead to disagreements and crises or linguistic unrest. This is true not just at a state level, but at a national level as well. Refusal to acknowledge the importance of access to ECA can be taken as an affront to the identity that Egyptians want to endow upon themselves.

In a country that has been more than once on the brink of sectarian strife, public discourse emphasizes the inclusion of both Christians and Muslims within the large Egyptian community. This inclusion relies on the fact that both groups are perceived as sharing access to the same linguistic resources, including geographic area and linguistic code.

In Egyptian novels that deal with the theme of identity, code-switching was used not to reflect reality, but as a stylistic device. Code-switching can also be explained in terms of access to resources. In *al-Ḥubb fī al-manfā* ("Love in exile") by Bahāʾ Ṭāhir (1995), the protagonist has access to both SA and ECA: he uses SA to converse with friends and acquaintances (not a depiction of linguistic realities), whereas he uses ECA only with his children. As a special resource, he does not make it available to all of the people around him, but rather only his children. There is shared knowledge of the indexes of this code between him and his children. The same is true for Jamāl al-Ghīṭānī's *Kitāb al-rinn* ("The book of names") (2008). The protagonist has access to both codes, but chooses to use ECA only to address the ancient Egyptian statue. Only the statue has access to this quintessentially Egyptian resource. Kīmī, the main character in *Awrāq al-narjis* ("The leaves of Narcissus") by Sumayya Ramaḍān (2001), uses ECA consistently only with her servant Āminah, who represents the typical Egyptian. On the other hand, the main female character, Fāṭimah, in *Qindīl Umm Hāshim* ("The saint's lamp") by Yaḥyá Ḥaqqī (1944) does not have access, except to ECA. Like Āminah in *The Leaves of Narcissus* and the protagonist's children in *Love in Exile*, she is not made to utilize SA as a resource, while there is emphasis on their access to ECA. The exclusion–inclusion pattern of display is manipulated to the utmost in literature. Time and again, one encounters the character of the "typical" Egyptian who only masters ECA or the distorted Egyptian with a conflicted identity and who either has access to a different code, such as SA, or to both codes, but does not utilize this access all the time. The protagonist, Ismāʿīl, in *The Saint's Lamp* may use different codes with his mother to reflect a disagreement about access and resources. However, what Ismāʿīl considers a resource may not be shared by his mother. This is an example of the dispute that involves shared resources and access to them.

When non-linguists, even psychologists, are disturbed about linguistic diversity within Egypt, such as the psychologist in Chapter 3, this disturbance is not about language, it is about the diversity in access to resources. For these intellectuals and media-makers, a coherent identity is associated with equal access to only "one" resource, rather than unequal access to many resources.

To reiterate, when the poet Īmān Bakrī wrote her satirical poem "Qualities of the future president," she asked for a president who is inclusive for all those who master ECA and not just those who master SA. She also wanted him to be an *"ibn balad,"* as Sawsan Messiri (1978: 1) calls the typical Egyptian—someone who speaks clearly so that "all" have access and all can understand. It is, again, the exclusion–inclusion game at play. This time, she demands an authentic, inclusive president, who does not exclude certain Egyptians because they do not understand or share his resources. Thus, it is not just language that she refers to. But, as usual, it is language that is mentioned—a symbol of entrenched conflicts and ideologies. This is, of course, true throughout the world, not just in Egypt or the Arab world.

This frame of analysis takes as its starting point the concept of access to resources and also straddles other sociolinguistic theories and frameworks. Discussion of language and order of indexicality is better explained when we are aware of the process of exclusion and inclusion at work in public discourse. In fact, throughout this section, examples discussed in this book were again mentioned in relation to this complimentary framework.

Stance and positioning is all about exclusion–inclusion. Access to codes is part of this process. In fact, it is the dynamo of this process.

In most of these cases, linguistic ideologies prevail over other social and political variables. In our study of the relationship between language and identity, we need to consider language a resource. As such, communities will struggle to gain access or deny access to resources.

Once we consider language in relation to the exclusion–inclusion pattern of display, we will also better understand political movements, social movements, revolutions, and sectarian struggles. We will, perhaps, reach a better understanding of how identity and language work together, not just in Egypt, but in many other countries as well.

On the July 24, 2012, an Egyptian satellite channel invited the writer Ṣunʿ Allāh Ibrāhīm to discuss the political situation after the first round of presidential elections (Fī al-Maydān 2012). The female interviewer asked him whether he thought there would be a second revolution. He replied that this was, indeed, possible. She then referred to the "Egyptian personality," as she called it, saying: "Don't you think this does not go with the Egyptian personality that yearns for stability?" His reply was short and simple: "Personalities change and Egyptians develop." In other words, "an Egyptian personality" is again referred to as one coherent identity encompassing all Egyptians—however, crucially, Ṣunʿ Allāh Ibrāhīm significantly points out that this coherent identity is subject to change. And yet, Egyptians are again lumped together, despite all their diversity, precisely as they were at the beginning of the twentieth century and throughout the twenty-first century. Whether identities of nations develop is essential, but it is not the main issue. However, people are still talked about, categorized, and stereotyped in public discourse—this fact will always remain.

This book has aimed at reaching a better understanding of the relation between language and identity in Egypt. It became clear throughout the process that language and identity cannot be fully understood through a study of linguistic practices alone. Language is at times abstracted and treated as a purely social variable, with no regard to its function. ECA is talked about as one coherent code; SA is talked about as pure and ideal, and so on. An ideology at work usually forms a complex pattern, especially with a sometimes contradictory attitude and different linguistic habits. What this book has demonstrated is how such a resource—language—can be employed in two different processes: a process of abstraction and a process of manifestation. Through a systematic analysis, the process of abstraction was exemplified and discussed in the form of talk about language in public discourse and, at times, conflict about access to language, again in an abstract, ideal form. The process of the manifestation of language refers to how language is used to connect an individual to a larger, coherent, and strong entity—an identity.

Notes

1. Mājdah al-Rūmī, a female, takes the stance of the male poet, who is infatuated with the Egyptian girl. This is not uncommon. Muḥammad ʿAbd al-Wahhāb, the classic Egyptian composer and singer, also took the stance of a woman in the SA song *ʔa-yaẓunnu* ("Does he think?"). This could happen in SA, but not in ECA.

APPENDIX: CHRONOLOGICAL LIST OF SONGS EXAMINED

1. *bila:d-i: bila:d-i:* ("My country, my country"), current national anthem; set to music by Sayyid Darwīsh (prior to 1923)
2. *ʔu:m ya: maṣri:* ("Rise up, Egyptian") by Sayyid Darwīsh (1919)
3. *ʔana l-maṣri:* ("I am the Egyptian") by Sayyid Darwīsh (1921)
4. *miṣr tataḥaddaθ ʕan nafsi-ha:* ("Egypt speaks about itself") by Umm Kulthūm (1921)
5. *ʔislimi: ya: maṣr ʔina-ni: il-fada: (la-ki ya: maṣr is-sala:ma)* ("Be safe, O Egypt, for I am the salvation [O Egypt, may you have peace]"), former national anthem (1921–36)
6. *maṣr al-lati: fi: xa:ṭir-i:* ("Egypt who is on my mind") by Umm Kulthūm (1952)
7. *ya: ʔaġla: ʔism fi: l-wugu:d* ("O, most beautiful name in existence") by Najāḥ Sallām (1956)
8. *al-waṭan il-akbar* ("My greater homeland") by ʿAbd al-Ḥalīm Ḥāfiẓ, Shādiyah, Sabāḥ, Wardah, Fāyizah Kāmil, and Najāt al-Ṣaghīrah (1960)
9. *bi-l-ʔaḥda:n* ("In the embrace") by ʿAbd al-Ḥalīm Ḥāfiẓ (1963)
10. *ṣu:ra* ("Sura") by Abd al-Ḥalīm Ḥāfiẓ (1966)
11. *ḥabibt-i: ya: maṣr* ("Egypt, my love") by Shādiyah (1967)
12. *ḥilwa: balad-i:* ("My beautiful country") by Wardah (1973)
13. *maṣr hiyya ʔumm-i:* ("Egypt is my mother") by ʿAfāf Rāḍī (1976)
14. *ḥilwa: ya: balad-i:* ("Beautiful, my country") by Dalīdah (1979)
15. *il-maṣriyyi:n ʔahumma* ("Here are the Egyptians") by Yasmīn al-Khayyām (1980)
16. *ṣo:t bila:d-i:* ("The voice of my country") by Various Artists (1980)
17. *si:na: ragaʕit ka:mila li:-na:* ("The Sinai has returned to us completely") by Shādiyah (1982)

18. *yaʕni: ʔe:h kilmit 'waṭan'* ("What does 'homeland' mean?") by Muḥammad Fu'ād (1983)
19. *balad-i:* ("My country") by Muḥammad Tharwat and Hānī Shākir (1984)
20. *maṣri:yit-na:* ("Our Egyptian") by Muḥammad Tarwat (approx. 1984)
21. *ʔidxilu:-ha: sa:limi:n* ("Enter her safely") by Shādiyah (1985)
22. *ʕaẓi:ma ya: maṣr* ("Egypt, you are great") by Wadīʿ al-Ṣāfī (approx. 1986)
23. *nifsi:* ("I wish") by Īmān al-Baḥr Darwīsh (1987)
24. *maṣr el-ḥabi:ba* ("Beloved Egypt") by Wardah and Muḥammad Yāsīn (approx. 1989)
25. *ʔumm id-dunya:* ("The mother of the world") by Laṭīfah (approx. 1995)
26. *samra:ʔ* ("Dark-skinned woman") by Mājidah al-Rūmī (1996)
27. *il-ḥilm il-ʕarabi:* ("The Arab dream") by Various Artists (1998)
28. *yibʔa ʔinta ʔaki:d il-maṣri:* ("Surely you are the Egyptian") by Laṭīfah (2001)
29. *yibʔa ʔinta ʔaki:d fi: maṣr* ("Surely you are in Egypt") by Various Artists (2001)
30. *ana: maṣri:* ("I am Egyptian") by Nānsī ʿAjram (2006)
31. *law kun-na: bi-niḥibb-ha:* ("If we loved her") by Midḥat Ṣāliḥ, Tāmir Ḥusnī, Bushrá, Shazá, Ḥusām Ḥabib, and Sūmah (2007)
32. *ma-ʃribt-iʃ min ni:l-ha:* ("Didn't you drink from her Nile?") by Shīrīn (2008)
33. *ma-tisʕali:-ʃ ya: maṣr* ("Don't ask, O Egypt") by Hishām ʿAbbās (2009)
34. *ʔagdaʕ na:s* ("The best people") by Ḥusayn al-Jāsimī (2010)
35. *balad-na: fi: l-ʔulu:b mitʃa:la* ("Our country is carried in our hearts") by Lu'ayy (2009)
36. *balad-i:* ("My country") by Muḥammad Fu'ād (2010)
37. *ʕasal ʔiswid* ("Black honey") by Rihām ʿAbd al-Ḥakīm (2010)
38. *alla:h alla:h* ("God, God") by Mashārī Rāshid al-ʿAffāsī (2010)
39. *fi:-ha: ḥa:ga ḥilwa* ("There's something beautiful about her") by Rihām ʿAbd al-Ḥakīm (2010)
40. *maṣr ʔumm id-dunya:* ("Egypt, mother of the world") by Dīnā Ḥāyik (2010)
41. *ya: ʔisra:ʔi:l* ("Oh, Israel") by Ḥamzah Namirah (2010)
42. *ʔumm id-dunya:* ("Mother of the world") by Muḥammad Ḥamāqī (2010)
43. *balad-na: (maṣri:ya w-ṭabaʕ-i: ʔa:si:)* ("Our country [I'm Egyptian and I'm harsh]") by Hishām al-Ḥājj and Amīnah (2010)
44. *b-aʃabbih ʕale:-k* ("I saw you before") by Muḥammed Fu'ād (2011)
45. *niḥlim* ("We dream") by a group of Tunisian and Egyptian artists (March 2011a)

46. *aḥla: ʃaba:b* ("The best youth") by a group of Tunisian and Egyptian artists (2011b)
47. *mazku:ra fi:-l-qurʔa:n* ("Mentioned in the Quran") by ʿĀyidah al-Ayyūbī (2011)
48. *irfaʕ ra:sak fo:ʔ inta maṣri:* ("Raise your head up, you're Egyptian") by Ḥamzah Namirah (2011b)
49. *ya: maṭar* ("Oh, rain") by Ḥamzah Namirah (2011a)
50. *qaṭar-i: ḥabi:b-i:* ("My beloved Qatar") by Cairo Opera, Bāsim Yūsuf (2013)

BIBLIOGRAPHY

ʿAbd al-Kāfī, Ismāʿīl. 1991. *al-Taʿlīm wa-baththʿal-hūwiyah al-qawmīyah fī Miṣr*. PhD thesis, Cairo University.

Abdel-Jawad, Hassan. 1986. "The emergence of an urban dialect in the Jordanian urban centres." *International Journal of the Sociology of Language* 61: 53–63.

Abdel-Malek, Zaki N. 1972. "The influence of diglossia on the novels of Yuusif al-Sibaai." *Journal of Arabic Literature* 3: 132–41.

Abdel Moneim, Amany. 2007. "Pickled tongue." *al-Ahrām Weekly*. Online. http://weekly.ahram.org.eg/2007/834/cu5.htm, accessed 4 September 2013.

Abu-Haidar, Farida. 1991. *Christian Arabic of Baghdad*. Wiesbaden: Harrassowitz.

Abu-Lughod, Lila. 1987. *Veiled Sentiments: Honor and Poetry in a Bedouin Society*. Cairo: American University in Cairo Press.

Abu-Lughod, Lila. 2002. "Egyptian melodrama—technology of the modern subject?" In *Media Worlds: Anthropology on New Terrain*, ed. by Faye D Ginsburg, Lila Abu-Lughod, and Brian Larkin, 115–33. Berkeley, CA: University of California Press.

Agar, Michael. 1985. *Speaking of Ethnography*. Beverly Hills, CA: Sage.

Ahmed, Rizwan. 2008. "Scripting a new identity: the battle for Devanagari in nineteenth century India." *Journal of Pragmatics* 40: 1163–83.

Ahmed, Rizwan. 2011. "Urdu in Devanagari: shifting orthographic practices and Muslim identity in Delhi." *Language in Society* 40: 259–84.

Aitchison, Jean. 2001. *Language Change: Progress or Decay?* Cambridge: Cambridge University Press.

Al-Anṣārī, Nāṣir and Maḥmūd Al-Anṣārī. 2002. *al-ʿUrūbah fī muqābil al-ʿawlamah: ʿAnāṣir li-naẓarīyah jadīdah*. Cairo: al-Hay'ah al-Miṣrīyah al-ʿĀmmah lil-Kitāb.

Al-Wer, Enam. 2002. "Jordanian and Palestinian dialects in contact: vowel raising in Amman." In *Language Change: The Interplay of Internal, External and*

Extra-Linguistic Factors, ed. by Mari C. Jones and Edith Esch, 63–80. Berlin: DeGruyter.
Al-Wer, Enam, Rudolf Erik de Jong, and Clive Holes. 2009. *Arabic Dialectology: In Honour of Clive Holes on the Occasion of his Sixtieth Birthday*. Leiden; Boston, MA: Brill.
Anderson, Kate T. 2008. "Justifying race talk: indexicality and the social construction of race and linguistic value." *Journal of Linguistic Anthropology* 18 (1): 108–29.
Androutsopoulos, Jannis. 2007. "Bilingualism in the mass media and on the internet." In *Bilingualism: A Social Approach*, ed. by Monica Heller, 207–30. Basingstoke: Palgrave Macmillan.
Androutsopoulos, Jannis. 2012a. "Introduction: language and society in cinematic discourse." *Multilingua* 31: 139–54.
Androutsopoulos, Jannis. 2012b. "Repertoires, characters and scenes: sociolinguistic difference in Turkish–German comedy." *Multilingua* 31: 301–26.
Armbrust, Walter. 1996. *Mass Culture and Modernism in Egypt*. Cambridge: Cambridge University Press.
Ashley, Evelyn. 1879. *The Life and Correspondence of Henry John Temple, Viscount Palmerston*. London: R. Bentley.
Auer, Peter. 2005. "Sprache, Grenze, Raum." *Zeitschrift Für Sprachwissenschaft* 23 (2): 149–79.
ʿAwaḍ, Luwīs. 1980. *Muqaddimah fī fiqh al-lughah al-ʿArabīyah*. Cairo: al-Hay'ah al-Miṣrīyah al-ʿĀmmah lil-Kitāb.
Badawī, al-Saʿīd Muḥammad. 1973. *Mustawayāt al-ʿArabīyah Al-muʿāṣirah Fī Miṣr: Baḥth fī ʿalāqat al-lughah Bi-al-ḥaḍārah*. Miṣr: Dār al-Maʿārif.
Bamberg, Michael G. W. and Molly Andrews. 2004. *Considering Counter Narratives: Narrating, Resisting, Making Sense*. Amsterdam: J. Benjamins.
Baring, Evelyn. [1908] 2000. *Modern Egypt*. London: Routledge.
Bassiouney, Reem. 2006. *Functions of Code-Switching in Egypt: Evidence from Monologues*. Leiden: Brill.
Bassiouney, Reem. 2007. "Leveling." In *Encyclopedia of Arabic Language and Linguistics*. Brill Online 2013. http://referenceworks.brillonline.com/entries/encyclopedia-of-arabic-language-and-linguistics/leveling-COM_vol3_0188, accessed 4 September 2013.
Bassiouney, Reem. 2009. *Arabic Sociolinguistics: Topics in Diglossia, Gender, Identity, and Politics*. Washington, DC: Georgetown University Press.
Basso, Keith H. 1996. "Wisdom sits in places: notes on a Western Apache landscape." In *Senses of Place*, ed. by Steven Feld and Keith H. Basso, 53–90. Santa Fe, NM: School of American Research Press.
Bastos, Liliana Cabral and Maria Oliveira. 2006. "Identity and personal/institutional relations: people and tragedy in a health insurance customer service." In *Discourse and Identity*, ed. by Anna De Fina, Deborah Schiffrin, and Michael Bamberg, 188–212. Cambridge: Cambridge University Press.

Bateson, Mary Catherine. 1967. *Arabic Language Handbook*. Washington, DC: Georgetown University Press.

Bauman, Richard. 2005. "Indirect indexicality, identity, performance." *Journal of Linguistic Anthropology* 15 (1): 145–50.

Bayat, Asef. 2010. *Life as Politics: How Ordinary People Change the Middle East*. Amsterdam: Amsterdam University Press.

Bean, Judith Mattsin and Barbara Johnstone. 2004. "Gender, identity, and 'strong language' in a professional woman's talk." In *Language and Woman's Place: Text and Commentaries*, ed. by Robin Tolmach Lakoff and Mary Bucholtz, 237–43. New York, NY: Oxford University Press.

Behnstedt, Peter and Manfred Woidich. 1985. *Die Ägyptisch-Arabischen Dialekte*. Wiesbaden: Reichert.

Beebe, Leslie M. and Howard Giles. 1984. "Speech-accommodation theories: a discussion in terms of second-language acquisition." *International Journal of the Sociology of Language* 46: 5–32.

Bell, Allan. 1984. "Language style as audience design." *Language in Society* 13 (2): 145–204.

Benrabah, Mohamed. 2007a. "Language-in-education planning in Algeria: historical development and current issues." *Language Policy* 6 (2): 225–52.

Benrabah, Mohamed. 2007b. "The language planning situation in Algeria." In *Language Planning and Policy in Africa*, ed. by Robert B. Kaplan and Richard B. Baldauf, 25–127. Clevendon: Multilingual Matters.

Bentahila, Abdelâli and Eirlys E. Davies. 2002. "Language mixing in Rai music: localisation or globalisation?" *Language & Communication* 22 (2): 187–207.

Benwell, Bethan and Elizabeth Stokoe. 2006. *Discourse and Identity*. Edinburgh: Edinburgh University Press.

Berque, Jacques. 1972. *Egypt: Imperialism and Revolution*. New York, NY: Praeger.

Blanc, Haim. 1953. *Studies in North Palestinian Arabic: Linguistic Inquiries among the Druzes of Western Galilee and Mt. Carmel*. Jerusalem: Israel Oriental Society.

Blanc, Haim. 1960. *Style Variations in Spoken Arabic: A Sample of Interdialectical Educated Conversation*. Cambridge, MA: Harvard University Press.

Blanc, Haim. 1974. "The Nekteb–Nektebu imperfect in a variety of Cairene Arabic." *Israel Oriental Studies* 4: 206–26.

Blommaert, Jan. 2003. "Commentary: a sociolinguistics of globalization." *Journal of Sociolinguistics* 7 (4): 607–23.

Blommaert, Jan. 2005. *Discourse: A Critical Introduction*. New York, NY: Cambridge University Press.

Blommaert, Jan. 2007. "Sociolinguistics and discourse analysis: orders of indexicality and polycentricity." *Journal of Multicultural Discourses* 2 (2): 115–30.

Blommaert, Jan. 2010. *The Sociolinguistics of Globalization*. Cambridge: Cambridge University Press.

Bolonyai, Agnes. 2005. "'Who was the best?': power, knowledge and rationality in bilingual girls' code choices." *Journal of Sociolinguistics* 9 (1): 3–27.

Bourdieu, Pierre. 2001. "Uniting to better dominate." *Items–Social Science Research Council* 2 (3–4): 1–6.

Boussofara-Omar, Naima. 2006. "Diglossia." In *Encyclopedia of Arabic Language and Linguistics*, ed. by Kees Versteegh, Mushira Eid, Alaa Elgibali, Manfred Woidich, and Andrzej Zaborski, I: 629–37. Leiden: Brill.

Brehm, Sharon S., Saul Kassin, and Steven Fein. 1999. "Social identity theory." In *Social Psychology*, ed. by Sharon S. Brehm, Saul M. Kassin, and Steven Fein, 145–50. Boston, MA: Houghton Mifflin.

Britto, Francis. 1986. *Diglossia: A Study of the Theory with Application to Tamil*. Washington, DC: Georgetown University Press.

Bucholtz, Mary. 2003. "Sociolinguistic nostalgia and the authentication of identity." *Journal of Sociolinguistics* 7 (3): 398–416.

Bucholtz, Mary. 2008. "All of the above: new coalitions in sociocultural linguistics." *Journal of Sociolinguistics* 12 (4): 401–31.

Bucholtz, Mary. 2009. "From stance to style: gender, interaction, and indexicality in Mexican immigrant youth slang." In *Stance: Sociolinguistic Perspectives*, ed. by Alexandra Jaffe, 146–70. Oxford: Oxford University Press.

Bucholtz, Mary and Kira Hall. 2010. "Locating identity in language." In *Language and Identities*, ed. by Carmen Llamas and Dominic Watt, 18–28. Edinburgh: Edinburgh University Press.

Burger, Rudolph. 1996. "Patriotismus und nation." In *Gesellschaft, Staat, Nation*, ed. by Rudolph Burger, Hans-Dieter Klein, and Wolfgang H. Schrader, 35–46. Wien: Verlag der österreichischen Akademie der Wissenschaften.

Cachia, Pierre J. E. 1967. "The use of the colloquial in modern Arabic literature." *Journal of the American Oriental Society* 87 (1): 12–22.

Cachia, Pierre J. E. 1992. "The prose stylists." In *Modern Arabic Literature [The Cambridge History of Arabic Literature]*, ed. by Muhammad M. Badawi, 404–16. Cambridge: Cambridge University Press.

Cachia, Pierre J. E. 1998. "Dialect in literature, modern." In *Encyclopedia of Arabic Literature*, ed. by Julie Scott Meisami and Paul Starkey, I: 190–1. London: Routledge.

Cameron, Deborah. 1997. "Demythologizing sociolinguistics." In *Sociolinguistics: A Reader*, ed. by Nikolas Coupland and Adam Jaworski, 55–67. New York, NY: St. Martin's Press.

Cameron, Deborah. 2005. "Language, gender, and sexuality: current issues and new directions." *Applied Linguistics* 26 (4): 482–502.

Cameron, Deborah and Don Kulick. 2005. "Identity crisis?" *Language & Communication* 25 (2): 107–25.

Casey, E. S. 1996. "How to get from space to place in a fairly short stretch of time: phenomenological prolegomena." In *Senses of Place*, ed. by Steven Feld and Keith H. Basso, 13–53. Santa Fe, NM: School of American Research Press.

Clackson, S. J. 2004. "Papyrology and the utilization of Coptic sources." In *Papyrology and the History of Early Islamic Egypt*, ed. by Petra Sijpesteijn and Lennart Sundelin, 21–44. Leiden: Brill.

Clark, Herbert H. 1997. "Dogmas of understanding." *Discourse Processes* 23 (3): 567–98.

Cohen, Anthony P. 1985. *The Symbolic Construction of Community*. Chichester: Tavistock Publications.

Coleman, Steve. 2004. "The nation, the state, and the neighbors: personation in Irish-language discourse." *Language & Communication* 24 (4): 381–411.

Collins, James. 2011. "Indexicalities of language contact in an era of globalization: engaging with John Gumperz's legacy." *Text & Talk* 31 (4): 407–28.

Connor, Walker. 1978. "A nation is a nation, is a state, is an ethnic group is a . . ." *Ethnic and Racial Studies* 1 (4): 377–400.

Cook, Rachel, Shelley Day Sclater, and Felicity Kaganas. 2003. *Surrogate Motherhood: International Perspectives*. Portland, OR: Hart Publishing.

Coupland, Nikolas. 2001. "Dialect stylization in radio talk." *Language in Society* 30 (3): 345–75.

Coupland, Nikolas. 2003. "Sociolinguistic authenticities." *Journal of Sociolinguistics* 7 (3): 417–31.

Coupland, Nikolas. 2007. *Style: Language Variation and Identity*. Cambridge: Cambridge University Press.

Coupland, Nikolas. 2010. "The authentic speaker and the speech community." In *Language and Identities*, ed. by Carmen Llamas and Dominic Watt, 99–112. Edinburgh: Edinburgh University Press.

Cromer, Evelyn Baring. 1908. *Modern Egypt*. London: The Macmillan Company.

Crystal, David. 1987. *The Cambridge Encyclopedia of Language*. Cambridge: Cambridge University Press.

Dajānī, Aḥmad Ṣidqī. 1973. *ʿAbd al-Nāṣir wa-al-thawrah al-ʿArabiyah*. Beirut: Dār al-Waḥdah.

Damari, Rebecca Rubin. 2010. "Intertextual stancetaking and the local negotiation of cultural identities by a binational couple." *Journal of Sociolinguistics* 14 (5): 609–29.

Danielson, Virginia. 1998. *"The Voice of Egypt": Umm Kulthum, Arabic Song, and Egyptian Society in the Twentieth Century*. Chicago, IL: University of Chicago Press.

Davies, Eirlys E. and Abdelali Bentahila. 2006. "Ethnicity and language." In *Encyclopedia of Arabic Language and Linguistics*, ed. by Kees Versteegh, Mushira Eid, Alaa Elgibali, Manfred Woidich, and Andrzej Zaborski, II: 58–65. Leiden: Brill.

Davies, Bronwyn and Rom Harré. 1990. "Positioning: the discursive production of selves." *Journal for the Theory of Social Behaviour* 20: 43–63.

Day Sclater, Shelley. 2003. "What is the subject?" *Narrative Inquiry* 13 (2): 317–30.

De Fina, Anna and Alexandra Georgakopoulou. 2012. *Analyzing Narrative: Discourse and Sociolinguistic Perspectives*. Cambridge; New York, NY: Cambridge University Press.

Deutsch, Harry. 1998. "Demonstratives and indexicals." In *Routledge Encyclopedia of Philosophy*, ed. by Edward Craig. London: Routledge. Online. http://www.rep.routledge.com/article/X010, accessed 4 September 2013.

Doss, Madiha. 2010. "Ḥāl id-Dunyā: an Arabic news bulletin in colloquial (ʿāmmiyya)." In *Arabic and the Media: Linguistic Analyses and Applications*, ed. by Reem Bassiouney, 123–40. Leiden: Brill.

Dragojevic, Marko, Howard Giles, and Bernadette Watson. 2013. "Language ideologies and language attitudes: a foundational framework." In *The Social Meanings of Language, Dialect and Accent: International Perspectives on Speech Styles*, ed. by Howard Giles and Bernadette M. Watson, 1–25. New York, NY: Peter Lang.

Du Bois, John W. 2007. "The stance triangle." In *Stancetaking in Discourse: Subjectivity, Evaluation, Interaction*, ed. by Robert Englebretson, 139–82. Amsterdam: John Benjamins.

Duffett, Mark. 2000. "Going down like a song: national identity, global commerce and the great Canadian party." *Popular Music* 19 (1): 1–11.

Eckert, Penelope. 2005. "Variation, convention, and social meaning." Conference paper presented at the annual meeting of the *Linguistic Society of America*, 7 January 2005, Oakland, California.

Eckert, Penelope. 2008. "Variation and the indexical field." *Journal of Sociolinguistics* 12 (4): 453–76.

Eckert, Penelope and Sally McConnell-Ginet. 2005. *Language and Gender*. Cambridge: Cambridge University Press.

Edwards, John. 2009. *Language and Identity: An Introduction*. Cambridge: Cambridge University Press.

Edwards, John R. 1985. *Language, Society and Identity*. Oxford: Blackwell.

Eickelman, Dale F. and Jon W. Anderson. 2003. "Redefining Muslim publics." In *New Media in the Muslim World: The Emerging Public Sphere*, ed. by Dale F. Eickelman and Jon W. Anderson, 1–18. Bloomington, IN: Indiana University Press.

Eid, Mushira. 2002a. *The World of Obituaries: Gender Across Cultures and Over Time*. Detroit, MI: Wayne State University Press.

Eid, Mushira. 2002b. "Language is a choice: variation in Egyptian women's written discourse." In *Language Contact and Language Conflict in Arabic. Variations on a Socio-Linguistic Theme*, ed. by Aleya Rouchdi, 203–31. London: Routledge Curzon.

Eisele, John. 1999. *Arabic Verbs in Time: Tense and Aspect in Cairene Arabic*. Wiesbaden: Harrassowitz.

Eisele, John. 2006. "Aspect." In *Encyclopedia of Arabic Language and Linguistics*.

Brill Online 2013. http://referenceworks.brillonline.com/entries/encyclopedia-of-arabic-language-and-linguistics/aspect-COM_0029, accessed 4 September 2013.

El-Hassan, Shahir A. 1978. "Variation in the demonstrative system in Educated Spoken Arabic." *Archivum Linguisticum* 9 (1): 32–57.

Englebretson, Robert, ed. 2007. *Stancetaking in Discourse: Subjectivity, Evaluation, Interaction*. Amsterdam: John Benjamins.

Fahmy, Ziad. 2011. *Ordinary Egyptians: Creating the Modern Nation through Popular Culture*. Stanford, CA: Stanford University Press.

Fairclough, Norman. 1989. *Language and Power*. London: Longman.

Fairclough, Norman. 2000. "Dialogue in the public sphere." In *Discourse and Social Life*, ed. by Srikant Sarangi and Malcom Coulthard, 170–84. Harlow: Pearson Education.

Fairclough, Norman and Ruth Wodak. 1997. "Critical discourse analysis." In *Discourse as Social Interaction*, ed. by Teun van Dijk, 258–84. London: Sage.

Fakhri, Ahmad. 2012. "Nominalization in Arabic discourse: a genre analysis perspective." In *Arabic Language and Linguistics*, ed. by Reem Bassiouney and Graham E. Katz, 145–56. Washington, DC: Georgetown University Press.

Faksh, Mahmud A. 1980. "The consequences of the introduction and spread of modern education: education and national integration in Egypt." *Middle Eastern Studies* 16 (2): 42–55.

Fasold, Ralph W. 1995. *The Sociolinguistics of Society*. Oxford: Blackwell.

Ferguson, Charles. 1959. "Diglossia." *Word* 15: 325–40. Reprinted in *Language and Social Context*, ed. by Pier Paolo Gligioli, 232–51. Harmondsworth: Penguin.

Ferguson, Charles. 1996. "Epilogue: diglossia revisited." In *Understanding Arabic: Essays in Contemporary Arabic Linguistics in Honor of El-Said Badawi*, ed. by Alaa Elgibali, 49–67. Cairo: American University in Cairo Press.

Fishman, Joshua A. 1967. "Bilingualism with and without diglossia; diglossia with and without bilingualism." *Journal of Social Issues* 23 (2): 29–38.

Fishman, Joshua A. 1977. "Language and ethnicity." In *Language, Ethnicity and Intergroup Relations*, ed. by Howard Giles, 15–57. New York, NY: Academic Press.

Fishman, Joshua A. 1996. "Summary and interpretation: post-imperial English 1940–1990." *Contributions to the Sociology of Language* 72: 623–41.

Fishman, Joshua A. 2002. "Endangered minority languages: prospects for sociolinguistic research." *International Journal on Multicultural Societies* 4 (2): 270–75.

Fought, Carmen. 2006. *Language and Ethnicity*. Cambridge; New York, NY: Cambridge University Press.

Frey, Hans-Peter and Karl Hausser. 1987. *Identität: Entwicklungen Psychologischer und Soziologischer Forschung*. Stuttgart: F. Enke.

Fridland, Valerie. 2003. "Network strength and the realization of the Southern vowel shift among African Americans in Memphis, Tennessee." *American Speech* 78 (1): 3–30.

Garner, Mark. 2007. "Techniques of analysis (III): discourse." In *The Routledge Companion to Sociolinguistics*, ed. by Carmen Llamas, Louise Mullany, and Peter Stockwell, 41–8. London: Routledge.

Garrett, Peter. 2010. *Attitudes to Language*. Cambridge: Cambridge University Press.

Gee, James Paul. 2010. *An Introduction to Discourse Analysis: Theory and Method*. London: Routledge.

Georgakopoulou, Alexandra. 2002. "Narrative and identity management: discourse and social identities in a tale of tomorrow." *Research on Language and Social Interaction* 35 (4): 427–51.

Georgakopoulou, Alexandra. 2006. "Small and large identities in narrative (inter) action." *Studies in International Sociolinguistics* 23: 83–102.

Glassé, Cyril, ed. 1989. *The Concise Encyclopedia of Islam*. San Francisco, CA: Harper & Row.

Goffman, Erving. 1974. *Frame Analysis: An Essay on the Organization of Experience*. Cambridge, MA: Harvard University Press.

Goffman, Erving. 1981. *Forms of Talk*. Philadelphia, PA: University of Pennsylvania Press.

Goffman, Erving. 1990. *The Presentation of Self in Everyday Life*. London: Penguin.

Goldschmidt, Arthur. 2008. *A Brief History of Egypt*. New York, NY: Facts on File.

Gordon, Joel S. 2002. *Revolutionary Melodrama: Popular Film and Civic Identity in Nasser's Egypt*. Chicago, IL: Middle East Documentation Center.

Guibernau, Montserrat. 2007. *The Identity of Nations*. Cambridge: Polity.

Gumperz, John. 1982. *Discourse Strategies*. Cambridge: Cambridge University Press.

Grice, H. Paul. 1975. "The logic of conversation." In *Syntax and Semantics, Vol. 3: Speech Acts*, ed. by Peter Cole and Jerry L. Morgan, 64–75. New York, NY: Academic Press.

Grosby, Steven. 2005. *Nationalism: A Very Short Introduction*. Oxford: Oxford University Press.

Haag, Michael. 2005. *The Timeline History of Egypt*. New York, NY: Barnes & Noble.

Haddington, Pentti. 2007. "Positioning and alignment as activities of stancetaking in news interviews." In *Stancetaking in Discourse: Subjectivity, Evaluation, Interaction*, ed. by Robert Englebretson, 283–317. Amsterdam: John Benjamins.

Haeri, Niloofar. 1994. "A linguistic innovation of women in Cairo." *Language Variation and Change* 6 (1): 87–112.

Haeri, Niloofar. 1996. *The Sociolinguistic Market of Cairo: Gender, Class, and Education*. London: Kegan Paul International.

Haeri, Niloofar. 1997. "The reproduction of symbolic capital: language, state, and class in Egypt." *Current Anthropology* 38 (5): 795–816.

Haeri, Niloofar. 2003. *Sacred Language, Ordinary People: Dilemmas of Culture and Politics in Egypt*. New York, NY: Palgrave Macmillan.

Hallman, Peter. 2009. "Quantifier." In *Encyclopedia of Arabic Language and Linguistics*, ed. by Kees Versteegh, Mushira Eid, Alaa Elgibali, Manfred Woidich, and Andrzej Zaborski, IV: 14–20. Leiden: Brill Academic Publishers.

Ḥamdān, Jamāl. 1981. *Shakhṣīyat miṣr: Dirāsah fī ʿabqarīyat al-makān, al-juzʾ al-thānī*. Cairo: ʿĀlam al-Kutub.

Hamilton, Heidi. 1996. "Intratextuality, intertextuality and the construction of identity as patient in Alzheimer's Disease." *Text* 16 (1): 61–90.

Ḥammūdah, Ibrāhīm. 2013. "Ḥilmī Ṭūlān: al-Ikhwān saraqū hūwiyat Miṣr . . . wa-al-Sīsī ḥaqqaqa ḥilm al-shaʿb." *Vetogate.com*, 31 July 2013. Online. http://www.vetogate.com/488770, accessed 20 August 2013.

Harré, Romano and Bronwyn Davies. 1989. *Gender and Education: Current Issues*. Abingdon: Carfax.

Harrison, Graham. 1998. "Political identities and social struggle in Africa." In *A Question of Identity*, ed. by Anne J. Kershen, 248–70. Aldershot: Ashgate.

Hawting, Gerald R. 2000. *The First Dynasty of Islam: The Umayyad Caliphate, AD 661–750*. London: Routledge.

Heller, Monica. 2007. *Bilingualism: A Social Approach*. Basingstoke: Palgrave Macmillan.

Heller, Monica. 2008. "Language and the nation-state: challenges to sociolinguistic theory and practice." *Journal of Sociolinguistics* 12 (4): 504–24.

Herman, David. 2010. "Multimodal storytelling and identity construction in graphic narratives." In *Telling Stories: Language, Narrative, and Social Life*, ed. by Deborah Schiffrin, Anna De Fina, and Anastasia Nylund, 195–208. Washington, DC: Georgetown University Press.

Hill, Jane H. and Bruce Mannheim. 1992. "Language and world view." *Annual Review of Anthropology* 21: 381–406.

Hoffman, Katherine E. 2006. "Berber language ideologies, maintenance, and contraction: gendered variation in the indigenous margins of Morocco." *Language & Communication* 26 (2): 144–67.

Holes, Clive. 1983a. "Bahraini dialects: sectarian dialects and the sedentary/nomadic split." *Zeitschrift für Arabische Linguistik* 10: 7–37.

Holes, Clive. 1983b. "Patterns of communal language variation in Bahrain." *Language in Society* 12 (4): 433–57.

Holes, Clive. 1984. "Bahraini dialects: sectarian differences exemplified through texts." *Zeitschrift für Arabische Linguistik* 13: 27–67.

Holes, Clive. 1986. "The social motivation for phonological convergence in three Arabic dialects." *International Journal of the Sociology of Language* 61: 33–51.

Holes, Clive. 1993. "The uses of variation: a study of the political speeches of Gamal Abd al-Nasir." *Perspectives on Arabic Linguistics* 5: 13–45.

Holes, Clive. 1999. "Socio-economic change and language change in the eastern Arab world." *Etudes Asiatiques* 53 (1): 45–74.

Holes, Clive. 2004. *Modern Arabic* (rev. edn). Washington, DC: Georgetown University Press.

Holes, Clive. 2011. "Language and identity in the Arabian Gulf." *Journal of Arabian Studies* 1 (2): 129–45.

Holmes, Janet. 1992. *An Introduction to Sociolinguistics*. London: Longman.

Holzinger, Wolfgang. 1993. *Identität als Sozialwissenschaftliches Konstrukt: Theoretische Grundlagen und Forschungsfragen*. Unpublished manuscript. Cited in Wodak, R., R. De Cillia, M. Reisigl, and K. Liebhart. 1999. *The Discursive Construction of National Identity*. Edinburgh: Edinburgh University Press.

Ibrahim, Muhammad H. 1986. "Standard and prestige language: a problem in Arabic sociolinguistics." *Anthropological Linguistics* 28 (1): 115–26.

Ibrahim, Zeinab. 2010. "Cases of written code-switching in Egyptian opposition newspapers." In *Arabic and the Media: Linguistic Analyses and Applications*, ed. by Reem Bassiouney, 23–46. Leiden: Brill.

Irvine, Judith T. 2009. "Stance in a colonial encounter: how Mr. Taylor lost his footing." In *Stance: Sociolinguistic Perspectives*, ed. by Alexandra Jaffe, 53–72. Oxford: Oxford University Press.

Ishaq, Emile Maher. 1991. "Coptic language, spoken." In *The Coptic Encyclopedia, Vol. 2*, ed. by Karen J. Torjesen and Gawdat Gabra: 604a–607a. Claremont, CA: Claremont Graduate University. Online. http://ccdl.libraries.claremont.edu/cdm/ref/collection/cce/id/520, accessed 6 June 2012.

Jaffe, Alexandra. 2007. "Codeswitching and stance: issues in interpretation." *Journal of Language, Identity & Education* 6 (1): 53–77.

Jaffe, Alexandra. 2009. "The sociolinguistics of stance." In *Stance: Sociolinguistic Perspectives*, ed. by Alexandra Jaffe, 3–28. Oxford: Oxford University Press.

Jaworski, Adam. 1987. "Attitudes to non-native Polish: a pilot study." *Multilingua* 6 (1): 77–83.

Jaworski, Adam. 2005. "Introduction: silence in institutional and intercultural contexts." *Multilingua* 24 (1–2): 1–6.

Jaworski, Adam and Dariusz Galasinski. 2000. "Vocative address forms and ideological legitimization in political debates." *Discourse Studies* 2 (1): 35–53.

Jibrīl, Muḥammad. 2009. *Miṣr fī qiṣaṣ kuttābihā al-muʿāṣirīn*. Cairo: al-Hay'ah al-Miṣrīyah al-ʿĀmmah lil-Kitāb.

Johnstone, Barbara. 1996. *The Linguistic Individual: Self-Expression in Language and Linguistics*. New York, NY: Oxford University Press.

Johnstone, Barbara. 2004. "Place, globalization, and linguistic variation." In *Critical Reflections on Sociolinguistic Variation*, ed. by Carmen Fought, 65–83. Oxford: Oxford University Press.

Johnstone, Barbara. 2007. "Linking identity and dialect through stancetaking." In *Stancetaking in Discourse: Subjectivity, Evaluation, Interaction*, ed. by Robert Englebretson, 49–68. Amsterdam: John Benjamins.

Johnstone, Barbara. 2009. "Stance, style and the linguistic individual." In *Stance: Sociolinguistic Perspectives*, ed. by Alexandra Jaffe, 29–53. Oxford: Oxford University Press.

Johnstone, Barbara. 2010. "Locating language in identity." In *Language and Identity*, ed. by Carmen Llamas and Dominic Watt, 29–36. Edinburgh: Edinburgh University Press.

Johnstone, Barbara and Daniel Baumgardt. 2004. "'Pittsburghese' online: vernacular norming in conversation." *American Speech* 79: 115–45.

Johnstone, Barbara and Scott F. Kiesling. 2008. "Indexicality and experience: exploring the meanings of /aw/-monophthongization in Pittsburgh." *Journal of Sociolinguistics* 12 (1): 5–33.

Johnstone, Barbara, Jennifer Andrus, and Andrew E. Danielson. 2006. "Mobility, indexicality, and the enregisterment of 'Pittsburghese'." *Journal of English Linguistics* 34 (2): 77–104.

Keisanen, Tiina. 2007. "Stancetaking as an interactional activity: challenging the prior speaker." In *Stancetaking in Discourse: Subjectivity, Evaluation, Interaction*, ed. by Robert Englebretson, 253–81. Amsterdam: John Benjamins.

Khalīfah, ʻAbd al-Karīm. 1977. "Majmaʻ al-lughah al-ʻArabīyah fī al-muʼtamar." *al-Lisān al-ʻArabī* 15 (3): 19–22.

Khan, Geoffrey. 1997. "The Arabic dialect of the Karaite Jews of Hît." *Zeitschrift für Arabische Linguistik* 34: 53–102.

Khiḍr, Muḥsin. 2006. *Min fajawāt al-ʻadālah fī al-taʻlīm*. Cairo: al-Dār al-Miṣrīyah al-Lubnānīyah.

Kiesling, Scott Fabius. 2009. "Style as stance." In *Stance: Sociolinguistic Perspectives*, ed. by Alexandra Jaffe, 171–94. Oxford: Oxford University Press.

Krämer, Gudrun. 1989. *The Jews in Modern Egypt, 1914–1952*. Seattle, WA: University of Washington Press.

Kristiansen, Tore and Nikolas Coupland, eds. 2011. *Standard Languages and Language Standards in a Changing Europe*. Oslo: Novus Press.

Krystyna, Warchał. 2010. "Moulding interpersonal relations through conditional clauses: consensus-building strategies in written academic discourse." *Journal of English for Academic Purposes* 9 (2): 140–50.

Lakoff, Robin. 2004. *Language and Woman's Place: Text and Commentaries* (rev. and expanded), ed. by Mary Bucholtz. New York, NY: Oxford University Press.

Lakoff, Robin. 2006. "Identity à la carte: you are what you eat." In *Discourse and Identity*, ed. by Anna De Fina, Deborah Schiffrin, and Michael Bamberg, 142–65. Cambridge: Cambridge University Press.

Lakoff, George, and Mark Johnson. 2008. *Metaphors We Live By*. Chicago, IL: University of Chicago Press.

Lempert, Michael. 2009. "On 'flip-flopping': branded stance-taking in US electoral politics." *Journal of Sociolinguistics* 13 (2): 223–48.

Le Page, Robert Brock, and Andrée Tabouret-Keller. 1985. *Acts of Identity: Creole-Based Approaches to Language and Ethnicity*. Cambridge: Cambridge University Press.

Levinson, Stephen C. 1983. *Pragmatics*. Cambridge: Cambridge University Press.

Levon, Erez. 2007. "Sexuality in context: variation and the sociolinguistic perception of identity." *Language in Society* 36 (4): 533–54.

Linell, Per. 2007. "Dialogicality in languages, minds and brains: is there a convergence between dialogism and neuro-biology?" *Language Sciences* 29 (5): 605–20.

Lister, Martin, Jon Dovey, Seth Giddings, Iain Grant, and Kieran Kelly. 2003. *New Media: A Critical Introduction*. London: Routledge.

Llamas, Carmen. 2007. "'A place between places': language and identities in a border town." *Language in Society* 36 (4): 579–604.

Llamas, Carmen and Dominic Watt, eds. 2010. *Language and Identities*. Edinburgh: Edinburgh University Press.

Lockman, Zachary. 2006. "Roger Owen. Lord Cromer: Victorian imperialist, Edwardian proconsul." *Harvard Middle Eastern and Islamic Review* 7: 215–18.

Luke, Allan, Carmen Luke, and Phil Graham. 2007. "Globalization, corporatism, and critical language education." *International Multilingual Research Journal* 1 (1): 1–13.

Maegaard, Marie, Frans Gregersen, Pia Quist, and J. Normann Jørgensen, eds. 2009. *Language Attitudes, Standardization and Language Change: Perspectives on Themes Raised by Tore Kristiansen on the Occasion of his 60th Birthday*. Oslo: Novus.

Mansfield, Peter. 2003. *A History of the Middle East* (2nd edn). NewYork, NY: Penguin.

Mazraani, Nathalie. 1997. *Aspects of Language Variation in Arabic Political Speech-Making*. Richmond: Curzon.

McConnell-Ginet, Sally. 2003. "'What's in a name?' Social labeling and gender practices." In *The Handbook of Language and Gender*, ed. by Janet Holmes and Miriam Meyerhoff, 69–97. Malden, MA: Blackwell.

McConnell-Ginet, Sally. 2004. "Positioning ideas and gendered subjects." In *Language and Women's Place: Text and Commentaries* (rev. and expanded), ed. by Mary Bucholtz, 136–42. Oxford: Oxford University Press.

McConnell-Ginet, Sally. 2011. *Gender, Sexuality, and Meaning: Linguistic Practice and Politics*. Oxford: Oxford University Press.

McFerren, Margaret. 1984. *Arabization in the Maghreb: Special Report*. Washington, DC: Center for Applied Linguistics.

Meiseles, Gustav. 1980. "Educated Spoken Arabic and the Arabic language continuum." *Archivum linguisticum* 11 (2): 117–48.

Mejdell, Gunvor. 1996. "Some sociolinguistic concepts of style and stylistic variation in spoken Arabic." In *Tradition and Modernity in Arabic Language and Literature*, ed. by Jack Smart, 316–26. Richmond: Curzon.

Mejdell, Gunvor. 1999. "Switching, mixing–code interaction in spoken Arabic." *Language Encounters across Time and Space: Studies in Language Contact*, ed. by Bernt Brendemoen, Elizabeth Lanza, and Else Ryen, 225–41. Oslo: Novus.

Mejdell, Gunvor. 2006. *Mixed Styles in Spoken Arabic in Egypt: Somewhere between Order and Chaos*. Leiden: Brill.

Messiri, Sawsan. 1978. *Ibn al-balad: A Concept of Egyptian Identity*. Leiden: Brill.

Miller, Catherine. 2003. "Linguistic policies and the issue of ethno-linguistic minorities in the Middle East." In *Islam in the Middle Eastern Studies: Muslims and Minorities*, ed. by Akira Usuki and Hiroshi Kato, 149–74. Osaka: Japan Center for Area Studies.

Miller, Catherine. 2004. "Variation and changes in Arabic urban vernaculars." In *Approaches to Arabic Dialects: A Collection of Articles Presented to Manfred Woidich on the Occasion of his Sixtieth Birthday*, ed. by Manfred Woidich, Martine Haak, and Kees Versteegh, 177–206. Leiden: Brill.

Miller, Catherine. 2007. "Arabic urban vernaculars." In *Arabic in the City: Issues in Dialect Contact and Language Variation*, ed. by Catherine Miller, Enam Al-Wer, Dominique Caubet, and Janet C. E. Watson, 1–31. London; New York, NY: Routledge.

Mills, Charles Wright. 1956. *The Power Elite*. Oxford: Oxford University Press.

Milroy, James and Lesley Milroy. 1999. *Authority in Language: Investigating Standard English*. London: Routledge.

Milroy, Lesley. 1987. *Language and Social Networks* (2nd edn). Oxford: Blackwell.

Milroy, Lesley and Matthew Gordon. 2003. *Sociolinguistics: Method and Interpretation*. Oxford: Blackwell.

Mitchell, Terence Frederick. 1980. "Dimensions of style in a grammar of Educated Spoken Arabic." *Archivum Linguisticum* 11: 89–106.

Mitchell, Terence Frederick. 1986. "What is Educated Spoken Arabic?" *International Journal of the Sociology of Language* 61: 7–32.

Mitchell, Timothy. 1991. *Colonising Egypt*. Berkeley, CA: University of California Press.

al-Muʿallim. 2012a. *al-Muʿallim fī al-lughah al-ʿarabīyah: al-ṣaff al-awwal al-ibtidāʾī, al-faṣl al-dirāsī al-awwal*. Cairo: al-Muʾassasah al-ʿArabīyah al-Ḥadīthah.

al-Muʿallim. 2012b. *al-Muʿallim fī al-lughah al-ʿarabīyah: al-ṣaff al-thālith al-iʿdādī, al-faṣl al-dirāsī al-awwal*. Cairo: al-Muʾassasah al-ʿArabīyah al-Ḥadīthah.

Muṣṭafá, Ḥusām. 2013. "Midḥat ʿAql: Lan nasmaḥ lil-Ikhwān bi-taghyīr hūwiyat

Miṣr." *Youm7.com*, 7 August 2013. Online. http://www1.youm7.com/News.asp?NewsID=1195254&SecID=319, accessed 20 August 2013.

Myers, Greg. 2010. "Stance-taking and public discussion in blogs." *Critical Discourse Studies* 7 (4): 263–75.

Myers-Scotton, Carol. 1986. "Diglossia and code switching." In *The Fergusonian Impact*, ed. by Joshua A. Fishman, Andrée Tabouret-Keller, Michael Clyne, Bh Krishnamurti, and Mohamed Abdulaziz, 403–15. Berlin: Mouton.

Myers-Scotton, Carol. 1993. *Social Motivations for Code Switching: Evidence from Africa*. Oxford: Oxford University Press.

Myers-Scotton, Carol. 1998. *Codes and Consequences: Choosing Linguistic Varieties*. Oxford: Oxford University Press.

Myers-Scotton, Carol. 2006. *Multiple Voices: An Introduction to Bilingualism*. Malden, MA: Wiley-Blackwell.

Nordquist, Richard. 2010. *Crossing Boundaries: Studies in English Language, Literature, and Culture in a Global Environment*. Frankfurt: Peter Lang.

Nydell, Margaret. 2006. *Understanding Arabs: A Guide for Modern Times* (4th edn). Yarmouth, ME: Intercultural Press.

Ochs, Elinor. 1992. "Indexing gender." In *Rethinking Context: Language as an Interactive Phenomenon*, ed. by Alessandro Duranti and Charles Goodwin, 335–58. Cambridge: Cambridge University Press.

Oliveira, Maria do Carmo Leite de and Liliana Cabral Bastos. 2002. "Immigration experience and situated construction of identities." *Veredas: Revista De Estudos Linguisticos* 6 (2): 31–48.

Omoniyi, Tope. 2006. "Hierarchy of identities." In *The Sociolinguistics of Identity*, ed. by Tope Omoniyi and Goodith White, 11–33. London: Continuum.

Oropeza-Escobar, Minerva. 2011. *Represented Discourse, Resonance and Stance in Joking Interaction in Mexican Spanish*. Amsterdam: John Benjamins.

Owen, Roger. 2004. *Lord Cromer: Victorian Imperialist, Edwardian Proconsul*. Oxford: Oxford University Press.

Pagliai, Valentina. 2003. "Lands I came to sing: negotiating identities and places in the Tuscan 'Contrasto'." In *Sociolinguistics: The Essential Readings*, ed. by Christina Bratt Paulston and G. Richard Tucker, 48–68. Malden, MA: Blackwell.

Palva, Heikki. 1982. "Patterns of koineization in modern colloquial Arabic." *Acta Orientalia* 43: 13–32.

Palva, Heikki. 2006. "Dialects: classification." In *Encyclopedia of Arabic Language and Linguistics*, ed. by Kees Versteegh, Mushira Eid, Alaa Elgibali, Manfred Woidich, and Andrzej Zaborski, I: 604–13. Leiden: Brill.

Pape, Helmut. 2008. "Searching for traces: how to connect the sciences and the humanities by a Peircean theory of indexicality." *Transactions of the Charles S. Peirce Society: A Quarterly Journal in American Philosophy* 44 (1): 1–25.

Paulston, Christina Bratt. 1994. *Linguistic Minorities in Multilingual Settings: Implications for Language Policies*. Amsterdam: John Benjamins.

Planchenault, Gaelle. 2012. "*Accented* French in films: performing and evaluating in-group stylizations." *Multilingua* 31: 253–75.

Reid, Donald Malcolm. 1998. "The 'Urabi revolution and the British conquest, 1879–1882." In *The Cambridge History of Egypt, Vol. 2*, ed. by Martin William Daly, 217–38. Cambridge: Cambridge University Press.

Ricento, Thomas. 2006. "Americanization, language ideologies and the construction of European identities." In *Language Ideologies, Policies, and Practices: Language and the Future of Europe*, ed. by Clare Mar-Molinero and Patrick Stevenson, 44–57. Basingstoke: Palgrave Macmillan.

Rosendal, Tove. 2009. "Linguistic markets in Rwanda: language use in advertisements and on signs." *Journal of Multilingual and Multicultural Development* 30 (1): 19–39.

Rosenbaum, Gabriel M. 2000. "Fushāmmiyya: alternating style in Egyptian prose." *Zeitschrift für Arabische Linguistik* 38: 68–87.

Russell, Michael E. 1994. *Cultural Reproduction in Egypt's Private University.* PhD thesis, University of Kentucky.

Ryding, Karin C. 2005. *A Reference Grammar of Modern Standard Arabic.* Cambridge: Cambridge University Press.

Sayyid-Marsot, Afaf. 1977. *Egypt's Liberal Experiment: 1922–1936.* Berkeley, CA: University of California Press.

Sayyid-Marsot, Afaf. 1985. *A Short History of Modern Egypt.* Cambridge: Cambridge University Press.

Sayyid-Marsot, Afaf. 2007. *A History of Egypt: From the Arab Conquest to the Present* (2nd edn). Cambridge: Cambridge University Press.

Sawaie, Muhammed. 1986. "Arabic language academies as language planners." In *Languages in the International Perspective: Proceedings of the 5th Delaware Symposium on Language Studies, October 1983, the University of Delaware*, ed. by Nancy Schweda-Nicholson, 56–65. Norwood, NJ: Ablex Publishing.

Sawaie, Muhammed. 2006. "Language academies." In *Encyclopedia of Arabic Language and Linguistics*, ed. by Kees Versteegh, Mushira Eid, Alaa Elgibali, Manfred Woidich, and Andrzej Zaborski, II: 634–42. Leiden: Brill.

Schieffelin, Bambi B., Kathryn Ann Woolard, and Paul V. Kroskrity, eds. 1998. *Language Ideologies: Practice and Theory.* New York, NY: Oxford University Press.

Schiffman, Harold F. 1998. *Linguistic Culture and Language Policy.* London: Routledge.

Schiffrin, Deborah, ed. 1984. *Meaning, Form, and Use in Context: Linguistic Applications.* Washington, DC: Georgetown University Press.

Scotton, Carol and William Ury. 1977. "Bilingual strategies: the social functions of code-switching." *International Journal of the Sociology of Language* 13: 5–20.

Secor, Anna. 2004. "'There is an Istanbul that belongs to me': citizenship, space, and identity in the city." *Annals of the Association of American Geographers* 94 (2): 352–68.

Shafik, Viola. 2007. *Arab Cinema: History and Cultural Identity*. Cairo: American University in Cairo Press.

Shraybom-Shivtiel, Shlomit. 1999. "Language and political change in modern Egypt." *International Journal of the Sociology of Language* 137 (1): 131–40.

Shohamy, Elana. 2006. *Language Policy: Hidden Agendas and New Approaches*. London: Routledge.

Silverstein, Michael. 1976. "Shifters, linguistic categories, and cultural description." In *Meaning in Anthropology*, ed. by Keith H. Basso and Henry A. Selby, 11–55. Albuquerque, NM: University of New Mexico Press.

Silverstein, Michael. 1985. "Language and the culture of gender: at the intersection of structure, usage, and ideology." In *Semiotic Mediation: Sociocultural and Psychological Perspectives*, ed. by Elizabeth Mertz and Richard J. Parmentier, 219–59. Orlando, FL: Academic Press.

Silverstein, Michael. 1996. "Indexical order and the dialectics of sociolinguistic life." In *Salsa III: Proceedings of the Third Annual Symposium about Language and Society*, ed. by C. B. Paulson and R. G. Tucker, 266–95. Austin, TX: University of Texas, Department of Linguistics.

Silverstein, Michael. 2003. "Indexical order and the dialectics of sociolinguistic life." *Language & Communication* 23 (3–4): 193–229.

Silverstein, Michael. 2005. "Axes of evals: token versus type interdiscursivity." *Journal of Linguistic Anthropology* 15: 6–22.

Somekh, Sasson. 1981. "The concept of 'third language' and its impact on modern Arabic poetry." *Journal of Arabic Literature* 12 (1): 74–86.

Somekh, Sasson. 1998. "Dialogue in literature, modern." In *Encyclopedia of Arabic Literature*, ed. by Julie Scott Meisami and Paul Starkey, I: 191–2. London: Routledge.

Soueif, Ahdaf. 2012. *Cairo: My City, My Revolution*. London: Bloomsbury Publishing.

Sperber, Dan and Deirdre Wilson. 1986. *Relevance: Communication and Cognition*. Oxford: Blackwell.

Spitulnik, Debra. 2009. "The social circulation of media discourse and the mediation of communities." In *Linguistic Anthropology: A Reader*, ed. by Alessandro Duranti, 93–113. Oxford: Blackwell.

Spolsky, Bernard. 2004. *Language Policy*. Cambridge: Cambridge University Press.

Spolsky, Bernard, Hanna Tushyeh, Muhammad Amara, and Kees de Bot. 2000. *Languages in Bethlehem: The Sociolinguistic Transformation of a Palestinian Town*. Amsterdam: Koninklijk Instituut Voor De Tropen.

Starkey, Paul. 1998. "Modern Egyptian culture in the Arab world." In *The Cambridge History of Egypt, Vol. 2*, ed. by Martin William Daly, 394–426. Cambridge: Cambridge University Press.

Suleiman, Yasir. 2003. *The Arabic Language and National Identity: A Study in Ideology*. Edinburgh: Edinburgh University Press.
Suleiman, Yasir. 2004. *A War of Words: Language and Conflict in the Middle East*. Cambridge: Cambridge University Press.
Suleiman, Yasir. 2008. "Egypt: from Egyptian to pan-Arab nationalism." In *Language and National Identity in Africa*, ed. by Andrew Simpson, 26–43. Oxford: Oxford University Press.
Suleiman, Yasir. 2011. *Arabic, Self and Identity: A Study in Conflict and Displacement*. Oxford: Oxford University Press.
Suleiman, Yasir. 2012. "Ideology and the standardization of Arabic." In *Arabic Language and Linguistics*, ed. by Reem Bassiouney, 201–14. Georgetown: Georgetown University Press.
Tajfel, Henri. 1978. *Differentiation between Social Groups*. London: Academic Press.
Tannen, Deborah. 2007. *Talking Voices: Repetition, Dialogue, and Imagery in Conversational Discourse*. Cambridge: Cambridge University Press.
Theodoropoulou, Irene. 2010. "From style to identity via indexicality." In *Proceedings of the Second Summer School of Sociolinguistics at the University of Edinburgh*, ed. by Miriam Meyerhoff, Chie Adachi, Agata Daleszynska, and Anna Strycharz. Edinburgh: University of Edinburgh. Online. http://www.lel.ed.ac.uk/sssocio/proceedings/Irene.pdf, accessed 14 September 2013.
Thompson, John B. 1995. *The Media and Modernity: A Social Theory of the Media*. Stanford, CA: Stanford University Press.
Tomiche, Nada. 1968. "La situation linguistique en Egypte." In *Le langage*, ed. by André Martinet, 1173–87. Paris: Encyclopédie de la Pléiade.
Trudgill, Peter. 1972. "Sex, covert prestige and linguistic change in the urban British English of Norwich." *Language in Society* 1 (2): 179–95.
Turner, John C. 1999. "Some current issues in research on social identity and self-categorization theories." In *Social Identity: Context, Commitment, Content*, ed. by Naomi Ellemers, Russell Spears, and Bertjan Doosje, 6–34. Malden, MA: Blackwell.
Turner, J. C. and R. Brown. 1978. "Social status, cognitive alternatives, and intergroup relations." In *Differentiation between Social Groups*, ed. by Henri Tjafel, 201–34. London: Academic Press.
Vallauri, Edoardo Lombardi. 2010. "Free conditionals in discourse: the forming of a construction." *Lingvisticae Investigationes* 33 (1): 50–85.
Van Dijk, Teun. 1998a. *Discourse as Structure and Process*. London: SAGE.
Van Dijk, Teun. 1998b. *Discourse as Social Interaction*. London: SAGE.
Van Dijk, Teun. 2008. *Discourse and Power*. Basingstoke: Palgrave Macmillan.
Van Leeuwen, Theo. 1996. "The representation of social actors." In *Texts and Practices: Readings in Critical Discourse Analysis*, ed. by Carmen Caldas-Coulthard and Malcom Coulthard, 32–70. London: Routledge.

Verbrugge, Sara and Hans Smessaert. 2010. "On the argumentative strength of indirect inferential conditionals." *Argumentation* 24 (3): 337–62.

Versteegh, Kees. 2001. *The Arabic Language*. Edinburgh: Edinburgh University Press.

Vuković, Milica. 2012. "Positioning in pre-prepared and spontaneous parliamentary discourse: choice of person in the parliament of Montenegro." *Discourse & Society* 23 (2): 184–202.

Walters, Keith. 1988. "Dialectology." In *Linguistics: The Cambridge Survey. Volume 4, Language: The Socio-Cultural Context*, ed. by Frederick J. Newmeyer, 119–39. Cambridge: Cambridge University Press.

Walters, Keith. 1996. "Diglossia, linguistic variation, and language change in Arabic." *Perspectives on Arabic Linguistics* 8: 157–97.

Walters, Keith. 2003. "Fergie's prescience: the changing nature of diglossia in Tunisia." *International Journal of the Sociology of Language* 163: 77–109.

Walters, Keith. 2006a. "Communal dialects." In *Encyclopedia of Arabic Language and Linguistics*, ed. by Kees Versteegh, Mushira Eid, Alaa Elgibali, Manfred Woidich, and Andrzej Zaborski, I: 442–8. Leiden: Brill.

Walters, Keith. 2006b. "Language attitudes." In *Encyclopedia of Arabic Language and Linguistics*, ed. by Kees Versteegh, Mushira Eid, Alaa Elgibali, Manfred Woidich, and Andrzej Zaborski, II: 650–64. Leiden: Brill.

White, Goodith. 2006. "Standard Irish English as a marker of Irish identity." In *The Sociolinguistics of Identity*, ed. by Tope Omoniyi and Goodith White, 217–32. London: Continuum.

Willmore, John Selden. 1905. *The Spoken Arabic of Egypt: Grammar, Exercises, Vocabularies*. London: D. Nutt.

Wilmsen, David and Manfred Woidich. 2012. "Egypt." In *Encyclopedia of Arabic Language and Linguistics*, ed. by Lutz Edzard and Rudolf de Jong. Brill Online 2013. http://referenceworks.brillonline.com/entries/encyclopedia-of-arabic-language-and-linguistics/egypt-COM_vol2_0001, accessed 6 May 2012.

Wodak, Ruth. 1999. *The Discursive Construction of National Identity*. Edinburgh: Edinburgh University Press.

Wodak, Ruth. 2007. "Pragmatics and critical discourse analysis: a cross-disciplinary inquiry." *Pragmatics & Cognition* 15 (1): 203–25.

Wodak, Ruth. 2008. "Introduction: discourse studies—important concepts and terms." In *Qualitative Discourse Analysis in the Social Sciences*, ed. by Ruth Wodak and Michał Krzyẓanowski, 1–29. Basingstoke: Palgrave Macmillan.

Woolard, Kathryn A. 2004. "Codeswitching." In *A Companion to Linguistic Anthropology*, ed. by Alessandro Duranti, 73–94. Oxford: Blackwell.

Wright, Sue. 2004. *Language Policy and Language Planning: From Nationalism to Globalisation*. Basingstoke: Palgrave Macmillan.

Yūsuf, Sa'd Allāh Suriyāl and Ṣubḥī Barsūm Wahbah, eds. 2012a. *al-Mu'allim fī al-dirāsāt al-ijtimā'īyah: al-Ṣaff al-awwal al-i'dādī, al-faṣl al-dirāsī al-awwal*. Cairo: al-Mu'assasah al-'Arabīyah al-Ḥadīthah.

Yūsuf, Saʿd Allāh Suriyāl and Ṣubḥī Barsūm Wahbah, eds. 2012b. *al-Muʿallim fī al-dirāsāt al-ijtimāʿīyah: al-Ṣaff al-thānī al-iʿdādī, al-faṣl al-dirāsī al-awwal.* Cairo: al-Muʾassasah al-ʿArabīyah al-Ḥadīthah.

Feature Films and Series

Bishārah, Khayrī (Dir.). [1983] ca. 1990. *Amrīkā shīkā bīkā* ("America: a fake dream"). Cairo: Raḥmah lil-Intāj wa-al-Tawzīʿ.

Bomba, Enrico and Andrew Marton (Dir.). [1961] ca. 2000. *Wā Islāmāh* ("Woe to Islam"). Cairo: Rūtānā.

Dhū al-Fiqār, Maḥmūd (Dir.). [1963] ca. 1980. *al-Aydī al-nāʿimah* ("The soft hands"). al-ʿAjūzah [Giza]: Bītsh Fīlm İjibt.

Ḥāmid, Saʿīd (Dir.). [1999] 2000. *Hammām fī Amstirdām* ("Hammām in Amsterdam"). Cairo: al-Subkī Vīdiyū Fīlm.

Ḥāmid, Saʿīd (Dir.). 2002. *Sāḥib ṣaḥbuh* ("A friend's friend"). Cairo: al-Judhūr Sintar.

Hunaydī, Muḥammad (Dir.). 2007. *ʿAndalīb al-Duqqī* ("Nightingale from Duqqī"). Cairo: Rotana Distribution.

Idrīs, ʿAlī (Dir.). 2010. *Thalāthah yashtaghalūna-hā* ("The three manipulate her"). Cairo: DVD Planet.

Iḥsān, Wāʾil (Dir.). [2008] 2009. *Ramaḍān Mabrūk Abū al-ʿAlamayn Ḥammūdah.* Cairo: Good News Group.

al-Imām, Ḥasan (Dir.). [1972] 2003. *Khallī bālak min Zūzū* ("Take care of Zūzū"). Cairo: Gamāl al-Laythī.

Imām, Rāmī (Dir.). 2008. *Ḥasan wa-Murquṣ* ("Hasan and Murqus"). al-Qāhirah: al-Subkī Vīdiyū Fīlm.

Jalāl, Aḥmad (Dir.). [2003] 2004. *ʿĀyiz ḥaqqī* ("I want my rights"). al-Qāhirah: al-Subkī.

Jalāl, Nādir (Dir.). 2011. *ʿĀbid Kirmān* ("Abid Kirman"). [Series]. Cairo: Kinj Tūt lil-Intāj al-Iʿlāmī.

al-Jindī, Aḥmad (Dir.). 2009. *Tīr inta* ("You fly"). al-Dukkī, al-Qāhirah: al-Subkī Fīdīyū Fīlm.

al-Jindī, Aḥmad (Dir.). 2010. *Lā tarājuʿ wa-lā istislām* ("No retreat, no surrender"). Cairo: Bird Eye Film Production.

al-Mājirī, Shawqī (Dir.). 2006. *Abnāʾ al-Rashīd* ("The sons of al-Rashid"). [Series]. ʿAmmān: al-Markaz al-ʿArabī lil-Khadamāt al-Samʿīyah wa-al-Baṣarīyah.

Marʿī, Khālid (Dir.). 2010. *ʿAsal aswad* ("Black honey"). Cairo: Brothers United for Cinema.

Rached, Tahani (Dir.). 1997. *Four Women of Egypt.* Montreal: National Film Board of Canada.

Shāhīn, Yūsuf (Dir.). [1959] 2000. *Jamīlah Būḥrayd* ("Djamila Bouhired"). Cairo: al-Subkī Fīdīyū Fīlm.

Shāhīn, Yūsuf (Dir.). [1963] 200–. *Nāṣir Ṣalāḥ al-Dīn* ("Saladin"). Seattle, WA: Arab Film Distribution.
al-Ṭawīl, 'Ārif (Dir.). 2008. *Ablah Nūrah* ("Sister Nurah"). [Series]. Kuwait: Bāsim 'Abd al-Amīr.
Wajdī, Anwar (Dir.). [1949] 2004. *Ghazal al-banāt* ("The flirtation of girls"). Cairo: al-Subkī Vīdiyū Fīlm.
Yāsīn, Muḥammad (Dir.). 2010. *al-Jamā'ah* ("The brotherhood"). Cairo: Kāmil Abū 'Alī.

TV Programs

ABC News. 2011. "Hosni Mubarak exclusive 2/3/2011." *ABC News*, 3 February 2011. Online. http://youtu.be/NtpamD9Jx3g, accessed 4 September 2013.
al-'Āshirah masā'an ("Ten o'clock"). 2010. "Interview with Iyād Naṣṣār." *Dream TV*, 22 September 2010. Online. http://youtu.be/nR9miLBuj8k, accessed 4 September 2013.
al-'Āshirah masā'an ("Ten o'clock"). 2011. "Interview with Buṭrus Ghālī." *Dream TV*, 8 February 2011. Online. http://youtu.be/Tml9rX9Uv78, accessed 4 September 2013.
Bakrī, Īmān. 2012. "Muwāṣafāt al-ra'īs al-qādim" ("Qualities of the future president"). *al-Ḥayāt TV Channel*. Online. http://youtu.be/YVdZ22imnYQ, accessed 4 September 2013.
Bi-tawqīt al-Qāhirah ("Cairo time"). 2013. "Interviews with Jews of Egypt." *Dream TV*, 3 January 2013. Online. http://youtu.be/WOrf35rPJbs, accessed 4 September 2013.
Fī al-Maydān ("In Tahrir Square"). "Interview with Ṣun' Allāh Ibrāhīm." *al-Taḥrīr TV*, 24 July 2012. Online. http://youtu.be/hGEBBPEqZQA, accessed 4 September 2013.
Kelani, Reem. 2012. "Songs for Tahrir." *BBC Video*, 18 January 2012. Online. http://www.bbc.co.uk/programmes/b019fxjf/, accessed 4 September 2013.
al-Ḥayāh al-yawm ("Life today"). 2011. "Talk show with 'Afāf Shu'ayb." *al-Hayāh TV*, 5 February 2011. Online. http://youtu.be/C3vhELQdk6k, accessed 4 September 2013.
'Īsá, Ibrāhīm. 2012. "Hunā al-Qāhirah" ("This is Cairo"). *Al-Qāhirah wa-al-Nās TV*, 2 June 2012. Online. http://youtu.be/RGv6sII7SZQ, accessed 4 September 2013.
Jukhkh, Hishām. 2010. "Juḥā" ("Goha"). *Drīm TV*. Online. http://youtu.be/z90qk08RKkM, accessed 4 September 2013.
Nile TV. 2011. "Tāmir bitā' ghamrah" ("Tāmir from Ghamrah"). *Nile TV*, 3 February 2011. Online. http://youtu.be/_bCuRfuj7vk, accessed 4 September 2013.
Nile TV. 2011. "Mashhad ra'sī min Mīdān al-Taḥrīr" ("A bird's eye view from

Tahrir Square"). *Abū Ẓabī TV Channel 1*. Online. http://youtu.be/Jcu0-MMpSI8, accessed 4 September 2013.

Literary works

al-Ghīṭānī, Jamāl. 1990. *Kitāb al-tajallīyāt: al-Asfār al-thalāthah*. Cairo: Dār al-Shurūq.

al-Ghīṭānī, Jamāl. 1996–2010. *Dafātir al-tadwīn*. Cairo: Markaz al-Ḥaḍāra al-ʿArabīya.

al-Ghīṭānī, Jamāl. 2008. *Kitāb al-rinn* ("The book of rinn"). Cairo: Dār al-Shurūq.

al-Ḥakīm, Tawfīq. 1934. *Shahrazād* ("Sheherazade"). Cairo: Maṭbaʿat Dār al-Kutub al-Miṣrīyah.

al-Ḥakīm, Tawfīq. 1938. *ʿUṣfūr min al-sharq* ("A bird from the East"). Cairo: Maktabat al-Ādāb.

Ḥaqqī, Yaḥyá. [1944] 1997. *Qindīl Umm Hāshim* ("The saint's lamp"). Cairo: al-Hayʾah al-Miṣrīyah al-ʿĀmmah lil-Kitāb.

Ḥaqqī, Yaḥyá. 1973. *The Saint's Lamp and Other Stories*. Leiden: Brill.

Ḥaqqī, Yaḥyá. 1986. *ʿItr al-aḥbāb*. Cairo: al-Hayʾah al-Miṣrīyah al-ʿĀmmah lil-Kitāb.

Ḥaqqī, Yaḥyá. 1989. *Ṣafaḥāt min tārīkh Miṣr*. Cairo: al-Hayʾah al-Miṣrīyah al-ʿĀmmah lil-Kitāb.

Ḥusayn, Ṭāhā. 1929. *al-Ayyām* ("The days"). Cairo: Maṭbaʿat Amīn ʿAbd al-Raḥmān.

Ḥusayn, Ṭāhā. 1938. *Mustaqbal al-thaqāfah fī Miṣr* ("The future of culture in Egypt"). Cairo: Maṭbaʿat al-Maʿārif.

Ibrāhīm, Muḥammad Ḥāfiz. 1980. *Dīwān Ḥāfiẓ Ibrāhīm* ("Collected poems of Hafiz Ibrahim") (2 vols), ed. by Aḥmad Amīn, Aḥmad Zayn, and Ibrāhīm Ibyārī. Cairo: al-Hayʾah al-Miṣrīyah al-ʿĀmmah lil-Kitāb.

Idrīs, Yūsuf. 1958. *al-Laḥẓah al-ḥarijah* ("The critical moment"). Cairo: al-Sharikah al-ʿArabīyah lil-Ṭibāʿah wa-al-Nashr.

Idrīs, Yūsuf. 1956. *Jumhūrīyat Faraḥāt* ("Farahat's republic"). Cairo: Dār Rūz al-Yūsuf.

Maḥfūẓ, Najīb. 2006. *Rasa'iluhu: Bayna falsafat al-wahdah wa-dirama al-shakhsiyah* ("Letters: between philosophy of unity and drama of the persona"). Cairo: al-Dār al-Miṣrīyah al-Lubnānīyah.

al-Qaʿīd, Yūsuf. 1994. *Laban al-ʿuṣfūr* ("Bird's milk"). Cairo: Dār al-Hilāl.

al-Qaʿīd, Yūsuf. 2004. *Qismat al-ghuramāʾ* ("The debtor's share"). London: Dār al-Sāqī.

Ramaḍān, Sumayyah. 2001. *Awrāq al-narjis* ("The leaves of Narcissus"). Cairo: Dār Sharqīyāt.

Ramaḍān, Sumayyah. 2002. *The Leaves of Narcissus*, trans. Marilyn Booth. Cairo: American University in Cairo Press.

Shalabī, Khayrī. 1986. *al-Watad* ("The tent peg"). Cairo: Dār al-Fikr.

al-Sharqāwī, ʻAbd al-Raḥmān. 1953. *al-Arḍ* ("The land"). Cairo: Dār al-Nashr al-Miṣrīyah.

Shawqī, Aḥmad. 1995. *Dīwān Aḥmad Shawqī*. Beirut: Dār al-Jīl.

Ṭāhir, Bahā'. 1995. *al-Ḥubb fī Al-manfā* ("Love in exile"). Cairo: Dār al-Hilāl.

Ṭāhir, Bahā'. 2001. *Love in Exile*, trans. by Farouk Abdel Wahab. Cairo: American University in Cairo Press.

al-Tūnisī, Bayram. 1987. *Dīwān Bayram al-Tūnisī* ("Collected poems of Bayram al-Tunisi"). Cairo: Dār Miṣr.

ʻUkāshah, Aḥmad. 2008. *Thuqūb fī al-ḍamīr: Naẓrah ʻalá aḥwālinā* ("Holes in our conscience: a look at our condition"). Cairo: Dār al-Shurūq.

al-Zayyāt, Laṭīfah. 1960. *al-Bāb al-maftūh* ("The open door"). Cairo: Maktabat al-Anjlū al-Miṣrīyah.

al-Zayyāt, Laṭīfah. 2000. *The Open Door*, trans. by Marilyn Booth. Cairo: American University in Cairo Press.

Music

ʻAbd al-Ḥakīm, Rihām. 2010a. "ʕasal ʔiswid" ("Black honey"). Online. http://youtu.be/hz3qPkZqGB0, accessed 4 September 2013.

ʻAbd al-Ḥakīm, Rihām. 2010b. "fi:-ha: ḥa:ga ḥilwa" ("There's something beautiful about her"). Online. http://youtu.be/yH-l0z23P3s, accessed 4 September 2013.

ʻAbd al-Wahhāb, Muḥammad. 1960. "ʔa-yaẓunnu" ("Does he think?"). Online. http://youtu.be/9KwajhwQn6A, accessed 4 September 2013.

al-ʻAffāsī, Mashārī Rāshid. 2010. "alla:h alla:h" ("God, God"). Online. http://youtu.be/IO6bp63I5kQ, accessed 4 September 2013.

ʻAjram, Nānsī. 2006. "ana: maṣri:" ("I am Egyptian"). Online. http://youtu.be/Jk-saBfQ2q0, accessed 4 September 2013.

al-Ayyūbī, ʻĀyidah. 2011. "mazku:ra fi:-l-qurʔa:n" ("Mentioned in the Qur'ān"). Online. http://youtu.be/rrvMMVaHJX8, accessed 4 September 2013.

Darwīsh, Īmān al-Baḥr. 1987. "nifsi:" ("I wish"). Online. http://youtu.be/EJ847olwWXU, accessed 4 September 2013.

Darwīsh, Sayyid. 1919. "ʔu:m ya: masri:" ("Rise up, Egyptian"). Online. https://www.youtube.com/watch?v=QIb_PvQ_kcE, accessed 4 September 2013.

Darwīsh, Sayyid. 1921. "ʔana l-maṣri:" ("I am the Egyptian"). Online. https://www.youtube.com/watch?v=QIb_PvQ_kcE, accessed 4 September 2013.

Fu'ād, Muḥammad. 1983. "yaʕni: ʔe:h kilmit 'waṭan'" ("What does 'homeland' mean?"). Online. http://youtu.be/YxlHBfHJhBU, accessed 4 September 2013.

Fu'ād, Muḥammad. 2010. "balad-i:" ("My country"). Online. http://youtu.be/IXHmuu4M3tg, accessed 4 September 2013.

Fu'ād, Muḥammad. 2011. "b-aʃabbih ʕale:-k" ("I saw you before"). In *Aḥlā again Fu'ād*. Cairo: Arabian Legends. Online. http://youtu.be/7ybNqUEZ44Q, accessed 4 September 2013.

al-Ḥājj, Hishām and Amīnah. 2010. "balad-na: (maṣri:ya w-ṭabaʕ-i: ʔa:si:)" ("Our country [I'm Egyptian and I'm harsh]"). Online. http://youtu.be/24VljXbywow, accessed 4 September 2013.

Ḥāyik, Dīnā. 2010. "maṣr ʔumm id-dunya:" ("Egypt, mother of the world"). Online. http://youtu.be/BlnsQrie6Eg, accessed 4 September 2013.

al-Jāsimī, Ḥusayn. 2010. "ʔagdaʕ na:s" ("The best people"). Online. http://youtu.be/Ek6XF7JG5F0, accessed 4 September 2013.

al-Khayyām, Yasmīn. 1980. "il-maṣriyyi:n ʔahumma" ("Here are the Egyptians"). Online. https://www.youtube.com/watch?v=B02ugbVSEhM, accessed 4 September 2013.

Kulthūm, Umm. 1921. "miṣr tataḥaddaθ ʕan nafsi-ha:" ("Egypt speaks about itself"). Online. http://youtu.be/itTFqKX8uBk, accessed 4 September 2013.

Laṭīfah. 1995. "ʔumm id-dunya:" ("The mother of the world"). Online. http://youtu.be/wBtEjqr5tX0, accessed 4 September 2013.

Laṭīfah. 2001. "yibʔa ʔinta ʔaki:d il-maṣri:" ("Surely you are the Egyptian"). Online. http://youtu.be/J1Fj_ordMds, accessed 4 September 2013.

Namirah, Ḥamzah. 2010. "ya: ʔisra:ʔi:l" ("Oh, Israel"). Online. http://youtu.be/QRMO5mYxFkA, accessed 4 September 2013.

Namirah, Ḥamzah. 2011a. "ya: maṭar" ("Oh, rain"). Online. http://youtu.be/IWxLDPX5DOM, accessed 4 September 2013.

Namirah, Ḥamzah. 2011b. "irfaʕ ra:sak fo:ʔ inta maṣri:" ("Raise your head up, you're Egyptian"). Online. http://youtu.be/EJvc96x1lWA, accessed 4 September 2013.

Rāḍī, ʿAfāf. 1976. "maṣr hiyya ʔumm-i:" ("Egypt is my mother"). Online. http://youtu.be/Sni2xldIyT0, accessed 4 September 2013.

al-Rūmī, Mājidah. 1996. "samra:ʔ" ("Dark-skinned woman"). Online. http://youtu.be/dtepzgazQE8, accessed 4 September 2013.

al-Ṣāfī, Wadīʿ. 1986. "ʕaẓi:ma ya: maṣr" ("Egypt, you are great"). Online. http://youtu.be/xJQYi7lrPS8, accessed 4 September 2013.

al-Ṣaghīrah, Najāt, ʿAbd al-Ḥalīm Ḥāfiz, Shādiyah, Sabāḥ, Wardah, and Fāyizah Kāmil. 1960. "al-waṭan il-akbar" ("My greater homeland"). Online. http://youtu.be/_ERFXIntNhQ, accessed 4 September 2013.

Shādiyah. 1967. "ḥabibt-i: ya: maṣr" ("Egypt, my love"). Online. http://youtu.be/8BvzxVVJhiE, accessed 4 September 2013.

Shīrīn. 2008. "ma-ʃribt-iʃ min ni:l-ha:" ("Didn't you drink from her Nile?"). Online. http://youtu.be/Ctfo7PtGYb8, accessed 4 September 2013.

Various Artists. 1980. "ṣo:t bila:d-i" ("The voice of my country"). Online. http://youtu.be/yS4-MtrpCyM, accessed 4 September 2013.

Various Artists. 1998. "il-ḥilm il-ʕarabi:" ("The Arab dream"). Online. http://youtu.be/PVgo9eCInSM, accessed 4 September 2013.

Various Artists. 2001. "yibʔa ʔinta ʔaki:d fi: maṣr" ("Surely, you are in Egypt"). Online. http://youtu.be/3tzMekew0I0, accessed 4 September 2013.

Various Artists (by a group of Tunisian and Egyptian artists). 2011a. *niḥlim*

("We dream"). Online. http://youtu.be/bl1w-74hvL8, accessed 4 September 2013.

Various Artists (by a group of Tunisian and Egyptian artists). 2011b. *aḥla: ʃaba:b* ("The best youth"). Online. http://youtu.be/b7YgEIdyDuk, accessed 4 September 2013.

Yūsuf, Bāsim. 2013. "qaṭar-i: ḥabi:b-i:" ("My beloved Qatar"). Online. http://youtu.be/bpDQNoshDK0, accessed 4 September 2013.

Articles and blog posts

ʿAbbūd, Ghādah. 2011. "Anā iskandirānīyah ḍidd al-irhāb." *Youm7*, 4 January 2011. Online. https://www.youm7.com/News.asp?NewsID= 330103, accessed 4 September 2013.

ʿAbd al-Salām, Karīm. 2008. "al-Shāʿir Yaḥyā Jābir: Uḥibbu al-jamāhīr athnāʾa nawmihim." *Youm7*, 31 July 2008. Online. http://www.youm7.com/NewsPrint.asp?NewsID=33898, accessed 4 September 2013.

Agha, Hussein and Robert Malley. 2011. "The Arab world is dead, but the Egyptians may revive it." *The Guardian*, 15 February 2011. Online. http://www.guardian.co.uk/commentisfree/2011/feb/15/arab-world-egypt-revolution, accessed 4 September 2013.

ʿAlī, Dāliyā. 2010. "Anā al-Miṣrī: Firʿawnī, ʿArabī, Hiksūsī anā Miṣrīyah wa-bi-jadārah." *al-Ḥiwār al-Mutamaddin*. Online. http://www.ahewar.org/debat/show.art.asp?aid=224348, accessed 4 September 2013.

Amin, Jalal. 2011. "Ahfād aḥfād Khūfū." *Shorouknews.com*, 23 December 2011. Online. http://www.shorouknews.com/columns/view.aspx?id= 732c8921-12ac-4c29-90ef-84b23c860159, accessed 4 September 2013.

Anazahra. 2011a. "Najwā Karam takshif asrār ʿadam ghināʾihā bi-al-lahjah al-Miṣrīyah." *Anazahra.com*, 16 October 2011. Online. http://www.anazahra.com/8934, accessed 4 September 2013.

Anazahrah. 2011b. "Najwā Karam bi-lā tārīkh min dūn al-lahjah al-Miṣrīyah." *Anazahrah.com*, 22 October 2011. Online. http://www.anazahra.com/122912-1, accessed 4 September 2013.

Bender, Daniel. 2011. "Egyptian national identity and prospects for democracy." *Policymic*. Online. http://www.policymic.com/articles/egyptian-national-identity-and-prospects-for-democracy, accessed 23 November 2011.

Central Intelligence Agency. 2012. "The world factbook: Egypt." *CIA*. Online. https://www.cia.gov/library/publications/the-world-factbook/geos/eg.html, accessed 4 September 2013.

Coptic History. n.d. "Ilghāʾ al-lughah al-qibṭīyah." *Coptichistory.org*. Online. http://www.coptichistory.org/new_page_509.htm, accessed 6 June 2012.

Danielson, Virginia. 1997. "Umm Kulthum Ibrahim." *Harvard Magazine*, July–August 1997. Online. http://harvardmagazine.com/1997/07/umm-kulthum-ibrahim, accessed 4 September 2013.

Davidson, Amy. 2011. "'Don't cry, Wael'." *The New Yorker*, 8 February 2011. Online. http://www.newyorker.com/online/blogs/closeread/2011/02/wael-ghonim.html, accessed 4 September 2013.

Dobson, William J. 2011. "'We are not going back.'" *The Washington Post*, 19 March 2011. Online. http://www.washingtonpost.com/blogs/post-partisan/post/we-are-not-going-back/2011/03/17/ABgXB2w_blog.html, accessed 4 September 2013.

Elbadil. 2011. "Najwā Karam: Ghinā' al-fannānīn al-Lubnāniyīn bi-al-lahjah al-Miṣrīyah lil-shuhrah wa jihāt bi-Misr tamna' al-Miṣriyīn bi-al-ghinā' bi-al-lahjah al-Lubnānīyah." *Elbadil.com*. Online. http://elbadil.com/% D9%86%D8%AC%D9%88%D9%89-%D9%83%D8%B1%D9%85-%D8%BA%D9%86%D8%A7%D8%A1-%D8%A7%D9%84%D9%81%D9%86%D8%A7%D9%86%D9%8A%D9%86-%D8%A7%D9%84%D9%84%D8%A8%D9%86%D8%A7%D9%86%D9%8A%D9%86-%D8%A8%D8%A7%D9%84%D9%84/, accessed 23 June 2013.

Elbendary, Amina. 2005. "Shubra-on-the-margins." *al-Ahrām Weekly*, 5–11 May 2005. Online. http://weekly.ahram.org.eg/2005/741/eg11.htm, accessed 4 September 2013.

Elcinema. 2011. "Najwā Karam: sa-ughannī bi-al-lahjah al-Miṣrīyah idhā ghannā 'Amr Diyāb aw Anghām bi-al-Lubnānīyah." *Elcinema*. Online. http://www.elcinema.com/news/nw678915001/, accessed 4 September 2013.

Encyclopedia Britannica. 2013. "Coptic Orthodox Church of Alexandria." *Encyclopedia Britannica Online Academic Edition*. Online. http://www.britannica.com/EBchecked/topic/136928/Coptic-Orthodox-Church-of-Alexandria, accessed 7 June 2013.

Faḍl, Ṣalāḥ. 2008. "Jamāl al-Ghīṭānī fī kitāb al-rinn." *al-Ahrām Weekly*, 7 January 2008. Online. http://www.ahram.org.eg/Archive/2008/1/7/WRIT1.HTM, accessed 4 September 2013.

Helmy, Mostafa. 2011. "Kayfa tatakhallaṣ min jārak al-masīḥī bi-aqall majhūd" ("How to get rid of your Christian neighbor with the least amount of effort"). *Werkstan*, 21 April 2011. Online. http://www.werakak.com/archives/8686, accessed 23 June 2013.

Ḥijjī, Aḥmad. 2012. "al-Aswānī: Hal yaqbal al-ikhwān istib'ād all-ummiyīn min istiftā' al-dustūr?" *Masrawy.com*, 9 December 2012. Online. http://www.masrawy.com/news/Egypt/Politics/2012/December/9/5455445.aspx, accessed 4 September 2013.

'Izz al-Dīn, Yūsuf. 2006. "Wājib qawmī wa-watanī yad'ūnā lil-taṣaddī li-hādhihi al-mu'āmarah: Al-'āmmīyah tuhaddid bi-indithār al-'Arab." *Akhbār al-Adab*. Online. http://www.akhbarelyom.org.eg/adab/issues/662/1001.html, accessed 23 June 2013.

Jack, Ian. 2012. "Schettino should have stayed aboard." *The Guardian*, 20 January 2012. Online. http://www.guardian.co.uk/world/2012/jan/21/schettino-should-have-stayed-aboard, accessed 7 June 2013.

Kamāl, Wisām. 2008. "Sāwīrus wa-rā'iḥat al-māl fī qanāt OTV." *Ikhwān*. Online. http://www.ikhwanonline.com/Article.asp?ArtID= 39000&SecID= 294. Google cache: http://webcache.googleusercontent.com/search?q= cache:5phKd1WXQhAJ:www.ikhwanonline.com/print.aspx% 3FArtID% 3D39000% 26SecID% 3D294+&cd= 1&hl= en&ct= clnk&gl= us, accessed 1 November 2008.

Mehrez, Samia. 2001. "A myriad of leaves." *al-Ahrām Weekly*, 20–6 December 2001. Online. http://weekly.ahram.org.eg/2001/565/cu4.htm, accessed 4 September 2013.

Nūr, Muḥammad. 2007. "Fārūq Shūshah: Miṣr Bi-lā Sulṭah Lughawīyah ... Wa-al-majma' 'yuhātī' Wa-lā Aḥad Yasma'." *Akhbār al-Adab 714*, 18 March 2007. http//www.akhbarelyom.org.eg/adab/, accessed 4 January 2008.

al-Sahrah taḥlá. 2008. "al-Fannān Iyād Naṣṣār fi barnāmaj al-Sahrah taḥlá." *Facebook*, 2 August 2008. Online. https://www.facebook.com/note.php?note_id=22504433455, accessed 23 June 2013.

Shadid, Anthony and David D. Kirkpatrick. 2011. "Promise of Arab uprisings is threatened by divisions." *The New York Times*, 21 May 2011. http://www.nytimes.com/2011/05/22/world/middleeast/22arab.html, accessed 4 September 2013.

Shūshah, Farouk. 2011. "Lughat shabāb al-thawrah." *al-Ahrām*. Online. http://www.ahram.org.eg/archive/The-Writers/News/69442.aspx, accessed 23 June 2013.

Surūr, Fatḥī. 2010. "al-Lughah al-'Arabīyah fī al-dustūr." *al-Ahrām*. Online. http://www.ahram.org.eg/archive/Issues-Views/News/12824.aspx, accessed 23 June 2013.

Tsotsis, Alexia. 2011. "Wael Ghonim's first interview after jail release." *TechCrunch RSS*, 7 February 2011. Online. http://techcrunch.com/2011/02/07/wael-ghonims-first-interview-after-jail-release-video/, accessed 4 September 2013.

INDEX

Page references in italics indicate an illustration or figure